The Geography
of Religion

The Geography of Religion

Faith, Place, and Space

ROGER W. STUMP

ROWMAN & LITTLEFIELD PUBLISHERS, INC.
Lanham • Boulder • New York • Toronto • Plymouth, UK

ROWMAN & LITTLEFIELD PUBLISHERS, INC.

Published in the United States of America
by Rowman & Littlefield Publishers, Inc.
A wholly owned subsidiary of The Rowman & Littlefield Publishing Group, Inc.
4501 Forbes Boulevard, Suite 200, Lanham, Maryland 20706
www.rowmanlittlefield.com

Estover Road, Plymouth PL6 7PY, United Kingdom

British Library Cataloguing in Publication Information Available

Library of Congress Cataloging-in-Publication Data

Stump, Roger W., 1951–
    The geography of religion : faith, place, and space / Roger W. Stump.
       p.   cm.
    Includes bibliographical references and index.
    ISBN-13: 978-0-7425-1080-7 (cloth : alk. paper)
    ISBN-10: 0-7425-1080-8 (cloth : alk. paper)
    1. Religion and geography.   I. Title.
  BL65.G4S78   2008
  200.9—dc22

                                      2007045921

Printed in the United States of America

♾ ™ The paper used in this publication meets the minimum requirements of American National Standard for Information Sciences—Permanence of Paper for Printed Library Materials, ANSI/NISO Z39.48-1992.

For Julia, Adam, and Owen

Contents

Illustrations

Maps

Photographs

Preface

Before launching into the main body of the text, I would like to make a few preliminary remarks regarding the content of this work and to acknowledge the contributions of various individuals to its completion. I should begin by acknowledging the possibility of a misconception arising from the main title of the book, *The Geography of Religion*, which suggests a definitiveness of scope and coverage that I have neither pursued nor attained. I have not intended this work to be a comprehensive survey of this subfield of cultural geography, much less the final word on the subject. Instead, in the following chapters I have chosen to address a specific set of themes that in my view are particularly salient in studying religion from the disciplinary perspectives of geography.

This approach clearly implies that the geography of religion differs in basic ways from, say, the sociology or economics or psychology of religion, an assertion that to me is more or less self-evident. At the same time, however, I have found in my academic interactions with sociologists, anthropologists, religious studies faculty, and even theologians that many of the geographical concerns on which I have focused are in fact relevant to their own work (and vice versa). The various disciplines concerned with religion have necessarily developed different emphases in their examinations of the topic, but those emphases do not preclude a good deal of overlap in the objects and methods of study. Despite the book's title, therefore, I have not focused in explicit terms on the "geographical," in opposition to the sociological, psychological, or anthropological. In effect, the geographical themes of spatiality and contextuality, around which much of this work is organized, are presented here without overt elaboration or validation in narrow disciplinary terms. I have, of course, put forward the discussion of these themes as a means of inquiring into the relationships between geographical concerns and religion. Indeed, this goal provides the rationale for the book's title (despite the caveats raised above and assuming that the reader will not put too much stress on the initial *The*). Nonetheless, I have aimed the discussion at an inclusively imagined audience, including readers who are new to the study of religion as well as readers who have addressed this topic from perspectives other than the geographical.

A further caveat regarding the title of this work centers on the use of the term *religion*, in the singular. This usage fell out of favor, to some extent, as scholars turned away from the idea of comparative religion in the later decades of the twentieth century. This trend in part reflected a questioning of the concept of religion, particularly in reference to two related points: that the term itself, in identifying a distinct category

xv

of cultural phenomena, tended to reify that category as a cultural universal form; and that the great variety of the specific phenomena associated with the concept of religion resulted either in imprecise definitions of the term or definitions too broad to be of much analytical use. A revival of interest in comparative religion around the turn of the century has in part reduced concerns with such issues, however. Within the latter context, two points are of particular importance from my point of view. First, the generic concept of religion continues to provide a useful construct for ordering a wide variety of comparable cultural phenomena, without requiring that religion per se be treated as an absolute, universal form. Second, despite certain points of contention, commonly used approaches to the study of religion provide the basis for a workable and useful definition of the concept, specific in its terms but widely applicable, as discussed in chapter 1. Together, these two points underlie the interpretation of religion expressed in the rest of this book.

In considering the geography of religion, finally, the following chapters generally focus on the relationships between various geographical concepts and central elements of religious belief and practice, primarily as expressed in empirical examples. I devote little attention to inquiring into cultural phenomena characterized as having religious dimensions that fall at the edges of or outside my definition of religion. Some such phenomena may be culturally significant, including certain types of environmentalism, nationalism, or unfocused spirituality. I have found, however, that these phenomena are better understood as substitutes for religion than as religion itself, as I have defined it, and therefore represent a different type of cultural expression. I also devote little attention to the actual details involved in "doing" the geography of religion. This decision represents a personal bias, as in general terms I have not found discussions of this type to be very useful. They often rely a bit too much on the philosophical or methodological fashions of the moment for my taste. As a corollary, they also tend to devalue previous work too readily, a practice that often impedes the overall development of particular areas of study. And such discussions frequently have difficulty finding a middle way between being too narrow or too general in their focus. In the case of this book, moreover, the objective of covering a great variety of empirical material does not leave room for more detailed examinations of "doing" the geography of religion. The concern with "doing" is certainly important but, in my view, is not as fundamental to a subfield this diverse as is an extensive familiarity with empirical and conceptual issues. In contrarian fashion, I prefer to reverse a well-worn phrase and assert that one should, in the long run, "do by learning."

Regarding some of the details of the text itself, the writing of a work as broad as this one in its geographical and cultural scope raises various difficulties. Perhaps most obviously, the transliteration or transcription of diverse languages into English represents a major issue. Different methods of converting a foreign system of writing into English, or of representing foreign phonemes as characters, may produce a variety of English written forms for the same foreign word or proper noun. Adding to the confusion, many foreign words and proper nouns have been assimilated into English using spellings that do not precisely match any organized system of transliteration or transcription. Like many authors in this situation, I have responded to these problems by avoiding rigid adherence to any particular system and instead emphasizing the goals of simplicity, readability, recognizability, and consistency in rendering foreign terms in English.

Because this text is global in scope, I have kept the transliterations and transcriptions as simple as possible. In general, I have retained diacritics only if they are essential to indicate the correct pronunciation of an unfamiliar term or if a diacritic appears in the common English rendition of a word (as in *Baha'i* or *Brother André*). I would have included all relevant diacritics if this work were a specialized treatise on, for example, Tibetan Buddhism. I assume, however, that most readers of this actual work would not find such diacritics useful and that specialists on Tibetan Buddhism will recognize relevant terms even without diacritics. On the other hand, I have rendered the names of the various Chinese schools of Buddhism in their Wade-Giles form, with diacritics included, because readers are very likely to encounter such names in this form in other academic writings on Buddhism.

Concerning recognizability, I have generally followed common usage if a foreign word or proper name has become popularized in English in a particular form (as in *matzo* or *Kaaba*). Along these lines, I have generally used the spellings of foreign words that are listed in *Merriam-Webster's Collegiate Dictionary* or the *Oxford English Dictionary*, and have used *Merriam-Webster's Geographical Dictionary* and the United States Board on Geographic Names via the GEOnet Names Server (earth-info.nga.mil/gns/html/index.html) for assistance with place names. I have made exceptions to all of the above patterns, however, when doing so would increase consistency in how a particular language is transliterated or would follow standard academic usage but would not raise problems of readability or recognizability (for example, using *Najaf* instead of *An Najaf* for the Iraqi city, or *ulama* in place of *ulema*). Finally, when a word has no widely used Anglicized form, or when it is introduced specifically as a word in another language, it first appears in the text in italics but is not subsequently italicized.

Regarding the photographs included in this book, I have made use of the growing collections of licensed photography available on the Internet, along with personal work, stock photography, and public domain images from the Library of Congress. Much of the licensed photography on the Internet is available without charge as long as certain licensing conditions are met. The licensing agreements most frequently encountered are the various Creative Commons licenses (creativecommons.org/licenses/) and the GNU Free Documentation License (www.gnu.org/copyleft/fdl.html). These licenses typically require that the photograph be accompanied by an attribution to the source, identification of and often a URL for the license involved, and often a URL for the photograph itself. Such information is provided as required in the photograph captions, and links to the relevant licenses provide access to information on specific license types and their terms. I would like to thank all of the observant and creative photographers whose work I have used by means of these licenses for their great generosity in making their images available. Note that all photographs remain under the copyright of the credited source unless they are identified as being released to the public domain. Also note that any deficiencies in the photograph captions are my responsibility, not that of the photographers.

Finally, I would like to thank the many individuals who have contributed to the successful completion of this project. Before writing my first book, I was under the impression that such a task represented an essentially single-handed endeavor. I discovered that I was wrong. I would therefore like to acknowledge all of the scholars, too many to name and including a large number whose work is not cited herein, whose work has informed and inspired my own efforts in the geographical study of religion. More specifically, I would also like to express my appreciation for Rowman & Littlefield, a determinedly independent academic publisher in a field increasingly dominated by media conglomerates and megacorporations. I am particularly grateful to Susan McEachern, my editor (as well as vice president of Rowman & Littlefield and its editorial director for international studies, geography, and history). Her enthusiasm, encouragement, patience, guidance, and reasonableness have all been invaluable to me. Susan deserves much credit and many thanks. Thanks go as well to Alden Perkins, production editor, for her stewardship as the book made its journey to publication; to Kimberly Ball Smith, copyeditor, for her close attention to issues of style and consistency within the text; and to editorial assistants Meg Tilton, Aubrey Brobst, and Jessica Gribble for their support during the final stages of the project. The production staff at Rowman & Littlefield also deserve recognition for their careful work on making this book a reality. And I thank two editorial readers who provided a wealth of thoughtful and constructive commentary on an earlier draft of this work. While the book benefited from their ideas, I again am solely responsible for all problems of fact and interpretation that may appear in the following pages.

Finally, I would like to thank my family for their indefatigable support. Special gratitude goes to my father, mother, and brothers—professors all—who have provided diverse models and standards for the progress of my own intellectual curiosity and academic pursuits over the years. Most significantly, however, I would like to thank Julia, Adam, and Owen, my wife and sons, for their understanding, patience, humor, endurance, and occasional quiet during the long process that produced this book. Words being inadequate, the actual effort that I have put into this project is dedicated first and foremost to them.

CHAPTER 1

Introduction

The Upper West Side *Eruv*

On the Upper West Side of Manhattan, in New York City, an inconspicuous boundary separates an area of roughly 200 city blocks from the surrounding urban landscape. Some sections of the boundary are made of cord, wire, or fishing line strung between light poles or trees; other portions are defined by existing building faces, walls, and fences. Ranging from 60th Street to 107th Street and from Central Park West to the West Side Highway and Riverside Park, the boundary stretches over six miles in circumference and encloses an area of 1.5 square miles containing approximately two hundred thousand residents. The boundary has little importance for most people living in the area, and because it is visually unobtrusive most residents ignore it or are unaware of its existence. For a significant minority of those who live within its limits, however, the boundary represents a basic fact of life, inextricably tied to the practice of their religion.

This obscure boundary defines an area known as an *eruv* ("mixture," pl. *eruvin*), a ritual space used by Orthodox Jews during observance of the Sabbath, from sundown on Friday to sundown on Saturday (map 1.1). The Sabbath plays a central role in Judaism, celebrating God's creation of the universe, commemorating the divine redemption of the Jewish people from slavery in ancient Egypt, and anticipating the perfection of the world to come. For Orthodox Jews, proper observance of the Sabbath requires adherence to a variety of restrictions laid out in Jewish religious law. According to these restrictions, the observant must refrain from all purposeful activity on the Sabbath, in emulation of God's day of rest following the six days of creation. Expressly forbidden activities fall into thirty-nine separate categories, including plowing, building, baking, weaving, and kindling a fire. Over time, these restrictions have been interpreted to forbid actions such as driving an automobile, turning electrical appliances on and off, and handling money. Among the most demanding of the Sabbath restrictions is the prohibition against carrying objects within public spaces or between public and private spaces. Those who observe this prohibition cannot leave their residences on the Sabbath carrying any object that they are not actually wearing, a rule that creates many practical difficulties. Eruvin like the one on the Upper West Side are spatial constructs specifically designed to alleviate such difficulties.

More precisely, an eruv (from the Hebrew for mixing or joining together) represents a conceptual merging of diverse public and private spaces to form a common private domain.[1] Within this communal home the restriction on carrying does not

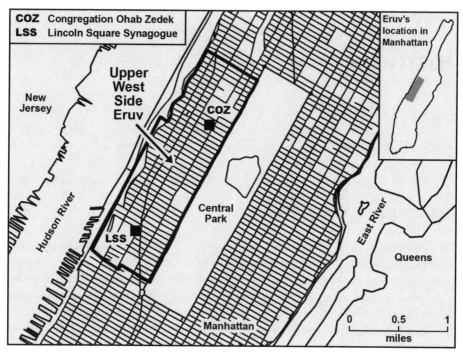

Map 1.1. The Upper West Side eruv, New York City. The Lincoln Square Synagogue and Congregation Ohab Zedek cooperated in establishing the eruv to serve the Jewish population of the Upper West Side.

apply, and thus inside the eruv observant Jews may carry any object that does not otherwise violate the law or spirit of the Sabbath. Tools used to perform prohibited activities cannot be handled, for example, but carrying small or easily transported necessities, such as house keys, handkerchiefs, reading glasses, medication, or extra clothing, is allowed. As in many other Orthodox Jewish communities, the presence of an eruv on the Upper West Side solves many of the difficulties that residents would otherwise face in observing the Sabbath. It permits them to carry their apartment keys to synagogue, to bring already prepared food to another person's house, to use strollers and diaper bags when taking young children to visit family or friends, or to use a cane or wheelchair in moving about the neighborhood. By extending the boundaries of private space beyond the individual household, the eruv spatially restructures the Sabbath ritual, fostering interaction among members of the Orthodox Jewish community on their day of rest.

As a form of ritual space, the Upper West Side eruv is a contemporary manifestation of a Jewish practice that originated in ancient Israel. The rabbinical literature attributes the concept of the eruv to King Solomon, and eruvin have been constructed in Jewish communities for well over two millennia. Rules concerning the creation of eruvin fill an entire section of the Mishnah, the codification of Jewish law. Those rules have guided the creation of eruvin as Jews have migrated to various parts of the world. Like many facets of Jewish law, however, the practice of creating an eruv has been subject to varied interpretations by authorities acting within different contexts. Some very conservative authorities have concluded, for example, that the complex structures and high population densities of contemporary cities preclude the creation of an eruv, and their followers do not use eruvin in metropolitan settings. Other authorities have declared urban eruvin valid as long as the rules for establishing them are rigorously followed.[2] In keeping with the latter position, Orthodox Jewish communities have set up eruvin in many cities around the world. More than one hundred eruvin currently exist within the United States, and their number continues to grow. The Upper West Side eruv was itself established in 1994, primarily through the efforts of Lincoln Square Synagogue and Congregation Ohab Zedek, two of the Orthodox Jewish synagogues located in the neighborhood (map 1.1).

To be considered valid, the creation of an eruv as ritual space must be carried out in strict accordance with Jewish law. This process includes three distinct components. First, the area of the eruv must be physically demarcated by a fixed boundary made up of tangible landscape features. Existing structures can be used to define the eruv's boundary. A major section of the Upper West Side eruv, for example, is defined by a wall that runs along the western side of Central Park. To make the boundary continuous, however, gaps between existing structures must be filled by symbolic "doorways" formed by two vertical poles joined by a horizontal lintel. Because the lintel need not be made of rigid material, doorways can be defined using existing telephone or utility poles and overhead cables, or created by erecting new poles and stringing a durable line between them. Although the boundary of the eruv may enclose both public and private land, it cannot include any heavily used public area, usually defined as space traversed by at least 600,000 people in a day, unless that area can be closed off during the Sabbath by symbolic "doors." These doors can be extended, at least theoretically, to block the movement of traffic into the eruv, while a doorway simply represents the shape of a doorframe and cannot be closed. On the Upper West Side, doors have been placed at several locations where the eruv boundary intersects with major thoroughfares that carry significant traffic on the Sabbath. The doors themselves are made of rolls of thin, durable material stored inside plastic canisters, which are affixed to light poles supporting the boundary wire. Finally, the eruv boundary must remain intact to be valid on the Sabbath, and so is regularly inspected and repaired. Many Jewish congregations have a telephone number by which members can verify the status of the eruv before the Sabbath begins.

After the boundary has been defined, a second step is required to make the eruv ritually effective. This step involves the performance of a ceremony, the "mixing of courtyards," through which the eruv acquires its religious meaning as a space shared by a community of observant Jews. In this ceremony, bread is placed in a designated location and a blessing is recited that grants a portion of the bread to every member of the observant Jewish community living within the eruv. This act symbolically unites the community as residents of the structure where the bread is stored, commonly a synagogue or the home of a rabbi. In the Upper West Side eruv, the bread is kept at the Lincoln Square Synagogue in the office of the senior rabbi. Because the bread must be edible to be effective, this ceremony must be repeated periodically.

The third stage in the creation of an eruv involves acquiring the right to use space within the eruv that is not owned by members of the observant Jewish community, including public streets and parks as well as private land. According to Jewish law, this right can be obtained by leasing permission to use the area in question. Establishing rental agreements with all landowners in an urban area may be impractical, so Jewish law allows this process to be performed symbolically as an agreement between a rabbi and civil authorities such as the mayor, police, or city council. The leasing process for the Upper West Side eruv, for example, was conducted with the New York City Mayor's Office. Such agreements are established for a fixed period and must be renewed upon expiration.

Although established according to widely accepted principles, the Upper West Side eruv is not universally accepted by Orthodox Jews living in New York City. As mentioned earlier, some Orthodox authorities do not accept the validity of neighborhood eruvin in densely populated cities, arguing that these spaces are too open to public traffic to be treated as private domains. The Satmar Hasidic neighborhood located in the Williamsburg section of Brooklyn, for example, does not have a communal eruv. Some Orthodox Jews living on the Upper West Side therefore do not use the eruv, preferring to adhere to stricter rules concerning carrying outside the home. According to other rabbinical authorities, the Upper West Side eruv is actually unnecessary, because under their more liberal interpretation the whole island of Manhattan is contained within an eruv, the boundaries of which are defined by the island itself. Disagreements over eruvin have developed in other places as well, and have often spread beyond the Orthodox Jewish community. In a number of cases outsiders have opposed the construction of an eruv because it promotes the social segregation of Orthodox Jews or makes religious use of public property such as utility poles and overhead cables. Such objections have not been raised on the Upper West Side, but they have emerged in response to eruv construction elsewhere in the New York metropolitan area and in other places as well.[3]

Once established, however, an eruv serves an important function in the lives of those who accept its efficacy, freeing them from some of the practical problems encountered in adhering to divine law while celebrating the Sabbath. Most importantly, it makes it easier for members of the Orthodox community to go to synagogue, the focus of Jewish religious life. The eruv also allows mothers with very young children to leave their residences on the Sabbath and in general supports a more active community life. As a result, the existence of an eruv in a neighborhood has a significant influence on the residential decisions of Orthodox Jews. Indeed, a major motivation for creating the Upper West Side eruv was to stem the migration of Orthodox Jews out of the area. The Upper West Side became an important Jewish residential area early in the twentieth century, and with its many synagogues and kosher businesses it served as the center of Orthodox life in New York.[4] In recent decades, however, Orthodox Jews began to move away from the neighborhood, often to other parts of the New York metropolitan area where eruvin already existed. Lincoln Square Synagogue and Congregation Ohab Zedek responded by establishing an eruv on the Upper West Side to make the area a more attractive place for Orthodox Jews to live. Synagogue leaders conclude, moreover, that this effort has been a success, particularly by attracting young Orthodox families to the area and encouraging them to remain there. By expanding the spatial domain of Sabbath observance, the eruv has thus contributed to the ongoing vitality of the Orthodox Jewish community on the Upper West Side.[5]

*   *   *

As a manifestation of Orthodox Jewish belief, the Upper West Side eruv provides a tangible illustration of the complex relationships between religion and the geographi-

cal motifs of space and place. Most obviously, the eruv exemplifies the common religious practice of defining ritual spaces with special meanings and uses. Within this
context, it reflects the significance of the spatial constraints placed on Orthodox Jews
by Jewish religious law, simplifying the specific religious act of going to synagogue
on the Sabbath by facilitating movement within the local community. As a socially
constructed space, the eruv also has the more general effect of expanding the activity
space of the elderly, the infirm, and families with young children. By delimiting a
shared Sabbath domain, the eruv thus establishes a communal space among Orthodox
Jews who live on the Upper West Side. In addition, the eruv is directly linked to the
spatial distribution of Orthodox Jews within New York City, marking an area that
contains a large Jewish community. More broadly, the presence of the Upper West
Side eruv reveals the ongoing diffusion of ancient religious practices as Jewish migration has spread to different regions of the world, while the adaptation of the laws of
eruv construction to the contemporary setting of New York City demonstrates how
religious traditions interact with the local contexts in which they are enacted and
reproduced. In sum, the Upper West Side eruv serves in various specific ways to
anchor Orthodox Jews' belief to this particular place, firmly grounding their conceptions of the sacred in the spaces and contexts of everyday life. In the process, the
various meanings and uses of the eruv demonstrate crucial connections between religion and central themes in cultural geography.

Those connections, relating the concepts of religion, place, and space, represent
the principal concern of this book. The study of religions has in fact been an important part of cultural geography since the middle of the last century. Its earliest systematic treatments appeared in seminal works by Pierre Deffontaines and David Sopher,
published in 1948 and 1967 respectively.[6] Since then, the geography of religion has
become a well-established field of study, the focus of professional specialty groups,
scholarly conferences, an online journal, and a growing academic literature.[7] Interest
in this topic among geographers derives from an appreciation of two factors: the fundamental importance of religion as an element of culture and the distinctly geographical character of various dimensions of religious belief and practice, as illustrated in the
example of the Upper West Side eruv. In exploring the spatiality of religious activity
geographers have analyzed a broad range of phenomena, from the diffusion of religious groups to the meaning and uses of sacred space.[8] This body of scholarship, while
quite varied in content and approach, has acquired increasing coherence in recent
decades, providing substantial insights into humanity's diverse religious traditions and
their relationships with the geographical contexts within which they have developed.[9]

This book elaborates upon such insights by examining the scope of the geographical study of religion through a conceptual synthesis of four interconnected
themes. The first of these themes addresses a key dimension of the spatiality of religions by focusing on the spatial dynamics of religious distributions. This theme
encompasses the processes through which religions have emerged in particular hearths
and then diffused to other locations through processes of migration and conversion.
The second theme centers on the inherent contextuality of religion. As religions have
spread to different places, their adherents have simultaneously influenced and been
influenced by the specific contexts in which they live. The result has been the perpet-
ual reworking of religions by communities of believers into distinct local expressions
linked to larger traditions. The third theme relates to relationships between religious

systems and the ways in which their adherents create, interpret, and use the social spaces that they inhabit. Such relationships arise from the conscious efforts of adherents to exert control over a territory as well as from the taken-for-granted customs through which religious tradition and daily life intersect. The book's final theme pertains to the meanings and uses of sacred space, treated here as a cultural construct defined by its meaning for believers. Sacred space in this sense differs from other forms of social space in that adherents ascribe religious meaning to it as a locus of interaction with the divine or the supernatural.

In examining these themes, the following chapters illustrate the contributions of geographical perspectives to the broader study of religion, an endeavor that crosses disciplinary boundaries.[10] A central point in this discussion is that geographical perspectives, focusing on the concepts of place and space, are crucial in understanding essential aspects of religion as an expression of human culture. The disciplinary concerns of geography are directly relevant, for example, to assessment of the deep connections between religion and place suggested in preceding paragraphs. They are equally relevant in analyzing the spatial dimensions of religious change and spatial patterns of religious diversity. More broadly, the lens of geography is useful in considering interactions between religion and diverse realms of human activity as expressed in social space. Religious belief in effect serves as an integrative factor within the cultural lives of adherents, establishing a paradigm through which they organize and interpret their existence. As an integrative science, geography provides an effective framework for analyzing the connection of religious belief to other spheres of thought and action at diverse scales.

In addition to appraising the uses of geography in studying religion, the examination of the four themes outlined above addresses the significance of religion as a focus of study within geography. Since its inception as a thematic field of study, the geography of religion has largely remained within the traditionally defined scope of cultural geography. It has not received sustained attention from scholars working in the other major subfields of human geography. It also appears to have generated little interest among practitioners of the new interpretations of cultural geography associated with the interdisciplinary field of "cultural studies" and other postmodern approaches.[11] The following chapters propose that this lack of attention is unwarranted (also see the section on "Studying Religion" in chapter 6). Religions serve as primary repositories of meaning and identity, and are used by believers to address issues of ultimate significance in their lives. As a result, the study of religion provides crucial insights into the structure and substance of human cultures. From a geographical perspective, moreover, religious belief and practice provide essential insights into the inherent spatiality of culture and the complex interactions between culture and place.

Through their engagement with issues of space and place, then, the four themes around which this book is organized illustrate essential connections between the disciplinary concerns of geography and the study of religion. Before proceeding to a more thorough introduction to each of the four themes, this chapter next lays the conceptual foundations for what follows by considering the nature of religion as an aspect of culture. The problem of defining religion as an object of study has yielded a variety of theoretical interpretations. The interpretation presented in this chapter provides a specific definition that conforms to prevailing currents in the cultural study of religion.

In addition, the interpretation presented here draws on a dynamic understanding of culture, reflecting recent work in cultural geography, as a foundation for examining the relationships between religion, space, and place.[12] After clarifying this conceptualization of religion, the discussion will return to the four themes outlined above and articulate in greater detail the topics addressed in subsequent chapters.

Religion as a Cultural System

Religion is interpreted throughout this volume as a cultural system, an integrated complex of meanings, symbols, and behaviors articulated by a community of adherents.[13] Like other elements of culture, religion encompasses a set of normative conceptions or "givens" that inform the ways in which people understand, act within, and influence the world that they inhabit. Religion differs from other elements of culture, however, in terms of its particular concerns. As defined here, a religion consists of a compelling set of beliefs and practices whose truth is presupposed by faith and that ultimately relate to superhuman entities postulated by adherents to possess transcendent attributes or powers superior to those of ordinary mortals.[14] These superhuman entities are most often represented as deities, but can take other forms as well, such as venerated ancestors, nature spirits, or persons who have achieved a state of spiritual perfection (photo 1.1). Whatever form they take, these entities are considered by adherents to exert crucial influences, directly or indirectly, for good or for ill, within and beyond the realm of human affairs. For believers, a religion offers a means of comprehending the nature of these entities as superhuman agents, their authority and effectiveness within the cosmos, and the ways in which they interact with humanity or provide archetypal models for human behavior.

The above definition has achieved widespread acceptance in the study of religions because of its specificity and broad applicability.[15] It asserts that religion as an identifiable element of culture differs explicitly in its concerns from other types of belief systems or models of reality. This definition of religion thus excludes vague or incidental notions of magic and superstition as well as ideological systems that are not primarily concerned with matters of spiritual faith, such as Marxism or nationalism. Its focus on conceptions of the superhuman also avoids the inherent ambiguity of approaches that represent religion in purely subjective terms, for example as an experience of transcendence or absolute dependence, or that expand the concept to include any perspective that involves a sense of reverence, such as some forms of environmentalism. At the same time, this definition identifies significant points of correspondence among spiritual belief systems articulated by culture groups throughout the world. Such belief systems take diverse forms, but the definition given above is sufficiently flexible to accommodate quite varied traditions and so remains useful in a comparative context.

Religious faith regarding the superhuman is generally organized around two central concepts: a religion's worldview and its ethos.[16] A worldview comprises a distinctive understanding of truth, reality, and the forces that shape worldly events. In the context of religion, a worldview represents an integrated system of beliefs that specify the essential order of existence and the ultimate sources of causality, particularly as

Photo 1.1.   A Theravada Buddhist image depicting superhuman aspects of the Buddha, including the *ushnisha* or bump atop his head signifying his supreme wisdom and attainment of complete enlightenment, and his right hand reaching down to touch the earth to call it to witness his defeat of Mara, the personification of evil and temptation. Wat Phra Sing temple, Chang Mai, Thailand, 2007.

Source: Akuppa (www.flickr.com/photos/90664717@N00/417341584/), under Creative Commons license (creativecommons.org/licenses/by/2.0/).

they relate to the nature and authority of the superhuman entity or entities recognized by the religion's adherents. As an expression of culture, a religion's worldview is socially produced and maintained, but adherents consider it to be absolute and incontrovertible. The understandings of reality defined in the worldview thus have vital repercussions for diverse areas of human thought and action, serving to unify the whole of human experience within a larger context. These repercussions are clearly revealed in a religion's ethos—the set of values, motivations, and emotions through which adherents realize consistency with their worldview. An ethos essentially represents an understanding of how people should think and behave given their faith in the worldview that they share. Together, the worldview and ethos of a religion explain in symbolic terms the relationship between human and superhuman, as well as the obligations on each side of that relationship, in terms that to the believer are both realistic and unequivocal. It is the authority of this explanation, which addresses the most basic ontological issues, that renders a religion compelling to its adherents as a belief system and that serves as the basis of its adherents' faith.

The ultimate veracity that adherents attribute to their belief system in turn underlies the profound importance of religion as an integrative factor in culture. Because they address crucial elements of reality and existence, religious beliefs become extensively involved in many different domains of daily life. The integration of religious belief into other aspects of culture appears most explicitly in conceptions of religious law, which formally define the obligations of believers to conform to various commandments or practices associated with the superhuman. In addition to mandated obligations, however, the worldview and ethos of a religion provide a general framework of beliefs and concepts within which adherents articulate or understand other cultural manifestations. These manifestations typically extend beyond the specific requirements of religious worship into more diverse cultural structures, including foodways, gender roles, personal appearance, family organization, house form, economic practices, the arrangement of time, and patterns of spatial mobility.[17] Through their associations with diverse cultural structures, the worldview and ethos of a religion serve as important sources of coherence within the cultural systems that adherents enact and reproduce.

As well as affecting varied aspects of cultural life, the fundamental meanings of any religion find expression in many different forms, including actions, rituals, symbols, texts, artifacts, and landscapes. A religion, as defined here, comprises all of these different expressions, not just the core beliefs on which they are based. This assertion runs counter to the view that culture is purely ideational, encompassing meanings, beliefs, and attitudes but not associated behaviors and objects. The latter are an integral part of the cultural environment, however, and can play significant roles as vehicles of cultural meaning. Moreover, behavioral and material expressions of culture are not merely the by-products of mental constructs; the former continually interact with the latter in a reciprocal fashion.[18] Normative patterns of behavior can reinforce the development and persistence of ideas among members of a culture group, for example, just as material artifacts and landscapes can place constraints on the symbolic structures within which individuals learn, enact, and reproduce particular ideas and behaviors. In the context of religion, religious behaviors and objects can strongly influence the ways in which adherents interpret religious meaning and its role in their daily lives. These behaviors and objects thus represent an essential part of the religious system as adherents experience it. As an example, the social expectation that all Muslim men will engage in weekly worship at a communal mosque will likely strengthen the religiosity of participants in this practice. The behavior of worship carried out in a specific material setting, the mosque, in effect reinforces religious orthodoxy.

As defined above, religion manifests several crucial characteristics as a cultural system. Like all of culture, religion is inherently communal, based on meanings and values collectively acknowledged by a group of believers. The religious experiences of all members of the group will not be identical, of course. Some individuals may be more devout than others or may adhere to mandated practices more precisely. Individuals may also develop their own idiosyncratic interpretations of group beliefs, or adopt elements of the beliefs of more than one religion. Moreover, a religion may prescribe different roles and experiences for individuals within the community of adherents based on factors such as age or gender. As a cultural system, however, a religion is an expression of the community rather than of the individual, rooted in shared understandings and reproduced through social interaction. Consequently, religion involves at least an implicit sense of identity and membership in a distinct community of believers. In some cases the concept of membership may be unarticulated, particularly within a relatively homogeneous society in which a single religion predominates. The individual's membership in a distinct community is recognized more explicitly in religiously diverse settings, or in religions that mandate an affirmation of membership such as baptism in many forms of Christianity or the *shahada* ("declaration of faith") in Islam. Whether implicit or explicit, the social bonds of membership foster conformity to the group's beliefs and practices.

Like other aspects of culture, religious systems are maintained over time through processes of cultural reproduction. Such processes arise out of the recurrent social interactions through which shared patterns of thought and action are conveyed and reinforced among members of a culture group. Many cultural givens are reproduced informally and un-self-consciously within the routine cycles and structures of daily life, but groups also develop more conscientious approaches in reproducing aspects of culture for which authenticity is a crucial attribute. Because religions encompass meanings of ultimate significance, their adherents have a particularly strong interest in ensuring that the authenticity of their beliefs and practices is preserved over time. As a result, the processes through which religions are reproduced are often highly formalized and exacting. Regular communal worship represents a primary expression of these processes, but they comprise a wide variety of other rituals, institutions, and social practices as well, from holidays to religious training to rites of passage. In religions that accentuate orthodoxy, or authenticity of belief, believers formalize processes of cultural reproduction through the use of sacred texts, confessions, creeds, or catechisms, which preserve faith in essential doctrines. Adherents of religions that emphasize orthopraxy, or authenticity of practice, focus on the social reproduction of sanctioned rituals and behaviors, for example through the development of systems of religious law such as the sharia of Islam or the *halakhah* of Judaism. Religious elites often play a central role in legitimizing and maintaining these processes, and so wield considerable influence over the reproduction of religious systems. Such processes may also persist, however, through the informal practices of everyday life among ordinary believers.

The Mutability of Religions

Processes of cultural reproduction are never exact, however, even when they are highly formalized. In response to changing cultural circumstances or the insights of influential individuals, members of a culture group can modify, reinterpret, or contest existing conceptions, or invent new ones, thereby transforming the culture in which they participate. Cultural patterns can also be altered as a culture group interacts with other groups or encounters new surroundings. Culture, in other words, is continually mutable, a dynamic mixture of tradition and innovation. As cultural systems, religions thus demonstrate an intrinsic mutability and are constantly susceptible to processes of change. Certain general conceptions may be relatively invariable, of course. Muhammad's role as God's final prophet remains a constant in Islamic belief, for example, as does the role of Jesus as the instrument of humanity's salvation in Christianity. Nonetheless, while adherents may consider their religion to be eternal and unalterable, that view does not prevent the development of often substantial variations in specific beliefs and practices as a religion is reproduced over time and space.[19]

Adherents may adapt elements of a widely dispersed religion to conform to local cultural practices, for example. Thus in the early history of Islam, different schools of Islamic law arose partly in response to the varied character of early communities of followers. To cite one instance, in the diverse and cosmopolitan community of Kufa, an early center of Islamic learning located in Iraq, Islamic jurists ruled that a husband could not marry into a family of higher socioeconomic status. In the more homogeneous and traditional community of Medina, where Muhammad formed the first Islamic society, such restrictions did not exist.[20] Adherents may also revise or reinterpret earlier traditions in response to changes in other aspects of their cultural circumstances. The adoption of prevailing modernist perspectives by liberal Protestants in Europe and North America during the late 1800s, for example, led to a substantial revision of certain of their beliefs, such as their reinterpretation of the Bible as parable and allegory rather than as the literal word of God. Change may also occur when believers participating in more than one religious culture seek some form of accommodation between disparate beliefs. The forced exposure of Africans to European culture in the Americas during the period of slavery, for example, led to the creation of new religious forms, such as Santeria in Cuba, Vodou in Haiti, and Macumba in Brazil, which fused elements of African religions and Christianity. More radical departures from tradition may develop through the introduction of new revelations that augment or supplant earlier religious givens, such as Buddhism's emergence out of the philosophical and cosmological contexts of early Hinduism. However they come about, changes in a particular belief or practice often produce a cascading effect, as adherents then modify other elements of their religious system to maintain its overall coherence. In this way, even highly formalized religious systems can develop distinctive expressions at different times and in different places.

The potential for change in the reproduction of religious beliefs and practices derives in part from the complexity of cultural communities. Such communities are neither homogeneous nor mutually exclusive. They typically contain a variety of subcultures based on factors such as gender, age, ancestry, education, and class; and in any given place a multitude of cultures may coexist or overlap. Individuals thus participate in various cultures at the same time, reflecting the different culturally defined groups to which they belong. Men and women living in a traditional patriarchy, for example, participate at one level in a common culture that assumes a male-dominated social hierarchy; but at another level, those men and women inhabit quite different cultural spheres, each with its own gendered assumptions and expectations. In the context of religion, individuals who share a common religious affiliation may differ considerably with respect to their participation in other cultural structures. As a result, they may develop quite different understandings of particular beliefs and practices. Cultural variations within a community of believers can in turn lead to conflict as individuals or groups contest the meanings of specific elements of their religious system, and the likelihood of conflict grows as such a community becomes increasingly diverse.[21]

The imperfect reproduction of religious systems derives as well from the spatial mobility of culture groups. Because adherents interpret their religion within the context of their immediate cultural surroundings, variations in belief and practice typically become increasingly pronounced as a religion diffuses to diverse places through processes of migration or conversion. Adherents living in different locations will experience distinctive cultural influences and circumstances and so will modify their understanding of religious meanings in distinctive ways. Some innovations that emerge in this manner will eventually spread out of their original hearth areas, and they too can generate conflict as adherents in other locations challenge their legitimacy. Through their interactions with diverse cultural contexts and perspectives, many religions have experienced repeated divisions or schisms.

As a result, most of the world's major religions are divided into distinct branches differing in key matters of belief and practice: Eastern Orthodoxy, Roman Catholicism, and Protestantism within Christianity; the Orthodox, Conservative, and Reform movements within Judaism; the Sunni and Shia branches within Islam; the Theravada and Mahayana schools within Buddhism; and Vaishnavism, Saivism, and Shaktism within Hinduism. As a matter of terminology, it is thus useful to distinguish between religious traditions and religious systems. A religious tradition, as defined here, represents a fundamental articulation of religious givens that are shared by a variety of specific religious systems. Hinduism, Buddhism, Judaism, Christianity, and Islam all represent religious traditions in this sense. The core beliefs of a religious tradition define a common identity for the various religious systems derived from it. At the same time, each branch of a religious tradition incorporates its own interpretations of particular matters of belief and practice, thereby producing distinct but related religious systems.

The impact of cultural variety on processes of religious change and adaptation is evident at more local scales as well. Many of the denominational divisions that have occurred within American Protestantism, for example, have grown out of cultural conflicts among coreligionists, such as the rift between Northern and Southern Baptists over the issue of slavery in the 1840s. Despite its unified institutional structure, Roman Catholicism also displays the impact of cultural variety on religious practice, as in the veneration of local or national saints and other forms of popular practice associated with particular places and ethnic groups (photo 1.2).[22] Differences in the interpretation of certain aspects of Islamic law, such as the manner in which women are expected to veil themselves in public, represent an even more explicit expression of the relationships between local cultural norms and religious practice.[23] Because communities of adherents participate in a multiplicity of local cultural structures and identities, then, religious beliefs and practices are frequently transformed as they are reproduced from place to place and from generation to generation.

The Multiformity of Religions

Another crucial feature of religion as a type of cultural system is its multiformity, or the variety of specific forms that it takes. The definition of religion given earlier identifies traits that all religious systems share in common, but specific religions manifest these traits differently. Most obviously, the world's religions display considerable diversity regarding specific matters of faith. Conceptions of the superhuman vary significantly, for example. As monotheistic religions, Judaism, Christianity, and Islam recognize a single, omnipotent deity as the ultimate superhuman force. Polytheistic religions, such as most forms of Hinduism, attribute divinity to a multitude of different entities. Still other religions focus on other kinds of superhuman beings, such as ancestors in Chinese folk religion or bodhisattvas ("enlightened ones") in Mahayana Buddhism. Differences appear as well in basic features of religious worldviews, such as the nature of time. Judaism, Christianity, and Islam, for example, support a world-

Photo 1.2. St. John Nepomuk, a fourteenth-century Catholic martyr, the most popular national saint of Bohemia, and an important saint in surrounding parts of Central Europe. Because he is also the patron saint of bridges, rivers, and floods, he became a principal figure in the river city of Heidelberg where this statue is located, placed in a corner niche of a building in the old city. The biretta, cassock, and surplice that he wears and the crucifix that he carries are his identifying symbolic attributes. Heidelberg, Germany, 2006.

Source: Author.

view based on a linear conception of time comprising a unique series of sacred events with a distinct beginning and end. Hindu and Buddhist worldviews, on the other hand, incorporate more varied conceptions of time in which the notion of recurring temporal cycles figures prominently. The nature of spiritual devotion also varies among religions. In religions that stress orthodoxy, such as most forms of Christianity, adherence to a particular set of doctrinal beliefs represents the believer's principal obligation. In religions that stress orthopraxy, on the other hand, proper observance of specific practices and rituals represents the primary obligation, as in traditional forms of Judaism.

Variations in social characteristics are a further expression of religion's multiformity. Again, in its social expression a religion is shared by a community of adherents. The nature of membership in that community varies, however. Such variations are perhaps most evident in the contrasts among tribal, ethnic, and proselytic religions. The membership of a tribal religion coincides with a specific tribal group whose members are typically united by their common ancestry, immediate social interactions with others in the tribe, and geographical proximity to one another. In an ethnic religion, such as Judaism or Hinduism, the community of adherents encompasses a much larger culture group that nonetheless possesses an exclusive identity and heritage. As in tribal religions, membership in an ethnic religion's community of believers is generally determined by birth. On the other hand, proselytic religions, such as Buddhism,

Christianity, and Islam, define membership essentially as a choice, in theory available to persons from any cultural or ancestral background. Missionary activity and processes of conversion thus play a major role in the proselytic religions. Variations in the nature of group membership also have implications for the geographical dispersion of communities of adherents. Some religions are highly localized in their distributions, practiced by communities that are limited in size and geographical extent. The animistic tribal religions traditionally practiced in parts of Africa, the Americas, and Asia exemplify this pattern, but so do many smaller sects and cults that have emerged within other religious traditions. The adherents of the larger ethnic and proselytic religions, on the other hand, can be quite widely dispersed, and may be quite diverse in terms of their other cultural characteristics, united only by their acceptance of certain basic matters of faith.

The internal organization of the community of adherents also varies among religions, for example in the distinctions made between religious specialists and the laity (photo 1.3). In some instances, religious specialists primarily provide religious interpretation and instruction to the rest of the community, as in the case of rabbis in Judaism and mullahs in Islam. In other cases, religious specialists are distinguished more sharply from the laity by their special sacramental roles, such as the consecration of the Eucharist by Roman Catholic priests. Along related lines, religious specialists may participate fully in the social life of the community, or they may live apart under more exacting conditions, as in the case of monastic communities. The institutional structures of religions take diverse forms as well. Some religions are structured around formal hierarchies through which a centralized authority theoretically provides direc-

Photo 1.3. Four rabbis of the Chernobyl dynasty of Hasidic Judaism. No location, no date.

Source: Azriell (commons.wikimedia.org/wiki/Image:Chernobil_rabbis.jpg), under Creative Commons license (creativecommons.org/licenses/by-sa/2.5/).

tion to all individual communities and adherents. The Roman Catholic Church exemplifies this pattern, organized as a single body under the leadership of the pope, and then divided into dioceses overseen by bishops, which are in turn subdivided into parishes overseen by priests. This hierarchical structure contrasts sharply with the local autonomy characteristic of many other religious systems, including Islam, Judaism, Hinduism, and those Protestant denominations that adhere to a congregational form of church government.[24]

As a key factor in the structuring of cultural communities, religion represents an important source of identity. This function is especially significant in pluralistic societies and other settings in which members of different religions come into frequent contact with one another. Within such contexts, a shared sense of religious identity reinforces conformity to group beliefs and practices, but it has other social implications as well. Religious identity provides a common means of marking the differences that separate one culture group from another, for example, and as a result has repeatedly played a role in ethnopolitical conflicts. Of course, religious affiliation represents only one possible source of cultural identity. Religion thus intersects with various other forms of identity, particularly at the local scales of daily life. Different adherents may attend the same place of worship but otherwise participate in different social identities organized, for example, by class or gender. In broader terms, religious identity helps to define the way in which adherents interact with others outside their own community. Some religious groups, like the Old Order Amish or ultra-Orthodox Jews, interpret their distinctive identity as a barrier to social interaction and seek to isolate themselves from outsiders as a means of preserving the integrity of their beliefs and practices. Other religious groups seek broader participation in society, for example by establishing institutions that perform social functions not exclusively tied to religious practice, such as schools or hospitals, or by trying to shape public policy or social mores to conform to their own beliefs. Activities of this type are most typical among religious groups positioned within the mainstream of society, but they may be undertaken as well by those seeking to expand their influence among outsiders, such as fundamentalist groups within various religious traditions.[25]

Along similar lines, religions differ widely in terms of their social and political status. Many political states have identified a particular religion as their official faith, thus assigning it a central role in public life. That role may be largely symbolic, as in Norway, where the constitution grants religious freedom to all citizens even though it recognizes the Church of Norway as the state church. The impact of an official religion can be more tangible, however, as in Saudi Arabia, which identifies Islam as the state religion and declares the Quran and the Sunna (traditions associated with the prophet Muhammad) to be its constitution and the basis for all law. In constitutionally secular states, religious groups vary in the extent of their influence on society: a dominant group may exert cultural hegemony by defining the norms of society in general, as in the observance of Sunday as a weekly holiday in predominantly Christian countries, while a small group may have little impact beyond its own membership. In pluralistic contexts, religious groups have often attempted to exert influence over secular society through the formation of political parties or organizations, such as the Christian Coalition in the United States, the Shas Party in Israel, the Muslim Brotherhood in Egypt, or the Bharatiya Janata Party in India. The politicization of religious interests has frequently led to hostilities between religious communities competing for status and power, and has often been an important factor in larger political conflicts. The position of individual religions in society can also be made difficult by public disapproval, such as that directed at secretive or eccentric cults in many countries, or by official persecution, such as actions by the Chinese government against Tibetan Buddhists, Falun Dafa, and other religious minorities.

*   *   *

Mutability and multiformity thus represent key characteristics of religions as cultural systems. As communal phenomena, religions exhibit considerable dynamism and diversity, both in particular matters of faith and in their social functions and identities. This variability derives from the complex interactions that take place between religions and the specific contexts in which they are practiced. Because religion plays a fundamental role in the lives of adherents, specific beliefs and practices become widely integrated into the structures and routines of existence. In the process, believers' understandings of religious meanings exert significant influence on various aspects of their daily lives, but are also continually shaped by the particular circumstances in which adherents live. Spatially dispersed religions that are practiced in different geographical contexts consequently appear in diverse local manifestations, each a unique variant of the commonalities that unite a larger religious tradition. Such diversity creates persistent tensions between the global and the local, between a shared heritage of belief and the circumstances of specific communities of adherents. Similarly, religions practiced in places that are undergoing processes of social change typically experience significant tensions between tradition and innovation, which again lead to the emergence of diverse religious forms. These patterns of diversification, in sum, reflect frictions between the coherence of the system of meanings encompassed by a religion and the various processes of change to which all religions are subject as elements of culture. In response to such frictions, believers place considerable emphasis on preserving the religious meanings that they consider to be of ultimate importance. Questions of authority and authenticity thus represent major religious concerns, and again are important sources of cultural conflict.

Religion, then, represents a core element of culture, highly variable in the ways in which it is manifested but crucial as a medium through which people understand the superhuman forces that in their view shape the nature of reality and human existence. Accordingly, religion represents an important object of study in disciplines concerned with cultural and social phenomena, including human geography. These disciplines approach the study of religion in different ways, of course, and provide distinctive insights into its many roles in human experience. The remainder of this chapter focuses on an examination of how the disciplinary concerns and perspectives of geography relate to the study of religion, and on the kinds of insights that geography contributes to the broader understanding of religion as a component of culture. This discussion further presents a more extensive overview of the specific themes around which following chapters are organized.

Faith, Place, and Space

The relevance of the disciplinary interests of geography to the study of religion derives from a number of factors. In the most general terms, as an integrative discipline concerned with the interactions among diverse phenomena in particular places and across space, geography provides a useful conceptual context for examining religion as an integrative element of culture. As discussed earlier, religion's complex involvement with other cultural structures and systems is one of its crucial features. The worldview and ethos of a religion have important connections to the ways in which believers understand and interact with the natural and cultural environments that they inhabit. Conceptions of religious obligation have explicit ramifications for the lives of adherents, for example; but even beyond these mandated responsibilities, adherents seek a broader coherence between their religious faith and other areas of thought and action. As a result, religious concerns inform many different realms of human existence. The integrative perspective of geography is useful in examining the varied relationships between religion and other dimensions of believers' lives. Such relationships have indeed been a recurring focus of geographical research on religion, as exemplified in studies of topics as diverse as the role of Jewish migration and religious practices on the cultivation of citron, the effects of religious affiliation on residential segregation in Northern Ireland and Israel, the impact of religious ideology on Mennonite church architecture, the role of the temple in the reconstruction of cultural identity among Hindus in the United States, and the meanings of veiling among Muslim women in contemporary Istanbul.[26] Geography's emphasis on the interactions among diverse phenomena within their spatial settings thus reveals a disciplinary affinity with the study of religion in its broader cultural context.

The thematic concerns of geography also coincide with more specific issues central to the study of religion as an element of culture. In this regard, one basic issue is the spatial variability of religious belief and practice. This variability is immediately evident in maps depicting the distributions of the world's major religions, but it appears as well in the intrinsic localism of religions as they are lived and practiced by their adherents.[27] Again, despite their representation as universal truths transcending the particular, religious systems are interpreted and realized by adherents in specific local contexts. As a result, the contextuality of place pervades the religious dimensions of cultural experience. The role of context finds expression, for example, in the development of religions through processes of cultural innovation that are situated or positioned within particular settings, such as Islam in western Arabia or Buddhism in northern India and Nepal. More generally, as religions spread out of their original hearths, they are typically transformed by tensions between received traditions and local practices and exigencies. The result of those tensions, again, is a strong association between the ways in which believers realize a religious system and the circumstances in which they live, as seen in the modification of Islamic burial rituals among some Muslim immigrants in Berlin or in the development of distinctive pilgrimage practices among Roman Catholics in Ireland.[28] The mutability and multiformity of religion thus possess inherent geographical dimensions as expressions of contextuality, the cumulative products of place-based processes of cultural reproduction set in diverse contexts.

At the same time, these patterns of diversification raise important questions of scale, another key geographical concern. Local religious expressions do not develop in complete autonomy; they influence and are influenced by cultural processes organized at a variety of scales. The formation of new Protestant denominations in the United States, for example, has emerged through interactions among innovations within local

communities, the essential voluntarism of American religious life, the broader transformation of the institutional organization of Western Christianity resulting from the
Protestant Reformation, and the even broader effects of the extensive diffusion of
Christianity itself. Local religious expressions, in other words, reflect the interaction
within a particular place of processes operating across a range of scales.[29] The issue of
scale figures as well in the complex relationship between place and religious identity.
Adherents have often used their religious affiliation in constructing local identities,
but a sense of membership in a widely dispersed religion has also served to integrate
adherents into transnational or global cultural structures. The relationship between
scale and religious identity takes on particular significance within the context of contemporary processes of globalization.[30] Finally, the concept of scale has important
implications for the comparative study of religion by providing a means of linking the
particularity of local religious expressions to trends occurring at wider scales.

   Religious concerns with space and place represent a further connection between
the thematic concerns of geography and the study of religion. Such concerns take
many different forms, but they appear in all religious systems, reflections of the intrinsic spatiality of social processes and the importance of place as a repository of cultural
meaning. Religious belief often influences the social construction of space, for example. Muslim belief in the concept of purdah, or seclusion of women from strangers,
thus produced in various locations house plans or tent layouts containing restricted
areas for the use of female household members.[31] At a broader level, the Hindu caste
system has played a central role in patterns of residential segregation within Indian
towns and villages, creating caste enclaves and isolated clusters of untouchables that
are necessary to maintain accepted practices regarding ritual purity.[32] Fundamentalist
Christians in the United States have similarly created a network of social spaces, such
as schools, youth camps, resorts, and businesses, where they attempt to create a social
environment consistent with their religious beliefs.[33] At the broadest level, religion has
been a key factor in the social construction and interpretation of political territory, as
in the partition of British India into the independent states of India and Pakistan or
the conflicts between Israel and predominantly Muslim states in the Middle East.

   In addition to their diverse concerns with the construction of social spaces generally, religious systems place profound emphasis on the special sanctity of particular
spaces and places. Adherents of various religions recognize the existence of a "holy
land," an area sanctified by divine action or defining events in the religion's development. Similarly, a diversity of shrines, holy sites, and places of worship marks points
of access to a manifestation of the divine or interaction between the human and the
superhuman. Pilgrimage routes assign sacred significance to movements through
space, and the concept of a sacred direction, such as the *qibla*, which points Muslims
toward the Kaaba ("Cube") in Mecca, places the adherent within a sacred orientation
(photo 1.4). Finally, the many ways in which adherents relate their faith to the meanings and uses of space lead to the creation of distinctive religious landscapes comprising features that are explicitly sacred as well as secular landscape elements that reflect
the influence of religious belief.

   These various connections between the disciplinary concerns of geography and
the study of religion suggest the specific themes on which this work will focus. Four
interrelated themes provide the basic structure for subsequent chapters: (1) the spatial
dynamics of religious distributions; (2) the contextuality of religious belief and prac-

Photo 1.4. The Kaaba within the Great Mosque at Mecca. Mecca, Saudi Arabia, 2005.

Source: Hisham BinSuwaif (www.flickr.com/photos/4444/417596839/), under Creative Commons license (creativecommons.org/licenses/by-sa/2.0/).

tice; (3) religious territoriality in secular space; and (4) the meanings and uses of sacred space. Together, these themes represent the ways in which adherents ground their faith in diverse places and spaces. The first two address the geographical dimensions of religion "from the outside," so to speak, using a spatial frame of reference to identify significant features of religious systems, processes, and communities. The other two themes focus on religion "from the inside," examining the relationships between religious belief and practice and the ways in which adherents imagine, construct, and use space. This chapter concludes with a more detailed introduction to each of these four themes and some of the issues that they encompass.

Religious Distributions

The discussion of the first of these four themes, the spatial dynamics of religious distributions, addresses perhaps the most basic geographical questions regarding religious traditions: where they originated and why, and how their spatial distributions have changed over time. The first of these questions focuses on the nature of religious hearths, those places where religions first arose in response to key religious innovations. To its adherents, a religion's hearth may be understood simply as the setting for sacred events: the revelation of God's law to Moses on Mount Sinai, the building of the first Jewish temple in Jerusalem, the life and death of Jesus in Palestine, the revelation of the Quran to Muhammad in Mecca and Medina, the enlightenment of the Buddha at Bodh Gaya. Many animistic, tribal religions relate the emergence of their tradition with a mythic prehistory through which the larger cosmos, the world of humanity, and patterns of religious obligation became linked. From the preceding points of view, the location of the religion's hearth derives from divine providence or some other supernatural force. In considering a religion as a cultural system, however, the hearth has significance primarily as a setting for social and cultural change. More specifically, a religion's hearth provides the context for processes through which believers first integrate a particular set of revelations or traditions into a coherent religious system, and through which that system achieves acceptance by a critical mass of followers. Religious hearths thus comprise two components: the sacred component linked to superhuman intervention in the world; and the social component linked to organization of a practical religious system by a community of adherents. These components need not overlap, moreover. Jews, for example, have placed greater emphasis on Jerusalem as the social hearth of Judaism than on Mount Sinai, where the tradition's most defining supernatural event occurred. Finally, the most prominent hearths, including the examples just cited, are associated with the emergence of an entire religious tradition. Religious hearths can also be conceptualized, however, as the setting of the innovations of religious systems within existing traditions, such as the development of Hasidic sects within Judaism, Sufi orders within Islam, or Protestant denominations within Christianity. Within this text, such patterns will be covered under the second main theme, contextuality.

The other basic question addressed in relation to the dynamics of religious distributions focuses on processes of spatial change. As with other expressions of culture, the spatial distributions of religions are not fixed. They constantly change as adherents move from one place to another and as the number of adherents in different places expands or contracts. Religions differ, however, in terms of how and to what extent their distributions change over time. All religions have the potential to spread through migration. Migration, in fact, represents the primary form of diffusion for tribal and ethnic religious groups, in which adherence is typically determined by birth into the group. As a result, the spatial distributions of these religious groups have often been limited over time, particularly in comparison with proselytic religions, which also expand through conversion, as discussed below.

The impact of migration on religious distributions varies significantly across religious groups, reflecting their experiences in particular places. The distribution of Christianity expanded significantly during the first waves of voluntary European migration to colonial settings, for example. In contrast, the diffusion of African religions occurred quite differently under the constraints of forced migration during the period of slavery. The rise of syncretistic religions merging African and European sources in the Western Hemisphere thus represents an important expression of the distinct African American experience. The varying role of migration in the diffusion of religions also derives from the religious meanings that some adherents associate with the act of migration itself. A primary example of this pattern developed in extensive Jewish migration to Palestine, beginning in the late 1800s and early 1900s. Although many Jews viewed the creation of an independent Jewish state of Israel as a secular enterprise, others known as religious Zionists believed that this process reflected the divine redemption of the Jewish people. Their migration to Israel therefore became an important act of religious devotion. Conversely, for many adherents migration has provided a means of preserving their religious system in the face of persecution in their place of origin. Many religious Jews, in fact, migrated to Israel for this reason, but a wide variety of other groups have followed this pattern as well.

Conversion represents another crucial factor underlying spatial changes in the distributions of religious groups, particularly for the proselytic religious groups who define their membership as being open to all peoples. Like migration, processes of conversion can be quite varied. In some cases they are the intentional product of organized missions, through which the resources of a religious group are focused on acquiring new converts in particular locations. Through such processes, conversion may become linked to forces or structures organized at regional or global scales, from the Roman Catholic Church's Sacred Congregation for the Propagation of the Faith to the international broadcasting networks of Protestant evangelicals. Conversion processes also develop in less formal ways as well, such as through spontaneous contacts between believers and potential converts. The hegemony of one religious group over an area, through which elements of its religious practice become accepted and normalized across society, can also create significant informal pressures for individuals to convert. This practice became widespread during the medieval period of Muslim rule in northern India, for example. In addition to variations in their modes of conversion, moreover, the success of proselytic religions in acquiring converts has varied considerably from place to place. The effects of conversion processes are likely to be especially pronounced in places that have few existing religious institutions, such as the American frontier during the early 1800s, or among local populations alienated from the surrounding dominant culture, such as untouchables in India or the urban poor in many developing countries.

Finally, the spatial distributions of religious groups may be transformed through factors other than diffusion. The enormous catastrophe of the Holocaust, to cite a uniquely grievous example, drastically altered the spatial distribution of Judaism in the middle of the last century through the murder of millions of European Jews. In less extreme fashion, processes of secularization have also contributed to the contraction of religious distributions in certain contexts, especially in some of the more developed countries in recent years.

Context and Faith

The second major theme of this work focuses on the intrinsic contextuality of religious belief and practice. One key dimension of this contextuality is the localism that emerges within religions as they are lived by their adherents in particular places. Again, like other elements of culture, religions are created and reproduced most immediately through processes of interaction that are primarily local in scale, taking place within spatially concentrated communities of adherents. Through such processes, local communities generate distinctive expressions of belief and practice: reverence for a local saint or pilgrimage site, adoption of a distinct interpretation of an older tradition, or the merger of beliefs from spatially overlapping religious systems, to list only a few possibilities. The integrative nature of religion as an element of culture furthers its harmonization with the local facts of daily life, and thus adds to the distinctiveness of local religious forms. As a result, even religions that aspire to universality or that emphasize the continuity of tradition find diverse expressions in different contexts.

In some cases, distinctive patterns of belief and practice emerge through intentional attempts at change or innovation, although individuals may in fact characterize their efforts as a reassertion of authentic traditions. The rise of Wahhabism as a religious and political movement in the Najd region of central Arabia during the eighteenth century illustrates this pattern. Although the Wahhabis insisted on absolute adherence to tradition and the complete rejection of heterodox beliefs, their brand of orthodoxy itself has distinguished them from other Muslims. Intentional efforts to adapt patterns of belief and practice have also developed as believers have sought to reconcile their religious system to the specific circumstances in which they live. To cite one example, the observation by Shiite Muslims of *Ashura*, the commemoration of the martyrdom of Muhammad's grandson Husayn, traditionally included rituals in which participants shed blood through self-flagellation. Some Shiites living as religious minorities in Pakistan and North America have abandoned this practice because it could meet with disapproval from outsiders. In its place they have adopted blood donation as a means of observing Ashura.[34]

Perhaps more commonly, though, the relationships between religions and local contexts have developed less reflexively as communities of believers have lived their faith at the scale of everyday experience. Whatever their origin, local variations in belief and practice represent an intrinsic feature of religion and clearly reveal the importance of place in understanding religions as cultural systems. After local variants of a religious system become established, moreover, they become an integral part of the surrounding cultural context and consequently structure the further local reproduction of both religious and secular expressions of culture.

Another issue related to the contextuality of religious systems is the importance of processes of interaction that develop within such systems across different geographical scales. Although rooted in the scale of experience, religious systems in general cannot be fully understood as purely local phenomena. Religious systems that take on diverse local expressions can at the same time share common patterns of belief and practice that lie at the heart of a broader tradition, such as the Five Pillars of Islam or the Christian concept of Jesus as savior. Similarly, although believers practice their religion at the scale of their own lives, they frequently understand their faith in more expansive terms, as embracing diverse local manifestations within a single, larger system. As a result, adherents often identify quite strongly with a widespread, imagined community of fellow believers, a perspective that necessarily connects them with cultural networks and forces beyond their own immediate experience. To cite one example, the Islamic concepts of *Dar al-Islam* ("Realm of Islam") and the Muslim *umma* ("community") reflect belief in an underlying unity among all Muslims and the lands where they rule, even though the localization of Islamic practice has in fact created many different "Islamic worlds," not just one.[35] Processes of change within religious systems also develop at scales other than the local, as is clearly illustrated by the historical differentiation of Europe into regions dominated by Eastern Orthodoxy, Roman Catholicism, or Protestantism, or by the regional associations of the major branches of Buddhism. The local expressions of a religious system, in other words, actually reflect the intersection of cultural processes operating at many different scales, from the local through the regional to the global. In this regard, localism in religion reveals the fundamental connectedness of place.

Interactions among contexts defined at different scales have varied implications within religious systems. Such interactions are a central concern in understanding the nature and effects of the organizational structures established by religious groups, for example.[36] Some organizational structures emphasize local authority, as in the congregational polity of many Protestant denominations, and thus foster the development of religious variations among different communities of adherents. In other cases, authority resides in a centralized hierarchy, as in the Roman Catholic Church, resulting in a much stronger tension between theoretically universal doctrines and local practices. The relationship between local and global contexts will clearly develop differently within these two types of organizational structure, although in both local heterodoxy may lead to conflict. More broadly, local expressions of a religious system often derive in part from processes operating at wider scales. Thus the emergence of the Church of Sweden as a national church in the sixteenth century was closely tied to the local rise of Swedish national identity, but also grew out of the broader reorganization of Christianity in northern Europe brought about by the Reformation. Through interactions among processes organized at different scales, local religious expressions may also have considerable influence beyond the contexts in which they originate. The continual emergence of new Protestant denominations in the United States, for example, reflects the influences of voluntarism and denominationalism within the American religious environment, but it has also had disproportionate effects on other parts of the world through the evangelistic activity of many of these new denominations. The nature of such interactions is particularly significant in understanding why some local religious expressions prove to be more widely influential than others.

*　　*　　*

The two remaining themes around which subsequent chapters are organized address the relationships between religious systems and the meanings and uses of space. The concern with these relationships is based on the recognition that religious groups do not simply exist in space; they also imagine and construct space in terms related to their faith. Indeed, an understanding of the nature and meaning of space and the places within it represents a fundamental component of the worldviews of religious systems. Such understandings may be quite abstract, as in the Hindu conception of the world as a series of seven continents concentrically arranged around Mount Meru and vertically located between the worlds of the gods above and various underworlds below. The spaces and places given meaning within a religion's worldview may also be more immediate or tangible, as in the Jewish concept of *Eretz Yisrael*, the sacred Land of Israel granted to the Jewish people by divine covenant, or Muslim belief in the Kaaba, located within Mecca's Great Mosque, as the center of the world and site of the first shrine erected by Adam after his expulsion from paradise.[37] The ethos of a religious system, as a model for the realization of religious belief and practice, likewise serves as a source of social concepts, behaviors, and structures with intrinsically spatial dimensions. These dimensions derive from the inherent spatiality of society itself, within which religious observance occurs. The creation of the Jewish eruv described at the beginning of this chapter effectively illustrates the conceptual intersection of space, social behavior, and faith. Further examples of this intersection range from the self-imposed segregation of certain religious minorities like the Old Order Amish and ultra-Orthodox Jews to the territorial expansionism of Christian and Islamic missionary organizations. Conceptions of the meanings and uses of space take on a fundamental importance in religious systems, in sum, because those conceptions relate directly to believers' comprehension of the world and their place within it.

Religious conceptions of space typically distinguish between two domains: sacred space, whose primary characteristics are defined in explicitly religious terms by the people who recognize and use the space, either materially or symbolically; and secular space, whose primary characteristics are not essentially religious in nature.[38] This distinction does not imply that secular space has no religious implications. Indeed, because religious systems may be integrated into diverse realms of existence, many actions and motivations based on religious belief are expressed by adherents within the context of or in relation to secular space, although without necessarily imbuing the space itself with a special transcendence or sacred meaning. Religious belief and practice, in other words, interact with both sacred and secular space, but in different ways and for different reasons. Consequently, both domains are relevant in understanding how religious systems inform and are informed by the spatial imaginations of their adherents.

Secular Space

The third broad theme examined in this work thus focuses on secular space, and in particular on the many varieties of territoriality by which adherents control the meanings and uses of secular space in relation to their religious system. In this context, religious expressions of territoriality primarily serve to integrate religious belief and practice into the structures of daily existence, but such efforts take diverse forms across a range of different scales. Religious expressions of territoriality frequently involve constraints on the creation and use of secular space. Often such constraints develop informally out of accepted beliefs and practices, and apply only to adherents themselves. Adhering to the New Testament admonition that believers should be separate from the world, for example, the Old Order Amish have in general preserved their isolation from the mainstream of North America by limiting their spatial patterns of settlement to rural colonies.[39] At the same time, many constraints on the use of secular space derive from the observance of codified systems of religious law, such as the sharia of Islam or the halakhah of Judaism, which define specific norms of thought and behavior in various realms of daily life. In such cases, the religious control of local social space may be imposed on adherents and nonadherents alike, in some instances by means of formal institutions. The state-funded Committee to Promote Virtue and Prevent Vice in Saudi Arabia, for example, enforces various Islamic standards within the context of secular space, including required patterns of gender segregation and the closing of businesses during prayer observances.[40] Other types of hegemonic practices also place general constraints on the use of space, such as the so-called blue laws enacted in various parts of the United States to restrict business and entertainment on Sundays in recognition of the Christian Sabbath.

In addition to imposing constraints, religious expressions of territoriality may also seek to appropriate secular space for religious ends. Proposals early in this century to post the Ten Commandments in public classrooms and courtrooms in Kentucky, North Carolina, and other states represent attempts to reshape the meaning of public space in this manner. The appropriation of space can also serve as a form of resistance to hegemonic practices, for instance through religious protests in public spaces. To cite one example, ultra-Orthodox Jews in Jerusalem have repeatedly staged demonstrations on Bar-Ilan Street, a major thoroughfare located near the ultra-Orthodox neighborhood of Meah Shearim, to protest use of the road on the Sabbath by secular Jews, a practice which ultra-Orthodox Jews consider to be a violation of Jewish law.[41] Various forms of social activism, from the Prohibition movement to liberation theology, have focused as well on the transformation of social space according to religious principles. Another less controversial form of religious territoriality involves the institutional organization of space. Through this process religious bodies create spaces that, while religious in origin, serve important social functions as well. Again, the Upper West Side eruv exemplifies the institutional use of spatial structures to address both the social and religious needs of a community of adherents. Other examples of this process include Roman Catholic parishes and the various Islamic Centers created by Muslim immigrants to North America.[42]

The various examples of religious territoriality discussed so far have all related to the intermediate scale of local social space or the community of adherents. Religious expressions of territoriality appear at other scales as well. At the scale of the political state, conservative and fundamentalist Muslims in a number of countries have sought to impose an explicitly Islamic identity on the secular state, typically through the establishment of an Islamic constitution. In Saudi Arabia, again, the government in fact recognizes the Quran and the Sunna as the country's constitution. At an even wider scale, the New Testament commission to spread the Gospel to all nations has led to the expansive territoriality of Christian missionary activity. On the other hand, the constitution of gendered spaces within traditional Islamic house forms, and its role in the creation of gendered subcultures, illustrates control over the meaning and use of space at the scale of the home.[43] The public use of the veil by Muslim women as a means of defining and protecting personal space can similarly be understood as an expression of territoriality at the scale of the body.[44]

Moreover, religious expressions of territoriality at these vastly different scales constantly interact with one another to produce complex relationships between religion and space. Returning to the example of the veil, its use in public is legally mandated or strongly supported by tradition for women in many Islamic countries, but is effectively optional in others. In still other countries, such as France and Turkey, wearing the veil has been discouraged and even banned in certain circumstances, and so can become an act of personal or communal resistance.[45] In all of these places, moreover, wearing the veil is a public matter that becomes irrelevant within the private domain of the home. Use of the veil therefore has meaning at the scales of the body, the home, the state, and possibly others as well, all of which intersect in defining the social and religious significance of the practice. In more general terms, the preceding examples together illustrate the depth and variety of the relationships between religious systems and so-called secular space, and suggest some of the implications of those relationships for diverse issues of identity, power, and meaning.

Sacred Space

The last of the four major themes of this work addresses the meanings and uses of sacred space. Returning to the definition given earlier, sacred space is considered here as space understood in explicitly religious terms by the believers who recognize and use it. This definition may appear to be tautological as it explains the sacred in terms of the religious without differentiating between those two concepts. More precisely, then, sacred space can be defined, from the adherent's perspective, as space that bears a direct connection to the superhuman entity or entities postulated to exist within a religious system, or that is directly involved in the interactions between humanity and such entities. This definition may suggest that certain commonalities exist among conceptions of sacred space in different religious systems, and in fact the investigation of such commonalities has been an important theme in the traditional field of comparative religion.[46] More recently, postmodern critiques of comparative religion have faulted such attempts at generalization, arguing that they ignore the genuine differences that distinguish superficially similar phenomena from one another.[47] Some scholars have gone on to assert that the intrinsic contextuality of religion in fact invalidates the use of universal categories, like sacred space, in analyzing religious phenomena. Such particularistic assertions are themselves problematic, however, in that they neglect the usefulness of general concepts in understanding both the structural similarities that exist among elements of different religions and the specific expressions of those elements in particular settings.[48] Sacred space can be most effectively understood, then, not as the expression of some sort of universal archetype, but rather as a religious component of the spatial imaginations of believers that takes different forms in different contexts.

A central concern in considering the varieties of sacred space is the manner in which believers relate space to superhuman entities and their interactions with human beings. Adherents may define sacred space as the explicit domain of the superhuman, as exemplified by the ancient Greek belief in Mount Olympus as the home of the Olympian gods, the Hindu conception of temples as divine habitations, or the Roman Catholic and Eastern Orthodox use of the altar as space containing the real presence of Christ in the Eucharist (photo 1.5). Adherents may also understand sacred space as the setting for direct manifestations or revelations of superhuman actions or intentions, such as divine apparitions or miraculous healings. In this context, adherents may view sacred space as a repository of superhuman power. For the believer, this power may be expressed by the actual presence of the superhuman in some form, as in Jewish belief in the presence of God at Jerusalem's Western Wall or Hindu belief that the god Shiva resides on Mount Kailas in the Tibetan Himalayas. Sites associated with the miraculous often become important centers of pilgrimage, as they represent unique points of contact between the human and the superhuman. Locations of sacred relics often serve a similar function. The concept of Eretz Yisrael as the Promised Land of Jewish tradition represents a somewhat different expression of sacred space as a manifestation of divine intentions.

The designation of a site as sacred space may result as well from its association with events in the sacred history of a religious group. As a holy city, Medina draws its significance within Islam from its role in the creation of the first organized Islamic society, founded in 622 CE after Muhammad's migration there to escape persecution in Mecca. Finally, distinctive sacred spaces may be defined primarily through their ritual contexts. For example, traditional Jewish observance of Sukkot, the Festival of Booths, requires the construction of small huts or enclosures, patterned after those used by Jews following the biblical Exodus from Egypt, in which adherents eat and

Photo 1.5.   Altar of the Mission San Francisco de la Espada, founded by the Spanish in 1690. San Antonio, Texas, 2002.
Source: Author.

perhaps even sleep during the festival. In Iran, Shiite rites held during Ashura in commemoration of the martyrdom of Husayn often take place in buildings specifically dedicated to this purpose, known as *husayniyas*.[49]

A final issue raised in connection with this theme addresses the efforts of adherents to establish various forms of control over the meanings and uses of sacred space. A common objective of such control is to prevent the desecration or violation of sacred space. Adherents may thus be required to enact a ritual of purification before entering the space, as in the Muslim practice of performing ablutions before entering a mosque; or specific standards of dress and behavior may be enforced within the space, as in the traditional Roman Catholic requirement that women wear head coverings when inside a church, or in the insistence of Orthodox Jews that men and women pray in separate areas in front of the Western Wall. Desecration of sacred space may also be prevented by controlling access to it. The Islamic prohibition against non-Muslims entering the sacred cities of Mecca and Medina serves such a purpose, as does the Hindu practice of restricting the entry of non-Hindus into a temple or certain portions of it. Similarly, within Roman Catholic and Eastern Orthodox churches only the clergy have access to the sanctuary, the church's most sacred area.

The issue of control extends as well to efforts to define or reclaim the meaning of sacred space. Such efforts have been a major concern of indigenous peoples seeking to regain access to sacred sites in the wake of European colonization and settlement. Control of the meaning of sacred space is also a key factor in disputes involving the Temple Mount or *al-Haram al-Sharif* in Jerusalem, which Jews and Muslims both claim as a sacred site.[50] Indeed, efforts to define the meaning of sacred space have been a recurring source of conflict within and between religious groups, and between religious groups and secular forces. And finally, the control of sacred space represents an important form of resistance for adherents contesting religious authority. Within Roman Catholicism, for example, unauthorized shrines and pilgrimage sites serve as an important source of local, lay resistance to the centralized ecclesiastical hierarchy.[51] The 1979 assault on the Great Mosque in Mecca by Islamic fundamentalists opposed to Western influences in Saudi Arabia provides a more extreme example of resistance through the control of sacred space.[52]

*   *   *

Together, then, the four major themes outlined above address some of the key issues relating to the contextuality and spatiality of religions. They illustrate various uses of geographical concepts in understanding the complexity of religious activity as well as the importance of religious belief and practice in understanding the relationships between faith, place, and space. These four themes also reveal the relevance of geographical perspectives in the comparative study of religions, an endeavor that has been hindered by postmodern concerns with difference and particularity. While inherently sensitive to place, the geographical perspectives adopted here also focus on the integration of local contexts through processes organized at wider scales, avoiding the limitations of atomistic points of view. The remainder of this text thus considers each of these major themes in turn, examining in detail their implications both for specific religious systems and, in a comparative sense, for religion as a realm of cultural meaning, power, identity, and experience.[53]

Notes

1. The term *eruv* refers in general to an approved practice that solves difficulties posed by Sabbath restrictions. Several kinds of eruvin exist. The spatial eruv described here is the most common expression of this concept.

2. The rules for constructing an eruv are quite complex and involve many issues not mentioned here. See Simon D. Eider, *A Summary of Halachos of the Eruv* (Lakewood, N.J.: Rabbi Shimon D. Eider, 1982); Yosej Gavriel Bechhofer, *Eruvin in Modern Metropolitan Areas*, 2d ed. (Skokie, Ill.: Hebrew Theological College Press, 1995).

3. For an analysis of an eruv controversy in London, see Davina Cooper, *Governing Out of Order: Space, Law and the Politics of Belonging* (London: Rivers Oram Press, 1998), 123–42.

4. Jenna Weissman Joselit, *New York's Jewish Jews: The Orthodox Community in the Interwar Years* (Bloomington: Indiana University Press, 1990), 14–16.

5. Personal communication, Rabbi Adam Mintz (Senior Rabbi, Lincoln Square Synagogue), February 26, 2001; Randy Kennedy, "Synagogues Propose a Ritual Fence," *New York Times*, May 29, 1994, 5(13); Jennifer Kingson Bloom, "'Enclosing' a Neighborhood with a Symbolic String," *New York Times*, February 5, 1995, 8(13).

6. Pierre Deffontaines, *Géographie et Religions* (Paris: Gallimard, 1948); David E. Sopher, *Geography of Religions* (Englewood Cliffs, N.J.: Prentice-Hall, 1967).

7. See *Geographies of Religions and Belief Systems*, gorabs.org/journal/index.htm (accessed June 25, 2007).

8. For an extensive review of this literature, see Chris C. Park, *Sacred Worlds: An Introduction to Geography and Religion* (London: Routledge, 1994).

9. Lily Kong, "Mapping 'New' Geographies of Religion: Politics and Poetics in Modernity," *Progress in Human Geography* 25, no. 2 (2001): 211–34; Catherine Brace, Adrian R. Bailey, and David C. Harvey, "Religion, Place and Space: A Framework for Investigating Historical Geographies of Religious Identities and Communities," *Progress in Human Geography* 30, no. 1 (2006): 28–43; cf. Yi-Fu Tuan, "Humanistic Geography," *Annals of the Association of American Geographers* 66 (1976): 271; Roger Stump, "The Geography of Religion: Introduction," *Journal of Cultural Geography* 7 (1986): 1–3.

10. For a cogent analysis of major theoretical interpretations of religion from diverse disciplines, see Daniel L. Pals, *Seven Theories of Religion* (New York: Oxford University Press, 1996); for useful summaries of different disciplinary approaches to the study of religion, see entries by field of study in Lindsay Jones, ed., *Encyclopedia of Religion*, 2d ed., 15 vols. (Detroit: Macmillan Reference USA, 2005).

11. Cf. Peter Jackson, *Maps of Meaning: An Introduction to Cultural Geography* (London: Unwin Hyman, 1989); Don Mitchell, *Cultural Geography: A Critical Introduction* (Oxford: Blackwell Publishers, 2000); David Atkinson et al., eds., *Cultural Geography: A Critical Dictionary of Key Concepts* (New York: Palgrave Macmillan, 2005).

12. Linda McDowell, "The Transformation of Cultural Geography," in *Human Geography: Society, Space, and Social Science*, ed. Derek Gregory, Ron Martin, and Graham Smith (Minneapolis: University of Minnesota Press, 1994), 146–73; Peter Jackson, *Maps of Meaning*, 171–86; William Norton, *Cultural Geography: Themes, Concepts, Analyses* (New York: Oxford University Press, 2000), 1–26

13. The most influential discussion of this approach to religion appears in Clifford Geertz, "Religion as a Cultural System," in his *Interpretation of Cultures: Selected Essays* (New York: Basic Books: 1973), 87–125; also see E. Thomas Lawson and Robert N. McCauley, *Rethinking Religion: Connecting Cognition and Culture* (Cambridge: Cambridge University Press, 1990). The terms *adherents* and *believers* are used interchangeably throughout this work to denote people who observe or practice a religious system of belief.

14. This widely used definition of religion is most clearly articulated in Melford E. Spiro, "Religion: Problems of Definition and Explanation," in *Anthropological Approaches to the Study of Religion*, ed. Michael Banton (London: Tavistock Publications, 1966), 85–126.

15. Pals, *Seven Theories of Religion*, 269–71; Jonathan Z. Smith, "A Matter of Class: Taxonomies of Religion," *Harvard Theological Review* 89, no. 4 (October 1996): 387–403; Rodney Stark and William Sims Bainbridge, *A Theory of Religion* (New York: Peter Lang, 1987), 39–40. Note that the definition given here is not universally accepted, and that the definition of religion remains a contentious issue; see, for example, Thomas Idinopulos and Brian C. Wilson, eds., *What is Religion? Origins, Definitions, and Explanations* (Leiden: Brill, 1998). Because of its non-theistic character, Theravada Buddhism is often cited as a recognized religion that does not fit a definition that refers to the superhuman. Even while recognizing the Buddha as a man, however, Theravada Buddhism does attribute characteristics to him that can be interpreted as superhuman in relation to ordinary experience (photo 1.1). For both sides of this argument, see Marco Orru and Amy Wang, "Durkheim, Religion, and Buddhism," *Journal for the Scientific Study of Religion* 31 (1992): 47–61; William Herbrechtsmeier, "Buddhism and the Definition of Religion: One More Time," *Journal for the Scientific Study of Religion* 32 (1993): 1–18.

16. Cf. Clifford Geertz, "Ethos, World View, and the Analysis of Sacred Symbols," in his *Interpretation of Cultures: Selected Essays*, 126–41. In defining the worldview and ethos as the core of a religious system, Geertz does not focus specifically on conceptions of the superhuman. He instead refers to religion as a source of comprehensive ideas of the order of reality, self, and society. Nonetheless, in slightly modified form, the concepts of worldview and ethos provide a useful means of interpreting essential religious beliefs within the definition of religion adopted here. For recent discussions supporting Geertz's approach, see Gregory R. Peterson, "Religion as Orienting Worldview," *Zygon* 36, no. 1 (March 2001): 5–19; Kevin Schilbrack, "Religion, Models of, and Reality: Are We Through with Geertz?" *Journal of the American Academy of Religion* 73, no. 2 (June 2005): 429–52.

17. See the many examples in Deffontaines, *Géographie et Religions*; Sopher, *Geography of Religions*; and Park, *Sacred Worlds*.

18. McDowell, "The Transformation of Cultural Geography," 148; Jackson, *Maps of Meaning*, 2; Marvin Harris, *Theories of Culture in Postmodern Times* (Walnut Creek, Cal.: AltaMira Press, 1999), 25–29.

19. Max Charlesworth, "Universal and Local Elements in Religion," in his *Religious Inventions: Four Essays* (Cambridge: Cambridge University Press, 1997), 81–104; Tracey Skelton and Tim Allen, "Culture and Global Change: An Introduction," in *Culture and Global Change*, ed. Tracey Skelton and Tim Allen (New York: Routledge, 1999), 2–4.

20. John L. Esposito, *Islam: The Straight Path* (New York: Oxford University Press, 1998), 76–77.

21. Jackson, *Maps of Meaning*, 180.

22. Roger W. Stump, "Pluralism in the American Place-Name Cover: Ethnic Variations in Catholic Church Names," *North American Culture* 2 (1986): 126–40; Ellen Badone, ed., *Religious Orthodoxy and Popular Faith in European Society* (Princeton, N.J.: Princeton University Press, 1990).

23. Helen Watson, "Women and the Veil: Personal Responses to Global Process," in *Islam, Globalization and Postmodernity*, ed. Akbar S. Ahmed (London: Routledge, 1994), 141–59.

24. Sopher, *Geography of Religions*, 56–58.

25. Roger W. Stump, *Boundaries of Faith: Geographical Perspectives on Religious Fundamentalism* (Lanham, Md.: Rowman and Littlefield, 2000), 85–156.

26. Eric Isaac, "The Citron in the Mediterranean: A Study in Religious Influences," *Economic Geography* 35 (January 1959), 71–78; F. W. Boal, "Territoriality on the Shankill-Falls Divide, Belfast," *Irish Geography* 6 (1969): 30–50; Sara Hershkowitz, "Residential Segregation by Religion: A Conceptual Framework," *Tijdschrift voor Economische en Sociale Geografie* 78 (1987): 44–52; Charles A. Heatwole, "Sectarian Ideology and Church Architecture," *Geographical Review* 79 (1989): 63–78; Surinder M. Bhardwaj and Madhusudana N. Rao, "The Temple as a Symbol of Hindu Identity in America?" *Journal of Cultural Geography* 17 (Spring/Summer 1998): 125–43; Anna J. Secor, "The Veil and Urban Space in Istanbul: Women's Dress, Mobility and Islamic Knowledge," *Gender, Place, and Culture* 9, no. 1 (March 2002): 5–22.

27. Charlesworth, "Universal and Local Elements in Religion," 81–82; McDowell, "The Transformation of Cultural Geography," 156.

28. Gerdian Jonker, "The Knife's Edge: Muslim Burial in the Diaspora," *Mortality* 1, no. 1 (March 1996): 27–43; Mary Lee Nolan, "Irish Pilgrimage: The Different Tradition," *Annals of the Association of American Geographers* 73, no. 3 (September 1983): 421–38.

29. This view of localism in religion corresponds to the broader concept of place as an expression of interactions among processes organized at wide scales, as discussed in Doreen Massey, "Power-Geometry and a Progressive Sense of Place," in *Mapping the Futures: Local Cultures, Global Change*, ed. Jon Bird et al. (London: Routledge, 1993), 59–69.

30. McDowell, "The Transformation of Cultural Geography," 165–68.

31. Amos Rapoport, *House Form and Culture* (Englewood Cliffs, N.J.: Prentice-Hall, 1969), 65–66.

32. J. Delvert, "Aspects Géographiques du Système des Castes en République Indienne," *L'Information Géographique* 45 (1981): 5–13.

33. Stump, *Boundaries of Faith*, 189–93.

34. Vernon James Schubel, "Karbala as Sacred Space among North American Shi'a," in *Making Muslim Space in North America and Europe*, ed. Barbara Daly Metcalf (Berkeley: University of California Press, 1996), 186–203.

35. Cf. V. S. Naipaul, *Among the Believers: An Islamic Journey* (New York: Vintage Books, 1982); V. S. Naipaul, *Beyond Belief: Islamic Excursions among the Converted Peoples* (New York: Vintage Books, 1998).

36. Sopher, *Geography of Religions*, 55–72.

37. A detailed explication of the concept of Eretz Yisrael appears in Gwyn Rowley, "The Land of Israel: A Reconstructionist Approach," in *The Impact of Gush Emunim: Politics and Settlement in the West Bank*, ed. David Newman (London: Croon Helm, 1985), 125–36.

38. In describing that which is not sacred, I prefer *secular* to *profane* because the former term is more neutral. The term *profane*, in addition to describing the non-sacred, can be used in a pejorative sense to denote that which actively desecrates the sacred. The non-sacred spaces of everyday life do not intrinsically oppose the sacred, however. As argued here, they may in fact serve important religious functions. A distinction between the sacred and the secular may thus be somewhat artificial since the two intersect with one another extensively, as discussed in Kong, "Mapping 'New' Geographies of Religion," 212–15.

39. William K. Crowley, "Old Order Amish Settlement: Diffusion and Growth," *Annals of the Association of American Geographers* 68 (June 1978): 249–64.

40. U.S. Congress, House, Committee on International Relations, and Senate, Committee on Foreign Relations, *Annual Report, International Religious Freedom, 1999*, 386.

41. Stump, *Boundaries of Faith*, 179.

42. On the role of Islamic Centers, see Yvonne Yazbeck Haddad and Jane Idleman Smith, eds., *Muslim Communities in North America* (Albany: State University of New York Press, 1994).

43. Regula Burckhardt Qureshi, "Transcending Space: Recitation and Community among South Asian Muslims in Canada," in *Making Muslim Space in North America and Europe*, ed. Metcalf, 46–64; Shahrbanou Tadjbakhsh, "Between Lenin and Allah: Women and Ideology in Tajikstan," in *Women in Muslim Societies: Diversity within Unity*, ed. Herbert L. Bodman and Nayereh Tohidi (Boulder, Colo.: Lynne Rienner Publishers, 1998), 180.

44. Claire Dwyer, "Veiled Meanings: Young British Muslim Women and the Negotiation of Differences," *Gender, Place, and Culture* 6 (March 1999): 5–26.

45. Secor, "The Veil and Urban Space in Istanbul," 10–11; Elaine Sciolino and Helene Fouquet, "French Muslims Protest Rule Against Scarves," *New York Times*, January 18, 2004, 10; Banu Gökariksel and Katharyne Mitchell, "Veiling, Secularism, and the Neoliberal Subject: National Narratives and Supranational Desires in Turkey and France," *Global Networks* 5, no. 2 (April 2005): 147–65.

46. A classic inquiry into such commonalities appears in the chapter on sacred space in Mircea Eliade, *The Sacred and the Profane* (New York: Harcourt Brace & Company, 1959), 20–65.

47. Jonathan Z. Smith, *Imagining Religion: From Babylon to Jonestown* (Chicago: University of Chicago Press, 1982), 19–35; Kimberly C. Patton and Benjamin C. Ray, eds., *A Magic Still Dwells: Comparative Religion in the Postmodern Age* (Berkeley: University of California Press, 2000).

48. A useful discussion of these issues in relation to the concept of pilgrimage appears in Simon Coleman and John Elsner, *Pilgrimage: Past and Present in the World Religions* (Cambridge, Mass.: Harvard University Press, 1995), 196–213.

49. Masoud Kheirabadi, *Iranian Cities: Formation and Development* (Austin: University of Texas Press, 1991), 74–75.

50. Stump, *Boundaries of Faith*, 159–66.

51. Carolyn V. Prorok, "Becoming a Place of Pilgrimage: An Eliadean Interpretation of the Miracle at Ambridge, Pennsylvania," in *Sacred Places, Sacred Spaces: The Geography of Pilgrimages*, ed. Robert H. Stoddard and Alan Morinis (Baton Rouge: Geoscience Publications, Dept. of Geography and Anthropology, Louisiana State University, 1997), 117–39.

52. Stump, *Boundaries of Faith*, 173–74.

53. Clifford Geertz, "'The Pinch of Destiny': Religion as Experience, Meaning, Identity, Power," *Raritan* 18 (Winter 1999): 1–19.

CHAPTER 2

The Spatial Dynamics of Religious Distributions

The spatial distributions of religious systems represent an essential concern in the geographical study of religion. At the most rudimentary level, religious distributions provide insights into basic spatial variations in cultural patterns (map 2.1). The contrasting prevalence of Christianity along the northern shore of the Mediterranean Sea and of Islam along the southern shore, for example, reveals a principal dimension of the cultural differences that separate the two regions. The transition from Hindu predominance south of the Himalayas to Buddhist predominance in the Tibetan Plateau to the north similarly indicates the presence of a significant cultural divide between these adjacent areas. At a different scale, the traditional contrast in Western Europe between a largely Protestant region in the north and a largely Roman Catholic region in the south comprises a major factor in the geographical differentiation of European cultures. Viewed simply as a set of locational facts, then, the spatial distributions of religious systems serve as useful indicators of cultural similarities and differences among diverse places.

The distributions of religions are not merely isolated empirical facts, however. At a more meaningful level, they are also manifestations of complex spatial and cultural processes. Contrasting patterns of religious adherence north and south of the Mediterranean, in areas that had both been part of the Roman Empire, thus reflect the social and cultural changes that transformed the Mediterranean world as Christianity and Islam diffused at different times out of their Middle Eastern hearths. The Himalayan boundary separating areas dominated by Hinduism and Buddhism likewise represents the outcome of a long sequence of religious developments in that part of the world. This sequence includes the ancient rise of Vedic religion in northern India, the eventual emergence of both classical Hinduism and Buddhism within this religious context, the gradual spread of Buddhism throughout much of the Indian subcontinent, and its later decline there as Hinduism underwent a period of revitalization. Along similar lines, the relative strength of Roman Catholicism and Protestantism in different areas of Western Europe is in part a product of the varied effects of the Protestant Reformation on the once-unified domain of Western Christianity. As articulations of underlying cultural processes, in other words, the spatial distributions of religious systems provide evidence of crucial patterns of cause and effect arising from interactions between particular religions and places. In this sense, such distributions possess an intrinsic dynamism, continually transforming and being transformed by the diverse contexts that they encompass.

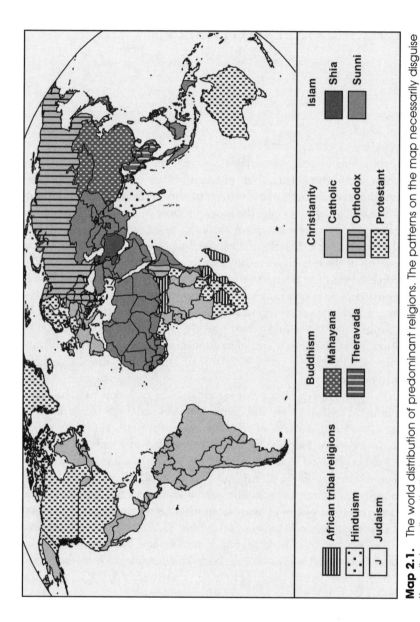

Map 2.1. The world distribution of predominant religions. The patterns on the map necessarily disguise the religious diversity that exists in many parts of the world. In some locations, moreover, popular practice incorporates both the predominant faith and other religious traditions, as in the cases of Buddhism and local folk religions in much of East Asia, of Buddhism and Shinto in Japan, of Catholicism and African traditions in the Caribbean and Brazil, and of tribal religions with various forms of Christianity in sub-Saharan Africa.

This chapter examines key expressions of that dynamism as a means of interpreting the broader significance of the spatial distributions of religious systems. Because many readily available sources have delineated the descriptive details of the distributions of specific religious groups at various scales, such particulars are not surveyed systematically here.[1] Instead, the discussion focuses on the processes of cultural change associated with the spatial distributions of religions. This chapter specifically addresses three general processes that shape the actual configuration of a religion's distribution over time. First, the development of a religion's distribution originates in the local cultural patterns through which places develop into religious hearths, which provide a setting for the emergence of a significant religious innovation or an effective reinterpretation of older traditions. Second, the distributions of many religions are shaped by processes of diffusion through which religious systems subsequently spread to diverse locations, through the migration of adherents as well as the conversion of new believers by formal missionary activity or everyday contacts with existing adherents. The spatial contraction of distributions, reflecting decline in the number of followers over time, represents a third general process that has affected the distributions of many religions.

As elements of the spatial dynamics of religious distributions, the processes addressed in this chapter have diverse effects both on the cultural development of religions and on the characteristics of specific places. The rise of a religious hearth in a particular place, for example, transforms the nature of the place itself, but it also impresses characteristics of the place on the new religion. Similarly, the spread of a religion through migration or conversion strongly influences the character of the regions and places involved. In sum, the continual changes that occur within religious distributions manifest the vital connections among religions, places, and patterns of cultural change. These processes thus reveal the basic cultural significance of the spatial configurations of religions, providing an important foundation for subsequent chapters.

Religious Hearths

As elements of culture, religions originate through processes of articulation and interpretation set in specific geographical hearths. Similar processes are involved in the more commonplace adaptation of existing religious systems to local circumstances, but the inception of a new religious tradition or system involves a more substantial departure from earlier beliefs and practices.[2] The number of distinct religions formed throughout human history is undoubtedly quite large, but most have been short-lived or confined to their places of origin. Of greater interest from a geographical perspective are those religions that have been successfully perpetuated and disseminated by their adherents, thus achieving influence at a wider scale. In such instances, the religious hearth takes on particular significance as the geographical source of the religion's subsequent spatial distribution, and at the same time provides insights into the religion's cultural vitality, its active and persistent expression by believers.

Religious hearths acquire their distinct identity through two stages.[3] The first involves the occurrence of initiating events that provide the basis for the articulation of new beliefs and practices or the extensive reinterpretation of existing ones. These initiating events typically focus on some form of superhuman intervention in the world but they take varied forms. They may develop quite abruptly in response to revelations or divine manifestations associated with specific individuals. The initiating events in Christianity, Islam, and other "revealed" religions follow this pattern, for example. In other cases, initiating events may develop through more gradual processes of cultural change, as in classical Hinduism's emergence through the coalescence of various traditions in the Indian subcontinent. For preliterate animistic groups, a religion's origins may relate to a mythic past associated, for example, with the group's story of creation. A religion's initiating events, it should be noted, are subject to quite different interpretations by adherents and "objective" outsiders. From the adherent's perspective, the initiating events of Islam began with the revelation of the Quran to Muhammad by the angel Jibril (or the archangel Gabriel), which is perceived as a natural, actual event. A rationalist account of the origins of Islam, on the other hand, by applying a different ontological perspective, might interpret Muhammad's revelatory experiences in psychological or political terms without acknowledging the involvement of superhuman agency. The conflicts between such divergent interpretations need not be resolved, however, to recognize the subsequent importance of Muhammad's revelatory experiences to the emergence of Islam. Whether it is literally true or not, the narrative of a religion's initiating events contains tremendous power for believers as a source of meanings.

Such meanings become the focus of the second stage in the development of a religious hearth as its founders begin to integrate their understanding of initiating events into a coherent system. In "revealed" religions this process may again develop rapidly, although usually not without some disagreements among early followers regarding specific matters of belief and practice, nor without later modifications to the system. In other religions, the integration of beliefs and practices into a coherent system may develop over a much longer time span, and the system's early adherents may be a less sharply defined group. As the central features of the new religion become more clearly defined, moreover, its continued vitality as a cultural expression depends on its acceptance by a critical mass of followers. Adoption of the religion by a broader community of adherents in fact represents the culminating step in the formation of a religious hearth, through which both the community and the hearth acquire distinctive religious identities. Again, adherents and outsiders may interpret this process of acceptance in different ways. Adherents may view acceptance of the new religion as the result of a divinely inspired conversion or as a natural consequence of the recognition of self-evident truths. Within the social sciences, on the other hand, religious adherence has generally been interpreted in terms of its material, psychological, or social benefits. From the latter perspective, prevailing social and cultural conditions are major factors in understanding believers' acceptance of a religious system. The survival of a new religion beyond its initiating events therefore depends in part on attributes of the hearth where it has originated. Geographical contexts characterized by broader patterns of cultural change are especially likely to sustain the consolidation of new religions.

Religious hearths differ, of course, in terms of the nature of the religious developments that they foster. In this regard, a crucial distinction exists between primary religious hearths, which support the emergence of radical innovations leading to the formation of a new religious tradition, and secondary religious hearths, which support conflictual processes resulting in schisms within existing traditions.[4] A primary hearth provides a setting for revolutionary change, where processes of innovation lead to the formation of a distinct religious tradition that differs in fundamental ways from existing traditions. Again, the emergent tradition may take shape very rapidly, within a single generation, or it may coalesce over a longer time span. In either case, the new tradition essentially comprises a set of basic religious givens that are synthesized by earlier adherents and then passed down in a more integrated form to later followers. It may have roots in an older tradition, as in the relationship between Christianity and Judaism or between Buddhism and Hinduism, but the new tradition deviates sufficiently from its precursor to develop a unique identity. The uniqueness of the new tradition derives from its innovative worldview and ethos, which incorporate a distinctive understanding of the superhuman and its relations with humanity. In literate societies, these conceptions are typically codified in a body of sacred texts. The core beliefs of the tradition also find expression in new ritual forms, patterns of social organization, and religious landscapes. In religiously pluralistic contexts, the new tradition contributes as well to a shared sense of identity among adherents.

A tradition that emerges in a primary hearth may subsequently engender any number of related religious systems as adherents living in different contexts continually reinterpret its beliefs. Early Christianity of the apostolic period, for example, subsequently evolved into various distinct systems in different contexts, including Roman Catholicism, Eastern Orthodoxy, and the various Protestant churches. Each of these religious systems also developed much internal variety in relation to particular contexts. Such divisions within a larger tradition originate in secondary hearths, where contextually based schismatic processes lead to the development of a new religious system within an existing tradition. The new system in some instances involves revisions to the worldview and ethos of its root tradition, and its adherents may create innovative ritual forms, organizational structures, and sacred writings. In other instances, schisms may develop as adherents reject modernizing tendencies and seek a return to more authentic beliefs and practices associated with the past. Secondary hearths, in other words, may accommodate either reformist or reactionary patterns of religious change. In either case, the newly defined system retains the most basic givens of the tradition from which it emerged and its adherents still consider themselves part of that tradition. The religious identities of believers become more complex, however, combining membership in a broader tradition with a more limited sense of adherence to the new religious system.

In addition to defining contexts for processes of religious change, primary and secondary hearths are both transformed by the consequences of those processes. The revolutionary changes associated with primary hearths generally have the most extensive effects, particularly in hearths dominated by followers of the new tradition, because they involve basic transformations in adherents' understanding of the nature of reality, agency, and authority. The Hejaz, that region of the Arabian Peninsula containing both Mecca and Medina, thus served as the setting for Islam's initial development but at the same time was transformed by that process into an area of great religious significance. The reformist and reactionary trends associated with secondary hearths may be less comprehensive in their effects, but they too may lead to a significant restructuring of broader social and cultural patterns within their hearth. The rise of Islam's Wahhabi movement in central Arabia, for example, played a key role in that area's political unification and led to the adoption there of stricter standards of Islamic orthodoxy. In sum, religious hearths of both varieties represent crucial intersections between the dynamic characteristics of religions and places.

In addressing the topic of religious hearths, this chapter focuses in particular on those of the primary variety, leaving the discussion of specific secondary hearths to chapter 3 as an expression of contextuality. Primary religious hearths have emerged in a great many places throughout human history as diverse culture groups have articulated distinctive religious traditions. At the global scale, however, a few of these hearths are especially significant because of the temporal persistence or extensive diffusion of the religions associated with them. These hearths represent the focus of the first part of this chapter. Two areas of the world in particular stand out as locations for such hearths: an Indic region located across the northern part of the Indian subcontinent, containing the hearths of Vedism, Hinduism, Buddhism, Jainism, and Sikhism; and a Semitic region located in southwestern Asia, containing the hearths of Judaism, Christianity, and Islam (map 2.2).[5] In both of these regions, diverse cultural processes contributed to a series of related religious developments over many centuries, from the beginnings of early Judaism and Vedism over three thousand years ago to the more recent emergence of Islam in the early seventh century CE and Sikhism in the early sixteenth century CE. In the process, both regions developed a number of primary hearths, each of which was associated with the origins of an enduring religious tradition.

These hearths differed from one another in terms of their defining characteristics, but their sequence of development reveals important relationships between early and later hearths in each of the two broader regions. The early hearths associated with Vedism and Judaism represented contexts for the gradual consolidation of religious elements into the common tradition of a people. Although these processes of consoli-

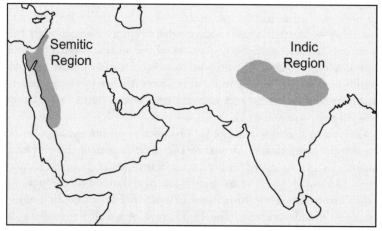

Map 2.2. The Indic and Semitic religious hearths. The Indic hearth gave rise to Vedism, Hinduism, Buddhism, Jainism, and Sikhism. The Semitic hearth gave rise to Proto-Judaism, Judaism, Christianity, and Islam.

dation developed over a long period of time, their results were nonetheless revolutionary in their articulation of distinctive religious beliefs, such as the concept of a divine covenant with the Israelites in the Judaic tradition or the complex concept of *brahman*, the sacred utterance that invokes superhuman power or the universal source of all power, in Vedism. At the same time, through their long processes of consolidation these early traditions became widely incorporated into patterns of cultural life within their hearths, a trend that contributed significantly to their persistence over time. As a result, the early primary hearths are strongly associated with the rise of enduring ethnic religions.

In contrast, the later primary hearths associated with Christianity, Islam, Buddhism, Jainism, and Sikhism developed far more rapidly, in response to the revelations or experiences of particular founding figures. The new religions that emerged in these hearths represented radical reinterpretations or extensions of existing ethnic religions. These new religions therefore had important connections to older traditions, but at the same time marked significant departures from prevailing patterns of more incremental religious change. An especially important component of the innovations associated with later hearths was the adoption of universalizing perspectives, which at least in theory made the new tradition accessible beyond the culture group in which it originated. The rapid articulation of these new traditions also brought about more immediate patterns of cultural and social change within the hearths where they developed. Thus, in both the Indic and Semitic regions, an early period characterized by the relatively gradual consolidation of ethnic religious traditions was later followed by more dynamic periods of religious transformation. In this sense, the specific primary hearths that emerged at different times can be seen as elements of more extended temporal processes through which related traditions developed within each region.

The Indic Region

The earliest identifiable stage in the emergence of enduring religious traditions in the Indic region appears to have developed in the ancient civilization that flourished in the Indus Valley between 2600 and 1600 BCE. Little is known about the details of Indus religion, but archaeological evidence suggests that it included elements later found in Hinduism. Scholars have often interpreted a three-faced or three-horned male figure depicted on Indus stamp-seals as a prototype of the Hindu god Shiva, for example. The presence of lingam stones at Indus sites also suggests the early worship of Shiva, whose primary symbol as a god of generative power is the phallic lingam. Similarly, the discovery of large numbers of small clay female figurines may be indicative of popular worship of a mother goddess, a practice that became an important focus of later Hindu devotion in the veneration of Shakti, the female expression of divinity, in her various manifestations. Validation of these suppositions will depend, however, on the definitive deciphering of the Indus script.[6] In any case, despite its possible connections to later developments within Hinduism, Indus culture underwent a significant period of decline around 1600 BCE, apparently as a result of catastrophic seismic events in the region.

Vedism

Around 1500 BCE, a second stage in the development of Indic religions appeared as Aryan nomads began to move from the west into the Indus Valley and across the Punjab. Some scholars have argued that Aryan influence in the Indus Valley is actually much older, and that the Indus civilization itself was the source of many elements of Indo-Aryan culture.[7] Whether that was the case or not, the expansion of Indo-Aryan settlement across northwestern and northern India produced a vital culture hearth after 1500 BCE, establishing a cultural environment that ultimately gave rise to the Sanskrit language and provided a context for enduring religious developments. The most important of these developments was the origin of the Vedas ("Books of Knowledge"), four collections of Sanskrit hymns and mantras that contain the core beliefs of Indo-Aryan religion, or Vedism, and that continue to serve as the ultimate foundation of Hindu belief and, less directly, as a major influence on other religions originating in this region.[8]

According to Vedism, the sacred knowledge of the Vedas was eternal and divinely revealed, and thus articulation of the Vedas represented an essential initiating event within this tradition. The hymns collected in the Vedas refer to a pantheon of nature gods who in many respects resemble deities associated with other early Indo-European traditions. The most important of these gods were Varuna, a sky god who maintained universal justice; Indra, the god of thunder and war, and benefactor of humanity; and Agni, the god of fire, who presided over the Vedic rituals. The practice of Vedism focused specifically on the rite of sacrifice, which was designed to celebrate or propitiate the gods as a means of maintaining cosmic order and gaining divine favor. The contents of the *Rig-veda*, *Sama-veda*, and *Yajur-veda*, the three original collections, were used by three different groups of priests involved in the public fire sacrifice, Vedism's key ritual. The *Atharva-veda* included mantras and incantations used in domestic rituals that were later incorporated into the fire sacrifice as well. Compilation of the *Rig-veda*, the earliest and most important of the Vedas, may have begun as early as 1500 BCE, but based on the hymns' geographical references, this process clearly originated after the Indo-Aryans had settled in the Punjab region.[9] Compilation of the other Vedas followed, ending around 1000 BCE with completion of the *Atharva-veda*. The Vedas were transmitted through oral traditions until around 600 BCE, when they began to be written out in Sanskrit.

The progressive integration of the oral traditions of Vedism took place over several centuries as Indo-Aryan culture flourished under relatively stable conditions in northern India. By the end of the second millennium BCE, the Indo-Aryans had spread across the Gangetic plain, assimilating various non-Aryan groups in the process, but they encountered no major challenges to their cultural dominance. As a result, Indo-Aryan religion continued to evolve into more orthodox forms within this broader hearth. As the primary focus of Vedism, the rite of sacrifice gradually developed increasing significance.[10] Instead of serving simply as a celebration or propitiation of the gods, the fire sacrifice came to be understood as an expression of power through which priests could compel the gods to act and through which the cosmos was maintained. In this sense, the power inherent in the ritual surpassed that of the gods themselves. Such power was represented in the concept of brahman, a term that came to signify the power itself, the sacred utterance used to invoke it, and the priest who recited such utterances. This reinterpretation of the sacrifice increased the status of the Vedic priests within Indo-Aryan society but also demanded of them a greater degree of ritual precision. The number of priests required for the rite of sacrifice therefore increased from three to four, with the additional *Brahmin* priest overseeing the entire ritual and preserving its integrity through the use of mantras from the *Atharva-veda*. The need for precision in performance of the rite of sacrifice also led to the development between 1000 BCE and 600 BCE of a new body of sacred texts, the *Brahmanas*, which explicated in detail the ritual elements associated with each of the four Vedas.

By the early centuries of the first millennium BCE, then, Vedism had become a highly formalized religious system, centered on the esoteric ritual power of the priesthood. At the same time, however, various trends began to emerge that challenged the power and wealth of the priests and the extreme formalism of their rituals. These trends were associated in particular with the cultural context of the eastern Gangetic plain, far from the original Indo-Aryan hearth of Vedism.[11] This region thus became the primary hearth for a number of new religious traditions. It provided a likely setting for religious innovation in part because of the strong presence of non-Aryan influences, which intersected with Vedic beliefs to produce new religious forms. In addition, the developing urban and political structures of Gangetic kingdoms early in the first millennium BCE fostered resistance among other social classes to the power of the Vedic priests. The ruling *Kshatriya* or warrior class in particular opposed the social and cultural dominance of the priests. The initial challenge in this hearth area to prevailing Vedic practices appeared in the early Upanishads, the culminating texts of Vedism composed between 800 BCE and 500 BCE. The Upanishads contain the teaching of various Vedic sages, mainly of the Kshatriya class, who had withdrawn from society to increase their religious understanding. The term *Upanishad*, usually interpreted as meaning "to sit close by," referred to the position of students in relation to the teachers imparting wisdom to them. During the sixth century BCE, more radical challenges to the Vedic past also appeared in the form of Jainism and Buddhism. These two traditions maintained some beliefs associated with later Vedism and Hinduism, but they rejected the sacredness of the four Vedas and each developed its own distinct worldview and ethos.

The Upanishads developed as commentaries on the Vedas, but they represented an important departure from earlier concerns with the Vedic gods and the practice of sacrifice. They focused instead on philosophical questions concerning the nature of reality and the self. In addressing these issues, the authors of the Upanishads retained the esoteric character of Vedism but introduced a number of insights. One of the most important of these insights was the reinterpretation of the concept of brahman, which in the Upanishads came to signify the essence of reality that pervades all of creation. Closely related to this new concept of *Brahman* was the idea of atman, the individual, eternal self that within every being is identical to Brahman.[12] The Upanishads further articulated the belief that this eternal self experiences a continual cycle of reincarnation based on the law of karma, which asserted that all past actions would have future effects. According to this belief, reincarnation in a new life would inevitably lead to suffering, and thus the goal of existence was to achieve *moksha*, or liberation, from the cycle of death and rebirth, after which the individual self would lose its identity in becoming one with Brahman. Significantly, the Upanishads did not focus on the rite of sacrifice as a means of achieving this ultimate goal. Rather, they asserted that moksha could be attained through individual understanding of Brahman and that such understanding could be achieved through ascetic and meditative disciplines, essentially internalizing the meanings of the older sacrificial rites. Thus, while they represent the culminating Vedic texts, the early Upanishads diverged in important ways from older beliefs and practices. By rejecting the ritualism of the sacrifice, the Upanishads weakened the influence of the Vedic priests as mediators of religious meaning and power. In place of the immediate but transient benefits of the sacrifice, the Upanishads focused on a more transcendent objective. Some of the innovations of the Upanishads may in fact have been rooted in non-Aryan beliefs, but they quickly became part of the broader Indic religious tradition. Indeed, the concepts of reincarnation, karma, and moksha, as well as the use of meditation rather than sacrifice to achieve knowledge, later became core ideas in Hinduism as it emerged as a religion distinct from Vedism.

Widespread acceptance of concepts articulated in the Upanishads helped to sustain the cultural revolt against Vedic ritualism in the middle of the first millennium BCE. Nonetheless, the esoteric knowledge of the Upanishads, particularly as it related to the attainment of moksha, was fully accessible only to the initiated few and thus did not provide a popular alternative to older religious forms, which survived in diverse folk expressions. During the sixth and fifth centuries BCE, moreover, northern India flourished as a hearth area for less esoteric forms of religious speculation and innovation. Most new religious movements devised during this period did not last, but two developed into enduring traditions: Jainism and Buddhism.[13] From their inception, these new religions shared certain characteristics related to conditions in their eastern Gangetic hearth. Reflecting conflicts between the Kshatriya and Brahmin castes, both religions rejected the authority of the Vedic priesthood, the Vedic emphasis on ritual sacrifice, and the formal class system of Indo-Aryan society. Indeed, the founders of both came from ruling Kshatriya families. Both religions also denied the divine revelation of the Vedas. They retained widely held beliefs regarding karma and reincarnation, with modifications, but rejected many other concepts from the Upanishads. Finally, in place of Vedic esotericism they offered a more direct, exoteric approach that in theory provided any believer with the means to progress toward and attain spiritual liberation. In a cultural sense, both religions thus represented responses to popular religious concerns and through their success in this regard both thrived in the eastern Gangetic region.

Jainism

Jainism developed from the insights of Vardhamana, born in the sixth century BCE, who sought liberation through strict ascetic practices. After attaining this goal, he became recognized by his disciples as a *Jina* ("Spiritual Victor") who had mastered and eliminated his own karma, and from that term his followers became known as Jains. Vardhamana himself became known as *Mahavira* ("Great Hero"), and was considered the last of twenty-four *tirthankaras* ("ford-makers"), great teachers who had crossed over the waters of existence and revealed a path for others to follow. In the worldview of Jainism, all objects were considered to have a soul that experienced the process of reincarnation as influenced by karma. Jainism produced a distinctive interpretation of karma, however, identifying it as a material substance that accumulates on the soul as a result of various kinds of actions. To be free of the cycle of rebirth, the soul must stop the process of karmic accretion and existing karma must be destroyed. The elimination of karma can only be achieved through a heroic asceticism, involving celibacy, mental discipline, physical inaction, ahimsa or nonviolence toward all living things, and the surrender of all possessions, including clothing and shelter. Suicide by starvation in a position of complete stillness represented an ideal death. Once free of karma, according to Jain belief, the purified soul would achieve an eternal state of bliss.

The extreme asceticism adopted by Jain holy men in the effort to destroy karma was beyond the abilities of most believers, however. Lay followers could nonetheless make progress toward purification in a subsequent lifetime by adopting a Jain ethos, for example by practicing ahimsa, avoiding the pursuit of pleasure, and providing support for the Jain ascetics who had withdrawn from worldly life. To avoid killing other living beings, Jains abandoned agriculture for occupations more compatible with their ethos, such as commerce. The Jain worldview rejected the concept of a divine creator of the universe, but as the practice of Jainism developed, it came to include the worship of various deities, including the tirthankaras and many lesser gods. Ultimately the austerity of Jainism prevented it from acquiring a vast following, but it did diffuse widely throughout the Indian subcontinent. An important early center of Jainism developed in the ancient city of Mathura in northern India, and somewhat later a significant following developed in western India.

Buddhism

Buddhism arose within the same general context as Jainism, but the two religions differed in significant ways. The initiating events of Buddhism focused on the life of Siddhartha Gautama, the son of a Kshatriya ruler born in the fifth or sixth century BCE (map 2.3). He also sought a solution to the suffering inherent in human existence. According to Buddhist tradition, this pursuit was inspired by Siddhartha's first exposure to the earthly effects of old age, illness, and death, realities from which he had been protected during a sheltered childhood. He looked for answers concerning the issue of suffering within existing religious systems, including those based on ascetic practices, but found none of them satisfactory. Then, seated under the *Bodhi* ("Enlightenment") tree, through profound meditation he came to see that the source of suffering was the endless cycle of rebirth, which was driven by the karmic effects of human desire and ignorance. Suffering could thus be ended by eliminating desire and ignorance; and this process would in turn require the realization that the individual self is illusory, merely an artifact of actions and desires tied to worldly existence. The Buddhist worldview thus denied the existence of an eternal soul underlying the self, in contrast to both Jainism and the Upanishads. The process of rebirth, in the Buddhist worldview, involved a continuity of identity without the presence of a discrete soul; and release from the cycle of rebirth could be achieved only by extinguishing the false sense of self that fostered desire and ignorance. The resulting enlightenment would occasion the attainment of nirvana, the true reality, an eternal and unitary state of absolute, immutable calm.

Siddhartha, having reached this stage, became the Buddha ("Enlightened One"), marking the central event in the founding of Buddhism. He then began teach-

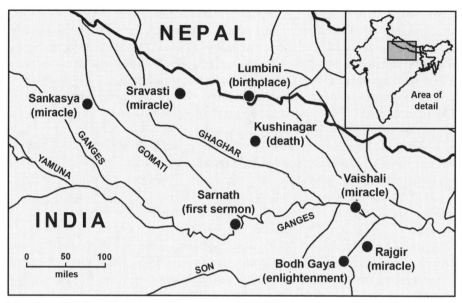

Map 2.3.   The hearth of Buddhism, based on locations associated with key events in the life of Gautama Buddha and with the major miracles attributed to him. These locations continue to be important pilgrimage sites for Buddhists. The four major miracles associated with the sites depicted here include the Buddha's creation of multiple representations of himself (the "Twin" miracle), at Sravasti; his descent from heaven after a period of retreat there, at Sankasya; his taming of a drunken elephant sent by his enemies to kill him, at Rajgir; and the offering of a bowl of honey to the Buddha by a band of monkeys, at Vaishali.

ing others about the way to enlightenment, expressed as the Four Noble Truths: that life is transient and full of suffering; that desire is the cause of suffering; that suffering ceases with the end of desire; and that the end of desire can be achieved through specific principles of thought and action. The Buddha's message rejected both the extreme asceticism of Jainism and the ritual punctiliousness of Vedism, instead describing a "Middle Way" based on mental discipline and ethical behavior. The goal of this process was to achieve the status of the *arahant* (Pali, "one who is worthy," also *arhat* in Sanskrit), one who has attained nirvana and will not be reborn. This Middle Way to salvation attracted a growing body of disciples who formed the original Buddhist monastic community, or *sangha*, which followed the Buddha in his wanderings across the Gangetic plain as he spread his message. The growth of the sangha marked the beginning of the second stage in the development of Buddhism's hearth.

Following the Buddha's death, members of the sangha maintained a strong sense of communal identity. A significant lay following began to emerge as well in northern India around Buddhism's original hearth, attracted by the accessibility of the moderate approach to belief and practice supported by the new tradition. The sangha also began to compile the Buddha's teachings to ensure their preservation, at first through oral recitation and memorization, and much later in written form. According to Buddhist tradition, a council of 500 monks composed these sacred texts in oral form shortly after the Buddha's death around 400 BCE, although modern scholarship questions the existence of such a council. During the next several centuries, however, the varied reproduction of this oral Buddhist tradition caused divisions to develop within the sangha over particular matters of faith. These schisms in turn led to the advent of a number of distinct schools and sects within Buddhism, discussed in chapter 3. Nonetheless, Buddhism continued to spread out of its Gangetic hearth, first across northern India and then more broadly throughout the subcontinent. A key event in the latter process was the conversion of the emperor Asoka of the Mauryan dynasty in the third century BCE. Asoka had played a major role in the expansion of the Mauryan Empire across much of India, but in remorse for the devastation he had caused in the process, he converted to Buddhism and helped to spread the religion across his empire. By the beginning of the Common Era, Buddhism had thus become one of the dominant religions of the Indian subcontinent.

Hinduism

Together, the rise of Jainism, Buddhism, and the innovations associated with the Upanishads significantly weakened the dominance of Vedic ritualism as a form of religious expression. The Vedic tradition itself persisted but in increasingly different forms as it underwent various local reinterpretations and absorbed external influences. The accumulation of such changes over time marked the beginnings of Hinduism. The term *Hinduism*, as used here, refers not to a single, discrete religion but rather to a whole constellation of related and overlapping religious systems rooted in Vedism.[14] The various systems that comprise Hinduism share some important features, but they do not constitute a uniform set of beliefs and practices. Hinduism thus emerged through processes very different from those involved in the articulation of Buddhism and Jainism. Hinduism did not spring suddenly from the insights of an individual founder, nor did its early followers possess self-conscious identity as members of a distinct religious movement. Instead, Hinduism developed gradually as believers in different places adopted various means of reconciling received Vedic traditions, such as belief in the sacredness of the Vedas or the authority of the Brahmin class, with local cultural practices and broader currents of religious change. Contributions to the development of Hinduism tended to be incremental rather than revolutionary. Moreover, Hinduism did not have a clearly defined local hearth. Its appearance took place throughout the subcontinent, from the middle of the first millennium BCE well into the Common Era. Hinduism as a result maintained the character of an ethnic religious tradition, but based on a diffuse sense of identity.

Despite its internal diversity, a number of common threads ran through Hinduism, reflections of the cultural context in which it emerged. Perhaps the most important was the doctrine that the Vedas and other early texts were divinely revealed, a belief that persisted even after the Vedas no longer served as the immediate focus of Hindu worship. Other beliefs and practices deviated from older sacrificial traditions, however, and in the process contributed substantially to the popularization of Hinduism. Again, the concepts of reincarnation, karma, and moksha articulated in the Upanishads became central to the worldview of emergent Hinduism. So too did the practice of yoga, in various forms, as a means of achieving liberation from the law of karma through mental discipline. Yoga may have existed as far back as the time of the Indus Valley civilization, but within a Vedic context its first detailed portrayal appeared in the late Upanishads, composed between 500 BCE and 200 BCE. The practice of yoga focused on establishing mental control over the body as a means of attaining higher states of consciousness and, ultimately, of eliminating the distinction between the self and Brahman, the absolute, undifferentiated reality. Yoga thus offered a path to liberation similar to that of Buddhist meditation but in a manner consistent with the worldview of the Upanishads. Over time the practice of yoga also incorporated a significant theistic dimension focusing on contemplation of the divine.

Within Hinduism, the law of karma also had important social implications, particularly in its relationship to the traditional caste system of Vedism, which had been rejected by Buddhism and Jainism (table 2.1). First articulated in the *Rig-veda*, this social structure originally comprised a hierarchy of four classes, or *varnas*: Brahmins (priests), Kshatriyas (rulers and warriors), *Vaishyas* (commoners), and a non-Aryan class of *Shudras* (serfs). Later, the hierarchy incorporated a fifth category of outcastes or untouchables. This system grew more elaborate as members of different varnas intermarried and as new culture groups were absorbed into Indo-Aryan society, and ultimately each varna became subdivided into numerous hereditary, endogamous castes, typically differentiated by occupation. The caste system did not become fully articulated until later in the first millennium CE. Its connections to the emerging

Table 2.1.   Varnas of the Vedic Caste System

Varna	Occupation	Status	Ethos
Brahmin	priests, scholars	Aryan, twice born[1]	learning guidance of others harmony kindness purity simplicity
Kshatriya	warriors, rulers	Aryan, twice born	courage power protection of others generosity justice nobility
Vaishya	merchants, artisans, farmers, herders	Aryan, twice born	productivity ethical treatment of others social responsibility
Shudra	serfs, servants	non-Aryan, once born	servitude obedience loyalty
Outcastes or Dalits[2]	spiritually polluted laborers	non-Aryan, once born	servitude in pollution

1. "Twice born" refers to a spiritual second birth achieved through a ritual initiation into the Vedic religion upon reaching adulthood. The initiate may then study the Vedas and conduct Vedic rituals, and may achieve final enlightenment in that lifetime.

2. The original Vedic system did not include outcastes, who technically have no varna. Outcastes, now generally known as Dalits ("Oppressed"), did not become a recognized category until the last half of the first millennium BCE.

Hindu tradition had been established much earlier, however, through the idea of dharma, which signified the proper duties, responsibilities, laws, or behaviors that adherents ought to observe. According to the law of karma, actions in past lives determined one's present station in life, including caste affiliation, and that station should therefore be accepted as fitting and just. Part of that acceptance involved fulfilling the dharma associated with one's current station. Fulfillment of the dharma into which one was born would in turn bring karmic benefits and rebirth into a higher station in the next lifetime. The *Dharmashastras*, explications of religious law compiled between 200 BCE and 400 CE, provided specific instructions concerning the various obligations associated with one's caste and stage of life. The concept of dharma thus integrated beliefs concerning karma and reincarnation into the social structure of the Indo-Aryan varnas, and in so doing reconciled the teachings of the Upanishads with older traditions. The exoteric nature of the observance of dharma also contributed significantly to the popular practice of Hinduism, establishing a connection to routine social life that Buddhism, Jainism, and late Vedism lacked. Moreover, the emerging Hindu interpretation of dharma and karma, by acknowledging the intrinsic diversity of society, legitimized in religious terms the ongoing incorporation of new tribal and regional groups into the Hindu tradition. Through its accommodation of diversity, this perspective helped to expand the cultural scope of Hinduism as an ethnic tradition.

Another important motif that ran through emergent Hinduism was the formation of new theistic traditions. In the early Upanishads, the conception of Brahman as the indescribable unity of reality diminished the significance of the Vedic gods. These texts did on occasion personalize Brahman in abstract terms, but not to the extent of identifying it as a deity. The later Upanishads supported a somewhat different worldview, however, in which Brahman became personalized as the anthropomorphic god Rudra, later identified as Shiva. The believer could achieve salvation, then, through meditative practices that focused on knowledge of and unity with this supreme, personal God as the manifestation of Brahman. This development significantly restructured older beliefs, in part by elevating Rudra, a minor Vedic storm god probably of non-Aryan origin, to a position of supremacy. The theistic approach to salvation detailed in the later Upanishads accorded well with the popular, exoteric worship of various gods, however, and over time became integrated into folk practice.

In the process, the specific focus of meditation on the divine expanded to include any god, not just Rudra, as in Hindu belief all gods were seen as expressions of the ineffable Brahman. Hinduism's theistic turn thus contributed to its widening ethnic scope because it ultimately allowed diverse groups to maintain folk devotion to local or regional deities within the broader context of a Hindu worldview. Because meditation on the divine had as its goal the visualization of a god's physical form, emergent Hinduism also incorporated a strong iconic dimension, possibly with pre-Aryan roots, that had not existed in Vedism. The great epics of Hinduism, the *Mahabharata* and *Ramayana*, compiled during the transition from Vedism to Hinduism, reinforced the developing theistic orientation, particularly with regard to the gods Vishnu, his avatars Krishna and Rama, and Shiva. The Puranas, collections of ancient narratives set down in written form starting around 200 CE to 300 CE, further advanced the theistic tradition, detailing the nature of Vishnu, Shiva, Brahma, the divine manifestations of Shakti, and other figures in the Hindu pantheon.[15] Two key features of Hinduism subsequently emerged from this growing focus on the divine:

the concept of bhakti, devotion to a particular deity; and the practice of *puja*, ceremonial worship based on bhakti (photo 2.1).

Over a period of two millennia, then, a series of religious hearths developed within the Indian subcontinent. Each of these hearths represented a context for local or regional processes of cultural change through which adherents established and reproduced distinctive patterns of religious belief and practice. The various hearths differed in their cultural dynamics, however, developing in three discernible phases. The earliest phase, associated with the hearth of Vedism, was defined by two key processes: the convergence of Aryan nomadic herders and surviving elements of the ancient Indus civilization, and the subsequent dominance of the Indus Valley and the Gangetic plain by an increasingly structured and settled Indo-Aryan society. These processes supported the gradual consolidation of older religious practices into a clearly defined system articulated in the oral traditions of Vedism and dominated by the Brahmin class. As the dominant Indo-Aryan society produced more complex social and political structures, reactions against the established Brahmin orthodoxy developed, particularly among the Kshatriya class. The resulting tensions produced the second phase in the development of the Indic region's religious hearths, centered in the eastern Gangetic plain. There, religious change unfolded in a more systematic fashion, through radical, philosophical reinterpretations of the existing Vedic tradition in the

Photo 2.1. Puja at the Kamakhya Temple in Assam state, India. Kamakhya is an aspect of Shakti and this temple ranks among the most important centers devoted to worship of the goddess. By tradition the temple marks one of the locations where portions of the body of Sati, Shiva's first consort and a manifestation of Shakti, fell to earth after being cut to pieces by Vishnu as a means of stopping the dance of destruction performed by Shiva while carrying Sati's corpse. In Hindu belief, Kamakhya specifically marks the location where Sati's sex organs fell to earth. Guwahati, India, 2006.

Upanishads and the development of distinct alternatives to Vedism in Buddhism and Jainism. These challenges to tradition, and Buddhism in particular, gained popularity over the next several centuries. At the same time, Indo-Aryan society continued to spread throughout the subcontinent, absorbing various local and regional cultural influences. These trends eventually led to a third phase of religious change defined by renewed processes of consolidation as a result of which the authority of Vedic tradition persisted but within the more diverse, exoteric context of emerging Hinduism. The hearth of Hinduism was geographically diffuse, however, reflecting its incorporation of local practices rooted in many different places.

Sikhism

The inclusive character of Hinduism as a religious tradition allowed for its expression in diverse forms, and as a result numerous secondary hearths developed within the broader Hindu tradition, as discussed in the following chapter. This flexibility in belief and practice was also a key feature of the cultural context within which the primary hearth of Sikhism emerged during the early sixteenth century CE. This hearth developed in the Punjab region several centuries after a significant Islamic presence had been established there through various Muslim conquests. Sikhism grew out of the encounter between Hinduism and Islam within this area. Its name derives from the Punjabi word *sikh*, meaning disciple. Its founder, the guru Nanak, was born a Hindu but also had frequent contact with local Muslim society, and was educated in Arabic and Persian as well as Sanskrit. According to Sikh tradition, at around the age of thirty Nanak had a profound religious experience and embarked on a lengthy spiritual journey that took him throughout the Indian subcontinent, north into Central Asia, and as far west as Mecca and Medina. After twenty years he returned to the Punjab and established a community of disciples at Kartarpur ("City of God") on the Ravi River. Guru Nanak's teachings retained Hindu beliefs concerning the law of karma and the goal of attaining salvation from the cycle of rebirth, but at the same time insisted upon a radical monotheism similar to that of Islam. Nanak also rejected the significance of the caste system. Instead, he proposed that all believers had equal access to the means of salvation, which could be reached, with the assistance of divine grace, through correct actions and meditation on the name of the one God. Correct actions did not imply asceticism, but rather ethical conduct within worldly social life. Although the egalitarian message of Sikhism attracted Hindu and Muslim followers from both urban and rural backgrounds, it appealed most strongly to the peasant classes of the Punjab. Because of this class association, along with the well-established hegemony of Islam, Buddhism, or Hinduism in surrounding regions, Sikhism did not spread significantly out of its hearth during its early history, but became an important cultural and political force within the Punjab.

The Semitic Region

As in the Indic region, the origins of the enduring religious systems associated with the Semitic region can be traced back to the integration of a key ethnic religious tradition. That tradition's earliest expressions, characterized here as Proto-Judaism, evolved over many centuries before giving rise circa the fifth century BCE to the beginnings of Judaism proper, which itself was not fully articulated until roughly the third century CE.[16] The gradual development of the Judaic tradition thus took place in a number of hearths as its adherents responded to changing circumstances through processes of religious innovation, interpretation, conflict, and consolidation.

Proto-Judaism

The initial hearth of Proto-Judaism likely developed during the second millennium BCE in an area located south and east of the Dead Sea, within the ancient regions of Moab, Edom, and Midian.[17] Within this hearth, nomadic proto-Israelites practiced a religious system focused on the worship of a national god identified as YHWH. This religion incorporated a set of beliefs concerning the earlier Hebrew people believed to have once inhabited Canaan to the north. The identity of the Hebrews remains unclear, but according to Judaic tradition they represented the descendants of Abraham, who was directed by God to settle in Canaan. There, as recounted in the biblical Book of Genesis, God made a covenant with Abraham, promising Canaan to his descendants. This covenant was reaffirmed with Isaac and Jacob (whom God renamed Israel). Proto-Judaism also drew on a second set of beliefs regarding the sacred history of the Israelites, the descendants of Jacob, as recounted in the Books of Genesis and Exodus: their enslavement and persecution in Egypt; their exodus and divine redemption as Moses led them out of Egypt into Sinai; and the revelation of divine law to Moses, reaffirming the Israelites' covenant with God (map 2.4). The historical sequence of these events as presented in the Torah is uncertain, and the biblical narra-

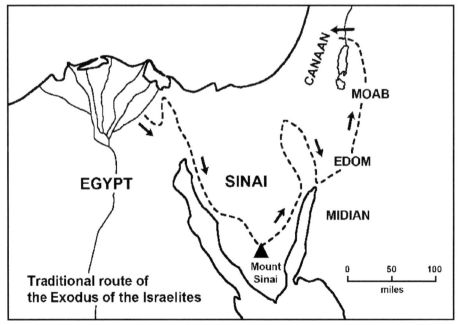

Map 2.4. The conventionally accepted route of the Exodus of the Israelites from Egypt in the second millennium BCE. By tradition, the area covered by this route represents the hearth of Proto-Judaism.

tive may represent a complex fusion of independent stories and legends.[18] Regardless, these mythic events defined the religious system that evidently prevailed among the proto-Israelites after arriving in their early hearth. Their worldview thus centered on belief in their covenant with YHWH, while their ethos focused on adherence to divine law.

Proto-Judaism became more fully integrated after the Israelites came to dominate a more significant hearth in Canaan. The Torah relates that process of domination to military conquest, but archaeological evidence suggests that it developed more gradually toward the end of the second millennium BCE, through patterns of migration and settlement. Such patterns focused primarily on the region's central highlands, where the Israelites likely settled in sparsely populated areas, adopting sedentary ways of life after first entering the region as nomadic pastoralists. After settling in Canaan, the Israelites formed a largely self-sufficient system of tribal societies whose common religion became the basis for a nascent sense of group solidarity. As settlement in the region expanded, the Israelites also absorbed other culture groups in the area, including indigenous Canaanites. Elements of Canaanite religion, such as the worship of local deities, thus persisted in the highlands alongside the religious system of Proto-Judaism. Nonetheless, the Israelites produced a common sense of identity that differentiated them from the older Canaanite society that persisted in nearby lowlands.[19]

The growing sense of cultural unity among the Israelite tribes, their conflicts with other groups, and their increasing agricultural specialization and social complexity ultimately gave rise to more formal political structures within their Canaan hearth, which in turn established the context for the culmination of Proto-Judaism's development. The first Israelite kingdom appeared in the eleventh century BCE, founded by Saul, but it was his successor David who unified the tribes of Israel within a single kingdom. During his reign, commonly dated from 1005 BCE to 970 BCE, David extended the kingdom's influence and established Jerusalem as its capital. Solomon, who ruled until around 930 BCE, furthered the centralization of religious practice by building the Jerusalem Temple, which became the primary ritual focus of Proto-Judaism as the center of sacrifice and the repository of the Ark of the Covenant (map 2.5).[20]

Later in the tenth century BCE, the Israelite kingdom divided into two parts: Israel in the north and Judah in the south. As the less isolated of the two, Israel first became a vassal state of Assyria and in the eighth century BCE was assimilated into the Assyrian empire. The dispersed indigenous population of Israel subsequently became identified as the "lost tribes" of Israel. Judah, on the other hand, remained somewhat isolated but intact; and its continued survival maintained its importance as the geographical focus of Proto-Judaism. Up to this time, despite the warnings of various prophets, worship of YHWH in Israel and Judah had existed alongside other Canaanite religious practices, including fertility rites, ancestral cults, and the worship of other gods. Starting around the end of the eighth century BCE, however, a reform movement emerged in Judah that stressed the worship of YHWH exclusively. Religious critics of Israel's heterodoxy, who fled to Judah after the northern kingdom's destruction, likely contributed to this process.[21] The Judahite emphasis on reform developed most fully during the reign of Josiah, toward the end of the seventh century BCE. Josiah initiated a reconstruction of the Jerusalem Temple, which purportedly led to the discovery of a book describing the divine code of law. Most scholars now iden-

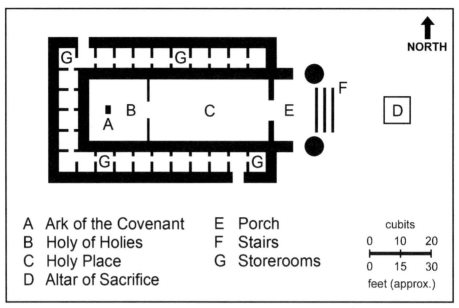

↑ NORTH

A Ark of the Covenant   E Porch
B Holy of Holies   F Stairs
C Holy Place   G Storerooms
D Altar of Sacrifice

cubits
0   10   20
0   15   30
feet (approx.)

Map 2.5. Reconstructed plan of the Temple of Solomon, the spatial center of Jewish practice erected in Jerusalem near the beginning of the first millennium BCE. Adapted from J. D. Douglas, ed., *The New Bible Dictionary* (Grand Rapids, Mich.: Wm. B. Eerdmans, 1962), 1243.

tify that text as an early form of the Book of Deuteronomy, most likely composed in the seventh century BCE and reflecting a distinct Judahite perspective. The book also articulated some of the principal beliefs that would inform Judaism proper as it emerged in the fifth century BCE. Most importantly, it systematized many existing beliefs and practices, including a monotheistic worldview and strict adherence to the terms of the covenant with YHWH, including a detailed code of social and personal ethics. It also defined the Jerusalem Temple as the sole legitimate center of worship, a departure from some earlier biblical sources; and it established Jerusalem as the setting for national ritual observances such as Passover. Based on the book's contents, Josiah instituted a campaign of religious orthodoxy in Judah, expelling idolatrous practices and foreign cults from the Jerusalem Temple, eliminating local shrines and altars, and allowing the rite of sacrifice only at the Temple.

Judah soon found itself in conflict with neighboring empires, however, and at the start of the sixth century BCE it was conquered by the Babylonians, who demolished Jerusalem and its temple and deported most of the city's upper classes to Mesopotamia. These events effectively destroyed the ritual center of Proto-Judaism. The worship of YHWH as articulated during Josiah's reign nonetheless survived, in somewhat altered form, within the context of the Babylonian exile as the Judahite aristocracy and priesthood assiduously maintained their religious identity and traditions. As they enacted and reproduced these traditions, however, they recast them to conform to their social and cultural circumstances in Mesopotamia; and in doing so, they initiated the cultural process through which Judaism later emerged out of Proto-Judaism. For example, they began to interpret YHWH as the universal God rather than as a national deity, and they adopted worship practices focusing on prayer, sermons, and the reading of scripture as a substitute for the Temple sacrifice. The first synagogues may have been established at this time to accommodate such practices. The exiles also began to interpret the divine covenant in more personal, ethical terms.

Judaism

Judaism proper did not become fully articulated, however, until after the Persian emperor Cyrus ended the Judahites' exile in 537 BCE. Some Judahites in fact remained in Mesopotamia at this time, while others returned to the vicinity of Jerusalem. This region was now a province of the Persian Empire, known by its Aramaic name of Yehud; and its inhabitants became the Yehudim, or Jews. Within Yehud, an influential Jewish elite arose among the repatriated exiles, loyal to the Persian Empire but committed to reestablishing the religious traditions that they had preserved in Mesopotamia. Over the next two centuries, the Jewish society in Yehud produced a revitalized but transformed religious system and Yehud became the hearth of Judaism as distinct from Proto-Judaism. A defining event of this period was the reconstruction of the Jewish Temple in Jerusalem, which initiated the so-called Second Temple era.

This revitalization of the Judaic tradition focused on three broad themes: the increasing decentralization of public worship, a renewed emphasis on the observance of divine law, and a greater concern with the ethnic exclusivity of the Jews as the chosen people. The decentralization of worship developed despite the repatriated Jews' rebuilding of the Jerusalem Temple upon their return. Based on their experiences in exile, they practiced synagogue worship as a legitimate alternative to the Temple, focusing on prayer and scriptural study rather than on the older ritual sacrifice. The term *synagogue* did not in fact become widely used until the first century CE, but archaeological evidence of such structures dates to the third century BCE, and synagogues probably originated much earlier than that. In any event, synagogues became increasingly common during the Second Temple era, particularly as the number of Jews living in Mesopotamia and other distant regions increased, and the Temple did not regain its central position in Jewish religious life.

A stronger emphasis on the observance of divine law also developed during this period, derived in part from Josiah's earlier reforms but reflecting conditions in Yehud as well, including the influence of the religious elite and continuing political uncertainties. The emphasis on orthopraxy was associated in turn with increasing reliance on the written law as expressed in the Torah. A scriptural tradition had already existed within Proto-Judaism, possibly as far back as the tenth century BCE. Following the Babylonian exile, however, scripture became the essential focus of Judaism. Starting in the fifth or sixth century BCE, priests in Jerusalem thus began to collate and expand upon the texts and narratives handed down by their predecessors. In the process, according to most scholars, they produced the Torah in its currently known form, drawing on earlier sources but reshaping them as the sacred history of the Jewish people from the perspective of post-exilic Yehud.[22] The Jewish Bible also came to include other scriptures, including those associated with the prophets and various speculative, poetic, and historical writings; but the Torah, containing the five books of Moses, remained the core revelation. As the Jews became increasingly dispersed in succeeding centuries, the Torah provided a means of preserving the integrity of Judaism in diverse locations.

Finally, along with the preceding trends, Judaism in the Second Temple era developed an increased emphasis on the ethnic exclusivity of the Jewish community. Injunctions against marriage outside the group had been a part of the Proto-Judaic tradition but had not been rigorously followed. Repatriated exiles in Yehud apparently found, moreover, that intermarriage had been widely practiced by Judahites who had not been exiled. Jewish leaders thus insisted on strict endogamy within the Jewish community, both to adhere to divine law and to preserve the identity of the Jews as a covenanted people. As a result, marriage outside the group became less common. Adherence to a more exclusive sense of communal identity also contributed to the survival of Judaism as it became more widely dispersed.

Early in the Second Temple era, then, Yehud served as the hearth of critical processes of religious interpretation and integration associated with the emergence of Judaism proper as a distinct ethnic religion. The context for such processes changed, however, as the hearth of Judaism entered a new period of conflict beginning with its conquest by Alexander late in the fourth century BCE. Known under the Greeks as Judea, this region was ruled for much of the next two centuries by Hellenistic empires, which unlike the Persians generally sought to impose their own culture on the lands that they conquered. The resulting tensions peaked in the second century BCE during the reign of Antiochus IV, a Greek Syrian ruler who sought to enforce control over Judea by eliminating the practice of Judaism. He therefore banned Jewish practices, took over Jerusalem, and erected an altar to Zeus within the Jerusalem Temple. These actions provoked the Jewish Maccabean rebellion in 165 BCE. The rebels retook Jerusalem and reconsecrated the Temple; and in 142 BCE Syria recognized Judea's independence.

Following the rebellion, however, political and religious divisions within Jewish society led to renewed internal conflict and ultimately contributed to the conquest of Judea by the Romans in 63 BCE. Within this context, a significant division existed between those Jews who insisted on strict adherence to cultural tradition and those more willing to adapt to Hellenistic influences and foreign rule.[23] Those accepting accommodation with external forces included the Sadducees, a group of hereditary priests, aristocrats, and merchants who comprised the upper classes of Jewish society. The Sadducees recognized the authority of the written Torah and emphasized Temple worship, but they also adopted elements of Hellenistic culture and later tended to compromise with Roman rule. Their main antagonists were the Pharisees, an influential group who asserted that piety and learning were more important than status and birth as sources of spiritual authority. The Pharisees believed that Mosaic law included two components: the written Torah, which was to be known to all; and the oral Torah, transmitted through scholarly teachings that preserved, interpreted, and adapted divine law as the contexts of Jewish society changed. The Pharisees also asserted that laws regarding ritual purity applied to everyone, not just the priesthood, and should be practiced in the home as well as in the Temple; and they espoused various eschatological beliefs, including the coming of a messiah, the resurrection of the dead, and the Last Judgment. The Essenes, a small sect that arose during the same period, shared some of the beliefs of the Pharisees but lived in isolated, ascetic communities. The Essenes strongly resisted the process of Hellenization and generally did not participate in Temple worship. Because most Jews did not belong to any of these sects, popular Judaism remained a mixture of these more formal systems.

Conditions worsened in Judea after the Roman conquest in 63 BCE, and within this context of conflict adherents furthered the articulation of Judaism in its primary hearth. Divisions within Jewish society persisted, as some Jews sought compromise with Roman rule while others opposed it. Cultural tensions between Jews and Gentiles also increased, and the Romans imposed various forms of economic and political constraints on Judea. Growing Jewish resistance to the status quo found expression in the formation of the Zealots, an anti-Roman sect that sought the restoration of an independent Jewish kingdom. At the same time, various sects supported belief in an impending apocalypse, possibly led by a messiah who would bring redemption from worldly evils. These circumstances ultimately led to a Jewish rebellion against the empire in 66 CE. The Romans put down the rebellion, however, capturing Jerusalem in 70 CE and destroying the Second Temple. The last Zealot stronghold, at Masada, fell in 73 CE with the mass suicide of nearly all of its inhabitants. By the end of the war, the Sadducees, Essenes, and Zealots had essentially ceased to exist.

In the course of the rebellion, however, a new element within Judaism had begun to take form. During the siege of Jerusalem, the Romans allowed a Jewish scholar named Johanan ben Zakkai to leave the city and establish a Jewish academy in the nearby town of Yavneh (now Yibna). By tradition, Johanan was the successor to a series of teachers of the oral Torah reaching back to Moses. He rejected the idea of armed resistance to Rome, focusing instead on the preservation and elucidation of the Torah. To this end, his academy established the ritual ordination of rabbis, scholars who had acquired knowledge of the written and oral Torah through their discipleship to a learned master. Johanan's academy, and others like it, became the source of Rabbinic Judaism, the final articulation of Judaic tradition in its primary hearth. Adherents of this form of Judaism centered authority in the rabbi as teacher of divine law rather than in the hereditary priest as performer of the sacrifice. In its challenge to priestly authority and its emphasis on the oral Torah, Rabbinic Judaism reflected Pharisaic influences; but Johanan and his followers were less sectarian than the Pharisees and accommodated a wide range of religious thought.

Following the destruction of the Second Temple in Jerusalem, the academy in Yavneh thus emerged as the primary center of Jewish authority, and as such it played a major role in preserving and reinterpreting Judaism. Johanan's followers came to see worship in the synagogue as fully replacing the Temple sacrifice, and prayer became the ritual focus of Judaism. In relation to communal synagogue worship, a strong liturgical tradition also developed during this period. The establishment of a synagogue required only a quorum of ten, however, and so the synagogue remained a highly decentralized institution. The trend toward decentralization was reinforced by the belief that rabbis should have a degree of freedom in interpreting the oral Torah to their followers. At the same time, the adherents of the Rabbinic system sought to maintain orthodoxy in the core beliefs of Judaism. They did so by compiling and systematizing existing teachings regarding the oral Torah in an early form of the Mishnah, the Jewish code of law ultimately assembled by the beginning of the third century CE. Johanan's successors also determined the canon of Jewish sacred scripture, excluding various apocryphal works and Christian writings.[24] Finally, with the Temple gone, the people themselves became seen as the primary vessel of Judaism. The early rabbis therefore promoted strict adherence to the details of divine law in all aspects of life, to preserve the distinctiveness of Judaism and the sanctity of the divine covenant.

Conflict between the Jews and the Roman Empire continued into the second century CE. The Roman emperor Hadrian tried to suppress Judaism by banning Sabbath observances, the teaching of Jewish law, and the ordination of rabbis; and on the site of the former Temple he erected a shrine to Jupiter. Amid new messianic expectations, another Jewish rebellion broke out in 132 CE. But despite some early Jewish triumphs the Romans again prevailed, inflicting massive casualties on the Jewish population. After the war the Jewish people no longer comprised a majority in the region, the survivors were temporarily banned from entering Jerusalem, and Judea was reorganized as Syria Palestina. In the subsequent Jewish diaspora, many survivors emigrated to Mesopotamia or other parts of the Roman Empire. The center of Jewish teaching relocated to Galilee, where Jewish scholars continued their work of systematizing and preserving tradition. By the beginning of the third century CE the Mishnah had been completed, ending the formative period of Rabbinic Judaism in its primary hearth. Rabbinic Judaism continued to develop over the next several centuries as scholars compiled commentaries on the Mishnah. These efforts produced the Jerusalem Talmud (actually compiled in Tiberias) by around 400 CE and the Babylonian Talmud by around 600 CE. By this time, however, the basic structure of Judaism was already in place, with the Rabbinic tradition at its core.

Like Vedism and Hinduism in the Indic region, the religious systems that originated in the primary hearths of Judaism and Proto-Judaism have had enduring influences. Judaism itself became a widely distributed religion despite the history of persecution suffered by its adherents. In addition, its traditions played an important role in the formation of Christianity and Islam within the Semitic region. These religions developed very differently from Judaism, however. They grew out of more clearly defined initiating events focused on a specific founding figure, and having originated in literate societies their core beliefs and practices became articulated in scripture more rapidly. Moreover, as abrupt departures from existing traditions they at first lacked substantial popular support. Their initial communities of believers adopted these religions deliberately rather than through the assimilation of received customs, and in doing so encountered much religious opposition. Through specific cultural processes unfolding within their hearths, however, Christianity and Islam each eventually acquired a critical mass of adherents and as proselytic religions both then spread rapidly to other areas.

Christianity

Christianity originated in the first century CE essentially as a movement within Judaism. It developed out of the life and message of Jesus, a Jewish religious teacher who came to be seen by his followers as the messiah, or Christ, and God incarnate (map 2.6). The teachings of Jesus accepted as given many elements of the worldview of Judaism, such as its monotheism and its ethical focus. The apocalyptic and messianic beliefs maintained by many Jews under Roman rule also had a formative influence on early Christianity, as did the tradition of the Judaic prophets who were believed to speak on behalf of God. Nonetheless, Jesus preached a radical reinterpretation of Jewish tradition. His message centered on belief in the coming of the kingdom of God on earth. Such a belief had some currency among Jews at the time, but was most often related to a future restoration of the united kingdom of Israel as once ruled by David.

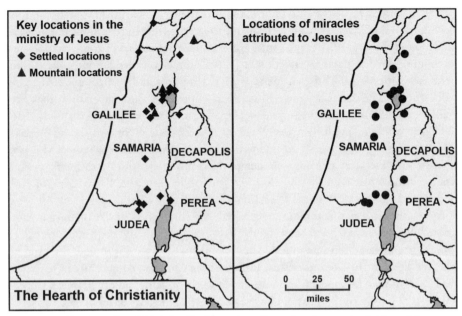

Map 2.6. The hearth of Christianity, based on the miracles and ministry of Jesus as recounted in the New Testament. Together the locations associated with these initiating events define a crucial sacred space within the Christian tradition.

The kingdom announced by Jesus was quite different, referring to the assertion of God's spiritual sovereignty on earth and the resulting redemption of humanity. According to the teachings of Jesus, moreover, strict adherence to Jewish law or to the rite of Temple sacrifice would be insufficient to achieve salvation in the kingdom of God. Rather, divine justice would favor those who had experienced an internal transformation based on an ethos of faith, repentance, humility, and love for God and one's fellow human beings. The Christian worldview later incorporated many beliefs about Jesus himself, including his birth to the Virgin Mary, his baptism by John the Baptist, his public ministry in and around Galilee, his performance of various miracles, his crucifixion, and his ascension to heaven from the Mount of Olives outside Jerusalem. The identification of Jesus as the incarnation of God became central to this worldview, as did the belief that as the messiah he died to atone for the sins of humanity. The twelve apostles, the leading disciples chosen by Jesus during his ministry, were crucial in articulating and spreading these beliefs, and thus also played a central role in the emergence of Christianity.

Jesus acquired an initial following in Galilee, but he also attracted considerable opposition as he became more widely known. In his teachings he had been highly critical of the Pharisees and Sadducees. In return, these groups had objected to his speaking in the name of God, to his diminution of the importance of sacred law and the Temple, and toward the end of his life to his messianic claims, which they considered heretical. Moreover, they feared that his growing popularity would incite rebellion and thus greater oppression by the Romans. Jesus was ultimately convicted of blasphemy by the religious authorities in Jerusalem and of treason by the Romans, and was crucified circa 30 CE. After his death, his disciples remained in Jerusalem where, according to Christian tradition, they experienced a spiritual inspiration on the Jewish festival of Pentecost and subsequently began actively to preach his teachings in and around the city. Within the context of Jewish messianic expectations, the apostles' account of the death and resurrection of Jesus acquired considerable authority. Moreover, the affirmative Christian message of redemption and justice attracted many adherents within the atmosphere of conflict, oppression, and uncertainty that prevailed under Roman rule in Judea, particularly from among the Jewish masses not affiliated with the Sadducees, the Pharisees, the Zealots, or one of the other sects. With its less rigid adherence to traditional Jewish law and its rejection of violence, Christianity also attracted many moderate, Hellenized Jews during this early period. In a cultural sense, then, the message of Christianity represented a rejection of both Jewish and Roman elements of the status quo in its early hearth.

As the Christian community expanded, the core beliefs of Christianity became more fully articulated. Most importantly, its adherents explicitly defined the teachings of Jesus in universal terms, applicable not just to Jews but to all people. Moreover, by the middle of the first century CE the leaders of the Christian community in Jerusalem had decided that, because salvation depended solely on faith and divine grace, Gentile converts to Christianity were not obliged to adhere to the laws of the Judaic covenant. The growing size and distinctiveness of the Christian community also led to renewed opposition from Jewish and Roman authorities, however, and a number of Christian leaders were put to death in Jerusalem. Jewish antagonism toward the Christian community increased during the rebellion against Rome beginning in 66 CE. Repudiating violence, the Christians in Jerusalem did not participate in the rebellion. Instead, in anticipation of the Second Coming of the messiah, they apparently left the city to seek refuge across the Jordan River near the Sea of Galilee. They also appear to have interpreted the destruction of the Second Temple as a fulfillment of prophecy concerning the Second Coming of Christ. As a result, many Jews who survived the rebellion considered the Christians to be traitors. The emerging leaders of Rabbinic Judaism subsequently labeled Christianity a heretical sect, based on its disregard for Jewish law and its beliefs concerning the messiah; and they banned Christian Jews from the synagogues that now became the center of Jewish religious life.

The influence of Christianity within its initial hearth was thus declining by the end of the first century CE. Beyond that hearth, however, Christianity had greater success. By the middle of the first century CE, Christian missionaries had begun to seek converts in other parts of the Roman Empire, particularly in Asia Minor and Greece. Paul, a Jew born in Asia Minor, played the leading role in this process. Raised as a Pharisee and once an antagonist of Christianity, he converted after experiencing a vision of Jesus on the road to Damascus; and some years later he became widely involved in missionary activity and in the articulation of Christian theology. His writings became an integral part of the New Testament and his ideas remained widely influential among later theologians. Paul advanced the development of Christianity as a universal religion through his success both in converting Gentiles and in convincing other Christian leaders that Gentile converts need not follow Jewish law. Through his efforts and those of other early missionaries, growing Christian communities emerged in various parts of the Roman Empire during the first century, despite official hostility toward the new religion. With this growth, the geographical center of Christianity moved away from its initial hearth, and its future development became linked to other places as discussed in chapter 3.

Islam

Islam, the third major tradition to develop in this region, emerged in the seventh century CE in a hearth distinct from those of Judaism and Christianity, located in the Hejaz region of the Arabian Peninsula (map 2.7).[25] Muhammad, its founder, explicitly identified Islam with the monotheistic, prophetic, and eschatological traditions of Judaism and Christianity. Nonetheless, from its inception Islam represented a discrete religious system. Its initiating event, according to Islamic belief, occurred in 610 in a cave near Mecca where Muhammad occasionally went to meditate. There, at the age of 40, he received from the angel Jibril the first of a series of divine revelations that would continue in Mecca and Medina until shortly before his death in 632. These revelations would later be recorded as the Quran. The revelations that Muhammad received while residing in Mecca established a worldview centered on belief in only one God (Allah, "the God") and an ethos of submission ("Islam") to God's mercy and justice that emphasized preparation for the Day of Judgment when God would reward good and punish evil. In the Islamic worldview, the God of Islam was identical to that of Judaism and Christianity, and the revelations given to Muhammad had also been received by earlier prophets, including Adam, Abraham, Moses, and Jesus. The recurring corruption of divine truth in past times, according to Islamic belief, made necessary its reiteration in the perfect form of the Quran to Muhammad, the final prophet.

The teachings of Muhammad based on these revelations constituted a significant

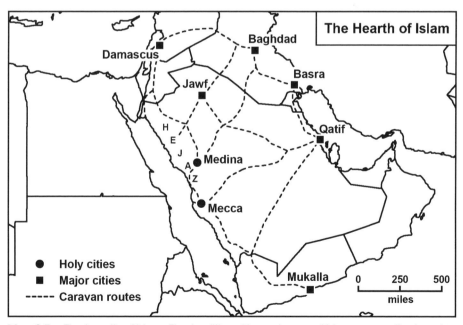

Map 2.7.   The hearth of Islam. The traditional importance of Mecca as a ritual center in pre-Islamic Arabia and the location of Mecca and Medina along major caravan routes both contributed to this region's success as a religious hearth.

break from prevailing traditions in Mecca and the Hejaz. In its strict monotheism, Islam diverged sharply from the Arab tribal religions in the region, which were rooted in polytheism and animism. Most tribes sought protection from a patron deity, but members also worshipped various minor deities and spirits. Allah appears to have been identified within this context as a remote, creator god but was not the object of tribal worship. More generally, however, the worldview and ethos preached by Muhammad challenged existing power structures centered in Mecca, and in particular the local dominance of the Quraysh tribe. Much of the Quraysh's cultural and political prestige derived from its status as protector of an important pre-Islamic sanctuary in the city, a responsibility especially associated with the tribe's Umayyad clan. This sanctuary or *Haram*, centered on the ancient structure known as the Kaaba, contained over three hundred idols of tribal deities and had become a well-established pilgrimage site by the fifth century CE. As sacred space, the Haram was also considered a neutral setting for trade and diplomacy between rival groups, and so was central to religious, political, and economic life. Muhammad's rejection of the tribal polytheism associated with the Haram thus threatened the influence of the Quraysh. Leaders of the Quraysh also objected to Muhammad's teaching that human history would end with a final judgment through which people would be rewarded or punished according to their individual merits. In its assertion of bodily resurrection and eternal reward or punishment, this doctrine contradicted prevailing religious beliefs. More importantly, Muhammad's concept of divine justice mandated an ethos of individual moral responsibility to God and this ethos clashed in a number of ways with the established social order headed by the Quraysh. The emphasis on individual devotion to God as the ultimate authority undermined the traditional social structures based on tribal and clan loyalties and hierarchies of status, both by applying the same standards of belief and practice to all people regardless of their position in society and by minimizing the importance of worldly power and allegiances. Muhammad also contested the social dominance of the wealthy elite, preaching that material riches would provide no advantage on the Day of Judgment, and that God would punish those who had accumulated wealth by taking unfair advantage of others or who had failed to help the needy.

For several years after the revelations began, Muhammad mainly spread his message privately and acquired only a limited following, including members of his household, and a few commoners, slaves, and members of minor clans. Muhammad himself belonged to the Hashim, a lesser clan within the Quraysh tribe, and this affiliation afforded him a measure of protection when he began to preach his message more widely. His public preaching in Mecca attracted few converts, however, mostly from lower status groups such as the minor clans, those lacking a tribal affiliation, and the poor. All the same, elements within the Quraysh tribe felt increasingly threatened by Muhammad's message and as their opposition grew stronger so did his attacks on them. Ultimately his own clan withdrew its protection, and the persecution of Muhammad and his followers by the Quraysh became more overt. As a result, Muhammad and about 200 followers migrated in 622 from Mecca to Yathrib, subsequently known as Medina (or "City" of the prophet), an agricultural community 200 miles to the north. That event, known in Islam as the *Hijra* ("Emigration"), represented a crucial initiating event, marking the beginning of an independent Islamic community and the starting point of the Islamic calendar.

Prior to the Hijra, Medina had been subject to social and political tensions typical of western Arabia at this time as nomadic groups became more settled and population densities increased. In Medina, such tensions had produced a struggle for power between two Arab tribes: the Aws, who had the support of three local Jewish tribes, and the Khazraj. Muhammad had ties to the Khazraj through his father's mother, and in 620 had converted several members of that tribe to Islam while they were on the customary pilgrimage to Mecca. In 622, members of both of the feuding tribes offered protection to Muhammad if he would come to Medina to arbitrate their differences, and he accepted. Once in Medina, Muhammad established a constitution that identified the Muslims as a distinct group within the city's diverse tribal society, defined by religious belief rather than lineage. The constitution also named Muhammad as the mediator of all disputes.

From this position of authority, Muhammad worked during the next several years to transform Medina into a unified Muslim community. This effort proved successful among the Arab tribes, who found in the emerging Islamic order a means of resolving their earlier divisions. Muhammad's support among Arabs was strengthened by his successes in raids against Meccan caravans and in subsequent battles with Meccan forces. At the same time, he dealt harshly with Medina's Jewish tribes, who resisted conversion and were therefore seen as potential enemies. He banished two of the tribes from Medina, and eliminated a third by killing its men and sending its women and children into slavery. Medina thus became increasingly unified under Muhammad's leadership. His divine revelations also continued in Medina, in this context outlining principles for the organization of Islamic social, legal, and religious practices. These revelations articulated two key elements of the Islamic religious system: belief in Islam as an integrated way of life, encompassing not just matters of ritual and worship but the entire spectrum of social, political, and economic concerns; and belief in a specific set of obligations, the Five Pillars of Islam, including the declaration of faith, charitable donation, regular prayer, fasting during Ramadan, and the Hajj or pilgrimage to Mecca. Muhammad had earlier stated that the act of prayer should be oriented toward Jerusalem, but following his conflicts with the Jewish tribes he mandated that prayer be oriented toward the Kaaba in Mecca.

Through these various processes, then, Medina became an Islamic state, based on the concept of a religious community rather than on tribal loyalty and ruled by a religious leader rather than by a hereditary chief. As Medina grew more powerful and extended its alliances with neighboring tribes, the Quraysh in Mecca became more conciliatory. In 628, Muhammad and the Quraysh established a truce that would allow the Medinans free access to Mecca to perform the Hajj; and the next year, Muhammad made the pilgrimage to Mecca with 2,000 Muslims from Medina. Muhammad continued to consolidate his power in the region, however, and in 630 he and his now formidable army marched on Mecca. There, he offered the city's residents amnesty if they surrendered peacefully and they accepted. Muhammad then entered the Haram and had the various tribal idols removed. The Haram and the Kaaba now became the central ritual space of Islam, which could no longer be entered by non-Muslims. The city's residents, including the leadership of the Quraysh, subsequently converted to Islam, and recognized Muhammad as ruler of the Hejaz. Increasing numbers of nomadic tribes in the region also allied themselves with Muhammad, even if they did not fully abandon their animistic religious practices. The Islamic state Muhammad had founded in Medina thus continued to expand; the revelations of the

Quran became the basis of law and social custom; and the umma, the community of Muslims, became the dominant social structure in the Hejaz.

Two years after taking control of Mecca, Muhammad performed his final pilgrimage to Mecca, which subsequently served as the model for the ritual of the Hajj. He died shortly after returning to Medina, with much of the Arabian Peninsula already under Muslim control. The unifying social ethic of Islam had fused with the emergence of a more settled, trade-oriented society in Arabia to form the foundation of a powerful empire that extended far beyond its original hearth. Muhammad's successors continued to enlarge the empire, and by the 650s it reached westward to Libya, northward to Armenia, and eastward through Persia. The Muslim community also continued to shape the religious system of Islam. In the decades following Muhammad's death the Quran was compiled in its final form, and oral traditions concerning Muhammad's life were preserved, later to be collected in writing as the hadith. As the empire grew, however, its geographical focus began to shift away from the primary Islamic hearth. Mecca and Medina retained their religious significance, but the empire's capital moved to Damascus in 661 and then to Baghdad in the middle of the next century. Religious divisions within Islam also developed, most importantly between the Sunni and Shia branches, but these too involved developments beyond the Islamic hearth in the Hejaz.

*   *   *

The preceding discussion of primary religious hearths could of course be extended to include many other specific examples, such as Shinto in Japan, Manichaeism and Zoroastrianism in southwest Asia, and a great variety of tribal, animistic, and ancient religions throughout the world. Nonetheless, the primary hearths examined here portray the general processes involved in the emergence of discrete religious traditions: the expression of religious meanings through a set of initiating events; the articulation of a distinct worldview and ethos, identifying the nature of the superhuman and its implications for humanity; the integration of corresponding beliefs and practices into a coherent system; and the consolidation of a community of adherents by which the emerging tradition is reproduced. At the same time, these primary hearths illustrate the contrasting forms that such processes can take. The founding expression of the religious meanings of Vedism, for example, unfolded over a long period of time through the incremental compilation and interpretation of the Vedas by many different authors. The initiating events of Buddhism, on the other hand, revolved more immediately around the specific story of its founder's experience of enlightenment. Likewise, in the hearth of Proto-Judaism the formation of a community of adherents explicitly involved the articulation of an exclusive sense of national identity, while in the hearth of Islam this process just as explicitly involved a rejection of the primacy of tribal loyalties.

Developments within these different primary hearths thus demonstrate the significance of contextual factors in the formation of religious traditions. Such factors obviously include the various influences of existing social and cultural structures on the emerging tradition. Of particular importance, however, is the connection of the tradition's worldview and ethos to the surrounding context within which it develops. More specifically, within these primary hearths the articulation of a distinct worldview and ethos provided believers with a structure of meanings from which to adapt and respond to underlying patterns of change or conflict within their cultural contexts. The connection of this structure of meanings to circumstances within the hearth strengthened the compelling nature of the religion's core beliefs, and thus was essential to the consolidation of a critical mass of initial adherents.

Processes of Spatial Change

Once a religious system has been articulated, various processes can affect its spatial distribution. Its adherents may spread the religion to new locations through migration or the conversion of others. Conversely, its presence may contract as believers adopt other religions or suffer the effects of persecution. A religion's spatial distribution at any point in time represents the cumulative outcome of such processes of spatial change, and such processes are thus central to an understanding of how a religion's distribution develops over time. These processes also have a number of broader implications, however. Processes of diffusion play a key role in the geographical differentiation of different branches within a common religious tradition, a topic considered in detail in chapter 3. Similarly, the expansion or contraction of a religion's distribution has diverse impacts on the people and places involved through the connections of religious faith to other social and cultural patterns. Perhaps most importantly, processes of spatial change can acquire important religious meanings for believers. Various groups have attributed religious significance to certain acts of migration, for example, just as adherents in a number of traditions interpret missionary activity as an essential religious obligation. Spatial change thus represents a complex theme in the geographical approach to the study of religion, focusing not only on the forces that have shaped a religion's distribution but on their underlying meanings and consequences as well. In examining the principal dimensions of this theme, the following discussion specifically addresses three crucial factors: processes of migration, involving the permanent relocation of existing adherents from one place to another; processes of conversion, involving the spread of a religion through its adoption by new adherents; and processes of contraction, involving the attrition of a religion's distribution brought about by a decline in the number of adherents.

Migration

As a basic form of spatial behavior, migration represents a major factor in the diffusion of religions. For tribal and ethnic religions, which generally do not seek converts, migration has been the primary mode of geographical expansion, but it has obviously played an important role in the spread of proselytic religions as well. The experience of migration has interacted with the lives of adherents in diverse ways, however. Most commonly, the spread of a religious system by migrants has occurred incidentally as part of a more general transfer of cultural traditions, through processes of migration prompted by secular rather than religious factors. Such processes vary, of course, in terms of migrants' motivations, their level of technological development, and the social, political, and economic structures with which they interact. The earliest forms of religious diffusion presumably developed though patterns of primitive migration involving the spread of preliterate tribal groups, usually in response to population pressures or changing environmental conditions. The initial movement of the Aryans into the Indian subcontinent exemplified this type of migration, as did the nomadic wanderings of the proto-Israelites who eventually settled in Canaan. Typically, little is known about a primitive migrant group's religion as it existed before the rise of a written tradition. It is likely, however, that such migrants continually adapted their traditions as they came into contact with new culture groups and environments. Vedism, for example, drew on the Indo-European traditions of the Aryans but also developed a distinct geographical focus on the Punjab region and may have incorporated influences from the prior Indus Valley civilization as well. Similarly, the isolation of primitive migrants from others practicing the same religion undoubtedly led to divergent religious expressions. Thus during the early peopling of Polynesia, lasting roughly from 1500 BCE to 800 CE, common religious elements like the ceremonial use of kava, the definition of tribal ritual space, and the concept of a priestly monarchy became augmented by more idiosyncratic local features, such as distinctive pantheons or creation myths, as migrants settled in different island groups.

Incidental Diffusion through Migration

The spread of religions through migration became somewhat more organized with the rise of more complex political and economic structures across the ancient world. Expanding civilizations brought their religious systems to nearby areas through conquest and colonization. Greeks moving westward during the seventh and eighth centuries BCE, for example, regularly built temples to the gods of their homeland as part of the planned settlements that they established in Sicily and Italy (photo 2.2).[26] The establishment of a state religion in many ancient empires reinforced this process, as seen in rules directing the observance of the Roman Empire's official cults by imperial legionnaires and Roman citizens outside of Italy.[27] The expansion of empires also led to the relocation or deportation of conquered peoples, such as the exile of Judahites to Babylon. At the same time, the economic integration of growing empires supported the spread of diverse religions through the migration of commercial classes. Within the Roman Empire, for example, Jewish migrants had established communities in Asia Minor, Egypt, Greece, Italy, and Spain by the middle of the first century CE, even before the destruction of the Second Temple in Jerusalem.

The incidental diffusion of religion via migration continued to follow such patterns until the early modern period, when the first wave of European colonialism began to produce radically different migration processes. These processes were marked by increases in both the geographical scope and the magnitude of migration. They emerged as European powers created permanent settlements in the Americas. In the aftermath of the Protestant Reformation, religious motives played a role in colonization as Protestant and Roman Catholic states competed in the effort to expand the domain of their version of Christianity. Some adherents also migrated to the colonies for specific religious reasons, such as to undertake missionary work or escape persecution. Most European migration to the Americas during the first wave of colonialism, however, was economically motivated and so contributed incidentally to the spread of religion.

Photo 2.2.   Temple of Athena built by Greek colonists in southern Italy around 500 BCE. Paestum, Italy, 2005.

Source: Michael Tomasello (commons.wikimedia.org/wiki/Image:Temple_of_Athena_at_Paestum.jpg), placed in the public domain.

The largest stream of European migrants comprised those moving from the British Isles to North America, where they constituted a strong Protestant presence. Although many of these migrants were nominally Anglican and the Church of England was at one time officially established in all of the southern colonies, Anglicanism did not dominate the British colonies. The dissenting Puritan church prevailed in most of New England, while other areas contained Presbyterians, Baptists, Quakers, and other British dissenters, along with various Protestant groups from continental Europe and a small number of Roman Catholics and Jews. Because the ecclesiastical infrastructure lagged behind the settlement process, moreover, only a small minority of British colonists regularly participated in organized worship. The Protestant character of the British colonies was thus founded on the persistence of generally held religious givens rather than on a strong institutional presence.

In the French, Spanish, and Portuguese colonies, on the other hand, the Roman Catholic Church represented a significant institutional presence. Its importance derived in large part from the emphasis that it placed on the conversion of indigenous peoples. In establishing Roman Catholic dominance, the emphasis on conversion thus compensated for the smaller number of European migrants who moved to the colonies of Roman Catholic powers rather than to British America. Nonetheless, European migrants to the French, Spanish, and Portuguese colonies provided a necessary foundation for the development of Roman Catholic hegemony.

Despite its importance in reshaping the world map of religious adherence, migration from Europe represented a small part of the total transfer of population to the Americas during the early colonial period. Over five times as many Africans, perhaps eleven million in all, were forcibly relocated to the Americas through the organization of the trans-Atlantic slave trade. The practice of slavery at this time forced the movement of Africans to other locations as well, but not on the same scale as to the Americas. Obviously for the enslaved Africans the transfer of religious beliefs and practices occurred under very different conditions than it did for European migrants. Supporting cultural expressions such as tribal structures and traditional social and religious roles were disrupted or destroyed. The inability to own land, for example, prevented the diffusion of cults of the earth.[28] The dispersal of members of local tribes to different locations further impeded the reproduction of their specific traditions. Over time, Africans in the Americas also had increasing contacts with the hegemonic traditions of Christianity, continuing a process of religious interaction that began in central Africa prior to relocation to the New World.[29]

Nonetheless, African religious beliefs and practices did survive in the Americas, albeit in modified form. These religious survivals reflected some of the common themes found among the traditions of groups from western and central Africa, including belief in a remote creator god, devotion to lesser deities and ancestors as active agents in the world, the propitiatory use of ritual and sacrifice, and the reliance on priestly mediators in contacting the divine. African religions thus underwent a process of cultural simplification as diverse slave communities came to focus on the common features within various traditions. In addition, syncretistic processes led to the gradual integration of African and Christian religious elements, and it was in this form that African religious traditions proved most durable in the Americas. These syncretistic religions generally merged the African worship of ancestors and various deities with the Roman Catholic veneration of saints. Such forms of syncretism developed a number of distinctive local expressions, most notably Vodou in Haiti, Santeria in Cuba, and Macumba and related traditions in Brazil.[30]

Starting in the 1800s, the incidental diffusion of religion further expanded through mass migration processes. Europe became the leading source of international migrants as perhaps seventy million people moved to other parts of the world between 1800 and 1914. Although religious concerns again motivated some of these migrants, most moved in response to changing economic conditions. Their leading destination was the United States, which consequently experienced significant changes in patterns of religious adherence. The Roman Catholic Church grew into the country's largest religious body, and a dominant presence in cities in the Northeast and Middle West, as adherents migrated first mainly from Ireland and Germany and later from southern and eastern Europe. Protestant denominations from continental Europe also grew rapidly, resulting most conspicuously in the predominance of Lutherans in much of the Upper Middle West. Jewish immigration increased as well, producing large communities in New York and other northeastern cities, although it was often motivated by religious concerns, as discussed below. The immigration of these and other religious groups contributed to the religious pluralism of the United States, with religious institutions providing both a source of cultural identity and a means of adapting to American society. This pluralistic context also brought together disparate ethnic groups within the same religious tradition, a pattern exemplified by the formation of national parishes within the Roman Catholic Church (photo 2.3).[31]

Mass migration to Latin America during the 1800s and early 1900s had a very different effect. Argentina and Brazil represented the primary destinations of that migration, most of which came from predominantly Roman Catholic countries in

Photo 2.3. St. Emerich's Roman Catholic Church, established by Hungarian immigrants in 1905. The church was deconsecrated and demolished in 2003 and the Hungarian parish was merged with St. Casimir's, formerly a Polish parish. Johnstown, Pennsylvania, 1988.

Source: Jet Lowe, photographer, Historical American Buildings Survey, U.S. Library of Congress.

southern Europe. This immigration thus reinforced the religious hegemony of the Roman Catholic Church that had been established in both countries during colonization. Immigrants came from other sources as well, particularly from Germany, but they did not transform the predominant religious landscape. A similar pattern developed in Russia, where eastward migration strengthened the preeminence of Russian Orthodoxy in parts of Asia controlled by the Russian empire. This migration, which eventually extended into northwestern North America, also brought a number of dissenting religious groups, but in much smaller numbers.[32]

Other notable instances of the incidental spread of Christianity in this period include the development of Anglican pluralities within Australia and New Zealand. In addition, the beginnings of mass migration from non-European sources began to contribute to the incidental diffusion of other religious traditions. Migration from India developed within the context of the British Empire as indentured workers replaced slaves as a source of labor and as middle-class Indians pursued economic opportunities in other colonies. This migration led to the growth of Hinduism, and to a lesser extent Islam, in British possessions in eastern and southern Africa, Southeast Asia, northeastern South America, and the Caribbean. Mass emigration from China in the middle of the 1800s arose largely in response to rapid population growth and the demand for indentured laborers in European colonies. Migrants also followed earlier movements of Chinese merchants and traders into Southeast Asia, or moved to the Americas, establishing Chinese religious traditions in widespread immigrant communities.

Over the past fifty years, new global patterns of migration have emerged in response to changing demographic and economic forces. The primary sources of this migration have shifted to parts of Asia, Latin America, and to a lesser extent Africa, while North America and Europe have served as the primary destinations. These migration patterns have had major impacts on the incidental diffusion of religions. Most importantly, recent migration to Europe and North America has supported the growth of religions that traditionally had a limited presence in these regions, such as Islam and Hinduism. The migration of Muslims from North Africa, Turkey, and South Asia to Western Europe has been especially significant.[33] Many came as labor migrants, on work visas of a specific duration, but remained as permanent immigrants and brought their dependents to Europe as well. By the early twenty-first century, Europe contained over thirty million Muslims by most estimates. In contrast, the United States contained approximately five million. The number of Hindu migrants to Europe and North America has been somewhat smaller. The United States and United Kingdom, their leading destinations, each contained more than one million Hindus by the early twenty-first century. Sikhs, Buddhists, and adherents of other Asian traditions have followed similar patterns of migration. Among all of these groups, migration has often led to the development of a diasporic culture of solidarity through which they have maintained their religious distinctiveness and promoted group interests (photo 2.4).[34]

Along with the changes brought about by preceding trends, religious patterns in northern Europe have been affected by labor migration from southern Europe, which has increased the Roman Catholic presence in many predominantly Protestant areas. Principally because of the large proportion of Roman Catholics among alien residents, Roman Catholicism had by 1970 become the leading religious affiliation in Switzerland, which a century earlier had a Protestant majority of nearly 60 percent. Both North America and the United Kingdom have also received migrants from the Caribbean, who have carried with them the syncretistic religions of that region. Finally, in recent decades the oil-producing states of the Arabian Peninsula have become important destinations for labor migrants, primarily from the Middle East, North Africa, and South and Southeast Asia. Much of this migration originates in predominantly Muslim countries, but it also includes many adherents of other religions. Over 90 percent of the 600,000 Filipinos working in Saudi Arabia in the late 1990s, for example, were non-Muslims.[35] Within the context of Islamic hegemony in these states, however, adherents of other religions have little social visibility and their religious activity generally takes place in private. The diffusion of religion by migration thus has had a more limited impact in this context than in more pluralistic settings.

Religious Meanings in Migration

The patterns of migration discussed thus far have contributed to the diffusion of religions in very different ways but they have done so incidentally, as they have been based primarily on secular motives. In many instances, however, migration processes contain explicit religious elements. The act of migration can take on a specific religious meaning for adherents, for example, either a priori as part of their understanding of religious obligation or sacred history, or a posteriori as they apply religious interpretations to key group experiences. More generally, religious issues may be central to the

Photo 2.4.   Masjid Bilal, a mosque in the East Ham district of London. As indicated on the main sign, the mosque belongs to the UK Islamic Mission, or UKIM, a group that focuses on a variety of Muslim concerns. The smaller sign asks visitors to the mosque not to gather in front of the building so that passersby and neighbors will not be inconvenienced, adding that causing nuisances for others is against the ethos of Islam. London, United Kingdom, 2005.

Source: Gren (commons.wikimedia.org/wiki/Image:Masjid_Bilal,_East_Ham.jpg), placed in the public domain.

push and pull factors that motivate adherents to migrate. Those issues may develop through the group's interactions with other elements of society, as in the persecution of a religious minority, or they may originate within the religious group itself, as in the decision of a community of adherents to limit external influences by settling in an isolated location. Migration processes that contain a clearly defined religious component are of particular interest, then, not only for their influence on the distributions of religions but because they also provide insights into the effects of religious belief and practice on this form of spatial behavior.

Migration itself acquires a transcendent religious meaning when adherents interpret the process of relocation as a religious act. The Islamic concept of *hijra* illustrates the religious meaning of migration. This concept derives from the Hijra of Muhammad, one of the founding events of Islam, in which the prophet and his followers migrated to Medina to escape persecution in Mecca. During Muhammad's rule, *hijra* to Medina also became an obligation for the faithful, a means of expressing their commitment to Islam.[36] Based on these precedents, Islamic jurists later interpreted hijra as the migration of adherents from *Dar al-Harb*, the "Realm of War" where non-Muslims ruled, to Dar al-Islam, the "Realm of Islam" where the principles of Islamic law prevailed. Some jurists considered hijra to be obligatory for adherents unable to engage in outward *jihad* ("struggle"), the effort to expand Dar al-Islam.[37] From at least the ninth century, however, many jurists ruled hijra to be mandatory only for adherents in Dar al-Harb who could not practice Islam freely.

The interpretation of hijra as a religious duty has affected Muslim migration in a variety of contexts. The emigration of millions of Muslims from Crimea and the Caucasus during the 1800s, following the Russian conquest of those regions, was based in part on an understanding of hijra through which migrants identified their primary destination, the Ottoman empire, with Dar al-Islam.[38] European colonial expansion during the 1800s also provoked calls to hijra among African Muslims. In response to the occupation of coastal Algeria by France in the 1830s, a confederation of Islamic tribal groups formed a separate polity in western Algeria based on the concept of hijra; and after the French defeated these groups and extended control over the interior of Algeria, many Muslims continued to undertake hijra to Morocco, Tunisia, and Syria.[39] Another variant of hijra emerged within the pan-Islamic Khilafat Movement in British India after World War I. This movement supported Muslim allegiance to the Ottoman Caliphate, a position complicated by the fact that the British and the Ottomans were adversaries during the war. Britain's role in dismantling the Ottoman empire after the war, which ended the Caliph's control over Mecca and Medina, led some within the Khilafat Movement to identify areas under British control as Dar al-Harb. As a result, in 1920 as many as 60,000 Indian Muslims undertook hijra to Afghanistan. Most were turned back by Afghanistan, however, while others settled in Turkey or Central Asia.[40] In more recent years, militant Islamists have reconceptualized hijra as the escape from settings where Islam predominates but in inauthentic forms. In Egypt during the 1970s, for example, the extremist Jamaat al-Muslimin ("Society of Muslims") called for members to isolate themselves through hijra from the corrupted mainstream of Egyptian society. In most cases they did so locally within certain outer suburban neighborhoods, but some migrated to sparsely populated areas of Upper Egypt.[41] For some Turkish Islamists, migration to Europe also represents a form of hijra, allowing them to practice their fundamentalist version of Islam more freely than they could in secular Turkey.

The transcendent meaning of migration has in other cases derived more specifically from the sacred significance of a chosen destination. The return to the Promised Land of Israel, for example, represents a central theme in traditional Jewish belief. In the worldview of Proto-Judaism, the Israelites' migration to the Promised Land following the exodus from Egypt served to validate the authority of the divine covenant. The return of exiled Jews from Babylon to Judah in the sixth century BCE took on similar religious significance through its parallels with the earlier migrations of the Israelites. The subsequent development of messianic doctrines within Judaism after other empires gained control of the region also focused on belief in a redemptive restoration to the Promised Land. In the late 1700s, small numbers of traditionalist Jews in Europe thus began to migrate to Palestine, motivated by the belief that they could most effectively realize an authentic Jewish life in the sacred land of Israel while awaiting the coming of the messiah.

Such beliefs acquired a broader significance with the rise of Zionism as a political movement late in the 1800s. Zionism expressed the belief that Jews would never be free from persecution until they had their own sovereign homeland, to be located in Palestine. Because Zionism was primarily a secular movement, however, its leaders did not articulate these objectives in religious terms; instead they proposed to create Israel as a modern nation-state. This secular vision provoked contrasting responses among religious Jews. The majority of Orthodox Jews viewed the creation of a Jewish state through human agency as heretical, since in their belief the restoration of Jews to sovereignty in the Promised Land could be achieved only through divine action. In addition, they rejected the secularism of the Zionists in Palestine, who did not follow the traditions of Jewish law. Nonetheless, the growing Jewish migration from Europe to Palestine during the late nineteenth and early twentieth centuries included many Orthodox Jews seeking religious fulfillment in the hearth of Judaism rather than the establishment of a new state. At the same time, the migration to Palestine included a separate group of Orthodox Jews who did support Zionism. These religious Zionists saw the creation of Israel as part of the divine plan for the redemption of the Jewish people, despite the largely secular nature of the Zionist movement; and thus they interpreted their relocation to the land of Israel as part of the completion of Jewish sacred history.[42]

Concern for a sacred destination also motivated the Europeans who migrated to the eastern Mediterranean region within the context of the early Crusades. Pope Urban II initiated the First Crusade in 1095 with the goal of freeing the Christian communities and pilgrimage sites of the Holy Land from Muslim control. In 1099 the crusaders captured Jerusalem and the most sacred Christian shrine, the tomb of Jesus. Between 1098 and 1109, they also organized a number of feudal states in the region that functioned essentially as religious colonies, ensuring Western Christian control of the Holy Land (map 2.8). These states developed significant communities of Western European migrants, some arriving with the crusade and others coming later as pilgrims to the Holy Land.[43] Migrants continued to arrive during the 1100s, moreover, as political and religious leaders sought to establish loyal populations of Western Europeans to maintain the crusader states' military and economic viability. Known locally as Franks, these migrants came from diverse origins, including various French provinces, Flanders, Italy, and Spain. By the middle of the twelfth century they had formed substantial communities within the existing towns controlled by the crusaders and had created a number of new settlements as well. These migrants were not motivated solely by religious concerns; various economic opportunities in the crusader states also served as pull factors. Nonetheless, the distinctive functions of the crusader states as defenders of the Christian Holy Land gave immigration an intrinsic religious meaning.[44] Despite this migration, however, the crusader states proved to be unsustainable. They went through a series of political reconfigurations as their conflicts with Muslim powers continued, and by the end of the thirteenth century they had ceased to exist as the Egyptian Mamluks asserted control over the region.

Persecution and Discrimination

The preceding examples of religiously motivated migration developed as expressions of beliefs relating to religious obligation or fulfillment and to the sacred character of certain places. Religious factors have also affected migration, however, through their interaction with other cultural factors. Adherents of many faiths have migrated in response to the persecution of their religious group, for example. Similarly, some believers have been motivated to migrate by their rejection of conditions in their place of origin and a corresponding desire to settle in a destination better suited to the

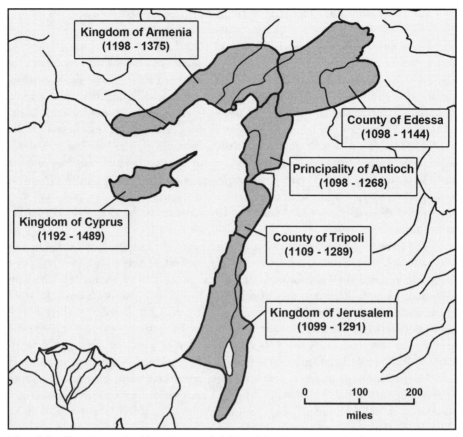

Map 2.8. The Crusader kingdoms established by Europeans in the Christian Holy Land early in the second millennium. These states represented a significant manifestation of the frequently changing boundary between the spatial domains of Christianity and Islam during the medieval period.

practice of their faith. Such migration processes essentially reflect the cultural significance of religious adherence. The practice of a particular religion enters into many dimensions of adherents' lives, including social interactions, personal behavior, and the formation of identity. Religious affiliation thus serves as one of the principal attributes through which adherents relate to broader cultural structures. As a result, religious adherence can be a key selective factor in migration as believers respond to specific conditions in their place of origin. Migration in such cases represents an outcome of the relationship between adherents and their surroundings rather than a religiously defined act. Nonetheless, the migration process may take on religious meaning for adherents as they interpret it within the context of their religious system.

Intolerance toward religious minorities has played a prominent role in these selective processes of migration. Patterns of persecution and discrimination have had conspicuous effects on the diffusion of Judaism. As a result of their diaspora across the Roman Empire and adjacent areas in southwest Asia, most Jews lived as members of a minority within a larger society by the third century CE. Their minority status exposed them to various forms of social exclusion and intolerance, especially in Europe where the Christian majority held strong anti-Jewish prejudices. This hostility was grounded in the traditional belief that blamed Jews for the death of Jesus, but it contained a social dimension as well, expressed as antagonism toward Jewish moneylenders or distrust of the exclusivity of Jewish society. A whole folklore of anti-Semitism developed out of these prejudices in medieval Europe, most clearly exemplified by the blood libels, accusations that Jews used the blood of Christians in Passover rituals.[45] Such animosity, later coupled to the religious fervor of the Crusades, produced a history of violent persecution and led to the expulsion or emigration of Jews from many locations. England expelled its Jewish population in 1290, for example, as did France in 1306. The Christian reconquest of the Iberian peninsula in the 1400s brought about the most massive of these expulsions, involving perhaps 200,000 Sephardic Jews, most of whom resettled in the Mediterranean region.

In other parts of Western and Central Europe, the persecution of Jews resulted in a general eastward migration, especially into Poland and Lithuania, which by the fourteenth century had granted legal protections to their Jewish populations. The Jews who settled in Poland and Lithuania were nonetheless subject to a series of massacres during the 1600s and 1700s. By the early 1800s, moreover, most of this region had been acquired by Russia through the partition of Poland and westward expansion following the Napoleonic wars. Russian authorities viewed the Jewish population as a potential threat, given its high growth rate, and therefore sought to contain it within a clearly defined region, the Pale of Settlement, located along Russia's western boundary. By the end of the nineteenth century, this region had become the world's leading center of Jewish settlement. A resurgence of anti-Semitism in the 1880s, however, incited a new period of violent persecution, resulting in the emigration of nearly three million Jews from western Russia and other parts of Eastern Europe by 1914.[46] A substantial majority of these migrants settled in the United States, while others went to Western Europe, South America, Palestine, and South Africa. Virulent anti-Semitism subsequently became a state policy of Nazi Germany in the 1930s, ultimately resulting in the murder of six million Jews, and the migration of hundreds of thousands to other parts of the world, particularly the United States and the Soviet Union. Persistent anti-Semitism in the Soviet Union and its constituent states subsequently led to significant Jewish emigration, primarily to the United States and Israel.

Religious intolerance contributed to the migration of other groups as well, especially in the context of broader social or political conflicts between majority and minority religious groups. The expulsion of Jews from Spain and Portugal in the late fifteenth century, for example, was followed in the sixteenth and seventeenth centuries by even more massive expulsions of Spanish Muslims, perhaps as many as 3.5 million, most of whom resettled in North Africa. Christian leaders, supported by the institution of the Spanish Inquisition, considered the presence of Muslims to be inimical to Christian hegemony and the preservation of authentic Christian beliefs and practices. Many of these Spanish Muslims had in fact converted to Christianity, at least publicly, but the continuing practice of Islam in private was perceived by Christians to represent a sufficiently grave danger to justify the expulsions. In other cases, religious minorities have been targeted by dominant groups as threats to political stability. Thus the aforementioned migration of Muslims from Crimea and the Caucasus to the Ottoman Empire developed in part through Russian efforts to eliminate possible sources of opposition in asserting control over those regions. Similarly, during the late nineteenth and early twentieth centuries the beleaguered Ottomans violently oppressed Christian minorities who sought independence or sided with the empire's enemies, resulting in the migration of hundreds of thousands of Armenians to the Soviet Union, other parts of the Middle East, Europe, and the United States, and the relocation of nearly a million Christian Syrians to Egypt, South America, India, and the United States.

Along somewhat different lines, the migration of religious groups can be motivated simply by fear of the consequences of minority status within a changing social context. A conspicuous example of such processes developed following the partition of British India into two independent states, predominantly Muslim Pakistan and predominantly Hindu India, in 1947. During the process of decolonization, political discord between Hindus and Muslims escalated into widespread violence, causing hundreds of thousands of deaths. Thus around eight million Muslims migrated from India to Pakistan, and an equal number of Hindus migrated from Pakistan to India. Approximately two-thirds of this cross-migration involved movement between India and West Pakistan, while the other third took place between India and East Pakistan.[47]

Migration in response to persecution and discrimination has repeatedly arisen out of interactions between adherents of different religious traditions, but similar patterns have also developed among groups sharing a larger, common tradition. Conflicts between adherents of different traditions are rooted primarily in the incompatibility of their worldviews, most often with regard to issues of revealed truth, religious authority, or the nature of the superhuman. Contention between religious groups within the same tradition, on the other hand, emerges more often from conflicting understandings of religious authenticity and the relative legitimacy of different readings of a shared faith. Again, migration represents an important spatial outcome of such conflicts, particularly when they develop between majority and minority groups.

The divisiveness brought about by the Protestant Reformation produced many examples of this type of migration. The spread of Calvinism during the 1500s, for example, resulted in persistent friction in France between the Calvinist Huguenots and the Roman Catholic majority. Many Huguenots thus migrated to Protestant states before and during the French religious wars of the late 1500s. The Edict of Nantes in 1598 provided Huguenots with a measure of protection, but their persecution resumed in the 1600s, and in 1685 the Edict of Nantes was revoked. By the end of the 1600s, as many as 400,000 Huguenots had left France for Protestant European states or North America. During the early 1500s, Protestants fleeing Spanish Roman Catholic rule in the Netherlands similarly moved to England and Germany; while in the late 1500s and early 1600s, Protestants in the Netherlands' southern provinces, still under Spanish control, migrated to the northern provinces where Protestants dominated. On the other hand, Protestant hegemony in the British Isles led to legal restrictions that provoked Roman Catholic emigration from England starting in the 1500s and from Ireland by the end of the 1600s. Many of these migrants relocated to nearby Roman Catholic regions of Europe, including France and the southern Netherlands, while others moved to North America. The colony of Maryland, intended by its original proprietors to serve as a refuge for British Roman Catholics, became an important colonial destination, although Roman Catholics remained a minority there. As a final example, the political fragmentation and religious diversity of the Holy Roman Empire prevented the universal establishment of either Protestant or Roman Catholic hegemony. Instead, the Diet of Augsburg in 1555 ruled that within the empire's local states inhabitants would follow the religion of the local ruler, either Lutheranism or Roman Catholicism, with the provision that adherents unwilling to change their religion would be allowed to emigrate. As a result, much cross-migration developed between Lutheran and Roman Catholic states.

The diverse interpretations of Christianity that arose from the Reformation also produced conflict within Protestantism as different groups asserted the legitimacy of their specific religious system. The migrations associated with such conflicts most often developed as adherents of the locally dominant form of Protestantism, usually the state church, sought to suppress other religious systems. The early migrations of Anabaptists, for example, derived largely from their persecution by other Protestants.[48] Founded in Switzerland and the Netherlands in the early 1500s, the Anabaptist movement sought a radical restoration of Christianity to its original principles, insisting on adult baptism, the rejection of violence, and the separation of church and state. The last of these beliefs posed an obvious threat to the hegemony of the state churches. The banning of Anabaptism by the Holy Roman Empire was thus supported by Lutherans as well as Roman Catholics. Anabaptists were also expelled during the 1500s from various Swiss Protestant cities and from England. Some found refuge in the more tolerant context of the Netherlands' northern provinces, while others moved eastward to rural districts in Moravia and Prussia. Many also migrated to colonial Pennsylvania, drawn there by both agricultural opportunity and religious tolerance.

Persecution by the established church played a key role as well in the emigration of many English Protestants during the 1500s and 1600s. These dissenters rejected various beliefs and practices of the Church of England, and as a result faced numerous sanctions. Separatists who advocated a complete break with the Church of England suffered the greatest persecution. An early community of Separatists thus moved to the Netherlands in the 1580s and in 1620 crossed the Atlantic to found the colony of Pilgrims at Plymouth. The Baptists and Quakers also emerged as conspicuous Separatist groups in the 1600s, and both groups had begun to migrate to North America by the middle of the century. The migration of Quakers, who were subject to harsh treatment in Britain, increased after the founding of Pennsylvania on Quaker principles in the 1680s. The more moderate Puritans experienced less persecution than other dissenters, as they had sought to reform the Church of England from within. Their inability to do so led many to migrate to the Massachusetts Bay colony in the 1630s, however, while a smaller number moved to Holland. The chances for Puritan reform in Britain increased between 1649 and 1660 under the Commonwealth established by Oliver Cromwell, but the restoration of the monarchy in 1660 resulted in a new period of discrimination and emigration that lasted until the legal enactment of religious tolerance in 1689.

Migration and New Beginnings

The role of religion as a selective factor in migration has not been limited to cases of overt persecution or discrimination, of course. Adherents have also been religiously motivated, at least in part, by the perception that some destination has distinct advantages for the practice of their religion and provides the site for a new beginning. The migration of Puritans to the Massachusetts Bay colony, for example, appears to have been more strongly motivated by the goal of organizing a new polity founded on their religious system than by a desire to escape conditions in Britain. They believed that their success in establishing a model society in New England, "a city upon a hill" for others to emulate, would validate their version of Christianity.[49] Puritan leaders thus encouraged their followers to migrate but at the same time sought to exclude other religious groups from entering their colony. William Penn and the early Quaker founders of Pennsylvania similarly viewed their colonial polity as a "Holy Experiment" through which their beliefs could be fully realized. Quaker migration to Pennsylvania thus continued even after religious tolerance became legally enacted in Britain. Pennsylvania's colonial policies providing inexpensive land, religious tolerance, and civil liberty also attracted adherents of dissenting Protestant groups from continental Europe.

Access to large tracts of land was an especially important incentive for sectarian groups seeking isolation from the outside world, including the Moravian Brethren, the Dunkers, and Anabaptists such as the Mennonites and Amish. Indeed, the search for both land and religious tolerance became a major factor in the migration of such groups in subsequent centuries, and various authorities used this situation to attract immigrants to sparsely settled agricultural regions. In the late 1700s, for example, Mennonite and Hutterite Anabaptists living in Central and Eastern Europe were invited by Russian authorities to settle in the Ukraine and in newly acquired areas along the Black Sea and the Volga River. Authorities at first accommodated these groups by allowing them to practice their religion freely and by excusing them from military service, but later in the 1800s Russian nationalism and increasing antagonism toward unassimilated German-speaking groups prompted the revocation of these privileges. Thus starting in the 1870s, Mennonites, Hutterites, and many others of German ancestry migrated in large numbers to the United States, particularly to the Great Plains. The prairie provinces of Canada became a major destination as well. Antagonism toward the pacifist, German-speaking Hutterites in the United States during World War I also resulted in their migration to Canada, where government policies were more accommodating. In addition, Mennonites formed migrant communities in various parts of Latin America during the twentieth century.[50]

Adherents may also interpret migration to a more auspicious setting a posteriori in religious terms. In such cases, the creation of a distinctive migrant society acquires religious significance after the fact, as a concrete expression of a belief system. The Massachusetts Bay region had no prior religious significance for the Puritans, for example, but their migration to that destination acquired religious meaning because of their efforts to create an ideal society there. Moreover, religious migrants may upon arrival invest the destination itself with religious meaning as a key location in their sacred history. The migration of Mormons to the Great Basin in the late 1840s represents a case in point.[51] This migration occurred after two decades of conflict in the eastern United States between the Mormons and antagonists who disapproved of their radical reinterpretation of Christianity. Following the murder of the group's founder, Joseph Smith, most of the Mormon community followed Brigham Young into the sparsely populated Great Basin, where they hoped to establish an isolated polity free from external interference. In 1847 Young selected the Great Salt Lake basin as the Mormons' new focus of settlement, identifying it as the Zion to which the faithful would finally gather to build a holy society in anticipation of the return of Jesus. This specific destination acquired religious meaning for the first group of Mormon migrants, then, only after they had arrived. For many later migrants, however, movement to the region had a priori religious significance, based on the sacred meaning already ascribed to the region. Tens of thousands of Mormon converts from Britain, Denmark, and other parts of Europe thus migrated to Utah later in the 1800s to participate in the gathering of the faithful. Indeed, the conceptualization of Utah and its primary Mormon centers as sacred space continues to attract Mormon migration to the region.[52]

*   *   *

The diffusion of religion through migration has taken various forms, then, in many cases developing incidentally but in others emerging from selective processes focusing on a specific religious group. The resulting movements of adherents have also had varied consequences. Most importantly, migration alters the social and cultural contexts in which a religion is practiced. It may have a major impact on the social status of adherents, for example. Migrants adhering to the majority religion in their place of origin may become a minority in their destination, while adherents of a minority religion may achieve local dominance in a new, more isolated setting. Similarly, migration typically brings believers into contact with new cultural influences. In some instances, migrant communities will respond to such influences by deliberately trying to maintain their religious boundaries. In other cases, migrants will gradually modify their existing beliefs and practices as they attempt to reproduce their religious traditions in a new and different environment. Migration processes may consequently add to the internal diversity of a religious tradition as spatially separate communities of adherents adapt to diverse contexts. At the same time, the religious beliefs and practices of migrants can have pronounced effects on the places where they settle, for example by redefining hegemonic cultural patterns or provoking social conflict and change. Processes of migration, in sum, have significant repercussions for adherents, their religious systems, and their destinations.

Conversion

Conversion is in many ways a more complex factor than migration in the spatial diffusion of religions. This complexity derives in part from variations in the meaning and importance of conversion in different religious traditions. The conversion of new followers typically represents a central concern in proselytic religions. Existing adherents frequently interpret the effort to convert others as a fundamental obligation, as in the Christian concept of mission or the Islamic concept of *dawah*. Proselytic religions also ascribe great importance to the rituals associated with conversion, such as baptism in Christianity or the shahada in Islam. Ethnic and tribal religions, on the other hand, typically do not emphasize conversion, and may lack a formal ritual for initiating others into the community of believers. Particular expressions of a religious tradition may depart from these general trends, however. Christian denominations vary widely in their involvement with missionary activity, for example; while proselytism is understood to be an essential activity by Jehovah's Witnesses, it is not a part of the religious culture of the Old Order Amish. In addition, conversion processes have been significant within ethnic religions in certain settings. Judaism incorporated formal conversion rites during the reconstitution of Jewish society after the Babylonian exile, for example, although in later times conversion to Judaism became increasingly uncommon.[53] More recently, Hindu fundamentalists have actively sought the reconversion of Hindu converts to Christianity or Islam, and of the descendants of such converts, even though proselytism did not exist in traditional forms of Hinduism. The meaning of conversion in a religious tradition may thus vary contextually.

Moreover, conversion does not always involve movement into an entirely new religious tradition. It may involve a shift to a different expression of the tradition to which the adherent already belongs. Conservative Protestant movements from the United States, for example, have acquired millions of converts from Roman Catholicism in Latin America over the past century. In postcolonial Africa, Islamic reform movements influenced by Wahhabism have, on a smaller scale, attracted converts from the local Sufi brotherhoods that have traditionally dominated African Islam.[54] Along similar lines, missionary work has focused as well on religious renewal among nominal adherents, as in the extensive religious revivals within American Protestantism during the 1700s and early 1800s.

The act of conversion itself entails complex processes of cultural, social, and psychological change. Conversion can be defined in abstract terms as acceptance of a particular religion accompanied by a perceived transformation in spiritual welfare and a redefinition of personal identity.[55] From a phenomenological perspective, however, this general definition encompasses a great variety of religious experiences, involving diverse motivations, emotions, and insights. Moreover, some individuals are more likely to convert than others, based on their specific personal traits or the nature of their interactions with existing adherents. In addition, conversion has implications beyond the narrowly defined domain of religious belief and practice. The adoption of a new religion with a distinct worldview and ethos often results in basic changes in the convert's cultural givens, although the extent of such changes varies. Converts may identify with a new religion through the participation in certain ritual practices, for example, without simultaneously recasting fundamental cultural values. The social effects of conversion tend to be more immediate, as the convert's redefined identity gives rise to new patterns of social interaction.

The nature of the conversion experience also raises complex issues of agency. From the believer's point of view, conversion may be interpreted primarily as the product of divine action. As a cultural process, however, conversion typically develops out of interactions, direct or indirect, between converts and existing adherents. Such interactions can be intentionally initiated by potential converts responding to personal motivations or by adherents seeking to spread their faith. Two very different expressions of human agency can therefore be at work, reflecting the distinct perspectives of the proselyte and the proselytizer. At the same time, the interactions that lead to conversion can be shaped as well by underlying social and cultural structures. The religious dimensions of local power relations or patterns of identity formation may produce indirect pressures for individuals to convert to a particular religion, for example. Context, in other words, plays a key role in the realization of conversion processes. And finally, efforts to promote conversion by existing believers have in various settings generated conflict. Established religious groups in an area have often sought to block the spread of other religions, and secular authorities have similarly attempted to limit conversion processes that appear to threaten the stability of existing social and cultural patterns. As a result, the meaning of the act of conversion can become contested among various interests, portrayed as a positive form of change or as a harmful disruption of the status quo.

Diverse factors have thus influenced the nature of conversion processes and their effects on the diffusion of religions. The significance of those spatial effects is in turn reflected in two broad themes. The first theme concerns the spatial processes through which religions have been transmitted from existing adherents to new converts. Of these processes, missionary activity has had an especially pronounced effect on religious diffusion. Driven by the intentional actions of existing adherents, this means of conversion often has explicit spatial objectives, as expressed in the concept of the mission field (photo 2.5). The establishment of religious hegemony in an area represents a very different type of process, but it too has strongly affected the spread of religions through conversion. More selective social factors have also influenced patterns of conversion among specific groups. All of these processes have had greater effects in some places than in others, however. The second theme thus focuses on the relationships between conversion and place. Given the selectivity of conversion, places differ in the number of potential converts that they contain. Moreover, existing adherents focus missionary activity on some areas more than others, in response to perceptions of need or likelihood of success. The influence of structural factors that foster or inhibit conversion varies spatially as well. Certain places have consequently emerged as important settings for the diffusion of religion through conversion. Together, then, these themes provide a framework for examining both the spatial effects of conversion processes and their diverse influences on specific places.

Photo 2.5. Sign at the exit of the parking lot of the Calvary Temple Church, a conservative Christian group with a strong evangelical program. This definition of the mission field as the entire world outside the group's own institutional space reflects both its sense of its own distinctiveness and its commitment to missionary activity as part of its Christian ethos. Kerrville, Texas, 2001.
Source: Author.

Spatial Effects of Missionary Activity

With regard to the first of the above themes, missionary activity again represents the most conspicuous spatial process in the diffusion of religions through conversion. Such activity has taken varied forms, from the local efforts of individuals to the global operations of formal institutions; but in all cases it involves efforts by existing adherents to persuade others to adopt a particular religion. The efficacy of missionary activity results partly from its importance to existing believers, either as an expression of their own faith or as an explicit religious duty. Within proselytic religions especially, such understandings of mission establish strong motivations for the support or participation of adherents. Mission, in essence, represents part of the religion's ethos. The institutional organization of much missionary work also represents a key factor in its widespread impacts on religious diffusion. Missionary institutions have varied in their effectiveness and in many instances have met with opposition. Nonetheless, they have influenced patterns of religious adherence in varied contexts by defining frameworks and providing resources for sustained proselytism. Institutional structures have been particularly important in the spread of proselytic religions into unfamiliar settings, often through explicit strategies of religious expansionism.

The diffusion of Christianity very clearly evinces the effects of systematic proselytism. The missionary journeys of Paul and other apostles were crucial to the spread of Christianity to Asia Minor, Greece, Egypt, and Italy during the first century CE. This activity at first focused on areas of Jewish settlement; but as Christianity's universal nature became more fully articulated, missionary work among Gentiles rapidly expanded. Despite intermittent persecution, Christianity became widespread throughout the Roman Empire over the next two centuries, and in the fourth century was established as the empire's official religion. Christian evangelism subsequently shifted toward northern and western Europe, still led primarily by the efforts of individual evangelists. Ireland thus became Christianized during the fifth century, and provided many of the missionaries who worked in England, Scotland, northern France, and Germany over the next several centuries. By the time the western and eastern branches of Christianity separated from one another in 1054, missionaries had brought the former to Scandinavia, Poland, and Hungary, and the latter to the Balkans, East-Central Europe, Russia, and scattered locations in Asia.

As the medieval period progressed, evangelism became more organized within the Roman Catholic Church, particularly through the formation of religious orders focusing on missionary work. With the founding of the Franciscans, Augustinians, Dominicans, and similar mendicant orders during the thirteenth century, itinerant friars undertook missions to various parts of northern and eastern Europe, northern Africa, southwest Asia and beyond, although generally with limited success. Starting in the 1500s, the rise of European colonialism significantly expanded the geographical scope of such activity as Roman Catholic missionaries sought to convert the indigenous inhabitants of Portuguese, Spanish, and French colonies in the Americas, Africa, and Southeast Asia. The older mendicant orders were joined in these efforts by the Jesuits, founded in the sixteenth century. The Jesuits also led Roman Catholic efforts to evangelize regions beyond the domain of European colonialism, particularly in China, Japan, and India. To maintain centralized control over an increasingly global missionary enterprise, the Roman Catholic Church created the Congregation for the

Propagation of the Faith in 1622. During the sixteenth and seventeenth centuries, the Roman Catholic emphasis on the conversion of indigenous colonial subjects had its greatest impact in Latin America and the Philippines, where the Roman Catholic Church became a dominant and enduring cultural institution. Elsewhere during this period, however, Roman Catholic missions were less effective and both missionaries and converts often faced persecution.

The emergence of Protestantism brought about a further expansion of Christian missionary activity. During the Reformation, Protestant proselytism operated mostly at local or regional scales, primarily with the goal of attracting adherents from within the existing Christian population, as in the spread of Calvinism in France or the rise of Anabaptism in Switzerland and the Netherlands. In the North American colonies, the Protestant churches placed little emphasis on the conversion of indigenous peoples, focusing instead on religious renewal among colonial settlers. This approach peaked during the Great Awakening of the early to mid-1700s. During the early 1800s, such activity again became a central concern of Protestant evangelical denominations on the American settlement frontier, producing rapid growth among Methodists, Baptists, and Disciples of Christ. By this time, Protestants in Europe and the United States had also begun to establish missionary societies in support of a broader involvement in evangelism. Some missionary societies were affiliated with a particular denomination, while others were interdenominational.

Although missionary societies at first tended to focus on domestic activities, they increasingly engaged in foreign work as well, particularly as Western colonialism and imperialism in the 1800s improved access to mission fields in Africa and Asia. The Roman Catholic Church likewise increased its missionary efforts in these regions. In the 1800s and early 1900s, new sources of Christian missionaries also emerged with the formation of a number of strongly evangelistic Protestant denominations, particularly in the United States. Such groups, including the Mormons, Seventh-Day Adventists, Jehovah's Witnesses, and various Holiness and Pentecostal churches, viewed proselytism as an obligation for all adherents and invested significant resources into both domestic and foreign missions. During the same period, the mainstream Protestant churches in the United States also became more widely committed to foreign missions and began to promote the concept of global evangelization. Through these developments, the United States took on an increasingly important role in the expansion of Protestant missionary activity, and during the twentieth century became the world's leading supplier of missionaries to foreign lands. The growth in Christian missionary activity during this period produced much competition, not only between Protestants and Roman Catholics but among different Protestant groups as well. To coordinate their efforts, many moderate and liberal Protestant churches thus adopted a more ecumenical approach to missionary work in the early 1900s. Conservative Protestant churches tended to work more independently, however, to prevent the dilution of their distinct messages. Moreover, many conservative Protestant groups supported missions to Roman Catholics as well as to non-Christians.

Christian evangelism from the 1800s onward varied significantly in its impacts on different places. Its influence remained limited in Asia, with the exception of Korea, where Protestantism in particular grew rapidly after World War II. Missionary efforts have had more extensive effects in sub-Saharan Africa, particularly since the mid-twentieth century; most estimates suggest that Christians now account for over

40 percent of the region's population and represent a clear majority in many countries. The relative growth of Roman Catholicism and Protestantism in colonial Africa varies to some extent according to the predominant religion of the ruling European power, although both groups are active in many parts of central Africa. During recent decades, however, much of the expansion of African Christianity has occurred through the growth of indigenous Christian churches rather than because of foreign missionary activity, as discussed in chapter 3. Protestant evangelism has also had dramatic effects on religious adherence in parts of Latin America through the conversion of millions of Roman Catholics. This process originated in the missionary work of mainstream Protestant groups in the late 1800s, but has increased in recent decades through the efforts of Pentecostal denominations, most notably the Assemblies of God, and other conservative evangelistic churches, principally of North American origin.[56] The foreign missions of such groups have been successful at gaining converts in other regions of the world as well. Consequently, within a number of denominations that originated within the United States a majority of adherents now live elsewhere. Over 90 percent of the adherents of the Assemblies of God and the Seventh-Day Adventists, for example, live outside the United States, as do over 80 percent of Jehovah's Witnesses and over 50 percent of Mormons.

Finally, an important recent trend in Christian missions has been the creation of global broadcasting networks to carry on evangelism by radio or television rather than through personal contact.[57] Estimates suggest that by the early twenty-first century Christian broadcasting reached more than a billion listeners in an average month, with perhaps a third of those residing in predominantly non-Christian regions. In areas where a religion is already present, broadcasting apparently serves more to reinforce the commitment of existing adherents than to effect new conversions. But broadcasting has also been used by Christian evangelists to reach many areas that have otherwise been relatively inaccessible to missionaries, particularly in Africa, Asia, and Latin America; and in these contexts religious broadcasts appear to be a factor in some conversions. Both Roman Catholics and Protestants have used broadcasting for this purpose, although Protestants have generally been more widely involved. Conservative and fundamentalist Protestants from the United States have been especially active. Their involvement in broadcasting derives in part from the belief that the Second Coming of Christ will occur once the Christian gospel has been preached to all peoples of the world. To this end, an association of conservative Protestant broadcasting networks formed the "World by 2000" project in 1985 to make the gospel available by radio in a sufficient variety of languages to reach every person on earth. Early in the twenty-first century, this group reasserted this goal as the "World by Radio" movement. These efforts have had a specific geographical target identified as the "10/40 Window," an area stretching across Africa and Asia between 10 degrees and 40 degrees north latitude, which contains the world's largest concentrations of non-Christians (map 2.9).[58]

Missionary activity in Islam was traditionally less formally organized than in Christianity. The ecclesiastical structures typical of most Christian denominations had no direct parallel in Islam. Belief in the responsibility of all Muslims to participate in dawah, the call of others to Islam, thus served as the impetus for individual proselytism, but during Islam's early history did not give rise to institutions devoted to that purpose.[59] Instead, the early spread of Islam in southwest Asia and northern Africa

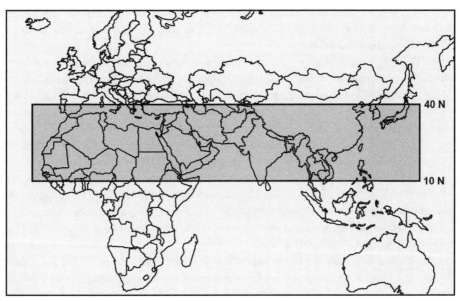

Map 2.9. The 10/40 Window, so-called because it lies between 10 degrees and 40 degrees north latitude. This area became a major target of Christian missionary activity during the twentieth century as it contains a large majority of the world's non-Christians. Evangelical Christians believe that spreading the Christian Gospel to all nations of the world, an endeavor known as the Great Commission, is a fundamental religious obligation.

occurred through more gradual processes of conversion that developed following the local establishment of Muslim hegemony, as discussed below. Islamic missionary activity eventually became more evident in areas beyond this early Muslim realm, however, especially through the growth of Sufism.[60]

Sufi approaches to Islam originated in the seventh century, emphasizing the mystical experience of the divine over the more worldly concerns of the expanding Muslim empire. Early Sufis focused on attaining insight through personal piety, a process that often involved ascetic or ecstatic practices. Islamic jurists disapproved of the movement, asserting that its emphasis on individual experience detracted from the authority of the Quran, but by the twelfth century Sufism had become widely integrated into Islamic religious life. It also began to acquire more of a social character through the formation of Sufi orders, communities of adherents organized around a particular school of Sufi teachings.[61] Sufi orders became involved in missionary work as their members began to seek converts as they traveled across Africa and Asia, along Muslim trade routes or in the wake of recent Muslim conquests. The success of Sufi missionary activity depended on the charisma of individual teachers, but it also arose from their doctrinal flexibility, as they frequently did not insist that new converts immediately abandon prior beliefs and practices. The conversion process might therefore include a syncretistic interval before converts fully adopted Islam. Sufi proselytism thus contributed to the spread of Islam across Central Asia after the conversion of Mongol rulers in the 1200s and 1300s. Sufism appeared in India at about the same time, although it had relatively little impact on the growth of Islam there until the 1500s and 1600s. Sufi teachers also supported the diffusion of Islam to parts of Southeast Asia by the 1500s. In Africa, Sufism had spread across the Sahara by the 1400s, and became a major factor in the growth of Islam through conversion, especially in West Africa, from the 1600s.[62]

During the past century, Islamic missionary work has become more systematic through the formation of organizations emphasizing dawah as part of their mission. Some organizations have focused on the revival of orthodoxy among nominal Muslims rather than on conversions from other traditions. The Tablighi Jamaat ("Missionary Society") or Tabligh, founded in northern India in 1927 by Muhammad Ilyas, exemplifies this approach. This group arose as a reaction against the prevalence of Hindu elements in the popular Islam of northern India. Its initial objective was to persuade Indian Muslims to abandon these syncretistic accretions, to adhere more closely to Islamic law and the teachings of the Quran, and to worship regularly in mosques. To this end, members of the Tabligh periodically went on missionary journeys, traveling in small groups to targeted locations to preach their message of Islamic renewal. This approach proved to be highly effective in promoting orthodox beliefs and practices among Indian Muslims. As a result the Tablighi Jamaat has grown into a significant Islamic movement, carrying on similar activities in Muslim communities around the world. It remains concerned with eliminating syncretistic elements from Islam in Africa and Asia, but has also addressed the secularization of Muslim migrants to Europe and North America. Similar Islamic reform movements have developed during the twentieth century in Africa, where Islamic syncretism is widespread. These movements have often contested the nature of Islam with the Sufi orders, which in recent centuries have been highly influential in various African settings. The Izala ("Eradication") movement in Nigeria, for example, organized in 1978 to purify the practice of Islam by eliminating un-Quranic Sufi innovations, such as pilgrimages to the tombs of Sufi saints and other Sufi rituals.[63] Contemporary Islamic organizations have also conducted missionary activity among non-Muslims. Most significantly, a number of pan-Islamic organizations founded in recent decades have supported the wider propagation of Islam. These organizations emerged as part of the resurgence in Islamic identity and solidarity that spread throughout the Muslim world toward the end of the twentieth century. Funded primarily by oil revenues from Arab states, they have supported a variety of Islamic causes including proselytism. The first of these organizations, the World Muslim League, was formed under Saudi leadership in 1962 to disseminate and defend orthodox Islam. In 1969, Saudi Arabia also sponsored the founding of the Organization of the Islamic Conference (OIC), an international association of Islamic states, with broadly similar goals. Much of the religious work of both organizations has promoted orthodoxy within existing Muslim communities, a goal that in part reflects the dominance of Wahhabism in Saudi Arabia. These groups have also sought to advance the spread of Islam, however, through the construction of mosques, cultural centers, and schools; through the publication of religious literature; and through Islamic religious broadcasting. Missionary work among non-Muslims has in addition been a major function of a third key organization, the World Islamic Call Society, founded in Libya in 1972. As well as funding local Muslim institutions and the teaching of Arabic, this group has focused on the training and mobilization of missionaries, particularly to work in African countries where Muslims represent a minority. Indeed, the activities of all three of these groups have been most conspicuous in Africa, now the major field of competition between Christian and

Islamic missionaries.[64] For the groups actively involved in dawah, countering the spread of Christianity in Africa represents a crucial objective.

Islamic missionary activity has developed, finally, in some parts of the world where Islam had little presence before the 1900s. In the United States and Japan, for example, members of the Tablighi Jamaat have begun to address the conversion of non-Muslims.[65] During the past century, Islam has also spread in the United States through the efforts of African American Muslims. Such efforts began with two black separatist groups supporting syncretistic forms of Islam: the Moorish Science Temple of America, founded in Newark in 1913, and the Nation of Islam, founded in Detroit in 1930. The Nation of Islam became the more influential of the two after World War II, but continued to deviate in many ways from traditional Islam. In the 1970s, however, its leaders began to emphasize adherence to orthodox Islamic beliefs and practices, in part through the influence of the Dar ul-Islam movement, an African American group centered in New York. This change in emphasis gave rise to an orthodox movement within African American Islam that ultimately abandoned its separate organizational identity as being un-Islamic, and identified instead with the Sunni Muslim community at large. A heterodox splinter group continued as the Nation of Islam, but its membership has remained small. The orthodox movement, on the other hand, has strongly influenced the growth of Islam through conversion in the United States, especially among African Americans.

Missionary activity has played a major role as well in the spread of Buddhism, beginning with the teachings of the Buddha and his early disciples in the Gangetic plain. Such activity acquired a distinctive institutional character in Buddhism, however, through its association with Buddhist monasticism. This monastic tradition originated during the Buddha's lifetime as his disciples renounced secular life and accompanied him on his missionary wanderings. After his death, monastic life gradually became more organized as itinerant monks regularly congregated in certain locations, especially during the monsoon season when travel became more difficult, and later began to settle in permanent monasteries. As they increased in number, monasteries became the institutional focus of Buddhism in India, providing lay adherents with models of piety and devotion to Buddhist teachings. As such, monasteries also became centers of missionary activity. Much of this activity took place at a local scale through interactions between the monastic community and local society. Buddhist monasteries typically located near existing settlements to have access to lay believers who could furnish needed material support, for which adherents accrued spiritual merit, and so that monks could provide religious guidance and perform ritual functions for the laity. In addition, nearby towns and cities served as important missionary fields. Monks fulfilled a religious obligation by spreading Buddhist teachings within the local vicinity and at the same time attracted new adherents and support for their monastery. Proselytism thus became a crucial form of interaction between monasteries and their local environs. As certain monastic settlements in India grew in size and influence, moreover, they became involved in proselytism at a wider scale, serving as principal centers of learning for those monks who carried Buddhism to distant locations. Many such missionaries subsequently established monastic communities at these destinations, which again supported the local spread of Buddhism.

Following his conversion to Buddhism in the third century BCE, the Mauryan emperor Asoka contributed to the early proliferation of Buddhist monasteries in India.

In addition, he instituted new patterns in the expansion of Buddhism by tying that process to the interests of the state. Although he maintained a policy of religious tolerance, he established Buddhism as the official religion and sought to spread its teachings by dispatching missionaries throughout his empire. To cultivate a unified social order throughout his empire, he also promulgated the principles of Buddhism through his "rock edicts," moral and ethical statements in local languages carved into stone pillars, cliff faces, and cave walls across India (map 2.10). Asoka also sent missionaries to locations outside his own empire. This endeavor proved most successful in Sri Lanka, where according to tradition Asoka's missionaries converted the king and much of the nobility. With the formation of local monastic communities and places of worship, Buddhism spread among the population at large and became a persistent element in the ethnic identity of the Sinhalese majority in Sri Lanka.[66]

This hierarchical pattern of proselytism, in which Buddhism was adopted first by the ruling class and later by broader segments of the populace, recurred in a number of Asian states during subsequent centuries. The early spread of Buddhism north and west of India into Central Asia, for example, was fostered by the conversion of the Bactrian-Greek ruler Menander during the second century BCE and by the support of missionary activity by the Kushana (or Yueh-chi) ruler Kanishka during the second century CE.[67] In sixth-century Japan, Prince Shotoku's adoption of Buddhism advanced its broader acceptance, leading to its establishment as Japan's official religion in the eighth century. After various early contacts, Buddhism likewise achieved sig-

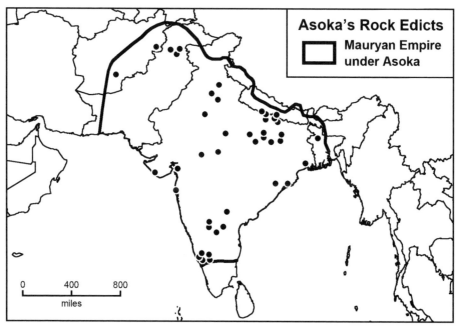

Map 2.10. The rock edicts of Asoka, the Mauryan emperor who ruled much of South Asia during the third century BCE. Rocks and pillars at these locations carried a variety of inscriptions expressing social and ethical principles reflecting Asoka's acceptance of Buddhism. These inscriptions supported the diffusion of Buddhism throughout much of South Asia at the time. The locations depicted include those sites where edicts have survived as well as those mentioned in historical sources.

nificant growth in Tibet during the eighth century under the reign of Trisong Detsen, who supported missionary activity and built the region's first Buddhist monastery. Similar patterns also developed in Southeast Asia, particularly as various rulers embraced a revival in Theravada Buddhism that originated in Sri Lanka early in the second millennium CE. Within these hierarchical patterns of expansion, concern for the growth of Buddhism presumably reflected the religious convictions of individual rulers, but the popular adoption of Buddhist precepts also served their political interests by creating a common ethical foundation for the ordering of society. Moreover, these patterns often produced important relationships between Buddhist institutions and the state, as discussed in chapter 3.

The spread of Buddhism outside of India did not occur solely through state sponsorship, of course. The independent missionary work of monks continued to be a crucial factor as well. In China, the early diffusion of Buddhism developed around the beginning of the Common Era through the eastward movement of monks and lay adherents following trade routes from Central Asia. By the second century CE monks from Central Asia and India had established a number of monasteries in eastern China and had begun translating Buddhist texts into Chinese. These monks also attracted growing numbers of Chinese converts, at first mostly educated people of moderate social standing.[68] Adherence to Buddhism broadened over time, however, and by the end of the fourth century extended into both the ruling class and the peasantry. Thus by the time Buddhism achieved significant imperial support in the seventh and eighth centuries, it had already diffused widely through the Chinese population.

Independent missionary patterns also developed in many parts of Asia through the proliferation of smaller, autonomous monastic communities serving limited local populations. These smaller monasteries, whose members generally adhered less strictly to orthodox doctrines, contributed to the spread of Buddhism in part through their ready accommodation of syncretistic tendencies. The merger of Buddhism with Taoism, Confucianism, and local folk traditions in popular religious practice in China and the incorporation of older shamanistic practices into Tibetan Buddhism both illustrate the effects of this flexibility. In more recent times, independent missions have also dominated conversion processes associated with the spread of Buddhism out of its traditional Asian domain, particularly to Europe, North America, and Australia. Among those involved in the emergence of this pattern, the thousands of monks who have fled Tibet since the Chinese takeover in the 1950s have been especially influential (photo 2.6).

Adherents of the major proselytic religions have thus organized missionary activity through a variety of institutional structures. The latter have differed with respect to the spatial scope of their operations and the extent to which they have been centrally administered. In the aggregate, though, they have been very effective in promoting the diffusion of the major proselytic religions over large areas. Much of that effectiveness derives from the substantial resources that larger religious bodies have been able to devote to proselytism. In addition, missionary activities within these religions have frequently advanced in association with other social and political processes, such as the expansion of empires, the unification of states, the growth of trade networks, or the extension of more general patterns of cultural influence. Consequently, the missionary efforts of prominent religious groups have often had secular as well as religious significance.

Photo 2.6.   The Karma Triyana Dharmachakra Center, a Tibetan Buddhist temple and monastery located atop Mead's Mountain north of Woodstock, New York. The center serves as the North American seat of the leadership of the Kagyu school of Tibetan Buddhism. It houses a permanent community of Kagyu monks and also serves as a missionary and educational center. Woodstock, New York, 2001.
Source: Author.

Among smaller or less established proselytic groups, on the other hand, proselytism tends to be tied more exclusively to religious concerns. Missionary activity is often crucial to the survival of such groups, including sects that have split off from a larger tradition and cults that have originated outside existing traditions. Their small size in most cases precludes the formation of specialized missionary institutions. Such groups typically consider proselytism to be an important expression of faith, however, and adherents may thus accept missionary work as a common obligation. This approach has been characteristic of many Protestant sects during their formative period, and has remained a defining attribute of some, such as Jehovah's Witnesses. The so-called new religious movements, the diverse cults that have proliferated throughout the world during the past century, also generally follow this pattern. The missionary activities of such groups initially tend to be organized at a local scale, but in some cases their geographical scope has broadened as the group has gained supporters. The Unification Church founded by Sun Myung Moon in 1954, for example, spread from Korea to the United States and Europe through persistent missionary campaigns during the 1970s.

Spatial Effects of Religious Hegemony

In contrast to missionary activity, patterns of religious hegemony have affected the diffusion of religions through conversion processes arising from general social and cultural influences rather than from direct appeals to individual converts by existing believers. Religious hegemony develops when adherents of a specific religion achieve a position of dominance through which their beliefs and practices acquire broader influence over an area. The dominant group's status may be based on its numerical superiority, but in such cases the local effects of its hegemony on conversion may be limited by the small number of potential converts. Patterns of hegemony have more extensive effects on conversion when the dominant group initially comprises a minority in the area over which its influence extends. In such cases, the group's status derives from its position of control within society.

As a factor in conversion, religious hegemony can take diverse forms. The establishment of a state religion represents an obvious expression of hegemony, linking religious affiliation and political identity. The conversion of a ruler may have similar effects, as discussed above. Less formally, a hegemonic religion may develop pervasive influences through its incorporation into ordinary realms of daily life, for example by determining the prevailing calendar of holidays or defining widely accepted behavioral norms. A dominant religious group may similarly exert influence through the prominence of its institutional infrastructure, especially if it encompasses secular functions such as education or health care. Participation in the dominant religion may also provide social or economic advantages, while nonadherents may face various types of discrimination or social exclusion. Through recurring interactions with existing believers, moreover, others will gain increasing familiarity with the dominant religion over time, and because of its associations with local power structures may gradually come to accept it as being normative. Together, such factors produce diverse pressures and incentives for individuals to convert to the hegemonic religion. As a result, these expressions of hegemony have had significant effects on patterns of religious adherence in various contexts.

The establishment of religious hegemony was highly influential in the early spread of Islam out of Arabia into other parts of southwest Asia and North Africa, for example. Muslim rulers placed little emphasis on the active conversion of indigenous peoples during the first several centuries of Islamic expansion. The Quran prohibits conversion by force (2: 256), an injunction that Muslim rulers generally followed; and at this time Islam lacked the necessary organizational structures to support extensive missionary activity. Moreover, the continuing subordination of non-Muslim populations preserved the higher status of Arab Muslims in newly conquered areas. Nonetheless, conversion to Islam gradually became widespread in these regions through the articulation of Islamic hegemony. This process developed principally through the reproduction of Islamic institutions, including formal entities such as mosques, schools, and courts of Islamic law as well as less formal structures such as those related to economic activity and social status. Within this institutional context, non-Muslims faced various disadvantages. They did not have the same rights as Muslims in the Islamic courts, were subject to higher rates of taxation, and had little access to political power. Because they were excluded from the Islamic system of credit, they could not participate on an equal footing with Muslims in trade and commerce. Islamic law also imposed certain restrictions, for example prohibiting non-Muslim men from marrying Muslim women. Conversion thus provided indigenous peoples with a means of improving their situation under Muslim rule; and for the poor in particular, it often brought a new sense of social status. Of course, the religious convictions of converts and proselytism by individual Muslims cannot be discounted as factors in the conversion process. Nonetheless, the establishment of hegemonic patterns clearly supported the spread of Islam through conversion in areas under the direct rule of the early Islamic empire, first in urban centers where the institutional presence was strongest and later in nearby rural districts.[69]

In addition, more limited expressions of hegemony had similar effects in contexts outside the early domain of Islam. In West Africa, for example, the international stature of Islam as a political and economic force had contributed to the conversion of numerous local rulers south of the Sahara by the thirteenth century. These rulers typically did not attempt to eliminate older animistic practices within their kingdoms, but they did cultivate connections with the larger Islamic world and thereby attracted growing numbers of Muslim merchants, scholars, and teachers. The subsequent development of economic systems dominated by Muslim trade networks thus encouraged conversions among the local merchant classes. The formation of Islamic schools in some parts of West Africa also had a major influence on conversion, as they dominated local systems of education through the nineteenth century.[70]

Patterns of hegemony have furthered the spread of other religions as well. After reconstituting the Mauryan Empire as a Buddhist state, for example, Asoka supported his missionary efforts by enacting laws intended to promote adherence to Buddhist principles, such as prohibitions against killing certain animal species.[71] Moreover, Asoka's public adoption of Buddhism imparted a broader legitimacy and prestige to the religion, which further supported its spread within his empire. Similar patterns developed in Japan, Thailand, Burma, and other parts of Asia following the conversion of local rulers, although missionary activity also contributed to the diffusion of Buddhism in these settings.

The rapid growth of Christianity following its establishment as the official religion of the Roman Empire also derived partly from hegemonic influences, including the social prestige associated with Christianity, the convergence of religious and political identity, and the state's support for Christian institutions. Later, various forms of Christian hegemony influenced conversion processes within the context of European colonialism. The dominant role of the Roman Catholic Church as a colonial institution in Latin America, for example, contributed significantly to the success of missionary efforts among indigenous peoples, which in turn reinforced European political control. In African colonies, Christian religious bodies set up a wide variety of institutions to strengthen and legitimate European rule, including schools, clinics, hospitals, and in many cases local industries. These institutions often engaged directly in missionary work, but they fostered conversion through broader social influences as well. Colonial educational systems in particular promulgated Christian ethical and behavioral norms.

Hegemonic influences have also affected the diffusion of ethnic religions in some contexts. As the Israelites came to dominate Canaan toward the end of the second millennium BCE, for example, many indigenous inhabitants of the region allied themselves with this emergent society by adopting the practices of Proto-Judaism. Similarly, the expansion of Hindu social and political hegemony into more isolated areas of India occupied by tribal animists traditionally resulted in the local spread of Hinduism, particularly among those having frequent contacts with the larger Indian society. The formation of Hindu kingdoms in parts of Southeast Asia during the first millennium CE also promoted the syncretistic spread of Hinduism, often together with elements of Buddhism.

Finally, while expressions of religious hegemony have generally affected processes of conversion through pervasive, underlying influences, they have in some contexts involved explicit coercion. Such instances have developed, for example, from the intolerance of some hegemonic forms of Christianity, either for other religions or for other Christian groups. Thus the assertion of Christian hegemony following the reconquest of Iberia, which caused massive Jewish and Muslim emigration, also led to the forced conversion of thousands of Jews and Muslims who initially chose not to leave. This process was supported by the Spanish Inquisition, which sought to suppress heresy first among these groups and later among Protestants. Patterns of religious coercion similarly emerged during the Protestant Reformation in those areas where a newly established state church insisted on either the conversion or exile of nonadherents. In Calvinist Geneva, for example, regular attendance at Protestant worship services became a civic obligation, while the practice of Roman Catholicism became a punishable offense; and inhabitants of local states within the Holy Roman Empire after 1555 were expected to conform to their ruler's religion or emigrate. Forced conversion to Islam has been less common because of the Quran's specific injunction against it and Muslim tolerance toward Judaism and Christianity as predecessors to the final revelation of Islam. Nonetheless, instances of forced conversion have occurred, particularly among animistic and polytheistic peoples conquered by Muslim empires.[72]

Spatial Effects of Selective Social Factors

In addition to religious hegemony and missionary activity, more selective social factors have also influenced the diffusion of religions. Such factors derive from social processes involving a specific set of potential converts. Most commonly, the affected group comprises individuals that have significant contacts with adherents of a foreign religion. The selective conversion of local rulers to Buddhism in different parts of Asia represents a special case of this more general pattern, but other instances have typically involved interactions between broader classes of individuals. To cite one important example, social interactions associated with international trade provided an important context for the spread of Islam among indigenous merchants in Southeast and East Asia early in the second millennium CE. As Muslim traders expanded their activities eastward, they generally operated with more freedom and over greater distances than most indigenous merchants and thus came to occupy a central position in the commercial networks that linked various coastal communities from India to China. As Muslims settled in these communities, their social and cultural norms came to permeate local mercantile society, standardizing and simplifying the process of economic exchange. In time, local merchants thus adopted the practice of Islam itself, thereby enhancing their status within the larger trade network. As a result, numerous Muslim communities had appeared around the Malay Straits and as far east as the southern coast of China by the thirteenth century. Hostility toward foreign influences ultimately limited Muslim influences in southern China, but the spread of Islam in the Malay Peninsula and Indonesia continued with the rise of Sufi missionary activity and the formation of various Muslim states.[73]

Selective conversion processes have developed in other ways as well, particularly through interactions between religious affiliation and other aspects of social identity.

Such processes are an important feature of the denominationalism that characterizes American religion, for example. Within this context, individuals have frequently changed religious affiliation based on their social circumstances.[74] One common pattern has been the movement of upwardly mobile Protestants into denominations of higher socioeconomic status, a trend exemplified by the growth of high-status mainline groups like the Episcopalians and Presbyterians in expanding suburban areas of the United States immediately after World War II.[75] At the same time, members of marginalized groups within American society have often sought to improve their position in society by affiliating with conservative Protestant denominations that emphasize strict behavioral norms, personal discipline, and a sense of moral community. This factor thus influenced the spread of various Holiness and Pentecostal churches to inner cities and to rural areas of the South and Midwest early in the twentieth century.

Many other specific factors have also influenced conversion processes, but because of their sporadic nature they have had less systematic impacts on wider patterns of religious diffusion. Intermarriage, for example, has been a factor in conversion in various settings where it is not hindered by religious law or custom. Within the pluralistic religious context of the United States, it represents a key factor in changes of affiliation between Protestant denominations and, more broadly, among Protestantism, Roman Catholicism, and Judaism.[76] The legitimacy in Islamic law of marriages between Muslim men and non-Muslim women has also affected patterns of conversion to Islam in certain contexts. Nonetheless, intermarriage has generally had limited effects on the expansion of religious distributions given its idiosyncratic pattern of occurrence. The same holds true for other factors related to the individual circumstances and concerns of potential converts. Although such factors have often developed within the context of broader influences such as religious hegemony or selective conversion, in themselves they have not generally had pronounced effects on diffusion processes.

Conversion and Place

The general processes that have influenced religious diffusion through conversion have varied among places in the magnitude of their effects, of course. These variations in part reflect patterns in the emergence of significant conversion fields, geographical contexts whose characteristics have fostered conversion processes. As discussed above, patterns of religious hegemony have in numerous instances created settings where social pressures have led to widespread conversion to the dominant religion. Conversion fields have also been defined in some cases primarily by the actions of existing believers engaged in missionary activity. The early colonial possessions of Spain and Portugal became important conversion fields, for example, through widespread proselytism among indigenous peoples by Roman Catholic religious orders. More broadly, Muslims and Christians have often targeted areas dominated by animistic or polytheistic religions as imperative contexts for proselytism. Much of the missionary work supported by adherents of these traditions has thus focused on sub-Saharan Africa over the past two centuries. In most cases, however, significant conversion fields have developed through the spatial intersection of missionary activity, either organized or spontaneous, with other factors related to prevailing social or religious conditions or the concerns of potential converts.

The absence of institutional expressions of religious authority may contribute to the growth of an active conversion field for proselytizing religious groups, for example. In the United States, the trans-Appalachian settlement frontier became an important conversion field in the early 1800s as population movements outpaced the reproduction of most religious institutions. That pattern resulted in a large unchurched population in newly settled areas, made up mostly of nominal adherents of Protestant versions of Christianity who initially had little or no contact with organized religion. Evangelical Protestant denominations, and most notably the Methodists, Baptists, and Disciples of Christ, subsequently adopted various means of advancing missionary efforts within this context. One common strategy was the organization of camp meetings, religious revivals usually held in the autumn that attracted participants to a central location from a large surrounding region (map 2.11). The camp meeting served important social functions within the context of frontier isolation, but it also became an essential institution in the widespread conversion of the unchurched to evangelical Protestantism. In addition, the evangelical churches developed diverse methods of maintaining a presence in the widely dispersed settlements west of the Appalachians. The Methodists made extensive use of circuit riders, itinerant preachers who regularly visited a series of settlements located along a circuit often hundreds of miles in length. These efforts were typically coordinated through the Methodists' national organiza-

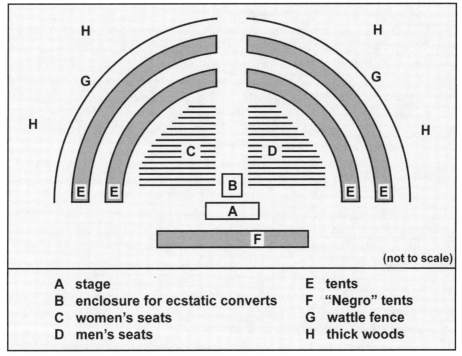

A	stage	E	tents
B	enclosure for ecstatic converts	F	"Negro" tents
C	women's seats	G	wattle fence
D	men's seats	H	thick woods

Map 2.11. Reconstruction of the layout of a camp meeting held in Fairfax County, Virginia, in 1809, adapted from a sketch of the site by architect Benjamin Latrobe. The enclosure set aside for ecstatic converts, filled with straw according to Latrobe's notes so that the converted ``might kick about without injuring themselves,'' reflects the fervent nature of the conversion experience in such contexts. Source: Journal of Benjamin Latrobe, August 23, 1806–August 8, 1809, Latrobe Papers, Manuscript Department, Maryland Historical Society, Baltimore.

tional structure. The Baptists' emphasis on local autonomy precluded the use of such a centrally organized approach. They instead achieved a presence in dispersed settlements primarily through the activities of so-called farmer-preachers, independent and self-supporting clergy more often inspired by their own conversion experiences than by formal training, who moved westward with the frontier. The Disciples of Christ, a movement that emerged in the Ohio River Valley during the revivalism of the early 1800s, largely depended on traveling evangelists to spread their message. Through such strategies, the evangelical churches acquired significant numbers of converts as the nineteenth century progressed, growing far more rapidly than the Protestant denominations that had dominated colonial America. As a result, the Methodists and Baptists became the leading Protestant denominations in the United States, and the Disciples emerged as one of the most prominent indigenous religious groups.

The decline of traditional sources of religious authority in an area may similarly lead to the development of conversion fields for innovative or sectarian religious groups. The challenges to existing ecclesiastical power expressed during the Protestant Reformation, for example, produced a cultural environment in northern Europe in which conversions to newly formed religious groups became commonplace. Most conversions in this context involved affiliation with a Protestant state church, but the broader challenge to centralized religious authority also contributed to the growth of many sectarian and dissenting groups, such as the Anabaptists, Baptists, Quakers, and Separatists. More recently, processes of secularization in many developed countries have led to a decline in the authority attributed to traditional religious institutions. As mainstream religious institutions have themselves become more secular in outlook, however, many of their followers have converted to smaller sects and cults that continue to emphasize the power of religious meanings. Highly secularized contexts, in other words, have often become important conversion fields for religious groups outside the established social mainstream.[77] This pattern developed within the United States during the 1970s with the rise of the Unification Church, the Hare Krishna movement, and many other new religious movements. It has perhaps been even more pronounced in Europe, where the effects of secularization have been more extensive, as seen in the rise of membership in unconventional or less formally organized religious movements (photo 2.7).[78] Along somewhat different lines, a society's acceptance of religious pluralism tends to weaken claims of exclusive authority by particular religious groups, making conversion less contentious and perhaps more frequent. Within the pluralistic and voluntaristic context of American religion, for example, changes in denominational affiliation occur with conspicuous frequency. According to most estimates, toward the end of the twentieth century at least 40 percent of American Protestants had changed affiliations during their lifetimes, as had 15 percent of American Roman Catholics and over 10 percent of American Jews.[79]

In more traditional settings, compatibility between an area's existing religious culture and a newly expanding religion may support widespread conversions. The early diffusion of Buddhism among the educated classes in China, for example, was fostered by correspondences between Buddhist doctrines and prevalent Taoist beliefs concerning the immortality of the soul and the role of asceticism in achieving enlightenment. The subsequent popularization of Buddhism in turn reflected the identification of Taoist and Confucian sages, as well as various folk deities, with different figures within the complex pantheon of Mahayana Buddhism. Similarly, various aspects of Christianity,

Photo 2.7. The Mormon Temple in Freiberg, Germany. When the temple was dedicated in 1985, Freiberg was located within the secularized setting of the German Democratic Republic, where unconventional religious groups had begun to flourish. This Mormon Temple was the first to be established in a communist country, a context viewed by evangelical groups of the time as a potentially important conversion field. Freiberg, Germany, 2006.

Source: Donny Wöllauer (commons.wikimedia.org/wiki/Image:Freiberg_Tempel.jpg), placed in the public domain.

including the concepts of salvation, resurrection, baptism, and the ritual of the Eucharist, had parallels in the Hellenistic mystery religions practiced within the Roman Empire. Most contemporary scholarship no longer regards these mystery religions as a direct source of Christian belief and practice, but the aforementioned parallels did likely contribute to the acceptance of Christianity in Hellenized regions of the empire, especially after Christianity achieved state recognition in the fourth century.

Widespread patterns of religious change have also occurred in settings where particular groups have used conversion as a means of challenging established social structures. In India, for example, conversion has repeatedly provided lower-status groups with a means of escaping the constraints of Hinduism's traditional caste system. This factor contributed to conversions to Buddhism in its early diffusion across northern India, and to conversions to Islam following the Muslim conquests in the subcontinent.[80] Over the past century, the selective conversion of outcastes, members of lower castes, and tribal peoples has played a role in the growth of Christianity, which now has tens of millions of adherents in India. The rise of a neo-Buddhist movement in northern India during the 1950s likewise attracted several million outcaste converts seeking to free themselves from their status as untouchables. In response to these trends, Hindu organizations like Arya Samaj ("Society of Noble Ones") that reject the caste system have tried with some success to attract converts to other religions back to Hinduism.

In similar fashion, the emergence of important conversion fields has in some cases reflected resistance to existing forms of secular power. In much of West Africa, for example, Islam grew rapidly under European colonialism during the twentieth century. This growth derived in part from increased interactions between existing Muslims and tribal animists, made possible by improved internal transport networks, urban migration and socialization, the introduction of mass media, and other similar factors. The same factors also brought animists into contact with Christian missionaries, but many animists adopted Islam rather than Christianity because the former had a stronger indigenous identity. Conversion to Islam thus provided a means of adapting to changing social circumstances while at the same time resisting the dominance of European cultural influences. In a very different context, urban African Americans have converted to various forms of Islam in part as an expression of resistance against the perceived Eurocentricity of Christianity and of American society. Much of the appeal of the Moorish Science Temple and the Nation of Islam lay in their separatist ideologies. These groups identified Christian hegemony as a factor in the continuing suppression of African Americans, and sought to contest the status quo by establishing separate social and economic structures based on a distinct Muslim identity. The subsequent turn toward orthodox Sunni Islam among many African Americans, first expressed in the Dar ul-Islam movement, similarly involved a rejection of racial discrimination as exemplified by the highly segregated character of Christian denominations in the United States.[81]

The weakening of the traditional secular order in an area can further support extensive religious change as conventional social and cultural structures give way to new adaptations. Within such contexts, religion systems have provided both a stable source of authority and a means of interpreting surrounding processes of change. This factor accounts in part for the early spread of Buddhism in China, for example. Most importantly, the political conflict and social disorder that followed the collapse of the Han dynasty in the third century CE undermined the legitimacy of the established doctrines of Confucianism. Buddhism, with its emphasis on universal law, enlightenment, moral responsibility, and immortality, attracted a growing number of believers within this atmosphere of uncertainty, particularly among the urban educated classes most affected by the breakdown in the traditional order.

Traditional social and cultural patterns may also be disrupted by the movement of individuals into unfamiliar settings, and in particular by rural to urban migration. As a result, rapid urban growth through migration has in many contexts produced significant conversion fields. Such a pattern has developed in recent decades in parts of Latin America, for example, where many migrants from the lower classes have adopted Pentecostalism or some other form of conservative Protestantism as a means of challenging their powerlessness within the alien and often hostile circumstances of the city. In adhering to these conservative Protestant movements, such converts typically find more immediate experiences of religious meaning and power as well as a morally and ethically demanding religious identity, both of which support their broader social aspirations and their engagement with a supportive community.[82]

*   *   *

Conversion processes, in sum, reflect the complex interaction of diverse social and cultural forces with the individual intentions of existing and potential adherents. Through their articulation within specific contexts, such patterns of interaction in turn represent a major factor in the diffusion of proselytizing religions. The preceding discussion has focused specifically on formative influences that have fostered diffusion through conversion. It should be noted, however, that various factors have inhibited the spread of religions as well. The hegemony of one religion over a region's social and cultural structures has often served as a barrier to the local spread of other religious systems, for example. Similarly, the key role of religion as a unifying element in the identities of particular ethnic groups has functioned as a strong structural deterrent to the conversion of group members to other faiths. Conversion processes have also been discouraged by more direct forms of human agency, such as the legal restrictions that different governments have placed on missionary work by foreigners or by groups labeled as undesirable cults. Active state suppression of specific religious groups has further limited patterns of conversion in diverse settings.

Contraction

The processes of spatial change discussed thus far have involved the diffusion of religions, either through the migration of existing adherents or through the conversion of new ones. The spatial distribution of a religion may also change, however, through a reduction in the number of its believers and a resulting contraction in its spatial extent. In extreme cases, such declines may lead to the extinction of the religious system as an active cultural expression. Like other forms of religious change, processes of contraction have significant consequences for the contexts in which they occur. In addition, they may take on important meanings for remaining members of the affected group. Because these processes can develop in quite different ways, though, the specific nature of their consequences and meanings varies considerably.

Contraction has often occurred through the extensive conversion of adherents from one religion to another. Most notably, the spread of universal religious traditions, and particularly of various forms of Buddhism, Christianity, and Islam, has resulted in the spatial contraction of tribal and ethnic religions in many parts of the world. In such cases, the declining religion typically undergoes a loss of status or influence that may in turn foster additional conversions. Such patterns of contraction have occurred rapidly in some contexts, especially in places where religious change has accompanied a broader, sudden transformation of the social or political order. The rapid rise of the early Islamic empire, for example, radically changed the political structure of the Arabian Peninsula in the seventh and eighth centuries, diminishing the role of traditional tribal identities and alliances. These changes contributed to the widespread decline of Arab tribal religions as adherents adopted the new personal and political meanings of Islam. To cite a more recent example, the practice of traditional syncretistic folk religions in Korea declined dramatically during the twentieth century as the country modernized and as it developed strong relations with the United States after the Korean War. By the end of the century only a small minority of Koreans continued to observe the old folk religions while a plurality identified themselves as Christian.

More commonly, though, religious contraction based on conversion has occurred through more gradual processes of attrition, as in the centuries-long decline of Hellenistic traditions and, somewhat later, of Germanic tribal religions with the spread of Christianity within the region encompassed by the Roman Empire. For the individual, the process of conversion itself may also involve a progressive shift from one religious system to another rather than an abrupt break with the past. Converts from tribal or ethnic traditions to universal, proselytic religions thus often adopt outward forms of the new system, including a new religious identity, while retaining some elements of traditional belief and practice. Following an initial period of syncretism, the process of contraction develops more fully as adherents either redefine older survivals to conform to the new religious system or discard them entirely in adopting a stronger commitment to orthodoxy. The contraction of animistic tribal religions in Africa during recent centuries has generally followed this pattern, for example, causing Islamic and Christian missionaries in various African settings to adopt gradualist approaches to their work. The survival of tribal religious elements in such contexts in part accounts for the strong emphasis placed on the elimination of unorthodox beliefs and practices by various Islamic movements in Africa during the past century. Religious survivals can be quite durable, however, persisting long after the religious system in which they originated has otherwise disappeared, as exemplified by the Christian use of pre-Christian icons like the Easter egg and Yule log.

Less commonly, processes of contraction based on conversion have occurred through the expansion of ethnic religions. This pattern has occurred primarily in contexts where an ethnic religious group exercises hegemony, and again frequently involves a period of syncretistic change. The rising hegemony of Proto-Judaism in Canaan toward the end of the second millennium BCE appears to have contributed to some extent to the contraction of Canaanite religion, for example, as indigenous inhabitants became incorporated into Israelite society. This process of incorporation did not initially eliminate Canaanite practices, but over time they became less prominent as various trends strengthened Jewish orthodoxy. In somewhat similar fashion, processes of contraction have occurred through the absorption of one religious system by another. A significant example of this pattern developed in India during the first millennium CE through the spatial intersection between Buddhism and Hinduism. By the beginning of the Common Era, Buddhism had become widely distributed across India, coexisting with Hinduism and in many locations surpassing it as the dominant religion. By the end of the first millennium, however, the popular practice of Buddhism came to be superseded by its incorporation into a revitalized Hindu tradition. This process led to the popular identification of the historical Buddha as one of the avatars of the Hindu god Vishnu, for example. Eventually this process effectively contributed to the disappearance of Buddhism as a distinct tradition in medieval India.

A second factor that has contributed to the contraction of religious groups is the inability of adherents to reproduce their religious system over time. This pattern is strongly associated with small sects and cults that have formed around the distinctive teachings of a charismatic founder. After the death of the founder, such groups frequently have difficulty in sustaining the cultural reproduction of their religious system. The distinctiveness of the group's beliefs may itself hinder efforts to acquire new members and the absence of the charismatic founder may cause existing believers to abandon the group. Most groups that follow this pattern never acquire large followings. A more successful example of such a religious group is the Shakers, a millennial sect originating in the eighteenth century. The Shakers believed that their founder, Ann Lee, represented the second incarnation of Christ and their religious system focused on creating the perfect society initiated by the Second Coming. Their ethos of sobriety and piety attracted many converts in the United States during the late 1700s and early 1800s, providing a pastoral sense of order within the dynamic social contexts of urban growth and frontier expansion; and Shakers continued to grow following the death of Ann Lee in 1784. Nonetheless, their continued expansion was limited by the Shaker ethos that banned sexual intercourse between believers. Their growth therefore relied on the recruitment of new converts and the adoption of orphans. The former process became increasingly difficult over time, however, as the strict, nearly monastic rural life of the Shakers became less appealing to potential converts. The group's membership had thus peaked by 1850, with around 6,000 members, and from that time forward its numbers gradually declined.

The process of contraction can also take more destructive forms through the forcible suppression of religious activity or the persecution of people belonging to a particular tradition. The Holocaust perpetrated by Nazi Germany against the Jews and other minorities represents the most massive occurrence within this category, a genocidal attempt to exterminate systematically an entire religious group. The Holocaust was driven by an extreme ethnic nationalism that focused on the creation of a unified, homogeneous German state. But while it reflected centuries of violent anti-Semitism in European culture, it was unique in its comprehensive scale of destruction. German policies of persecution led to the migration of hundreds of thousands of Jews out of Nazi territories. Nonetheless, the Holocaust led to the deaths of six million Jews, nearly two-thirds of Europe's Jewish population in 1939, through mass murders in Jewish communities and the Nazi death camps (photo 2.8). The devastation was particularly widespread in Poland, which contained Europe's largest concentration of Jews before World War II. There, the Holocaust eliminated approximately 95 percent of the Jewish population.

Although not on the same scale, violence and oppression directed at religious groups have occurred in many other contexts as well. The dispersal of Jews throughout the Roman Empire after the failed rebellions of the first and second centuries CE represents one early example of this pattern. Buddhists in China experienced a similar period of oppression in the ninth century when China's ruling class sought to suppress Buddhism because of its drain on local economies and its competition with Taoism. Several hundred thousand monks and nuns were forced to return to secular life during this period of oppression. In modern times, Armenian Christians faced severe persecution from the Muslim Turks during the final years of the Ottoman Empire, a reaction against rising Armenian nationalism during World War I. Hundreds of thousands of Armenians were relocated from their traditional homeland and at least as many more, possibly numbering more than one million, were killed. More recently, in Cambodia during the 1970s the Maoist Khmer Rouge carried out a massive campaign of violence, killing roughly a fifth of the country's Buddhist population, including most of its monks and nuns, and more than half of the country's Muslims. Finally, the destruction of religious groups has not always been carried out in such systematic fashion. During the European colonization of North America and the subsequent expansion westward in the United States, the practice of many Native American reli-

Photo 2.8.   The Memorial to the Murdered Jews of Europe, dedicated to the Jews killed during the Holocaust. The memorial opened to the public in 2005. It comprises a large field of 2,711 stelae of varying heights. Berlin, Germany, 2006.

Source: Zutalegh (www.flickr.com/photos/fear_and_loathing/264754755/), under Creative Commons license (creativecommons.org/licenses/by-sa/2.0/).

gions declined or died, particularly in the eastern states, through the devastating effects of disease, starvation, and war on indigenous populations.

A final factor in the contraction of religious distributions has been the rise of secularization, the diminishing role of religion in people's lives as the process of modernization supported more rationalist worldviews. Until the 1980s, many social scientists saw the process of secularization as the inevitable outcome of modernization, but since then the universality of this theory has been widely rejected. In many places with a long history of modernization, such as the United States, religion remains a potent force in many people's lives. Nonetheless, processes of secularization have changed the religious character of some locations. In some cases, secularization has produced a decline in traditional forms of institutional religion but has also been accompanied by greater interest among some people in new religious movements or less formal expressions of religiosity, as discussed above. In other cases, the rise of secularism has been accompanied by the persistence of religious activity simply as normative social behavior without a strong underlying foundation of belief. And in still other cases, secularization has been associated with the widespread abandonment of religious activity and the adoption of an entirely secular worldview and ethos. Various communist regimes have sought to encourage or impose secularization, although with uncertain effects. The significant resurgence of religious activity over the past decade in states formerly part of the Soviet Union illustrates the persistence of religious belief that may occur under such circumstances (photo 2.9). Secularization has proceeded more generally in some contexts, however, as an informal process of cultural change. This pattern has been most evident in Europe. A century ago, relatively few Europeans identified themselves as having no religious affiliation, but estimates suggest that 15 percent of Euro-

Photo 2.9. Kazan Cathedral, located in Moscow's Red Square. The cathedral was originally built during the seventeenth century but was demolished during Stalin's rule to expand Red Square as a state-centered political space. The cathedral was restored during the early 1990s, immediately following the demise of the Soviet Union, as an expression of the resurgent social importance of Russian Orthodoxy. Moscow, Russia, 2007.

Source: Jack Versloot (www.flickr.com/photos/jackversloot/905583424/), under Creative Commons license (creativecommons.org/licenses/by/2.0/).

peans do so now. The proportion of Europeans who do not regularly participate in religious worship is actually much higher.

Conclusions

This chapter has examined key influences on the spatial dynamics of religions, including the emergence of religious traditions in primary hearths and the subsequent processes of diffusion and contraction that shape a religion's distribution over time. These influences and their effects represent basic facts regarding the geography of religions, providing insights into how the complex distributions of the world's religions came into being and continue to evolve. At the same time, they also illustrate a number of important spatial dimensions within religious belief and practice. One significant spatial dimension is the association between religious hearths and the concept of a holy land, a region sanctified by its role in a religion's formation. For Christians, the sites associated with the life of Jesus represent more than a simple set of historical artifacts. They instead comprise a sacred region in which the interactions between the human and the divine found their most significant expression, providing the basis for conceptions of sacred history, faith, and salvation. Similarly, Jerusalem and the biblical Promised Land encompass crucial meanings within Judaism regarding the divine covenant and divine law, and for Muslims the sacred cities of Islam represent the original context for the realization of an ideal Islamic society. In the Indic region, Hindus have typically characterized all of India as a holy land through its unique association with a great variety of divine manifestations and expressions, while Buddhists have focused more narrowly on the region of Nepal and northern India where the key events in the life of the Buddha took place. Seen from the outside, in sum, the hearths of religious traditions represent specific contexts in which the conjunction of various cultural and social processes produced the conditions necessary for a particular religious innovation to thrive. Seen from the perspective of the believer, on the other hand, such hearths also manifest transcendent meanings that relate the human and the superhuman to core beliefs within a tradition's worldview and ethos.

Believers also attribute religious meanings to the processes through which the spatial distributions of religions have evolved over time. Processes of migration frequently have taken on religious significance for adherents, for example through their relationships to religious obligation as in the Islamic concept of hijra. Conversion processes have taken on even more explicit religious significance, both for adherents seeking to spread their religion and for converts adopting a new religious identity. Within the proselytic religions especially, the conversion of others frequently represents a crucial dimension of the ethos of believers. The contraction of religions has also acquired significant religious meanings. In the process of secularization, for example, the rejection of a religious worldview represents a major transformation for the former adherent. To cite a more far-reaching example, the destruction of the Holocaust generated an entire body of theological thought seeking to reconcile the event to concepts of evil, humanity, and the role of the divine in Jewish and Christian belief systems.[83] Some religious scholars have argued that the Holocaust had no religious meaning, or perhaps arose from an absence of faith, but others have asserted that it represented a divine punishment of heterodoxy or reflected the special religious role of Jews in suffering on behalf of the rest of the world.

Finally, the spatial dynamics of religions have important implications in relation to the concept of contextuality. Religions that have spread out of their hearths to diverse places, developing widespread spatial distributions, have continually undergone processes of adaptation in relation to the particular cultural environments to which they have diffused. The religious tradition initiated in a particular hearth may thus give rise to a variety of different religious systems as it spreads by means of migration and conversion to disparate locations. Such patterns reflect a crucial relationship between the complex spatial dynamics of religious traditions and the impacts of contextuality on how believers articulate those traditions in particular places. Chapter 3 now directs the discussion toward a more detailed examination of the role of contextuality and its effects on the world's religious traditions.

Notes

1. Ninian Smart, ed., *Atlas of the World's Religions* (Oxford: Oxford University Press, 1999); Isma'il Ragi al Faruqi and David E. Sopher, eds., *Historical Atlas of the Religions of the*

World (New York: Macmillan, 1974); for detailed data by country, see David B. Barrett, George T. Kurian, and Todd M. Johnson, eds., *World Christian Encyclopedia: A Comparative Survey of Churches and Religions in the Modern World* (Oxford: Oxford University Press, 2001); for distributions of religious groups in the United States, see Edwin Scott Gaustad and Philip L. Barlow, eds., *New Historical Atlas of Religion in America* (New York: Oxford University Press, 2000); Wilbur Zelinsky, "An Approach to the Religious Geography of the United States: Patterns of Church Membership in 1952," *Annals of the Association of American Geographers* 51 (1961): 139–93.

2. A useful interpretation of processes involved in the formation of new religions appears in Rodney Stark and William Sims Bainbridge, *A Theory of Religion* (New York: Peter Lang, 1987), 121–94. They are primarily concerned with the formation of cults and sects, but their ideas apply as well to the development of religious traditions and the division of those traditions into distinct religious systems.

3. Stark and Bainbridge, *A Theory of Religion*, 155–56.

4. Cf. Stark and Bainbridge, *A Theory of Religion*, 124.

5. By current estimates, followers of the religions that originated in these hearths now account for 85 percent of all adherents worldwide; see "The 2005 Annual Megacensus of Religions," *Britannica Book of the Year, 2006*, 2007, Encyclopædia Britannica Online, search.eb.com/eb/article-9432655 (accessed July 1, 2007).

6. Stanley Wolpert, *A New History of India*, 5th ed. (New York: Oxford University Press, 1997), 14–23; Gavin Flood, *An Introduction to Hinduism* (Cambridge: Cambridge University Press, 1996), 27–30.

7. See, for example, Subhash C. Kak, "The Indus Tradition and the Indo-Aryans," *The Mankind Quarterly* 32 (Spring 1992): 195–213.

8. The Indo-Aryan religious tradition has also often been labeled Brahmanism (or Brahminism). *Brahmanism* is a problematic term, however, as it is has been used as a synonym for Vedism, as a description of only the later phases of Vedism, and even as a distinct tradition situated between Vedism and Hinduism. To avoid confusion, I have adopted the term *Vedism* to denote the entire Indo-Aryan tradition up to the emergence of Hinduism, discussed below.

9. Manohar Lal Bhargava, *The Geography of Rgvedic India* (Lucknow: The Upper India Publishing House, 1964).

10. A detailed interpretation of this transformation appears in Thomas J. Hopkins, *The Hindu Religious Tradition* (Encino, Cal.: Dickenson Publishing Company, 1971), 17–35.

11. Wolpert, *A New History of India*, 44–54.

12. Following common practice, I have capitalized *Brahman* when it is used in its Upanishadic sense but have not capitalized it when used in reference to earlier Vedic beliefs.

13. Of the movements that subsequently disappeared, the most durable was the Ajivaka movement. Adherents of this movement followed an austere form of asceticism similar to that of Jainism and believed in reincarnation, but they did not accept the concept of karma. They believed that human action could not influence the cycle of reincarnation, which would continue until it was destined to end. Although influential for a time, despite strong opposition from Buddhists, the Ajivaka movement disappeared by the fourteenth century CE.

14. The concept of Hinduism as a discrete religion dates back only to the nineteenth century, when it was first used by the British to characterize Indian religion.

15. The Puranas dealt with many other topics as well, including cosmological themes and the genealogies of kings and sages.

16. The distinction between Proto-Judaism and Judaism is adopted from Phillip Sigal, *Judaism: The Evolution of a Faith* (Grand Rapids, Mich.: William B. Eerdmans Company, 1988), 6–30.

17. Donald B. Redford, *Egypt, Canaan, and Israel in Ancient Times* (Princeton, N.J.: Princeton University Press, 1992), 272–73; Baruch Halpern, *The Emergence of Israel in Canaan* (Chico, Cal.: Scholars Press, 1983), 102–3.

18. A concise discussion of these issues appears in Baruch Halpern, "The Exodus from

Egypt: Myth or Reality?" in *The Rise of Ancient Israel*, ed. Hershel Shanks et al. (Washington, D.C.: Biblical Archaeology Society, 1992), 87–113; see also Israel Finkelstein and Neil Asher Silberman, *The Bible Unearthed: Archaeology's New Vision of Ancient Israel and the Origin of Its Sacred Texts* (New York: The Free Press, 2001), 48–71.

19. Useful discussions of these various explanations appear in Finkelstein and Silberman, *The Bible Unearthed*, 97–122, 240–43, 329–39; Halpern, *The Emergence of Israel*, 47–63, 101–3, 241; Redford, *Egypt, Canaan, and Israel in Ancient Times*, 255–80; William G. Dever, "How to Tell a Canaanite from an Israelite," in *The Rise of Ancient Israel*, ed. Shanks et al., 54; P. Kyle McCarter, Jr., "The Origins of Israelite Religion," in *The Rise of Ancient Israel*, ed. Shanks et al., 131–34.

20. Recent scholarship casts doubt on the spatial extent of a unified kingdom under David and Solomon and on the growth of Jerusalem into a major urban center in the tenth century BCE. Archaeological evidence does indicate, however, that David was a historical figure and the founder of a dynasty known to other groups in the region. See Finkelstein and Silberman, *The Bible Unearthed*, 123–55.

21. Halpern, *The Emergence of Israel*, 247–48; Finkelstein and Silberman, *The Bible Unearthed*, 246–48.

22. Finkelstein and Silberman, *The Bible Unearthed*, 280–81, 310–13.

23. Sigal, *Judaism*, 44–53.

24. Sigal, *Judaism*, 93–95.

25. For detailed but accessible analyses of the origins of Islam, see Malise Ruthven, *Islam in the World* (New York: Oxford University Press, 1984), 49–100; John L. Esposito, *Islam: The Straight Path*, 3d ed. (New York: Oxford University Press, 1998), 1–31.

26. Irad Malkin, *Religion and Colonization in Ancient Greece* (Leiden: E. J. Brill, 1987), 135–86.

27. Mary Beard, John North, and Simon Price, *Religions of Rome,* 2 vols. (Cambridge: Cambridge University Press, 1998), I:320–39.

28. George Brandon, *Santeria from Africa to the New World: The Dead Sell Memories* (Bloomington: Indiana University Press, 1993), 76–78.

29. The African roots of New World conversion to Christianity are discussed in John Thornton, *Africa and Africans in the Making of the Atlantic World, 1400–1680* (Cambridge: Cambridge University Press, 1992), 235–71.

30. Margarite Fernandez Olmos and Lizabeth Paravisini-Gebert, *Creole Religions of the Caribbean: An Introduction from Vodou and Santeria to Obeah and Espiritismo* (New York: New York University Press, 2003).

31. Roger W. Stump, "Patterns of Survival among Catholic National Parishes, 1940–1980," *Journal of Cultural Geography* 7 (Fall/Winter, 1986): 77–97; Roger W. Stump, "Pluralism in the American Place-Name Cover: Ethnic Variations in Catholic Church Names," *North American Culture* 2 (1986): 126–40.

32. Susan Wiley Hardwick, *Russian Refuge: Religion, Migration, and Settlement on the North American Pacific Rim* (Chicago: University of Chicago Press, 1993), 1–48.

33. A useful overview of this migration appears in the introduction to Steven Vertovec and Ceri Peach, *Islam in Europe: The Politics of Religion and Community* (New York: St. Martin's Press, 1997).

34. See, for example, Barbara Daly Metcalf, ed., *Making Muslim Space in North America and Europe* (Berkeley: University of California Press, 1996); Richard Burghart, ed., *Hinduism in Great Britain: The Perpetuation of Religion in an Alien Cultural Milieu* (London: Tavistock Publications, 1987); Darshan Singh Tatla, *The Sikh Diaspora: The Search for Statehood* (Seattle: University of Washington Press, 1999).

35. U.S. Congress, House, Committee on International Relations, and Senate, Committee on Foreign Relations, *Annual Report, International Religious Freedom, 1999*, 386.

36. Daoud S. Casewit, "Hijra as History and Metaphor: A Survey of Quranic and Hadith Sources," *The Muslim World* 88 (April 1998): 105–28; Sami A. Aldeeb Abu-Sahlieh, "The Islamic Conception of Migration," *International Migration Review* 30 (Spring 1996): 37–57.

37. The term *jihad* ("struggle") can be used in various senses, from an inward effort to strengthen one's faith to missionary activity aimed at convincing nonbelievers to accept Islam to overt warfare against the enemies of Islam; see Sachiko Murata and William C. Chittick, *The Vision of Islam* (St. Paul, Minn.: Paragon House, 1994), 20–22.

38. Brian Glyn Williams, "Hijra and Forced Migration from Nineteenth-Century Russia to the Ottoman Empire: A Critical Analysis of the Great Tatar Emigration of 1860–1861," *Cahiers du Monde Russe* 41 (2000): 79–108.

39. Rudolph Peters, *Islam and Colonialism: The Doctrine of Jihad in Modern History* (The Hague: Mouton Publishers, 1979), 53–62; Charles-Robert Ageron, "L'Émigration des Musulmans Algériens et l'Exode de Tlemcen," *Annales: Économies, Sociétés, Civilisations* 22 (1967): 1047–68.

40. John Keay, *India: A History* (New York: Atlantic Monthly Press, 2000), 477–79.

41. Roger W. Stump, *Boundaries of Faith: Geographical Perspectives on Religious Fundamentalism* (Lanham, Md.: Rowman and Littlefield, 2000), 145.

42. Stump, *Boundaries of Faith*, 40–48.

43. Jonathan Phillips, "The Latin East: 1098–1291," in *The Oxford Illustrated History of the Crusades*, ed. Jonathan Riley-Smith (Oxford: Oxford University Press, 1995), 112–13.

44. Jean Richard, *The Crusades, c. 1071–c. 1291* (Cambridge: Cambridge University Press, 1999), 94–97.

45. Daniel Cohn-Sherbok, *Atlas of Jewish History* (London: Routledge, 1994), 86–89.

46. Cohn-Sherbok, *Atlas of Jewish History*, 162.

47. Victor Kiernan, "The Separation of India and Pakistan," in *The Cambridge Survey of World Migration*, ed. Robin Cohen (Cambridge: Cambridge University Press, 1995), 356–59.

48. Calvin Redekop, *Mennonite Society* (Baltimore: The Johns Hopkins University Press, 1989), 3–29; Frank H. Epp, *Mennonites in Canada, 1786–1920: The History of a Separate People* (Toronto: Macmillan, 1974), 23–63.

49. John Winthrop, the colony's first governor, described the Puritan's mission in New England using the biblical imagery of a city upon a hill, taken from Matthew 5:14.

50. Sydney E. Ahlstrom, *A Religious History of the American People* (New Haven, Conn.: Yale University Press, 1972), 230–44; Epp, *Mennonites in Canada, 1786–1920*, 49; John A. Hostetler and Gertrude Enders Huntington, *The Hutterites in North America* (New York: Holt, Rinehart, and Winston, 1967), 3.

51. D. W. Meinig, "The Mormon Culture Region: Strategies and Patterns in the Geography of the American West, 1847–1964," *Annals of the Association of American Geographers* 55 (June 1965): 191–220; Richard H. Jackson, "Mormon Perception and Settlement," *Annals of the Association of American Geographers* 68 (September 1978): 317–34.

52. Richard H. Jackson and Roger Henrie, "Perception of Sacred Space," *Journal of Cultural Geography* 3 (Spring/Summer 1983): 94–107; Michael B. Toney and Carol McKewen Stinner, "Mormon and Non-Mormon Migration In and Out of Utah," *Review of Religious Research* 25 (December 1983), 114–26.

53. Sigal, *Judaism*, 4–5.

54. David Westerlund, "Reaction and Action: Accounting for the Rise of Islamism," in *African Islam and Islam in Africa: Encounters between Sufis and Islamists*, ed. David Westerlund and Eva Evers Rosander (Athens: Ohio University Press, 1997), 308–33.

55. Robert W. Hefner, "World Building and the Rationality of Conversion," in *Conversion to Christianity: Historical and Anthropological Perspectives on a Great Transformation*, ed. Robert W. Hefner (Berkeley: University of California Press, 1993), 3–44.

56. Daniel R. Miller, ed., *Coming of Age: Protestantism in Contemporary Latin America* (Lanham, Md.: University Press of America, 1994).

57. Roger W. Stump, "Spatial Implications of Religious Broadcasting: Stability and Change in Patterns of Belief," in *Collapsing Space and Time: Geographic Aspects of Communication and Information*, ed. Stanley D. Brunn and Thomas R. Leinbach (London: HarperCollins Academic, 1991), 354–75.

58. Stump, *Boundaries of Faith*, 223–24.

59. Marshall G. S. Hodgson, *The Venture of Islam: Conscience and History in a World Civilization*, 3 vols. (Chicago: University of Chicago Press, 1974), II:533–35.

60. Larry Poston, *Islamic Da'wah in the West: Muslim Missionary Activity and the Dynamics of Conversion to Islam* (New York: Oxford University Press, 1992), 17–19; Ruthven, *Islam in the World*, 262–64; Hodgson, *The Venture of Islam*, II:201–4.

61. J. Spencer Trimingham, *The Sufi Orders in Islam* (New York: Oxford University Press, 1971).

62. Trimingham, *The Sufi Orders in Islam*, 90–98; Hodgson, *The Venture of Islam*, II:544–51; Mervyn Hiskett, *The Development of Islam in West Africa* (London: Longman, 1984), 258–59.

63. Muhammad Khalid Masud, ed., *Travellers in Faith: Studies of the Tablighi Jama'at as a Transnational Islamic Movement for Faith Renewal* (Leiden: Brill, 2000); Barbara D. Metcalf, "New Medinas: The Tablighi Jama'at in America and Europe" in *Making Muslim Space*, ed. Metcalf, 110–27; Roman Loimeier, "Islamic Reform and Political Change: The Example of Abubakar Gumi and the Yan Izala Movement in Northern Nigeria," in *African Islam and Islam in Africa,* ed. Westerlund and Rosander, 286–307.

64. John Hunwick, "Sub-Saharan Africa and the Wider World of Islam: Historical and Contemporary Perspectives," in *African Islam and Islam in Africa,* ed. Westerlund and Rosander, 28–54.

65. Marc Gaborieau, "The Transformation of Tablighi Jama'at into a Transnational Movement," in *Travellers in Faith*, ed. Masud, 121–38.

66. Trevor Ling, *The Buddha: Buddhist Civilization in India and Ceylon* (London: Temple Smith, 1973), 175–82.

67. Keay, *India*, 107–12.

68. E. Zürcher, *The Buddhist Conquest of China: The Spread and Adaptation of Buddhism in Early Medieval China*, 2 vols. (Leiden: E. J. Brill, 1972), I:23–38.

69. Hodgson, *The Venture of Islam*, II:533–39; Ruthven, *Islam in the World*, 144–45; Albert Hourani, *A History of the Arab Peoples* (New York: MJF Books, 1991), 46–47.

70. Hiskett, *The Development of Islam in West Africa*, 106.

71. Ling, *The Buddha*, 159–60.

72. Jeff Haynes, *Religion in Third World Politics* (Boulder, Colo.: Lynne Rienner Publishers, 1993), 51–52.

73. Hodgson, *The Venture of Islam*, II:543–48; Ira M. Lapidus, *A History of Islamic Societies* (New York : Cambridge University Press, 1988), 467–70; Ross E. Dunn, *The Adventures of Ibn Battuta: A Muslim Traveler of the 14th Century* (Berkeley: University of California Press, 1986), 248–50.

74. Roger W. Stump, "Regional Variations in Denominational Switching among White Protestants," *Professional Geographer* 39 (November 1987): 438–49.

75. Wade Clark Roof and William McKinney, *American Mainline Religion: Its Changing Shape and Future* (New Brunswick, N.J.: Rutgers University Press, 1987), 163–64.

76. Stump, "Regional Variations in Denominational Switching," 438–49.

77. Stark and Bainbridge, *A Theory of Religion*, 279–313.

78. Cf. Stark and Bainbridge, *A Theory of Religion*, 279–313; some have argued that Stark and Bainbridge have overstated the extent of cult formation and growth, however, as discussed in Steve Bruce, *Religion in the Modern World: From Cathedrals to Cults* (Oxford: Oxford University Press, 1996), 187–91; on the decline of conventional religious activity in Germany, see Edgar Wunder, "Was Geschieht in Deutschland mit der Religion?" *Berichte zur Deutschen Landeskunde* 78, no. 2 (2004): 167–92.

79. Roof and McKinney, *American Mainline Religion*, 165.

80. Hodgson, *The Venture of Islam*, II:557.

81. Ernest Allen, Jr., "Identity and Destiny: The Formative Views of the Moorish Science Temple and the Nation of Islam," in *Muslims on the Americanization Path?,* ed. Yvonne Yazbeck

Haddad and John L. Esposito (Oxford: Oxford University Press, 2000), 163–214; R. M. Mukhtar Curtis, "Urban Muslims: The Formation of the Dar ul-Islam Movement," in *Muslim Communities in North America*, ed. Yvonne Yazbeck Haddad and Jane Idleman Smith (Albany: State University of New York Press, 1994), 51–73.

82. Everett A. Wilson, "The Dynamics of Latin American Pentecostalism," in *Coming of Age*, ed. Miller, 89–116; Jeff Haynes, *Religion in Global Politics* (London: Longman, 1998), 53–54.

83. Dan Cohn-Sherbok, ed., *Holocaust Theology: A Reader* (New York: New York University Press, 2002).

CHAPTER 3

The Contextuality of Religions

Religions are generally understood by their adherents as representations of universal truths relating to the nature of reality, conceptions of the superhuman, and associated ideas of right human thought and behavior. From the adherent's point of view, religious beliefs and practices derive from certainties that transcend the contingencies of particular moments in space and time. Moreover, followers of many religions identify, at least at some level, with an imagined community of fellow believers encompassing all of the adherents of a particular tradition. Perceptions of religious unity appear, for example, in the traditional notion of Christendom as the integral domain of Christianity, or in the Islamic concept of the umma as the unified community of all Muslims. Rituals common to an entire tradition, such as the pilgrimage to Mecca in Islam, reinforce this sense of commonality among diverse groups of believers. Religious movements and organizations have also sought to promote unity within a shared tradition, from the various expressions of ecumenism that have emerged within Christianity over the past century to international associations like the World Fellowship of Buddhists, founded in 1950 to foster solidarity among all adherents of Buddhism.

As cultural systems, however, religions continually develop in relation to the specific places in which they are articulated and lived by communities of believers. The reproduction of active patterns of religious faith takes place primarily through social and cultural processes organized at the scale of everyday experience, such as communal worship or the performance of customary rituals. Through these processes, adherents routinely interpret, negotiate, contest, and adapt their religious system within the context of their particular circumstances. Religious systems consequently possess intrinsic connections to the situations in which they are enacted. Although they may draw on an idealized and absolute body of doctrine, religions in practice find expression through distinct manifestations rooted in the life and character of particular places. At a certain level of abstraction, Buddhism, Christianity, or Islam can each be characterized as a single religious tradition, for example, but as vital religious systems each has taken diverse forms in different locations. This inherent contextuality represents a crucial characteristic of religions as cultural systems and, given geography's disciplinary sensitivity to place and context, a fundamental concern in the geographical study of religion.

The contextuality of religious belief and practice is perhaps most immediately evident in the primal religions of traditional tribal societies. Such religious systems typically manifest direct ties to their followers' homeland through the worship of localized deities, spirits, and ancestors. Adherents interpret these entities as being integral to the local realm of lived experience, frequently identifying them with specific environmental features or ritual spaces. The Ganda religious system traditionally practiced by the Baganda people in southern Uganda, west of Lake Victoria, provides a representative example of the contextual associations inherent in tribal religions (map 3.1).[1] Like other belief systems indigenous to East Africa, traditional Ganda religion postulates the existence of a remote creator god, but its primary emphasis is on relationships between adherents and various categories of superhuman beings linked to local customs and concerns. The primary objects of worship are the *lubaale*, hero gods associated with particular phenomena central to Baganda life, such as fertility, wealth, the hunt, the elements, war, hunger, and disease. The Baganda conceptualize the lubaale as primal ancestors, inhabitants of the region whose exceptional characteristics or actions resulted in their deification. Temples and shrines link the presence of these deities to specific places, thus making them accessible to adherents and their propitiations. Some of the lubaale represent national gods significant to the entire tribal group, while others have more localized identities defined in relation to particular clans or places.

In addition to the lubaale, Ganda religion recognizes a large variety of spirits associated with local features of the natural environment. The Baganda thus believe that the spirits of individual rivers should be invoked to ensure a safe crossing, and that large trees contained spirits that had to be appeased before the tree could be felled for timber. They also consider certain hills to be sacred, possessed by the spirits of lions or leopards. Ghosts of the deceased represent another important category of localized superhuman entities. According to Ganda belief, the ghosts of humans and wild animals linger near the places where they had lived or were buried, where they could either harm or assist the living. The Baganda place particular importance on seeking assistance from ancestors, and to this end they typically maintain household shrines for making offerings to deceased relatives. In sum, Ganda understandings of the superhuman and related religious practices are inseparable from the context of the Bagan-

Map 3.1. The lands of the Baganda people of Uganda.

da's physical surroundings and patterns of daily existence. In invoking and propitiating various deities, spirits, and ghosts, the Baganda give expression to religious conceptions explicitly defined in terms of local experience. These conceptions reveal an inherent connectedness between ritual, belief, and place that is typical of tribal religions practiced within a traditional tribal domain.

Contextuality also represents a key factor in patterns of adherence to more widespread religious traditions, but in such cases it takes on a more complex aspect. As religious traditions spread from their primary hearths to other locations, they are reproduced by their adherents within an expanding variety of contexts. As a result, the practice of widely distributed religions tends to acquire a distinctive character in particular places, for example through the reinterpretation of existing beliefs in response to local circumstances or through the development of local accretions to existing rituals. At the same time, these local religious customs typically remain expressly connected to the larger tradition from which they derive. In most such instances, adherents do not recognize their local patterns of belief and practice as a categorical departure from their source tradition, and they identify not only with the local community of believers in which they directly participate but with a more extensive, imagined community of coreligionists as well. Thus in Morocco and other parts of North Africa the veneration of local saints or marabouts as transmitters of divine grace is a distinctive feature of popular Islam, rooted in local customs, but adherents understand this practice as being integral to their broader identity as Muslims. Similarly, devotion to shrines with local territorial associations is an important feature of folk expressions of Roman Catholicism in some parts of Europe, but it occurs largely within the universalizing institutional structure of the Roman Catholic Church. Local manifestations of geographically dispersed religions in effect develop in relation to places characterized by the interaction of processes, structures, and meanings constituted at various scales, from the local to the global. In this sense, the contextuality of such manifestations mirrors the nature of places themselves as intersections of differently scaled processes.[2] The realization of a larger religious tradition by a particular community of adherents therefore reflects a dynamic relationship between local influences and more widely established patterns of belief and practice.

Religions differ, of course, in the ways in which they are affected by such processes. Pluralistic religions, those whose worldview and ethos allow for varied forms of worship, are most susceptible to processes of diversification in their articulation by believers in distinct contexts. Hinduism most notably exemplifies such a tradition, fundamentally recognizing diverse paths to the ultimate goal of salvation. As a result, it encompasses a striking variety of expressions distinguished by their different emphases on particular deities or ritual practices. Among religions that stress orthodoxy and orthopraxy, in contrast, the diversification of belief and practice tends to be more problematic. Significant tensions may develop between local heterodoxies and orthodox conceptions of a tradition, particularly when widely accepted beliefs and practices have been doctrinally or institutionally formalized. Returning to preceding examples, some Islamic authorities in North Africa have thus discouraged the veneration of marabouts as a deviation from authentic Islam, and the Roman Catholic Church has at times encouraged the adoption of more generalized forms of devotion in place of older, localized practices. More generally, the core features of the worldview and ethos of a tradition typically provide a unifying conceptual framework from which most

local religious expressions develop. Specific articulations of widespread religious traditions generally take place, then, within contexts distinguished by the convergence of
both localized and dispersed influences.

In some instances, moreover, processes of cultural reproduction may introduce
more extensive changes into a religious tradition, resulting in the emergence of an
explicitly distinct religious system. This pattern characterizes secondary religious
hearths, places where adherents purposefully establish a discrete religious system
within a larger, existing tradition. In doing so, believers identify themselves as a separate religious community and define their interpretation of their source tradition as
being manifestly different from other versions. Their worldview and ethos will retain
key features of the larger tradition, but may be distinguished by the emphasis placed
on particular beliefs and practices or by the incorporation of unique innovations. The
formation of a new religious group typically involves the contesting of correct belief
and practice, either with competing groups or with central authorities. The innovations that develop within secondary hearths thus tend to be schismatic in character,
based on a deliberate departure from beliefs and practices that prevail among other
groups rooted in the same tradition. Such departures can be expressed in different
ways, from the revision of a tradition in accordance with secular cultural trends to a
fundamentalist return to a tradition's core principles. The religious systems associated
with secondary hearths also differ from other local religious variants in the breadth of
their impact, based on the new group's distinct identity. Adoption of the new religious
system may have far-reaching repercussions for the ways in which believers live their
daily lives, for example, or for their interactions with other members of society. If
adherents of the new system dominate the society in which they live, their innovations
may affect other inhabitants of the hearth as well. More to the point, innovations of
this type are more likely to have significant impacts beyond the context of their original hearths, either by spreading to new locations or by provoking counteractions elsewhere.

As a result of these different manifestations of contextuality, widely distributed
religious traditions are typically characterized by significant geographical diversity, a
product of the inherent mutability of religions as cultural systems. Patterns of spatial
diversification appear across different geographical scales, moreover, linking local articulations of a common tradition with larger, nested sets of related religious systems.
Adherents of an Episcopal congregation in Ohio thus share religious commonalities,
to different degrees, with other Episcopalians in the United States, with the Anglican
community worldwide, with Protestantism generally, and ultimately with Christianity
as a whole. Through variously scaled contexts, moreover, the spatial diversification of
religious traditions also occurs at a variety of scales. In the case of widely distributed
religious traditions, adherents reproduce their religious systems most immediately at
the scale of their own experience, but in the process they also draw on diverse elements
of the larger tradition that ties them to adherents in other places and times. The
variations in belief and practice that arise through such processes in turn reflect the
nature of the relevant contextual effects in different locations. Religious systems reproduced in closely related settings therefore tend to be quite similar to one another. The
most pronounced differences among particular expressions of a religious tradition, on
the other hand, tend to correspond to other major cultural boundaries.

The major regional divisions that exist within many of the major world religions thus represent the broadest consequences of contextuality, typically emerging out of distinct secondary hearths and marking the division of a religious tradition into separate branches that are both doctrinally and spatially different. The division of Christianity into Eastern Orthodoxy, Roman Catholicism, and Protestantism illustrates this pattern, as does the division of Islam into its Sunni and Shia branches or of Buddhism into its Theravada and Mahayana branches. Such divisions are particularly significant in that they correspond to the most substantial differences in matters of belief and practice among religious systems within the same tradition. At the same time, an appreciation of the role of scale in contextual processes leads to the conclusion that more localized patterns of diversification have also transformed religious traditions in important ways. The religious lives of Sunni Muslims in Morocco and in Indonesia differ substantially, for example, as do the religious lives of Protestant Christians in northern Europe and in the southern United States. At even more local scales, down to the level of the individual congregation, distinct groups of adherents may practice a common faith in different ways. In total, the related factors of scale and context produce a complex web of relationships between religious traditions and the diverse geographical settings in which their adherents live out specific religious systems.

Such relationships and their impacts on the world's major religious traditions represent the primary concern of this chapter. The following discussion focuses in particular on the spatial diversification of religious belief and practice within Hinduism and Judaism, as key examples of ethnic religions, and within Buddhism, Christianity, and Islam, as key examples of proselytic religions. In examining these traditions, the text addresses both the development of specific patterns of religious belief and practice within particular geographical contexts, and the contextual relationship of religious systems to a variety of other social processes, structures, and meanings.

Hinduism

The emergence of the Hindu tradition took place gradually, from the last few centuries BCE through most of the first millennium CE; and it emerged not within the confines of a discrete hearth but in a multitude of locations across South Asia to which the older religious tradition of Vedism and its offshoots had spread. In the process, Hinduism took shape as a variety of related religious systems rather than a unitary, homogenous religion, combining certain widely accepted religious givens with a multitude of local beliefs and practices. Common features of the emergent Hindu tradition included belief in the divine origins of the Vedas and in various Upanishadic concepts, such as reincarnation, karma, dharma, and moksha. The *Ramayana* and the *Mahabharata*, the major Sanskrit epics, also provided a foundation for the theistic elements of most expressions of early Hinduism. These common features had become integrated with local religious elements through the process of Sanskritization, the largely unreflexive merger of the written traditions of Vedism and early Hinduism with the folk religion of local communities. Through this process, for example, a variety of local deities became identified with the deities of the formal, Sanskrit sources, thus preserving local religious expressions within the context of the larger Hindu tradition. The different approaches to religious practice that had emerged in the first millennium

BCE, including the surviving ritualism of the Brahmin caste, the philosophical speculation of the Upanishads, and the mental disciplines of yoga, also persisted into the Common Era. All of these factors combined to produce a highly diverse and inclusive religious tradition; and adherents of this emergent Hindu tradition accepted as natural the diversity of belief and practice that it encompassed.

Within this inclusive context, processes of diversification did not take on the schismatic character that they have acquired in other religious traditions. The extensive mixing of local customs with more broadly recognized textual sources to some degree worked against the development of significant spatial rifts within Hinduism. At the same time, local contexts themselves typically contained considerable religious diversity, for example in the contrasting practices of different castes or theistic traditions, which in turn inhibited the development of a unitary religious identity among adherents in a given locale or region. The spatial concentration of early Hinduism also facilitated the diffusion of religious innovations from their local hearths to other parts of South Asia, preventing most innovations from taking on an exclusively local or regional association. Nonetheless, important spatial contrasts did appear during the emergence of early Hinduism, and such contrasts continued to develop as Hinduism became more fully articulated in the second millennium CE.

Within early Hinduism, one major source of regional diversification was the cultural variety of India itself, particularly as expressed in the contrast between the Indo-Aryan culture of the north and the Dravidian cultures of the south. The Indo-Aryans spoke Sanskrit or related languages of the Indo-European family and were descended in part from pastoral nomads who entered the subcontinent from southwestern Asia. The people of southern India, on the other hand, spoke languages in the Dravidian family and were likely descended from inhabitants present on the subcontinent before the Aryan migrations. As early Hinduism developed into a source of commonality between these two major culture groups, and among various smaller ones as well, it clearly differed from most other ethnic religions in that it possessed a much more diffuse ethnic character. That diffuse character was in turn reflected in regional contrasts within the emerging tradition. In northern India, and particularly in the Gangetic plain, early Hinduism in many ways represented an elaboration of the older Vedic tradition established in that area during the second millennium BCE. In the south, on the other hand, Hinduism emerged through the merger of Dravidian and Indo-Aryan traditions during the more recent process of Sanskritization, which lasted into the first centuries of the Common Era.[3]

Southern India

By the first several centuries CE, the theistic tradition developing within Hinduism thus focused in the north on Vishnu and Shiva, gods associated with the older Vedic tradition who had been personalized and raised to positions of supremacy in the Hindu epics and the later Upanishads. Devotion to Vishnu and Shiva had also begun to emerge as part of the theistic traditions of southern India but in more syncretistic forms, incorporating distinct elements of local traditions. The important Tamil gods Mudalvan and Tirumal, for example, became identified with Shiva and Vishnu, allowing worship of the older deities to become part of the Sanskritized tradition.[4] Simi-

larly, the Tamil war goddess Korravai became identified with Durga, one of the principal forms of Shakti, the supreme goddess in Hinduism. Such processes took place at
a more local scale as well. In the major temple complex in Madurai, the goddess
Meenakshi and her consort represented local deities associated with older Dravidian
traditions, and much of the mythology surrounding them had explicitly local elements, but eventually they became identified with the pan-Indian deities Parvati and
Shiva.[5] Some deities were less clearly transformed by Sanskritization in southern India,
however. Most importantly, Tamils continued to worship Murugan, their chief indigenous god, who was associated with youth and beauty as well as war. Worship practices
associated with Murugan included a distinctive ritual form of ecstatic sacred dance.
At some point this deity became linked to Skanda, the northern Indian war god and
a son of Shiva, but this connection did not become fully accepted in southern India
and Murugan continued to be worshipped in native forms. In sum, the process of
Sanskritization had engendered complex religious contrasts between northern and
southern India by the first millennium CE, a pattern mirrored on more local scales in
countless interactions between the formal sources of Hinduism and local religious
customs.

As the Sanskritization of India's religious cultures became more fully realized,
their spatial diversity continued to develop through certain regional innovations. The
Tamil-speaking region of southern India again exemplified this pattern in its approach
to the concept of bhakti, or personal devotion to a particular deity. This concept had
roots in the Vedas, the theistic elements of the Upanishads, and the Hindu epics, and
was closely related to the growing Hindu emphasis on the worship of Vishnu and
Shiva. In southern India, however, bhakti underwent a significant reinterpretation,
starting around the middle of the first millennium CE.[6] The Tamil approach to bhakti
identified intense, emotional, and selfless love for a personal deity as the primary goal
of religious practice, a sign of and appeal to divine blessing. Through this intimate
relationship with a personal god, the adherent sought refuge and salvation. This more
impassioned and intimate understanding of bhakti found expression by the sixth or
seventh century in the form of ecstatic, devotional poetry composed in Tamil by various mystics and saints. Two major schools of Tamil devotional poetry developed: that
of the Alvars (the "Immersed"), devoted to Vishnu; and that of the Nayanars ("Masters"), devoted to Shiva. The devotional works of these poet-saints represented the
first major body of Hindu literature composed in a language other than Sanskrit.
These works eventually came to be regarded as the Tamil Vedas, and they remain
an important part of Hinduism in Tamil-speaking regions. Similar poetic traditions
subsequently developed in other parts of the Dravidian linguistic region of southern
India as well.

The Tamil tradition of bhakti poetry arose in part from the theistic dimension
developing within Hinduism generally, particularly as expressed in two widespread
forms of devotion: Vaishnavism, focusing on Vishnu, and Saivism, focusing on Shiva.
But the Tamil bhakti movement also reflected the effects of distinctive regional influences in southern India. Most importantly, the resurgence of Hinduism in the first
millennium CE, and the subsequent decline of the competing traditions of Buddhism
and Jainism, occurred somewhat earlier and in more complex fashion in the Dravidian
south than in most other parts of India. A crucial feature of the Hindu resurgence in
the south was the emergence of overtly Hindu kingdoms, such as those of the Pandya

and Pallava dynasties, whose rulers favored Hindu institutions and practices. This pattern contrasted with that of the dominant Gupta Empire in northern India, for example, in which Hinduism, Buddhism, and Jainism all benefited from royal patronage.

After the fall of the Gupta Empire in the sixth century, moreover, the migration of Brahmin priests to the southern kingdoms strengthened the presence there of the orthodox Vedic elements of Hinduism. Brahmin influences thus furthered the process of Sanskritization, but without diminishing the vitality of Tamil culture. The result was a greater, if unreflexive, sense of Tamil identification with emerging trends within Hinduism, but expressed within the context of Tamil traditions and in vernacular form rather than in Sanskrit. Older Tamil forms of love poetry that predated Sanskritization thus provided an important foundation for the later development of bhakti poetry and contributed to its distinctive emotional character.[7] At the same time, the Hindu resurgence in southern India at the popular level encouraged the growth of more egalitarian forms of devotion, accessible to all adherents rather than just the priestly caste. In this sense, the bhakti movement represented an important reaction against the orthodoxy of the Brahmins and the often oppressive social order that it supported.[8] Significantly, the Alvars included a woman and lower-caste men among their numbers, as well as Brahmins and scholars. The Vaishnavist and Saivist groups that came to venerate the Alvars and Nayanars thus placed little emphasis on caste or gender, supporting a view of salvation that stressed the primary importance of divine grace.

The rise of the bhakti movement had important consequences for Hinduism, both within southern India and beyond. In southern India, it became a significant vehicle for the conversion of Jains and Buddhists from all strata of society, offering an emotional form of religious practice absent from the more ascetic traditions.[9] The bhakti movement was also linked to the growth of temple construction in the south. The construction of permanent Hindu temples apparently originated around the fourth century CE in the Gupta Empire of northern India, in association with emerging theistic trends; temple worship had not been present in traditional Vedism, whose ritual focus was the sacrificial altar. By the sixth century, the Hindu temple had diffused to southern India as well, where it became a principal setting for the practice of bhakti. Moreover, because temple construction came to be considered an important act of devotion, the growth of the bhakti movement led to a considerable increase in the number of temples in the region, which in turn led to the development of a distinctive style of temple architecture characterized by elaborate towers or pyramids (photo 3.1). The Alvars and Nayanars were likewise linked to the establishment of pilgrimage sites in southern India, including the major Vaishnavist center at Srirangam and the major Saivist center at Chidambaram. After the works of the Tamil poet-saints had been compiled into canonical forms in the tenth and eleventh centuries, they also contributed to the development of two important devotional sects concentrated in southern India, the Saiva Siddhanta and Sri Vaishnava. Both of these sects drew on older religious influences from the north, but their attachment to Tamil bhakti poetry distinguished them from similar Saivist and Vaishnavist groups elsewhere in India. At the same time, however, the Tamil bhakti movement came to influence theistic practices beyond southern India, both through the migration of adherents and more grad-

Photo 3.1.   Chamundeswari Temple dedicated to Durga, an aspect of Shakti. The structure illustrates the Dravida architectural style characteristic of temples in southern India, with a tower made up of a stacked series of ornately decorated tiers that decrease in size from base to apex. Mysore, India, 2007.

Source: Zach Casper (www.flickr.com/photos/zcasper/500450824/), under Creative Commons license (creativecommons.org/licenses/by-sa/2.0/).

ual processes of contact diffusion.[10] The intense emotionality of Tamil bhakti thus became an increasingly common feature of Hindu devotion in other regions as well.

Muslim Conquests and Regional Diversity

As the Hindu tradition became more completely articulated in the early centuries of the second millennium CE, another major source of regional diversity emerged as Muslim empires began to invade the Indian subcontinent from southwestern Asia.[11] The subsequent period of Muslim conquest and rule significantly changed the contexts within which Hindus practiced their religion in much of India, not only through the imposition of Muslim political control but also through the assertion of new cultural norms. Perhaps the most basic factor in the resulting confrontation between Hinduism and Islam was the contrast in their worldviews, one rooted in Vedic polytheism and the other in strict monotheism. This contrast established a fundamental tension between the two traditions, precluding any widespread synthesis of their beliefs. Muslims also brought a strong missionary tradition to India and in some places actively sought Hindu converts. The Muslim conquests had important social consequences as well, typically establishing Muslims at the top of a new social order that traditionally had been defined by the Hindu caste system. The spread of Muslim rule in sum effected widespread changes in Hindu religious and social customs. Such changes did not occur to the same degree throughout India, however. The impacts of Muslim rule varied spatially and in some areas they remained fairly limited, especially in the south. As a result, the continuing reproduction of Hinduism by its adherents had distinct outcomes in different regions during the medieval period, producing a number of significant regional contrasts.

The most extensive effects of Muslim rule appeared throughout India's northern plain, from Punjab across the Gangetic plain to Bihar. Central Asian Muslims had begun making incursions into this region by the eleventh century and by the late twelfth and early thirteenth centuries, under the Ghurid dynasty, had established extensive territorial control. This conquest led to the formation of the Delhi sultanate, an empire that lasted under successive dynasties into the sixteenth century. It came to an end with the invasion of northern India by a new dynasty of Central Asian Muslims, the Mughals, who dominated the region until the early eighteenth century. Both the Delhi sultanate and the Mughal Empire expanded and contracted over time, but they maintained more or less continuous control over most of the northern plain of India. For over five centuries, then, Hindus in this region reproduced their religion largely within the context of Muslim rule.

The migration of Turks, Afghans, and Persians into the Muslim empires of northern India brought new cultural influences to the region, but again the disparate worldviews of Islam and Hinduism prevented much direct influence of the former over the latter. Some conversion of Hindus to Islam did occur, most notably through the missionary efforts of Sufi orders, although these conversion processes primarily developed among Hindus of low caste who could raise their status by joining Muslim society. More significant effects developed through the assertion of Muslim hegemony over the region, which brought about a corresponding decline in Hindu institutions, social structures, and cultural expressions. Muslim rulers destroyed Hindu temples in locations across northern India, for example, often erecting mosques on the same sites as an expression of Muslim dominance. The Muslim empires also commonly banned the construction of new temples.[12] These practices had a devastating effect, as by this time temple worship had become central to most expressions of Hinduism. The temples themselves were not merely physical structures; they represented complex sacred spaces and cultural institutions, serving as centers of ritual, learning, and social interaction. Their destruction thus impoverished Hindu culture and society. The establishment of a Muslim ruling class similarly weakened the traditional social order associated with most forms of Hinduism. Many Brahmins and Kshatriyas thus left northern India, while others turned to agriculture. The result was again a regional decline in the more learned traditions of Hinduism.

Of course, rulers in the northern empires differed in their treatment of the Hindu majority. The Mughal emperor Akbar, ruling from 1556 to 1605, established tolerant policies, allowing the construction of Hindu temples and eliminating taxes on non-Muslims and Hindu pilgrims. On the other hand, his great-grandson Aurangzeb, ruling from 1658 to 1707, sought to impose Islamic law throughout the empire, outlawed Hindu festivals, reinstated the taxes rescinded by Akbar, banned temple construction or repair, and ordered that temples built since Akbar's rule be destroyed.[13]

The overall effect of Muslim hegemony in the northern plain was a gradual simplification of Hindu belief and practice. Hinduism in the region lost much of its philosophical sophistication and ritual complexity as knowledge of Sanskrit declined, and the region no longer served as a major center of Hindu learning. In effect, Hinduism became largely a folk religion rooted more in local customs than in written tradition. Moreover, in the Gangetic plain, certain important religious developments flourishing in other regions during this period declined or remained weak, including Tantrism and Shaktism, both discussed in more detail below.

The simplification of Hinduism in India's northern plain contrasted most sharply with the ongoing development of Hinduism in southern India, where Muslim influences remained weaker. At their greatest extent the Delhi sultanate and the Mughal Empire each extended well into the south, but their control was often superficial and relatively short-lived. Various independent Muslim kingdoms also emerged in central India, but their cultural hegemony over the Hindu majority also proved to be limited. In the far south of India, moreover, direct Muslim rule was never fully established. As a result, reproduction of the Hindu tradition in the south remained largely unaffected by the constraints that had arisen in the north. The higher castes generally maintained their elite status within the social and cultural structures of daily life. Brahmins continued to dominate the formal dimensions of religious life, preserving the continuity of the Hindu tradition through their knowledge of Sanskrit and of older ritual practices. The continued strength of the traditional social order, in combination with a weaker Muslim presence in the south, also made conversions of lower-caste Hindus to Islam less common than in the north. Some destruction of Hindu temples by Muslim forces did occur but not on the same scale as in the Gangetic plain and with little long-term effect given the extensive pattern of temple construction that developed in the south. Temple worship thus retained its sophistication and complexity, accommodating the formal Vedic traditions of the Brahmin priests as well as more popular expressions of bhakti. The frequency of temple construction in the south also produced a distinctive and elaborate architectural style, continuing to reflect ritual divisions of space associated with the ancient Vedic altar while incorporating a strong iconic element in the form of vivid statuary associated with bhakti devotion (photo 3.1).[14] Hindu temples in southern India also retained their importance as social institutions, integrating the political, social, economic, and religious dimensions of daily life. The major temple towns and cities of Tamil Nadu perhaps most clearly reflected this pattern, but it also appeared through the role of Brahmins as both major landowners and the custodians of formal temple ritual.[15] In the south, then, secular life continued to be grounded in the encompassing context of Hinduism as a cultural system.

In religious terms, the relative autonomy of southern India during the medieval period allowed for the articulation of a much more diverse tradition than existed in the north. Again, Brahmins in the south, and especially in Tamil Nadu, adhered more closely to Vedic tradition than did many northern Brahmins. At the same time, Brahmins in the south tended to be relatively tolerant of more popular, heterodox expressions of Hinduism. This tolerance reflected both the Brahmins' certainty of their elite position within society and the absence of the external threat to their position that Muslim hegemony could bring. The bhakti movements focusing on Shiva and Vishnu thus flourished alongside older ritual practices, resulting in a distinctive regional synthesis of formal and popular strands within Hinduism.

Regional and Local Developments

Various other developments in Hinduism during the early medieval period, of relatively minor importance in the Gangetic plain, also became more fully established in the south. One such development was Shaktism, a devotional movement similar to Saivism and Vaishnavism that focused on Shakti, the female aspect of divinity, in various forms and under various names. The worship of local goddesses had many precedents in India and before the medieval period appears to have been quite common in the south.[16] References to a principal goddess became increasingly frequent in Hindu writings by the seventh century, however, reflecting the emergence of Shakti as a key figure within the Hindu tradition. Indeed, as the medieval period progressed Shakti in her various forms came to rival Vishnu and Shiva as the object of popular devotion. This development most likely originated in eastern India, and spread rapidly to other parts of the subcontinent. Its influence remained weakest in the Gangetic plain, but in the south it became an important part of the region's increasingly diverse tradition.

A similar pattern emerged in the spread of Tantrism, a Hindu religious system closely associated with Shaktism. Tantrism has been defined in various ways, but here the term refers to beliefs and practices associated with the Tantras, writings that describe practical physical and mental processes for accelerating the attainment of enlightenment. In these writings Shakti frequently appears as the feminine expression of divine creative energy. Tantric practices had become influential across much of India by the tenth century, but thereafter declined in importance in the north. In contrast, Tantrism remained an important current of thought in southern India, and gradually became integrated into the region's complex synthesis of Hinduism.

Through the active commingling of these various elements of Hinduism, southern India and Tamil Nadu in particular became the primary center for the development of Hindu thought during the medieval period, reinforcing the divergence between the complex Hinduism of the south and the folk Hinduism of the Gangetic plain.[17] Between the extremes of these two regions, other parts of India had taken on a degree of distinctiveness as well, reflecting local patterns of belief and practice and varying interactions with Muslim rule.[18] In regions of northern India peripheral to the Gangetic plain that were not as extensively dominated by Muslim hegemony, the more formal elements of the Hindu tradition persisted more or less intact. The simplification of the Gangetic plain was thus less pronounced in Bengal, Kashmir, Rajputana, and other surrounding areas. Developments such as Shaktism and Tantrism also found more frequent expression in these areas. Shaktism in particular became important in Bengal, where a strong tradition of devotion to the more fearsome manifestations of Shakti developed.

The contrast between other parts of the north and the Gangetic plain were less pronounced than those between the latter and the peninsular south, however, largely because the social impacts of Muslim rule were more strongly felt than in the south. In the northern regions surrounding the Gangetic plain, the conversion of low-caste Hindus to Islam was more common than in the south, for example. Many of these converts continued to adhere to some elements of Hinduism, however, as formal means of ensuring conformity to Islamic orthodoxy for the most part did not exist. High-caste Hindus in the northern periphery also were not widely displaced by a

Muslim upper class, in contrast to patterns in the Gangetic plain, but they did experience pressures to accommodate Muslim hegemony in their public lives. In response, the higher castes maintained strict adherence to ritual orthodoxy in their private religious lives and were much less tolerant of popular heterodoxy than were high-caste Hindus in the south. In Bengal, this insistence on Hindu orthodoxy found expression in the emergence of new, strict codes of religious law by the end of the medieval period.

Many other regional variations in the practice of Hinduism have developed throughout the tradition's history, at geographical scales down to the level of the individual village. Of particular note, because they developed quite differently from the patterns described above, are the distinct expressions of Hinduism that have emerged in the regions dominated by the tribal peoples of central and eastern India. These groups are culturally distinct within India, speaking languages unrelated to the Indo-European and Dravidian linguistic families. They primarily inhabit hilly and forested areas, and traditionally possessed less complex social and economic systems than did other parts of India. Because of their relative isolation, the process of Sanskritization came to these groups relatively late and developed less completely. Their religious practices, in turn, clearly manifest processes of syncretism combining Hindu elements with traditional tribal religions rooted in animism and ancestor worship.[19]

Judaism

Judaism, like Hinduism, represents a complex ethnic religious tradition, encompassing a variety of different strands. The contrasts among those different strands are perhaps not as pronounced as they are within Hinduism, given the centrality of certain specific concepts within Judaism. Jewish belief is strictly monotheistic, for example, and thus adherents of all Jewish religious systems worship the same divine being. Judaism also focuses unambiguously on the Torah as the principal source of religious insight and on the distinct identity of the Jewish people established through their covenant with God. Traditional expressions of Judaism have also stressed the importance of adhering to the requirements of Jewish law, the halakhah. Together, these common elements of the Jewish tradition have produced an emphasis on orthodoxy and orthopraxy in most forms of Judaism. Nonetheless, Judaism has been transformed throughout its history by spatial processes of diversification, and those processes have produced a variety of distinct religious systems within the larger tradition.

Indeed, regional divisions had emerged even within Proto-Judaism in contrasts between the kingdoms of Israel and Judah and somewhat later between the Judahites exiled to Babylonia and those who remained in Judah. During the early centuries of Rabbinic Judaism, after the destruction of Jerusalem's Second Temple in 70 CE, regional differences again arose between Jews who migrated to Mesopotamia and those who remained in Palestine, eventually finding expression in the contrasting schools of Jewish scholarship that produced the Babylonian and Palestinian Talmuds. Regional diversification within Judaism developed on a broader scale, however, through the dispersion of Jews throughout the Mediterranean world and into Western Europe early in the Common Era. Through this Jewish diaspora, two major regional groupings emerged during the first millennium CE: the Sephardim concentrated in Spain, and the Ashkenazim concentrated in the Rhineland and adjacent areas of France and Germany (map 3.2). The Sephardim eventually came to be defined more broadly to include Jews throughout the Mediterranean region and the Middle East, while the Ashkenazim included Jews throughout northern, central, and eastern Europe. As in the case of the major geographical contrasts within Hinduism, the distinction between Sephardim and Ashkenazim was largely the product of uncontested processes of change as Jews reproduced their religion in different contexts. The division did not arise from schism or dissent within the tradition of Judaism, but rather through the emergence of distinct Jewish cultures in different circumstances.

As these regional forms of Judaism arose during the early medieval period, they continued to share much in common. Both groups drew much of their understanding of Jewish doctrine and law from the Jewish academies in Mesopotamia, which from the sixth to the eleventh centuries were the primary centers of Jewish learning. Jewish migrants to different areas also shared basic culture traits, such as a common ethnic identity and use of the Hebrew language. Over time, however, the regional forms of Sephardic and Ashkenazic Judaism became increasingly distinct, through both their isolation from one another and their interactions with different surroundings. The Sephardim and Ashkenazim diverged linguistically, for example, as the languages they used in daily life came to mix elements of Hebrew with European influences. This process produced Ladino, a mixture of Hebrew and Spanish, among the Sephardim and Yiddish, a mixture of Hebrew, German, and Slavic sources, among the Ashkenazim. Both groups retained Hebrew as their ritual language but developed different

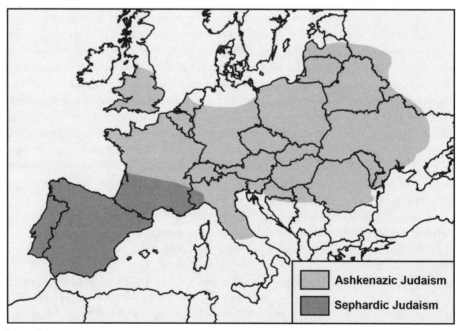

Map 3.2. The distribution of Sephardic and Ashkenazic Judaism within medieval Europe. Adapted from Dan Cohn-Sherbok, *Atlas of Jewish History* (New York: Routledge, 1994), 83.

Hebrew dialects in matters of pronunciation. In religious terms, the worship services of the Sephardim closely adhered to the Babylonian liturgy codified in the Mesopotamian Jewish academies. Ashkenazic Jews drew in part on this same tradition, but also incorporated somewhat older liturgical practices developed in Palestine, including a variety of distinctive hymns and prayers in the public worship service. This Palestinian tradition diffused to northern Europe with the migration of Jews from Palestine through Italy to Germany by the seventh and eighth centuries. The liturgical tradition of the Ashkenazim also differed from that of the Sephardim in the order and wording of specific prayers, in the manner of reciting biblical texts, and in the melodies used in biblical recitation. Differences emerged as well with regard to ceremonial practices relating to marriage and death.

Sephardic Judaism

Contrasts between Sephardic and Ashkenazic Judaism reflected the dissimilar social settings in which they lived. Sephardic Judaism arose within the context of relatively tolerant Muslim rule in the Iberian Peninsula. Jews had experienced intense persecution in Spain under the Visigoths during the seventh century, but their position improved dramatically after Muslims came to power in the eighth century. The Quranic acceptance of Christians and Jews as "People of the Book," those who recognize the biblical tradition from which Islam also derived, generally allowed for the participation of Jews within Muslim society and the free expression of Jewish culture. Jewish writers and thinkers produced a variety of important literary, philosophical, and scholarly works, which over time had considerable influence beyond Iberia. The writings of the twelfth-century philosopher Maimonides represent the most significant intellectual product of this period. At the same time, the spatial continuity of Muslim rule from Spain to southwestern Asia helped to keep the Sephardic community in contact with the Babylonian academies, preserving forms of religious practice associated with the latter. The circumstances of Jews in Spain deteriorated, however, after a less tolerant Muslim dynasty, the Almohads, came to power in the 1100s. The Almohads' persecutions caused many Jews to migrate to more tolerant Muslim regions along the eastern Mediterranean, while others moved to parts of Spain that by that time were controlled by Christians.

As Christian rulers expanded their control over the Iberian Peninsula during the next several centuries, the Jews who remained in Spain faced changing circumstances. In some areas, they retained certain economic and religious rights and Sephardic religious culture continued to thrive. An important development during this period was the flourishing of Kabbalah, a mystical expression of Sephardic Judaism. This innovation had diverse origins, possibly dating to the Second Temple period, and had emerged in various forms during the twelfth century in southern France and northern Spain. A systematic articulation of Kabbalah first appeared, however, in northern Spain during the thirteenth century with the appearance of Moses de Leon's *Sefer ha-Zohar*. The *Zohar* comprises various commentaries based on the Torah that examine the nature of the divine, of creation, and of evil, and that address the consequences of prayer and obedience to divine law. This approach represented a departure from the earlier Talmudic emphasis on the meticulous explication of religious law. By the

1300s, the mystical teachings of this work and the pietistic forms of religious experience that it supported had become an important part of Sephardic Judaism. During the same period, however, Christian hostility toward the Jews in Spain had increased and many Jews converted to Christianity to protect their position in society. Conditions worsened in the fifteenth century, as Christians accused Jewish converts of continuing to practice Judaism in private. The Spanish Inquisition, established in 1478, institutionalized the expanding pattern of persecution, resulting in the deaths of approximately 2,000 Jews; and in 1492, after the Christian reconquest of Iberia had been completed, the Spanish monarchy issued an edict expelling Jews from Spain. The Sephardim subsequently migrated to various areas largely dominated by Muslims in North Africa, southeastern Europe, and the Middle East.

As the adherents of Sephardic Judaism spread across the Mediterranean region into southwestern Asia, they continued to reproduce the distinctive Judaic culture that had taken shape in Iberia. The strong scholarly tradition of the Sephardim contributed to the rise of new centers of Jewish thought, most notably the community of Safed located in the north of present-day Israel. A key figure in that process was Joseph Karo, a scholar born in Spain in 1488, four years before the expulsion of the Jews. As an adult, Karo settled in Safed where he produced a definitive codification of Jewish law that synthesized and explicated the scholarship of earlier legal authorities. He later wrote a condensation of this work for popular use, which thereafter provided the foundation for the popular practice of Sephardic Judaism. Karo's relatively liberal reading of halakhah, in part a reflection of the Sephardic background of his major sources, supported the flexibility and openness that had typified much of the Sephardic tradition. Karo concluded, for example, that the absence of a practice in the past did not necessarily mean that it was forbidden and that adherence to halakhah therefore did not preclude some forms of innovation. Alongside the scholarly tradition, the contrasting approach of Kabbalah also flourished at Safed, from whence it became widely disseminated throughout the Mediterranean region and other parts of Europe by traveling scholars and the circulation of homiletic writings.[20] The ongoing vitality of Kabbalistic thought thus helped to maintain a pietistic emphasis on personal religious experience among the Sephardim. Through the preservation of both scholarly and mystical traditions at Safed, the Sephardim continued to reproduce their distinctive religious culture as they resettled throughout the Mediterranean region and southwestern Asia; and in places where they settled in large numbers their traditions typically became dominant within the Jewish community. The flexibility of Sephardic Judaism allowed a degree of local adaptability, but at the same time it preserved a general sense of commonality among its adherents based on the observance of Jewish law and Sephardic customs.

Ashkenazic Judaism

Ashkenazic Judaism developed within a very different set of contexts. Jewish traders and merchants had become established within the Christian Frankish Empire in northern Europe by the ninth century, and by the tenth century a number of active Jewish communities existed in cities along the Rhine. The settlement of Jewish migrants from Palestine in the Rhineland contributed from an early date to contrasts with Judaism in Iberia, especially through the reproduction of portions of the Palestinian liturgy in Ashkenazic worship. Contrasts with the Sephardim increased as Jews moved into other parts of Christian Europe during this period, including various areas of France, Germany, the Netherlands, England, and northern Italy. Within these settings, Jews generally did not participate widely in the surrounding society. Christian rulers valued the trade connections to the Middle East that Jewish merchants could provide, but in most areas of daily life, Christians and Jews remained segregated from one another (photo 3.2). This pattern in part grew out of Jewish concerns for the preservation of their tradition, but it also reflected fundamental Christian animosity toward Judaism. This animosity grew out of the widely held belief that Jews were accountable for the death of Jesus, and would remain so until they accepted Christianity. Ashkenazic Judaism thus emerged within a context where, by necessity, Jewish society functioned largely in isolation from the surrounding Gentile world. The interactions between Jewish, Arabic, and classical traditions that had characterized Sephardic culture had no parallel among the Ashkenazim. Instead, their religious culture during the early medieval period remained more inward-looking, focused on the observance of Jewish law and traditional study of the Torah and the Talmud.[21]

Increasing Christian antagonism further affected the isolation of Ashkenazic society by the end of the eleventh century. Christian hostility toward Jews reached an early climax in 1096 when participants in the First Crusade, on setting out to liberate the Holy Land of Christianity, massacred thousands of Jews in various cities in northern France and the Rhineland. Such massacres recurred on a smaller scale during the

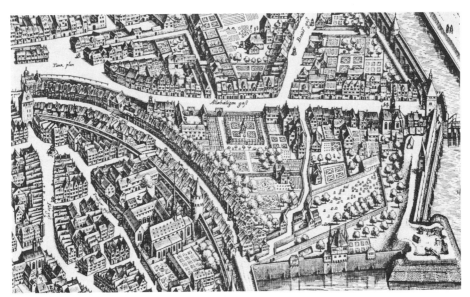

Photo 3.2.   Detail from a city map of Frankfurt am Main, Germany, produced by Matthäus Merian in 1628. The city's segregated Jewish quarter, the Judengasse or Jews Street, curves through the lower left quadrant of the image. Note the depiction of a much higher building density within the confines of the Judengasse than in surrounding parts of the city. The church to the right of the lower end of the Judengasse is part of a Dominican monastery.

Source: Public domain (commons.wikimedia.org/wiki/Image:Frankfurt_Judengasse_1628.jpg).

Second Crusade beginning in 1147. During the twelfth and thirteenth centuries, so-called blood libels, accusations that Jews had used the blood of Christians in Passover rituals, repeatedly provoked anti-Semitic violence in England, northern France, and Germany. Similar allegations that Jews had desecrated wafers used in the Christian Eucharist also incited attacks on Jewish communities in thirteenth-century France and Germany.[22] Antagonism toward Jews in northern Europe developed as well in reaction to their role in moneylending, an activity in which Christians did not participate because of a religious prohibition against charging interest. Jewish involvement in moneylending had increased in the early medieval period, as they were excluded by the hegemonic Christian society from many other forms of economic activity. Moreover, Christian rulers had benefited from Jewish financial activity through the taxes that they imposed on it. Over time, though, resentment toward Jewish creditors became widespread among Christians and at various times Christian rulers cancelled the debts owed to Jews or seized their wealth.

Together, these various sources of Christian hostility produced a prolonged period of often violent persecution of the Ashkenazic Jews, resulting in many thousands of deaths. They also led to the periodic expulsion of Jews from locations in the region. England expelled its Jewish population in 1290, an edict not rescinded until the 1600s. The French monarchy, in contrast, expelled Jews numerous times during this period, in 1182, 1254, 1306, and 1394, repeatedly allowing them to return only to banish them once again after seizing their wealth. Various cities and states in Germany also expelled their Jewish populations, although often only temporarily, and many confined the Jewish population to clearly defined ghettoes within specific cities.

This context of persecution reinforced pre-existent elements of Ashkenazic Judaism, including both its independent, inward-looking nature and its emphasis on strict adherence to traditional law. Local Jewish communities, or *kahals*, were largely self-governing entities, headed by elected councils and judicial courts. The kahals in northern Europe did depend on external sources in interpreting Jewish law, at first including the Babylonian academies. Over time, however, the cultural and geographical isolation of the Ashkenazim strengthened the importance of local authority in establishing and enforcing the regulations that ruled Jewish life. The role of local authority in interpreting Jewish law in turn reinforced the Ashkenazic emphasis on study of the Torah and Talmud. This emphasis produced a strong tradition of religious scholarship in the region and in many communities led to the formation of rabbinic academies, which became the final authority on legal matters for the Ashkenazim.

The most important of these institutions was the academy in Mainz, where the eleventh-century rabbi Gershom ben Judah produced influential rulings that his students spread to kahals across northern Europe. By promoting a meticulous observance of sacred law, Gershom and his followers sought to preserve Jewish tradition within a context of Christian hegemony and recurring persecution. Significantly, though, Gershom's rulings deviated in some ways from those of the Babylonian academies and thus contributed to the articulation of Ashkenazic Judaism as a distinct branch within the larger Jewish tradition. He formed new rules banning polygamy and nonconsensual divorce, for example, and insisted on the binding authority of local Jewish courts. By the end of the eleventh century, then, Jewish scholars in northern Europe recognized Gershom's teachings as part of the foundation of their particular understanding of Judaism. It was also around this time that Jewish writers began to use the term

Ashkenaz to denote Germany, providing the basis for the name later ascribed to this distinct branch.

As the distinct emphases on strict observance and local authority flourished among the Ashkenazim, the continuing threat of Christian persecution and a desire to improve their economic circumstances contributed to the beginnings of their migration eastward.[23] By the end of the thirteenth century, some Jews had migrated to Palestine to live under more tolerant Muslim rule, but a greater number had begun moving into Poland, Lithuania, and adjacent areas of Eastern Europe. Various rulers in Eastern Europe at this time sought to develop their territories by encouraging immigration, and to this end established statutes granting Jews certain legal protections. Such statutes were in effect by 1244 in Austria, by 1264 in Poland, and by 1388 in Lithuania. Outbreaks of anti-Semitism did occur in Eastern Europe as the Jewish population grew. Nonetheless, migration into the region continued, and increased rapidly after the mid-fourteenth century, when Jews faced renewed persecution in many parts of Western Europe based on accusations that they had caused the Black Plague by poisoning water sources. Over the next several centuries, through the combined effects of migration and natural increase, Eastern Europe emerged as the new geographical focus of the Ashkenazim and eventually contained the world's largest concentration of Jews. Ashkenazic Judaism consequently interacted with an increasing variety of contexts within Europe, from more urbanized settings in the west to more rural areas in the east.

The distinctive elements of Ashkenazic Judaism persisted as the Ashkenazim themselves became more dispersed. Many Ashkenazim were dissatisfied, for example, with the Sephardic codification of the halakhah compiled by Joseph Karo, which paid little attention to Ashkenazic customs and in some ways interpreted the law with greater flexibility than Ashkenazic scholars did. Karo's work did not achieve widespread acceptance among the Ashkenazim, therefore, until it was supplemented by a commentary written by Moses Isserles, a sixteenth-century rabbi and founder of an influential yeshiva in Krakow. Isserles's commentary incorporated Ashkenazic practices, interpreted the law more strictly, and placed a strong emphasis on the observance of established customs. The Ashkenazim's emphasis on local authority also persisted as they spread to diverse locations and thus local communities similar to the kahals in Western Europe appeared throughout Eastern Europe as well.

Again, these characteristics contributed to the survival of Ashkenazic Judaism in disparate, often hostile, contexts. These attributes also gave rise, however, to increasing religious divisions among the Ashkenazim. Unlike the Sephardim, who maintained a sense of commonality through the flexibility of their religious culture, the Ashkenazim developed a variety of different religious expressions based on their tradition of adherence to local authority. As a result, by the early modern period the Ashkenazim had produced a number of secondary hearths where distinct interpretations of Judaism flourished. In the process, the diversification of Ashkenazic Judaism also took on an increasingly reflexive character as adherents more consciously identified with particular articulations of Jewish tradition.

Hasidic Judaism

The first of these secondary hearths, associated with the rise of Hasidism, originated during the 1700s among Jews in the Polish Ukraine, a context characterized by considerable social and political instability. Jewish society in this region had been devastated during the 1600s by nearly two decades of warfare set off by a Cossack rebellion against the Polish aristocracy, which had escalated into a broader conflict involving Poland, Russia, and Sweden. The Cossacks massacred thousands of Jews, whom they viewed as allies of the aristocracy. Russian and Polish combatants in this conflict also considered the Jews to be a threat and expanded the violence against them. By the end of the war, perhaps a fourth of the region's Jewish population had been killed. Further massacres of Jews in the Ukraine occurred during the 1700s. Moreover, the established system of Jewish self-government was weakened in the 1760s when the Polish government abolished the Jews' governing council. The partition of Poland by surrounding empires during the late 1700s further intensified regional uncertainties.

Within this context, Hasidism emerged as a striking departure from the established patterns of Rabbinic Judaism.[24] It grew out of the teachings of Israel ben Eliezer, also known to his followers as the *Baal Shem Tov*, or "Master of the Good Name," abbreviated in acronymic form as the Besht. He was born and lived in the Polish Ukrainian province of Podolia where he followed in the Eastern European tradition of itinerant Jewish healers. According to tradition, these healers could effect cures and exorcise spirits and demons through the use of various folk remedies and their esoteric knowledge of the ineffable name of God. The Besht's followers credited him with possessing such abilities, but he also articulated a distinctive interpretation of Judaism that became the basis for Hasidism. The Besht's teachings focused in particular on the experience of communion with God through spontaneous, joyful prayer. He rejected the formalism of traditional Jewish worship, instead emphasizing the use of ecstatic practices like singing and dancing to achieve a state of bliss. Although he drew inspiration from Kabbalah, he opposed the asceticism often associated with Kabbalistic practices. He believed that all of creation continually derives from the will of God, and that Jews must enthusiastically cling to God not only in worship but also in the performance of ordinary daily activities. Through this process the individual could ultimately achieve salvation. The Besht's teachings thus supported a worldview that emphasized the proximity of God in daily life and an ethos based on joy and hope as well as on adherence to Jewish law.

After settling in the Podolian village of Medzhibozh in 1736, the Besht attracted a large following drawn by the hopefulness of his message and by the otherworldly power evident in his performance of miraculous healings (map 3.3). Over the next two decades his ideas spread to other villages in neighboring provinces. His successor, Dov Baer ben Samuel, further advanced the wider diffusion of Hasidism. During the late 1700s, his disciples thus established Hasidic communities in Ukraine, Poland, and Lithuania. By the early 1800s, most Jews in central Poland, Galicia, and Ukraine were adherents of Hasidism, and the movement had spread into Lithuania and Hungary as well. The diffusion of the movement depended in part on a reinterpretation of religious leadership focusing on the zaddik, the model of Jewish behavior in the Talmud. In Hasidism, however, this term was applied to specific leaders who, like the Besht, were believed to have achieved spiritual superiority and magical abilities through a union with God. Zaddikim thus served as models of Hasidic devotion, but they also provided spiritual leadership by acting as intermediaries between their followers and God. The zaddik, also known by the title of rebbe, as a result became the central figure within a community of followers, known as Hasidim or loyalists.

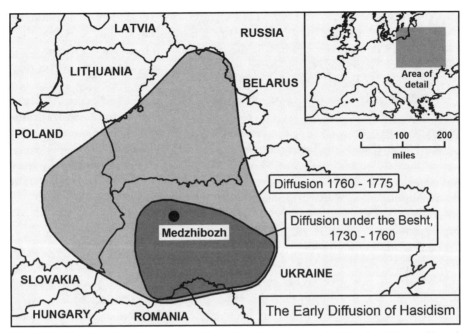

Map 3.3. The hearth of Hasidic Judaism. Hasidism grew out of the teachings of Israel ben Eliezer, or the Besht, in western Ukraine and spread from there into the areas of dense Jewish settlement to the north and west. Adapted from Dan Cohn-Sherbok, *Atlas of Jewish History* (New York: Routledge, 1994), 130.

Because the zaddikim had autonomy within their own communities, Hasidism became increasingly diverse as it spread during the late 1700s and early 1800s. At the same time, although Hasidism insisted on observance of the halakhah and Ashkenazic customs, it attracted opposition from traditional Jewish leaders in Eastern Europe, who accused the Hasidim of excessive emotionalism during worship, of neglecting the study of the Talmud, and of separating themselves from the rest of the Jewish community.

Reform Judaism

The mystical character of Hasidism also drew criticism from adherents of Reform Judaism, a movement that originated in Germany during the early 1800s as an attempt to modernize and liberalize the Jewish tradition. It developed within the context of broader transformations within Jewish life, particularly in Western Europe, that had been brought about by the Jewish Enlightenment and the Emancipation. The Enlightenment represented an effort to expand the scope of Jewish culture to incorporate developments in mainstream European thought and knowledge. Supporters of the Enlightenment sought to introduce secular disciplines into traditional Jewish education, rejected the traditional cultural practices of Jewish ghetto life, favored the use of the language of the surrounding society rather than Yiddish, and de-emphasized the authority of religious custom. They also worked to free Jews from the traditional laws of exclusion imposed on them by European states, which restricted Jewish involvement in mainstream structures of political, economic, and social life. This effort ultimately contributed to the Emancipation, the revocation of such laws of exclusion beginning in the late 1700s in France and spreading to other parts of Europe during the 1800s and early 1900s.[25] By increasing opportunities for Jewish participation within European society, the Emancipation reinforced the modernizing perspective of the Enlightenment.

Reform Judaism applied that modernizing perspective to religious belief and practice. It originated during the early 1800s in a hearth in northern Germany encompassing Berlin and areas to the west, where the Enlightenment had achieved a wider currency among well-educated Jews and where the influence of Napoleonic France had weakened restrictions on Jewish society. Because opposition from traditionalists at first excluded Reform ideas from the synagogues, Reform Jews concentrated instead on establishing modern Jewish schools.[26] Israel Jacobson, a lay Reform leader, played a key role in this process, founding a number of schools throughout Westphalia, starting in the town of Seesen in 1801. In 1810, he also established the first Reform synagogue next to his school in Seesen. He later moved to Berlin, but efforts to create a Reform synagogue there in 1815 were frustrated by Jewish traditionalists who persuaded the Prussian government to intervene based on the traditional practice of defining the Jews as a single, undivided community. Nonetheless, the first major Reform temple was founded in 1818 in Hamburg and despite traditionalist opposition the Reform movement continued to expand. By the 1840s Reform congregations existed in Berlin and Frankfurt, and in 1844 the first Reform rabbinical conference met in Braunschweig to standardize practices within the movement.

The early Reform congregations specifically emphasized the reorganization of Jewish worship. The movement's proponents argued that traditional worship practices had become obsolete and would drive away Jews who had adopted modernist or assimilationist views. They also disapproved of the ecstatic character of Hasidism. Reform worship thus incorporated distinct innovations, including prayer and sermons entirely in German, prayer in unison rather than individually, the use of organ and choral music, the mixed seating of men and women, and disuse of the prayer shawl. Many of these practices in fact resembled those of the Lutheran church, the dominant religious body in northern Germany. Adherents of Reform also abandoned Jewish dietary laws, allowed work on the Sabbath, and rejected belief in the messianic redemption of the Jews.

By the middle of the 1800s, Reform scholars had also begun to articulate the philosophical foundations of their religious system in greater detail, going beyond the earlier Reform focus on worship practices.[27] In doing so, they distinguished between eternal, divinely inspired elements of Judaism, such as the biblical emphases on monotheism and ethical behavior, and the accretions of traditional custom, such as certain Sabbath restrictions, dietary laws, and patterns of dress. They saw such accretions as expressions of belief rooted in a particular time and place rather than as universal obligations. They therefore believed that external religious practices should be continually adapted to changing circumstances so that the underlying principles of Judaism would remain relevant. The worldview of Reform Judaism recast Jews as a religious community rather than the chosen nation of God. Reform adherents thus saw themselves not as a chosen people in exile but as citizens of the states in which they lived, a view particularly associated with Abraham Geiger, an influential Reform rabbi. Based on this new understanding of Jewish identity, the Reform ethos in turn focused

on the general concepts of morality, reason, and justice rather than on strict observance of Jewish law.

Ultra-Orthodox Judaism

As the Reform movement spread during the nineteenth century, however, it encountered considerable resistance, and most Ashkenazic Jews remained committed to traditional beliefs and practices. Traditionalist leaders saw the Reform movement as a threat
to the survival of authentic Judaism as expressed in the halakhah. The traditionalists
were also suspicious of the new freedoms effected by the Emancipation, fearing that
assimilation into Gentile society would weaken the integrity of the Jewish community.
The rise of the Reform movement was thus accompanied by a significant resurgence
in orthodoxy among the Ashkenazim during the 1800s. In Germany, the proponents
of orthodoxy did make some accommodations to modernity, including the adoption
of secular education and the use of German in worship. In Eastern Europe, however,
the reassertion of orthodoxy was more uncompromising, contributing to the rise of
the ultra-Orthodox movement within Judaism.[28]

The initial hearth of ultra-Orthodoxy developed in Hungary.[29] The influence of
the Jewish Enlightenment and the Reform movement appeared somewhat later there
than in German states and provoked a much stronger reaction. The leading critic of
Jewish modernism at the time was Moses Sofer, a rabbi born in Germany who served
as the leader of the Jewish community in Pressburg (now Bratislava) during the early
1800s. Sofer rejected all forms of innovation in Jewish life or worship, based on his
belief that the Torah expressly prohibited any deviation from established traditions.
He thus supported the continued segregation of Jews from the rest of society and
opposed the secularization of Jewish education, the revision of worship practices, and
the translation of sacred texts into vernacular languages. In his view, strict and thorough adherence to traditional customs provided the only means of preserving Judaism
and fulfilling halakhic obligations. In the decades following Sofer's death in 1839,
however, the effects of the Enlightenment became more widely felt in Hungary, particularly in the larger urban centers, where the supporters of modernization promoted
changes in synagogue worship, education reform, and Jewish participation in the
larger society. In response, some Orthodox leaders began to accept a degree of accommodation to change.

These trends, reinforced by the impending Emancipation of Hungarian Jews in
1867, led to a backlash among strict traditionalists, and by the 1860s ultra-Orthodoxy
had emerged as a recognizable movement. Its followers resided primarily in a largely
rural region northeast of Budapest that extended into present-day Slovakia. This area
contained a higher density of Jews than did other parts of Hungary, and because of its
relative isolation had been less affected by modernizing influences. It had also absorbed
influences from Hasidic Judaism, whose adherents supported Sofer's rejection of the
Reform movement. The ultra-Orthodox movement that flourished here opposed any
compromise with modernity. Its leaders insisted on the preservation of Jewish separateness and adherence in every detail to the customs of traditional Jewish life in the
region. In matters not explicitly covered by the halakhah, they asserted that Jews
should avoid any imitation of Gentile culture. The use of Yiddish and the preservation
of traditional patterns of dress and personal appearance thus became important sym-

bols of ultra-Orthodoxy. The ultra-Orthodox saw their movement, in sum, as the authentic continuation of the Jewish tradition rather than a departure from it. Their worldview identified the Jews in traditional terms as a distinct people whose purpose was the realization of divine law, and their ethos in turn stressed the observance and study of the Torah. The ultra-Orthodox did diverge in some ways from the mainstream of European Judaism, however, for example in their adherence to established customs and their reliance on obscure textual authorities. More importantly, the ultra-Orthodox departed from tradition in separating themselves from less traditional Jews, forming their own social and institutional structures. This practice differed markedly from the customary organization of the Jewish inhabitants of an area as a single, unified community.

*   *   *

The movements that emerged within these three secondary hearths thus represented distinct reinterpretations of a common source tradition. The ultra-Orthodox identified themselves as the authentic core of Judaism, in opposition to an increasingly deviant mainstream, while the Reform movement grew out of a more reflexive process of enlightened innovation. Hasidism also incorporated innovations concerning worship practices and religious leadership, but retained a strong adherence to Jewish tradition and the observance of the halakhah. Tensions therefore existed among all three groups, although over time the ultra-Orthodox and Hasidim became increasingly allied through their opposition to the effects of modernity. They are often grouped together as the *haredim* ("those who tremble" at the word of God), distinguished by their adherence to traditional customs, observance of the halakhah, and uncompromising stance toward modern secular culture. Nonetheless, the Hasidim and ultra-Orthodox maintained separate social and institutional structures. The contrasts among these three groups persisted, moreover, after they became established in other areas, the Reform movement primarily in North America, and the ultra-Orthodox and Hasidim primarily in North America and Israel. Despite their differences, however, all three movements shared a common concern with defining themselves in relation to the broader context of European society. That process of definition was in fact central to the emergence of each group. Adherents of the Reform movement essentially adopted an assimilationist approach, seeking greater accommodation with Gentile culture and society while maintaining their religious identity as Jews. The ultra-Orthodox and Hasidim were more isolationist, stressing their distinctiveness from surrounding cultures and focusing on strategies for resisting external influences.

Again, the diversification of Ashkenazic Judaism within these hearths contrasted with the sense of commonality that generally persisted among the Sephardim, who for the most part adhered to their traditional orthodoxy wherever they settled. In addition, the earlier differences between Ashkenazic and Sephardic Judaism continued to distinguish the Orthodox expressions of each from one another. These differences thus had a significant effect on the religious life of Israel during the twentieth century as immigrant Ashkenazim settled in greater numbers among the Sephardim already living there. Although the Orthodox communities of the two branches shared much in common, they believed that their contrasting religious cultures could not be accommodated under a single religious authority. As a result the Office of the Chief Rabbinate, the primary religious authority for Israeli Jews, was divided between two Chief Rabbis, one Sephardic and the other Ashkenazic.

The differences among the different branches of Ashkenazic Judaism also persisted as their adherents migrated to other regions of the world. This migration brought Reform and Orthodox Jews into more extensive contact with one another than they had experienced in their European hearths, but with varying results. In the United States, interactions between Reform Judaism and various forms of Orthodoxy led to the emergence of Conservative Judaism during the late nineteenth and early twentieth centuries. This movement represented a compromise of sorts between Reformism and Orthodoxy. While it continued to emphasize adherence to the halakhah, it also stressed the role of human insight in adapting divine law to changing circumstances. In contrast, the encounter between Reform and Orthodox Judaism in Israel has proven to be more contentious, with many Orthodox leaders challenging the basic legitimacy and Jewish identity of the Reform movement.

Buddhism

In the centuries following the Buddha's death, during the latter half of the first millennium BCE, Buddhism underwent a significant period of sectarianism. Different groups of monks within the sangha sought to formalize the Buddha's teachings, creating a variety of schools defined by their distinctive interpretations of doctrine and monastic practice. Adherents of these early schools also began to compile the oral traditions of Buddhism in written form. The earliest and most widely accepted of these scriptures was the *Tipitaka* ("Three Baskets"), which was compiled during the final centuries BCE. The Tipitaka comprised three major components: the *Vinaya pitaka*, describing ethical principles and the rules of monastic life; the *Sutta pitaka*, describing the Buddha's discourses as reproduced through oral tradition; and the *Abhidhamma pitaka*, providing analyses of various aspects of Buddhist thought. According to early tradition, the Buddha had prohibited the recording of sacred writings in Sanskrit because doing so would make them accessible only to the educated rather than to all people. The Tipitaka was therefore compiled in Pali, a vernacular Indo-European language, and in this form is known as the Pali canon. The early schools of Buddhism reproduced the Tipitaka in somewhat different forms, however, and so each had its own version. Some schools also eventually reproduced the Tipitaka in Sanskrit, in which it is known as the *Tripitaka*, and its parts as the *Vinaya*, the *Sutra*, and the *Abhidharma*. These scriptural differences thus reinforced the persistent sectarianism that had developed within early Buddhism by the beginning of the Common Era. This sectarianism did not at first have a significant spatial dimension, however. Many different schools existed side by side in northern India; and after the conversion of Asoka, discussed in chapter 2, most of them spread more widely across India. Early monasteries often housed monks from more than one school, and monks of different schools frequently traveled together.[30] Moreover, although they differed on certain philosophical points, the early schools shared a common understanding of the Buddha's teachings as representing both the truth of existence and the means of achieving nirvana.

Origins of Mahayana Buddhism

Distinct spatial variations within Buddhism first developed early in the Common Era with the emergence of the Mahayana or "Great Vehicle" school, so named because it focuses on the salvation of all beings rather than on the individual believer. The Mahayana school departed from Buddhist tradition both in its reinterpretation of existing doctrines and its introduction of new ones. Most importantly, it transformed the ethos of Buddhism from the ideal of the arhat, a perfected adherent who had achieved freedom from rebirth, to the ideal of the bodhisattva, a near-perfect individual who forgoes nirvana to remain in the material world and help others attain salvation. This revision added an important new emphasis on compassion to the traditional Buddhist concern with wisdom. The Mahayana school also introduced a more explicit theistic dimension into the Buddhist worldview. Earlier doctrines had depicted the Buddha as a human being who had attained ultimate perfection through a process of enlightenment. The Mahayana school attributed a more complex character to the Buddha, comprising three elements: his oneness with truth itself, his identity as a supreme celestial deity, and his bodily manifestation in the material world. Moreover, the Buddha took different celestial and material forms, and the celestial domain contained a multitude of bodhisattvas who could intervene in worldly affairs. Mahayana scholars also developed new emphases on the unitary emptiness of reality and the intrinsic falsehood of all human efforts to explain it. In addition, they established the concept of "skill in means," the doctrine that Buddhist teachings may legitimately vary among different contexts, taking whatever form will prove most effective in advancing human enlightenment. The latter doctrine legitimized the Mahayana school's reflexive differentiation of itself from other branches of Buddhism. In asserting their distinctiveness, however, Mahayana Buddhists depicted their innovations as a more complete expression of the Buddha's teachings and thus came to characterize earlier schools in derogatory terms as Hinayana ("Lesser Vehicle") Buddhism.

Elements of Mahayana thought had appeared before the Common Era in various parts of India, but adherents articulated the school's doctrines more systematically during the first several centuries CE in an active hearth located in the upper Indus Valley.[31] By tradition this process began following a first-century Buddhist Council held at Jalandhar or possibly in Kashmir, which resulted in the formal articulation of Mahayana Buddhism's distinct identity. At about this time, Sanskrit became the primary written language of the Mahayana school, further distinguishing it from older expressions of Buddhism. The Gandhara region in the upper Indus Valley similarly became an important center in the development of Mahayanist themes in Buddhist art. Mahayana Buddhism continued to flourish in northern India with the rise of the Gupta dynasty in the fourth century, but its geographical focus shifted eastward into the mid Ganges valley, the new empire's core. Under Gupta patronage, the city of Nalanda became the principal center of Mahayana Buddhism, the site of a major monastic community and the first Buddhist university. Among Nalanda's leading scholars during this period were early proponents of the Yogacara school of Mahayana thought, which posits that consciousness represents the only reality.

Mahayana Buddhism's success during this period derived in part from the popular expressions that developed alongside the school's often-abstruse philosophical innovations. This popular dimension included a broader spiritual role for the laity as well as a growing emphasis on devotional worship. In contrast to the Buddhist schools that linked salvation to the observance of strict monastic discipline, Mahayana doctrines asserted that all beings had the potential of attaining the status of a bodhisattva, and further asserted that this goal could be achieved in various ways, not solely through a single, prescribed path. Early Mahayana writings thus included various lay figures among the bodhisattvas they depicted, the most important being the householder Vimalakirti, who was characterized as the ideal lay Buddhist. The theistic aspect of Mahayana Buddhism in turn focused on a great variety of celestial beings believed to be capable of influencing the material world. The Buddha remained the central figure but in a variety of manifestations, including the historical Siddhartha as well as other celestial Buddhas of the past, present, and future. The Mahayana pantheon also came to include a large number of celestial bodhisattvas and by the second or third century CE the worship or invocation of these bodhisattvas had become one of the distinguishing characteristics of this school. Mahayana devotion focused especially on Maitreya, the bodhisattva and future Buddha who will return to earth to teach the way to enlightenment; on Manjusri, the bodhisattva of wisdom; and on Avalokitesvara, the bodhisattva of compassion (photo 3.3).

Mahayana Buddhism, in sum, represented a distinctive mixture of metaphysical speculation and lay devotion, both of which contributed to its active reproduction by adherents in northern India. This process of reproduction was supported, moreover, by various northern dynasties, such as the Guptas from the fourth to the sixth century and the Palas from the eighth to the twelfth century. As a result of these factors, an extensive commingling of Hinduism and Mahayana Buddhism developed in northern

Photo 3.3. Second- or third-century relief from Gandhara, located in northern Pakistan and eastern Afghanistan. The relief depicts the complex pantheon that had developed within Mahayana Buddhism by this time, with the Buddha at the center and the bodhisattvas Maitreya and Avalokitesvara to the left and right, respectively. In addition, a Buddhist devotee appears at the far left and a Buddhist monk at the far right. Musée Guimet, Paris, France, 2005.

Source: PHGCOM (commons.wikimedia.org/wiki/Image:BuddhistTriad.jpg), under Creative Commons license (creativecommons.org/licenses/by-sa/2.5/).

India, particularly at the level of folk practice. The rise of Tantrism in the middle of the first millennium CE represented another important link between Mahayana Buddhism and Hinduism. Mahayana expressions of Tantrism, also known as Vajrayana, incorporated a more pronounced philosophical component, however, focusing on the attainment of Buddhahood in the present lifetime. In contrast to Hindu Tantrism, Tantric Buddhism also remained stronger in northern India than in the south and became strongly identified with the major Buddhist universities. Finally, the diverse and dynamic religious context of northern India contributed to cross-influences between Mahayana Buddhism and the surviving Hinayana schools, so that the former gradually came to absorb the latter within this region.

Origins of Theravada Buddhism

While the Mahayana school emerged as the dominant form of Buddhism in northern India, a somewhat different pattern developed in places where more conservative schools maintained a greater influence.[32] These more conservative forms of Buddhism were descendants of the Sthavira school established following the council that had produced the original schism within Buddhism between traditional and progressive factions. The conservative descendants of the Sthavira school retained the use of Pali as the language of sacred texts and, following the example of the historical Buddha, continued to emphasize strict monastic discipline as a means of attaining the status of arahant and achieving salvation. This interpretation of Buddhism later came to be known as the Theravada ("Way of the Elders") school, because its adherents claimed to follow the traditions of the sangha as practiced during the Buddha's lifetime. This school also represented one component of what Mahayana adherents called Hinayana Buddhism; but because the latter term also included a variety of more liberal, early schools, the term *Theravada* is more precise. In addition, the latter term lacks the derogatory connotation originally associated with the term *Hinayana*.

The exact origins of Theravada Buddhism remain somewhat obscure. Descendants of the older Sthavira school survived in various parts of India into the Common Era, and Theravada most likely derived from one or more of these conservative branches of Buddhism. The Theravada school first acquired a clearly defined identity, however, in Sri Lanka. By tradition, Buddhism became established in Sri Lanka in the third century BCE through the missionary efforts of Asoka. Buddhism subsequently became the dominant religion there, and adherence to Buddhism became a central element of the identity of Sri Lanka's Sinhalese majority. At the start of the Common Era the Sinhalese followed various forms of Buddhism, but by this time Sri Lanka had already become an important hearth for the emerging Theravada school. Most significantly, in 29 BCE the Sinhalese king Vattagamani by tradition ordered the preservation of Buddhist traditions in written form as the Tipitaka. These writings became the primary scriptures of Theravada Buddhism and maintained the use of Pali as a sacred language even as schools in northern India began to shift to the use of Sanskrit. Compilation of the Pali canon provided the Theravadans in Sri Lanka with a more thorough written account of early Buddhist traditions than existed among other schools. As a result, the study of canonical scripture became an essential element of Theravada Buddhism, and by the first century adherents placed greater emphasis on study of the Tipitaka than on earlier approaches to worship based on meditation and other monastic practices.[33] This trend in turn produced a large number of commentaries on the Tipitaka in the Sinhalese language, which by the fifth century had been translated into Pali by Theravadan monks from South India. In the fifth century a council of such scholars also produced a final revision of the Tipitaka, which since then has served as the definitive expression of Theravadan doctrine.

Despite the above developments, the Theravada and Mahayana schools competed for influence within Sri Lanka through the first millennium CE. Both had important monasteries on the island and both found favor at different times under different rulers. The main Mahayana monastery gained considerable prestige in the fourth century when it acquired custody of one of the Buddha's teeth, his only surviving relic. Buddhist authorities considered this monastery to be a suitable location for the tooth given the Mahayana emphasis on devotional worship of the Buddha. Later in the first millennium, some Sri Lankan monks and lay practitioners also began to adopt elements of Tantric Buddhism. Theravadan dominance became firmly established in the twelfth century, however, through the efforts of the Sinhalese king Parakramabahu to foster social stability, eliminate religious heterodoxy, and promote traditional Buddhist values within this kingdom.[34] His efforts strongly favored the Theravada school, in part because of its links to the "pure" Buddhism of the Pali canon, which itself was strongly linked to early Sinhalese traditions, but also because of the Theravadan emphasis on the social role of the sangha, an important feature of Sri Lankan society throughout the first millennium. Parakramabahu's rule thus led to the emergence of the Theravada school as the definitive form of Buddhism in Sri Lanka.

Diffusion in Central and East Asia

The spatial divergence that developed between the Mahayana and Theravada schools through the above processes had significant implications as Buddhism spread to other parts of Asia. According to tradition, the diffusion of Buddhism out of South Asia began before these schools developed their distinct identities, as missionary envoys traveled into Central and Southeast Asia during the reign of Asoka. More clearly documented patterns of diffusion began in the first and second centuries CE, however, as missionary monks traveled north into Central Asia from the upper Indus Valley. The trade routes of the Silk Road that traversed Asia provided a crucial channel for the early spread of Buddhism by these missionaries, first to the northwest into various Central Asian kingdoms and then eastward into China (map 3.4). Competition from other religious traditions, and especially the later rise of Islam, impeded diffusion to the west, but Buddhism quickly became widely dispersed across East Asia. Mahayanists tended to dominate this process, in part because of their strong footing in the upper Indus region. By the middle of the first millennium, the influential universities and monasteries of the Ganges valley provided a second major source of missionaries, again more often associated with Mahayana than with other schools.

As it spread into Central and East Asia, Mahayana Buddhism benefited significantly from its tolerance of innovation relative to the Hinayana schools. While the latter generally insisted on literalist adherence to scripture and tradition, the Mahayana

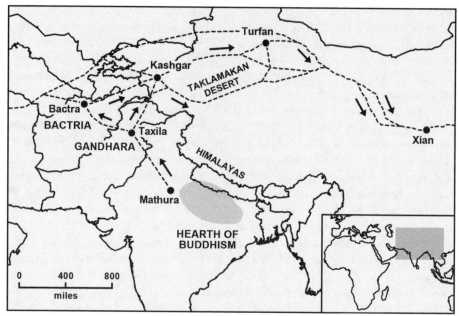

Map 3.4. The diffusion of Mahayana Buddhism into Central Asia and China early in the first millennium CE, following the trade routes of the Silk Road. Greek Bactrian artistic traditions in Central Asia became an important influence on Mahayana art early in this process (photo 3.3).

school allowed for some latitude in doctrinal interpretation and monastic rules, based on the concept of skill in means. This flexibility, for example, allowed Central Asian nomads to adopt Buddhism without giving up the consumption of meat, a key element of their diet. Mahayana monks also engaged in various medical practices that had not been allowed under older monastic rules, providing them with a means of reaching potential adherents at all levels of society. Perhaps most importantly, Mahayana Buddhism's flexibility allowed it to coexist alongside and interact with other traditions, including Taoism and Confucianism in China, Shinto in Japan, and Bon in Tibet.

In contrast to patterns of diffusion into Central and East Asia, the spread of Buddhism into Southeast Asia reflected a broader extension of Indian cultural influence through political and economic contacts, dating from the beginning of the Common Era. This process also brought Hinduism into Southeast Asia, but over time Buddhism developed a more widespread and lasting presence in the region. The Mahayana school, including elements of Tantric Buddhism, initially competed for influence, but over time the Theravada school became dominant in most areas.

These processes of diffusion led to the emergence of distinctive expressions of Buddhism in various locations outside of India. The geographic variation that developed within Buddhism in part reflected the diverse character of the locations to which it spread. This variation was reinforced, however, by the significant decline of Buddhism in India that had begun by the end of the first millennium. As key Buddhist institutions in India died out, so did their influence on the practice of Buddhism elsewhere. The decline of Buddhism in India thus supported the autonomy of different expressions of Mahayana across Central and East Asia, especially in areas where Buddhism flourished fairly late. This trend also reinforced the growing Theravadan connections between Sri Lanka and Southeast Asia by removing alternative Mahayana sources of influence (map 3.5).

Various factors contributed to the disappearance of Buddhism as a major religion in India. Toward the end of the first millennium, the differences between Mahayana Buddhism and Hinduism gradually faded, each embracing related theistic and Tantric forms. In folk worship especially, the contrast between the two traditions began to lose its significance as believers came to associate the Mahayana pantheon with Hindu gods. Ultimately, much of Buddhist practice in India essentially became absorbed into the broader Hindu tradition, which had itself been reshaped over many centuries by the rise of Buddhism. A second factor in Buddhism's decline was the loss of support from royal patrons, which weakened the monasteries and universities considerably. This trend was reinforced by ongoing antagonism toward Buddhism from many in the Brahmin caste, who saw Buddhist influence as a threat to their privileged status. The lack of distinct communal boundaries separating lay Buddhists from Hindus further weakened the social functions of the monastic system, particularly within the context of Mahayana Buddhism. Finally, the Muslim invasions of northern India that began early in the second millennium, previously discussed in relation to Hinduism, had a devastating effect on Buddhism in the region. Invading Muslim rulers strongly opposed monasticism, based on a passage in the Quran (57: 27) rejecting the monastic life as a human invention not prescribed by God. As a result, these rulers vigorously attacked the Buddhist monastic system, destroying mon-

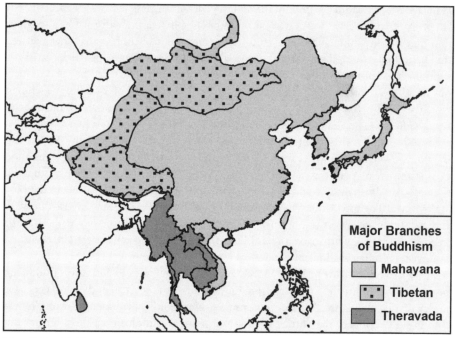

Map 3.5. Distribution of the major branches of Buddhism. Note that some scholars treat Tibetan Buddhism as a distinct branch rather than as a subbranch of Mahayana Buddhism, often under the name of Vajrayana or Tantric Buddhism.

asteries and universities and killing thousands of monks. By the thirteenth century, such actions had effectively eliminated Buddhist institutions from areas under Muslim control. Invading Muslims had also been hostile toward Hinduism, destroying temples across northern India, but Hindu belief and practice were so inextricably tied to other dimensions of Indian life that Hinduism remained a vital religion. Buddhism, on the other hand, depended more directly on the presence of monastic institutions, and so did not survive the destruction of the latter.[35]

China

The continual reproduction of Buddhist belief and practice in diverse parts of Asia thus proceeded as the tradition disappeared from its early hearth, allowing localized expressions of Buddhism to flourish in the absence of universal, centralizing institutions. In East and Central Asia, this pattern led to a recurring process of adaptation between Mahayana Buddhism and local cultures. This process typically began with the introduction of Buddhism by missionary monks or converted rulers, followed by the local translation of Buddhist texts. Over time, elements of Mahayana belief and practice would also gradually interact with local customs, including patterns of popular worship, ultimately resulting in a distinct expression of the larger Buddhist tradition among lay believers.[36]

In China, this process in fact began while Buddhism was still a vital force in India. Buddhist monks had likely arrived in China by the beginning of the Common Era, and by the second century had begun to translate key texts into Chinese. Nonetheless, Buddhism as such remained largely a foreign religion under the third-century Han dynasty, spreading primarily through a general synthesis with Taoism. After the fall of the Han dynasty, however, Buddhism became increasingly distinct as a religious tradition within China. The social uncertainty and political conflict that characterized this period contributed to the wider appeal of Buddhism's concerns with transitory suffering and spiritual justice, and by the fifth century adherents had become numerous at all levels of society. Some rulers remained suspicious of Buddhist teachings, which seemed to challenge the traditional emphases in Chinese culture on duty to family and state; but few rulers saw Buddhism as a threat, given its adherents' pacifist ethos and disinterest in political affairs, and some actively supported it. As a result, the popularization of Buddhism in China proceeded rapidly. The ongoing translation of Buddhist texts played a key role in this process, as did the ordination of the first Chinese Buddhist monks and the subsequent proliferation of monasteries, temples, and shrines. The growth of Chinese Buddhism also spurred ongoing interaction with Indian Buddhism. Most importantly, Chinese monks made numerous visits to India in search of learning and sacred texts. This practice declined after the eighth century, however, as Indian Buddhism entered its period of decline.

During this same period, moreover, distinctly Chinese forms of Buddhism began to arise, flourishing most conspicuously during the seventh and eighth centuries under the Tang dynasty. Within this context, two significant dimensions of Chinese Buddhism developed: the "little" tradition of popular Buddhism and the "great" tradition associated with various philosophical schools. The popular tradition focused on the promise of rebirth in a paradise where nirvana could easily be attained and on the assistance of various Buddhas and bodhisattvas in reaching such a place. In Mahayana

belief, numerous such paradises existed across the cosmos, each associated with a principal Buddha. The most important of these were the western paradise ruled by Amitabha, the eastern paradise ruled by Akshobhya, and the future paradise ruled by Maitreya. These "Pure Lands" and the Buddhas who ruled them became a central concern
of popular devotion in China, particularly that overseen by Amitabha. Popular devotion focused as well on a larger pantheon of Buddhas and bodhisattvas derived from
the Mahayana scriptures. Adherents worshipped these figures in much the same way
that traditional Chinese gods had been worshipped, as divine sources of material good
fortune as well as spiritual salvation.

With time, believers therefore came to identify particular bodhisattvas with figures in traditional Chinese folklore. The most widely worshipped bodhisattva was
Kuan-yin, the bodhisattva of infinite compassion, known in Sanskrit texts as Avalokitesvara. Although Buddhists in India conceived of this figure as a male deity, by the
end of the first millennium the popular tradition in China increasingly recast Kuan-
yin in female form as a compassionate mother goddess; and in this form she later
became widely associated with the princess Miao-shan, worshipped as a mythical
embodiment of mercy and self-sacrifice.[37] Adherents also believed that Kuan-yin could
bring sons to devotees and would protect their children, thus reconciling this figure
with traditional Confucian values. Kuan-yin became absorbed as well into the pantheon of Taoist folk religion. This reconception of Kuan-yin illustrates the unreflexive
syncretism characteristic of popular Buddhism at this time, through which diverse
traditions merged into an undifferentiated fusion of Buddhism, Taoism, Confucianism, and older folk practices.

In contrast to popular traditions, the great tradition in China emphasized the
exegesis and refinement of Buddhist philosophy, producing a number of distinct
schools of thought during the middle centuries of the first millennium (map 3.6). The
earliest schools relied closely on Indian thought for their understanding of Buddhism.
The San-lun or Three Treatises school, for example, focused on Indian Mahayana
thought concerning the emptiness of reality. Similarly, the Fa-hsiang or Dharma-char-
acter school derived directly from the Indian Yogacara school. Another early group,
the Lu ("Law") school, focused primarily on the rules of monastic life and had little
influence on broader philosophical concerns. With time, however, the philosophical
schools of China's great tradition became more distinctive. Indian influences persisted
for a time within the Mi ("Secret") school of Tantric Buddhism, introduced by Indian
missionaries in the eighth century, but this school prospered for little more than a
century. Of more lasting importance were the schools that reflected a distinctly Chinese character.

The influential T'ien-t'ai school, named for the mountainous region of southern
China where it originated in the sixth century, proposed an affirmative conception of
reality in place of the absolute negation of phenomenal experience typical of Indian
Mahayana thought.[38] This school grew out of the teachings of Chih-i, who sought to
systematize the whole of Buddhist thought. He judged the Lotus Sutra, composed in
India between the first century BCE and the second century CE, to be the culmination
of Buddhist doctrine, but he reconciled its teachings with a Chinese emphasis on the
fundamental duality of reality. He taught that all phenomena exist equally on two
levels, the temporary level of distinct material appearances and the eternal level of
undifferentiated emptiness realized by the Buddha, and that all material phenomena

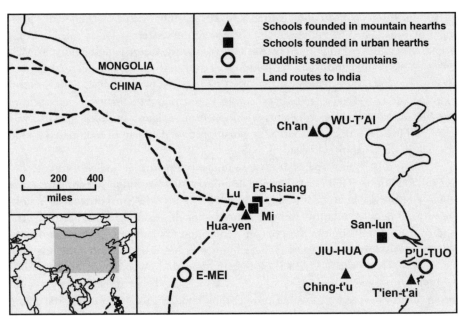

Map 3.6. Hearths of the leading schools of Chinese Buddhism. The cluster of locations around Xian reflects that city's importance as a political center as well as its situation at the western end of the Silk Road. Together these hearths reflect the competing role of urban centers, associated with worldly power, and mountainous regions, associated in traditional China with spiritual power, as centers of religious innovation.

can thus attain the Buddha's ultimate perfection. The T'ien-t'ai school, which stressed enlightenment through practical methods of contemplation, had become the predominant school of Buddhism in southern China by the eighth century.

In northern China, the Hua-yen or "Garland" school developed a similar emphasis on the affirmation of reality. This school too regarded itself as the ultimate articulation of Buddhist thought, taking as its primary scripture the *Avatamsaka* (or Garland) *Sutra* compiled in India by the second or third century CE. Hua-yen thought systematically articulated a doctrine that all material phenomena are interdependent with and inseparable from one another and are ultimately identical as expressions of the Buddha-nature. From this perspective, even the smallest particle of dust contained the essence of the entire cosmos, including all of the Pure Lands, and all beings shared traits that would ultimately lead them to Buddhahood. Again, this affirmation of reality reflected a distinct departure from the negation of reality characteristic of Indian thought. Together, the Hua-yen and T'ien-t'ai schools thus reflected the development of a Chinese approach to Buddhist philosophy within the great tradition.

The philosophical dimension within Chinese Buddhism did not develop in isolation from the popular tradition, however; and ultimately the most enduring schools of Buddhist thought in China, the Pure Land or Ching-t'u school and the Meditation or Ch'an school, brought together formal and popular elements. The Pure Land school grew out of the popular cult of Amitabha, which had become widespread by the fifth century. During the seventh century, popular beliefs associated with this cult became systematized into a formal school of thought even as they continued to spread among the masses. The Pure Land master Tao-ch'o laid the foundation for this systematization, teaching that the world had entered a period of spiritual decay that impeded the process of enlightenment. Salvation could be achieved only through rebirth in Amitabha's Pure Land, whose environment intrinsically fostered movement toward enlightenment. Shan-tao, the successor to Tao-ch'o, articulated a more formal system of doctrine defining the specific practices necessary to achieve rebirth in the Pure Land. These practices centered on constant meditation on Amitabha, particularly through the invocation of his name, which would assure rebirth in his domain. The simplicity of the Pure Land school's approach contributed to its rapid diffusion throughout China over the next several centuries.

The Ch'an school also advocated a simplification of Mahayana doctrine, focusing on the use of practical meditation techniques in attaining enlightenment. By tradition Ch'an teachings were introduced to China in the fifth or sixth century by an Indian monk, but the historicity of this event remains in doubt. Ch'an doctrine was first systematized in southern China by Hui-neng, recognized as the school's sixth patriarch, in the seventh century. Ch'an doctrine opposed the philosophical diversity and complexity of other formal schools and deemphasized the importance of scriptural analysis. Instead, it directly addressed the goal of enlightenment and the practical means by which it could be achieved in the adherent's current lifetime. The Ch'an school focused specifically on the practice of meditation, incorporating various novel approaches that diverged from traditional Indian methods. One such approach involved the contemplation of paradoxical anecdotes or koans, passed from teacher to pupil, which required the adherent to abandon conventional modes of thought and accept the ineffable nature of truth.[39] Teachers might also shout at or strike pupils immersed in meditation to break any conscious effort to realize truth. The purpose of such methods was to move the adherent toward enlightenment without conscious striving, with the guidance of an enlightened teacher rather than through the study of texts. According to Hui-neng, when enlightenment did occur it would be sudden and complete, again a departure from Mahayana thought in India. A rival school of Ch'an thought in northern China posited that enlightenment must take place gradually but that school proved short-lived. Eventually Ch'an adherents considered Hui-neng's sermons to be a new sutra, a term previously applied only to the Buddha's teachings, thus expanding the Buddhist scriptures to include local Chinese sources.

The period of growth reflected in the emergence of the various schools of Chinese Buddhism also led, over time, to increasing opposition from China's ruling class. The Buddhist monastic system, which usually did not involve productive labor by monks or nuns, required significant lay support to survive and thus absorbed significant amounts of wealth and labor. So too did the expanding infrastructure of Buddhist temples and shrines.[40] The growth of Buddhism also challenged the influence of Taoism, to which most of the ruling class adhered. In response to these developments, the Taoist emperor Wu-tsung in 845 initiated a period of widespread persecution against Buddhist institutions, during which 1,600 formal temples were deconsecrated and more than 250,000 monks and nuns were obliged to return to secular life.[41] Later in the ninth century the restrictions placed on Buddhist institutions were removed, and in the tenth century Buddhism regained a measure of imperial support under the Sung dynasty. Nonetheless, it never fully recovered its earlier position of influence in China.

The doctrinal diversity of earlier centuries also began to decline during this period. The Ch'an school absorbed much of the Hua-yen and T'ien-t'ai schools, and after 1000 CE only the Ch'an and Pure Land schools maintained distinct identities. The Ch'an school remained particularly influential among the more educated classes, while the Pure Land school maintained a stronger connection to popular practices. In time, however, the differences between these schools also began to fade and many adherents drew on elements of both. The resulting fusion combined the belief that all beings had the potential to achieve Buddhahood, the concept of sudden enlightenment, and a concern with practical methods of attaining salvation. In more general terms, Chinese Buddhism ultimately became incorporated as well into a complex syncretism with Taoism, Confucianism, and Chinese folk religion.

Korea

From China, Buddhism spread eastward into Korea and Japan, where it again acquired distinctive forms. It arrived in northern Korea in the fourth century and spread throughout the peninsula over the next several hundred years. Its impact was originally greatest among the ruling classes; and when the Silla dynasty unified Korea as a single kingdom in 668, it established Buddhism as the state religion. From these beginnings Korean Buddhism gradually developed a strong nationalistic character. Members of the ruling class and nobility frequently undertook extensive religious training, and ordained monks frequently played important roles in secular and political affairs. Within folk practice, Buddhist beliefs and practices underwent an extensive synthesis with indigenous forms of shamanism, resulting in a vital popular tradition as well. Over time the more formal elements of Korean Buddhism drew on all of the Chinese schools but ultimately merged various elements from these different Chinese sources. This fusion took place largely within an indigenous expansion of the Ch'an school, or Son school in Korean, which reconciled the practical methods of the meditation-based schools with the scriptural orientation of the philosophical schools. This synthesis became the dominant form of Korean Buddhism under the Koryo dynasty, from the tenth to the fourteenth century. The secular influence of the Buddhist establishment during this period had corrupting effects, however, provoking opposition from a rising neo-Confucian movement. When the Yi dynasty took control in 1392, it thus established Confucianism as Korea's state religion and enacted a number of anti-Buddhist policies. Thereafter Buddhism survived mainly as a rural, popular tradition in Korea, combining the more formal teachings of the Son and Pure Land schools with the folk syncretism of earlier centuries.

Japan

Buddhism spread to Japan by the sixth century as part of the broader diffusion of Chinese cultural influences. Some members of the Japanese court saw Buddhism's arrival as an affront to the indigenous Shinto deities, whose wrath would bring disaster to the nation; but others readily accepted Buddhism as a superior expression of Chinese culture. As Buddhism spread with the court's support, however, most adherents focused on its magical elements and on forms of devotion aimed at producing worldly benefits, in a manner similar to Shinto practice. A greater degree of doctrinal sophistication emerged during the seventh and eighth centuries with the transplantation of specific Chinese schools of Buddhism to Japan. The status of Buddhism also grew after the emperor established it as the state religion during the Nara period of the eighth century. Japanese Buddhism nonetheless adhered closely to Chinese models at this time; and it remained primarily a religion of the ruling class, for whom it represented both a spiritual means of protecting the state and a worldly means of attaining material ends.

Japanese Buddhism acquired a more distinctive character during the Heian period, from 794 to 1185. The major development of this period was the rise of the Shingon and Tendai schools, founded in the early 800s by Japanese monks returning from study in China. Both schools sought to replace the worldly practices of the Nara period with more authentic forms of Buddhism. In doing so, they reflected strong Chinese influences: the Shingon ("True Word") school followed the esoteric teachings of the Mi school, and the Tendai school was rooted in T'ien-t'ai (from which it took its name). Both schools exhibited a degree of independence from their Chinese sources, however. Shingon, for example, developed a comprehensive theory of religious consciousness that identified other Buddhist schools as steps toward its own ultimate revelations. Similarly, Tendai instituted a new ritual of ordination with no Chinese precedent and incorporated various esoteric and magical elements.[42] Both Shingon and Tendai also came to acknowledge the older Shinto deities, at first by characterizing them as guardians of Buddhism, mirroring the protective role that they played in Shinto. With time the Shinto deities also came to be seen as manifestations of celestial Buddhas and bodhisattvas who had visited ancient Japan, acknowledging their continuing national importance. Most importantly, Shingon adherents identified the sun goddess Amaterasu, Shinto's principal deity, with the Buddha Vairocana, the primary object of Shingon devotion (again making such an association across genders, as in the case of Kuan-yin in China).[43] Finally, Tendai belief developed an important patriotic element, characterizing Buddhism itself as a protector of the Japanese nation.

During the Kamakura era, from 1192–1333, the Japanization of Buddhism became more complete as new indigenous schools of thought emerged. These schools still reflected mainland influences, but they articulated the Buddhist tradition in more distinctive forms and achieved broader popular appeal than the older schools had. These new schools also expressed disillusionment with the older schools' worldly outlooks and their relative inaccessibility to the common people. While the new schools derived primarily from Tendai, they rejected the latter's philosophical abstractions in favor of more pragmatic and attainable approaches to achieving personal enlightenment or salvation.

The Jodo or Pure Land school, founded in the late 1100s, identified devotion to Amida (Japanese for Amitabha) as the core of Buddhism. It asserted that the present time represented a period of decay and corruption, and that adherents could achieve salvation only by being reborn in Amida's Pure Land. Rebirth there in turn depended solely on the grace of Amida, which could be achieved through *nembutsu*, the constant repetition of his name in the phrase *Namu Amida Butsu* ("I take refuge in Amida Buddha"). Jodo was the first school of Japanese Buddhism to be founded without imperial authority and initially it faced opposition from the Buddhist establishment. Nonetheless, it attracted a widespread popular following through its promise of salvation in a period dominated by warfare, feudal oppression, and social instability. In the process, Jodo also gave rise to a number of distinct sects. The most important of these was the Jodo Shin (True Pure Land) school or Shin for short, founded in the early thirteenth century, which taught that invoking Amida's name only once, if done in sincerity and faith, would bring salvation through rebirth in paradise. The Shin school thus viewed the practice of nembutsu as a means of giving thanks for salvation already assured rather than as a prayer for grace. Shin also rejected the concept of monastic celibacy and thus evolved essentially as a form of lay religion. Through its radically simplified approach to Buddhism, Jodo Shin achieved even wider popularity than Jodo, and the Pure Land sects together comprised the leading expression of Japanese Buddhism.

The Rinzai Zen or Meditation school, the Japanese extension of Ch'an teachings, emerged as a second major branch of Japanese Buddhism during this period. Rinzai Zen adhered to the Ch'an doctrines that the Buddha-nature inherent in all beings could be realized through disciplined practice resulting in enlightenment, and that this process depended on sudden intuitive insights rather than scriptural learning or formal rituals. These teachings met with resistance from Japan's Buddhist establishment and the educated elite, reflecting the declining interest in Chinese culture within Japan at the time. The samurai warrior class, however, found these methods adaptable to military training and discipline, resulting in a distinctive fusion between Rinzai Zen and Japanese martial arts. As the school's adherents began to present Zen as a force that would protect and preserve Japan, it developed a strong following among the aristocracy as well.

As interest in Zen spread during the thirteenth century, other Zen sects also began to appear. The most important of these was Soto Zen, founded in the thirteenth century, which taught that all human beings possessed an enlightened nature, but that their own ignorance prevented them from grasping their inherent enlightenment. This school thus saw Zen as a means of realizing one's existing nature rather than of entering a new enlightened state. It also stressed quiet sitting in meditation, rejecting the more active approaches to meditation in Rinzai Zen. Soto Zen further departed from Ch'an thought by asserting that, because people are born enlightened, all of the normal expressions of daily life are expressions of enlightenment and should be enacted with thanks to the Buddha.[44] Soto Zen grew rapidly in the 1300s as its adherents interacted more outwardly with Japanese society, as in the performance of esoteric rituals for the upper classes or through public works for the benefit of the common people. Together, Soto, Rinzai, and other smaller sects contributed to the rise of Zen as a significant force in Japanese culture, informing the Japanese tea ceremony, Noh drama, and other artistic forms. In the process, Soto Zen ultimately acquired the largest following and became the dominant form of Zen in Japan.

The third major development of the Kamakura period was the rise of the Nichiren school, named for the Tendai monk who founded it in 1253. This school rejected the complexity and diversity of the other schools, instead emphasizing the original Tendai focus on the Lotus Sutra as the supreme Buddhist teaching. Nichiren went a step further, however, by deemphasizing study of the scripture itself, asserting that a simple declaration of faith in the power of the Lotus Sutra would be sufficient to gain salvation. Like the Pure Land school, Nichiren characterized the present as a period of decay, making it impossible for adherents to achieve enlightenment except through a declaration of faith in the Lotus Sutra. Despite its similarities to Pure Land thought, the Nichiren school was highly intolerant of the Pure Land school, and of Zen and the various other schools as well. Nichiren characterized other interpretations of Bud-

dhism as heresies that would bring ruin to those who followed them and to the Japanese nation as a whole. These views provoked much opposition from the Buddhist
establishment and the government, but adherents of Nichiren considered their beliefs
to be strongly patriotic and essential to the protection of Japan. In the fourteenth
century, the contentious nature of the Nichiren school gave rise to a variety of separate
sects, a process that has continued to the present. Despite these recurring divisions,
however, Nichiren remained a vital force, and together the various Nichiren sects
represent the second largest branch of Japanese Buddhism, following the Pure Land
school.

The innovations of the Kamakura period expanded the importance of Buddhism
among the common people over the next several centuries. For ordinary adherents
unwilling to accept the monastic life, Pure Land, Zen, and Nichiren Buddhism each
presented a means to achieve personal salvation. Buddhist beliefs and practices thus
became incorporated into various aspects of Japanese culture, and during the medieval
period various Buddhist schools received considerable government support. Support
for Zen was particularly strong during the Ashikaga shogunate, from 1333 to 1568.
The sectarian character of Japanese Buddhism ultimately limited its authority, however, and eventually the political influence of Buddhism declined. The Tokugawa
period, from 1603 to 1868, saw revivals of both Confucianism and a nationalistic
strain of Shinto, reducing the public role of Buddhism. During the Meiji period, from
1868 to 1912, this trend continued with the institution of Shinto as the state religion
and a brief period of persecution against Buddhism. As a popular religion Buddhism
remained influential throughout these periods, however, and in the twentieth century
experienced a significant revival. As a result, Japanese Buddhists subsequently played
an important role in the more recent popularization of Buddhism in Europe and the
Americas.

Tibet

A final stage in Buddhism's diffusion north of India began in the seventh century with
its entry into Tibet. The spread of Buddhism to Tibet lagged behind its arrival in other
regions of Central and East Asia primarily because of Tibet's geographic isolation. The
trade routes that facilitated the diffusion of Buddhism across Central Asia early in the
first millennium CE did not extend into Tibet, a region of scarce resources, access to
which was hindered by the physical barriers of the Himalayas and other mountain
ranges and by the high elevation of the Tibetan Plateau. The sparse population and
political fragmentation of Tibet also limited external contacts. By the seventh century,
however, a more unified Tibetan kingdom had begun to interact with adjacent areas
of Central, East, and South Asia and as a result Tibetans came into increasing contact
with Buddhism.

By tradition, Buddhism was introduced to Tibet at this time through the marriages of King Songtsen Gampo to Nepalese and Chinese princesses, who in turn
established the first temple in Lhasa, the royal capital. Thus began the so-called first
diffusion of Buddhism into Tibet, lasting into the ninth century. Although Buddhism
did not spread extensively among the people, many of the basic features of Tibetan
Buddhism became established during this period. Tibetan leaders saw Buddhism as a
means of developing their state, for example by spreading basic ethical principles, and

thus provided significant support for the construction of temples and monasteries. This period thus set an important precedent for later relationships between monastic institutions and the royalty and for the central institutional role of monasteries in Tibetan culture. Tibetan rulers also initiated connections with centers of Buddhist learning in India, and to a lesser extent China, and invited a number of Indian scholars to help establish Buddhism more fully, especially through the translation of Buddhist texts into Tibetan and the establishment of traditional forms of monastic rule. These interactions led to a strong dependence in early Tibetan Buddhism on Indian versions of Mahayana, including Tantrism, but without the dominance of any single school. At the popular level, the first diffusion period also saw the syncretistic merger of Buddhism with Bon, the indigenous shamanistic tradition. But despite these trends, many members of the ruling class rejected Buddhism as an alien religion, and most of the populace remained ignorant of it. Buddhism thus declined in significance from the mid-800s to the late 900s, as Bon experienced a resurgence while Tibet underwent a period of political fragmentation.

The "second diffusion" of Buddhism began late in the tenth century in western Tibet, where a local ruler sought to strengthen his kingdom by bringing monks from northern India to restore Buddhist orthodoxy. This effort led to the establishment of numerous temples and monasteries in western Tibet and to the translation of additional Buddhist texts into Tibetan. The earlier pattern combining traditional monastic rule, Mahayana philosophy, and Tantric practices thus began to flourish again.[45] Of the scholars who came to Tibet at this time the most influential was Atisha, a Bengali monk who sought to reform Buddhism and articulate it in a manner accessible to the population at large.

Atisha's teachings treated the different branches of Buddhism as sequential stages within a single path, Hinayana being the most basic, Mahayana the middle stage, and Tantric Buddhism the most advanced. A key element of his teachings, however, was that this sequence did not imply the superiority of one stage over another. Because Atisha considered monastic discipline to be a core element of Buddhism, he sought to reform monastic life, banning marriage, travel, and the possession of money. At the same time, he preached a broader Mahayana ethos with three emphases: the study of sutras to understand the nature of reality, the use of meditation to focus the mind on emptiness and compassion, and the altruism of the bodhisattva to work toward the salvation of all beings. Atisha also espoused Tantrism, but as a means of achieving the bodhisattva's way rather than as a separate practice. He thus rejected many aspects of Tantrism, including those involving sexual elements, the use of intoxicants, and a focus on worldly gain. In Atisha's construction of Buddhism, the observance of monastic rule while on the bodhisattva's way represented the supreme form of religious life.[46] For the common people, however, he preached a simpler form of Buddhist practice centered on seeking refuge in the Buddha, adhering to one's dharma, accepting leadership from the sangha, and consistently practicing compassion and basic ethical principles. He also promoted theistic devotions that became widely integrated into popular Tibetan Buddhism. These practices focused primarily on the bodhisattva Avalokitesvara and on Tara, a savior goddess believed to be an emanation of the former. Both subsequently became worshipped as celestial patrons of Tibet. Through these various elements, then, Atisha's synthesis of different traditions established the core of Buddhism in Tibet.

The religious renewal associated with the "second diffusion" and Atisha led to the flourishing of Buddhism in Tibet during the eleventh and twelfth centuries. An important outcome of this process was the emergence of a number of distinct schools of monasticism that provided an enduring institutional framework for Tibetan Buddhism. The Kadam school adhered to the entire breadth of Atisha's synthesis of Buddhism, but placed particular importance on moral discipline and monastic rule, including strict adherence to monastic celibacy. The similar Sakya school placed particular emphasis on monastic scholarship and thus balanced the practice of Tantrism with continuing inquiry into Buddhist literature and philosophy. In contrast to the first two, the Kagyu school focused more exclusively on a fusion of Tantrism and advanced meditative practices derived from Indian sources. During the twelfth century, various subdivisions within the Kagyu school also appeared, each forming its own monastic institutions. Finally, many Tibetan Buddhists adhered to older beliefs and practices associated with the period of the "first diffusion," and especially to the syncretistic mixture of Tantrism and Bon practices. These believers ultimately became organized as the Nyingma or Old Translation school, which focused on rapid, intuitive enlightenment through heterodox Tantric practices.

The development of these schools and their monastic lineages marked the inception of a more fully realized Tibetan Buddhist tradition. Over the next several centuries, moreover, three major factors further strengthened the distinctive character of Tibetan Buddhism: belief in the reincarnation of key religious leaders, or lamas; the growing integration of religious and secular authority; and the development of a new, dominant school of Tibetan Buddhism. The first of these factors became established during the thirteenth century through the concept of successive reincarnation. In the years following the death of an important lama, members of his monastic order would use various means to identify him in reincarnate form as a child. The reincarnated lama thus identified, known as a *tulku*, would be trained to adulthood to resume the place of authority he had occupied in his previous life. The tulkus played a crucial role in maintaining the legitimacy of Tibet's monastic lineages; and because adherents believed in the tulkus' continuing accumulation of merit and prestige over many lifetimes, they possessed considerable authority. Leading tulkus also came to be seen as manifestations of key Buddhas and bodhisattvas.

The second major development in Tibetan Buddhism at this time, the integration of religious and secular authority, grew out of Tibet's interactions with the Mongol dynasty that ruled much of Central Asia and China. Seeking to solidify his control over Tibet, the Mongol ruler Godan Khan in 1244 summoned the Tibetan lama Sakya Pandita to his court for political negotiations. After Sakya Pandita converted Godan to Buddhism, the two reached an agreement whereby Tibet would submit to Mongol authority in exchange for Mongol protection. In addition, the Sakya school headed by Sakya Pandita would provide religious guidance to the Mongol court and its head would serve as Tibet's political representative. Later in the 1200s Kublai Khan appointed Phagpa, Sakya Pandita's successor, as the regent of a unified Tibet, establishing him as Tibet's first governing lama. Phagpa thus embodied the merger of religious and secular authority, a pattern rooted in the early relationship between Tibetan kings and the arrival of Buddhism. For several generations the leaders of the Sakya school continued to rule Tibet as regents of the Mongols. By the middle of the fourteenth century, however, declining Mongol power in China and competition from other Buddhist schools in Tibet led to the end of Sakya dominance and the increasing fragmentation of secular rule.

Finally, a third defining transformation of Tibetan Buddhism occurred late in the 1300s with the establishment of the Gelug ("Virtuous") school. Tsongkhapa, the school's founder, had been widely educated in the teachings of the Kadam, Sakya, and Kagyu schools but was disillusioned by their growing laxity regarding monastic practice and scholarship. He founded the Gelug school as a reform movement intended to restore the integrity of Buddhist practice. He drew in part on the teachings of Atisha, but recast those teachings within an original synthesis of Buddhist tradition comprising three key ideas: the ideal of the scrupulously observant ordained monk as the supreme expression of Buddhist practice; the central role of textual study, scholarship, and philosophical debate in Buddhist religious life; and the restriction of Tantric practice to a monastic elite that had undergone extensive scholarly study and training.[47] Again, this integration of monastic, scholarly, and Tantric elements reflected the characteristic breadth of Tibetan Buddhism, but compared to other schools it deemphasized the role of Tantrism in ordinary monastic practice and excluded it from lay practice.

Each of the above developments contributed to the distinctiveness of Buddhism in Tibet during the thirteenth and fourteenth centuries. Their impact increased in importance, however, as they converged in the institution of the Dalai Lama during the 1500s and 1600s. This process arose from renewed ties between Tibetan religious leaders, now of the Gelug school, and eastern Mongol rulers. In 1576 Altan Khan invited the chief Gelug lama, Sonam Gyatso, to reintroduce Buddhism to the Mongols. Following Kublai Khan's rule, Buddhism had declined among the Mongols and traditional shamanism prevailed as their dominant religious system. Altan sought to change this pattern as a means of reviving Mongol prestige. He gave Sonam Gyatso the title of Dalai Lama, dalai being the Mongolian word for ocean, used here to describe the breadth of the Dalai Lama's wisdom. The title was also applied to Sonam Gyatso's two immediate predecessors, of whom he was the incarnation in Tibetan belief. Sonam Gyatso in turn identified Altan as the reincarnation of Kublai Khan.

At the time of these developments, the Gelug school did not play a significant political role in Tibet, its status deriving primarily from its strict standards of monastic rule and scholarship. Connections with the Mongol khanate, however, led to the political dominance of the Gelug school. After the death of Sonam Gyatso in 1587, the Mongols identified a great-grandson of Altan as the tulku of the Dalai Lama, reinforcing the status of the ruling dynasty. This decision met with considerable opposition from within Tibet, however, and during the early 1600s contributed to Kagyu persecution of the Gelug school. That persecution ended with the rise of the fifth Dalai Lama, Losang Gyatso, who was again of Tibetan origin, as have been all of his successors. He is also known as the Great Fifth because of his profound influence on Tibetan history. Most importantly, he reconfirmed the alliance with the Mongols. The Mongol ruler Gushri Khan in return offered military backing to the Gelug school and subsequently supported the unification of Tibet, which by the early 1600s had fragmented into a number of different kingdoms. In 1641 Gushri also established the Great Fifth as the religious and secular ruler of all of Tibet. The fifth Dalai Lama thus represented the union of Gelug preeminence, the institution of the tulku, and the integration of religious and political power.

The rule of the fifth Dalai Lama led to a renaissance in Tibetan Buddhism and Tibetan culture and reinforced the central role of Buddhist institutions in daily life. It also provided a religious and political model for Tibet that lasted into the twentieth century, until China's invasion of Tibet in the 1950s (photo 3.4). Elements of that model remain intact, moreover, in the role of the fourteenth Dalai Lama as leader of the Tibetan community in exile. Under the rule of the Dalai Lamas, conflicts between the various schools of Tibetan Buddhism also gradually gave way to a greater degree of tolerance. A distinctive expression of this trend appeared in the eighteenth century with the emergence of the Rime or Eclectic movement, which recognized the value of all of the different Tibetan schools. This movement originated primarily within the Kagyu and Nyingma schools, but it gradually spread to other schools as well.

Mongolia

As the preceding discussion suggests, Tibetan Buddhism had a strong influence in Mongolia, the final region north of India in which Buddhism became widely adopted. The Mongols had encountered Buddhism prior to their expansion as a major power in Asia, but with little effect. Contacts with Tibetan Buddhists during the reigns of Godan and Kublai Khan led to conversions among the ruling class but again had little influence on the Mongol people as a whole. The broader diffusion of Buddhism among the Mongols began during the 1500s through the relationship between Altan

Photo 3.4.   Potala Palace, the traditional center of the Dalai Lamas' political power in Tibet. The palace embodies three distinctive elements of Tibetan Buddhism: belief in the reincarnation of key religious leaders such as the Dalai Lama, the integration of religious and political authority, and the dominance of the Gelug school starting in the seventeenth century. Lhasa, Tibet, 2006.

Source: Nat Krause (commons.wikimedia.org/wiki/Image:Potala_from_square.jpg), placed in the public domain.

Khan and the Dalai Lama. Missionary activity among Mongol commoners developed on a wider scale and the first Mongolian monastic communities were established. The Mongols under Altan's rule also adopted various laws that supported the spread of Buddhist beliefs and limited older shamanistic practices. Such laws prohibited killing humans or animals in funerary and sacrificial rituals, for example, and banned the possession of shamanistic idols. Nonetheless, Buddhist missionaries often used Tantric magic to demonstrate their religion's superiority to indigenous shamanism, thus incorporating some traditional folk beliefs concerning the supernatural into a new Buddhist synthesis. The mass conversion of Mongol tribes close to Altan Khan, which did not necessarily produce a full acceptance of Buddhism among individuals, also ensured the survival of some traditional religious forms among the Mongol people. During the 1600s, however, orthodox Buddhism became more widespread through the missionary efforts of Mongol converts. The continuing creation of monasteries also produced centers of Buddhist learning that began the translation of the Tibetan canon into Mongolian.[48] All of the Tibetan monastic schools participated in the spread of Buddhism in Mongolia during this period, but the Gelug school ultimately dominated.

The practice of Buddhism in Mongolia thus adhered closely to the Tibetan model, incorporating the various Tibetan monastic schools and relying on the Tibetan canon as its source of scriptural authority. As in Tibet, monastic institutions also came to be a dominant force in Mongolian society. Hundreds of Mongol monasteries were built as Buddhism became established, and by the early twentieth century perhaps a third of the male population had taken monastic vows, although many lived outside of monasteries. Within the monasteries, Tibetan remained in widespread use as the language of religious practice; and scholars continued to study Tibetan texts despite the existence of Mongolian translations. In part this pattern reflected the ongoing movements of both Tibetan and Mongolian monks back and forth between the two regions. Mongolian Buddhism did acquire a degree of distinctiveness in the realm of folk practice, primarily through the persistence of syncretistic practices rooted in traditional shamanism. The worship of ancestral guardian spirits, for example, merged with the worship of protective Buddhist deities, most commonly Mahakala, the wrathful manifestation of the bodhisattva Avalokitesvara and defender of the Buddhist faith. Similarly, a wide variety of Buddhist mantras replaced older shamanistic rituals as a means of addressing everyday concerns such as the protection of livestock or warding off disease.[49] For the most part, however, Buddhism in Mongolia has reflected the continuing primacy of Tibetan religious influence.

Diffusion in Southeast Asia

As Buddhism diffused northward from India into Central and East Asia, then, it acquired a variety of different forms within the general context of Mahayana belief and practice. Many factors contributed to the distinctive character of the diverse Buddhist communities that developed in these regions, but they shared the Mahayana emphases on the compassion of bodhisattvas, the cultivation of wisdom concerning the nature of reality, and belief in the celestial Buddhas and bodhisattvas. In contrast, the Theravada branch emerged as the dominant form of Buddhism in Southeast Asia (map 3.5). This pattern developed long after the initial diffusion of Buddhism to the area, which occurred as part of a broader transmission of Indian cultural, political, and economic influences. Within the latter context, the Mahayana Buddhism, including its Tantric forms, flourished alongside Theravada, as did Hinduism and various indigenous animistic traditions. Only later did Theravada Buddhism become the most prominent religious system in mainland Southeast Asia. The specific processes that led to Theravada's preeminence varied, but they generally reflected the intersection of three related factors: the declining religious influence of India on the region by the second millennium CE; a corresponding increase in the religious influence of Sri Lanka, the primary center of Theravada thought; and the adoption of Theravada Buddhism by various Southeast Asian monarchs.

According to the Pali tradition recorded in the *Mahavamsa*, Sri Lanka's early Buddhist chronicle, the Indian emperor Asoka sent two Buddhist missionaries to Southeast Asia in the third century BCE. The destination of these missionaries was Suvannabhumi, a region interpreted by most scholars as being part of the mainland inhabited by the Mon people, most likely in southeastern Burma, central Thailand, or both. The historicity of this early missionary activity is uncertain. Nonetheless, the Mons were one of the first peoples to adopt Buddhism in Southeast Asia, and they may have had significant contact with Indian and Sri Lankan missionaries by the early centuries of the Common Era. A more widespread diffusion of Indian cultural influences in the region developed by the third century CE, with the rise of significant maritime trade between India and China. Following this increase in maritime traffic, Indian culture attained a position of prestige within less advanced, indigenous societies across Southeast Asia. Various kingdoms established during the first millennium in Southeast Asia thus incorporated significant elements of Indian religious and political culture.

Within this context, Hinduism and Buddhism each flourished in different places at different times, although where the two overlapped Hinduism typically predominated. Nonetheless, a number of factors supported the expansion of Buddhism in Southeast Asia during this period. Because of an earlier accommodation in Indian society between commerce and the practice of Buddhism, Buddhists participated extensively in the maritime trade that linked India with China. Buddhism in turn came to represent a shared cultural connection among those involved in this trade, including Southeast Asians along the trade routes. The maritime routes also gave Buddhist missionaries ready access to Southeast Asia and supported a constant flow between China and India of monks on pilgrimage or in search of sacred texts. India exerted a much greater influence than China on Southeast Asian Buddhism, however, because of its more extensive contacts with the region. Accordingly, all of the major branches of Indian Buddhism spread to Southeast Asia during the first millennium, although their relative influence varied among Indic kingdoms in the region.

Burma and Thailand

Among the earliest Indic kingdoms of Southeast Asia, such as the Funan and Champa empires, Hinduism generally acquired a more central cultural role than did Buddhism. Various forms of Buddhism were practiced within these settings, but initially with limited impact. By the middle of the first millennium, however, predominantly Buddhist kingdoms began to appear in Southeast Asia. The region's earliest Buddhist kingdoms emerged in areas dominated by the Mon and Pyu peoples, located in present-day Burma and Thailand. Theravada Buddhism had come to the Mon kingdom of Thaton along the Burmese coast through interactions with Theravadan centers in southeast India and Sri Lanka, including early missionary activity from the latter.[50] In contrast to the early diffusion of Hinduism to the region, however, Theravada Buddhism's spread was less closely tied to issues of status and was therefore adopted more widely throughout Mon society. In the interior of northern Burma, Buddhism also became dominant within the Pyu kingdom. Through their overland contacts with India and Nepal, however, the Pyus had more exposure to Mahayana than to Theravada Buddhism, and so the former became more common, often along with Tantric practices. To the east, in present-day Thailand, two other Mon Buddhist kingdoms emerged in the seventh century, Dvaravati in the south and Haripunjaya in the north. With support from Thaton and royal patronage, Theravada Buddhism became Dvaravati's prevailing religion; and from there it spread as well into Haripunjaya. At this time, Buddhist kingdoms also began to appear as well on the Southeast Asian islands, although they contained a more diverse mixture of Hindu and Buddhist influences.

From these beginnings, mainland Southeast Asia differed sharply from the islands and the Malay Peninsula in the further development of Buddhism. In the latter regions, a syncretistic mixture of Hinduism and Mahayana Buddhism had become prevalent by the end of the first millennium, but over the next several centuries increasing Arab dominance of trade routes through the islands, along with the Muslim invasions of India, led to the wider introduction of Islam to the region, fostered by the conversion of local rulers. By the 1500s, Malaya and the islands had become predominantly Muslim, with the older Hindu-Buddhist syncretism persisting mainly in Bali. On the Southeast Asian mainland, on the other hand, Buddhism became widely established as the dominant religious system, eliminating older expressions of Hinduism and blocking the spread of Islam. In most parts of the mainland, moreover, Theravada Buddhism became predominant. This trend in part reflected the declining cultural influence of India, first as trade patterns shifted and later as the Muslim invasions of India began and the major centers of Indian Buddhism disappeared. The cultural significance of contacts between mainland societies and Sri Lanka therefore increased, as the latter now provided the primary focus of interaction with the sources of South Asian culture. Most importantly, in its role as the prevailing religious system of Sri Lanka by this time, Theravada Buddhism dominated religious exchanges between the two regions. The development of new kingdoms in mainland Southeast Asia during this period led, moreover, to the more widespread integration of Theravada Buddhism into regional political and social structures. That process in turn marked the emergence of Southeast Asian Buddhism as a distinct regional expression of the larger Buddhist tradition.

The Pagan kingdom in Burma played an important part in the regional expansion of Buddhism during this period. This kingdom arose during the ninth century as the Burman people moved out of the northern interior, gradually absorbing the Pyu and Mon populations of central Burma. The Pagan kingdom initially favored Mahayana Buddhism, including its Tantric expressions, but in the eleventh century the Burman king Anawrahta converted to Theravada Buddhism. Subsequently he sought to eliminate heterodox expressions of Tantrism and establish the primacy of Theravada orthodoxy within his kingdom. At the same time, Anawrahta brought about through conquest the first political unification of Burma and under his rule Theravada Buddhism became the state religion. His capital, the city of Pagan, became a major center of religious activity, providing missionaries to areas farther east; and in 1065 he supplied monks and Pali texts to support the reestablishment of the Theravadan ordination lineage in Sri Lanka. From this time forward Theravada Buddhism became the dominant religious system of Burma. In the process, Burmese Buddhism absorbed some indigenous folk beliefs and practices, particularly the propitiation of local spirits and guardian deities, known as *nats*. Theravada orthodoxy nonetheless remained central to Buddhism in Burma, a trait reinforced through continuing contacts with Sri Lanka. In the late 1400s, for example, in response to growing heterodoxy a group of Burmese monks traveled to Sri Lanka to be reordained by Theravada masters there; and those who returned reinstated this ordination lineage across Burma. Burmese Buddhism thus developed a primary emphasis on Theravadan authenticity and scriptural orthodoxy as defined by the Pali canon, which in turn discouraged the development of sectarian divisions.

From the time of Anawrahta, missionaries from Burma also contributed to the spread of Theravada in Thailand. Theravada was already widespread among the Mon people there, but by the eleventh century a new group, the Thai people, began to spread southward into the region. The Thais apparently arrived as adherents of Mahayana Buddhism, including its Tantric forms, which dominated their source region to the north; and their adherence to Mahayana Buddhism and Tantrism may have been supported by their early encounters with the Khmer Empire, where these forms of Buddhism were prevalent by this time. Nonetheless, the influence of Burmese missionaries and the religious customs of the Mon people led to a rapid increase in Theravada adherence among the Thais. When they began to establish new states in the region during the 1200s, Thai rulers thus established Theravada Buddhism as their state religion. Seeking to ensure orthodoxy within their kingdoms, various Thai rulers also initiated close contacts with Sri Lanka, bringing monks from Sri Lanka to help purify local Buddhist practice and to establish an authentic Theravadan ordination lineage. Moreover, royal patronage provided continuing support for temples, monasteries, and centers of learning in the Thai kingdoms, resulting in a close relationship between the monarchy and the Buddhist sangha and in the widespread integration of Theravada Buddhism into Thai society. As in Burma, Theravada orthodoxy thus became an essential feature of Thai Buddhism. Because Thailand was not subject to European colonial rule, moreover, it grew in importance as a center of the Theravada tradition. Thus in the mid-1700s, when Sri Lanka sought to renew its Buddhist institutions in the wake of Portuguese and Dutch rule, its king sent for Thai monks to reestablish an authentic ordination lineage on the island. Heterodox elements did persist in some aspects of Thai Buddhism, of course. Thai folk religion retained a significant animistic element, for example. Later kings tried to diminish these heterodox elements, however, particularly following the Chakri dynasty's reorganization of Thailand (then known as Siam) starting in 1782. One expression of this effort was the founding in 1833 of the Thammayut ("Those who adhere to the Dharma") monastic order, which came to define Thai orthodoxy.

Cambodia and Laos

The predominance of Theravada Buddhism in Burma and Thailand affected religious patterns in Cambodia and Laos as well. The predominance of Hinduism over Buddhism within the Cambodian Khmer Empire continued into the early second millennium. As the Khmer Empire expanded during the 1100s, however, royal patronage of Mahayana Buddhism increased significantly. At the same time, Mon missionaries from Burma and Thailand were helping to spread Theravada Buddhism among the Cambodian peasantry and lower classes. Buddhism thus began to thrive in two forms within the Khmer Empire: a more elaborate Mahayana form among the ruling classes, which preserved the traditional concept of divine royalty; and a simpler Theravada form among the common people. With time, however, Mahayana Buddhism declined in significance. The founding of Thai kingdoms in what had been the western portion of the Khmer Empire furthered the adoption of Theravada among Cambodians during the thirteenth century. In the fourteenth century, moreover, Khmer rulers adopted Theravada Buddhism and established it as the court religion, relinquishing the title of god-king. At this time, significantly, Pali replaced Sanskrit as the language used in inscriptions on Khmer Buddhist monuments.

As the Khmer Empire disintegrated over the next two centuries, Theravada Buddhism remained the most prominent religious system within Cambodia, the core of the older Khmer region. During the fifteenth century, Cambodian monks ordained in Sri Lanka thus established the orthodox Theravadan monastic lineage in Cambodia. Relative to Burma and Thailand, Buddhism in Cambodia had a more syncretistic character, retaining both Hindu and animistic elements, and the role of the Buddhist sangha in Cambodian society has been constrained by repeated periods of political instability. The main body of Theravada monks in Cambodia, the Mohanikay order, thus did not develop a strong association with the ruling class. When the Thammayut movement spread from Thailand to Cambodia in the mid-1800s, on the other hand, it received widespread support from Cambodia's rulers. This contrast distanced the Mohanikay and Thammayut orders from one another, and thus in recent times the smaller Thammayut order has had less influence in promoting orthodoxy in Cambodia than in Thailand.

The Lao people, closely related to the Thais, began to migrate from southern China into Southeast Asia toward the end of the first millennium. Like the Thais, they apparently arrived in the region as adherents of Mahayana and Tantric Buddhism. Early in the second millennium most Laos inhabited the northern reaches of the Khmer Empire, but starting in the 1200s some were likely exposed to the spread of Theravada within the Thai kingdoms that expanded into the region. By the time the independent Lao kingdom of Lan Xang appeared in the mid-1300s, moreover, Theravada had become well established in the Khmer Empire as well. Lan Xang thus absorbed Theravada influences from both Thailand and Cambodia, and as the kingdom's official religion Theravada Buddhism was widely adopted by the Lao people. As in Thailand and Burma, strong ties developed in Lan Xang between the monarchy and the Buddhist sangha. These ties helped to preserve a unified monastic order in Lan Xang and, later on, in Laos. The relationship between king and sangha was weakened, however, by the breakup of Lan Xang in the late 1600s and by the centuries of political instability and foreign rule that followed. Theravada Buddhism nonetheless remained the dominant religious system, although again in folk practice it incorporated animistic beliefs concerning local spirits.

*   *   *

By the middle of the second millennium CE, then, Buddhism within Burma, Thailand, Cambodia, and Laos had developed a distinctive regional character. Because Theravada dominated the societies of this region, they looked to the Pali tradition of Sri Lanka as the principal source of religious authenticity and they accepted the Pali Tipitaka as their canonical scriptures. Buddhists in the region also followed Sri Lankan patterns of monasticism, including the exclusion of nuns from full ordination. Within the context of mainland Southeast Asia, however, the practice of Theravada Buddhism also acquired significant distinguishing characteristics. The relationship that commonly existed between royalty and the sangha had particularly important effects. Theravadan kings on the mainland frequently used their authority to reinforce Buddhist orthodoxy within their domains, acting in the role of *cakkavatti* ("wheel-turner"), the ideal of Buddhist kingship based on the model of the Indian ruler Asoka. Royal patronage also provided a major impetus for the spread of Theravada among mainland societies. Within this context, Theravadan kings considered their guardianship of the Buddhist community to be an essential duty, and the sangha in return served to legitimize the monarchy, although it rarely became directly involved in politics. This pattern of interaction between king and sangha has remained fully intact only in Thailand; elsewhere, it did not survive the political changes wrought by colonialism and postcolonial conflict. The early dominance of this pattern, however, established an underlying concern in the mainland Theravadan societies with adherence to a well-defined orthodoxy. As a result, Buddhism within these societies experienced relatively little in the way of sectarianism. By way of contrast, Theravada Buddhism in Sri Lanka came to comprise a number of distinct monastic orders; and sectarian divisions became a principal feature of Mahayana Buddhism in East Asia and Tibet.

The early connections between king and sangha in mainland Theravadan states also strengthened the sangha's social role. Monastic communities became essential institutions, providing religious and secular education, giving various forms of assistance to those in need, and overseeing rituals such as weddings and funerals. The resulting ties between the sangha and the laity contributed to the development of the distinctive and nearly universal custom of temporary ordination in the mainland Theravadan states. In this custom, young men acquire merit by entering the monkhood and living in a monastery for a short time, usually lasting from several days to three months. This custom has in turn strengthened the role of the laity in religious affairs, particularly where changing political conditions eliminated royal support for Buddhism.

Vietnam

The one mainland region of Southeast Asia in which the above pattern did not develop was its eastern coast, corresponding to present-day Vietnam. China exerted significant influence there and the area thus developed a more diverse religious character. Chinese influence was strongest in northern Vietnam, which was under Chinese rule by the first century BCE. This region was inhabited by the Vietnamese proper, who emerged as a distinct ethnic group in the middle of the first millennium BCE. By the second century CE, Buddhism had spread to northern Vietnam as part of the broader diffusion of Chinese culture; and in subsequent centuries various Mahayana schools became established, mirroring religious developments in China. Beginning in the sixth century Chinese monks brought the Ch'an and Pure Land schools to northern Vietnam; and these schools ultimately became the most influential forms of Buddhism in the region, although Taoism, Confucianism, and Tantric forms of Mahayana Buddhism were also present by this time. By 939 CE, when the Vietnamese Dai Viet kingdom achieved independence from China, Buddhism thus had a strong but diverse presence in northern Vietnam, which continued to flourish under royal patronage in the centuries that followed. From the eleventh to the thirteenth century, Buddhism also achieved broader popular support as missionaries recast local deities as guardian figures within the Mahayana pantheon.

As these developments occurred in the north, however, very different religious patterns unfolded along the southern Vietnamese coast. Much of the southern coast was first dominated by the Cham people; and farther south, in the Mekong River delta, ethnic Cambodians predominated. As discussed above, Indian influences played an important role in the formation of the Funan and Champa empires in this region, and those influences persisted within the Khmer Empire. Within this context, Hinduism and various forms of Buddhism became established. Hinduism remained the dominant religious system in Champa through most of the first millennium, supported by a concept of divine kingship. By the ninth century, however, Champa rulers began to promote Buddhism, as did Khmer rulers by the twelfth century. During this period, Theravada Buddhism became established in the region but it did not supplant Mahayana traditions. As Dai Viet expanded southward from the 1400s to the 1700s, it thus incorporated areas where diverse forms of Buddhism again prevailed.

By the beginning of the French colonial period, then, Vietnam comprised a unique mixture of Mahayana and Theravada Buddhism, reflecting the regional intersection of Chinese and South Asian influences. Although Mahayana remained the dominant form, Theravada increased in importance during the twentieth century as adherents built Theravada temples, established an authentic Theravada ordination lineage, and translated the Pali canon into Vietnamese. As a result, a growing number of ethnic Vietnamese adopted Theravada, particularly in the south. At the same time, the religious diversity of Vietnam contributed to the development of new Buddhist expressions during the twentieth century, most importantly the Hoa Hao sect, which espoused a simple form of Buddhism characterized by an emphasis on ethics, a de-emphasis on ritual, and the incorporation of elements of Taoism and Confucianism. Elements of Buddhism also appeared in the Cao Dai sect, a syncretistic union of the world's religions incorporating beliefs in reincarnation with monotheism and a Christian ecclesiastical structure.

*   *   *

The introduction of Buddhism to different parts of Asia thus led to the emergence of significant geographical variations in belief and practice. Through a long history of proselytism, Buddhism spread to many different cultural and social contexts, giving rise to a variety of specific religious systems, each characterized by distinct articulations of the basic concepts of Buddha, dharma, and sangha. A primary contrast developed between the domains of Mahayana and Theravada, which differed in their under-standing of the Buddha and in the texts included within their canonical scriptures. Within each of those larger domains, moreover, considerable variation existed. Fre-quently such variations arose in part from the capacity of Buddhism to subsume older, local traditions, as in its incorporation of elements of Bon in Tibet or of animistic worship in Southeast Asia. More to the point, though, Buddhism itself was continu-ally reshaped by its adherents in accordance with specific contexts and circumstances. In China, for example, Buddhists practiced within the context of a diverse and com-plex religious landscape in which Confucianism and Taoism also prevailed as "great" traditions. The philosophical traditions of its surroundings contributed to the sectari-anism characteristic of Chinese Buddhism, a trait transmitted as well to Japan. Sectari-anism also became a feature of Buddhism in Tibet, but there the incorporation of Tantric practices into Mahayana Buddhism developed to a much greater extent than in China. Because Buddhism came to dominate Tibet, however, the monastic orders had a more significant social role there than in other Mahayana countries, ultimately combining secular and religious authority through Tibet's interactions with external powers. In the Theravada states of Southeast Asia, Buddhist monastic orders lacked direct political influence but they too played significant social roles as authentic trans-mitters of dharma as codified in the Pali canon. The emphasis on authenticity in this context also often reflected an integral relationship between Buddhism and the state, and more generally tended to suppress the development of sectarianism. In these and many other ways as well, Buddhism thus took on distinctive traits as it spread beyond its initial hearth into diverse culture regions.

Christianity

The diffusion of Christianity out of its hearth in Palestine proceeded rapidly during the first several centuries CE as missionaries introduced it to locations across the Roman Empire. In the process, the relative independence of individual congregations under local bishops fostered the diversification of Christianity and the rise of hetero-dox interpretations of Christian belief. In the second century, for example, the Alexan-drian scholar Valentinus articulated an esoteric theology that distinguished between the material Jesus who suffered crucifixion and the divine Christ who did not, and between the ineffable supreme deity and the inferior god who created the evil world of matter. His teaching that redemption could come only through the transmission of esoteric knowledge, or gnosis, attracted communities of followers in both Alexandria and Rome, and from those cities spread into neighboring areas. Marcion of Pontus, on the Black Sea, represented another prominent example of heterodox thought at this time. He taught that the Gods of the Old and New Testaments were actually different entities, the New Testament God representing good and the Old Testament God evil; and thus he rejected the validity of the Old Testament itself and issued his own redactions of early Christian texts to remove Old Testament influences. Marcion first articulated his teachings in Rome, but they later spread to Asia Minor, Egypt, and Persia.

Such variations in early Christian belief were countered, however, by three significant influences: the concept of a unified Christian Church, the establishment of canonical scriptures, and the concern for maintaining universal Christian doctrines. The first of these influences derived from belief in the unity of all Christians, as "one body in Christ" (Romans 12:5). This sense of the universal Church was supported by the idea of apostolic succession, the belief that the authority of bishops was transmitted through an uninterrupted ordination lineage that began with the original Apostles. Through their bishops, local congregations thus possessed a direct link to a shared religious source. The importance of the sense of unity in early Christianity was evident as well in the process of excommunication through which transgressors and heretics, such as Valentinus and Marcion, could be excluded from the community of Christians.

The definition of the scriptural canon of Christianity provided another source of consistency in belief and practice. In contrast to Buddhism, accounts of the founding of Christianity were recorded in written form by early generations of adherents. Within a century of the Crucifixion, the four gospels recounting the life of Jesus and thirteen letters by Paul had been widely accepted as authoritative. In 382 a synod meeting in Rome formally defined the Christian canon, although various bodies have since defined it in slightly different ways.

Finally, early Christian leaders sought to formalize universal doctrines as a means of discouraging heterodoxy. This effort resulted in a series of ecumenical councils organized to address particular doctrinal concerns. The first such council, held at Nicaea in 325, dealt primarily with the divinity of Jesus. It rejected the belief known as Arianism that Jesus was a created being and thus not divine, and it instead asserted that the Godhead comprised God the creator and Christ, the Son of God. The First Council of Nicaea also established the hierarchical relationship between the principal metropolitan sees, areas overseen by metropolitan bishops or metropolitans, and the smaller sees of surrounding regions overseen by ordinary bishops. The second major council, held in Constantinople in 381, again rejected Arianism; defined the Godhead as comprising the trinity of Father, Son, and Holy Spirit; and approved the Nicene Creed, the most widely accepted statement of Christian faith. Subsequent councils held in Ephesus (431), Chalcedon (451), Constantinople (533 and 680–681), and Nicaea (787) focused largely on doctrinal complexities relating to the nature of Christ as both divine and human. The first four councils are considered authoritative by most Christian bodies, and Roman Catholicism and Eastern Orthodoxy both accept the authority of the next three.

As a result of these influences, a significant degree of unity existed within Christianity for several centuries. Its adoption by the Roman emperor Constantine early in the fourth century and its subsequent establishment as the empire's official religion also supported the internal unity of Christianity. Changing political circumstances, however, worked against this unity. By the fourth century, internal discord had weakened the Roman Empire, as had conflicts with Persia and various Germanic tribes. To lessen the complexity of ruling the empire, in 286 Diocletian subdivided it into two parts, the Latin-speaking west and the Greek-speaking east, a division that became permanent at the end of the fourth century. Moreover, a combination of cultural, economic, and political factors, including continuing pressure from the Germanic tribes, led to the disintegration of the Western Empire into a number of smaller kingdoms by the end of the fifth century. This situation restructured the context within which Christianity was practiced: the connections among diverse communities of adherents, which had been supported by the Roman Empire, were now much weakened by political fragmentation in the west. In addition, cultural differences between Greek- and Latin-speaking regions fostered a growing divergence between east and west, as did the west's growing mixture of Germanic and Roman influences. The prevalence of Arianism among the Germanic tribes especially complicated religious patterns in the west. Within the Ostrogothic, Visigothic, and Vandal kingdoms of the early sixth century, for example, adherence to Arianism served as an important distinction between Germanic inhabitants and indigenous Christians. Nonetheless, processes of assimilation ultimately led to the Germanic adoption of elements of the more complex Roman culture, including Latin-based dialects and the prevailing Christian orthodoxy.

Eastern and Western Christianity

The separation between the eastern and western halves of the Christian world had more significant consequences as further religious differences began to develop between the two regions. One major source of division was the status of the bishop of Rome, later known as the pope. Within early Christianity, the bishop of Rome had generally been recognized as "first among equals" in relation to the other leading bishops, a position deriving from the role of the apostle Peter as the first bishop of Rome and the city's role as capital of the Roman Empire. In the fifth century, however, the Council of Chalcedon challenged this status. Because by this time the empire's capital had been relocated to Constantinople, the council accorded equal privileges to the bishops of Constantinople and Rome, while still recognizing the latter's position as first among equals. Leo I, then the bishop of Rome, opposed the council's decision but could not prevent it from being approved. From this time forward, the relative status of the bishops of Rome and Constantinople became a recurring source of discord between eastern and western Christianity. By the fifth century various bishops of Rome, including Leo, had in fact begun to assert that they possessed ultimate jurisdiction over the entire Christian Church, an idea rejected by eastern Christians. In the sixth century the emperor Justinian recognized five Christian patriarchs—the bishops of Rome, Constantinople, Antioch, Jerusalem, and Alexandria—and eastern Christians believed that each patriarch held exclusive authority over a separate territory. The fact that four of the five patriarchs presided in the east had various implications. In 533 at the Council of Constantinople, for example, Justinian accorded each patriarch equal representation, reducing the western, Roman presence to a small minority of the delegates. The bishop of Rome thus refused to attend. Finally, the conflict over the authority of the bishop of Rome also had a significant political dimension. The fall of the Western Empire gave the bishop of Rome a degree of independence, freeing him from direct imperial control. The patriarchate of Constantinople, in contrast, functioned in many ways as part of the imperial apparatus of the Eastern Empire, resulting in a strong interdependence between patriarch and emperor. During the sixth century Justinian tried to bring the bishop of Rome back under his control as he expanded his empire westward, but distance from Constantinople, relationships with the Germanic kingdoms, and the gradual contraction of the

Byzantine Empire all enabled the bishops of Rome to preserve some of their autonomy under Byzantine rule.

The contesting of religious authority also informed the competing missionary activities of eastern and western Christianity, most notably among the Slavs. This competition arose during the ninth century in the kingdom of Moravia. Missionaries from the kingdom of Germany, representing western Christianity, entered the region first but had little success, in part because they insisted on the use of Latin in liturgy and scripture. The Byzantine emperor subsequently sent two brothers to the region, Cyril and Methodius, who had previously conducted missions in southern Ukraine among the Khazars. They proved to be more successful in gaining converts, and undertook the translation of the Bible into Slavonic using a Greek-influenced system of writing devised by Cyril. This Cyrillic alphabet later became the basis for the written forms of many of the Slavic languages. Nonetheless, alliances with the Germans caused the Moravian ruler to expel eastern Christianity from his kingdom. When the kingdom of Bohemia supplanted Moravia in the tenth century, it too came under the influence of the German kingdom, and its rulers gave their support to western Christianity.

From these beginnings, western Christianity thus became dominant among the western Slavs, including Moravians, Bohemians, Slovaks, and Poles, as well as among the neighboring Hungarians. Among the southern Slavs, on the other hand, the competition between east and west resulted in the expansion of both forms of Christianity in the earlier borderland between the Western and Eastern Roman Empires. The Croats and Slovenes, who migrated to areas traditionally under western control, converted to western Christianity between the seventh and ninth centuries. The Byzantine Empire had greater influence farther to the south, and its missionaries had converted the Serbs and Bulgarians by the ninth century. Among the eastern Slavs, finally, eastern Christianity dominated. In the tenth century, the Russian princess Olga converted to eastern Christianity. In 988 Vladimir, Olga's grandson, also converted, according to tradition after having also examined the teachings of western Christianity, Islam, and Judaism. His conversion established eastern Christianity as the dominant religious system in Russia, while also serving to reinforce political connections between the latter and the Byzantine Empire. Eastern Christianity subsequently prevailed among the various eastern Slavic peoples, including the Ukrainians and Belarusians. By the end of the tenth century, then, the competition between eastern and western Christianity had produced a distinct religious boundary across Eastern Europe, the western church and Latin alphabet dominant on one side and the eastern church and Cyrillic alphabet on the other.

In addition to conflicts over religious authority, the growing division between eastern and western Christianity involved important differences in religious belief and practice. The popular worship of icons, images of sacred figures or events, had become widespread within eastern Christianity by the middle of the first millennium but remained uncommon in the west. In the eighth century the iconoclast movement within the Byzantine Empire sought to eliminate this practice, citing it as a weakness that contributed to losses to the expanding Muslim empire, which itself strongly opposed the worship of idols. Byzantine emperors thus outlawed icon worship as idolatrous and ordered the destruction of all icons. The bishop of Rome, seeking to expand his authority in the east, declared his support for icon worship and excommunicated the emperor who outlawed the practice; but while this act contributed to the decline of Byzantine power in Italy, it had little impact on Roman influence among eastern Christians. Late in the eighth century, however, a Byzantine empress revoked the ban on icons and in 787 convened the Second Council of Nicaea, which defined the place of icons in Christian worship, stating that as representations of faith they deserved the same veneration accorded to crucifixes or the Bible. A second imperial ban on icons occurred in the ninth century, but in 843 the worship of icons was again restored and thereafter remained a distinguishing element of eastern Christianity.

Other religious contrasts developed between east and west as well. Monasticism began to flourish in the east by the fourth century and in the west a century later. Eastern monasticism comprised two distinct forms: an older idiorrhythmic form in which monks lived in isolation and a cenobitic form organized around monastic communities. In the west, on the other hand, the cenobitic form dominated. Monastic communities in the east also frequently drew support from the laity, while in the west they tended to be self-supporting. Western Christianity in addition had stricter requirements for celibacy among the clergy, requiring it of all ordained clergymen. Eastern Christianity required celibacy only of bishops, allowing married men to be ordained as priests. And eastern clergy wore beards, reflecting their understanding of the image of Jesus, while western clergy did not. In terms of church ritual, eastern Christians performed the liturgy in vernacular languages and used leavened bread for the Eucharist, the rising of the bread symbolizing Jesus' resurrection. Western Christians, in contrast, used Latin as their liturgical language and unleavened bread for the Eucharist. With regard to theology, a major division occurred regarding the nature of the Holy Spirit as articulated in the Nicene Creed, which was central to the liturgy in both east and west. Eastern Christians held to the original view that the Holy Spirit proceeds from the Father, God the creator. Starting in the sixth century, Spanish Christians revised the Nicene Creed to read that the Holy Spirit proceeds *filioque* (Latin: from the Son) as well. This interpretation of the Holy Spirit became widely accepted in the west and was formally adopted by the western church in 1014, but it provoked strong opposition in the east.

In 1054, growing tensions between east and west produced a formal division between the two regional forms of Christianity as the leaders of the two branches excommunicated one another from the Christian Church. The proximate causes of the Great Schism of 1054 focused on the filioque controversy and the dispute over the leavening of the Eucharistic bread. Clearly, though, the rift between east and west had developed over many centuries. Two distinct Christian bodies thus emerged from the schism: the Roman Catholic Church and the Orthodox Catholic Church (map 3.7). Both bodies considered themselves to be catholic or universal in character. The Roman Catholic Church recognized the authority of the bishop of Rome, or pope, over all of its adherents and in liturgy followed the Latin rite, based on western practices and conducted in Latin. The Orthodox Catholic Church, or more commonly the Orthodox Church or Eastern Orthodoxy, considered the patriarch of Constantinople to be its honorary head but recognized the authority of the other patriarchs over their respective domains; and it followed the liturgy of the Byzantine rite, conducted in vernacular languages. In addition, a small number of eastern churches that followed the Byzantine rite but also recognized the authority of the pope came to be known as the Eastern Catholic or Eastern Rite churches. Shortly after the schism, the pope

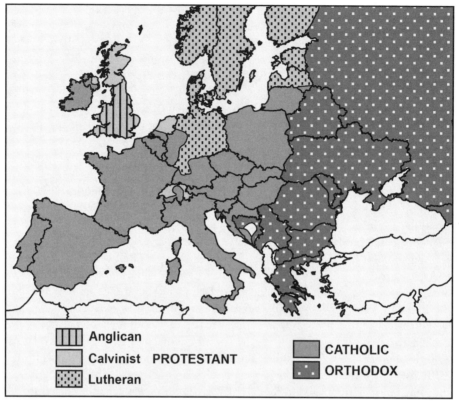

Map 3.7. Distribution of the major branches of Christianity in Europe. The patterns depicted here emerged over a number of centuries, from the formal division of Christianity into its Roman Catholic and Orthodox branches in the eleventh century to the separation of the major branches of Protestantism from Roman Catholicism in the sixteenth century during the Reformation.

decreed that future popes must be elected by a group of cardinal bishops. In the Byzantine Empire, on the other hand, the emperor formally selected the patriarch of Constantinople; and political factors influenced the selection of Orthodox patriarchs in other contexts as well. More broadly, Roman Catholicism emphasized doctrinal conformity, maintained through a strong tradition of scholarship and an authoritarian, hierarchical church structure. In contrast, Eastern Orthodoxy placed less emphasis on theological homogeneity, instead claiming religious authenticity through the preservation of orthodox worship practices; and over time it allowed the development of separate national churches under their own patriarchs. The translation of the Bible into vernacular languages and the use of those languages in the liturgy also strengthened the role of the laity in Eastern Orthodoxy relative to Roman Catholicism.

Eastern Orthodoxy

Following the split between eastern and western Christianity, the two branches developed very differently. Spatial variety developed within Eastern Orthodoxy through the formation of autocephalous, or independently headed, churches organized by nationality or geographical location. These churches remained in communion with one another, each recognizing the legitimacy of the others. The ancient patriarchates of Constantinople, Antioch, Jerusalem, and Alexandria represented the primary bodies within Eastern Orthodoxy at the time of the Great Schism, although a number of metropolitan bishops under these patriarchs had a degree of autonomy. Over time, however, church-state relations within the Byzantine Empire provided a model for the creation of new independent churches within emerging states. For example, the Georgian Orthodox Church, which had a degree of autonomy by the fifth century, became organized as an independent patriarchate in the eleventh century after the unification of the kingdom of Georgia. Similarly, the formation of an autocephalous Bulgarian church followed the establishment of a Bulgarian state in the thirteenth century. The Russian Orthodox Church, in contrast, remained under the jurisdiction of the patriarch of Constantinople until asserting its autocephalous status in 1448, five years before the conquest of Constantinople by the Ottoman Empire. When the bishop of Moscow received the title of patriarch in 1589, however, he was ranked by the Orthodox churches as fifth in honor behind the four ancient patriarchs, a position of status that reflected Russia's importance as largest Orthodox Christian state at the time. Throughout the history of Orthodoxy the independent existence of individual national churches has been continually subject to political vicissitudes, and many of them were dissolved or placed under other jurisdictions at certain times. In recent centuries, however, the rise of modern states has contributed to a significant structural reorganization of Orthodoxy, which now comprises fourteen mutually recognized autocephalous churches. Eastern Christianity also continues to be represented by a variety of smaller churches, some independent and some recognizing the authority of the Roman Catholic pope.

Within these various contexts, the Orthodox churches maintained their shared liturgy and similar institutional structures. Nonetheless, the national churches developed many distinctive attributes. Each has particular saints that it venerates, for example. These figures were often linked to a group's conversion to Christianity, as in Russia's St. Vladimir, or to crucial events in a nation's history, as in Serbia's St. Lazar, who was martyred in unsuccessfully opposing the advance of the Ottoman Empire in the 1300s. The veneration of national saints reflects a broader connection between church and national identity, a relationship that has continued to provoke controversy among Orthodox groups. Since the Soviet era, for example, the Russian Orthodox Church has strongly opposed the formation of autocephalous churches by non-Russian nationalities once within the jurisdiction of the patriarch of Moscow, including Ukrainians, Belarusians, Estonians, and Latvians. With regard to matters of religious practice, a split occurred between Russian Orthodoxy and the other Orthodox churches during the 1500s over the correct manner of making the sign of the cross. The Russians argued for the use of two fingers symbolizing God and humanity in place of the more common usage of three fingers symbolizing the holy trinity. The Russian Orthodox council that approved the use of two fingers also decreed that all adult male adherents should wear beards and that icon painters should only reproduce approved images. The tensions resulting from the accretion of such local practices have in turn produced reform movements seeking more authentic articulations of Orthodoxy. Returning to the example of Russia, during the 1600s the patriarch of

Moscow sought to reform the church by eliminating some of its idiosyncratic practices. He took the Greek-speaking Orthodox as his model, decreeing that the clergy should dress as the Greek clergy did and that one should make the sign of the cross with three fingers instead of two. These decrees in turn provoked a schism within the Russian Orthodox Church in the 1660s as opponents of reform split off to become a distinct group known as the Old Believers. This group's insistence on retaining distinctly Russian forms of practice again reveals the great importance of local religious accretions to believers. As these brief examples suggest, then, the Orthodox churches have undergone various processes of diversification throughout their history, reflecting the continuing interaction between Orthodox tradition and the specific contexts in which adherents have practiced their faith.

Roman Catholicism

In contrast to the Orthodox churches, Roman Catholicism remained institutionally unified under a single church hierarchy. Indeed, the centralization of religious authority represented one of the defining characteristics of the Roman Catholic Church. The Roman Catholic organizational structure thus discouraged local or regional variations in belief and practice. Still, such variations did develop and in many contexts became an important part of the religious lives of adherents. As in the Orthodox east, the veneration of local saints had become widespread within western Christianity by the early medieval period and remained an important element of Roman Catholicism. Local saints and their relics provided a concrete link between adherents and more abstract dimensions of faith. Believers typically viewed local saints as the immediate protectors of the local community and as the source of cures and other miraculous events.[51] But again, such practices existed in tension with the universal identity of the Roman Catholic Church. By the twelfth century, church institutions had thus begun to emphasize doctrinal and ritual conformity. The Cistercian monastic order, formed in 1098, played an important role in this process by seeking to restore the church's authentic traditions and universal character. The Cistercians in particular contributed to two key trends: emphasis on devotion to Mary rather than local saints; and emphasis on the mass as the church's central ritual.

The latter trends initially promoted greater uniformity within the church, but over time they began to acquire local accretions as well. Devotion to Mary often became linked to local manifestations, apparitions, or shrines. From the late fourteenth century, for example, an icon of Mary known as Our Lady of Czestochowa, named for the city where it is located, became widely venerated in Poland as a source of miracles and spiritual protection. Similarly, by the twelfth century devotion to Our Lady of the Pillar had become established in Zaragoza, Spain, where by tradition this apparition of Mary atop a pillar carried by angels had appeared in the first century to the apostle James. The liturgy of the mass also acquired local elements, such as the veneration of local saints in brief musical passages, known as melismas. During the 1500s, the Roman hierarchy again sought to establish greater uniformity of practice in response to these trends. In 1570 the church issued a standard missal or mass book, in part to eliminate the incorporation of local saints into the liturgy; and in 1588 the pope established the Congregation of Rites to regulate the canonization of saints. The

Roman hierarchy also required that the addition of local saints' feasts to the calendar of specific dioceses or parishes receive approval from Rome. Such actions did not eliminate local variations in practice, of course, but rather shaped the contexts within which such variations occurred. Indeed, the veneration of local and national patron saints remained an important and widespread part of Roman Catholic practice. Eastern European groups, for example, continued to venerate national saints associated with both the adoption of Christianity and the formation of national identity, such as St. Wenceslaus of Bohemia, St. Stephen of Hungary, and St. Stanislaus of Poland. Marian apparitions, including Our Lady of Guadalupe in Mexico (1531) and more recently Our Lady of Lourdes in France (1858) and Our Lady of Fatima in Portugal (1917), have also acquired significance as national patrons.

In some instances, moreover, local worship practices ultimately became common to the Roman Catholic Church as a whole. A particularly important example of this process involved belief in the Immaculate Conception of Mary, the doctrine that Mary was conceived free from the stain of original sin. Belief in the purity of Mary had its roots in early Christian thought, particularly in the east; and by the eighth century the eastern church celebrated a feast honoring the conception of Mary but without reference to its immaculate character. In the west, the commemoration of Mary's conception did not begin to flourish until the eleventh century, when it became the object of a feast day celebrated in England; and at this time, English belief in the Immaculate Conception began to emerge. The feast subsequently became widely celebrated in England and by the end of the twelfth century was also well established in Normandy. Roman Catholic theologians opposed belief in the Immaculate Conception, arguing that it contradicted the doctrine that Christ had redeemed all of humanity from original sin. Nonetheless, the growing emphasis on Marian devotion led to widespread popular acceptance of the Immaculate Conception during the medieval period. Over time church institutions adopted the belief as well, and in 1476 the pope approved the Feast of the Immaculate Conception for the entire church. The eleventh-century English commemoration of the conception of Mary had thus evolved into a universal Roman Catholic doctrine.

The Roman Catholic Church did not accommodate all doctrinal variations, however. During the medieval period the church hierarchy expelled and persecuted a number of heretical groups in various parts of Europe (map 3.8). One such group was the Waldenses, a twelfth-century reform movement founded in southern France that sought to return to the simplicity of early Christianity. Its adherents advocated living in poverty without possessions and in place of the Latin Bible they used a version translated into the dialect of southern France. Because they preached their message without church permission, they were excommunicated in 1184. The Waldenses then began to deviate more sharply from Roman Catholic doctrine, rejecting the concept of purgatory, the veneration of saints, and the sacramental role of the priesthood. The group was most successful in attracting followers in southeastern France and northwestern Italy, but it also spread to other parts of Europe. The Waldenses met with various forms of persecution, however, and by the 1400s they were limited mostly to their area of origin.

Another notable heretical movement, the Cathars ("Pure Ones"), also emerged in the twelfth century in northern Italy and southern France. The French branch of the movement was known as the Albigenses, after the city of Albi where it was cen-

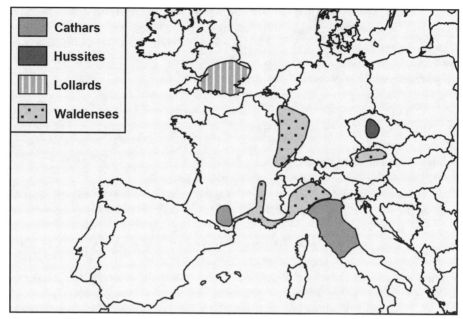

Map 3.8.   Hearths of heretical groups within medieval Christianity.

tered. The Cathars emphasized an intrinsic dualism between good and evil, stressed asceticism based on their belief in the evil of the material world, and rejected many elements of Roman Catholic doctrine, such as the virgin birth and the incarnation of Jesus in a material, human body. They also strongly opposed the institution of the Roman Catholic Church, which they characterized as an expression of the material world. The Roman Catholic Church responded with vigorous persecution, including the Albigensian Crusade targeting Cathars in southern France, and by the fifteenth century the movement had disappeared.

Heterodox groups also appeared in northern Europe, albeit somewhat later than in the south. The Lollards, a movement that developed in the late fourteenth century among the working class and small landowners in southern England, held various controversial views largely derived from the English theologian John Wycliffe. They rejected the doctrine of transubstantiation, which held that the bread and wine in the Eucharist are transformed into the actual body and blood of Christ. They also opposed the veneration of saints, pilgrimages, church wealth, the sacrament of confession, clerical celibacy, and various other Roman Catholic practices. They further held that the Bible, accessible through translation into vernacular languages, represented the primary source of religious authority. The church hierarchy and the English monarchy vigorously suppressed the Lollards, however, and by the sixteenth century the movement had effectively dispersed.

A similar movement developed on the mainland in the early fifteenth century around Jan Hus, a Bohemian church reformer. Hus too supported the dissemination of the Bible in vernacular languages and believed that religious authority lay in the Bible, not in the church. He further advocated that all communicants receive both bread and wine in the Eucharist, a departure from Roman Catholic practice in which only the priest received the wine. Hus was convicted of heresy and executed, but his supporters, known as the Hussites, continued to spread his views. The Hussite movement, which comprised both commoners and members of the Bohemian nobility, entered into prolonged conflict with the Roman Catholic Church. Despite efforts by some members to reach some form of compromise with Roman Catholicism, however, the movement did not last beyond the early 1600s.

Protestantism

By the early sixteenth century, the spreading concern for religious reform had led to more far-reaching divisions within western Christianity, articulated through the Reformation and the rise of Protestantism, the third major branch of Christianity. The Reformation comprised a variety of different movements associated with particular reformers and specific places.[52] The most widely influential of these reformers were Martin Luther and John Calvin, but various figures contributed to the emergence of Protestantism at more local scales, including secular rulers as well as theologians. Despite their differences, the Reformation movements had certain features in common: openness to change in doctrine and ritual, dissatisfaction with the institutional hierarchy of Roman Catholicism, an emphasis on the Bible as the only infallible source of authority, a corresponding interest in translation of the Bible into vernacular languages, and belief that salvation comes through faith in divine grace rather than through good works. Regarding specific matters of doctrine and ritual, the Reformation movements generally opposed the practice of confession, monasticism, clerical celibacy, the concepts of transubstantiation and purgatory, and the veneration of the saints and of Mary.

The Reformation movements also shared a similar geographical distribution, originating in northern and central Europe at a distance from the center of papal authority in Rome (map 3.7). As in the earlier division between eastern and western Christianity, cultural differences played an important role in the rise of the Reformation. Protestantism tended to flourish in the parts of Europe dominated by Germanic languages and Roman Catholicism in areas dominated by Romance languages, although exceptions to this pattern did exist. Universities in northern Europe also became more open than those in the south to the questioning of church doctrines, particularly in light of a growing interest in early Christian writings. Political factors also contributed to the development of the Reformation in northern Europe as various rulers in the region rejected the temporal authority of the pope and the involvement of the church hierarchy in political matters. Within the weakening Holy Roman Empire, the Reformation provided support for the growing independence of local states from imperial control. In addition, northern European rulers resented the wealth accumulated by the Roman Catholic Church, ultimately leading the kings of England and Sweden and the princes of various German states to dissolve the monasteries within their domains and confiscate their property. The emphasis on the individual in Reformation thought also agreed with the economic concerns of the merchant class as capitalism began to emerge in northern Europe. At the same time, the promise of a radical restructuring of society advanced the appeal of the Reformation among the peasantry. Finally, older patterns of religious distinctiveness in northern Europe may have fostered the development of Reformation movements. In contrast

to southern Europe, popular religious practice in the north tended to be more individualistic, stressing personal piety over communal expressions of universal church doctrine, such as the veneration of Mary. The celebration of local saints also differed
between northern and southern Europe: local saints in the north had often been significant leaders linked to a group's national identity, while in the south local saints
were more commonly exemplars of ascetic devotion to the church. Such trends in
northern Europe supported the spread of the Reformation emphasis on the individual
believer and the rise of national Protestant churches.[53]

Lutheranism

By most accounts the initiating event of the Reformation took place in 1517 when
Martin Luther, a theologian and ordained Roman Catholic priest, issued his ninety-
five theses disputing the legitimacy of papal indulgences. In Roman Catholicism, an
indulgence is granted to remit the punishment imposed by divine justice on an individual for having sinned, after the sin has been forgiven through confession and penance. Indulgences came into widespread use during the twelfth century when popes
granted them to Christians participating in the Crusades. The practice of collecting
contributions from those granted indulgences also emerged at this time as a means of
funding the construction of churches. By the early 1500s, however, the expanding
traffic in indulgences by professional pardoners had led to a variety of abuses and
increasing opposition from reformers. Much of this opposition was directed specifically at the papal decision in 1507 to finance the construction of St. Peter's Basilica
in Rome through the sale of indulgences.

Luther objected most immediately to the noncanonical claims made by local
sellers of indulgences: for example, that purchasers were automatically absolved of
guilt or ensured of salvation or that they could buy the release of the deceased from
purgatory. But he also challenged more basic church doctrines, asserting that the
repentance of sins depended on the inner transformation of the adherent rather than
on church ritual. By 1520, moreover, Luther had published writings that articulated
a broader reconception of Christian practice. At the center of his theology was the
concept of justification by faith, the belief that adherents receive divine grace and thus
salvation through faith alone. In his view human works could not bring about salvation, while faith, instead of causing divine grace to be granted, served as the means by
which grace, freely offered, could be received. He thus rejected the role of the priest
as intermediary in the individual's salvation, arguing instead for a priesthood of all
believers. The second essential feature of his theology was belief in the exclusive
authority of the Bible as the source of religious truth. Based on this belief he rejected
nonscriptural innovations, including the authority of the pope, the Roman Catholic
mass, clerical celibacy, the doctrines of transubstantiation and purgatory, the veneration of Mary and the saints, and the infallibility of various church councils. The
Roman Catholic Church viewed him as a heretic and excommunicated him in 1521.
The Holy Roman Empire subsequently declared him an outlaw and banned his writings.

Luther had the support of a number of the princes of German states within the
Holy Roman Empire, however, and they provided him with protection, allowing him
to publish his German translation of the New Testament in 1522 (photo 3.5). In

Photo 3.5.   Wartburg Castle in Eisenach, Germany, where Frederick the Wise, Elector of Saxony, provided Martin Luther with protection after the latter's excommunication from the Roman Catholic Church. As the site where Luther produced his German translation of the New Testament, during late 1521 and early 1522, Wartburg Castle represents a key location in the practical development of the Reformation. Eisenach, Germany, 2006.

Source: Robert Scarth (www.flickr.com/photos/robert_scarth/241708183/), under Creative Commons license (creativecommons.org/licenses/by-sa/2.0/).

1526, moreover, the Diet of the Holy Roman Empire rescinded the earlier action against Luther and granted each state within the empire the right to determine its own religious identity. This decision was revoked in 1529, however, provoking a formal protest by Lutheran members of the Diet. When the Diet met in Augsburg the following year, the Lutherans presented the emperor with a formal statement of their beliefs, subsequently known as the Augsburg Confession, which became the basis for Lutheran doctrine. The Diet declined to accept this statement of faith, however, and reinstituted the ban on Luther's teachings. Various Lutheran princes and cities responded in 1531 by forming the Schmalkaldic League to defend themselves against the emperor, Charles V. Over the next decade, the league formed alliances with France and Denmark and helped to spread Lutheranism throughout much of northern Germany. Luther also published his complete German translation of the Bible in 1534, and within forty years more than one hundred thousand copies had been sold. Charles V ultimately defeated the Schmalkaldic League, in 1547, but by this time Lutheranism had become well established in many areas and new alliances emerged to defend its interests. Finally in 1555, with the signing of the Peace of Augsburg, individual states and cities within the Holy Roman Empire acquired religious independence, allowing local rulers to determine a place's religious identity. Approximately half of the empire, mostly in the north and east, became identified as Lutheran at this time. Local control of religious identity was later reconfirmed in the Treaty of Westphalia, in 1648, which more firmly established the sovereignty of the German states.

During the religious conflicts within the Holy Roman Empire, Lutheranism spread rapidly in areas to the north. The Duke of Prussia helped to introduce Lutheranism to that region as he established a hereditary state there in 1525, with assistance from the king of Poland. A similar pattern developed farther north along the Baltic Sea with the establishment of Lutheranism in Livonia and Courland by the 1550s, but these areas were soon absorbed by other states and Lutheranism declined in significance throughout the Baltic region. In Scandinavia, on the other hand, Lutheranism flourished, ultimately becoming the state religion of Denmark, Sweden, Norway, Finland, and Iceland. It reached Denmark in 1520 and, after a period of political instability and religious conflict, became the official religion in 1536, with the king of Denmark as its head. Early support for Lutheranism in Denmark intersected with various political alliances and economic interests, and once established Lutheranism continued to dominate there and in Danish-controlled Norway and Iceland. The establishment of Lutheranism in Sweden also occurred at this time as part of a broader assertion of nationalism as the Swedes, led by Gustav Vasa, asserted their independence from Denmark in 1523. As king, Gustav sponsored the publication of a Swedish translation of the New Testament and in 1527 the Swedish parliament transferred control of all church property to the king, prohibited the sacrament of confession and papal confirmation of bishops, and defined biblical teachings as the only valid subject of sermons. Lutheranism was established as the state's official religion in 1544, and became prevalent in Swedish-controlled Finland as well.

Zwinglianism

As Lutheranism spread northward, a second major branch of Reformation thought was developing to the south in Switzerland. The Swiss Reformation comprised two phases, the first led by Ulrich Zwingli in Zurich and the second by John Calvin in Geneva. Calvin ultimately had greater influence, but Zwingli initiated the development of distinctive trends within Switzerland. Zwingli's popularity as a Roman Catholic parish priest led to his appointment as pastor of the cathedral in Zurich in 1519. Based on his study of the New Testament, however, he preached against various Roman Catholic practices for which he found no scriptural basis, such as fasting during Lent and tithing; and in 1520 at his request Zurich's ruling council banned the teaching of nonscriptural doctrines. His departures from Roman Catholic dogma led to a public disputation between Zwingli and a member of the Roman Catholic hierarchy in 1523, at which Zwingli presented his basic teachings: that the Bible was the sole source of religious authority, that Christ alone was the head of the church, and that salvation came only through divine grace. He also spoke against the concept of purgatory, the doctrine of transubstantiation, the mass, the veneration of saints and religious images, and clerical celibacy. The disputation concluded with the Council of Zurich adopting Zwingli's ideas and withdrawing Zurich from the jurisdiction of the Roman Catholic Church. Zurich in effect became a theocracy, with Zwingli advising the council on religious matters. By 1525, the mass and confession had been banned, organs and religious images had been removed from churches, worship services were held in German, and monasteries had been dissolved. Moreover, Zwingli's teachings had also begun to spread to other Swiss cantons. By 1529 his form of church polity, known as the Reformed church, had been established in Bern, Basel, Schaffhausen, and St. Gall.

During this time contacts had also developed between Zwingli and Luther, but the two remained divided over the meaning of the Eucharist. Luther held that in the Eucharist the substance of the bread and wine coexisted with the presence of Christ, while Zwingli held that the bread and wine commemorated the body and blood of Christ but did not contain his real presence. Zwingli also supported a closer relationship between civil and religious authority than did Luther. The Reformed and Lutheran branches of the Reformation thus remained distinct from one another. Zwingli's further impact on Reformed Protestantism was cut short, however, by his death in 1531 during civil war between the Reformed and Roman Catholic cantons in Switzerland.

Calvinism

The focus of the Swiss Reformation subsequently shifted to Geneva, where John Calvin established a theocratic polity by the 1550s. Calvin, born in France, studied law until a conversion experience in 1532 led him to focus on religious concerns. He rapidly absorbed the main currents of religious reform, particularly regarding the authority of the Bible. Growing hostility toward reformers in France caused him to move to Basel, Switzerland. There, in 1536, he produced the first edition of his *Institutes of the Christian Religion*, which in later editions became the defining text of Reformed Protestantism. In this work he focused on the fundamental concepts of divine grace and scriptural authority. His theology posited a worldview in which salvation depended solely on the unearned grace of God, and thus he rejected the redemptive power of the Roman Catholic sacraments. He further believed that comprehension of the Bible, based on direct examination rather than on the traditions of the Roman Catholic Church, provided the only means of attaining union with Jesus as the divine savior. Based on these doctrines, he asserted that baptism and the Eucharist were the only valid sacraments. He rejected the mass, and like Zwingli asserted that the bread and wine of the Eucharist did not contain Christ's physical presence. He also opposed the use of religious images and even crucifixes as expressions of idolatry. More distinctively, he supported the concept of predestination as an expression of divine will. Luther had also accepted predestination, but merely as an expression of divine foreknowledge. Calvin's view of predestination gave rise to the concept of the elect, those who are predestined to achieve salvation. Calvin finally insisted that the teachings of the Bible should inform all aspects of life. He argued specifically that the New Testament had not invalidated many of the divine injunctions concerning moral law that had been articulated in the Old Testament and that Christians were therefore obliged to adhere to them. More generally, he asserted that believers had an absolute religious obligation to promote the common good through hard work and moral discipline. To this end, Calvin argued for a union of church and state, with the church responsible for defining the correct patterns of Christian life and the state responsible for enforcing adherence to those patterns.

Calvin gained the opportunity to put his ideas into practice in Geneva starting in the late 1530s. At that time the city was emerging from a period of conflict during which its rising bourgeoisie asserted its independence from the Duke of Savoy and the

Roman Catholic bishop of Geneva, a prince of the Holy Roman Empire. In this context, Geneva had also sought protection through an alliance with the Reformed city of Bern. These events led to prolonged conflict over control of the city and the establishment of Protestantism there. The conflict ended in 1536 with the city's governing council committing itself to the Reformed church. Calvin arrived several months later, and was invited to remain in the city and help establish religious reform. In response he developed a set of ordinances and a confession of faith for the church in Geneva. He and his supporters also sought to impose regulations requiring adherence to the Reformed creed and to strict moral codes. Edicts regulating moral behavior, commerce, and other aspects of public life had in fact been issued as early as the late 1400s in Geneva. Nonetheless, many residents of Geneva resisted these new regulations, and in 1538 Calvin was forced to leave the city after his leading supporters were removed from public office.

Calvin's supporters regained control in Geneva in 1541, however, and invited him to return. He did so and remained in Geneva until his death in 1564. Upon his return, the city fully accepted his Ecclesiastical Ordinances for governing the church. Calvin's ordinances established various bodies to realize church objectives. Perhaps the most prominent of these was the Consistory, a group made up of clergy and lay elders that was charged with maintaining discipline in religious worship and moral behavior. Many residents of the city continued to oppose Calvin's ideas, and the status of Geneva's political independence remained precarious during the 1540s. Calvin gradually consolidated power, however, backed by the bourgeoisie and a continuing influx of Protestant refugees from France and other parts of Europe. The last major reaction against Calvin in Geneva was suppressed in 1555.

Calvin's influence in Geneva therefore came to be realized in the form of a Christian commonwealth organized in accordance with his theology. Geneva under Calvin and his successors was not a strict theocracy, as the clergy had no legislative authority. Nonetheless, the clergy exerted considerable influence, particularly through the Consistory, and typically with the support of civil law. The practice of Roman Catholicism was banned, and the city's inhabitants were subject to various restrictions on both public and private behavior. Calvin's Reformed ideas thus achieved a pervasive influence on Genevan society, supporting a communal ethos of piety, industriousness, and sobriety. As this Calvinist transformation developed, moreover, Geneva's significance as a center of the Reformation increased (photo 3.6). The city itself came to be known as the Protestant Rome. Calvin and his supporters saw themselves as the new chosen people of God, and Protestants across Europe considered Geneva to be the model of a Christian polity. As a result, the city continued to attract Protestant immigrants, many of whom later carried Calvinist views back to their homelands. In 1559 Calvin founded the Academy of Geneva to educate pastors and scholars who would spread his teachings. The flourishing printing industry in Geneva also helped to disseminate Calvin's works across Europe.

Within Switzerland, moreover, Calvinism quickly merged with the Zwinglian tradition to form a single Reformed tradition. In 1549 Calvin met with Zwingli's successor, Heinrich Bullinger, to sign the *Consensus Tigurinus*, which placed the two branches of the Swiss Reformation in communion with one another and outlined their common doctrines. The desire for a stronger church union resulted in the establishment of the Second Helvetic Confession in 1566 (the first, from 1536, having

Photo 3.6.   The centerpiece of the International Monument to the Reformation, or Reformation Wall, in Geneva. The monument, located in the Parc des Bastions, runs along the wall of the old city. It features, from left to right, Guillaume Farel (who first invited Calvin to Geneva), John Calvin, Theordore Beza (Calvin's successor), and John Knox (who helped spread Calvinism to Scotland). Geneva's coat of arms lies in front of the statues. Geneva, Switzerland, 2006.

Source: John Eckman (www.flickr.com/photos/jeckman/418507746/), under Creative Commons license (creativecommons.org/licenses/by-sa/2.0/).

unified various Zwinglian churches). This document provided a more complete artic-ulation of Reformed belief and unified the Swiss Reformed churches under a single confession. The institutional organization of the Swiss Reformed churches remained essentially local in character, however, with a separate church structure in each canton. In the Protestant cantons these local churches functioned essentially as state churches, a pattern that persisted through the 1800s and in some cantons continues to exist.

During the 1500s the Reformed tradition, particularly as articulated by Calvin, diffused to other parts of Europe as well. It became widely accepted in the Netherlands after its introduction in the 1540s, again despite the suppression of Protestantism by the ruling Spanish monarchy. In the long Dutch revolt against Spanish rule, lasting until 1648, Calvinism became increasingly integral to the Dutch cause and steadily attracted new adherents. Thus in 1618 the Dutch Synod of Dordrecht established Dutch Reformed theology along Calvinist lines and banned public worship by Roman Catholics; and after independence the Dutch Reformed church effectively became the state religion.

The Reformed tradition spread to Scotland through the efforts of John Knox, a Roman Catholic priest who converted to Protestantism and studied with Calvin in Geneva. Knox returned to Scotland in 1559 to lead the growing party of reform against the Roman Catholic monarchy. With the promise of support from Protestant England, the Scottish parliament in 1560 established Reformed Protestantism as the national religion. The Church of Scotland used a confession of faith drafted by Knox that incorporated Calvinist theology with a Presbyterian church organization. Presbyterianism, church governance by a community of pastors and lay elders, thus became a distinctive feature of the Reformed tradition in Scotland.

Elsewhere in Europe, Calvin had less influence. In France, his ideas spread rapidly among the Huguenots, despite repeated periods of persecution; and Calvin himself helped to produce a French Reformed creed approved as the Confession of La Rochelle by a Huguenot synod in 1571. The Reformed tradition also spread to Germany, but its effects were limited by Lutheranism's dominance of German Protestantism. The Reformed tradition diffused as well to Hungary, leading to the formation of the Hungarian Reformed Church, although Roman Catholicism remained Hungary's dominant faith. Finally, the Reformed tradition had a significant influence on the Puritan movement in England, which sought to reform a third major tradition arising from the Reformation, Anglicanism.

Anglicanism

The establishment of Anglicanism in 1534 occurred primarily for political reasons. Henry VIII had sought a papal annulment of his marriage to Catherine of Aragon, who had failed to produce a male heir. In 1533, lacking the pope's approval, Henry secretly married Anne Boleyn; and Thomas Cranmer, as archbishop of Canterbury, annulled Henry's marriage to Catherine. The pope declared Henry's new marriage to be illegitimate and excommunicated both Henry and Cranmer. Henry in turn acted to remove England from the jurisdiction of the Roman Catholic Church; and in 1534 the English parliament passed the Act of Supremacy, which declared Henry to be the supreme head of the Church of England. At its inception, the Church of England thus differed little from the Roman Catholic Church in terms of doctrine or practice. The first major changes occurred later in the 1530s, when the parliament dissolved the English monasteries and Cranmer persuaded Henry to order that a newly authorized English Bible be chained to an accessible location within every church. More significant doctrinal change occurred after Cranmer issued an Anglican liturgy, the *Book of Common Prayer*, in 1549. The first form of the liturgy received much criticism from supporters of reform, but a second version issued in 1552 had a more distinctly Protestant character. Changes incorporated into the second version included a rejection of the doctrine of transubstantiation, use of a communion table in place of the altar, and support for the doctrine of salvation through grace.

In 1553 the ascension to the English throne by Mary I resulted in the reestablishment of Roman Catholicism; but five years later she was succeed by Elizabeth I, and under her rule the Parliament restored the *Book of Common Prayer* as the sole source of religious practice in the Act of Uniformity of 1559. To ensure uniformity of belief and practice, the Church of England issued the *Thirty-Nine Articles of Religion* in 1571; and the parliament subsequently required acceptance of that document by all English clergy. The *Articles* asserted the basic Protestant principles of the authority of the Bible and salvation through grace, but in many specific matters they did not adhere solely to the views of any other school of Reformation thought. Regarding predestination, for example, the Anglican position accepted the role of divine choice, as in Calvinism, but focused only on the predestination of salvation, as in Lutheranism, rather than on the predestination of both salvation and damnation, again as in Calvinism. Anglicanism also retained certain aspects of Roman Catholic practice, including a centralized hierarchical structure and the use of all seven Roman Catholic sacraments, although the *Articles* identified only baptism and the Eucharist as essential. Anglicanism thus developed a stronger emphasis on liturgical ritual than did other Protestant traditions. Finally, in contrast to the Lutheran and Reformed churches, the Church of England remained under the jurisdiction of the English monarchy. Anglicanism thus did not spread to other areas until England began to establish overseas colonies.

*   *   *

The organization of new state churches articulating Lutheran, Calvinist, and Anglican principles represented one of the primary outcomes of the Reformation (map 3.7). This process reinforced the significance of these three major expressions of Reformation thought and at the same time contributed to the spatial diversification of Christian belief and practice. In addition to the state churches, however, the Reformation comprised a great variety of smaller movements. The rise of the predominant schools of Reformation thought produced an atmosphere conducive to further innovation in many places. This atmosphere of reform legitimized religious change, fostered the questioning of tradition, and in some contexts introduced the concept of freedom of religious conscience. The result was a proliferation of religious movements within the regions of Europe dominated by Protestantism. These smaller movements tended to fall into two broad categories: those seeking continuing reform within a larger Protestant church; and those seeking more radical reforms, rejecting certain elements of mainstream Reformation thought. Although the local influence of these movements varied considerably, they too added a significant dimension to the growing spatial diversity within Christianity.

Puritanism and Pietism

Puritanism in England exemplified efforts to reform established forms of Protestantism. The Puritans emerged during the sixteenth century as a diverse group seeking to purify Anglicanism by eliminating traditions rooted in Roman Catholicism. Most Puritans advocated a closer adherence to Calvinist teachings, a position supported by the experiences of those who had lived in exile in Geneva during the rule of Mary I. The Puritans specifically opposed practices that lacked a scriptural basis, including the episcopal structure of Anglican governance, the wearing of vestments by ministers, the use of the sign of the cross in baptism, and the ornamentation of churches. They supported a Calvinist interpretation of predestination and stressed the importance of conversion as a sign of membership among the elect. They further believed that Anglicanism's liturgical ritual should be replaced by biblically inspired preaching and a greater concern with personal morality. Some supported a church polity similar to that of the Church of Scotland, while others sought congregational independence rather than a national church.

The opposition of Anglican bishops to these reforms and the resulting persecution of reformers led a minority of Puritans, including some emigrants to North America, to abandon the idea of reforming Anglicanism and adopt the Separatist objective of forming their own church. Those who continued to seek reform within the Church of England gradually gained influence, however, particularly among the middle class and some members of the nobility. Growing Puritan strength in the English parliament led to civil war during the 1640s, resulting in the establishment of a Puritan Commonwealth under the rule of Oliver Cromwell. The Puritan parliament eliminated the authority of the bishops and approved the Westminster Confession of Faith, based on Calvinist theology. The Puritans banned the *Book of Common Prayer*, the celebration of Christmas (as a nonbiblical innovation), and the use of maypoles (as a pagan survival); and they sought to regulate public morality, for example by closing theaters, banning horse races, and making adultery a capital crime. After Cromwell's death in 1658, however, the Puritans lacked a sufficiently strong political leader to remain in power, and the English monarchy was restored two years later. During the 1660s, the parliament reestablished the episcopal Church of England, enforced conformity to the *Book of Common Prayer*, and banned religious assemblies outside the established church. The resulting persecution of dissenters ended in 1689 with the Toleration Act, but Anglicanism remained the state religion. Although the Puritans' attempt to reform the Church of England proved unsuccessful, some of them remained within the church while others formed distinct denominations.

Similar efforts at reform developed on the European mainland. The most influential of these movements, broadly known as Pietism, arose within German Lutheranism. It drew part of its inspiration from English Puritanism and in some ways resembled similar trends in the Netherlands, but it remained more Lutheran than Calvinist in orientation. Pietism developed essentially as a reaction against the increasing dogmatism and perceived moral laxity of Lutheranism in the 1600s. In place of the liturgical emphases of Lutheranism, it supported more immediate forms of religious experience. In particular, it stressed individual Bible study, personal morality, and good works as an expression of faith. Pietists also favored greater tolerance for differences of belief, an emphasis on devotional life in the training of ministers, a greater role for the laity in church governance, and a focus in preaching on promoting faith rather than articulating doctrine.

The early leader of the Pietist movement was Philipp Jakob Spener, a theologian who held various prominent positions in German Lutheran churches during the seventeenth century. Although strongly opposed by orthodox Lutheran theologians, Spener's ideas became widely influential, particular in northern Germany, and continued to influence German Lutheranism even after Pietism began to lose its identity as a Lutheran movement later in the 1700s. Spener influenced developments outside of Lutheranism as well. One of his followers, Count von Zinzendorf, in the 1720s provided refuge on his estate in Saxony to some of the remaining radical Hussites. There, the group reorganized as the Moravian Church, largely along Pietist lines, and became active in missionary activity throughout Protestant Europe and in North America. In the process, the Moravians influenced the leader of an eighteenth-century reform movement within the Church of England, John Wesley.

Wesley, an Anglican priest, had first organized a small study group to examine Christian teachings in 1729. Because of its methodical approach to attaining holiness, the group came to be known as the Methodists. After a period of missionary work in

North America, he became increasingly influenced by Moravian Pietism, resulting in a conversion experience in 1738 that convinced him of the personal nature of salvation. He subsequently became committed to preaching his new understanding of salvation by faith, which in contrast to the Calvinist doctrine of selective salvation by divine grace held that salvation was accessible to all believers, a view known as Arminianism. Wesley thus rejected predestination, and instead believed that the free will of believers played a role in their salvation. Wesley continued to consider himself an Anglican and sought to reform the Church of England from within. Therefore, while the church hierarchy rejected Wesley's ideas, he initially organized his followers into Methodist "societies" without splitting from the Church of England. In the late 1700s, however, he established the Methodist Church as a distinct denomination so that he could ordain ministers to serve Anglicans in the new United States. From that time, Methodism grew rapidly in the United States.

Radicals and Separatists

Alongside such efforts to reform the established Protestant churches, various groups advocated more radical interpretations of the Reformation. The Anabaptist movement played a particularly important role in this regard. It began in Zurich during the 1520s among radical reformers who found Zwingli's reforms to be too moderate. This group, later known as the Swiss Brethren, rejected any connection between church and state, including state collection of taxes or tithes to support the church. They instead sought to create a "gathered church" of believers who had fully accepted the teachings of the New Testament and had deliberately sought membership in the Brethren. Because they believed that the acceptance of faith could occur only in adulthood, through free will, they further opposed infant baptism, which was widely practiced by both Protestants and Roman Catholics. The rejection of infant baptism led early adherents to be baptized a second time, as adults, as they joined the Swiss Brethren, producing the term *Anabaptist* or baptized again. The Swiss Brethren also departed from Reformed orthodoxy in their belief in free will and rejection of predestination, and they opposed military service and the swearing of oaths as un-Christian.

These beliefs led to the persecution of the Swiss Brethren in Zurich, and most migrated to other parts of Europe where similar groups were emerging at this time. Anabaptist refugees from Switzerland and southern Germany, for example, formed a distinct group in Tyrol and Moravia in the late 1520s. Known as the Hutterites, from its early leader Jakob Hutter, this group adhered to a distinctive belief in the communal ownership of property. They faced severe persecution in Austria during the 1500s and were expelled from Moravia in the early 1600s, resettling in various parts of Eastern Europe and Russia before migrating to North America during the 1800s. In the Netherlands and northern Germany, Anabaptist groups also appeared during the early 1500s. Anabaptist thought in this region initially contained a significant millennial component, which served as the basis for an Anabaptist rebellion in the city of Münster in 1534. The rebels declared the city to be the New Jerusalem where the kingdom of God would be established; but the Roman Catholic bishop of Münster, the city's feudal ruler, recaptured the city in 1535 and executed the Anabaptist leaders. These events also provoked a significant increase in the persecution of Anabaptists elsewhere as local rulers came to see them as political threats as well as heretics. Anabaptists thus distanced themselves from the Münster rebellion and consequently millennialism no longer played a major role in Anabaptist thought. In addition, they sought to maintain a more inconspicuous presence within society (photo 3.7). Menno Simons, a Dutch Roman Catholic priest who converted to Anabaptism in 1536, became the leader of a new Anabaptist movement, the Mennonites, which explicitly embraced pacifism and rejected involvement in politics. This movement grew rapidly in the 1600s and 1700s, but continuing opposition caused many to emigrate to Russia and later to North America. Various divisions also occurred among the Mennonites, giving rise for example to the stricter Amish in the late 1600s.

Radical approaches to reform also developed in England during the 1600s, partly through the influence of the Anabaptist movement. Puritan Separatists, who sought to establish a church outside the Church of England, faced significant persecution in the early 1600s; and many went into exile in the more tolerant Netherlands, where they encountered other expressions of radical reform, including Anabaptism. One such exile was John Smyth, a former Anglican priest, whose contacts with Mennonites convinced him of the illegitimacy of infant baptism. Most of his followers eventually became Mennonites, but those who did not returned to England and founded the first Baptist church. The Baptists differed most clearly from Separatist

Photo 3.7. Former Mennonite church and cemetery in Friedrichstadt, Germany. The local Mennonite congregation acquired the building in the mid-1600s; but in keeping with their ethos of simplicity and separateness, they did not restructure the plain exterior of the building to indicate the religious use of its interior space. This strategy of inconspicuousness appeared in many Anabaptist churches in the period following the failed Münster rebellion of the 1530s. Friedrichstadt, Germany, 2007.

Source: Dirk Ingo Franke (commons.wikimedia.org/wiki/Image:Friedrichstadt_mennonitenkirche_und_al te_boerse.jpg), under Creative Commons license (creativecommons.org/licenses/by-sa/2.5/).

Puritans in the matter of baptism, which they believed should be administered only to those who had declared their faith and should involve immersion of the adherent. In addition, these early Baptists espoused the Arminian view that salvation was accessible to any believer. Over time, however, this view was rejected by some Baptists, who held to the Calvinist view that Jesus had atoned only for the sins of the predestined elect. Those holding the Arminian view came to be known as General Baptists and those holding the Calvinist view Particular Baptists. Both groups grew rapidly during the 1600s, but ultimately became far more successful in the United States.

Puritan Separatism in England also contributed to the rise of Congregationalism. The Congregationalists were English Calvinists who believed, like the Baptists, that church governance should be strictly local in character. Not all Congregationalists were Separatists; some, including Cromwell, sought to impose their form of church polity on the Church of England. Separatist Congregationalists, however, strictly adhered to the concept of the gathered church of true believers. In colonial Massachusetts, the Pilgrims of Plymouth Bay were Separatist Congregationalists, the Puritans of Massachusetts Bay non-Separatist Congregationalists. Perhaps the most radical reform movement of seventeenth-century England, finally, was the Society of Friends, or Quakers. The Quakers rejected all attempts at reform within existing organized Christianity. They asserted instead that Christian belief and practice should focus on a direct relationship with God unmediated by clergy or sacraments. Like the Anabaptists, they were pacifists and would not swear oaths. They faced intense persecution in England, from Puritans and Anglicans alike, but had a strong influence in colonial Pennsylvania.

*   *   *

The Reformation thus produced complex changes within the religious character of the Protestant regions of Europe, introducing new state churches often closely linked to national identity while at the same time increasing religious diversity through the rise of distinct sectarian movements. The Reformation influenced Roman Catholicism as well through its impact on the Counter-Reformation of the 1500s and early 1600s. The various trends that comprised the Counter-Reformation, in fact, represented more than just a response to Protestantism. The standardization of the liturgy and of procedures for canonizing saints, for example, grew out of older concerns for uniformity within Roman Catholicism, as discussed above. Nonetheless, the Reformation likely contributed to Roman Catholic responses to abuses within the church, as in the decision to outlaw the sale of indulgences in 1567. And the Reformation clearly provoked the statements of Roman Catholic belief issued by the Council of Trent, documented as a series of anathemas against those who would deny given doctrines. Finally, the diversification of Christianity in Europe continued into later times as well. New Protestant denominations continued to develop, for example, as did local diversity within the practice of Roman Catholicism.[54]

At the same time, geographical patterns of diversification continued to arise through the expansion of Christianity beyond Europe and adjacent areas, first to the Americas and then to Africa and Asia. A wide variety of innovations developed through these processes of diffusion, too many for a comprehensive survey here. The following discussion therefore focuses on some significant examples of the ways in which adherents have articulated Christianity in particular contexts during its diffusion to diverse regions in recent centuries. Together, these examples address two central themes: the ongoing integration of Christianity into specific cultural and political settings, and the interactions between Christianity and other religious traditions.

Christianity in the Americas

The development of Christianity in the United States clearly reveals the significance of the first of these themes. During the colonial period the Church of England was legally established at some point in all of the southern colonies and Puritanism functioned as a state church in Massachusetts. Nonetheless, through the migration of various religious groups during the colonial period, the United States already contained a degree of religious diversity by the time of independence. With the constitutional proscription against the legal establishment of religion, that diversity became fully integrated into the structure of American society. Churches that in Europe had depended on state support now relied exclusively on the support of their members, and smaller churches now existed on an equal footing with those that had dominated different parts of Europe. At the same time, organized religion in its various forms, predominantly Protestant, remained a central institution within American society, serving as the focus of communal activity and social identity. Through these trends, a strong tradition of religious voluntarism developed within the United States. One consequence of that tradition was the denominationalism of American Protestantism in which no single group dominated and different churches competed with one another for members. Such competition strongly favored the evangelical denominations, those that actively sought new members through missionary work. The impact of evangelical groups was furthered by periods of widespread religious revival within the United States, typically within contexts of significant social change, during which heightened popular interest in religion resulted in rapid church growth. The Baptists and Methodists, and to a lesser extent the Disciples of Christ and Presbyterians, achieved dramatic increases in membership through revivalism on the American frontier during the early 1800s. As a result, the Baptists and Methodists became the nation's largest Protestant groups, in clear contrast to membership patterns in Protestant Europe. Revivalism among the growing urban populations of the late 1800s and early 1900s similarly led to growth in various conservative Protestant churches, including those of the new Holiness and Pentecostal movements. Finally, American society generally maintained higher levels of religious activity than did European societies, including foreign missionary work.

The tradition of religious voluntarism in the United States also contributed to the frequent division of existing groups into separate denominations, a process that over time produced hundreds of distinct denominations and independent churches. In some instances, these divisions contained a significant social dimension. Prior to the Civil War, for example, the major Baptist, Methodist, and Presbyterian denominations each split into separate northern and southern bodies. More often, though, denominational divisions had a religious foundation. By the late 1800s, for example, several major evangelical denominations became increasingly divided between conservative and liberal factions. Many liberals challenged the traditional doctrine of biblical inerrancy. Instead, liberals argued, the Bible should be reinterpreted in terms of contemporary thought and the findings of modern science. Liberal rejection of the biblical account of creation became an especially significant point of contention. By this time, many conservative evangelicals had also adopted the doctrine of dispensational millennialism, which asserted that the millennium during which Jesus would rule on earth was close at hand. Liberal evangelicals, whose worldview increasingly de-emphasized supernatural elements, rejected this doctrine. Because of these disputes, conservatives among the Northern Baptists, Northern Presbyterians, and Disciples of Christ split off from their parent bodies to form new denominations. This outcome underscored a significant regional contrast within evangelical Protestantism between a more liberal North and a more conservative South. It also led to the rise of a Christian fundamentalist movement within the United States. Crossing denominational boundaries, the fundamentalist movement comprised conservative Protestants who believed that modernism and secularism in American culture posed a threat to fundamental Christian values and beliefs.[55]

The American tradition of religious voluntarism also contributed to an atmosphere of religious pluralism that supported the continuing introduction of new forms of belief and practice. Immigrants were free to reproduce their own religious traditions after arriving in the United States, although non-Protestants often initially faced various forms of discrimination. The vast immigration from continental Europe thus introduced many different forms of European Christianity and significantly expanded the presence of Roman Catholicism. In this context, the Roman Catholic Church had to adapt to being viewed as one denomination among many. Moreover, while most immigrant groups formed church structures independent of their homeland, Roman Catholics remained under the ultimate spiritual jurisdiction of the pope. This situation gradually produced various tensions over issues such as birth control, abortion, divorce, and clerical celibacy as American adherents began to adopt positions inconsistent with Roman Catholic doctrine.

In addition to fostering immigrant churches, the atmosphere of religious pluralism has supported the development of new religious movements within the United States.[56] The Disciples of Christ became the first major indigenous denomination during the early 1800s, a product of frontier revivalism and efforts to organize a simpler form of Christianity based directly on the New Testament. As the nineteenth century progressed, newly formed American denominations included such distinctive groups as the Mormons, Seventh-Day Adventists, Christian Scientists, and Jehovah's Witnesses. The Holiness movement, characterized by belief in the sanctification of true converts, also produced numerous denominations during the late 1800s. Similarly, many denominations arose in the early 1900s from the Pentecostal movement, sharing the belief that, following conversion, spiritual baptism by the Holy Spirit could give adherents the ability to heal, prophesy, speak in unknown tongues, or exorcise evil. In addition to major groups like the Assemblies of God and the Church of God in Christ, Pentecostalism gave rise to a large number of local denominations and independent churches. Most of the indigenous denominations founded in the United States shared a significant commitment to proselytism, clearly a necessary trait for them to compete with religious organizations having a longer institutional history. As a result, the indigenous denominations have also contributed substantially to the distinctive emphasis in the United States on foreign missions.

Equally distinctive characteristics emerged within Christianity in Latin America, but in response to different social circumstances. The initial diffusion of Christianity to Latin America established the Roman Catholic Church as a dominant cultural institution, a privileged position that brought it considerable wealth and political influence during the colonial period. As a result, Roman Catholicism became widely integrated into the region's colonial cultures. One expression of this process was the emergence of indigenous shrines and saints, such as Our Lady of Guadalupe and St. Rose of Lima. Within various Latin American countries distinctive rituals also took on national importance. One prominent example of this process was the development of the Day of the Dead in Mexico, which mixes traditional folk practices commemorating the dead with a significant nationalist element.[57]

At the same time, the cultural hegemony of Roman Catholicism contributed to the development of syncretistic religions among persons of African descent, particularly in Brazil and the Caribbean, where Africans were most heavily concentrated.[58] These religions were basically instrumental in character, focusing on the immediate problems of daily life. Within this context they often preserved traditional animistic practices by linking them with the Roman Catholic veneration of saints, attributing African and Christian names to the same supernatural being. These religions also drew on both African and Roman Catholic ritual and in some cases related African traditions of revelation to analogous traditions within Roman Catholicism.

In Cuba, the most common form of syncretism became known as Santeria. It fashioned a Roman Catholic framework around the traditions of the Yoruba people regarding the worship of orishas, animistic deities associated with forces of nature and human concerns. Santeria worship retained African elements such as spirit possession, divination, and propitiatory animal sacrifice but linked these practices to the veneration of particular Roman Catholic saints. Specific associations included St. Peter with Ogun, the Yoruba god of war; St. Barbara with Shango, god of fire and lightning; St. Francis of Assisi with Orunmila, god of wisdom and divination; and Our Lady of Charity, the patron saint of Cuba, with Oshun, goddess of love and marriage. Adherents recognized their link to Christianity and typically were baptized Roman Catholics, but the Roman Catholic hierarchy strongly opposed the practice of Santeria. It thus remained an expression of folk religion in Cuba and among Cuban emigrants to the United States, although in the 1990s some adherents proposed organizing a Yoruba Catholic Church. A similar syncretistic sect emerged as Vodou in Haiti, although it drew on a somewhat broader variety of African tribal traditions. Brazil produced a variety of syncretistic religions, often collectively labeled as Macumba, that combine African and Roman Catholic elements to varying degrees. Candomblé, concentrated in northeastern Brazil, most closely resembled Santeria and Vodou. An urban sect, Umbanda, has become especially influential in Brazil over the past century, mixing African, Roman Catholic, and Native American elements with nineteenth-century French spiritualism.

The hegemony of the Roman Catholic Church in Latin America had other consequences as well. During the colonial period the wealth and influence of the Roman Catholic Church tied its interests to those of ruling elites. After independence, the political and economic power of the Roman Catholic Church declined, but it maintained its alliance with the ruling classes as a means of preserving its social influence. The resulting conservatism of the church hierarchy contributed to the disaffection of many adherents who subsequently converted to various forms of evangelical Protestantism, primarily deriving from the United States. Within Roman Catholicism, on the other hand, disaffection with the church's traditional conservatism gave rise to a significant reinterpretation of its role in Latin American society, characterized as liberation theology. This movement originated in the 1960s among Latin American clergy who asserted that the church should focus on the problems of the poor. The supporters of liberation theology linked concern for the poor to the core teachings of the New Testament, but they also believed in the particular relevance of this concern to the Roman Catholic Church in Latin America because so many of its adherents in fact lived in poverty. They argued that Roman Catholicism in Latin American differed in this regard from Roman Catholicism in Europe or North America. The liberation theologians questioned the ability of the conservative church hierarchy to address the structural sources of inequality in Latin American society, and so instead they supported the development of popular church structures aligned to the people's needs. At the center of that effort were the so-called base communities, small groups of lay adherents that combined Bible study with practical attention to the basic material needs of members. The base communities manifested a core tenet of liberation theology: that the Roman Catholic Church should place less emphasis on doctrinal orthodoxy and instead stress orthopraxy through the enactment of Christian ideals. Although many local clergy accepted the relevance of liberation theology to Roman Catholicism in the developing countries, the church hierarchy generally opposed the movement, concluding that it drew too heavily on Marxism and neglected the church's primary focus on spiritual salvation. Despite opposition from the church hierarchy, however, liberation theology remains a distinctive feature of Roman Catholicism in Latin America.

Christianity in Africa

In addition to the United States and Latin America, Africa has seen the development of distinctive expressions of Christianity, particularly over the past century. Despite an early period of Roman Catholic missionary activity, African conversions to Christianity did not become widespread until the period of European colonialism beginning in the late 1800s. European and American churches originally dominated this process, but African Christians began to establish their own distinct denominations early in the colonial era, a pattern that became increasingly common in the twentieth century. This process of religious innovation in part represented a response to European colonial hegemony, serving as a means of reconstituting newly introduced cultural models in locally meaningful forms. At the same time, it reflected indigenous efforts to assert control within changing social contexts, such as urbanization, that inhibited adherence to traditional religions. The denominations formed by Africans were first collectively described as "African Independent Churches" (or AICs), but some adherents reject that label as it implicitly defines these bodies in relation to non-African churches, and instead describe them as "African Instituted Churches." The AICs are primarily Protestant in orientation. A few closely resemble the varieties of Protestantism established by European and American missionaries, but most comprise more distinctly African interpretations of Christian tradition. They generally share a strong emphasis on experiential religion, particularly in forms consistent with biblical narratives and older indigenous customs, such as prophecy, revelation, and healing.[59]

Among the different types of AICs, the most common are the Holy Spirit churches, so called because of their Pentecostal emphasis on baptism in the Holy Spirit, a practice that in some ways corresponds to indigenous beliefs in spirit possession. Most Holy Spirit churches are based on the revelatory experiences of a founder-prophet. They typically practice enthusiastic forms of worship, such as singing and dancing, which focus on the workings of the Holy Spirit. They also emphasize healing, divination, prophecy, and other expressions of Pentecostalism. Many of these churches have established their own holy cities to serve as pilgrimage centers for those seeking healing. They tend as well to profess a legalistic ethos, banning certain forms of behavior such as the consumption of alcohol and tobacco and, in some churches, the traditional practice of polygamy. Finally, the Holy Spirit churches strongly condemn witchcraft, along with many other traditional religious practices, but in general they do not deny the efficacy of witchcraft in inciting evil spirits. In response, they therefore practice exorcism through the Holy Spirit. The Holy Spirit churches are generally limited in their geographical extent. Among the largest are the Aladura ("Prayer") churches in western Africa and the Zionist churches in southern Africa. More local examples include the African Israel Church Nineveh in Kenya and the Musama Disco Christo Church ("Army of the Cross of Christ") in Ghana.

A second category of AICs includes the various non-Pentecostal prophetic churches. These churches in some ways resemble the Holy Spirit churches, in some instances incorporating healing and the creation of a distinct holy city into their belief system; but they do not practice most Pentecostal forms of worship. They also frequently place a stronger emphasis on ethical behavior, and are less likely than the Holy Spirit churches to allow traditional forms of polygamy or ceremonial dance. The leading movement in this category, Kimbanguism (named for its founder-prophet, Simon Kimbangu), is the largest single AIC with more than three million members, mainly in Central Africa.

Ethiopianism represents a third category of AICs. It draws its name from biblical references to Ethiopia and the early Christian kingdom of Ethiopia, which adherents cite as evidence of the legitimacy of African institutions. The distinguishing characteristic of Ethiopianism is the explicit assertion that Africans should control their own churches. The churches within this movement generally originated by separating from colonial missionary churches, and thus theologically they tend to resemble their parent denominations. In practice, however, they have sought to promote an African identity through the preservation of cultural traditions like polygamy.

Finally, a fourth significant group of AICs are the syncretistic churches, which combine Christian elements with a traditional African worldview and ethos. Many of these churches have retained some aspects of ancestor worship, for example. Syncretistic churches have also preserved traditional forms of ritual dancing in their worship practices, but recast as representations of New Testament events. One prominent syncretistic group, the Bwiti movement in Gabon and Cameroon, has retained the use of the iboga plant to induce visions of Jesus, Mary, and the Christian saints as well as dead and revered ancestors. In recent decades, however, many of the syncretistic churches have given greater attention to more orthodox Christian beliefs and practices.

*   *   *

As the preceding examples illustrate, in sum, the diffusion of Christianity in recent centuries has been accompanied by ongoing processes of innovation and contextualization, a pattern that has in fact developed over two millennia. As Christianity has emerged as the world's largest religious tradition, believers have continually reproduced it in reference to their own local circumstances. For many adherents, of course, this process of reproduction has been largely unreflective, involving the observance of received traditions within the framework of Christian practice. For many others, though, the obligations of faith have included attention to the legitimacy and relevance of their particular forms of worship. Within Christianity, the questioning of belief and practice has generally developed around a key set of related issues, including the meaning of salvation, the basis for religious authority, the relative importance of religious ritual versus religious experience, the meaning of the church, and the relationship between church and state. Christian efforts to define, or redefine, orthodoxy and orthopraxy have been most obviously the work of theologians and other church leaders, and the insights of such individuals should not be discounted in understanding the diversification that has occurred within Christianity. Nonetheless, these thinkers have developed within and been shaped by particular social and cultural contexts and their efforts have been successful only to the extent that they have resonated with larger groups of adherents. The major divisions within Christianity thus often derive from abstract theological differences, but they also reflect geographical variations in believers' acceptance of particular understandings of Christian tradition.

As Christianity has diversified, it has differed from the other major proselytic religions in the particular importance that adherents have placed on the character and organization of formal institutional structures. This organizational emphasis has taken different forms within the three major branches of Christianity, however. Roman Catholicism has maintained the concept of a single, universal church under a common hierarchy of leaders. Sustaining that unity remains a principal objective of the Roman Catholic Church, which has thus emphasized the concepts of authority and doctrinal orthodoxy. Local variations in the practice of Roman Catholicism have been accepted by the church hierarchy, as in the veneration of local saints, but only when they are consistent with Roman Catholic doctrine. This approach has produced a constant tension in the Roman Catholic Church between local and universal elements. By controlling that tension, however, the church hierarchy has preserved the Roman Catholic Church as a unified organization spread across highly varied contexts. The organizational context of Eastern Orthodoxy, in contrast, has followed a less centralized pattern. This decentralization originated in the tradition of equality among the early Orthodox patriarchs, but it acquired a national character as Eastern Orthodoxy spread through the organization of new churches to serve the needs of specific language groups. Leaders of the Orthodox churches continued to seek uniformity within the tradition, which they maintained primarily through common use of the Byzantine Rite liturgy, albeit in different languages. The diversity within Eastern Orthodoxy therefore became institutionalized along cultural lines. Lastly, Protestantism has yielded a highly particular pattern of institutional structures, partly based on the formation of national churches, but deriving more generally from hermeneutic disagreements as to the meanings of Christianity. The church structures of Protestantism tend to assert difference and distinctiveness in place of the universality of Roman Catholicism or the looser cohesion of Eastern Orthodoxy. Indeed, the consequent proliferation of separate church bodies represents one of the distinguishing features of regions where Protestantism predominates. The diversification of Christianity has thus emerged within three contrasting organizational contexts, each accommodating diversity in different ways. The result has been a complex variety of interactions between Christianity and the places where it is practiced.

Islam

The processes of geographical diversification within Islam have differed somewhat from corresponding processes within the other major proselytic religions. In part these differences reflect the more recent emergence of Islam and the more immediate documentation of its historical beginnings. Most importantly, the canonical form of the Quran was widely accepted at an early date, as were many of the basic components of Islamic orthodoxy. The rapid articulation of Islam as a religious system therefore precluded to some degree the sorts of theological and philosophical debates that emerged during the early centuries of Buddhism and Christianity. Muslims were further united through the concept of the Islamic umma, the community of believers, and through participation in the Hajj. At the same time, Islam lacked the institutional structures that became central to Buddhism and Christianity. Islam has no ordained clergy, based on rejection of the need for an intermediary between the adherent and God, nor does it have a tradition of organized monasticism. It also did not develop governance structures to regulate religious practice. As a result, diversification within Islam has generally been less schismatic than within Buddhism and Christianity, although the division between Sunni and Shia Islam represents a significant exception. Instead, processes of diversification have more often arisen from variations in the reading of a shared orthodoxy or the accretion of local practices. Such variations have tended to focus on three broad concerns: sources of authority within the Islamic tradition, the interpretation of Islamic law, and forms of Islamic worship. The issue of authority has produced the sharpest divisions, while Muslims have commonly accepted the legitimacy of different methods of interpreting Islamic law. Variations in worship practices have occasionally produced tensions between movements seeking orthodox reform among local communities of believers, but in the absence of formal structures of religious governance such tensions have typically gone unresolved.

The major schism within Islam, between the Sunni and Shia branches, occurred early on in a dispute over authority. All Muslims accept the Quran as the primary source of authority in Islam, but the early Muslim community became divided over the issue of human authority, specifically in reference to leadership of the umma following Muhammad's death. The majority, later known as Sunnis ("Traditionalists"), asserted that the umma should elect Muhammad's successor, the caliph, who would provide both secular and religious leadership. The Sunnis chose Abu Bakr, a member of Muhammad's Quraysh tribe, as the companion of the prophet most capable of preserving unity among the umma. A minority faction argued, however, that Muhammad had designated as his successor his cousin and son-in-law Ali, a choice that conformed to Arab patterns of hereditary leadership; and thus they supported Ali as their Imam or leader. This group came to be known as the Shiites, or "Partisans" of Ali. Shiite leaders initially accepted Abu Bakr as caliph to prevent division within the umma and the Sunnis eventually accepted Ali as their fourth caliph in 656. Nonetheless, the two groups remained divided over the concept of leadership and Ali was the only caliph whose legitimacy was fully recognized by both sides. The final break between the two groups came in 680 through conflict between Yazid, the sixth elected caliph, and Husayn, son of Ali and Muhammad's daughter Fatima. Husayn rejected the election of Yazid and left Mecca with his family and followers to seek refuge in the Mesopotamian city of Kufa, where Shiites had become a majority. Sunni forces pursued and massacred Husayn's party, however. The massacre of Husayn provoked two Kufan rebellions against the Sunnis, but both were suppressed. Together, these events reflected a significant polarization within the Muslim world and marked the beginnings of Shiism as a separate branch of Islam.

Early conflicts over leadership of the umma, in addition to dividing Shiites from Sunnis, also gave rise to a third, much smaller group, the Kharijites ("Seceders"). This group comprised former supporters of Ali who took exception to his negotiated peace with Syrian Sunnis who had opposed his election as caliph. The Kharijites viewed this compromise as un-Quranic and as a result they rejected both Ali and his opponents. Most of the early Kharijites were killed in 658 during a rebellion against Ali, but the movement persisted in southern Iraq and gradually spread to more remote areas, including Oman, the East African coast, and the interior of Algeria. Over time, the Kharijites developed a distinctive form of Islam incorporating a strict ethos of piety and a democratic polity. They rejected all caliphs except the first three, but believed that any spiritually perfect Muslim could serve as Imam. In selecting an Imam, they believed that divine will was expressed through the free will of the umma. They viewed proselytism as an obligation and treated any deviation from Quranic behavior as apostasy. Over time the Kharijite movement divided into numerous sects. The most extreme of these, the Azariqa, advocated death for all non-Kharijite Muslims and their families, but more moderate sects advocated greater tolerance toward other forms of Islam and forbade the killing of non-Kharijites. One such sect, the Ibadites, represents the only surviving Kharijite group.

Most of the Muslim world, however, remained divided between Sunni and Shia, and the further development of diverse forms of Islam took place primarily within these two branches. The two developed differently, however. Sunni Islam remained broadly unified. While Sunni Muslims came to interpret Islamic tradition in a variety of ways and reproduced Islamic practices differently, such diversity continued within a larger, often implicit concept of the Muslim umma. Shiism, on the other hand, was more schismatic. The sectarianism of Shiism arose partly from its minority status, which fostered more explicit concerns with identity among its adherents than among the Sunni majority. The Shiites' focus on meanings attached to the succession of leadership also repeatedly gave rise to divisions, however.

Sunni Islam

Within Sunnism, the persistence of the Abbasid dynasty of caliphs from the eighth to the sixteenth century nominally contributed to the sense of commonality shared by the Sunni umma. Over time, however, the religious influence of the Abbasid caliphs declined. After the fall of the Abbasid Empire in the tenth century, the caliphs lost political control as they came under the rule of various secular dynasties; and their influence declined further after the Mamluk Empire relocated the caliphate to Cairo in the 1200s. By the early 1500s, when the Ottoman sultans assumed the title of caliph, the office no longer represented a primary source of religious leadership. Sunni religious authority had instead become more decentralized, exercised primarily through local religious jurists, or *qadis*, serving under secular rulers. As this pattern developed, the methodology of legal interpretation became a major issue within Sunni Islam. Concern with the latter issue in turn contributed to the spatial diversification of Sunnism through variations in adherence to particular schools of Islamic law. A variety of distinct legal schools developed early in Sunni history, but only four attained enduring influence. All four emerged during the eighth and ninth centuries, primarily from the work of scholars in Baghdad, Medina, and Cairo. Again, the rise of these schools did not lead to overt schisms within Sunnism, as the legitimacy of each school came to be recognized by followers of the others. Through popular support and the influence of local qadis and secular rulers, however, individual schools came to dominate Sunni practice in particular regions (map 3.9).

Sunni Legal Schools

The emergence of the first two schools took place as the Sunni community expanded to include significant non-Arab populations. In the process, Muslim society formed a distinction between Arabs and non-Arab converts.[60] Because of their secondary status,

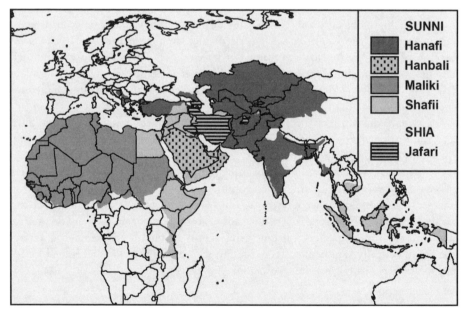

Map 3.9. Distribution of predominant Islamic legal traditions, including the four Sunni legal schools and the Jafari tradition of Twelver Shiism. More than one tradition may be present in an area but one usually dominates. Most Sunnis recognize the validity of schools other than the one that they follow.

non-Arabs faced various social and economic disadvantages and many were in fact attracted to Shiism as a reaction against the Arab majority. Non-Arab Sunnis, however, incorporated concerns with their status into their view of religious law, which they sought to reconcile with their own traditions. Such efforts produced the Hanafi school, which derived from the teachings of Abu Hanifa, an eighth-century scholar from Kufa. The Hanafis acknowledged the primary authority in legal matters of the Quran and the hadith, but they also accepted the local role of legal reasoning by analogy and the qadi's use of personal judgment in matters not covered by precedent. Abu Hanifa argued in effect that legal rulings should take local circumstances into account. In his view the rulings that applied to desert nomads, for example, might be inappropriate when applied to an urban society. He thus concluded that the qadi should rule based on the spirit of the sharia rather than on its literal interpretation, particularly when the latter would contradict local traditions. As one example, within the socially diverse context of urban Mesopotamia, Hanafi judges promoted social stability by enforcing the local tradition that allowed marriage only between social equals, even though this practice did not have a specific Quranic source.[61] By permitting the incorporation of local custom into the administration of sharia, the Hanafi school facilitated the incorporation of non-Arab societies into the Sunni umma. The Hanafi school eventually became the official system of religious law employed by the Abbasid caliphs. In later centuries, the Hanafi school served as the legal system of the Seljuk and Ottoman empires and it spread eastward into other Turkic Muslim states in Central and South Asia. In all of these regions it remains the most influential legal school.

Within the Arab communities of the Hejaz, in contrast, the rival Maliki school prevailed. Its founder, the eighth-century Medinan scholar Malik ibn Anas, deemphasized individual judgment and discretion in interpreting the sharia. Instead, he focused on the practices of the Muslim community of Medina, which could trace its origins to Muhammad, as a source of insight into the law. Only if the Quran and the established consensus in Medina did not provide a solution did Malik allow for the use of individual reasoning by the qadi. He further asserted that legal rulings must reflect the qadi's understanding of the intentions of Quranic injunctions concerning the common welfare. In emphasizing the primacy of communal consensus in Medina, the Maliki school in effect incorporated various Arab customs into its reading of Islamic law. Again using marriage as an example, the Maliki legal school followed Arab tradition in insisting that the parents or guardians of those to be married must approve of the union, a practice that the Hanafis did not follow. The Maliki school diffused widely beyond its hearth in Medina, particularly into North Africa as part of the spread of Arab culture with the expansion of the Islamic empire. A major center of Maliki thought thus developed in the Tunisian city of Kairouan by the ninth century. Although various legal schools were introduced into Spain, the Maliki school prevailed there as well through popular support. The Almoravid dynasty that arose in Morocco during the eleventh century further reinforced the regional dominance of the Maliki school.[62] Since that time, the Maliki school has remained dominant throughout Muslim Africa except in the lower Nile Valley and some eastern coastal areas. Although it dominated parts of the Arabian Peninsula early in its development, it has remained the principal legal school only in Kuwait and Bahrain.

The contrasting perspectives of the Hanafi and Maliki schools initially led the

adherents of each to challenge the other's validity. This source of division was reconciled through the teachings of Muhammad al-Shafii, the founder of the third major
legal school. In early ninth-century Cairo, al-Shafii undertook a synthesis of Islamic
legal traditions, systematized by his followers as the Shafii school. Al-Shafii identified
four valid sources for Islamic law: the Quran; the Sunna, or traditions associated with
Muhammad as revealed in hadith; *ijma*, the consensus of scholars; and *qiyas*, reasoning
by analogy based on the Quran and hadith. He did not accept the Malikis' emphasis
on prevailing customs in Medina, and he placed less emphasis on juridical discretion
in regard to local custom than did the Hanafis. He did, however, recognize the possibility of different applications of the sharia based on legitimate sources. His definition
of the four sources of law, which became widely accepted by Sunnis, thus provided a
framework within which different legal schools could exist without denying one
another's legitimacy. The Shafii school subsequently flourished in Cairo and the lower
Nile Valley, and from that hearth it gradually spread eastward. It also spread throughout Arabia, replacing the Maliki school as the primary legal tradition into the eighteenth century. It was particularly important in southern and eastern Arabia, where it
remains influential. From Egypt and Arabia the Shafii school also diffused along the
east-central coast of Africa, and from these locations it spread via maritime trade routes
to Southeast Asia, where it became the primary legal school.

The fourth major school of Islamic law developed partially as a reaction against
the accommodating perspectives of the Shafiis. It derived from the teachings of Ahmad
ibn Hanbal, a ninth-century scholar from Baghdad, who wholly rejected the legitimacy of personal opinion and communal tradition in the interpretation of religious
law. Ibn Hanbal argued that legal rulings must depend solely upon the Quran and
hadith; other approaches, in his view, would lead to inauthentic innovations. His followers used his teachings as the foundation for the most literalist legal school, but they
had little early success in competing with the more established schools. The Hanbali
school achieved a measure of influence in Iraq and Syria during the early medieval
period, but it existed essentially as a sectarian movement separate from the larger
Sunni community.[63] It became more fully developed, however, when it was adopted
by the Wahhabi movement in central Arabia during the eighteenth century, as discussed below. The strict literalism of the Hanbalis accorded well with the Wahhabi
emphasis on Islamic authenticity and strict adherence to the Quran. Through the
spread of Wahhabi influence, the Hanbali school supplanted the other legal schools as
Saudi Arabia came into being, and it also became the dominant legal school in Qatar
and Oman.

As the major legal schools spread to different regions, they became integral to
local expressions of Sunni practice. Beginning in the tenth century, they acquired an
important, local institutional role through the establishment of madrassas, religious
schools in which scholars, or ulama, taught Islamic law, theology, Arabic grammar,
theology, and other subjects.[64] Through the bonds that developed between the ulama
and their students, madrassas came to define the religious identity of the communities
that they served. In addition, the madrassas were typically funded by an endowment,
or *waqf*, consisting of income-producing donations from local supporters. Donors
often retained control over properties granted to the waqf, allowing families to avoid
the subdivision of estates mandated by Islamic laws of inheritance.[65] The latter practice
reinforced the ties between donors and the madrassas, while giving the ulama a mea-

sure of economic influence within their communities. The ulama also played a central role in local mosques and charitable institutions, and those who served in the role of qadi oversaw the local administration of justice. The integration of the madrassas and ulama into local social structures thus produced significant relationships between the legal schools and Sunni communities. As a result, the legal schools gradually evolved into broader religious movements that attained widespread popular support and involvement; and the influence of the legal schools extended into many dimensions of local social life. The local dominance of particular legal schools thus became a key expression of the spatial diversification within Sunnism as a cultural system.

Alongside the broader regional divergence in the influence of the major legal schools, the spatial diversification within Sunni Islam developed as well through the emergence of a variety of local and regional religious movements. Again, such movements generally did not arise as overt schisms within Sunnism. They instead represented distinctive articulations of received Sunni tradition, defined by their particular interpretations of religious authority, authenticity, and experience. In most cases these movements produced distinctive patterns of individual religious practice, but they frequently had significant effects as well on society and the state. They thus represent a major source of the contextuality of Sunnism and more generally of Islam as a whole.

Sufism

Perhaps the most influential factor in this process of contextualization was the rise of Sufism as a distinct expression of Islam.[66] The term *Sufism* in fact comprises a diverse array of institutions, practices, and organizations. Although the various manifestations of Sufism share certain historical connections and metaphysical concepts, they differ in many ways and typically have strong connections to the particular contexts in which they are practiced. Sufism most likely derives its name from the Arabic word *suf* ("wool"), after the woolen garments of early Sufis. The movement originated partly as a response to the great success of the early Islamic empire, whose rapid expansion had led many Muslims to focus more on temporal concerns than on issues of faith. Early Sufis thus perceived a conflict between the worldliness of the new political order and the religiosity of the original Muslim community. Even in religious matters, the rapid growth of Islamic society led to a predominant emphasis on matters of religious law rather than faith. The early Sufis did not reject the sharia, but they asserted the importance of more direct forms of religious experience rather than simple adherence to the law. Basra emerged as the center of this movement during the seventh and eighth centuries, particularly through the teachings of Hasan al-Basri, who promoted an ethos of humility based on the fear of divine judgment, an important theme in the Quran. Al-Basri taught that Muslims should put aside worldly concerns and commit themselves to a life of ascetic devotion to God. This combination of asceticism and devotionalism was further advanced during the eighth century by Rabia al-Adawiyya, a leading female Sufi in Basra, who taught that the believer should love God for God's sake alone, without concern for any possible material or spiritual benefit.

Over the next several centuries, Sufis developed these early teachings into more elaborate systems of belief, generally focusing on four elements: humility and love of God as a means of accepting divine grace; self-purification to achieve unity with God; the use of esoteric practices, such as repetition of the names of God, to achieve divine communion; and belief in the miraculous powers of those who fully know God. As these elements developed, however, Sufism acquired a degree of internal diversity. By the ninth century, regional differences had already emerged in the relative emphasis placed on different aspects of Sufi belief. Baghdad became the center for one of the two original regional variants. Baghdadi Sufism emphasized strict asceticism as well as observance of the sharia. This emphasis on both devotion and law produced an ethos of renunciation, self-discipline, and love of God. Through its emphasis of the sharia, Baghdadi Sufism also maintained strong ties to the mainstream of the region's Muslim society. Farther to the east, a second major center developed in the region of Khorasan in western Iran and eastern Afghanistan. There, Sufism developed a very different character, in many ways resembling the asceticism of Hinduism and Buddhism. Khorasanian Sufism emphasized complete resignation to the will of God, including withdrawal from society into a life of poverty. The goal of this resignation was ecstatic union with God, in which the self would be annihilated through its rapturous communion with the divine. By focusing on the esoteric dimensions of Sufism, and in particular on the surrendering of the self, the Khorasanian branch placed little emphasis on observance of the sharia. Khorasanian Sufis thus existed in tension with mainstream Muslim society, a pattern that reappeared in some other expressions of Sufism in later centuries as well.

As Sufism continued to evolve, it also developed distinct institutional structures that contributed to its further diversification. This process began in the tenth century with the development of more formal relationships between Sufi masters, or *shaykhs*, and their disciples. Based on these relationships, disciples came to regard their shaykhs not only as teachers but also as *walis*, saint-like figures who possessed superhuman abilities and served as repositories of *baraka*, or divine blessing.[67] Proximity to the shaykh, in Sufi belief, became a means of receiving the divine grace transmitted through him. In articulating their authority, shaykhs placed great store in defining their spiritual lineage, tracing it back through generations of earlier teachers to Muhammad. The more formal relationship between shaykhs and disciples also led to the rise of the local Sufi lodge, or *zawiya*, as an institution. The earliest zawiyas mainly provided shelter for traveling Sufis, but by the eleventh century they had been transformed into the primary local focus of Sufi activity. They often served as monastic centers and thus became the established setting for interaction between a shaykh and his disciples. In addition, they provided contact between Sufi initiates and lay Muslims who had integrated Sufism into their practice of Islam. In the process, zawiyas developed into influential social institutions, serving as places of communal worship, religious instruction, and proselytism. The zawiyas also became the burial places of local shaykhs, whose tombs often became pilgrimage sites based on the belief that the shaykh's baraka could continue to be transmitted to believers at the site.

The expansion of Sufism as a form of popular Islam created significant tensions between Sufis and the ulama, particularly in locations where Sufis did not stress adherence to the sharia. Sufis believed that the ulama were too concerned with worldly affairs, while the ulama saw the Sufi shaykhs as threats to their religious authority. Conflict between the two groups was lessened, however, by the Islamic synthesis expressed in the teachings of Abu Hamid al-Ghazali, a twelfth-century Iranian theologian and legal scholar who sought to reconcile mystical religious experience with theological reasoning and Islamic law. Al-Ghazali in effect asserted that faith and reason represented compatible expressions of the totality of Islam. He thus wrote extensively about mystical forms of devotion, but he also produced important legal and theological analyses. In his view, each of these elements played a legitimate role within a common belief system. His teachings achieved widespread influence among Sunnis, earning him the epithet of the "Proof of Islam." His synthesis of Islamic thought therefore contributed to a general revival within Islam at the time, but it also gave new legitimacy to Sufism within the larger Islamic mainstream.

Within the context of this new legitimacy, Sufism continued its institutional growth with the formation of the first Sufi orders, or *tariqas*. The term *tariqa* ("path") originally applied to the specific means used by mystics to achieve unity with God. Starting in the twelfth or thirteenth century, its meaning broadened to comprise the whole system of methods, rules, ceremonies, and prayers taught by shaykhs to their followers. These systems were typically associated with the lineage of mystics to which a shaykh belonged. Because the practices of early mystics varied, their lineages developed different systems of Sufism and the latter evolved into the different tariqas. Over time, as these systems became more formalized, the term *tariqa* came to signify not only the system itself but the body of adherents who followed it. The tariqas did not exist as formal organizations, however; the local associations headed by individual shaykhs remained the primary institution of Sufism. Nonetheless, the tariqas provided a basic sense of shared culture and identity for dispersed but related Sufi communities.

The original development of the tariqas generally occurred within three broad regions: in the early Sufi hearths in Mesopotamia and Khorasan, and in North Africa (map 3.10).[68] The early tariqas that arose in these regions established the basic patterns for subsequent orders, all of which claimed derivation from one or more of these early models. Three early tariqas developed in Mesopotamia with significant influence from the teachings of al-Ghazali. The Qadiriya order originated in Baghdad early in the twelfth century based on the teachings of a Hanbali preacher who emphasized a moderate form of Sufism expressed through an ethos of sobriety, humility, and philan-

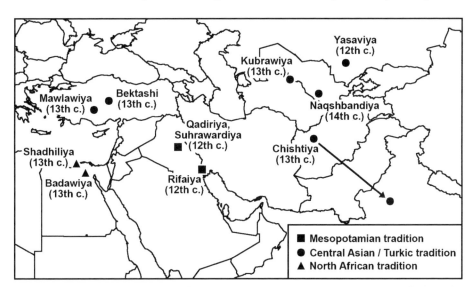

Map 3.10.   Hearths of the major Sufi tariqas established during the twelfth, thirteenth, and fourteenth centuries.

thropy. The order initially remained limited in its impact but by the fifteenth century had started to diffuse widely in North Africa and Central and South Asia. The Suhrawardiya order, which originated in Baghdad later in the twelfth century, adhered closely to the Shafii legal school and thus also stressed a sober approach to Sufism. It placed particular emphasis on strict spiritual discipline, including repetition of the epithets of God as a means of achieving enlightenment. This order's center later shifted to Afghanistan, but its various offshoots remained widespread throughout the Middle East. The Rifaiya order, the third of the early Mesopotamian orders, differed significantly from the other two. Originating in the rural surroundings of Basra, it espoused a more heterodox understanding of Sufism involving severe asceticism as well as worship through ecstatic trance states. The Rifaiya order remained concentrated in the Middle East, but declined in importance as the popularity of the Qadiriya order began to increase during the fifteenth century.

As in Mesopotamia, the tariqas that originated in and around Khorasan professed varied interpretations of Sufism. The Naqshbandiya order, founded in Bukhara, was the most orthodox, stressing strict observance of the sharia. Its worship practices were also subdued, focusing on silent repetition of the order's ritual prayers. At the same time, its members remained actively involved in proselytizing, typically by drawing parallels between other religions and Islam. This order diffused widely, eastward into China, westward into Turkey and Kurdistan, and southward into India and Southeast Asia. The Kubrawiya order possessed a similar commitment to Islamic orthodoxy, but it placed particular emphasis on the role of Sufism as a universal approach to Islam. It thus included both Sunnis and Shiites, and like the Shiites accepted the veneration of Ali. Although the Kubrawiya order did not spread to a significant degree beyond Central Asia, it played an important role in the conversion of animists and Buddhists on the northeastern peripheries of Islam's domain. The Chishtiya order first developed in Afghanistan and primarily spread into South Asia, where it became one of the leading Sufi orders. In the process it developed a distinctly austere character, mirroring ascetic practices within Hinduism. The order's initiates rejected material possessions, espoused pacifism, and lived apart from the rest of society.

In contrast to the three preceding orders, several tariqas that flourished among the Turkic people produced more heterodox expressions of Sufism. The Yasaviya order, founded in southern Kazakhstan, played a major role in adapting Sufism and Islam to Central Asian nomadism and became widely influential among Turkish nomads by the fourteenth century. It downplayed the mystical elements of Sufism and focused instead on incorporating Islamic worship into existing cultural patterns. Through its relation to nomadic groups, it also had relatively few permanent zawiyas and was spread mainly by wandering preachers. The other two Turkic tariqas grew out of the traditions of the Khorasan hearth but became formally organized after the westward extension of that hearth's influence into present-day Turkey. The Mawlawiya order, which originated in thirteenth-century Anatolia, also diverged from the other tariqas. Its most distinctive feature was its central worship practice, during which adherents induced ecstatic trance states by spinning repeatedly on their right foot while praying, typically to music. This practice lent the group the epithet of the whirling dervishes, a dervish being one who practices Sufi rituals. The group remained concentrated in Turkey and Syria; and while banned by Turkey's secular government in 1925, it still persists in that country. The Bektashi order similarly originated in Anatolia, but it did not become formally organized until the fifteenth century, under Ottoman rule. This order adopted various heterodox beliefs and in the sixteenth century essentially became a Shiite group, emphasizing the veneration of Ali. As it spread to the European possessions of the Ottoman Empire, it placed less emphasis on adherence to sharia and gradually absorbed some elements of Christianity, including confession and the ritual use of wine. It also allowed greater female participation in its rituals. Although banned by Turkey in 1925 and by Albania in 1967, it too remains active.

Finally, two of the major early tariqas developed in North Africa, where the core of their following has since been concentrated. The Badawiya order originated during the thirteenth century in the vicinity of Cairo.[69] Its founder was originally initiated in the Rifaiya order and maintained the spirit of severe asceticism characteristic of that group. Initiates of the Badawiya order generally withdrew from society and typically sought enlightenment through difficult physical tests, such as staring at the sun, fasting, or remaining silent for extended periods. The order also gained a large lay following based on the reputed baraka and associated miracles of its founder. Despite political opposition and the disapproval of the ulama, it became one of the most popular tariqas in Egypt. It also developed offshoots that diffused elsewhere within and beyond Africa. The other major North African order, the Shadhiliya, was founded by a Moroccan Sufi theologian in Alexandria. Its teachings emphasized the patient acceptance of events both good and bad, reverence toward God that mixed fear and thankfulness, and complete indifference toward other people as a means of eliminating worldly concerns and achieving unity with the divine. At the same time, the order stressed participation in the larger society and strict adherence to Sunni orthodoxy. The Shadhiliya order spread across North Africa and the Sudan, becoming the region's dominant tariqa and giving rise to many different offshoots. It spread as well into Arabia and Syria, but remains most closely associated with North Africa.

The formation of the early tariqas led to the greater systematization of Sufism's mystical practices. The tariqas also provided an institutional structure for the broader diffusion of Sufism, which proceeded rapidly from the twelfth century onward. In the process, the tariqas also contributed to the diffusion of Islam generally, especially on the periphery of the Muslim world. Sufism's incorporation into diverse Muslim societies led to its gradual transformation, however, in part through the emergence of many distinct local branches and offshoots but, more importantly, also through an extensive process of popularization. Because most adherents chose not to follow the strict rules of initiates, the number of lay associates of the tariqas increased rapidly. For these lay members, Sufi worship focused on the veneration of shaykhs whose baraka, they believed, could bring them blessings. The result was the proliferation of popular cults of Sufi sainthood beginning during the fifteenth century. While some of these cults developed around major figures in Sufism's development, popular devotion concentrated primarily on local saints whose baraka was accessible through worship at their tombs. The shrines of local saints thus became key elements of the landscape of Sufism, often rivaling the local mosque as a center of popular worship. Sufi initiates would worship at shrines to enter into spiritual communion with venerated saints as an aid in seeking unity with God, while lay worshippers would seek more direct intercession from saints in both temporal and spiritual matters. The latter practice provided a crucial means for female Muslims to become more directly involved in Sufism. The transformation of the focus of Sufism from the asceticism of initiates to popular devo-tionalism provoked opposition from the Sunni ulama, who held that the veneration of saints violated the basic Islamic tenet that adherents should worship God alone. Popular Sufism nonetheless flourished, becoming a significant element of popular Islam generally. Indeed, by the start of the nineteenth century half of all male Muslims belonged to one or more tariqas, according to most estimates. The Sunni worship of saints became a particularly important feature of popular worship in North Africa, where it is known as maraboutism.

Sufism therefore came to represent a second major source of diversity within Sunni Islam, alongside the major legal schools. Sufism played an important role in local patterns of worship, although the historical ties of local Sufi associations to the early tariqas also reflects broader regional connections as well, expressed in the overlap-ping distributions of the North African, Baghdadi, and Central Asian traditions within Sufism.[70]

Reformism and Revivalism

A third major factor in the diversification within Sunnism has been the emergence of various reformist movements. The reassertion of fundamental beliefs and practices has been a recurring trend within Sunni Islam throughout its history and concerns with orthodoxy have produced distinctive movements in many different contexts. Most such movements have taken one of two general forms: a "jihadist" form emphasizing the purification of Islamic society generally, and Sufi reformism emphasizing the indi-vidual believer's closer adherence to Islamic orthodoxy.[71] Jihadist movements have commonly taken Medina under Muhammad's rule as their ideal and thus have sought to re-create a contemporary version of that model. Such movements have conse-quently tended to have a strong political dimension, often expressed through the for-mation of new Islamic states. Some jihadist movements have additionally contained a messianic component, identifying their founder as the Mahdi, the messiah who with divine guidance and authority would restore authentic Islam and justice to the world.[72] In contrast, Sufi reform movements have arisen as Sufi shaykhs have encouraged the more careful observance of traditional Islamic practices among their followers. Such movements have been especially common in the peripheries of the Muslim world. Rather than seeking to restructure society as a whole, these movements have focused on personal religious discipline, typically based on the model of early Sufi ascetics. As a result, they have played an important role in linking local religious practice to the larger Islamic tradition. Some Sufi revivalist movements have also taken on some ele-ments of jihadism, however, particularly in Africa under European colonialism.

Among the earliest jihadist movements were the Almoravids and Almohads, groups that developed among Berbers in North Africa during the eleventh and twelfth centuries. The Almoravids (from the Arabic al-Murabitun, loosely translated as the defenders of Islam) originated among Sanhaja Berber tribes in southern Mauritania. The movement arose when a tribal leader sought to strengthen the position of his people relative to competing kingdoms and tribes by purifying their practice of Islam, based on the orthodox teachings of a Moroccan Maliki scholar, Abdallah ibn Yasin. Ibn Yasin imposed a strict code of religious purity on Sanhaja society, calling on adher-ents to carry out an internal jihad against sin and error. He closed taverns, banned musical instruments, and instituted Islamic criminal punishments. The Almoravids also changed their conduct of warfare to conform to Quranic models of closed-ranks fighting.[73] As a result of this restructuring of Sanhaja society, the Almoravids became a major political force in the region, first controlling much of southern Mauritania, then gaining control of Morocco, and finally conquering southern Spain.

Early in the following century, however, the Almohads emerged as a reaction against the decline in religious discipline that had occurred among the Almoravids as their political power grew. The leader of the new movement was Muhammad ibn Tumart, a Berber scholar who declared himself the Mahdi. Like most jihadists who claimed the title of Mahdi, Ibn Tumart followed the model of Muhammad's Hijra by first withdrawing to an isolated location in the Anti-Atlas Mountains where he gathered popular support. The militant following that he developed there eventually succeeded in removing the Almoravids from power, establishing an Almohad state in their place. Ibn Tumart's teachings focused on the orthodox Islamic avowal of the oneness of God, a belief from which the group took its Arabic name, *al-Muwahhidun*, or "Believers in Unity." He insisted as well on strict adherence to Islamic law, insisting on the veiling and social segregation of women and banning alcohol and music. The Almohads ruled parts of North Africa and Spain into the thirteenth century, but over time their messianic fervor fell into decline and they gave way to later dynasties in North Africa. Their strict construction of Islamic life nonetheless had a lasting effect on religious practice in much of North Africa.

Revivalist movements began to develop on a broader scale during the seventeenth and eighteenth centuries, as both the ulama and Sufis began to promote more authentic forms of Islam. This reformist ideology had both political and personal dimensions, emphasizing the model of Muhammad's Muslim state but also stressing the purification of personal religious observance. From its centers in Arabia and Cairo, the reformist ideology was disseminated to Muslim societies across Africa and Asia by scholars, Sufi shaykhs, traders, and pilgrims returning from the Hajj. The most influential jihadist movement to emerge from this context of reform emerged within Islam's Arabian hearth. This movement, commonly known as Wahhabism, originated in the Najd region of central Arabia during the eighteenth century. Its founder, Muhammad ibn Abd al-Wahhab, taught and studied in various parts of Arabia and southwest Asia; and in the process, he concluded that much of the Muslim world lived in a state of ignorance, a situation that had weakened Arab society and Islam itself. In Najd, he composed the *Kitab al-Tawhid*, or "Book of Unity," to lay out the principles for a return to authentic Islam. These principles centered on absolute monotheism, expressed as the *tawhid* ("unity") of God, and on the exclusive authority of the Quran and the Sunna. Abd al-Wahhab believed that the reform of Arab society and the practice of Islam depended on rigorous adherence to these principles, and thus he rejected any form of religious innovation. He particularly opposed beliefs concerning any superhuman agent other than God and so condemned practices involving spiritual intermediaries such as popular Sufi saints, animistic spirits, and the Shiite Imams. In matters of law, Abd al-Wahhab supported the strict Hanbali school, particularly as expressed by Ibn Taymiya, a Hanbali reformer in the thirteenth and fourteenth centuries.

Abd al-Wahhab's attack on what were widespread religious practices provoked much antagonism, leading him to seek the protection of local political leaders. A local

Arab emir, Muhammad ibn Saud, was receptive to his ideas regarding Islamic reform and the two formed an alliance with the goal of creating an Islamic state organized in conformity with the Quran and the Sunna. Within this state, Abd al-Wahhab would control the implementation of Islamic principles under the secular leadership of Ibn Saud. This goal of religious reform provided a strong rationale for the expansion of the incipient Saudi state, and by the end of the eighteenth century Saudi rulers had established control over all of Najd and adjacent areas of central Arabia. In the process, Abd al-Wahhab's Islamic reforms became widely adopted by the region's inhabitants. These adherents called themselves Muwahhidun ("Believers in Unity") or *ahl al-tawhid* ("people of unity"), emphasizing their strict monotheism.[74] They were vigorous opponents of animism, the cults of popular saints, the use of ornamentation in mosques, the adoption of foreign customs, and the erection of tombs and shrines dedicated to individuals. Even their leaders were buried in unmarked graves.

As the Saudi state expanded beyond its central Arabian hearth during the early 1800s, it continued to impose its uncompromising interpretation of Islam. In 1801, Saudi forces captured Karbala in Iraq, the site of the martyrdom of Husayn and thus a holy city to Shiites. After taking the city, the Wahhabis destroyed Husayn's tomb to prevent its use in devotions that they defined as idolatrous. In 1803 they began to focus their attention on the Hejaz region of western Arabia and its sacred cities, Mecca and Medina; and within several years they had established control over the region. They again destroyed or dismantled many shrines and tombs, including Muhammad's sepulcher in Medina, and removed all ornamentation from the Kaaba in Mecca. They also prevented those performing the Hajj from traveling afterward to Medina to visit Muhammad's tomb, characterizing this practice too as idolatrous. Expansion into the Hejaz led to conflict with the Ottoman Empire, however, resulting in the temporary dismantling of the Saudi state. Nonetheless, Wahhabism remained the dominant religious force in central Arabia and in 1824 the Saudis established a new state in Najd. After the fall of the Ottoman Empire, the Saudis again expanded out of this core area with Wahhabi support and regained control of most of the Arabian Peninsula, including Mecca and Medina. In 1932 the Saudi ruler Ibn Saud organized his kingdom as Saudi Arabia, with the doctrines of Wahhabism defining its religious character and the Hanbali school serving as the foundation of its legal system.

The spirit of reform expressed in the rise of Wahhabism contributed as well to the rise of jihadist movements in Africa, which in turn produced a number of Islamic states.[75] Because these movements developed in contexts where Islamic orthodoxy competed with the widespread practice of indigenous tribal religions, they combined the goal of purifying Islam with a broader emphasis on proselytism. The political dimension of these movements was also shaped by the slave trade, which benefited some traditional elites at the expense of more marginal groups. The jihadist movements responded to this injustice by defining themselves as opponents of what they viewed as the unjust kingdoms in the region. Most of the states arising from these movements proved to be short-lived, but the movements themselves have had persistent regional influences, and in West Africa in particular they have been an important factor in reinforcing Islamic orthodoxy.

The earliest of these movements established the Boundou state in Senegambia in the late 1600s, but Boundou rulers did not require religious conformity and some continued to observe animistic practices. Two subsequent jihadist states in Senegambia, Fouta Djallon and Fouta Toro, promoted Islam more actively and placed particular emphasis on Islamic education as a stabilizing social force. Fouta Djallon arose in 1726 out of a popular movement unified by Islamic identity in opposing the region's non-Muslim elites. It was governed by an imam who provided both political and religious leadership.[76] Fouta Djallon was particularly committed to extending its influence through outward military jihad against surrounding states, which also provided a source of slaves for the slave trade. In the 1770s the Islamic state in Fouta Toro similarly developed out of a popular movement against local elites, partly in defense against the slave trade. This movement's leaders again emphasized Islamic authenticity and sought to expand into surrounding non-Muslim regions. All three of these states eventually declined, however, especially after the rise of France's colonial presence.

Perhaps the most important of the West African jihadist movements developed somewhat farther to the west in a region extending across northern Nigeria and Cameroon. There, the Fulani Muslim scholar Usman dan Fodio established a major jihadist movement during the late 1700s and early 1800s. Usman preached adherence to Islamic orthodoxy and rejection of both traditional animism and syncretistic forms of Islam. His preaching attracted significant opposition from the dominant Hausa tribe but attracted many followers from less influential groups, including Fulani pastoralists from the north, Hausa peasants, and escaped slaves. Hausa attempts to suppress Usman's movement led him to declare a jihad in the early 1800s; and during the subsequent rebellion he overcame various Hausa states, founding in their place the Caliphate of Sokoto. Within Sokoto religious and political authority were united and Islamic law became widely established. The Sokoto caliphs also constructed large numbers of mosques and religious schools. The influence of Usman's Islamic orthodoxy remained strong in the region under British colonial rule and has continued to play a significant social role in northern Nigeria.

In addition, Usman's successful creation of a jihadist state inspired similar efforts by followers in neighboring areas of West Africa. Shortly after the creation of Sokoto, jihadists founded similar states in Fombina, south of Lake Chad, and in the region of Air in southern Niger. In both, rulers imposed strict adherence to Islamic law and sought to suppress animistic practices. Farther to the east, a jihadist state inspired by Usman emerged in the Masina region of Mali in 1818. In addition to imposing Islamic law, rulers there required the conversion of pagans. In 1852, al-Hajj Umar Tal conducted a similar jihad in what had been Fouta Toro, but in addition to traditional animism and syncretistic Islam he included European influences among his targets. The state that he founded, centered in Kaarta in southwestern Mali, later absorbed Masina to the east. He too imposed the sharia and banned animistic practices, creating an Islamic polity that lasted to the end of the century when it came under French colonial control.

A significant jihadist movement developed in Sudan as well, but it differed from those to the west in its more explicit messianic character. It was founded by Muhammad Ahmad, who in 1881 declared himself the Mahdi and claimed a divine mandate to create an authentic Islamic state. He based his strategy on the model of Muhammad, first withdrawing to southern Sudan to consolidate power, and then undertaking a jihad against the ruling Egyptian regime, nominally part of the Ottoman Empire, which he considered to be unjust and un-Islamic. His followers interpreted his defeat of Egyptian forces in 1883 as proof of divine support, and his movement subsequently gained widespread backing from Muslim Sudanese tribes. The defeat of British forces seeking control of the region and the taking of Khartoum in 1885 in turn led to the establishment of a jihadist state. This state was defeated by the British in 1898, but in the interim it succeeded in establishing a strict interpretation of Islamic orthodoxy within Sudanese society and in defining a common Islamic identity that transcended tribal loyalties. Support for the Mahdists' interpretation of Islam remained widespread even after the fall of their state and has continued to shape Islam in Sudan to the present.

In contrast to the various jihadist movements, the Islamic revivalist movements that emerged specifically within the context of Sufism generally had a less pronounced political dimension, focusing instead on the promotion of orthodoxy in personal religious practice. Many such movements arose with the diffusion of the ideology of reform beginning in the seventeenth century; and several had a pronounced influence on the practice of Islam in certain regions, particularly in parts of Africa and Asia. Sufi expressions of Islamic revivalism in Africa were initially represented by the Tijaniya, a reform order founded in the 1780s in Fez, Morocco, by Ahmad al-Tijani. Al-Tijani belonged to various Sufi orders, but after a revelatory experience he claimed the authority to found a new tariqa. The primary concern of his new order was individual adherence to Islamic tradition, with a particular emphasis on purity of thought and action. He de-emphasized the role of esoteric ritual, and the order's worship practices focused primarily on the simple recitation of prayers. Contrary to widespread practice, al-Tijani also ruled that followers of his order could not belong to other Sufi orders and must call only on him and other walis of the order for intercession with God. He further taught that his followers should respect established political authority and focus on their own spiritual development rather than social change. Because al-Tijani forbade devotions to earlier saints outside his order, the Tijaniya did not at first become widely popular. The order's influence grew during the 1800s, however, as it spread from North Africa into West Africa and across the Sudan. Al-Hajj Umar Tal was a member of the order, giving it a local jihadist character in the formation of his state in Kaarta; but the order generally remained uninvolved in broader social and political issues.

The Sanusiya, another reformist order in Africa, more clearly mixed jihadism with the Sufi focus on individual piety. The order's founder, Muhammad ibn Ali al-Sanusi, studied extensively in Cairo and Mecca, where he came to oppose the Islamic establishment supported by the Ottoman Empire. He thus founded his order to reform both Sufi practice and the application of Islamic law. Forced to leave Mecca by local authorities, he reestablished his order in coastal Libya where he proselytized among various coastal and interior tribes. He endeavored to promote Islamic unity over tribal identity among these groups but he sought as well to establish strict adherence to a primitive Islam free from the accretions that it had accumulated through centuries of interpretation. In addition, he advocated the elimination of the more esoteric aspects of Sufi worship, focusing again on ritual prayer. Beyond these efforts to reform worship practices, however, he also sought to establish an Islamic state. To that end, he organized his followers as militant associations in fortified zawiyas associated with particular tribes. The militancy of his followers subsequently became a major asset in Libya's struggle for independence from Italian colonial rule, and al-Sanusi's grandson became the first king of independent Libya after World War II.

The primary Sufi expressions of Islamic revivalism in Asia originated in the Naqshbandiya order. In seventeenth-century India, the shaykh Ahmad Sirhindi initiated a movement to rid Islam of the syncretistic elements it had absorbed from Hindu culture. In particular he opposed the concept of the unity of all existence with God, a belief that he saw as an expression of Hindu pantheism. Sirhindi argued that God was distinct from the created cosmos and that the Sufi experience of unity with God was purely subjective. He further preached strict adherence to sharia and separation from Hindu patterns of life. The widespread popularity of his teachings among Muslims had a marked effect on Islam in India, countering earlier tendencies toward syncretism and furthering the development of a distinct Indian Muslim community. Antagonism between Muslims and Hindus provoked a different Naqshbandiya response in the 1700s in the teachings of the shaykh Shah Wali Ullah. Wali Ullah taught that Muslims in India must interpret Islamic tradition in light of the realities of their surrounding context, arguing for an emphasis on the spirit of the Quran rather than on literalist readings. He also promoted familiarity with the Quran by translating it into Persian, the most widely used language among literate Muslims in India. The sense of Muslim unity emphasized in Wali Ullah's teachings contributed in the 1800s to an unsuccessful military jihad by his followers against the Sikhs and the British. The teachings of Sirhindi and Wali Ullah also provided a foundation for Islamic fundamentalist movements in South Asia in the twentieth century.[77]

The Naqshbandiya order also played a central role in Islamic revivals in other parts of Asia, again by promoting conceptions of Muslim unity. The order thus contributed to the conflict against Dutch colonialism in Indonesia and against Christian hegemony in the Philippines. In Turkey, it promoted Islamic identity in opposition to the secularism enacted by the government under Mustafa Kemal Atatürk in the 1920s. Similarly, in the former Soviet Union the order sought to provide a more authentic Islam as an alternative to the official Islam supported by the state. In China, members of the order participated in the founding of an Islamic revivalist group known as Xinjiao ("New Teaching") in the 1700s. It emphasized the preservation of Islamic identity among Chinese Muslims alongside external accommodation of Chinese cultural patterns. A member of this group thus produced the first translation of the Quran into Chinese. At the same time, the group's militant defense of the Muslim community resulted in a series of rebellions against Chinese authorities between the late 1700s and early 1800s.[78]

Sunni Fundamentalism

Reformist movements have continued to influence Sunni Islam in contemporary contexts. Over the past century, however, such movements have developed more explicit concerns with modernity and its consequences, concerns that have in turn lent these movements a more self-reflexive character. Their adherents have again sought to promote purified forms of Islam, in some cases by focusing on individual religious practice but more commonly by addressing Islam as a totalizing ideology informing all aspects of life. Through such concerns, these movements have tied their objectives to a wide range of contemporary phenomena, including nationalism, secularism, and pluralism. Together they have been characterized by various descriptive terms, most commonly *Islamic fundamentalism* and *Islamism*, to distinguish them from earlier expressions of reformism. These general terms should not mask the diversity among contemporary reformist movements, however. Sunni fundamentalism is not a monolithic entity. Individual fundamentalist groups have arisen as responses to specific local and regional contexts and as a result they vary in their essential characteristics.[79] Connections have developed among fundamentalist groups in different locations, to be sure, but their diverse attributes represent an important characteristic element of Sunni fundamentalism broadly defined.

Two major hearths have been particularly influential in the development of Sunni fundamentalism. The first centered on Egypt, which has produced a series of important movements since the late 1800s. The earliest of these was the Salafiya movement, which grew out of the teachings of Muhammad Abduh. Abduh's primary concern was that Christian Europe had surpassed the Muslim world in social, economic, and technological terms. He thus sought to modernize Islam, asserting that the Islamic system was entirely compatible with contemporary science, technology, and social thought. He argued for a return to the Islam of the early Muslim community, but reinterpreted with regard to the contingencies of modern life. He thus supported a greater emphasis on science in education, for example, and greater freedom for women. The Salafiya movement became influential across North Africa and the Middle East, and from there spread eastward into Asia.

Some Muslims disapproved of the Salafiya movement, however, because it focused on emulating European developments. This opposition became more pronounced after World War I in response to two perceived threats to Islam. First, after the war the victorious allies dismantled the Ottoman Empire, leaving no major Islamic empire still in existence. Second, and more seriously, the secular government of Turkey in 1924 abolished the office of the caliph, a title that the Ottoman sultans had claimed since the late 1700s, thus eliminating the spiritual figurehead of Sunni Islam. These events provoked a strong backlash against modernist efforts to reform Islam, resulting in the rise of militant Islamic fundamentalism in the 1920s and 1930s. Again, Egypt was the initial hearth of this fundamentalist response, which first found expression in the Muslim Brotherhood, a jihadist group formed in 1928 that eventually developed offshoots throughout the Muslim world.[80] The group's founder, Hasan al-Banna, sought to reconstitute Islam in its own terms, not in emulation of European models, and thus advocated the return to an authentic Islam based strictly on the Quran and the Sunna. The Muslim Brotherhood rejected existing religious institutions as corrupt and established its own network of mosques and religious schools. The group further supported the jihadist objective of establishing an authentic Islamic state and as a result participated in the conflict for Egyptian independence from British control. At the same time, the group sought to provide an alternative to the perceived corruption within society and thus formed an extensive network of social institutions, including various business, clinics, and charities. These institutions played a major role in the popular acceptance of the Muslim Brotherhood in Egypt.

After the constitution of Egypt as an independent republic, the unwillingness of secular leaders to establish a fundamentalist Islamic state produced repeated conflicts between the Muslim Brotherhood and the Egyptian government. The resulting suppression of the Muslim Brotherhood ultimately produced an internal division by the

1970s between the mainstream membership and a highly radical group. The mainstream of the Muslim Brotherhood restructured itself as a more moderate organization during the 1970s, remaining committed to an abstract conception of jihad based on a strategy of gradual reform instead of revolutionary change. It remained committed to its core emphasis on authentic Islam based on the Quran and the Sunna, maintaining its own mosques and religious schools. At the same time, it continued to expand its institutional system of social support, in many locations serving the populace more effectively than parallel government institutions; and it used legitimate political action to promote stricter Islamic practices. Through these efforts, the Muslim Brotherhood continues to have a wide following in Egypt. The radical offshoot of the group, on the other hand, adopted a very different interpretation of jihad based on isolation from society. The radicals drew their inspiration from the writings of Sayyid Qutb, a militant executed by the government in 1966. Qutb had argued that true Muslims should form a revolutionary vanguard separate from society and carry out a militant jihad to destroy the existing government. The radical followers of Qutb organized as a loose confederation of separate militant groups in the 1970s and 1980s and since then have been active participants in terrorist activity in the name of Islam in Egypt and other parts of the world. Their membership has remained small, however, relative to the Muslim Brotherhood.

The second major hearth of Sunni fundamentalism developed in South Asia. The groups that emerged there represented responses to contexts significantly different from that of Egypt. The minority status of Muslims in much of South Asia had significant consequences, as did the contrasting settings for Sunni fundamentalism in India and Pakistan after independence. In India, the concept of a broader social or political jihad was rendered irrelevant by Muslims' minority status. Fundamentalists therefore focused primarily on issues of Islamic identity, much as Naqshbandi reformers had in previous centuries. A key expression of this focus is the Tablighi Jamaat, or Tabligh, founded in northern India in 1927. Founder Muhammad Ilyas and his followers did not try to convert non-Muslims. Rather, they proselytized exclusively among their fellow Muslims, encouraging them to adhere to the sharia rather than to local Hindu custom or syncretistic practices and to observe the religious duties defined by the Quran and the Sunna, such as communal prayer in local mosques. Because Ilyas believed that active proselytism reinforced the faith of the proselytizer, participation in grassroots missionary activity became a central obligation of the Tabligh's adherents. The Tabligh attracted a wide following among Muslims in India and from there it expanded to other areas, becoming one of the largest international Muslim organizations. Other Islamic fundamentalist groups have emerged in India in recent decades, but they too have focused primarily on the purification of religious practice and the defense of Muslim interests within Indian society.

In Pakistan, on the other hand, Sunni fundamentalism possessed a strong jihadist element as adherents sought to create an authentic Islamic state. This element was founded on the teachings of Abul Ala Mawdudi, a journalist and politician from southern India. Mawdudi asserted the superiority of Islam over Western ideologies, arguing that Islam could accommodate technological advances and scientific knowledge on its own terms without borrowing from the West. Like other Islamic reformers in South Asia, he was concerned with maintaining Muslim identity, but he linked identity to the obligation to live Islam as a total way of life. That obligation had two elements, in his view: the observance of authentic Islamic practices in daily life, and the broader social and political application of Islam principles to promote the interests of the Muslim community. Mawdudi further believed that an elite devoted both to political action and religious purity could best achieve this second goal. He founded such a group in 1941 as the Jamaat-i-Islami ("Islamic Society"). The group's efforts to define Pakistan in strict Islamic terms after partition generally met with opposition from secularist leaders, although at times those in power have supported some elements of the Jamaat-i-Islami's program of Islamization, such as greater incorporation of the sharia into Pakistan's legal code. The absence of any permanent resolution of the Jamaat-i-Islami's concerns eventually contributed to the rise of more radical, populist forms of Islamic fundamentalism, particularly in relation to the Soviet occupation of neighboring Afghanistan and the ongoing conflict with India over control of Kashmir. These radical fundamentalists, comprising a variety of splinter groups, have also sought to purify Islamic practice in Pakistan through conflicts with Shiites and more heterodox Islamic sects.

Innovations from the hearths of Sunni fundamentalism in Egypt and South Asia have spread to most Muslim countries, often alongside the strict form of Islam promoted by the Wahhabis. Local versions of the Muslim Brotherhood, the Jamaat-i-Islami, and more radical offshoots have therefore become widespread. Most local expressions of Islamism have adopted moderate approaches advocating conformity to the Quran and the Sunna in personal Islamic practice while also seeking a more explicit role for Sunni Islam in larger social and political structures. Recent efforts by Muslims in northern Nigeria to establish the sharia as the basis for civil law typify this approach. In some locations, however, Sunni fundamentalists have established Islamic states through political jihad. A significant example of this process occurred in Sudan, where local members of the Muslim Brotherhood began to push for the creation of an Islamic state in the late 1970s. This objective became more fully realized following a coup in 1989, after which the ruling regime established the sharia as the basis for civil law. Opposition to this move by secularists and non-Muslims subsequently led the government to adopt a more moderate policy, applying the sharia only among Sudanese Muslims. Nonetheless, Sudan has become an important center for the promulgation of Sunni fundamentalism in other parts of Africa. Another significant example of the establishment of a fundamentalist polity developed in Afghanistan in the 1990s as the Taliban took over most of the country following the end of Soviet occupation. The Taliban enforced a particularly rigid form of Sunni fundamentalism, banning most Western innovations and severely curtailing the rights of women. Although Taliban beliefs drew on the Quran and the Sunna, they also incorporated many distinctive Afghan traditions, such as the complete bodily veiling of women. As a result, the Taliban movement remained highly localized in its religious influence. Its commitment to political jihad allied it with more militant expressions of fundamentalism such as al-Qaeda, however. That alliance ultimately led to the destruction of the Taliban state early in the twenty-first century as the United States and various allies responded to the al-Qaeda attacks of September 11, 2001.

Again, an important feature of Sunni expressions of fundamentalism, as well as of the earlier revival movements, has been an underlying belief in the intrinsic unity of Sunnism. Even those groups that have isolated themselves from society, such as militant Islamists and terrorist movements, hold to the view that Islam should represent a single, unified system. One of the stated objectives of al-Qaeda, for example, is the reestablishment of the caliphate to rule over the Sunni umma. This conception of religious unity has emerged as well in the different Sunni legal schools and Sufi tariqas, which over time have rejected the sectarianism that characterizes the other major proselytizing religions. Despite this conception of unity, however, considerable diversity exists in the practice of Sunni Islam in different contexts; and this diversity represents an essential characteristic of Sunni Islam as a lived religion.

Shia Islam

A very different pattern developed within Shia Islam, which diversified over time through schisms that produced a number of discrete sects. This sectarianism in part reflected the Shiites' origins as a schismatic minority within Islam, but it also grew out of their emphasis on the Imamate, which at various times led to the contesting of leadership. As discussed above, Shiism arose as a distinct movement late in the seventh century as Muslims who had supported Ali as Muhammad's successor unified behind Husayn as their Imam. The Shiites became divided almost immediately after the martyrdom of Husayn, however. One faction, originally in the minority, insisted that the Imam must be descended directly from Muhammad through Ali and Fatima and their son Husayn. This group thus supported Ali Zayn al-Abidin, Husayn's only surviving son, as the next Imam. It also rejected the idea that the Shiite Imam should serve as caliph, maintaining instead that he should be a religious leader serving only God. This group has thus been characterized as Imami Shiism, as it rejects the importance of the caliphate. The majority Shiite faction, on the other hand, sought to unify the Imamate and the caliphate; and they gave their support to more distant relatives of Muhammad who had stronger political backing. Recurring conflicts between this second group and the Umayyad caliphate ultimately resulted in the latter's downfall and the establishment of the Abbasid dynasty of caliphs in 750. The Abbasids were descended from Abbas, an uncle of the prophet Muhammad, but not directly from Muhammad himself. The Imami Shiites therefore rejected the Abbasids' leadership in religious matters. After taking power, moreover, the Abbasids aligned themselves with the Sunni majority, in effect abandoning the cause of Shiism. The Imami Shiites thus became the dominant force within Shiism in the eighth century.

By this time, Shiism had developed beliefs and practices that diverged more explicitly from those of Sunnism. Commemoration of the anniversary of Husayn's martyrdom, incorporated into the older feast of Ashura, became a key holy day in the Shiite calendar. The theological meaning of the Imamate also became more fully developed in the middle of the eighth century by Jafar al-Sadiq, the great-grandson of Husayn. Jafar articulated a number of key doctrines: that God had conferred on the direct descendants of Muhammad the right to serve as Imam; that each Imam passed on his authority through the divinely guided designation (*nass*, in Arabic) of his successor; and that in doing so each Imam also passed on his comprehensive knowledge (*ilm*) of religious matters to his successor. Together, nass and ilm defined the legitimacy of the Imam as religious leader, and Jafar declared that he was the sole recipient of both in a lineage tracing back to Muhammad. These doctrines became the basis for belief in the spiritual perfection and infallibility of the Imam. Moreover, they confirmed the belief that the Imam should have no concern for secular issues: his mandate came from God and focused on religious matters. Nonetheless, Jafar's claims to religious authority posed a threat to the Abbasids who came to power at about the same time. Jafar thus also promulgated the doctrine of dissimulation, allowing his followers to disguise their adherence from outsiders to avoid persecution. Together, these doctrines provided the basis for the survival of Shiism within a complex and often hostile political environment.

By the eighth century, the spatial distributions of Shia Islam had also started to diverge from that of Sunnism. At the time of Husayn's death, Shiism was still predominantly an Arab phenomenon. Shiite resistance to the Umayyad caliphate, however, attracted increasing support from non-Arab converts to Islam. Because non-Arabs faced various disadvantages within Muslim society, they adopted Shiism as a reaction against the Arab majority. Many Persians inhabiting the eastern reaches of the growing Islamic empire thus espoused Shiism. An especially important Shiite concentration subsequently developed in Iran south of the Caspian Sea, later spreading eastward across Central Asia to Samarqand. Shiism also diffused from Kufa to other cosmopolitan urban centers in Mesopotamia, and from the latter region into Syria. Various concentrations of Shiism thus developed within the more extensive domain of the Sunni majority.

Twelver Shiism

Antagonism between the Shiites and Sunnis persisted after the fall of the Umayyads as the Abbasid caliphs too saw the Shiite Imams as a threat and sought to limit their influence. Most of the Imams following Jafar were imprisoned or kept in isolation, and most apparently died by poisoning while in custody. This pattern ended, however, with the twelfth Imam, Muhammad al-Mahdi, who became a central figure in Shiite belief. By tradition, his birth in 868 was hidden from the authorities and he remained in seclusion after becoming Imam at the age of five. He communicated with his followers through a series of *babs* ("gates") or deputies until 939, when a letter presumably from the Imam announced that there would be no further babs. This letter also indicated that Muhammad al-Mahdi was the final Imam: no others would follow him, and he himself had entered into occultation, or divine concealment, from which he would reemerge at the divinely appointed time as the Mahdi, initiating the final judgment day. These pronouncements became central to the mainstream body of Shiism, whose adherents came to be known as Twelver Shiites based on their emphasis on the twelfth Imam. Twelver Shiites accept the twelve Imams as the primary sources of religious authority and as essential intermediaries in salvation. As a result, pilgrimages to the shrines of the Imams became a central part of Shiite practice, equal in importance to the Hajj.

With its culmination in the Hidden Imam, the Imamate ceased to pose a threat to the secular rule of Sunni leaders and the Twelver Shiites became a less immediate threat to the Sunni caliphs. Moreover, the Twelver Shiites achieved some respite from Sunni opposition under the regional Buyid dynasty, which from its origins in the Persian Shiite region south of the Caspian Sea came to rule much of Iran and Iraq from 945 to 1055. Although the Buyids recognized the religious authority of the Abbasid caliphate over the Sunnis under their control, they provided legitimacy to the

Twelver Shiites within their domain. The dominance of this region by subsequent Turkic and Mongol empires again brought the Twelver Shiites under Sunni rule until the sixteenth century, when the Turkic Safavid dynasty established Twelver Shiism as the state religion of its empire. The Safavids had been Sunnis, but adopted Shiism as a means of garnering local support in Iran. The Safavids' official support of Shiism also served to assert their independence from the Ottoman Empire emerging in Turkey, although it also contributed to a protracted series of conflicts with the Sunni Ottomans. Later, the Safavids also used conformity to Shiism as a means of exerting territorial control over their own empire, authorizing Shiite ulama to promote and enforce popular observance of Shiite beliefs and practices.

Twelver Shiism thus became dominant in Iran and an integral part of Iranian culture. After the Safavids lost power in the early 1700s, moreover, the Shiite ulama retained their influence as a source of authority within Iranian society. The ulama became divided, however, over the nature of their authority. Some argued that the ulama should hold strictly to the Quran and the Sunna, while others asserted that the ulama served as representatives of the Hidden Imam and had the right to use personal judgment in interpreting sharia. The latter group prevailed and came to be known as the *mujtahids*, who alone possessed the right to interpret Islamic tradition. The mujtahids became central figures in Iranian society, providing religious guidance to local communities and in return receiving revenues from a religious tax that supported mosques, schools, charities, and other institutions. The mujtahids themselves came to be directed by a hierarchical structure of senior leaders known as ayatollahs ("sign of God"), who served as the ultimate religious authorities. This system persisted under the Qajar dynasty, from 1779 to 1925, during which the mujtahids exercised considerable power at local scales.

After coming to power in 1925, the Pahlavi dynasty sought to strengthen the central government by limiting the influence of the mujtahids; but the latter nonetheless retained control of various local religious institutions. Through these local bases of support, the mujtahids played a central role in the popular movement opposing the Pahlavi shah in the 1970s. The senior ayatollah, Ruholla Khomeini, became the leader of the opposition, and after the fall of the shah reorganized Iran as a Shiite Islamic republic. In the process, Khomeini reinterpreted the Shiite tradition that had separated religious and secular rule, asserting instead that both secular and religious authority should be placed in the hands of a supreme religious jurist, or *Faqih*, who would govern as representative of the Hidden Imam until the latter returned as the Mahdi. This union of secular and religious rule, while rooted in the messianic beliefs of Shiism, reflected a new interpretation of the relationship between Islam and the state. Khomeini himself became the first Faqih, overseeing all branches of Iran's Islamic government. The latter included an elected president and parliament, but these officials ultimately remained under the jurisdiction of the Faqih.

Shiite Sects

Iran thus emerged as the dominant Shiite state, containing a majority of Twelver Shiites. The latter also formed a majority in much of present-day Iraq. Elsewhere, the distribution of Shiism remained more fragmentary. Various schisms within Imami Shiism, again focusing on issues of authority, further contributed to that fragmented pattern. The earliest significant division had developed over the successor to Ali Zayn al-Abidin, the son of Husayn. Most of Ali's followers supported his son Muhammad al-Baqir as the fifth Imam, as he continued his father's disengagement from secular affairs. Muhammad's brother Zayd opposed the latter position, however, and in 740 led a rebellion against the Umayyad caliphate. Some of the Shiites who supported the unification of the Imamate and the caliphate thus recognized Zayd as their Imam. After Zayd was killed in battle near Kufa, his followers became organized as a distinct movement, later known as the Zaydis, which gradually articulated distinctive doctrines concerning the Imamate. Although they acknowledged that the Imam must be descended from Ali and Fatima, they asserted that Imams drew their legitimacy from their own learning and abilities rather than from designation by their predecessor. They also denied that Imams had any supernatural qualities, characterizing them instead as skilled leaders and scholars. The Zaydis were originally concentrated around Kufa, but conflict with the Abbasids in the ninth century drove them to more remote, mountainous areas. One group became established in Iran south of the Caspian Sea, but they later became absorbed into Twelver Shiism under Safavid rule. A second group of Zaydis settled in northern Yemen, where they established a theocracy under the rule of their Imams. This polity persisted in various forms into the twentieth century, and the Zaydis remain the dominant religious group in much of northern Yemen.

A further division occurred within Imami Shiism in 765 after the death of Jafar al-Sadiq, the son of Muhammad al-Baqir. Jafar's oldest son, Ismail, was already deceased, and most Shiites thus recognized a younger son, Musa al-Kazim, as the seventh Imam. Their view became the orthodox position within Imami Shiism. A smaller group asserted that Ismail was Jafar's true successor, and that the Imamate would past next to Ismail's son Muhammad. This group, known as the Ismailis, developed distinct doctrines that contrasted the exoteric religiosity of most believers with the superior but guarded esoteric knowledge of Ismaili initiates. In addition, they placed particular importance on allegiance to the Imamate as an expression of faith, on purity and cleanliness, and on jihad, understood as activism in the spread of true belief. The Ismailis became highly schismatic over time, producing a number of separate sects. They first split over the issue of the continuing succession of Imams. Most accepted the ongoing continuity of the Imamate, but a minority believed that Ismail represented the final Imam in the current historical era. This minority later revised its beliefs, identifying Ismail's son as the final Imam, who would return as the Mahdi. Like some other Ismailis, this group counted Ismail's son Muhammad as the seventh Imam, and through their emphasis on his role as Mahdi they became known as Seveners.

Through their emphasis on jihad, both groups of Ismailis rejected the disengagement from politics typical of other Shiites, and both established political dynasties. The Seveners achieved their greatest influence through the Qarmatian movement, founded in Kufa by Hamdan Qarmat at the end of the ninth century. The Qarmatians, based on millennial beliefs concerning the seventh Imam, strongly opposed other Muslim regimes, which they considered to be in error. Early in the tenth century, they seized the island of Bahrain from the Abbasid caliph and from that base they extended their influence over adjacent areas of the Arabian Peninsula and into Iraq. Constant conflict with surrounding tribes and states led to their decline, however, and after the eleventh century they were no longer influential. The larger body of Ismailis, who recognized the continuing succession of Imams beyond Ismail and his son, had a more significant impact. Their view of the Imamate as an ongoing institution provided strong leadership for their efforts to establish Ismaili political rule.

Such efforts found expression in the tenth century in the rise of the Fatimids, an Ismaili dynasty that claimed descent from Ali and Fatima and sought to eliminate the Abbasid caliphate. The Fatimids originated in Syria but came to focus their territorial objectives on North Africa, away from the major centers of Sunni power. Starting from a base in Tunisia, they conquered northern Algeria and Libya, and the dynasty's founder, Ubayd Allah, declared himself the Mahdi, reuniting the Imamate and caliphate. Under succeeding rulers, Fatimid control spread across North Africa and into Sicily. In 969 they captured Egypt and founded Cairo as their capital, from which they gradually extended their control over Palestine, Syria, and western Arabia, including the holy cities of Mecca and Medina. Eventually, though, both internal and external conflict weakened the Fatimid empire, and in 1171 it was absorbed into the Ayyubid empire of Saladin, who abolished the Fatimid caliphate.

The rule of the Fatimids had only limited effects on religious patterns among their subjects, and Sunnis remained in the majority in most parts of their empire. Nonetheless, the Fatimids contributed to the spread of Ismaili Islam and they gave rise to several enduring Ismaili groups. Two of these groups, the Mustalis and the Nizaris, arose at the end of the eleventh century. They diverged over which of two brothers, Mustali or Nizar, would succeed their father, the eighth Fatimid caliph. As the Fatimid empire collapsed during the twelfth century, Yemen emerged as the main center of the Mustalis, who believed that Mustali's descendants would preserve the Imamate in hiding until some future time. This group later became established in parts of India as well. The Nizaris persisted in Iran and Syria, where they maintained the Imamate as an ongoing institution. By the thirteenth century the Nizaris had begun missionary activity in Sind and Gujarat, located in southeastern Pakistan and western India, and during the nineteenth century the Nizari Imamate relocated to Bombay. At present, this group represents the largest of the Ismaili sects.

The development of local schisms within Shiism produced more heterodox sects as well. The Druze, one of the principal surviving expressions of this heterodoxy, emerged in the eleventh century in the Egyptian court of the Fatimid caliph Hakim. Its early adherents were dissatisfied by the failure of previous caliphs to reform Islam. In 1017 two missionaries appointed by the caliph, Hamza ibn Ali and Muhammad al-Darazi (from whom the Druze take their name), began to preach that this reformation would be brought about by Hakim, whom they characterized as the incarnation of divine intellect. Hakim himself used this belief as justification for his autocratic and often eccentric behavior, which provoked growing opposition to his rule. In 1021 Hakim disappeared, presumably having been assassinated, but the Druze believed that he had merely concealed himself to test their faith. Following the disappearance of Hakim, the Druze adopted the belief that he would return in the future as the Mahdi and final Imam.

Subsequent persecution by the succeeding caliph forced many of the Druze to migrate to more remote areas. Followers of the movement subsequently established a permanent presence in mountainous areas of southern Lebanon and southwestern Syria, where they formed a highly segregated, exclusivist society. In the areas under their control they destroyed the existing mosques and established their own system of religious law. Their religious system emphasized strict monotheism, but they also believed in the recurring incarnation of divine intellect, culminating in the caliph Hakim. They further believed that Hakim, through Hamza, had replaced the Five Pillars of Islam with a new set of obligations focusing on commitment to the Druze community and acceptance of the beliefs laid out in various Druze scriptures. They also developed a tradition of secrecy concerning their religion and thus came to reject proselytism. That tradition of secrecy ultimately led to a division within the Druze community between the lay majority and an initiated elite that fully comprehends the group's most esoteric doctrines. The ethos of the Druze has focused primarily on the distinctiveness and isolation of their community. They forbid apostasy and marriage outside the group, and require all adherents to be truthful with one another and to support and defend the community. Through these beliefs and practices, the Druze have remained a distinct religious body in Lebanon and Syria.

Another surviving heterodox sect, the Alawites, became established in northern Syria and Lebanon and adjacent areas of southern Turkey during the tenth century. This group's most distinctive beliefs concern divine incarnation. Possibly borrowing from Christianity, the Alawites identified a divine trinity, made up of Ali, Muhammad, and Salman al-Farsi, a companion of Muhammad. Within this trinity, Ali represents God incarnate, Muhammad represents the creation of Ali, and Salman represents the archangel Gabriel who in Islamic belief revealed the Quran to Muhammad. The Alawites also denied the literal truth of the Quran, believing instead that it contains allegorical meanings accessible only to the initiated. Like the Druze, the Alawites sought to maintain the secrecy of these esoteric meanings, and established a process of initiation for young men as they reached adulthood. Women were not initiated and generally played little role in formal religious practices. The Alawites also believed in reincarnation, but again of men only, asserting that women do not have eternal souls. The radical heterodoxy of this group subjected it to recurring persecutions by various Muslim regimes and the group survived primarily in the mountains of northwestern Syria. In the twentieth century, however, it became more widely integrated into Syrian society. The Alawites unsuccessfully tried to establish their own state during the period of the French mandate, but after Syrian independence they became a dominant political force, particularly after Hafiz al-Assad, an Alawite, took control of the government in 1970.

Modern Heterodox Sects

The heterodoxy of the Druze, Alawites, and other smaller groups represented an important expression of Shiite sectarianism during the first several centuries of the movement's history. This pattern stood in clear contrast with the diversity within unity that has been more characteristic of the historical development of Sunnism. For most of Islam's history, then, its spatial diversification has developed primarily within these two contrasting frameworks. In recent centuries, however, new forms of Islamic diversity have emerged in a number of different geographical contexts. These recent expressions of diversity involve more significant departures from the established world-view and ethos of Islam, in some cases to the extent that they represent essentially new religious systems with only historical ties to Islamic tradition. As a result, these heterodox movements have typically experienced significant conflict with more orthodox Muslims and some have faced severe persecution.

These recent heterodox movements generally fall into two broad categories: those signifying a particularistic reinterpretation of Islam within a specific local context, and those reinterpreting Islam as one element of a broader, more universalistic worldview. Several instances of the first type developed in Africa during the European colonial period. The Mouride brotherhood of Senegal and Gambia, for example, was founded in 1886 by Amadou Bamba, a Sufi shaykh who with members of the local Wolof aristocracy sought to fashion a society that could flourish within the context of French colonialism. Bamba thus discouraged resistance to colonial power and rejected the jihadism of some earlier West African movements, teaching instead that his followers should focus on piety and work under the leadership of their religious leaders. Despite initial suspicion of the group's popularity, the French eventually supported the Mourides and the group grew rapidly during the later colonial period. The Mourides founded a number of villages where followers settled, providing part of their labor to the movement.

In religious terms, the Mourides dropped many elements of orthodox Islam. They considered Bamba to be a messenger from God and accorded him greater veneration than they did Muhammad. After Bamba's death, the group developed a strict hierarchical structure, led by a *khalifa* and, under him, several hundred local shaykhs; and these leaders also acquired great significance to their followers. The Mourides abandoned the Hajj to Mecca as a religious obligation, replacing it with the Magal, an annual pilgrimage to the city of Touba, one of the communities established by the group and the site of its primary religious shrine, Amadou Bamba's tomb. The Mourides also replaced traditional Islamic patterns of almsgiving with tithing to the local shaykhs. Similarly, the teachings and rulings of the local shaykhs, and of the khalifa above them, replaced the sharia as the primary source of religious authority. Through these practices, the Mourides formed a distinctive expression of Islam, organized around a strongly localized worldview and ethos.

A somewhat similar movement, Hamallism, developed in Mali during the early twentieth century among adherents of the reformist Tijani order of Sufism. This group organized around Hamallah, a shaykh who broke away from the Tijani order. Hamallah's basic message was one of equality among believers. His movement therefore attracted a diverse following of escaped slaves, members of the lower classes, persons without tribal standing, and women without family support. Through its appeal to such believers, Hamallism diffused to various parts of the interior and coastal regions of French West Africa. In the process, Hamallah did not actively oppose French colonial rule but he refused to recognize its authority and many of his followers consequently became involved in the struggle for independence. French colonial authorities thus exiled Hamallah to various parts of Africa and later to France. Hamallism's active proselytism drew strong opposition as well from the Tijani order itself, which felt threatened by the success of the splinter group. As a countercultural movement the Hamallists became increasingly unorthodox over time. They established a number of communal villages in Mali and the Ivory Coast, and like the Mourides they established their own holy city at Nioro in Mali. When in prayer they faced

Nioro rather than Mecca. They also abandoned various aspects of Islamic tradition, such as performance of the Hajj.

These Islamic sects reflected responses to their specific contexts, most notably to the social and economic dislocations associated with colonialism. Social and economic uncertainties also gave rise to a heterodox Islamic sect among African Americans in the United States early in the twentieth century. This group, the Nation of Islam, grew out of the convergence between black nationalist ideologies and the Islamic preaching of Wallace D. Fard, an orthodox Muslim born in Mecca who came to the United States in 1930. Fard established a mosque in Detroit and proselytized among African American migrants from the southern states, preaching that they would overcome white society and achieve social and economic dominance. His followers considered Fard to be the latest messenger from God and perhaps a divine incarnation. The movement became more formally organized under the leadership of Georgia-born Elijah Muhammad and it grew rapidly in the years after World War II. The Nation of Islam's primary message was the superiority of those of African descent. Its leaders characterized Christianity as a white religion that would only suppress black aspirations. They argued for the isolation of the African American community within their own institutions, to serve their own needs and to prepare for the final conflict between good and evil from which they would emerge victorious. The Nation of Islam's strict moral order and emphasis on personal discipline attracted a significant following among African Americans seeking to improve their status in American society, but it initially placed relatively little emphasis on adherence to Islamic orthodoxy. By the 1970s, however, influential members of the group, including Elijah Muhammad's son, Warith Deen Muhammad, began to seek stronger ties to the global Muslim community and gave greater attention to orthodox Sunni practice. To this end, the group largely disbanded in the 1980s as most followers came to identify with the Sunni community as a whole rather than with a separate sect, although a smaller splinter group continued as the Nation of Islam under the leadership of Louis Farrakhan.

In contrast to these particularist trends, some heterodox movements have reflected an extension of Islam's universalism by accommodating the integration of other religious traditions. The Baha'i faith arose from such an accommodation during the nineteenth century. Baha'i grew out of an earlier Shiite sect, Babism, which arose in Iran during the 1840s based on the teachings of Sayyid Ali Muhammad. Ali Muhammad at first claimed to be the *Bab*, the sole "gate" or intermediary between Twelver Shiites and the Hidden Imam, and later revealed himself to be the actual Imam and a manifestation of the divine. He codified his teachings in the *Bayan* ("Exposition"), a new scripture that he introduced as a replacement for the Quran. His heterodox teachings and his support for various social reforms attracted a significant Shiite following, known as Babis. At the same time, the Bab's claims to religious authority provoked strong opposition from the Shiite ulama and persecution by Iran's ruling Kajar dynasty. After Babis had taken part in a series of rebellions against the Kajars, Ali Muhammad was executed in 1850, as were many of his followers.

Following his death, the Babi community became divided. A small group of militants continued to support radical political action, but under intense persecution this group gradually lost influence. Most Babis instead followed Husayn Ali Nuri, who promoted a nonmilitant revival of the movement in Baghdad during the 1850s.

By the 1860s, however, Husayn began to reformulate Babism as a distinctly new sect, first claiming to be a new messenger from God and ultimately declaring himself the Mahdi, acquiring the honorific *Baha'u'llah* ("Glory of God"). These claims led to his banishment by authorities to various locations, lastly to Acre. There he began to develop Bahaism, which he claimed superseded Islam as the unification of all of the world's faiths in a single religion of God. The worldview of Bahaism focused on the continuity of a series of divine manifestations, including Abraham, Moses, Zoroaster, the Buddha, Jesus, Muhammad, the Bab, and Baha'u'llah, through which God's will was revealed to humanity. Bahaism emphasized the essential unity of all of humanity and the need for the continuing spiritual development of each individual's eternal soul. It therefore rejected racial, class, or religious distinctions, instead emphasizing social justice and equality. Bahaism places little emphasis on ritual, does not possess specific sacraments or an ordained priesthood, and incorporates scriptures from all world religions into its worship services. The religious obligations of Bahaism include regular prayer and fasting, abstention from the use of alcohol or narcotics, monogamy, participation in a communal feast every nineteen days, and missionary activity. It attracted a significant following in various parts of the Middle East, including Iran where it became the largest religious minority, and later in Europe and North America. Although the Baha'is' ethos stresses disengagement from politics, they have nonetheless faced various forms of government opposition, particularly in predominantly Muslim states where they are considered guilty of apostasy. The persecution of Baha'is has been particularly intense in Iran, where in recent decades hundreds of Baha'is have been executed for practicing their religion and engaging in missionary activity.

A similar universalist movement emerged from Islam in the Punjab region of South Asia during the 1800s. The movement was founded by Ghulam Ahmad in the Punjabi town of Qadian, where he had been born; and the movement is commonly referred to as Ahmadism or Qadianism. Ghulam Ahmad first began to acquire followers as an Islamic reformer, especially after he declared himself the Mahdi in the early 1890s. Over time, however, his teachings became increasingly unorthodox as he recast his movement as the one universal religion. By the early 1900s, he thus claimed to be the second coming of Christ and the reappearance of both Krishna and Muhammad. In his teachings he strongly opposed Western influences, arguing for example that Jesus had not died on the cross but had migrated to India where his true teachings had been passed on. He also rejected the concept of violent jihad against unbelievers. Because of these extreme views, which attributed all religious authority to Ghulam Ahmad, the Ahmadis met with continual, sometimes violent opposition from orthodox Muslims. Following Ghulam Ahmad's death, his followers thus divided into two principal groups: a more orthodox Islamic group, concentrated in Lahore, which recognized him as an important reformer but nothing more; and a more heterodox group centered in Qadian that maintained belief in its founder's supernatural identity. After the partition of British India, the heterodox Ahmadis faced significant opposition from orthodox Muslims who saw them as heretics. Most of them consequently lived in isolation from the mainstream of Pakistani society, and many eventually emigrated to Europe, North America, India, and former British colonies in Africa.

*   *   *

Through its history, then, Islam has undergone significant processes of diversification. A unitary "Islamic world," even among Sunnis, has no more reality than does a unified "Christian world" or "Buddhist world." This diversity has not undermined the sense of an imagined community maintained by many Muslims, particularly Sunnis, but the practice of Islam as a religious system has been reproduced by adherents in widely different contexts with distinctly different results. The Muslim diaspora of recent decades has continued this process, as Muslim communities in Europe, North America, and elsewhere have adapted to settings in which they do not represent the majority religion (photo 3.8). Within these settings, tensions between received traditions and the circumstances of daily life have produced a new reflexivity regarding orthodoxy and its meaning to adherents, particularly with regard to maintaining a separate identity within a largely non-Muslim society.

Conclusions

As the preceding patterns illustrate, the processes through which religions take on new expressions in diverse contexts develop in varied ways. Adherents of orally transmitted religions may adapt or restructure their beliefs and practices unreflexively, without acknowledging a significant break from older traditions. This pattern is most likely to

Photo 3.8. Marchers in the United American Muslim Day Parade, proceeding down Manhattan's Fifth Avenue. Staged annually since the 1980s by the Muslim Foundation of America, the parade brings together Muslims from diverse backgrounds to reinforce their identity as a cohesive religious community. The parade thus draws significant participation both from Muslim immigrants and from Muslim African Americans, who together form a distinctly American version of the Muslim umma. Manhattan, New York, 2000.

Source: Author.

develop in tribal religions and early ethnic religions, where the integration of religious belief and practice into all aspects of daily life supports a tacit naturalization, or unquestioning acceptance, of gradual changes that take shape in response to varying circumstances. Diversification processes become more complex when believers reflexively recognize that they are in some way deviating from earlier religious patterns. Such reflexivity among adherents reflects a more conscious awareness of the continuity of religious tradition, as expressed for example in the form of religious writings or institutions. The awareness of tradition does not preclude changes in belief and practice, however, as adherents enact a religion in disparate contexts. The major universal religions have thus displayed significant tensions between received tradition and local innovation as they have spread to different settings. Similar tensions have developed as well within widely dispersed ethnic religions, such as Judaism.

Adherents often seek to reconcile the tensions between tradition and innovation, of course, and this reconciliation therefore becomes a central feature of diversification processes. In traditional settings, the conflict between tradition and innovation has typically been resolved through references to superhuman agency. Believers in such cases frequently understand change as a matter of divine inspiration or authority. In this way the acceptance of change, as revealed expressly to true believers, acquires intrinsic legitimacy as an absolute religious obligation. For Protestants during the Reformation, for example, the adoption of certain innovations in belief and practice became a hallmark of genuine religious commitment. In other cases, and especially in more modern settings, believers may consider religious change to depend more on human agency, as a hermeneutic process based on reflexive interpretations of religious tradition in particular circumstances. The rise of Reform Judaism, involving the abandonment of traditions perceived to be outdated and incidental as a means of preserving more basic and universal religious truths, exemplifies this pattern. Adherents may in fact believe that divine inspiration contributes in some way to such processes of interpretation, but without denying the role of human agency. In certain circumstances, greater tolerance may exist between those adherents who adopt new patterns of belief and practice and those who do not because the new patterns are understood to be of human rather than divine origin. In other cases, reflexive departures from tradition may be strongly contested by those adhering to older patterns of belief and practice.

The patterns discussed in this chapter also focus on the relationship between the diversification of belief and traditional spatial variations in the distributions of religions. Within modern settings, however, various trends have contributed further to processes of diversification, particularly within increasingly pluralistic social and cultural contexts. Within such settings, for example, diverse interpretations of a common tradition have frequently emerged as an expression of social stratification or fragmentation.[81] A common form of this pattern is the division of a tradition as liberal and conservative movements split off from existing mainstream institutions. The various forms of fundamentalism discussed earlier in the chapter illustrate this pattern. A second widespread spatial trend in religious diversification has emerged from the rise of various diasporic cultures in contemporary contexts. This trend typically involves complex reconstructions of religious identities in diverse forms, based on reflexive attempts by immigrant adherents both to maintain ties to a common tradition and to adapt to local circumstances.[82] The rise of diasporic cultures thus contributes significantly to the diversity within widely dispersed traditions, but at the same time it may serve to reinforce a sense of community among adherents in different locations.

Finally, as particular religions have come to dominate certain contexts and as growing religious pluralism has affected others, religious groups in all traditions have commonly sought to express their distinctive identity through the control of space at various scales. Such expressions of religious territoriality in fact represent a central feature of religious systems as lived expressions of culture. Chapter 4 now takes up this characteristic of religious systems in detail, focusing in particular on religious concerns with secular space.

Notes

1. See John Roscoe, *The Baganda: An Account of Their Native Customs and Beliefs*, 2d ed. (New York: Barnes and Noble, 1966), 271–345; a classic ethnography first published in 1911 that provides a detailed empirical account of the Baganda prior to European colonization.

2. Doreen Massey, "Power-Geometry and a Progressive Sense of Place," in *Mapping the Futures: Local Cultures, Global Change*, ed. Jon Bird et al. (London: Routledge, 1993), 59–69.

3. Gavin Flood, *An Introduction to Hinduism* (Cambridge: Cambridge University Press, 1996), 129.

4. Klaus K. Klostermaier, *A Survey of Hinduism* (Albany: State University of New York Press, 1989), 279–80.

5. David Dean Shulman, *Tamil Temple Myths: Sacrifice and Divine Marriage in the South Indian Saiva Tradition* (Princeton, N.J.: Princeton University Press, 1980), 4; the goddess Parvati represents the manifestation of Shakti as a consort of Shiva.

6. J. L. Brockington, *The Sacred Thread: Hinduism in Its Continuity and Diversity*, 2d ed. (Edinburgh: Edinburgh University Press, 1996), 130–50.

7. Flood, *An Introduction to Hinduism*, 128.

8. Flood, *An Introduction to Hinduism*, 170.

9. Flood, *An Introduction to Hinduism*, 131.

10. Brockington, *The Sacred Thread*, 151–72.

11. Nirad C. Chaudhuri, *Hinduism: A Religion to Live By* (New York: Oxford University Press, 1979), 124–36.

12. Chaudhuri, *Hinduism*, 125–26.

13. Stanley Wolpert, *A New History of India*, 5h ed. (New York: Oxford University Press, 1997), 157–58; John Keay, *India: A History* (New York: Atlantic Monthly Press, 2000), 342–43.

14. Brockington, *The Sacred Thread*, 202; Margaret Stutley, *Hinduism: The Eternal Law* (Wellingborough, U.K.: Aquarian, 1985), 132.

15. Keay, *India*, 218–19.

16. Brockington, *The Sacred Thread*, 123–26.

17. Flood, *An Introduction to Hinduism*, 129.

18. Chaudhuri, *Hinduism*, 129–33.

19. Chaudhuri, *Hinduism*, 133–35.

20. David Biale, "Jewish Mysticism in the Sixteenth Century," in *An Introduction to the Medieval Mystics of Europe: Fourteen Original Essays*, ed. Paul E. Szarmach (Albany: State University of New York Press, 1984), 328.

21. Dan Cohn-Sherbok, *Atlas of Jewish History* (London: Routledge, 1994), 84.

22. Cohn-Sherbok, *Atlas of Jewish History*, 86–89.

23. Israel Bartal, *The Jews of Eastern Europe, 1772–1881*, trans. Chaya Naor (Philadelphia: University of Pennsylvania Press, 2005), 14–15.

24. Gershon David Hundert, ed., *Essential Papers on Hasidism: Origins to Present* (New York: New York University Press, 1991).

25. Cohn-Sherbok, *Atlas of Jewish History*, 132–43.

26. Joseph L. Blau, *Modern Varieties of Judaism* (New York: Columbia University Press, 1966), 31–32.

27. Blau, *Modern Varieties of Judaism*, 34–39.

28. Many adherents of ultra-Orthodoxy consider the latter term to be pejorative, but its use here conforms to general academic practice and is intended only to distinguish this movement within the larger context of traditional Judaism from which it arose.

29. An excellent analysis of developments in this hearth appears in Michael K. Silber, "The Emergence of Ultra-Orthodoxy: The Invention of a Tradition," in *The Uses of Tradition: Jewish Continuity in the Modern Era*, ed. Jack Wertheimer (New York: Jewish Theological Seminary of America, 1992), 23–84.

30. Kenneth W. Morgan, ed., *The Path of the Buddha: Buddhism Interpreted by Buddhists* (New York: Ronald Press, 1956), 40.

31. Edward Conze, *Buddhism: A Short History* (Oxford: Oneworld Publications, 2000), 26.

32. Morgan, *Path of the Buddha*, 39.

33. Conze, *Buddhism*, 59.

34. Trevor Ling, *The Buddha: Buddhist Civilization in India and Ceylon* (London: Temple Smith, 1973), 191–94.

35. Conze, *Buddhism*, 107–10.

36. Conze, *Buddhism*, 62–63.

37. Morgan, *Path of the Buddha*, 231.

38. Morgan, *Path of the Buddha*, 198–202; Conze, *Buddhism*, 92–93.

39. An influential collection of Chinese koans compiled during the twelfth century appears in *The Blue Cliff Record*, trans. Thomas Cleary and J. C. Cleary (Boston: Shambhala, 2005).

40. Conze, *Buddhism*, 101.

41. Morgan, *Path of the Buddha*, 220–21.

42. Morgan, *Path of the Buddha*, 326–27.

43. Heinrich Dumoulin, ed., *Buddhism in the Modern World* (New York: Macmillan, 1976), 220; Conze, *Buddhism*, 102; Morgan, *Path of the Buddha*, 323–24.

44. Conze, *Buddhism*, 126.

45. Peter A. Pardue, *Buddhism* (New York: Macmillan, 1971), 105.

46. Reginald A. Ray, *Indestructible Truth: The Living Spirituality of Tibetan Buddhism* (Boston: Shambhala, 2000), 133.

47. Ray, *Indestructible Truth*, 194–96.

48. Walther Heissig, *The Religions of Mongolia* (Berkeley: University of California Press, 1980), 30.

49. Heissig, *Religions of Mongolia*, 36–45.

50. Morgan, *Path of the Buddha*, 56–57.

51. William A. Christian, Jr., *Person and God in a Spanish Valley* (New York: Seminar Press, 1972); Peter R. L. Brown, *The Cult of the Saints: Its Rise and Function in Latin Christianity* (Chicago: University of Chicago Press, 1981).

52. Peter G. Wallace, *The Long European Reformation: Religion, Political Conflict and the Search for Conformity, 1350–1750* (New York: Palgrave Macmillan, 2003).

53. Lionel Rothkrug, "Popular Religion and Holy Shrines: Their Influence on the Origins of the German Reformation and Their Role in German Cultural Development," in *Religion and the People, 800–1700*, ed. James Obelkevich (Chapel Hill, N.C.: University of North Carolina Press, 1979), 20–86; André Vauchez, *Sainthood in the Later Middle Ages* (New York: Cambridge University Press, 1997).

54. See, for example, Ellen Badone, ed., *Religious Orthodoxy and Popular Faith in European Society* (Princeton, N.J.: Princeton University Press, 1990).

55. Roger W. Stump, *Boundaries of Faith: Geographical Perspectives on Religious Fundamentalism* (Lanham, Md.: Rowman and Littlefield, 2000), 25–35.

56. Paul Keith Conkin, *American Originals: Homemade Varieties of Christianity* (Chapel Hill: University of North Carolina Press, 1997).

57. Juanita Garciagodoy, *Digging the Days of the Dead: A Reading of Mexico's Dias de Muertos* (Boulder: University of Colorado Press, 1998), 67–107.

58. For a useful comparative survey of these religions, see Margarite Fernandez Olmos and Lizbeth Paravisini-Gebert, *Creole Religions of the Caribbean: An Introduction from Vodou and Santeria to Obeah and Espiritismo* (New York: New York University Press, 2003).

59. A detailed comparative study of AICs within their surrounding religious and political contexts appears in Paul Gifford, *African Christianity: Its Public Role* (Bloomington: Indiana University Press, 1998).

60. Ira M. Lapidus, *A History of Islamic Societies* (New York: Cambridge University Press, 1988), 50.

61. Malise Ruthven, *Islam in the World* (New York: Oxford University Press, 1984), 157.

62. Lapidus, *History of Islamic Societies*, 372–76.

63. Lapidus, *History of Islamic Societies*, 166.

64. Lapidus, *History of Islamic Societies*, 165–67.

65. Ruthven, *Islam in the World*, 171.

66. Lapidus, *History of Islamic Societies*, 109–15, 168–71; J. Spencer Trimingham, *The Sufi Orders in Islam* (New York: Oxford University Press, 1971).

67. Trimingham, *Sufi Orders*, 13.

68. Trimingham, *Sufi Orders*, 31–66.

69. This tariqa is also known as the Ahmadiya order, but because that name has also been used to signify various unrelated groups, the more specific term *Badawiya* is preferable; Trimingham, *Sufi Orders*, 45.

70. Ninian Smart, ed., *Atlas of the World's Religions* (New York: Oxford University Press, 1999), 178–79.

71. Ruthven, *Islam in the World*, 266–67.

72. The concept of the Mahdi is less well developed in Sunnism than in Shiism. In the latter, the coming of the Mahdi signals the approach of the final day of judgment. Sunni beliefs regarding the Mahdi's arrival, on the other hand, are less explicitly eschatological and focus primarily on the divine mandate for the re-creation of a just society.

73. Lapidus, *History of Islamic Societies*, 372.

74. Although the term *Wahhabism* is commonly used to describe this movement, the Muwahhidun do not use it because they believe it places too much emphasis on one man when in their view all emphasis should be placed on God.

75. Lapidus, *History of Islamic Societies*, 508–23; John H. Hanson, *Migration, Jihad, and Muslim Authority in West Africa: The Futanke Colonies in Karta* (Bloomington: Indiana University Press, 1996).

76. When not capitalized, the term *imam* refers to a local ruler or other important leader in Sunni Islam, while when capitalized it refers to the supreme religious leader of Shia Islam or of some Kharijite groups.

77. John L. Esposito, *Islam: The Straight Path*, 3d ed. (New York: Oxford University Press, 1998), 121–24; Ruthven, *Islam in the World*, 280–84.

78. Ruthven, *Islam in the World*, 284–85.

79. Stump, *Boundaries of Faith*, passim.

80. Stump, *Boundaries of Faith*, 52–56.

81. The classic examination of this process in the United States is H. Richard Niebuhr, *The Social Sources of Denominationalism* (New York: Henry Holt and Company, 1929).

82. Cf. Steven Vertovec, *The Hindu Diaspora: Comparative Patterns* (New York: Routledge, 2000); Darshan Singh Tatla, *The Sikh Diaspora: The Search for Statehood* (Seattle: University of Washington Press, 1999); Haideh Moghissi, ed., *Muslim Diaspora: Gender, Culture and Identity* (New York: Routledge, 2006).

CHAPTER 4

Religious Territoriality in Secular Space

In enacting and reproducing their religious systems, believers necessarily imagine and construct a variety of places and spaces of religious significance. Such geographical entities are an essential part of religious systems, both within abstract conceptions of doctrine and faith and in the more immediate contexts of lived religious experience. The resulting spatiality of religious systems represents a primary concern in the geographical study of religion, particularly with regard to understanding religious belief and practice from the "inside," from the perspective of the believer. The intrinsic spatial elements of religious systems derive from various factors. Such concerns in part reflect the general spatiality of cultural systems and the human behaviors associated with them. In essence, all social and cultural activities contain inherent spatial dimensions that give rise to distinctive spaces and places. Throughout their daily lives, people in turn reproduce distinctive time-geographies within diverse social spaces organized at various intersecting scales, from the bodily to the global.[1] Within the context of such processes, believers continually integrate the practice of their religion, just as they do other cultural expressions, into the spatial patterns of their worldly existence.

Perhaps more significantly, however, religious belief informs the basic meanings that adherents attribute to many of the spaces that they construct and use, so that the spaces themselves represent articulations or extensions of the adherents' faith. This process occurs most clearly in relation to sacred space, to which believers ascribe explicit, often transcendent, religious meaning. Sacred space in essence manifests the imagined supernatural cosmos that is encompassed by the worldview of adherents. In reproducing the ethos of their religious system, however, adherents also assign religious import to the meanings and uses of secular space. Indeed, although it lacks special transcendence, secular space provides the primary context within which believers live their religion. For this reason, their worldview and ethos play essential roles in the structuring of the secular spaces of everyday life. Concerns with the meanings and uses of both secular and sacred space contribute, therefore, to the inherent spatiality of religious systems. It should be added here that in many religious systems sacred and secular space do not represent discrete phenomena and adherents may not in fact distinguish between them. Nonetheless, the distinction does provide heuristically valuable concepts for understanding the diverse meanings and uses that adherents attribute to space and in this sense underlies the structure of the following discussion.

This chapter focuses in particular on relationships between religious systems and secular space, leaving the discussion of sacred space to chapter 5. In addressing these relationships, the following discussion takes as its organizing theme the concept of territoriality. Territoriality is considered here not as an atavistic biological instinct but as a form of cultural strategy through which individuals and groups seek to exert control over the meanings and uses of particular portions of geographical space.[2] The most explicit forms of territoriality involve the assertion of political or economic control over space, but the social ordering of space involves the development of a complex network of implicit expressions of control rooted in family responsibilities, the pressure of peer groups, social norms and expectations, and a wide variety of other cultural influences. Territoriality in sum represents an intrinsic product of the spatiality of human activity. In reference to the relationships between religious systems and secular space, expressions of territoriality serve as the means by which adherents integrate their religious beliefs and practices into the spatial structures of their daily lives. In some cases this process is reflexive, based on intentional efforts to organize social space in harmony with specific readings of religious faith and obligation. In other cases, expressions of territoriality develop less by conscious design than by adherents' reproduction of meanings and behaviors that they simply take for granted. In either case, religiously informed expressions of territoriality have profound influences on the construction of the landscapes of daily life and on social spaces organized at diverse scales.

Religious expressions of territoriality differ from other forms, however, in that they possess a distinctly compelling character rooted in the certainties of the worldview and ethos of believers. Those certainties, based on adherents' understanding of the indisputable truth of their religious system, link the organization and control of space to essential issues of meaning, experience, power, and identity.[3] Again, such issues may appear most obviously in adherents' concerns with sacred space, but they clearly pertain to the relationship between territoriality and secular space as well. Religious territoriality in secular space in effect represents the application of the ultimate truths accepted by believers to the spaces of their everyday world.

Broadly speaking, the resulting expressions of territoriality involve four primary functions. At the most basic level, such expressions serve to maintain consistency between daily life and the religious meanings comprising adherents' worldview. Territoriality in this context supports the coherent accommodation of particular religious beliefs within secular space. Efforts to establish legal structures that accord with religious belief represent a common expression of this function, as seen in the goal of Islamic fundamentalists to incorporate the sharia into civil law in various Muslim societies, or in the goal of many Roman Catholics and conservative Protestants to enact legal restrictions on abortion.

Expressions of religious territoriality secondly structure secular space to provide worldly contexts for the realization of the ethos of a religious system, including the performance of commonplace religious practices, the fulfillment of religious obligations, and the pursuit of religious goals. This function has extensively shaped the living spaces, social institutions, and settlement patterns of diverse religious groups. Representative examples include Muslim house forms that accommodate the social segregation of women, local stores and restaurants that provide for the dietary restrictions of Orthodox Jews, and the communitarian settlements of sectarian Christian groups like the Hutterites or Shakers.[4]

The third function, closely related to the preceding two, is to maintain the continuing reproduction of a religious group's system of beliefs and practices, both by reinforcing the faith of existing adherents and by communicating that faith to children and, among proselytic religions, to converts. Institutions providing religious education represent the most obvious manifestation of this function but it finds expression in many other ways as well, from the self-imposed segregation of certain religious minorities to the establishment of various outreach institutions by proselytic religious groups.

Finally, religious groups frequently assert their distinctive identity, in social as well as religious terms, through manifestations of territoriality. This function is perhaps less important than the others in homogeneous societies, whose members take for granted adherence to the dominant religion. In pluralistic contexts, however, its effects are often widespread. The assertion of identity has, in addition, become increasingly reflexive in recent centuries, revealing the intentional demarcation of religious boundaries between groups. The adoption of particular styles of dress represents an obvious expression of this function at the scale of the body, for example.[5] Some expressions of religious nationalism, such as Sikh efforts to create an autonomous state, articulate the same function at a wider scale.

As the preceding examples suggest, each of the major functions of religious territoriality in secular space has been articulated in diverse ways by different religious groups. The remainder of this chapter focuses primarily on the variety of such expressions of territoriality and the distinctive social and spatial structures that they have produced. In addressing this theme, the discussion distinguishes between two major approaches through which adherents articulate religious territoriality: internal processes focusing on the community of adherents itself; and external processes involving interactions with larger social structures that extend beyond the community of adherents. Through internal processes, adherents link the religious norms and expectations that they hold for themselves to the secular places and spaces that they inhabit, articulating their beliefs and practices in relation to their own religious community. Through external processes, on the other hand, adherents fashion their position within a larger social context, defining, adapting, and contesting secular places and spaces that are also inhabited or used by other religious and secular groups. These two approaches to territoriality, internal and external, are not mutually exclusive, of course. Many expressions of religious territoriality involve both internal and external dimensions, with implications for both believers and outsiders. Many religious systems implicitly distinguish between the two approaches, however. More generally, this distinction again provides a useful heuristic approach to understanding the diverse ways in which adherents articulate religious territoriality.

The following examination of internal and external processes of religious territoriality in secular space is not exhaustive, of course. Rather, it offers an assessment of the varied ways in which adherents articulate their religious beliefs by shaping meaning and action within the spaces of everyday life. As mentioned above, many expressions of territoriality have arisen unreflexively from the daily practices of believers and are rooted in the unchallenged conventions of custom. In other cases, manifestations of territoriality involve deliberate, calculated efforts by believers to organize space in accordance with their faith. Thus, internal and external processes may involve informal communal practices or they may reflect the influence of formal religious institutions and structures with specific, defined objectives. And finally, internal and external forms of territoriality both occur within contexts defined at a variety of geographical scales, examined in detail below. Perhaps the primary scale of religious territoriality in secular space is that of the local community of adherents, but from that level expressions of territoriality extend to the more local scales of body and home as well as to the wider scales of the imagined community of all believers, the state, and the world generally. As a result, adherents typically participate in a multitude of territorial processes organized at diverse, intersecting scales within secular space. In doing so, they both reproduce and transform the various contexts in which they enact their religious systems. Expressions of territoriality in secular space in this sense represent an important link between the contextuality of religious systems and the spatiality of religious practice.

Internal Expressions of Religious Territoriality

Adherents of religious systems exercise many different forms of territoriality, intentional and unintentional, over the secular spaces that they inhabit. They exercise territoriality internally when they shape or define secular spaces specifically in relation to their own religious group. They do so by organizing their secular surroundings in religious terms, by attributing religious meanings to particular places and spatial behaviors, and by imposing constraints on the specific activities that they allow within secular spaces. Through these processes, they continually integrate their religious system into their secular surroundings, from the immediate settings of daily life to the broader contexts of the imagined body of coreligionists to which they belong. These expressions of territoriality thus play a crucial role in the expression of believers' religious identity and in the realization and reproduction of their faith.

The Communal Scale

Of the various scales at which internal expressions of territoriality develop, the most fundamental is the communal, the scale that comprises the spaces inhabited by a local community of believers. It is at this scale that the most significant interactions among adherents take place, group interactions that are essential for the immediate enactment and reproduction of religions as cultural systems. Such interactions arise from adherents' identification with a common religion; but like other direct forms of human contact, they are also spatially constrained by the effects of distance. The interactions that bind together a community of believers thus produce a network of local spaces that serve as the primary contexts for the expression of the group's religious system. The communal scale at which such spaces are organized encompasses crucial elements of the religious lives of believers, including their collective worship practices, the realization of shared norms and expectations concerning religious belief and behavior, and group participation in local institutions and social structures. In transforming and reproducing local settings to accommodate these elements, adherents inevitably exert control over the meanings and uses of particular communal spaces; and such expressions of territoriality in turn represent a central feature of the community's religious character. Most importantly, social and cultural processes operating at the communal scale represent the principal means through which believers promote orthodoxy and orthopraxy within their group, typically through the intersecting influences of familial and peer pressures, community sanctions, formal institutions, and local religious and lay leaders. At the same time, the scale of the local community serves as an important context for the development of innovations within or deviations from a larger religious tradition, which gain significance as they become incorporated into the meanings and uses of local communal spaces.

Communal Spaces

The religious focal point of most communities of adherents is the communal place of worship, although other religious institutions may possess central social functions as well. In many religions, adherents understand places of worship as manifestations of sacred space, as discussed in chapter 5. Commonly, though, adherents also understand temples, churches, mosques, and similar structures as centers of the totality of communal life, not just as the site of ritual activity and other explicitly religious practices. The links between places of worship and the communities that use them may be defined in explicitly spatial terms, as in parishes within the Roman Catholic Church. The Orthodox Jewish eruv serves a somewhat similar function. More commonly, the ties between a place of worship and a local community arise informally through custom or religious practice. In many settings, the social meanings centered on the place of worship find expression in associated institutions, such as schools, charities, or community centers.

As an example, the Sufi zawiyas of North Africa arose as ritual centers, but over time they also came to serve multiple social functions. Zawiyas contained a school, provided medical and charitable assistance, and served as a place of social gatherings for lay adherents. Many zawiyas also had connections to craft or commercial guilds, and some hosted annual fairs that attracted trade from surrounding regions.[6] Similarly, in eighteenth-century Iran Shiite mujtahids began to form institutional complexes that became a dominant factor in local social life. Such complexes centered on communal mosques but also included charities, religious schools, and other institutions supported by regular donations from the mujtahid's local followers. Analogous patterns have emerged in many other religious contexts. Such patterns have become increasingly reflexive in modern settings, moreover, as adherents have deliberately expanded the meaning and uses of their places of worship to encompass a wide range of social functions. Among Muslims living in diasporic communities in North America and Western Europe, for example, this process has led to the widespread formation of local "Islamic Centers" or "Islamic Cultural Centers," purposefully named to reflect the secular purposes that they serve in addition to the religious functions of the mosques that they contain (photo 4.1).[7] In the United States, the expanding secular meanings of places of worship perhaps finds clearest expression in the so-called megachurches, large Protestant congregations that provide adherents with services as varied as child care and employment counseling.[8]

Among institutional settings organized at the communal scale of secular space, schools typically rank second in importance. Most of the world's major religions have a tradition of placing education under the control of religious institutions. In many places, such institutions in fact dominated the rise of educational systems. Following

Photo 4.1. The Islamic Center of New England in Sharon, Massachusetts. The text from the Quran (49: 13) displayed across the front of the building explains that God divided people into different nations so that they could identify one another, not to promote hatred, and that God most honors those who are most pious. Sharon, Massachusetts, 2001.

Source: Author.

the spread of Theravada Buddhism across mainland Southeast Asia, for example, Buddhist monks played a central role in the development of schools for commoners, providing education to lay pupils as early as the 1200s in central Thailand. Moreover, Buddhist monks directed public education in Thailand and Burma into the 1800s and in Laos and Cambodia into the 1900s. Again, similar patterns have occurred among many other religious groups. The rising secularization of public education over the past two centuries has constrained the role of religious institutions in this sphere, with varied results. In some instances, religious groups have responded by establishing their own private educational systems. This trend has been widespread in the United States, beginning in the 1800s with the growth of Roman Catholic schools and expanding in recent decades with the formation of conservative Protestant schools. Together, religiously affiliated schools thus educated approximately one in twelve elementary and secondary students in the United States in 2001.[9] These schools represent a crucial expression of territoriality for some religious groups. For many fundamentalist Christians, for example, private educational spaces ensure that secular subjects will be taught in accordance with their literal interpretation of the Bible, as in the teaching of creationism. For immigrant or minority communities in various contexts, private schools provide a means of reproducing their culture systems, including religions, in an alien or pluralistic environment.[10] For other religious groups, however, the secularization of public education has led to the dissociation of secular and religious education, the latter typically being provided at the place of worship.

Because of their importance as sites of cultural reproduction, schools have often become contested spaces, particularly where the objectives of a religious community clash with those of secular authorities. Such conflicts arise from competing efforts to control the social space of children. Traditionalist Anabaptists like the Amish and Hutterites, for example, have contested the role of schools as the spatial setting for integration into the larger society, seeking instead to ensure that their children's schools foster identification with their distinctive religious communities. As a result, these groups have repeatedly contested the schooling of their children with secular authorities in the United States. The Amish have traditionally opposed secular education beyond early adolescence as a worldly distraction that exposes their children to unwanted influences. They have thus challenged the enforcement of compulsory education laws by various states, forming their own schools where children typically complete their education at the eighth grade. Hutterites have similarly resisted sending their children to public schools. Their communities have thus typically contained two schools: an "English" school for state-mandated secular education, and a "German" school, using the Hutterites' German dialect, which focuses on traditional religious and moral education.

For quite different reasons, fundamentalist Islamic schools have become contested spaces in Turkey in recent decades.[11] In the 1920s, after the dismantling of the Ottoman Empire, the secular regime established by Mustafa Kemal Atatürk closed religious schools as part of a campaign to promote secular nationalism. Ultimately the restrictions on religious schools were eased, but growth in the number of Islamic schools in the 1980s and 1990s provoked the government to establish new controls, increasing the period of compulsory public education for all children and banning religious schools from operating when public schools were not in session. In addition, the government denied university admission to graduates of Islamic high schools. For Turkey's secular elites, the public schools represented spaces for reproducing the values of secular nationalism. Islamic fundamentalists have contested this objective, establishing religious schools to reproduce their children's principal devotion to Islam. As fundamentalists have gained in political power in recent years, they have also sought to weaken the restrictions placed on religious education in the 1990s.

In addition to places of worship and schools, the communal spaces of religious groups typically comprise many other institutions and activities. Some institutions, such as charities, hospitals, or child-care centers, may be formally established by religious organizations; but the contexts of everyday life typically contain less formal expressions of religious territoriality as well. Private businesses that serve the specialized needs of adherents represent a common feature of the communal religious landscape. The Hasidic Jewish neighborhoods of Brooklyn, New York, for example, are identifiable by many such features: kosher groceries and restaurants conforming to dietary laws; wig stores for women following the religious practice of covering their own hair in public; hat stores for men; clothing stores selling goods that accord with traditional Hasidic forms of dress; and bookstores selling both secular and religious works in the Yiddish language (map 4.1). Likewise, stores selling halal meat butchered according to traditional Islamic rules represent a common feature in the city's Muslim neighborhoods (photo 4.2). More generally, communities in many Muslim countries possess Islamic banks that adhere to the Quranic injunction against charging interest. In India, the Hindu belief in ahimsa accounts for the presence of thousands of *goshalas* or cattle homes housing infirm or nonproductive cattle, a reflection of the sanctity of

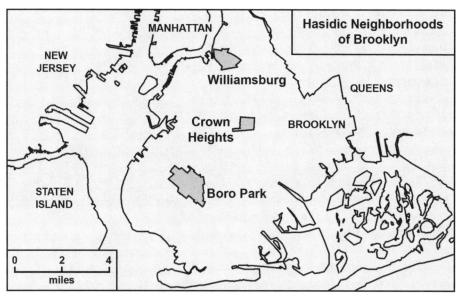

Map 4.1. The major Hasidic neighborhoods of Brooklyn, New York. The Satmar Hasidim predominate in Williamsburg and the Chabad-Lubavitch Hasidim predominate in Crown Heights. The Bobov Hasidim are the largest groups in Boro Park, but this neighborhood includes many smaller groups as well, including the Ger, Belz, Karlin-Stolin, Munkacs, and Skver Hasidim, in addition to many non-Hasidic Orthodox Jews. Neighborhood boundaries derive from the author's fieldwork and U.S. Census data on the speaking of Yiddish in the home, Yiddish being the usual language of Hasidic Jewish migrants from Eastern Europe. Within a number of census tracts in Williamsburg and Boro Park, a large majority of the population speaks Yiddish at home. The use of Yiddish has declined within the Chabad-Lubavitch branch of Hasidism, however, which has adopted a less isolationist stance than have other branches.

the cow in Hindu belief. Some goshalas are run by temples, but many are maintained by local merchants as charitable endeavors.[12]

In rural settings, agricultural land uses frequently reflect religious meanings through associations with the dietary laws followed by adherents. The ritual use of certain crops has influenced agricultural landscapes as well. Early in the first millennium BCE, Greek adherents of the cult of Dionysus likely contributed to the westward diffusion of vineyards producing wine grapes from Greece to Italy and Sicily. Over a millennium later, the spread of viticulture in Europe, and later to the Americas, followed the diffusion of Christianity partly through the use of wine as a sacrament. The spread of citron cultivation along Europe's Mediterranean coast early in the first millennium CE similarly reflected demand for the crop by diasporic Jews for use in the Sukkot festival commemorating the wandering of the Israelites after their exodus from Egypt.[13] More recently, the cultivation of marijuana has emerged as a form of religious territoriality among Rastafarians, adherents of a syncretistic religion that emerged in Jamaica in the mid-twentieth century combining elements of African nationalism and Old Testament symbolism, who understand the smoking of marijuana or ganja to be a sacrament.[14] Finally, expressions of territoriality in communal secular space may not arise from their relationship to specific religious practices but rather from an effort to articulate a larger sense of community among believers. In the United States, for exam-

Photo 4.2.   The Bismillah (''In the Name of God'') Deli, located in a South Asian neighborhood on Manhattan's East Side. The deli prominently advertises the sale of halal meat, from animals that have been slaughtered according to Quranic directives. Believers generally interpret these directives as requiring that a Muslim butcher the animal, invoking God's name during the act of slaughter and using a sharp instrument that immediately dispatches the animal. According to its owner, the Bismillah Deli acquired its halal meat from a specialist Muslim slaughterhouse in Pennsylvania. Manhattan, New York, 2000.
Source: Author.

ple, Christian fundamentalists have frequently used the ichthus, a stylized fish drawn from New Testament imagery, as a symbolic marker in advertisements or store windows to attract fellow adherents who prefer to give their business to other Christians.[15]

Hegemonic Religious Groups

The specific manner in which a community of adherents articulates control over local secular space partly depends on its relationship to its surrounding social environment. Dominant groups exercising hegemony over an area will articulate communal territoriality in ways different from those of minority communities. Groups that dominate a local setting will necessarily have much more extensive and pervasive influences on the secular spaces and landscapes of a locale than will minority groups. Such influences are often articulated through formal institutions, through which adherents reflexively assert control over social space. For example, the Consistory in Calvinist Geneva, acting with the authority of civil law, asserted territorial control over both public and private spaces. Its concerns focused in part on religious behavior, enforcing adherence to Reformed principles and banning the practice of Roman Catholicism or any of its outward expressions, such as wearing a crucifix or using a rosary. The Consistory also regulated many forms of behavior in secular space, however, enforcing bans on dancing, playing cards, fornication, and the disobedience of children toward their parents.[16] The enforcement of religious orthodoxy and moral sobriety became a feature of later Calvinist communities as well. The theocratic structures of early Puritan settlements in New England, which banned the practice of other religions and maintained strict communal standards of behavior, represent one notable instance. Similar patterns have also developed in other religious communities that emphasize adherence to a strict moral order. In Saudi Arabia, for example, local officers of the government-sponsored Committee to Promote Virtue and Prevent Vice enforce obedience to Islamic law throughout the community, in both public and private space, often with the assistance of lay informants. Similar institutions have existed in Sudan and, during the period of Taliban rule, in Afghanistan. More generally, the formal enforcement of religious orthodoxy and orthopraxy within local communities has occurred in many other contexts as well.

The control of communal secular space by hegemonic groups also finds many less formal expressions. These expressions often reflect believers' habitual acceptance of customs, which over time become deeply engrained within local social structures. Such forms of territoriality often become naturalized from the perspective of the hegemonic group, unreflexively taken for granted as part of the natural social order. In many traditions, for example, local communities organize elements of social space in accordance with their religious holidays, transforming the secular landscapes that they inhabit through the use of religious symbols, structures, and other forms of decoration. Wreaths, decorated trees, and crèches representing the nativity of Jesus thus represent typical landscape features during Christmas within many Christian communities. In Jewish communities, the construction of a sukkah (pl. sukkot) or "booth" represents a central part of the celebration of Sukkot, providing the setting where believers eat their meals during the weeklong festival (photo 4.3).

Adherents may also exert territoriality over secular space in reference to shorter time scales, for example by restricting the use of space on a designated day of worship or rest. The closing of businesses during the Sabbath exemplifies this form of territoriality among Orthodox Jewish communities. The naturalization of such restrictions within local communities may be reinforced by legal structures. Such a pattern had developed within Christian communities by the fourth century CE when the Roman emperor Constantine banned nonagricultural labor on the Sabbath. Similarly, in colonial North America this practice became naturalized through the enactment of so-called blue laws, which restricted local business activity on Sundays. Many states and localities in the United States subsequently adopted such laws, although in recent decades the latter have often been relaxed or repealed. Nonetheless, their legacy persists in the shorter hours of operation of many businesses on Sundays.

The naturalization of the community's hegemony may be reinforced as well by the unquestioned incorporation of its religious system into local institutions. Again, the role of religion in schools represents an important example of this process. Another common example is the incorporation of communal prayer into the rituals of public life, such as invocations at the beginning of civic events or the use of religious oaths

Photo 4.3. Sukkah booth built adjacent to Goldsmidt House, a leading Jerusalem hotel, for the festival of Sukkot in 1934. The sukkah is built of organic materials, normally with a roof of palm fronds or other types of greenery. During the weeklong festival, observant Jews eat all of their meals within the sukkah and may sleep there as well, commemorating the life of the Israelites during the Exodus. The sukkah is built adjacent to the permanent dwelling so that the observant may move back and forth between the two on the Sabbath without leaving their own private space. Jerusalem, Israel, 1934.

Source: G. Eric and Edith Matson Photograph Collection, Prints and Photographs Division, U.S. Library of Congress.

in legal proceedings. Through such practices, the dominant group confirms the centrality, and ultimately the authority, of its religion in the communal spaces that it inhabits. All of the expressions of hegemonic territoriality outlined above have an internal dimension as they reinforce observance of the hegemonic religion by its adherents. Their influence frequently extends beyond the boundaries of the hegemonic group itself, however, and thus they come to have an external dimension as well.

Religious Minorities

In contrast to hegemonic groups, minority religious communities typically cannot exert such extensive patterns of territoriality. As a result, their exercise of secular territoriality generally involves strategies that differ from those of dominant groups. Frequently these strategies are explicitly reflexive, deliberately focusing on the preservation of group identity or defending against the effects of assimilation or discrimination. Minority territorial strategies have varied considerably, however, as groups have responded to diverse local contexts. Minority expressions of territoriality within such circumstances partly reflect the character of the larger society in which the minority group is situated. In most traditional settings, minority communities have inhabited contexts dominated by a hegemonic group, a pattern that constrains their ability to control secular space. In many parts of medieval Europe the restrictions placed on Jews regarding occupation or place of residence followed this pattern. In more pluralistic societies, on the other hand, minority religious communities have often had greater territorial control through accepted patterns of communalism, as in the Ottoman Empire's *millet* system, which gave local religious communities a degree of autonomy over their own affairs. In recent centuries, secularized societies have generally provided more liberal contexts for the exercise of territoriality by religious minorities.

Within all of these contexts, of course, the ability of religious minorities to control secular space depends on their relationship with the larger society. A sectarian community inhabiting an area dominated by adherents of the same larger tradition may participate in and support some of the dominant group's territorial expressions in secular spaces. Many Christian fundamentalists in the United States, for example, support broader expressions of Christian hegemony such as the erection of nativity scenes in public spaces during the Christmas season. On the other hand, the exercise of territoriality in secular space by a dominant group will be less likely to coincide with the interests of religious minorities adhering to a wholly different tradition. Finally, expressions of territoriality by religious minorities will be further influenced by the latter's treatment by the dominant group, which may vary from positive acceptance to active persecution.

A minority religious community's efforts to exercise control in secular space will thus be supported and constrained by various factors. When a minority community does not feel strongly at odds with the surrounding society, its efforts to exert communal territoriality will most likely remain limited. Adherents of smaller mainline Protestant denominations in the United States, for example, have generally made few efforts to assert separate control over secular space because they participate comfortably within the larger society. On the other hand, the greater the social and cultural distance between a minority and the surrounding society, the more a minority feels marginalized or threatened, or the stronger a minority's sense of its own separate identity, the more likely minority adherents will be to seek overt control over the secular spaces that they inhabit or use. Such efforts will be especially pronounced when the minority asserts the need for true believers to separate from society or to adhere to a distinctive way of life.

Among religious minorities, the most radical strategy for the control of communal space has traditionally been the formation of isolated settlements. Believers seek to achieve a degree of self-sufficiency by organizing such settlements, which traditionally have been agriculturally based. A minority community's desire for separateness and self-sufficiency may reflect sectarian or fundamentalist views that the surrounding society has abandoned the basic religious principles of a tradition. The Santi Asoke movement, a Buddhist fundamentalist group that arose in Thailand during the 1970s, typifies this pattern.[17] Asoke adherents believed that Thailand's Buddhist establishment had come to focus more on bureaucratic and political issues than on authentic Buddhism; and they rejected the increasingly secular character of Thai society, which, in their view, subverted Buddhist values. As a result, they formed a number of self-sufficient, rural communities where they could enact their interpretation of Buddhism in isolation. Within these isolated spaces, group members have articulated a way of life characterized by simple dwellings and clothing, the practice of organic agriculture, and strict adherence to vegetarianism.

The formation of isolated settlements has in some cases arisen from more explicit doctrines requiring true believers to remain separate from the rest of society. This pattern has emerged among various Anabaptist groups within Christianity, for example. Their formation of isolated settlement patterns derived from passages in the New Testament that direct believers to separate themselves from non-Christians, as in 2 Corinthians 6:17: "Do not be yoked together with unbelievers." Anabaptists have organized secular space in various ways to conform to this belief in separation from worldly society. The creation of distinct settlements first became widespread among Anabaptists driven into Central and Eastern Europe by persecution from other Protestants. The Hutterites formed small, collective villages in which adherents held their goods in common, a practice that persists in the Bruderhofs they have established in the United States and Canada. The Amish adopted a somewhat different settlement pattern made up of individual farms, often inhabited by extended families. Their commitment to remaining separate in secular space found expression in other ways, such as their rejection of electricity and telephone networks that would connect them to the outside world. Because of the religious significance of remaining separate, these groups strongly emphasize the acquisition and control of land over successive generations.

The creation of communal spaces by religious minorities has also arisen from more overt efforts to merge civic and religious life, often in the form of a local theocracy. This strategy has commonly appeared among sectarian groups who adhere to beliefs at odds with those of society and whose ethos places strict limits on behavior. The Druze exemplify this pattern. As a heterodox Islamic group, they sought to preserve their distinct identity in the eleventh century by taking refuge in isolated communities in the mountainous regions of Lebanon and southwest Syria. Local religious leaders enforced strict adherence to their faith and its system of religious law, loyalty to the group, the practice of endogamy, and mutual defense.

Similar patterns, though less extreme in their isolation, developed among various sectarian groups that emerged from the Protestant Reformation. The Moravian Brethren, for example, sought to create local communities independent from the influences of hegemonic state churches. Herrnhut, a village formed by Brethren in the early 1700s on the estate of a sympathetic nobleman in Saxony, became the original model for self-sufficient Moravian communities. The group subsequently replicated this model in various parts of Europe and North America, the latter including early settlements in Bethlehem, Nazareth, and Lititz in Pennsylvania, and in Salem, North Carolina. These communities served as a foundation for further evangelism, but they also provided a context within which the group could enact its ethos focusing on personal piety, equality among adherents, charitable work, education, and industry. The communities founded in the early 1600s by Puritans in the Massachusetts Bay colony and Pilgrims in the Plymouth colony represented analogous expressions of communal territoriality in which religious authority became widely integrated into the meanings and uses of secular space.

The formation of communal spaces by religious minorities has also developed, in some instances, in connection with conceptions of sacred space. During their early history, Mormons in the United States conceptualized the secular settlements that they created as sacred sites as well.[18] They based their major settlements in Jackson County, Missouri; Nauvoo; and Salt Lake City on the model of a new Jerusalem to serve as their primary ritual centers. As their settlement patterns became increasingly dispersed, however, they came to associate their communal spaces in a more general sense with Zion, a new, earthly Eden in which the Mormons would dwell. On this model they constructed hundreds of local communities across the interior of the western United States after arriving in Utah in the late 1840s. The Shakers similarly viewed the communitarian settlements that they created in New York, New England, and the Middle West as landscapes of redemption, reflecting the transformation of the secular world through the second coming of Christ in the person of founder Ann Lee. Similar patterns have developed in many other settings. A number of Christian and Islamic sects in Africa, for example, have established communal settlement patterns focusing on newly defined holy cities. Among Christian groups, various African Instituted Churches created settlement patterns focusing on a holy city associated with the group's founder. Examples include Mozano and New Mozano in Ghana, associated with the Musama Disco Christo Church; Ninevah, Kenya, associated with the African Israel Church Ninevah; and N'kamba, Zambia, associated with Kimbanguism. Such cities serve ritual functions as pilgrimage centers but they also represent settings for communal secular life and institutions.

The creation of secular settlements may also be linked to the conceptualization of sacred space at wider scales. A significant contemporary example of this pattern has emerged in the formation of settlements by religious Zionists in Judea and Samaria, based on the belief that creation of the modern state of Israel was linked to the eschatological redemption of the Jews. As part of this process, religious Zionists have emphasized the importance of reclaiming control over ancient Jewish territory; and with Israel's occupation of the West Bank after the Six-Day War, they thus began an aggressive campaign of settlement in the region, forming well over a hundred local communities.[19] These settlements in effect reflect two expressions of territoriality: immediate control over local secular spaces as well as a foothold for expanding control over the sacred space of the biblical Promised Land.

Finally, religious minorities that have established isolated communal spaces have done so through strategies of land control, maintaining the integrity of the community by seeking isolated settings and retaining control of the land within the community itself. The continuing integrity of communal spaces further derives from the establishment of institutional structures, both religious and secular, that bind the group together. In some cases, external sources of discrimination or persecution may also reinforce the persistence of isolated minority communities. Early antagonism toward the Mormons, for example, contributed to their decision to relocate to the isolation of the Great Basin, although their own religious beliefs also played a central role in their settlement patterns. In any case, efforts to form isolated communal spaces can be very effective. The Druze, to cite an obvious example, have succeeded in maintaining their distinct identity in isolated rural villages in Lebanon and Syria for nearly a millennium.

The expression of territoriality by religious minorities tends to be more complex in urban settings. Strategies of land control in urban contexts are more difficult to implement, and religious minorities may face competition from other groups for the use of secular space. Nonetheless, the organization of urban secular spaces by religious minorities represents an important form of communal territoriality. Such groups have often asserted control over the spaces of their daily lives by concentrating in particular urban neighborhoods, in many cases reflexively using such spaces to express their distinct identity. In contrast to more isolated rural settings, however, urban settings place religious minorities into closer proximity to other social groups, producing more diverse forms of interaction. Most importantly, processes of urban segregation tend to develop out of two factors: a religious minority's territorial strategies for maintaining its distinct character, and attitudes of other groups toward it.

The diverse forms of segregation associated with urban Jewish communities exemplify the complexity of such processes. Relatively distinct Jewish quarters had appeared in Egyptian cities by the tenth century, reflecting Muslim accommodation of "People of the Book." Similarly, Jews and other religious minorities developed distinct quarters in Jerusalem beginning in the twelfth century, under the accommodating policies of Saladin. During the Middle Ages, distinct Jewish ghettos also began to appear in European cities. The Jewish ghettos of Europe in part grew out of the discriminatory practices of local governments, which confined Jews to specific urban districts, often located beyond the city walls. This pattern reflected the broader antagonism of Christian Europe toward Jews, frequently expressed in explicitly religious terms. Tragically, this medieval pattern recurred in more destructive form during the twentieth century under the rule of the Nazis, who enforced Jewish residential segregation as part of broader policies of persecution and genocide.

Despite the association of Jewish ghettos with patterns of discrimination, however, the neighborhoods themselves functioned as vital communal spaces for European Jews. The importance of these communal spaces to many of their inhabitants became evident during the Jewish Enlightenment and Emancipation of the nineteenth century, as various cities and states removed restrictions on their Jewish populations. Reform Jews, who embraced a liberal outlook, abandoned the older patterns of segregation to achieve greater participation in European society. Most early adherents of Orthodox and Hasidic Judaism, on the other hand, remained committed to the inward-looking life of their traditional neighborhoods and maintained their segregation from the larger society. For these groups, the communal organization of secular space remained essential to the enactment and reproduction of their religion. Orthodox and Hasidic Jews who subsequently emigrated from Europe continued to establish distinct urban neighborhoods as they settled in new locations. Hasidic Jews formed several such neighborhoods in Brooklyn, New York, for example, each area associated with a Hasidic sect identified by its place of origin in Eastern Europe (map 4.1). These neighborhoods reflect conscious efforts by Hasidic immigrants to maintain their communal isolation through the control of secular space.

Within urban settings, the residential separation of religious groups has also intersected in complex ways with other segregation processes. Antagonisms between ethnoreligious groups, for example, have contributed to patterns of religious segregation. In such cases, religious conflict may contribute to the rise of segregation, but the process typically involves issues of identity and historical conflict that extend beyond religious concerns. The conflict in Northern Ireland between Protestants and Roman Catholics, to cite one example, produced rigid patterns of residential segregation; but in this case, group concerns focused less on establishing local contexts of religious meaning than on asserting historical claims to primacy within the surrounding region.[20] Again, the Nazis' ghettoization of Jews represented a more egregious expression of the consequences of ethnoreligious conflict. In some pluralistic contexts, however, patterns of segregation have developed differently, as a means of limiting conflict between different groups. The Ottoman Empire's millet system had such an effect, permitting each religious community to function under its own laws and communal leaders. In diverse urban settings, moreover, each millet typically occupied its own quarter of the city, which contained a variety of secular and religious institutions to serve the local group and operated in accordance with the group's customs. This system enabled the Ottomans to rule over potentially fractious, heterogeneous societies and at the same time provided religious minorities with a degree of control over their own communal spaces.

Various social processes have also contributed to the subdivision of secular space among different elements of a single religious group. Again, such patterns have often reflected the influence of ethnic identity. The settlement of Roman Catholic immigrants in American cities during the 1800s and early 1900s, for example, produced complex patterns of segregation, isolating Roman Catholics from Protestants but also separating Roman Catholic ethnic groups from one another. The rise of separate neighborhoods for German and Irish Roman Catholics became commonplace during the mid-1800s. By the end of the century, this pattern repeated itself with the emergence of distinct neighborhoods for Roman Catholic immigrants from Italy, Poland, and other origins in Southern and Eastern Europe. The subdivision of secular space may also reflect the importance of more narrowly defined religious communities within a single tradition. Again, the aforementioned Hasidic neighborhoods in Brooklyn emerged as Hasidic communities rooted in particular European centers sought to establish separate secular domains. Contrasts in social status within religious groups may as well produce distinct secular spaces within urban settings. Perhaps the most complex instance of this pattern exists within Hinduism, in the intersection of social and religious status with traditional patterns of caste segregation.

In various recent settings, narrowly defined communities of mutual support and self-interest have also developed within larger religious traditions. The "base communities" associated with the rise of liberation theology in Roman Catholicism exemplify this process. The concept of base communities developed during the 1960s as part of the movement toward grassroots empowerment of the poor through personal liberation.[21] This movement linked secular well-being, self-determination, and social change to the process of spiritual redemption. The base communities thus provided contexts both for religious activity, particularly Bible study, and for mutual aid. The latter focused on communal activism, especially with regard to political participation and community development. The base communities themselves came to number in the tens of thousands across South America during the 1970s and 1980s. They typically comprised local groups of fifteen to twenty families who provided mutual forms of support, integrating religiosity with secular needs. In most regions they accounted for only a small portion of the Roman Catholic population, however. Because they frequently operated beyond the supervision of the church hierarchy, they also tended to develop locally distinctive religious practices. As a result they often functioned as minority religious communities even within predominantly Roman Catholic societies.

Their initial success in South America contributed to their diffusion to other Roman Catholic countries, especially Haiti and the Philippines; but because of their early associations with revolutionary social aims, they have become less prominent in recent decades.

The broad strategy of the base communities, integrating secular forms of mutual support into a religious system, has recent parallels in some fundamentalist communities in other religious traditions. Christian fundamentalists in the United States, for example, have in many locations established communal networks of businesses and services to provide both financial and religious support for one another. These local networks are often spatially dispersed within a surrounding city, so participating enterprises have commonly identified themselves using Christian symbolism, such as the ichthus, on store fronts and in advertisements. Fundamentalist groups have similarly created local Christian yellow pages to direct adherents to the businesses of coreligionists. In recent decades, Muslim fundamentalists in various settings have also created networks of communal spaces to promote the concept of Islam as a total way of life. The Muslim Brotherhood in Egypt typifies this pattern, having established a variety of local communal spaces including hospitals, clinics, schools, charitable organizations, and small businesses. While the Muslim Brotherhood has sought to serve large segments of Egypt's population, the smaller Jamaat al-Muslimin ("Society of Muslims") has pursued a strategy of isolation, residing in the outer suburbs of Cairo and in upper Egypt where they have shared a variety of more confined local communal spaces.[22]

A common feature of most of the aforementioned examples of urban religious communities is their visibility. In certain situations, however, persecution has driven minority religious communities underground, out of the sight of local authorities. For such communities, the structuring of secular space can involve significant risks and thus their communal spaces are often highly fragmentary and limited in size, function, and usage. Despite the dangers involved, however, such spaces provide the group with the necessary contexts for maintaining a functioning community within hostile surroundings. In some instances, the persecution of religious minorities derives from their characterization as heretics. The Baha'i communities of Iran provide a case in point. Since the nineteenth century, various regimes in Iran have sought to suppress Bahaism as heretical. Thus the current Islamic government in 1983 banned Baha'is from assembling in public and from operating administrative offices or other communal institutions, activities that are allowed for other religious minorities in the country. The government has also confiscated many of the group's properties. As a result, Baha'is must conduct their communal life covertly, primarily in private homes.[23] Adherents of Ahmadism (or Qadianism), also considered heretics by orthodox Islamic authorities, have similarly faced persecution in Pakistan. The Pakistani government has, for example, banned Ahmadis from using Islamic terms or phrases in public speech and has prevented Ahmadis from holding religious conventions within the country. Orthodox antagonists have also destroyed a number of Ahmadi places of worship, forcing communal religious activity into more private settings.

Religious minorities have also been forced underground by secular authorities seeking to limit their social influence. In the former Soviet Union many orthodox Muslims rejected the limitations placed on officially sanctioned expressions of Islam and instead formed their own clandestine communal spaces, such as local mosques.

Such activity was particularly common among adherents of the Naqshbandiya Sufi order in the Caucasus region.[24] A government ban on the Falun Dafa sect in China since 1999 has similarly forced adherents to establish a covert network of communal institutions and worship spaces.

Monastic Spaces

Finally, the various types of communal spaces discussed so far are largely inhabited, used by, and reproduced by adherents at large. Christianity and various Eastern religions have given rise, however, to specialized communal spaces reserved for distinctive religious orders.[25] The communal spaces of such religious orders have taken varied forms, but for the sake of convenience they are identified here in generic terms as monastic spaces. In most traditions, monasticism first took the form of individual hermits living in isolation, but communal or cenobitic forms of monasticism ultimately became more significant. Communal monasticism became widely established early in the development of Buddhism and Jainism. In Christianity it developed more slowly, emerging in the fourth century but increasing in importance after Benedict, the sixth-century founder of the Benedictine order, defined the basic patterns of Christian cenobitic life. Communal monastic spaces in some cases have functioned as places of withdrawal, where inhabitants focus largely on personal expressions of piety. Such spaces are generally established in isolated locations and have limited contact with the outside world (photo 4.4). Because of their separate identity, they may ultimately

Photo 4.4. La Grande Chartreuse monastery, located in an isolated valley on the edge of the French Alps. La Grande Chartreuse is the primary monastery of the cloistered Carthusian order. Members of the order live apart from the outside world and spend most of their time in solitary prayer, study, and labor. Isère department, France, 2006.

Source: Eusebius (commons.wikimedia.org/wiki/Image:La_Grande_Chartreuse.jpg), under Creative Commons license (creativecommons.org/licenses/by/2.5/).

take on some of the characteristics of sacred space, serving for example as pilgrimage destinations.

More commonly, though, monastic spaces possess important connections to lay society. In Buddhism and Jainism, and to a lesser extent Christianity, monasteries serve in part as centers of religious activity for lay adherents, who gain merit through their involvement with monastic institutions. This pattern appears explicitly in Theravada Buddhist communities, where young men frequently spend a short time as novices in monasteries before fully entering adult life. Moreover, monastic spaces have often served central functions within lay society. Some of these functions, such as missionary work and the performance of rituals, are distinctly religious in character; but others involve secular activities, from education to health care to charitable work. In various traditional societies, monasteries also often functioned as important cultural and economic institutions, serving as centers of learning and controlling large surrounding estates. The traditional role of monastic institutions as centers of political power in Tibet reflects a more distinctive pattern of involvement in secular affairs. Through their diverse roles at the communal scale, monastic spaces thus represent important expressions of religious territoriality in secular space.[26]

*   *   *

The varied ways in which adherents organize secular space at the communal scale, in sum, define the contexts for the interactions between their religious faith and their daily lives. Some of these spaces simply reflect the religious identity of the group, while others take on more explicit religious significance. In either case, the formation of these spaces provides believers with the means to enact and reproduce their communal religious culture. Such spaces are thus necessary to the grounding of religions as cultural systems in the immediate, shared experiences of group members. Consequently, such spaces also provide the foundation for the assertion of territoriality at both narrower and wider scales, topics to which the discussion now turns.

Narrower Scales

Forms of religious territoriality constituted at scales narrower than the local community focus primarily on the traits and behaviors of individual believers. Such expressions of territoriality interact extensively with communal processes, however, and thus they connect individuals to their local communities. Among the various narrower scales of religious territoriality, two are particularly significant: those of the body and the home.[27] Territorial processes constituted at these narrower scales necessarily differ from those organized at communal scales, even though the former frequently intersect with the latter. Most importantly, narrower expressions of territoriality relate more immediately to the specific details of adherents' lives. As a result, religious territoriality at narrower scales frequently has more direct connections to a religion's ethos, and more specifically to conceptions of the religious obligations of the individual adherent.

Body Space

Religious territoriality at the scale of the body reflects a complex set of issues relating to individual appearance, behavior, and worship. Perhaps the most basic of these issues is the assertion of religious identity. The body provides an essential medium for articulating the religious character of the self, for example through dress, ornamentation, and other aspects of personal appearance. A second crucial issue focuses on personal purity. This concern addresses purity in a social sense, expressed in the adherent's relations with others, as in prohibitions against adultery or premarital sex; but it also involves spiritual purity, for example through dietary practices or ritual bathing. Thirdly, the body represents the most immediate focus of concerns with the observance of orthodoxy and orthopraxy. Control of body space in this sense provides a fundamental means of promoting accordance with group expectations regarding adherence to religious law or a religion's ethos. Finally, concerns with individual worship and expressions of faith converge at the scale of the body. Prayer, baptism, fasting, and faith healing, to cite a few examples, all manifest explicit intersections between body space and belief.

These issues underlie a great variety of bodily expressions of territoriality among the world's religious traditions. Many such expressions focus on personal appearance. Patterns of dress represent a common example of this form of territoriality. Various religious groups have manifested their religious ethos through distinctive dress, while others have used dress to mark the religious boundaries that separate them from others. After Orthodox Judaism emerged as a distinct entity in Eastern Europe, for example, adherents maintained traditional dress as a means of signifying their strict observance of tradition and their difference from Jewish proponents of reform. These patterns of dress, such as hats, beards, and dark overcoats for men and long sleeves and head coverings for women, remain an important element of Orthodox Jewish culture. Many Sikh men adopted distinctive patterns of dress following the rise of the concept of the Khalsa, or community of the pure, a seventeenth-century movement within Sikhism that promoted a stronger sense of religious obligation and identity among adherents. As a sign of their distinct identity, male Khalsa Sikhs adopted the so-called five *kakars* ("articles of faith"): *kesh*, uncut hair and beard; *kanga, kara*, and *kacha*, a wooden comb, an iron bracelet, and breeches worn by the adherent; and *kirpan*, a small sword carried by the adherent. In contrast, various religious groups have emphasized simplicity of dress as an expression of an ethos of piety and humility. English Puritans during the 1600s emphasized plain dress, for example, as did various smaller Protestant groups, such as the Quakers and Anabaptist groups. Many male Anabaptists also adopted the practice of wearing beards without mustaches, by tradition an expression of their opposition to the German military class with which the wearing of mustaches had been associated. The wearing of beards by Muslim males similarly reflected a concern with identity, apparently deriving from Muhammad's concern that believers distinguish themselves from nonbelievers who did not wear beards.

Many religious groups have also adopted distinctive dress for women. Typically this pattern manifests the individual's acceptance of an ethos of modesty or sobriety, but in many contexts it has also been used as a means of asserting social control over women.[28] Perhaps the most well-known example of this pattern is the wearing of veils by Muslim women, based on a Quranic injunction (24: 31) that a woman should disguise her beauty from men outside her family. This practice takes widely different forms, however, from the complete veiling of the body by the traditional Afghan burqa to less obscuring forms of headscarves used merely to cover the hair. In addition, the practice of veiling holds quite different meanings for Muslim women in different contexts, not always related to issues of social control. Indeed, for many Muslims this practice represents an important expression of identity, personal respectability, or resistance to a dominant non-Muslim culture.[29]

Dress relates as well to the meaning of body space in reference to specific religious practices. Adherents often use special dress to articulate the role of the body in particular rituals. When Muslims participate in the Hajj, for example, they begin by performing *ihram* or purification in preparation for the pilgrimage rites. For men, this ritual involves adopting simple white clothing, comprising two rectangular pieces of fabric, which symbolizes both their purification and the equality of all believers before God. The adherent may also shave his head and trim his beard at this time, and he continues to wear the ihram clothing throughout the pilgrimage. Although not a requirement, women also often wear white clothing during the Hajj. The use of special clothing during rites of passage also occurs in many religions. In Christianity, adherents undergoing the rite of baptism frequently wear special white clothing, again a symbol of purification, such as a christening gown for infants or a baptismal robe for adults. The wearing of certain types of clothing may in itself be associated with particular religious states. Jewish men have traditionally observed morning services wearing a prayer shawl based on belief in a divine revelation to Moses that this practice would keep believers mindful of God's commandments. When inside a temple, Mormons wear white temple clothing to symbolize reverence and purity. The ancient Jewish tradition of wearing sackcloth in expressing grief became adopted as well by Christians in the wearing of hair shirts as an expression of repentance, a practice that remained commonplace into the medieval period. In the Vodou religion, clothing serves to link adherents to particular nations or tribes of deities, or *loa*. In worshipping the generally benign Rada, loa adherents traditionally wear ritual white clothing, for example, while in the less common worship of the more fearsome Petro, loa adherents wear red clothing.

In addition to its relationships to specific religious practices, dress can symbolize more general elements of a religious group's distinctive ethos. In traditional forms of Judaism, for example, men have customarily worn some form of head covering as a sign of respect for God and as a reminder that their worldly existence lies below a greater divine presence. The kippah or yarmulke, usually a small, round skullcap, represents a common type of Jewish head covering. Male headgear takes more elaborate forms in some Jewish groups, however, especially among the Hasidim. The adherents of the different branches of Hasidism wear various types of hats, usually dark in color, in some cases made of rabbit (or, more traditionally, beaver) fur, and mostly based on traditional East European styles. The hat store therefore represents an important feature of the local business landscape of most Hasidic neighborhoods (photo 4.5). Hasidim also generally tend to distinguish hat styles associated with normal daily wear (as in photo 4.5) from styles worn on the Sabbath and holidays, such as the large, round *shtreimel* (photo 1.3).

In many religions, distinctive dress and physical appearance also define a significant boundary, at the scale of the body, between the laity and religious elites. The symbolism of such clothing may focus on issues of identity and piety, manifesting the special personal status of religious leaders, priestly classes, and monastic orders. Examples include the traditional black-and-white habit of Roman Catholic nuns, the tradi-

Photo 4.5. Store sign for Feltly Hats, located in the Hasidic neighborhood of Williamsburg. The sign depicts two distinctive hat types: the flat style, worn primarily by the Satmar Hasidim who dominate the Williamsburg neighborhood, and the tall style, worn by most Hasidic groups. Brooklyn, New York, 2000.

Source: Author.

tional clerical tonsure in Roman Catholicism and Eastern Orthodoxy, the shaved heads and saffron robes of Buddhist monks, or the distinctive headgear and robes of Shinto priests. Within the Digambara ("sky-clad") sect of Jainism, monks manifest their sacred identity by living entirely without clothing. The special dress of religious orders or elites may have more complex meaning, however, indicating the wearer's legitimacy in the performance of religious ritual. Within Roman Catholicism, for example, vestments manifest the authority of the priest in celebrating the mass and administering other sacraments. The vestments are blessed by the priest's bishop, and according to tradition denote the priest as a representative of the divine. Ritual dress may also serve to induce certain sacramental states, such as trance or spirit possession, by religious elites. This pattern appears in Tibetan Buddhism in the rituals of the Nechung oracle, the chief priestly medium and since the 1600s the state oracle in Tibet, who wears an elaborate costume and, to designate the actual trance state, a massive sacred helmet. Similarly, a common feature of animistic religions is the use of masks by shamans to enhance their spiritual vision or achieve possession by a spirit.

The wearing of religious symbols by lay adherents represents another overt assertion of religious meaning in body space. The wearing of amulets and charms appears in many religious traditions as a means of protecting body space, but the use of religious symbols has various other functions. The wearing of a crucifix, symbolizing the death and atonement of Christ, is a commonplace but diverse practice in Christian cultures. The wearing of a crucifix in part reinforces the religious identity of the adherent, particularly among Protestants who generally represent the cross in symbolic form without the body of Christ. Within Roman Catholicism, the crucifix more commonly includes the body of Christ, and serves more as a form of personal devotion. In some traditional Roman Catholic cultures, adherents in addition view the crucifix as a source of spiritual and physical protection.

A common form of bodily religious symbolism in Hinduism is the wearing of a *tilak* or mark on the forehead or other parts of the body (photo 4.6). During the ancient Vedic period tilaks had associations with caste affiliation, but in classical Hinduism they became associated with specific devotional patterns. The *bindi*, a red dot usually of vermillion worn on the foreheads of women, traditionally represented the goddess Parvati, the principal consort of Shiva and benign manifestation of Shakti. It served to indicate that a woman was married, but as a manifestation of the divine power of Shakti it also provided protection to the woman and her spouse. In more recent years, the bindi has become more purely decorative in function, and is often worn by unmarried women. Sectarian devotional groups also wear tilaks to specify their religious identity and acquire divine protection. Devotees of Shiva typically wear a tilak comprising three horizontal lines on their foreheads, for example, while those devoted to Vishnu apply a tilak consisting of two vertical lines connected in a U shape, sometimes with a third central line.

A more particular practice of wearing religious symbols developed within traditional Judaism in the form of tefillin, small leather cases containing texts from the Torah, which are strapped to the arm and the forehead. This practice derived from a scriptural commandment to bind the divine law to the body. Tefillin are placed on the inside of the arm to be close to the heart and on the forehead to be close to the mind, in both instances to keep the adherent focused on divine law and the Jewish covenant with God. Orthodox Jews and some Conservative Jews wear tefillin during morning services, except during the Sabbath, and on specific festivals. Traditionally

Photo 4.6. A Hindu man with a tilak painted on his forehead, the three horizontal lines indicating devotion to Shiva. Kathmandu, Nepal, 2006.

Source: Pål Anders Martinussen, under Stock.xchng image license (www.sxc.hu/txt/license.html).

only males wore tefillin, but in recent years some Conservative and Reform women have adopted the practice as an expression of Jewish feminism relating directly to female body space.

Along with matters related to physical appearance, religious territoriality at the scale of the body frequently focuses on the meaning and conduct of specific bodily processes. Everyday dietary patterns represent a common expression of religious control at this scale. Many religious traditions include prohibitions against certain foods, such as the ban on pork consumption in Islam, the avoidance of meat observed by many Hindus and Buddhists, or the *Book of Mormon*'s injunction against consuming strong or hot drinks. Dietary restrictions may be quite complex, not only banning particular foods but also specifying how allowed foods must be prepared, as in Jewish rules concerning the kosher diet and Muslim rules concerning the preparation of halal meat. In some instances dietary rules support the consumption of specific foods, such as the traditional Roman Catholic practice of eating fish in place of meat on Fridays or the promotion of nuts and whole grains as substitutes for meat among Seventh-Day Adventists. Of course, many religions prohibit the consumption of various nonfood products, such as tobacco, alcohol, and other intoxicants. The imposition of dietary restrictions has various rationales, in some cases reflecting concerns with bodily health or purity but in others involving ethical concerns, as in vegetarianism among Eastern religions supporting belief in reincarnation, or obedience to divine law, as in Judaism.

Spiritual benefits also provide a rationale for periodic departures from ordinary dietary practices, usually through fasting or the adoption of a modified diet during a portion of the religious calendar. Fasting during the Christian period of Lent, for example, replicates in the believer's person the fasting of Christ in the wilderness and expresses repentance, humility, and religious discipline in advance of the celebration of Easter. The Muslim observance of Ramadan, lasting throughout the lunar month called by that name in the Islamic calendar, requires fasting during the daylight hours to commemorate the origins of the divine revelation of the Quran to Muhammad. In Muslim belief, fasting also strengthens religious discipline and gratitude while promoting an ethos of humility and atonement for the believer's sins. The end of Ramadan is marked by one of Islam's major feasts, *Eid al-Fitr*. Yom Kippur, the Jewish Day of Atonement, similarly incorporates fasting as a means of achieving spiritual purity and discipline and as a mark of repentance. Adherents modify their dietary patterns differently for the Jewish festival of Passover, marking the flight of the Israelites from slavery in Egypt. During Passover, adherents eat unleavened matzo in place of bread, as the fleeing Israelites did according to tradition.

The preceding examples illustrate that fasting in various traditions provides a physical means of expressing humility and penitence, but it has had other functions as well. In various ancient religions, for example, fasting served as a means of purification for religious elites in their interactions with the divine. Adherents of various religions have also used fasting to achieve elevated spiritual states, as in the extreme asceticism of some Hindu and Jain holy men. Adherents of tribal religions have also frequently used fasting to achieve trances or visions. Many Native American traditions, for example, have incorporated this practice into the vision quest through which young men become initiated into adulthood. Conversely, the ingestion of intoxicants has been a common means for shamans to achieve visionary states in various tribal religions. Examples include the use of peyote by the Native American Church in the western United States, the use of iboga in the Bwiti religion in West Africa, and the use of ayahuasca by various groups in South America.

At the scale of the body, religious groups also exert territoriality in relation to issues of health, sickness, and medicine. Religious elites play a significant role in healing in many religious traditions, typically as the medium through which divine or spiritual forces influence or transform the body. The role of the shaman as healer is common in animistic religions, with the shaman serving as the intermediary between the spirit world and supernatural processes organized in body space. The healing practices rooted in the syncretistic animism of Santeria, comprising a complex system of charms, herbs, and rituals, represent a typical example.[30] Conversely, animistic religions often include beliefs in the possible malevolent use of spiritual influences to infect or harm the body, requiring the shaman's protection. More generally, religious traditions have frequently associated sickness with sin or demonic possession, a commonplace view in early Judaism and Christianity, for example.

Concern with the control of body space has also engendered a diversity of healing cults in world religious traditions, through which bodily maladies are treated through religious means. These cults may focus on the healing powers of a particular individual or substance, as in the Muslim practice of seeking cures by acquiring baraka at the tombs of Sufi saints or in the Christian use of holy water to cure or prevent illness. Such cults have often produced significant pilgrimage traditions, discussed in chapter 5, focusing on specific environmental settings, such as springs, rivers, or mountains, believed to have intrinsic curative powers.[31] An emphasis on faith healing has also appeared in the beliefs of certain Protestant groups. Christian Science is perhaps most distinctive in this regard, emphasizing the spiritual healing of physical ailments through the ministry of "practitioners." The use of faith healing, administered by ministers at local religious revivals or, more recently, via radio and television, has also become a common feature of various conservative Protestant denominations.

Finally, religious belief may intersect with health and the control of body space through adherents' avoidance of certain medical procedures. Jehovah's Witnesses, for example, banned the use of vaccinations up until the early 1950s, based on the belief that inoculation with vaccines derived from animal sources violated a biblical injunction against consuming blood. Although the group eventually dropped this ban, in the 1940s it established a similar ban against blood transfusions, which remains a part of the group's doctrines.

Processes relating to sexuality and gender are another common focus of religious territoriality at the scale of the body, but one that has found expression in highly divergent forms. Most importantly, the meanings attached to sexual activity vary widely among different religious groups. In many religions of the ancient Mediterranean world, for example, adherents viewed sexual union as a manifestation of divine union, a belief that found direct expression in the practices of temple prostitutes in various traditions. Many forms of Hinduism represent sexual pleasure as an integral part of the experience of life, and within the context of Tantrism sex may provide a means of achieving enlightenment for those with the necessary esoteric knowledge. Within Roman Catholicism and some forms of conservative Protestantism, in contrast, the meaning of sexual activity derives primarily from its association with biological reproduction. Most forms of Buddhism, on the other hand, depict sexual activity as a common impediment to spiritual progress toward enlightenment.

Such diverse interpretations of the meaning of sexual activity have in turn produced varied expressions of territoriality in relation to body space. Generally these expressions include prohibitions against some forms of sexual behavior, most commonly incest and adultery. Many religious groups also ban premarital sex or homosexuality, but others do not. Certain groups have enforced various forms of gender segregation to restrict even casual bodily contact between unmarried men and women. Some ultra-Orthodox Jewish businesses in Jerusalem, for example, have separate shopping hours for men and women to prevent contact between them. Similar patterns of gender segregation in public space occur in many conservative Muslim societies, a pattern that became particularly pronounced in Afghanistan under Taliban rule. Gender segregation may find expression as well in visual terms, as in the veiling of women in Islam or the use of wigs by Orthodox Jewish women to keep their own hair from public view.

Abstinence from sexual activity has also taken on specific religious meanings. Such meanings are perhaps most explicit in the practice of celibacy by religious elites, who are expected to accept sexual abstinence as a means of achieving higher states of enlightenment or unity with the divine. This practice is particularly common in Christianity and Buddhism, but has appeared among ascetics in other religious traditions as well. Religious traditions may also place sexual restrictions on lay adherents in particular religious contexts, as in the Islamic prohibition against sex during Ramadan in the daylight hours and the Jewish proscription of sex on Yom Kippur.

Regarding reproduction, opposition to artificial birth control may have a religious foundation, as in traditional Judaism, following the biblical commandment to be fruitful and multiply, or in Roman Catholic doctrine, which views birth control as contrary to the workings of divine law. Many religious groups also ban or discourage abortion, which they typically characterize as the taking of a life. Such groups differ greatly, however, in their understanding of the conditions under which an abortion is justifiable, a complex issue encompassing practical, moral, and theological concerns ranging from the health of the mother to the moment at which an embryo acquires a soul.

Practices concerning the sexual organs and their functions finally represent a common expression of religious territoriality at the scale of the body. Rituals regarding menstruation are widespread, usually based on concerns with issues of bodily purity. As an example, in traditional Judaism the laws of *niddah*, rooted in the belief in the sins of the biblical Eve, require that women must purify themselves following menstruation by performing a ritual bath or *mikveh*. The practice of circumcision has acquired religious meaning in some traditions, particularly Judaism, in which it represents a mark of the covenant with God, and in Islam, in which it follows rules of cleanliness based on hadithic traditions. Some Muslims, especially in Africa and the Middle East, also practice female genital cutting (also known as female genital mutilation or female circumcision) as part of the Sunna of Islam, although most Muslims oppose the practice (map 4.2). Both circumcision and female genital cutting appear to have ancient origins and are found as well in diverse tribal religions.

Along with matters relating to physical appearance and bodily processes, the place of the body in ritual represents an important expression of religious territoriality in individual patterns of worship. The body again represents a focus of purification rituals in diverse religious traditions. The Islamic performance of ablutions before

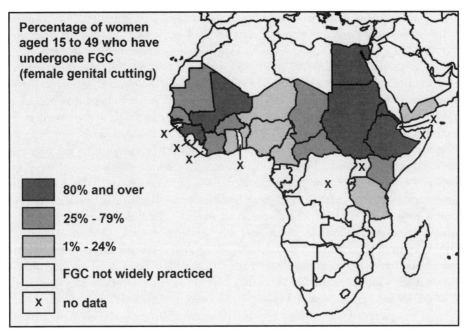

Map 4.2. Distribution of the prevalence of female genital cutting among women aged 15 to 49. Based on data from *Female Genital Mutilation/Cutting: A Statistical Exploration* (New York: UNICEF, 2005).

entering the mosque exemplifies such rituals, as do the aforementioned ritual of ihram before the Hajj, the practice of fasting in many traditions, and the use of the traditional mikveh in Judaism. The body also often plays an important symbolic role in religious ritual. The practice of marking adherents' foreheads with ash on Ash Wednesday, as a reminder of sin, death, and divine grace, represents such a practice in Roman Catholic, Anglican, and Lutheran branches of Christianity. A Hindu example appears in *Holi*, the saturnalian Festival of Colors that celebrates the coming of spring, during which adherents throw colored powder and water onto the bodies of other celebrants.

In various traditions, finally, the use of the body in worship and ritual centers at times on physical forms of penance, such as the fasting practices discussed above. Physical penance may also take more severe forms, such as self-mortification and flagellation. Such practices are most characteristic of ascetic monasticism but they have also appeared among the laity in various traditions. Flagellant brotherhoods, devoted to public displays of penance, emerged among Christians in Italy during the thirteenth century, for example, providing believers with both a means of atonement and a personal, physical connection to the sufferings of Christ. This practice became widespread across Europe during the following century within the context of uncertainty arising from the diffusion of the plague.[32] Although suppressed by the Roman Catholic Church, such brotherhoods also later developed in various locations in Latin America.[33] The Shiite Muslim observance of Ashura, a day of grief commemorating the martyrdom of Muhammad's grandson Husayn, also traditionally incorporated public processions of flagellants. In some contemporary Shiite communities the practice of self-flagellation has been abandoned and replaced by another practice centered on the body, the donation of blood to a local blood bank.[34] Further relationships between body space, ritual, and religious experiences are examined in chapter 5.

Religious territoriality pertaining to body space and worship also finds expression in concerns involving the location of the body. Such concerns appear in many traditions in the practice of communal worship, which incorporates the expectation that believers will regularly and directly participate in group religious activity. Participation in communal worship, as in a temple, church, or mosque, serves as a primary link between the scales of the body and the community by establishing ties between personal experience and a broader religious identity. Within the context of worship, believers may also apply more specific restrictions on the location of the body, often as an expression of adherence to religious tradition or law. In Islam, orientation during prayer toward the qibla, in the direction of Mecca, illustrates this pattern, as does observance of the boundaries of an eruv during the Sabbath in Orthodox Judaism. Bodily location plays a role in more exceptional forms of worship as well. The meaning of pilgrimage, for example, depends directly on the placement of an individual's physical self within a distinctive location, or set of locations, typically associated with a particular conception of sacred space, as discussed in chapter 5.

The concept of the religious retreat represents a different but equally widespread expression of the interactions among location, worship, and the body. The retreat, like many prayer and meditation rituals, serves as a means of enhancing religious concentration, but it also involves the actual relocation of the body to a place of isolation apart from the world at large. The retreat is often part of a specific worship ritual. During the final days of the Islamic celebration of Ramadan, for example, Muslims typically perform *itikaf*, a nighttime retreat to a mosque for concentrated prayer. Many tribal religions include retreats in particular rites of passage, such as those associated with the attainment of adulthood, during which believers seek individual visions through isolation and fasting. The retreat may also serve as a more exceptional practice, however, adopted by individuals seeking spiritual renewal or enlightenment. Christianity has a strong tradition of this practice based on the model of Christ's forty days of isolation in the wilderness, and institutionalized in idiorrhythmic forms of monasticism. Different forms of physical relocation have taken on religious significance in many other traditions as well. The concept of hijra in Islam, for example, which grew out of Muhammad's original emigration from Mecca to Medina, later came to signify any migration of any adherent from a non-Muslim to a Muslim society, often considered a religious obligation as discussed in chapter 2.[35]

Finally, the control of body space in terms of various aspects of bodily appearance, processes, and ritual uses has taken on special significance in relation to religious concerns with death. Territoriality in this context focuses both on the proper treatment of the body itself and on its proper disposition within the larger contexts of social and sacred space. Religious traditions have generally emphasized the respectful treatment of the dead, but the diverse practices of different traditions reflect their multifarious understandings of death and the role of the body after death.[36] Regarding treatment of the body itself, washing the corpse represents a practice common to many traditions, in some contexts serving to purify the dead and in others to guard the living against the pollution of death. Many traditions also maintain the practice of dressing the corpse in special clothing, either as a sign of purity or respect or to prepare the dead for the afterlife. Death may also be associated with more elaborate bodily rituals, such as anointing the body with oil in Roman Catholicism or with sandalwood paste in Hinduism. Furthermore, preparation of the body for disposition may incorporate connections to broader spatial structures, as in the display of the dead in the home or a place of worship during a wake or similar ritual, or in the public procession of the body to the site of its final disposition. Through such practices, believers transform social space as a means of marking the significance of death. In many traditions, adherents also understand such practices as the initial stages of the dead's journey into the afterlife.

The final disposition of the body, in turn, reflects beliefs concerning the relationship between the body and the individual's self or soul. Such beliefs generally fall into two major categories: those based on unitary conceptions of the human individual, which posit that the body is not separable from the self; and those based on dualistic conceptions, which posit that the body serves only as the temporary vessel for a nonmaterial essence, such as a spirit or soul, that survives death. Among religious groups adhering to a unitary view of the individual, burial represents the primary means of disposition of the corpse, as it leaves the body intact. This practice has been widespread in Judaism, Christianity, and Islam, all of which developed a unitary view of the individual based on eschatological beliefs concerning the physical resurrection of the dead. Reform Jews, Protestants, and, since 1963, Roman Catholics, have also accepted cremation, but among traditionalists burial remains the primary means of disposition. The treatment of the body in burial practices varies widely, however. Orthodox Jewish belief prohibits embalming, to ensure that the body will return to dust in accordance with scripture. Islamic belief also prohibits embalming in most cases. Within Christianity, on the other hand, embalming has become widely practiced in recent centuries, although previously the practice was relatively uncommon. These traditions also have developed various concerns with burial and the location of the body relative to sacred space, as discussed in the next chapter. Religious groups that adhere to a dualistic view of the individual, in contrast, have typically adopted methods of disposition that involve the destruction of the corpse itself. Cremation, as practiced widely in Hinduism, Buddhism, and many archaic religions, represents the most common method, although some forms of Buddhism and Zoroastrianism practice exposure of the corpse to predators. Issues of location again play an important role in these funerary practices, discussed in chapter 5.

Although they take multifarious forms, the abovementioned expressions of territoriality at the scale of the body generally share an underlying emphasis on the religious identity, duties, and obligations of the believer. These practices therefore provide an essential link between the individual's personal existence and the larger framework of a religious tradition. In more immediate terms, they are particularly important in situating the individual within the context of a surrounding religious community. Observance of the meanings and uses of body space is one of the principal means by which adherents associate themselves with a religious community. At the same time, such expressions of territoriality enable the community to assert control over individual adherents, through standards of behavior and practice that reinforce the community's reproduction of its religious system. Territoriality over body space thus intersects in important ways with territoriality at the broader scale of the community.

Home and Family Space

A similar pattern exists for religious territoriality at the scales of the home and family. Indeed, the meanings and uses of domestic space frequently mediate relationships between the scales of the body and the community, especially through the basic rules and structures of the family.[37] The significance of territoriality at the scale of the home derives in particular from the central role of home and family, in most religious systems, as the foundation of the larger social order and as the immediate setting for the reproduction of core beliefs and practices. In accordance with that role, religious groups have generally developed specific expressions of territoriality to foster family stability and to define the religious obligations and activities of the believer in relation to home and family.

Perhaps the most basic expressions of religious control of home or domestic space focus on concerns with the structure of the family itself. Diverse traditions relate the character of the family unit to religious doctrine, especially through the practice of marriage. As the foundation of family and home, marriage may take on symbolic meanings through its associations with larger spiritual unions, such as the union of Christ and the church in Christianity or the covenant between God and the Jews in Judaism. In more concrete terms, however, the religious dimensions of marriage reflect various forms of social control expressed through specific practices concerning wedding rituals, the choice of partner, and the meaning of marriage itself. Among contemporary world religions, such rules have most often asserted a preference for monogamy. Islam represents the primary exception, the Quran (4: 3) allowing a man to have up to four wives providing that he can treat them with equal justice. Polygamy is also allowed by some African Instituted Churches within the Christian tradition, and was traditionally common in ancient and tribal religions. Control at the scale of the family has focused as well on the choice of marriage partner. Because they have linked marriage to procreation, most religions have discouraged or banned homosexual unions, although some contemporary religious groups, particularly within the context of liberal Protestantism, have abandoned this stance. More generally, religious groups have typically articulated restrictions concerning marriage between particular individuals, including bans on marriage between close relatives, individuals belonging to different social groups, or adherents of different religious traditions. Religious controls at the scale of the family also commonly address divorce, either banning it outright or defining the circumstances under which it is allowed. The concern with divorce again reflects the representation within most religious traditions of the importance of family and home in fostering social stability.

Religious concerns with family structure extend as well into beliefs regarding the organization of family roles. Perhaps the most common expressions of such beliefs relate to issues of gender, especially with regard to the expected roles of husband and wife. Patriarchal family structures have had an explicit religious foundation in most of the major world religions, rooted either in scripture or in custom. In Christianity and Judaism, for example, belief in the obedience of wife to husband derives from a divine commandment to Eve in Genesis (3:16). In addition to power relations within the family, religious control may focus on the division of labor and the domestic role of women. This pattern appears in contemporary settings, for example, among ultra-Orthodox Jews and many conservative Christians. As a further example, the Quranic injunction (4: 34) that men should serve as guardians over women, who should in turn be obedient, has traditionally been interpreted by Muslims as restricting the social role of women primarily to domestic responsibilities. Another Quranic injunction (33: 53), indicating that Muhammad's wives should remain isolated from men to whom they were not related, has served as the basis for the traditional spatial seclusion of women within the household, reinforcing their domesticity. As this example illustrates, control of family thus intersects significantly with territoriality at the scale of the body. It should be noted, of course, that patriarchal family structures have declined in influence in some contemporary societies.

Religious belief informs a wide variety of other functions organized at the scale of the family. Control over such functions focuses both on the reproduction of religious systems and on the observance of religious obligation centered in the family. With regard to cultural reproduction, most traditions constitute the family as the primary context for the religious education of children, especially early in life. This function often has a gendered character with mothers playing the primary role, through ethical instruction and the encouragement of religious practice. As children age, formal religious instruction may take place outside the home, but the inculcation of a basic religiosity typically remains a parental responsibility. The maintenance of a religiously authentic household by parents thus represents a primary expression of religious territoriality at this scale. Within the context of the family, children also bear religious responsibilities toward their parents, for example with regard to the care of elderly parents or the performance of funerary rituals. In Islam, for example, the Quran and hadith represent caring for elderly parents as a basic religious act; and in Hinduism, the eldest son typically plays a central role in funerary rites for his parents. Patterns of inheritance linking different generations of adherents represent another familial function that may have distinct religious meanings. This function is especially clear in Islam, in which religious law explicitly defines the proper means of handling matters of inheritance.

In addition to concerns with family structure and function, religious territoriality at the scale of the home encompasses diverse practices related to the dwelling itself. In some traditions, religious belief finds expression in the siting and layout of dwellings. To cite one widely observed example, religious groups whose worldview attributes a specific spatial orientation to the cosmos have typically laid out their dwellings in line with a cosmologically significant direction. Within the context of animistic religions, the effort to propitiate or conform to spiritual forces commonly introduces magical elements into the construction of dwellings. The use of feng shui in traditional Chinese religion as a factor in locating and constructing houses, and other landscape features as well, exemplifies such practices. Dwellings also may incorporate significant ritual functions in the actual practice of a religious system. Household shrines represent an important focus of religious activity in varied traditions, as discussed in chapter 5. Adherents may also ascribe religious meanings to their homes through the use of decorations, such as religious symbols, which identify the religious character of the family and in some traditions protect it from harm. This pattern appears among many Christians, for example, in the display of a cross or crucifix in the home. Within traditional forms of Judaism, adherents view the religious identification of the house as a divine commandment, based on the Torah. Adherents observe this commandment by attaching a mezuzah, a text from the Book of Deuteronomy (6:4–9; 11:13–21) contained within a small case, to the doorpost of a house or room. Finally, control of the religious meanings of the home appears in some traditions through the use of the dwelling to articulate religious conceptions of household structure. This pattern may find expression implicitly, as in the division of domestic space into masculine and feminine portions based on religious beliefs concerning gender roles. In the case of many traditional forms of Islam, adherents have made such divisions more explicit through the creation of a distinct portion of the house reserved for the women of the household (map 4.3). Along different lines, the dwelling may reflect the relationship between the individual family and the larger community, for example by linking the family home to a larger communal settlement. Such a pattern appears in the communal settlements of the Hutterites, in which groups of families occupy separate apartments within a shared dwelling or longhouse.

Wider Scales

Internal expressions of territoriality organized at scales wider than the local community, over a particular country or across the globe, represent a crucial feature of spatially dispersed religions. Such expressions serve a number of functions. Most importantly, they connect the local community to a larger, shared tradition. Wider articulations of religious territoriality provide essential means of maintaining orthodoxy among dispersed adherents and thus are central to the reproduction of a religious

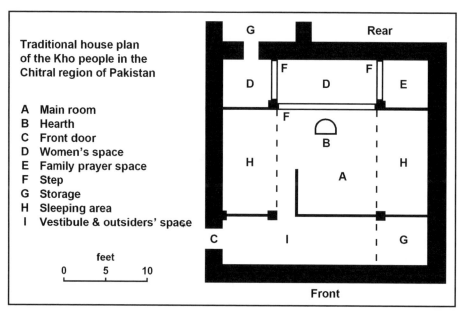

Map 4.3. Generalized plan of the traditional rural house of the Kho, a Muslim people living in the Chitral region of northern Pakistan. The main room is reserved for household members, relatives, and perhaps close friends. Regarding the household's pets, cats have the run of the house while dogs, like outsiders, are restricted to the vestibule. Adapted from illustrations and descriptions in Shahzada Hussam-Ul-Mulk and John Staleym, ``Houses in Chitral: Traditional Design and Function,'' *Folklore* 79, no. 2 (Summer 1968): 92–110.

system in diverse contexts. In this sense, expressions of territoriality at wider scales strongly influence the organization of processes of control at the scales of community, home, and body. Religious groups also exercise territoriality at wider scales by unifying separate communities as a larger, imagined body of adherents. The existence of this larger body provides an extended sense of fellowship and serves as the foundation for shared identity and institutions. In addition, it establishes a context for the articulation of religious authority and of broader religious objectives, such as missionary activity or social activism. Wider expressions of territoriality serve as well to define religious practices that acquire meaning from the participation of believers from beyond a single community, as in the organization of major pilgrimages.

Imagined Communities of Believers

At the most extensive scale, the conception of imagined communities of believers, which links specific religious systems to a larger tradition, contains at least an implicit element of territoriality. This element has been made explicit in some cases through the symbolic identification of a religious tradition with its spatial domain. The concepts of Christendom and Dar al-Islam exemplify this pattern, each defining a territory in which one tradition exercised hegemony. The concept of Christendom played a central role in medieval European political geography, providing an image of cultural unity as well as establishing the discourse governing relations between Europe and neighboring Islamic states. Belief in the obligation to defend Christendom thus became a major expression of territoriality at a regional scale. Dar al-Islam, signifying those parts of the world where Islamic law prevailed, was a somewhat more complex concept in medieval Islam, as some jurists argued that observant Muslims could lead a true Islamic life only within Dar al-Islam's boundaries. The concept thus referred in part to obligations at the scale of the individual adherent.

Even when the conception of a universal community of adherents is not linked to a geographical region, moreover, the sense of common identity may imply the authority of a particular tradition across diverse spaces. The concepts of world Jewry and of a global Buddhist sangha, for example, imply a form of territoriality by asserting that a tradition's unity has meaning and authority across different spaces, transcending local contingencies. Adherents have reflexively promoted such global conceptions of a community during the modern era through the establishment of institutions supporting worldwide ecumenism within a tradition, such as the World Council of Churches (founded in 1948), the World Buddhist Sangha Council (1966), and the Organization of the Islamic Conference (1969) (map 4.4).

Religious Institutions

The linking together of dispersed communities of believers generally focuses on narrower conceptions of religious identity, however. The most basic institutional expression of such efforts is the denomination, a union of local groups adhering to a common religious system within a larger tradition. Although individual denominations may allow internal diversity, they typically draw their identity from a specific set of beliefs, often codified in a formal text or confession, and from standardized religious practice. As institutions, denominations exercise a dispersed form of territoriality over

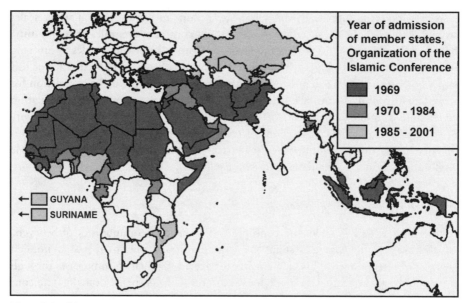

Map 4.4. Member states in the Organization of the Islamic Conference (OIC) by year of admission. The OIC seeks to foster solidarity among Muslims and member Muslim states.

the local spaces articulated by adherents in different communities. They have influence over specific worship spaces, of course, but in many ways denominational discourses also affect the control of the spaces of adherents' daily lives. In organizing denominational institutions, many groups have also established territorial structures under the control of specific bodies or leaders. This practice appears commonly within Christianity, as in the division of space into parishes, dioceses, and archdioceses within Roman Catholicism or into synods and presbyteries by some Protestant denominations.

With regard to organizational structure, denominations have adopted very different forms of polity. Some have implemented highly centralized polities, in which a denominational hierarchy exercises significant control over spatially dispersed adherents. Again, the Roman Catholic Church represents a primary example of this type of structure, but the centralization of authority appears as well among the various Orthodox churches, the Mormons, the Church of England, and numerous other Protestant groups. Although less formally defined in a denominational sense, Tibetan Buddhism reflects such a pattern in the leadership of the Dalai Lama. Hasidic Judaism has also traditionally been characterized by the centralization of leadership within a Hasidic court in the person of the rebbe. In contrast to the aforementioned groups, many denominations have adopted more decentralized forms of polity, placing greater control in the hands of local leaders or individual adherents. In such cases the denomination as a whole exerts influence by articulating basic commonalities in belief and practice, but local communities have a degree of autonomy in realizing the larger group's religious system. This pattern represents a fundamental matter of faith among many Protestant groups, who view Jesus as the only legitimate religious leader. Similarly, within most forms of Buddhism the local monastery has served as the immediate source of religious authority. An emphasis on local autonomy may also reflect the absence of centralized denominational institutions within branches of a larger tradition, as in the cases of Sunni and Shia Islam or of Saivism, Vaishnavism, and Shaktism in Hinduism.

Along with denominational organizations, various more specialized institutions have linked local groups of adherents to a larger imagined community. Religious orders are a common example. Institutions of this type again vary in their degree of centralization. Some have clearly defined, hierarchical structures of authority and administration, as in the monastic orders of Roman Catholicism. Others are more loosely structured, however, comprising relatively autonomous local communities united by a common lineage. The monastic traditions of Buddhism tend to follow the latter pattern, for example. In either case, the unity of the larger association represents a source of authenticity and in this sense articulates a form of territoriality over dispersed networks of monastic or clerical spaces.

Specialized organizations focusing on particular religious concerns represent another unifying influence over dispersed communities. Some such organizations focus primarily on fostering adherence to orthodoxy. Orthodox Jews, for example, have established a great variety of local, regional, and national kosher certification agencies in the United States to guarantee that commercially marketed foods satisfy Jewish dietary laws. These organizations, and especially the national agencies like the Orthodox Union and OK Kosher Certification, in effect contribute to the standardization of religious practice within distributed Jewish communities (photo 4.7). As another example, since the 1970s Muslims in various countries have formed Islamic

Photo 4.7. כשר שלום or Shalom Kosher Pizza, located in midtown Manhattan. According to the sign in the upper right corner of the window, the kosher character of the restaurant's food is certified by the Organized Kashrus Laboratories, or OK Labs, under the supervision of Rabbi Don Yoel Levi. Headquartered in Brooklyn, the OK Labs use a K inside a circle as their *hechsher* or symbol of kosher certification. Manhattan, New York, 2001.

Source: Author.

banks founded on the Quranic principle banning the use of interest in financial deal-ings. The multinational Islamic Development Bank further seeks to promote eco-nomic development in keeping with the broader principles of Islamic law.

Other organizations have focused on the revival of religious activity among fol-lowers of a particular tradition. This pattern is reflected in the Tablighi Jamaat, the Indian Islamic group that has sought to advance authentic Islam in place of the syncre-tistic practices common among Indian Muslims. Starting in the 1940s, adherents of the Chabad-Lubavitch branch of Hasidic Judaism established a similar outreach movement, eventually global in scope, aimed at promoting orthodox observance among all Jews. Revivalism also has a significant recent history within Protestant Christianity, although focusing more on personal salvation than on specific ritual practices.

Finally, adherents of different traditions have formed organizations aimed at furthering religious objectives more broadly within society. These organizations may in part express external forms of territoriality to the extent that their influence extends beyond the adherents' own religious group, but they also function as sources of inter-nal unity and religious authority among coreligionists. Various popular religious movements have reflectively adopted this approach in the past century as a means of promoting social and political change. In Egypt, the Muslim Brotherhood has created an extensive network of institutions in its effort to reform society along authentic Islamic lines. Similarly, the Rashtriya Swayamsevak Sangh ("National Union of Vol-unteers"), a Hindu fundamentalist organization founded in India during the 1920s, fostered the development of a number of organizations in India to promote the influ-ence of Hindu nationalism. To a more limited extent, the Christian men's movement known as the Promise Keepers, founded in 1990, has sought to expand the role of traditional Christian values within American society.[38]

Less Formal Sources of Interaction

Less formal institutions and processes also may exert influence over the dispersed adherents of a particular religious system. Although lacking formally defined institu-tional structures, distinctive schools of religious thought in some contexts represent a significant factor in the unification of religious identity among believers. Within Sunni Islam, for example, the major schools of Islamic law and the various Sufi orders have contributed to a distinct sense of commonality across dispersed adherent populations. That sense of commonality in turn has a strong effect on local patterns of belief and practice, linking the latter to more widespread conceptions of religious doctrine and obligation. The sense of identity associated with a particular legal school or Sufi order in essence places an implicit form of territoriality on the religious lives of adherents and the specific spaces that they inhabit. The various schools of Mahayana Buddhism display a similar pattern, tying believers in dispersed locations to the doctrines and obligations of a shared religious lineage.

Less formal expressions of territoriality also develop through periodic interac-tions or associations among adherents. One such association, the communal retreat that brought together itinerant monks and nuns during the rainy season, played a significant role in early Buddhism, maintaining a sense of solidarity among otherwise solitary practitioners and eventually leading to the establishment of formal monasteries. More generally, in many religions traditional forms of periodic association have developed in relation to special worship practices. In ancient Judaism, for example, adherents from scattered settlements traveled to the temple in Jerusalem three times a year to celebrate the festivals of Passover, Pentecost, and Sukkot. Periodic assemblies of dispersed adherents have frequently developed around communal rites of pilgrimage, as in the participation of Muslims in the Hajj and of Hindus in the *Kumbh Mela* pilgrimages. Lay retreats and revivals, such as the camp meetings held on the nineteenth-century settlement frontier of the United States, further exemplify this pattern. In contemporary settings, religious groups have organized a great variety of periodic councils and conferences focusing on particular matters of belief and practice. Although quite different in character, these periodic associations share the effect of bringing together adherents from diverse locations. This process of interaction again represents an implicit form of territoriality in which adherents articulate a unified sense of religious obligation or commitment, reinforcing the internal commonalities of the larger religious group to which those adherents belong.

Religion and Secular Social Structures

Beyond the effects of explicitly religious institutions and processes, the integration of religious belief and practice into broader social structures has also contributed to the expression of religious territoriality at wider scales. Such patterns develop primarily at the scales of region, nation, and state; and they typically produce more explicit expressions of territoriality, from legal controls to widely accepted social norms. These expressions of territoriality have been commonplace in societies where a single religious group has predominated. Through the hegemony of the dominant group, the integration of its religion into diverse social structures has largely developed unreflexively, with the group's worldview and ethos taken for granted as the basis for social order. In the process, believers' acceptance of particular religious doctrines and obligations affects diverse forms of social behavior. In homogeneous religious settings, the resulting expressions of territoriality again are essentially internal in character. In more diverse societies, however, the widespread social integration of the majority's belief system has often been imposed on other populations. The latter pattern is characteristic of external patterns of territoriality, and is addressed in more detail later in this chapter.

The integration of religion into broader social structures finds varied expression, both informal and formal, as a factor in internal religious territoriality at wider scales. Informally, religiously homogeneous societies generally integrate religious belief and practice into their fundamental mores and customs. Through this often unreflexive process, believers tacitly reproduce their daily lives in accordance with their religious system. Many different practices fit this pattern, including phenomena as diverse as the structuring of time and work in accordance with a religious calendar, the organization of agriculture in a manner consistent with dietary laws, or the application of given ethical rules in the conduct of economic activity. As such patterns develop, the direction of causality between religious belief and secular behavior may be ambiguous. To cite a common example, the Hindu veneration of cows is associated with various cultural and social behaviors, such as prohibitions against the consumption of beef or the wearing of leather items. These behaviors have traditionally been explained as a product of the more basic veneration of life and of the cow's symbolic significance in Vedic belief. Cultural materialists, on the other hand, have explained them as the outcome of an adaptation to a context in which cattle are more valuable as draft animals and sources of milk and manure than as sources of meat and leather.[39] According to the latter point of view, cow veneration ultimately derived largely from those more practical, material concerns. This point remains arguable, however. Regardless of the direction of causality, moreover, Hindus have traditionally reproduced behaviors associated with cow veneration from one generation to the next on religious grounds, thus asserting an informal expression of religious territoriality concerning the treatment of cattle in areas where Hinduism predominates. More generally, in such situations the informal integration of religious and social structures produces a tacit religious discourse that, for believers, naturalizes particular social phenomena within the framework of their worldview and ethos.

More direct expressions of religious territoriality through the integration of religious and social structures have emerged from the fulfillment of social and political roles by religious institutions. Again, such processes have often developed unreflexively, based on adherents' acceptance of organized religion as an integral part of the social order. In such cases believers may not separate a religious institution's secular and sacred roles, considering both to be expressions of its social function. As discussed above, education represents one of the principal social roles that have been taken on by religious institutions. Adherents have frequently organized this role at the scale of the individual community, but within larger, homogeneous societies religious institutions have often taken responsibility for the principal system of public education. In various traditional contexts this pattern developed as a matter of course out of the traditions of learning associated with religious elites, but in some contexts it has been more formalized, as in the national responsibility of religious institutions for public education in the Theravada Buddhist states of Southeast Asia or in some predominantly Roman Catholic states.

The broader integration of religious and social structures has also often found expression in the political roles of religion. In a wide variety of contexts religious beliefs or doctrines have served as an important source of political legitimacy, providing validation for particular leaders or states to exercise territoriality over political regions. This pattern commonly characterized ancient states, in which the state cult provided an unquestioned link between divine mandate and political action. The development of the ancient Greek city-states, for example, contained a significant religious dimension, focusing on the central temple. The city-state governed the construction and maintenance of the temple; and in turn the temple, recognized as the city's most important public building, defined the identity and authority of the city-state itself.[40] Similarly, many ancient and traditional cultures have attributed religious meanings to the institution of kingship, again tying territorial control to divine will. Such meanings have taken diverse forms. Kings in some contexts have been seen as the mortal representatives of God, as in ancient Israel, or as ruling by divine right, a notion that became commonplace in medieval Europe. In other settings, divinity has been attributed to kings themselves, as in the traditional Japanese belief in the descent of the royal family from the Shinto goddess Amaterasu.

Over time, religious and political forms of territoriality have intersected as well through the efforts of secular rulers to draw political support and legitimacy from religious institutions. The broader diffusion of Tibetan Buddhism in Mongolia beginning during the sixteenth century, for example, had considerable political significance, strengthening the status of the Mongol ruling class as some of its members became identified as reincarnated lamas within the Tibetan tradition. Connections to influential monastic schools of Tibetan Buddhism remained an important source of legitimacy for Mongol rulers into the twentieth century. Within the context of medieval Islam, after the fall of the Abbasid empire in the tenth century, the secular rulers of successive Middle Eastern empires continued to rely on Islamic institutions as a source of political legitimacy.[41] From the thirteenth to the sixteenth century, to cite one instance, the Mamluk Empire that ruled Egypt, Syria, and western Arabia sought legitimacy by reestablishing the Abbasid caliphate in Cairo.[42] Along somewhat different lines, an important political dimension of Buddhism within medieval Japan was the perceived role of Buddhist deities as protectors of the state, a view particularly associated with the early Nara period and later with adherents of the Tendai and Nichiren schools. Practitioners of Shinto ascribed the same role to their deities. Through this perceived role, Buddhism and Shinto both reinforced the territoriality of the state.

Religious institutions' political roles have not been organized only within the context of the state, however. They have also functioned as independent political forces, in some cases operating across wider regions. This pattern is clearly illustrated by the role of the Roman Catholic Church in medieval Europe. The Church not only provided legitimacy to individual rulers but also asserted its authority over states in matters of church law, clerical appointments, and the collection of revenue from church lands. It further asserted the primacy of loyalty to the Church over loyalty to the state. The Roman Catholic Church in essence exerted various forms of political territoriality alongside those exercised by secular states. On a more limited scale, religious institutions have frequently functioned as independent political forces within a state. The political activities and agendas of religious fundamentalist groups in recent decades, including conservative Christians in the United States, religious Zionists in Israel, and Hindu nationalists in India, exemplify this pattern.[43]

In addition to the tacit processes discussed above, the broader social integration of religious beliefs and practices has frequently been more reflexive, merging the social and political roles of religion in relation to specific social institutions. One widespread expression of this pattern is the inclusion of compulsory religious instruction in public school curricula. Again, in homogeneous societies this practice may derive from the unreflexive acceptance of religion as part of a larger cultural tradition, but the practice has also been adopted more reflexively to promote given social and ethical norms rather than to reproduce a specific religious system. In Thailand, for example, the government has mandated religious instruction in primary and secondary public schools, but the classes themselves may focus on either Buddhism or Islam. Similarly, Egyptian public schools require students to receive instruction in Islam or Christianity. In other cases, though, the homogeneity of the larger society has led to the focus of religious instruction on a specific tradition. In Greek public schools, for example, Greek Orthodox students receive compulsory religious education, although students from other traditions are exempt. Likewise the public schools of Saudi Arabia are required to provide instruction in Islam.

Through the formal integration of religious doctrines into civil law, legal systems represent another important social institution contributing to religious territoriality in many homogeneous societies. The sharia provided a comprehensive foundation for the legal systems of many traditional Muslim societies, defining basic legal principles; specific behaviors to be encouraged, allowed, or prohibited; and punishments to be applied. The sharia in part focuses on matters of religious obligation but it also addresses such social concerns as criminal, family, and commercial law. In modern settings, the integration of the sharia into civil law has often been highly controversial, but this practice persists in religiously conservative states such as Saudi Arabia and Iran. In other contexts, the religious dimensions of civil law have tended to focus on specific matters of belief rather than on comprehensive systems of religious law. Such matters may explicitly involve the reinforcement of religious practices. After converting to Buddhism, Mongol clans in the 1500s established various laws in accordance with Buddhist beliefs, such as prohibitions against the ritual sacrifice of humans or animals. As a reflection of Hindu cow veneration, most of India's individual states have passed laws governing the protection of cows or the prevention of cow slaughter. In Europe and North America, the Christian proscriptions against activity on the Sabbath have traditionally been reflected in the enactment of Sunday closing laws. Laws based on a foundation of religious belief have also addressed various social issues, such as marriage, divorce, inheritance, and similar family-related issues. Similarly, laws against activities defined as violations of moral standards, such as abortion and homosexuality, have frequently reflected underlying religious meanings.

Religion and Political Structures

In addition to their integration into specific social institutions, religious systems have also become formally linked to the overarching political structures of state and nation. This process has its roots in the long-standing connections between religion and nationalism among many peoples of the world, a pattern that implicitly fostered the concept of the religious legitimacy of the state and its rulers, as discussed above. With the rise of the modern state system, the connections between religion and nationalism have become more reflexive. Most importantly, adherents in a variety of contexts have integrated their religious identity into their ideology of nationalism, using the former to legitimize both their sense of distinctiveness and their national political objectives. Religious identity in this context has thus frequently contributed to the raison d'être of particular states. As an example, the Greek Orthodox Church played a central role in the rise of modern Greek nationalism by defining a common cultural basis for Greek identity and by lending its support to the cause of Greek independence from Ottoman rule. Greek independence in fact complicated the status of Orthodox Greeks since their nominal leader was still the Patriarch of Constantinople, who remained under Ottoman rule. This situation thus led to the formation of the autocephalous Church of Greece, an independent Orthodox body, and that outcome in turn further reinforced Greek national identity.

Diverse political objectives and strategies have arisen from the intersection of religious and nationalist ideologies, however. Religious nationalism has contributed to various secessionist ideologies, as in Sikh efforts in India's Punjab state to form the independent state of Khalistan. During the 1980s, a radical Sikh religious movement aggressively pursued this objective through violent confrontations with Indian authorities, but was ultimately suppressed by aggressive government action. Ideological issues rooted in religious nationalism have also contributed to conflicts over territorial control. In the 1990s following the disintegration of Yugoslavia, for example, conflict over the control of Kosovo was fueled by Serbian Orthodox nationalism. Serbs viewed Kosovo as the hearth of their religious identity and an integral part of their national homeland, as the site of the martyrdom of their national hero, St. Lazar.[44] Religious nationalism has also played a significant role in the ideology of state identity. This pattern appears in the use of religious symbols in national iconography, such as versions of the Christian cross in the flags of the United Kingdom, the Scandinavian countries, Switzerland, and Greece, and the crescent and star or the color green in the flags of various predominantly Muslim states, including Algeria, Azerbaijan, Libya, Malaysia, Pakistan, Saudi Arabia, Tunisia, Turkey, Turkmenistan, and Uzbekistan.

Often in association with religious nationalism, religious and political structures intersect in the concept of a state religion. The primary characteristic of a state religion is that it receives institutional support from the civil government, although the relationship between the government and state religious institutions can take various forms. A single institutional structure may possess both governmental and religious functions, the pattern found in strict theocracies, as discussed below. More commonly, however, state religious institutions operate with a degree of autonomy, in some instances with complete independence from civil authorities but in other cases under government jurisdiction or as an office of the government. The status of state religion represents a position of privilege for religious institutions, providing them with material support but also strengthening their capacity for exercising control within the state. State religions typically play a prominent role in state rituals, ceremonies, and holidays; and as suggested above, reproduction of the state religion frequently represents an objective of state-run educational systems. In traditional settings the presence of a state religion also frequently precluded the practice of other religions, at least in public, although that pattern has become less frequent in contemporary contexts. The state religion's hegemony has often been further expressed through the association between religious affiliation and citizenship. Such an association is quite explicit in Saudi Arabia, for example, where all citizens must be adherents of Islam and no other religions may be practiced in public. Similar associations have existed in many other contexts. In Sweden, prior to the formal separation of the Church of Sweden from the state in 2000, all children were registered at birth as members of the Church of Sweden if either parent was a member. Similarly, in Norway citizens are considered to be adherents of the Church of Norway unless they explicitly join a different group. In many other homogeneous societies, membership in the state religion has served as the default affiliation for citizens. Through their monopolies in religious matters and their access to state support, state religious institutions have typically had considerable influence on the state and its policies. This influence may be exercised through the immediate authority of religious leaders, as in theocratic contexts, or it may develop less directly as state institutions maintain policies consistent with the doctrines of the state religion. At a global scale, however, the power of state religions has generally declined over the past century as states have expanded constitutional freedoms of religious expression or, as in Sweden, have actually disestablished the state church.

A final expression of the formal intersection between religion and politics appears in the concept of theocracy. A theocracy can generally be defined as a polity that is organized as a religious entity based on a political ideology associated with an official religion. This definition comprises many different forms of government, however. A strict theocracy possesses a government that is directly administered by religious leaders. In this form of polity, no division exists between spiritual and secular authority, and thus all government actions and policies have complete religious legitimacy. Many states characterized as theocracies, however, have not possessed this absolute unity of spiritual and secular authority. It is useful, therefore, to define a second category of theocratic state, termed here a limited theocracy. In a limited theocracy, religious principles provide the foundation for the ideology and governance of the state, but secular and religious authority to some extent remain distinct. The theocracy itself thus comprises two dimensions: a state religion that defines the legitimacy of political doctrine and a secular government that puts that doctrine into effect. In such contexts, religious institutions have a greater influence over the state itself than do state religions in nontheocratic settings, but they lack the complete integration with governance structures as found in strict theocracies.

Although not as common as limited theocracies, strict theocracies have developed in many contexts. Strict theocracy characterized the Islamic empire established by Muhammad, who combined the roles of religious and secular leadership. The concept of Islam as a complete way of life in part derives from the model of this early Islamic polity, in which religious and political territoriality coincided. Strict theocracy persisted for several centuries through the institution of the caliphate, but ended when the Abbasid caliphs lost political power in the tenth century. A strict theocracy also emerged in Tibet under the rule of Buddhist lamas. This pattern existed in the thirteenth and fourteenth centuries as the hereditary leaders of the Sakya monastic lineage governed Tibet; and after a period of political fragmentation, the Mongol ruler Gushri Khan reestablished theocratic rule over Tibet under the leadership of the fifth Dalai Lama, whose successors governed Tibet into the twentieth century. Within the context of Christianity, the Papal States of central Italy in theory constituted a strict theocracy from the eighth to the nineteenth centuries, although the secular authority of the Roman Catholic Church over much of this territory remained limited before the 1500s. Most of the territory of the Papal States became incorporated into Italy in the 1800s, but Vatican City retained its sovereignty and continues to function as a strict theocracy. Many smaller strict theocracies have arisen as well in different parts of the world, particularly in association with sectarian groups. Imams of the Zaydi Shiite sect ruled northern Yemen from the ninth to the twentieth centuries, for example, although nominally under Ottoman jurisdiction for several centuries. In North America, the early Mormon settlements in the interior West initially functioned as a strict theocracy until Utah became formally organized as part of the United States. More recently, the Taliban movement established a strict theocracy in Afghanistan in the 1990s, governed in accordance with a traditional conception of Islam rooted in the country's ethnic Pashtun villages.

Limited theocracies have also emerged in diverse contexts, where they have taken varied forms based on the nature of the relationship between religious and secular leadership. In some instances, religious leaders maintain significant control over the state despite a partial separation of religious and secular authority. The current Islamic Republic of Iran exemplifies this pattern. Iran's constitution defines the state in religious terms, but it also establishes a secular administrative structure including an elected executive and legislature. Nonetheless, the executive and legislative branches ultimately remain under the control of the Faqih, the supreme jurist. The Faqih is further assisted in legislative matters by a Guardian Council, made up of other jurists and elected officials, which he oversees. Thus while secular officials have a degree of freedom in carrying out the ordinary business of government, the Faqih ensures that the Islamic character of the state is not contravened.[45] Somewhat analogous patterns developed within the Swiss branch of the Protestant Reformation during the sixteenth century, in which key reformers became the de facto leaders of local communities. In Zurich, Ulrich Zwingli regularly advised the city council on matters of religious concern; and in Geneva, John Calvin articulated basic principles for the secular administration of the city as a Christian commonwealth. One significant outcome of Calvin's influence was the organization of the Consistory as a civil institution that enforced laws concerning religious and moral behavior that had been enacted by the secular government.

In many other instances, however, limited theocracies have been characterized by the less extensive involvement by religious leaders in government matters. Religious leaders in such contexts may articulate basic religious doctrines, but they are not directly involved in the actual running of the state. The Puritan state established by Oliver Cromwell in seventeenth-century England adhered to this form of limited theocracy. As leader of the Puritan army and later as Lord Protector, Cromwell exercised authoritarian rule over England, enforcing Puritan regulations in an effort to transform the state into a religious polity. He did not act as a religious leader, however, and the Puritan clergy did not have a direct role in state affairs. A similar pattern developed in Puritan New England during the 1600s. Puritan colonial leaders explicitly sought to establish a polity founded on biblical principles, in which religious and civic obligations would be united through a shared adherence to Calvinist theology; but the Puritan clergy again played little direct role in matters of administration.

An authoritarian form of limited theocracy has also characterized the kingdom of Saudi Arabia, in which the Saud family maintains exclusive rule over the state. While the king is charged with the protection of Islam, he does not function as a religious leader. Matters of doctrine are instead the responsibility of the state's ulama. The ulama have no direct role in governing the state, however, influencing royal policies primarily through indirect pressure and informal means. Most conceptions of the Islamic state proposed by Sunni fundamentalist groups also fall into this category of limited theocracy. Although such groups generally take the Islamic polity established by Muhammad as their model, they focus less on rule by religious leaders than on the adoption of the sharia as the legal system and the incorporation of Quranic principles into the administration of the state. This approach in part reflects the lack of a clerical hierarchy within Sunni Islam, but in some contexts, such as Egypt and Pakistan, it also derives from the antagonisms between fundamentalists and the established ulama linked to existing secular governments. A less radical Islamic interpretation of the religious state appears in the concept of theodemocracy articulated by the twentieth-century Islamic reformer Abul Ala Mawdudi.[46] Mawdudi defined the state as a divine instrument, created with the purpose of establishing the sharia, but he further proposed that this could be achieved through democratic institutions acting in accordance with divine will. Again, Mawdudi's model defines the state in religious terms but does not require the worldly union of religious and political leadership.

In all of their forms, theocratic political structures represent a significant expression of internal religious territoriality. By connecting religious and political control, they establish a religious system's hegemony across the state and thereby strengthen orthodoxy among adherents. The homogenization of belief and practice promoted by a theocracy arises both from informal pressures and from the influence of formal institutions. The legal apparatus of the theocratic state also provides formalized procedures for suppressing heterodoxy or heresy. Theocracies have often devised specific state institutions for this purpose, such as the Consistory in Calvinist Geneva or the Committee to Promote Virtue and Prevent Vice in Saudi Arabia. The enforcement of orthodoxy within theocracies has generally been directed internally at adherents of the state religion itself, since they typically dominate the state's population. In some instances, however, theocratic states have actively persecuted nonadherents, thus creating an external dimension to this form of territoriality. The persecution of Quakers and Baptists in Puritan New England and of Baha'is in contemporary Iran typifies this pattern. The establishment of a theocracy as a result has both internal and external religious implications.

Indeed, most of the aforementioned expressions of religious territoriality at wider scales do not remain wholly internal in orientation as they extend beyond the boundaries of individual communities. The distinction between internal and external forms of religious territoriality thus becomes somewhat blurred at wider scales. Nonetheless, some wider expressions of territoriality clearly have a stronger internal focus and others a stronger external focus. The discussion will return to the latter in the second half of this chapter.

Intersections among Scales

Finally, a crucial feature of all internal expressions of religious territoriality is their interconnectedness across different scales. Factors that affect adherents' behavior at the scale of the body or home cannot be separated from processes and institutions organized over communal space, and the latter in turn interact extensively with influences that tie together coreligionists over wider scales. It is through these intersections across different scales that the control of personal, communal, and social spaces acquires its full, complex meanings. As an example, the wearing of a traditional *abaya* and *hijab*, or black cloak and head covering, by a Saudi woman clearly represents an expression of territoriality at the scale of her body space (photo 4.8). This practice protects her body from public view by men outside her family, in accordance with Hanbali interpretations of Quranic principles, and it serves as a mark of her personal commitment to Islam. Many Saudi women further believe that the veil extends their personal activity space by allowing them to move about in public unmolested. At the same time, the act of veiling has implications at the scale of the home and family. The family represents the primary context of socialization within which adolescent girls take on the practice of veiling. Acceptance of this practice also reflects a somewhat broader form of territoriality involving power relations within the patriarchal family structure. Social pressures encourage husbands to enforce the veiling of their wives and daughters to protect the honor and religious reputation of their household. The *mutawwa*, the agents of the Committee to Promote Virtue and Prevent Vice, also may

Photo 4.8. Saudi women traditionally dressed in black abayas and hijabs. The two women are leaving a polling station after voting in local elections that for the first time included women on the ballot for the board of the Eastern Province Chamber of Commerce and Industry, although none of the female candidates was in fact elected. The expanding participation of women in Saudi public life may appear to contrast with the survival of traditional forms of dress, but it also reveals the complex, intersecting meanings of the latter at a variety of scales. Qatif, Saudi Arabia, 2006.

Source: AFP/Getty Images.

admonish husbands for allowing their wives to be seen in public without being properly veiled.

The various formal and informal pressures to adhere to accepted norms concerning veiling in turn derive from the family's situation within a larger, local community. The community has an inherent interest in supporting adherence to those norms as a means of maintaining the local social order, based on a shared commitment to religious orthodoxy and a common interpretation of religious obligation. In public, strangers may thus take offense at seeing a woman not properly veiled. As the primary context for the realization of religious identity, the community also reinforces the naturalization of the practice of veiling as part of the unquestioned routine of daily life. Because in this sense they are expressions of communal expectations, however, specific veiling practices vary among local contexts. Women in rural settings within Saudi Arabia are more likely than urban dwellers to cover their face with a *niqab* or face veil; and they may wear cloaks made of a variety of traditional textile patterns rather than simple black. In Saudi urban centers, on the other hand, young and well-to-do women have increasingly taken to wearing more fashionable, professionally designed cloaks.

Nonetheless, the varied practices of local communities all conform to expectations articulated at wider scales. The Saudi state requires Muslim women to wear an abaya and hijab; and again it enforces that requirement through the mutawwa. Saudi veiling practices further represent a manifestation of the prevailing religious ideology of Wahhabism and the Hanbali legal school on which it is based. Wearing a veil thus links a woman both to Saudi Arabia as an Islamic theocracy and to broader legal and theological identities within Islam. And in a more general sense wearing a veil establishes a connection between a Saudi woman and both Dar al-Islam and the global Muslim umma, within which the practice of veiling exists in many different forms. Through all of these scales, then, the wearing of a veil reflects the influences of intersecting layers of religious territoriality, both formal and informal, relating the lived spaces of believers to a complex system of religious customs, norms, expectations, and obligations.

External Expressions of Religious Territoriality

In shaping the meanings and actions associated with secular spaces, a religion's adherents inevitably exert various forms of influence beyond the boundaries of their own tradition. These external forms of religious territoriality develop through interactions within secular space between adherents and others outside their group. Such expressions of territoriality are somewhat less commonplace than the internal forms discussed above, as the concerns of religious groups tend to focus more extensively on their own members than on outsiders. Nonetheless, the exercise of external territoriality represents an important aspect of the diverse ways in which adherents realize their religious systems. In particular, it is a significant product of the relationship between adherents and the broader social contexts in which they practice their religion, and in this sense it is crucial in understanding the contextuality of religions as lived cultural systems.

External expressions of religious territoriality arise in diverse ways. Within traditional societies they have often developed unreflexively through the hegemony of a dominant religion. Over time the hegemonic religion's tacit influence on society results in the naturalization of its beliefs and practices, so that the latter become widely embedded in secular space. Nonadherents thus face widespread exposure to the dominant religion's influence, in some cases resisting accommodation but in others adjusting to or adopting certain hegemonic patterns. In other instances, religious groups have asserted external forms of religious territoriality more reflexively, through purposeful efforts to promote the group's interests. Dominant religious groups have frequently articulated such expressions of external territoriality as a means of asserting or protecting their hegemonic status. This objective may lead to periods of heightened religious intolerance as the dominant group seeks to eliminate other religious systems from the spaces over which it prevails. This form of territoriality has also developed in less aggressive forms, however, in response to a rise in pluralism, secularism, or religious heterodoxy that the dominant group sees as a threat.

Conversely, religious minorities have often adopted external forms of territoriality to defend or preserve their own religious system. Such groups may seek to reinforce boundaries in secular space between their members and outsiders, but their success will depend in part on the response of society at large. Official suppression of a religious minority, for example, may undermine such attempts. Religious minorities may also exert territoriality outside of their own group boundaries in an effort to transform larger social structures in ways that better accommodate the minority's religious practices.

Finally, both minority and majority religious groups have often seen external assertions of territoriality as a religious obligation based on their worldview or ethos. A notable expression of this pattern is the commitment to missionary work in proselytic religions, through which believers specifically seek to spread their religious system in secular space. Many religious groups have also felt an obligation to transform society in general, in an effort to realize their ethos or in accordance with belief in a divine plan of redemption. That obligation typically involves reorganizing larger social spaces in religious terms. Such efforts represent a characteristic trait of fundamentalist movements, for example, although other groups have adopted them as well, such as advocates of liberation theology.

As religious groups extend their influence beyond their own spatial boundaries, they inevitably create the potential for conflicts with others. Through such conflicts, external forms of religious territoriality are commonly associated with the contesting of secular spaces by opposing groups. Traditionally the groups embroiled in such conflicts have both had religious motivations, but in modern settings the contesting of space has increasingly involved opposition between religious groups and secular influences. The conflicts engendered by external articulations of religious territoriality have focused on a great many issues relating to religious meaning, practice, reproduction, and identity. They have also taken varied forms, from informal disagreements to open warfare. For religious minorities, conflict often emerges from patterns of resistance to the hegemony of dominant groups, while the latter have often provoked conflict through the suppression or persecution of minorities. In all of these cases, believers assign considerable significance to conflicts rooted in the control of secular space because from their perspective their position is grounded in incontrovertible religious truths. For this reason such conflicts often resist easy resolution and may persist over long periods of time.

As with internal expressions of territoriality, religious groups articulate external expressions at varied but interconnected scales. The issue of scale becomes more complex in considering external forms of territoriality, however. In one sense, all such forms of territoriality occur at scales wider than the local community of adherents, since by definition their influence extends beyond the local group itself. It is thus more useful to categorize external expressions of territoriality by the scales of the actual spaces on which adherents focus their concerns. Even from this perspective, however, it can prove difficult to separate the scales of territoriality, since a process may need to operate at one scale to produce change at another. As an example, efforts by conservative Christians to ban most abortions in the United States represent a form of religious territoriality at the scale of the body, but to achieve this goal abortion opponents have sought change at the scale of the state, through legislation or a constitutional amendment.

Regarding the different scales at which adherents articulate external territoriality in secular space, the scale of the local community is again significant as the context for the most immediate interactions between religion and daily life. Narrower scales tend to be less important in reference to external forms of territoriality, largely because adherents of a religious system generally have little influence on the activities of outsiders organized at the scales of body and home. Significant exceptions do exist, however, particularly in regard to certain areas of individual moral and ethical behavior, as in the aforementioned example of abortion. Scales wider than the local community take on considerable importance, on the other hand. The tacit influences of a hegemonic religion typically extend over large areas, especially if that religion has some formal standing, such as that of a state religion. Moreover, believers frequently organize their actions at wider scales when they reflexively seek to exercise external territoriality. Adherents aiming to achieve social change within a state, for example, often adopt strategies focusing on state-level electoral and legislative processes. Violent conflicts between religious groups have often been organized as well at even wider scales, beyond that of the individual state.

The Communal Scale

The scale of the community again represents the primary context within which religious groups relate their faith to the patterns of daily life. In the process, believers enact various forms of territoriality beyond their own group, alongside the internal controls applicable solely to the group itself. In considering internal expressions of territoriality, however, the communal scale relates essentially to local spaces as they are used and organized by group members. The scale of the community takes on a different character in relation to external territoriality, encompassing the entirety of a local social context rather than the communal spaces of a single group. As seen from this perspective, the concerns of more than one group may overlap at the communal scale, again resulting in the potential for conflict.

Public Space

One principal concern of external forms of territoriality at the communal scale is the relationship between public space and religion. Believers have articulated this relationship in two ways: by seeking to incorporate elements of their religious system into public space and by seeking to exclude phenomena inconsistent with their beliefs from public space. The exercise of territoriality in public space in effect provides adherents with a means of ensuring consistency between their beliefs and the structures of social life. It also serves to protect a group's religious identity and supports the reproduction of its religious system. Religious majorities have most easily realized territoriality over public space, but smaller groups have exerted such efforts as well. For hegemonic groups, these processes have often developed unreflexively through the naturalization of their religious system. Dominant groups have also reflexively sought to shape the role of religion in public space, however, especially to counter the influence of secularism or pluralism. For religious minorities, on the other hand, efforts to control public space have largely been reflexive, and often defensive, in character.

The hegemonic exercise of external territoriality within local spaces appears in part through the incorporation of religion into the rituals and routines of public life.

Again, the incorporation of prayer into public events represents a widespread expression of this practice in many parts of the world. As communities have become more self-conscious of their internal diversity, public prayer has often become increasingly generic or ecumenical, but the roots of this practice in most cases developed in reference to a single hegemonic tradition. The integration of religious belief into the character of public institutions also reflects the hegemonic exercise of territoriality. Again, this process appears in the formulation of the curricula of public schools around the teachings of the dominant religion, as in state and local bans on teaching evolution in public schools in various parts of the United States early in the 1900s or the required instruction in Islam in public schools in Saudi Arabia.[47] The incorporation of religious elements in public landscapes represents a further form of hegemonic territoriality. The depiction of religious figures or inscriptions in public monuments exemplifies this pattern. In many locations in the United States, for example, county courthouses and city parks contain displays of the Ten Commandments as a symbol of the divine origins of the law. During the late twentieth and early twenty-first centuries, efforts to promote this practice have expanded in parts of the country dominated by conservative Christianity, whose adherents consider the Ten Commandments to be central to the cultural traditions of their communities.[48]

Although adherents of hegemonic groups have traditionally taken for granted their control of public space, in contemporary settings such adherents have become more reflexive in their efforts to maintain that control. At the same time, religious minorities have also sought to shape the character of public space, often in response to hegemonic practices, while secular forces have challenged the legitimacy of religious influences generally within public contexts. The result has been an increase in controversies over the role of religion in public space in various parts of the world. The rise of religious fundamentalism in diverse traditions has contributed significantly to the proliferation of such conflicts, but so have growing commitments to pluralism and civic secularism in many modern societies. Conflicts have arisen in some cases from the efforts of adherents to strengthen the influence of their religion, based either on a dominant group's claim of social preeminence or on the desire of religious minorities to ensure public accommodation of their faith. In other cases, conflicts have developed out of efforts to remove religious influences from public space, either by adherents of minority religions or by proponents of religiously neutral or secular conceptions of the public sphere.

Many of these conflicts have focused on the presence of religion in official public spaces such as government buildings, parks, and schools.[49] Such conflicts tend to be largely symbolic, emphasizing issues of identity and tradition rather than the practical advantages of one group over another. This pattern has recurred in numerous forms in the United States, for example, where the naturalized hegemony of Christianity has persisted alongside the constitutional separation of church and state. Especially in recent decades, the Christian majority's influence over public spaces has been contested both by religious minorities and by those professing no religion. The aforementioned practice of displaying the Ten Commandments in public spaces has been one focus of controversy. Although various court rulings have decided against this practice in recent years, Christian fundamentalists have continued to promote it. One notable example of such efforts took place in 2001 when the chief justice of Alabama's state supreme court installed a monument to the Ten Commandments in the state courthouse, an action that federal courts subsequently disallowed.[50] A more widespread example of such conflict involves the traditional practice of erecting Christmas decorations, such as decorated trees and nativity scenes, in local public spaces. Christians have argued that the use of such decorations represents a cultural tradition rather than an assertion of religious superiority. Non-Christians have argued, on the other hand, that such decorations represent a misuse of public space through the promotion of one particular faith. Courts have generally ruled against the use of more explicitly religious symbols, such as nativity scenes, but have allowed less overt symbols, such as Christmas trees. Similar conflicts have emerged in recent years over the traditional incorporation of Christian symbols, such as the cross, into the official seals of local communities. Religious minorities and secularists have again argued against the association of religious symbols with the identity of the secular space of a town or county. And local groups have challenged the use of sectarian opening prayers in town meetings. In 2004, for example, a federal court ruled in favor of an adherent of the Neo-Pagan Wiccan religion who had sued the town of Great Falls, South Carolina, for opening official meetings with specifically Christian prayers.[51]

Schools have also frequently emerged as contested public spaces as adherents have sought the accommodation of their faith within public education systems. Concern over the role of religion in public schools has again produced a number of controversies within the United States. Starting in the early twentieth century, Christian fundamentalists have sought various means of ensuring that public school curricula conform to the literal interpretation of the Bible. They initially focused on banning the teaching of evolution, which contradicted the traditional biblical account of creation. They pursued this goal through legislation and local school board decisions, but the negative publicity generated by the so-called Scopes Monkey Trial in 1925 largely discredited the fundamentalist position within American popular culture. Christian fundamentalists took up this cause once more during the 1980s and 1990s, however, again by trying to take control of local public school boards. They also sought to limit instruction that in their view challenged biblical values, such as coursework expressing tolerance for homosexuality, the use of contraception, and illegal drug use. The overall impact of this strategy remained limited, however, and by the late 1990s some fundamentalist leaders called for concerned parents to abandon the public school system altogether in favor of private schools or home schooling.[52] A somewhat broader issue of concern to conservative Christians in the United States involves prayer in public schools, a practice banned by the U.S. Supreme Court in 1962. Again, many conservative Christians have sought to define public schools as valid settings for religious expression, while the courts have largely ruled against such uses of public space.

The contesting of schools as public spaces has also appeared in recent years in conflicts involving Muslim minorities in different parts of the world. Muslims in India have repeatedly challenged articulations of Hindu hegemony in public space. Such challenges in part reflect broader concerns with the constitutional secularism of India as a state, but at the local scale they have found specific expression in concerns over Hinduism within public schools. Muslims have objected to the adoption of textbooks that, in their view, contain pro-Hindu and anti-Islam elements. They have also opposed efforts to incorporate Hindu nationalism into the routine of public schools. A prominent example of this concern emerged in 2004 when members of the Hindu fundamentalist Shiv Sena party in Mumbai sought to make the singing of the nationalist hymn *Vande Mataram* mandatory in all publicly funded schools. Originally composed in the nineteenth century, *Vande Mataram* became a nationalist anthem prior to independence, but because it compares India to the Hindu deities Durga and Lakshmi (Shakti manifested as the consorts of Shiva and Vishnu respectively), Muslims have opposed the hymn's use in civic contexts.[53]

In recent years a different type of controversy has developed in France over personal displays of Islamic affiliation in public schools. This conflict has focused specifically on the wearing of headscarves by Muslim girls. This issue addresses the right of the state to ban religious activity in public space, a particular concern in France because of the state's explicitly secular identity. The controversy over wearing headscarves began in 1989 when school officials in Grenoble banned the practice as a violation of a law against proselytizing in schools. French courts upheld the ban, and in 1994 the French Ministry of Education prohibited any ostentatious display of religious symbolism in public schools, a policy enacted into law by the French national assembly in 2004. The law affects all religious groups, not only Muslims, but conservative Muslims have voiced the strongest opposition to it, arguing that the ban on headscarves prevents the free practice of their religion.[54] Muslims have also opposed a ban on wearing headscarves in public schools in Singapore. According to the government, the ban in Singapore reflects a policy of promoting social harmony within the state's highly diverse population. Singapore in fact lacks a dominant religion; the largest tradition, Buddhism, accounts for little more than a fourth of the population. Ethnically, however, three-fourths of inhabitants are of Chinese ancestry while most Muslims are ethnic Malays. Similar bans on wearing headscarves in public spaces have been enacted in other locations as well. In recent years a number of local states within Germany have banned civil servants, including teachers, from wearing headscarves or other religious articles of clothing, for example.

Territorial controversies have developed as well in reference to less formal public spaces. In various instances, religious minorities have contested control over less formal spaces in seeking the accommodation of their religion. In Israel, for example, ultra-Orthodox Jews have sought to establish gender segregation in public settings, in accordance with their belief that adults should not come into contact with members of the opposite sex outside their own family. Although opposed by secularists, such efforts have led to gender segregation in some health care facilities, at certain beaches, and on bus routes serving ultra-Orthodox neighborhoods. Use and control of public space has also emerged as an issue in relation to Amish religious practices in the United States. Because of their dispersed rural settlement patterns, the Amish use public roads to travel within and between their local communities. In adhering to tradition, however, they do so using black horse-drawn buggies. Numerous states and localities have sought to require the Amish to place triangular orange reflectors on their buggies when driving on public roads, but many Amish have resisted this effort (photo 4.9). A number of court rulings have allowed those opposed to the use of triangular reflectors to use gray reflecting tape as a compromise.[55]

In addition to efforts to reproduce elements of their religion in public space, religious minorities have sought to prevent uses of public space that interfere with their private religious practices. Ultra-Orthodox Jews in Jerusalem, for example, have demanded since the early 1990s that authorities close major public roads near their neighborhoods during the Sabbath, arguing that traffic on the Sabbath not only vio-

Photo 4.9. An Amish buggy with a required triangular reflector, an accommodation to legal constraints on the use of social space. Pataskala, Ohio, no date.

Source: Kenn Kiser, under morgueFile license (morguefile.com/archive/terms.php).

lates Jewish law but also generates noise that interferes with their observance of the Sabbath. Their effort to control this use of public space has focused in particular on Bar-Ilan Street, a major road located adjacent to the principal ultra-Orthodox neighborhood of Meah Shearim. The government's refusal to ban traffic on this road has produced repeated demonstrations by ultra-Orthodox Jews. A parallel controversy of somewhat longer standing, dating at least to the nineteenth century, has developed in various Indian cities around the use of public streets adjacent to Islamic mosques. This controversy has focused on the use of music in Hindu religious processions that pass by mosques during periods of Muslim worship. Muslims have argued that the Hindus' processional music interferes with their ability to pray in peace; and over time they came to view this practice as an intentional provocation. As a result, for more than a century local conflicts over the issue of "music before mosques" and similar intrusions on religion in secular space have sporadically erupted in communal riots.[56] Many localities with large Muslim communities have thus banned processional music in front of mosques, and local police often redirect Hindu processions so that they do not pass by mosques. Such bans have been contested and in some instances lifted in recent decades, however, and the issue remains a source of conflict.

Social Space

The external territorial concerns of religious groups at the local scale are not limited to issues involving public space narrowly defined. Frequently they extend into social space generally, focusing on wider concerns of religious groups within local society. At the broadest level, such concerns comprise the goal of structuring all of society in accordance with one group's religious law. Adherents may view that goal primarily in internal terms, in relation to their own group, but in many contexts it has an external dimension as well. As an example, the ordinances that Calvin and his followers established to regulate society in Geneva, discussed above, did not focus solely on enforcing conformity to Calvinist principles among adherents of the Reformed church. They also sought to eliminate other religious practices, and in particular those associated with Roman Catholicism, among all inhabitants of the city in both public and private space. The territorial assertion of religious law by a dominant group can of course generate significant conflict. Such conflict has emerged in northern Nigeria in recent years, for example, where Islamic fundamentalists have sought to incorporate the sharia into civil law.[57] Since 1999 they have succeeded in this effort in twelve northern states (map 4.5). Although Muslims have claimed that this process would not affect non-Muslim minorities, the latter have strongly opposed these changes to local legal systems. The resulting conflict has led to thousands of deaths in local riots and other forms of violence.

The contesting of religious law in local social space may also occur among adherents of the same tradition. The hegemony of a larger tradition does not guarantee homogeneity in belief and practice. Adherents of a dominant tradition may differ in terms of how they understand the application of religious law in social space, and those differences may in turn lead to conflict. Again, the emergence of religious fundamentalism in various settings during the past century has produced many such conflicts. Fundamentalist adherents typically express far stricter and more literal understandings of religious law than do their nonfundamentalist coreligionists. As a result, fundamentalists commonly view the application of religious law in social space in distinctively ideological terms. A striking example of conflict over social space within a hegemonic tradition developed in Afghanistan during the 1990s with the rise of the Taliban. Through local ruling councils, the Taliban imposed a strict interpretation of sharia on the portions of Afghanistan that they controlled. In the process, they redefined the meanings and uses of social space in urban settings like Kabul, where many Afghan Muslims had previously followed less rigid interpretations of sharia. The Tali-

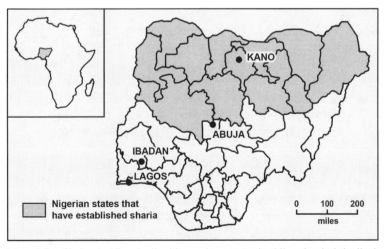

Map 4.5.   States in Nigeria that have incorporated the sharia into their legal systems, as of 2004.

ban banned movies, television, dancing, and playing football, all of which had been commonplace. They also instituted severe spatial constraints on women, prohibiting them from leaving the home unless completely veiled by a burqa and accompanied by a male relative. They further prohibited girls from attending school and dictated that women and men be treated at separate medical facilities. These rules represented a sharp departure from previous articulations of social space in Kabul; and after the removal of the Taliban from power in 2001, more liberal interpretations of Islamic tradition again began to emerge in local social space.

In contrast to the above examples, the pluralistic or secular character of many modern states precludes the general implementation of systems of religious law. Within such contexts religious groups have sought to shape specific dimensions of local society to conform to their beliefs. This focus on selected social issues is a commonly observed characteristic of fundamentalist movements, but it appears among other religious groups as well. At the scale of the local community, adherents' efforts to control activity within social space have focused primarily on phenomena that are inconsistent with their religious values. Again, adherents often view such efforts reflexively as a religious obligation, ensuring wider conformity to their core religious beliefs. In the United States, the 1973 Supreme Court ruling against the constitutionality of most state abortion laws generated significant opposition from conservative Christians who viewed abortion as a violation of their religious beliefs. Religious groups expressed this opposition at the local scale through picketing and other forms of public protest directed at facilities that provided abortions. Operation Rescue, a Christian fundamentalist organization founded in the 1980s, established a nationwide network of local groups organized to block local access to abortion clinics through public demonstrations, a strategy that has been strongly contested in the courts. In response the U.S. Congress passed the Freedom of Access to Clinic Entrances Act in 1994.[58] In recent decades Christian fundamentalists in various locales have also staged protests against adult book stores, gay nightclubs, and gay and lesbian festivals, again citing the incompatibility of those phenomena with their local religious values.

Islamic fundamentalists in various parts of the world have similarly sought to assert religious law in social space, for example through efforts to limit or ban the consumption of alcohol. In some countries, such as Pakistan, such efforts have largely been internal, focusing on the use of alcohol by Muslims. In other locations, however, fundamentalists have attacked the use of alcohol generally. Beginning in the 1980s, the expansion of more violent forms of Islamic fundamentalism in Egypt and Lebanon led to frequent attacks against businesses selling alcohol, such as liquor stores and nightclubs. Islamic fundamentalists have also protested against violations of their religious standards of female modesty. Such protests in Nigeria, for example, ultimately prevented the staging of the Miss World beauty pageant there in 2002.[59]

Ultra-Orthodox Jews in Israel have similarly expressed concern with the observance of the Sabbath in social space. They believe that Jewish law obliges them to rebuke Jews who violate restrictions on Sabbath activity. In addition to protesting street traffic on roads near their neighborhoods, they have thus protested the opening of various businesses, such as movie theaters and restaurants, on the Sabbath. Observance of Jewish dietary laws represents another concern of this group, which has led them to object to the presence of stores and restaurants that sell non-kosher food in Jerusalem.

In addition to concerns with religious law, various forms of social activism have been central to the external territoriality of religious groups in local social space. Activism in this context emphasizes enacting a religion's ethos within society at large. Instead of trying to make society conform to specific religious principles, adherents seek to use or control local spaces as a stage on which to express their own religious values. This form of territoriality has typically produced less controversy than have concerns with religious law. Perhaps the most common expression of religious activism in local social space is charitable work, through which adherents articulate values of compassion, benevolence, and social responsibility. Although much of the charitable activity of religious groups focuses on fellow adherents, in many contexts such basic efforts as providing food, shelter, and clothing extend beyond the group as well.

Other forms of social activism have developed through more complex efforts to restructure society. The Social Gospel movement in liberal American Protestantism exemplified this pattern during the late nineteenth and early twentieth centuries. It asserted that Christians had a religious responsibility to work for the improvement of society in anticipation of the coming of God's kingdom on earth. The movement was generally concerned less with millennial theology, however, than with the social ethos of the New Testament. Its primary concern was to promote the interests of the poor and the working classes, emphasizing practical responses to material conditions rather than the process of personal salvation. Adherents thus became involved in various forms of social service within local urban spaces, focusing on issues such as housing, education, sanitation, and health care. More recently, various religious groups in the United States played a key role in the civil rights movement of the 1950s and 1960s. African American Protestant churches provided the primary source of leadership for the movement, particularly based on the writings of Martin Luther King, Jr., but they also served as the foci of grassroots efforts to promote civil rights in local social space (photo 4.10).

Religious groups in other parts of the world have also become extensively involved in social action as well, especially over the past century. The "Engaged Buddhism" movement emerged in Vietnam during the 1960s, within the context of decolonization, as an effort to apply the Buddhist principle of right effort to practical matters of social injustice and suffering. The movement's adherents have in part focused on issues organized at wider scales, such as disarmament and globalization, but they have also addressed a variety of concerns in local social space, including community development, domestic violence, environmental problems, and hospice work.[60] The Baha'i religion also supports a strong commitment to local social action, based on the belief that service to others represents a form of religious devotion; for example, Baha'i adherents have established projects promoting economic development in locations around the world. More generally, charitable organizations within all of the world's major religious traditions have carried out local humanitarian and development projects.[61]

Concerns with religious law and social action largely emphasize the transformation of society, either to establish social conformity to certain beliefs or to provide adherents with a means of enacting their own religious values. External expressions of religious territoriality can have other functions, however. In many contexts, religious groups have exerted a degree of control over social space in defining their place in society. This process occurs unreflexively in hegemonic settings, where the dominant

Photo 4.10.   Participants in the civil rights march from Selma to Montgomery, Alabama, in 1965. African American ministers such as Martin Luther King, Jr., led the civil rights movement, but this cause also drew widespread support from various Christian and Jewish groups, as the marcher's sign indicates. Alabama, 1965.

Source: Prints and Photographs Division, U.S. Library of Congress.

group asserts its preeminence through its tacit control over local social space. In more diverse settings, this process develops more reflexively through the articulation of social boundaries or barriers inhibiting interactions between groups. Those social boundaries have significant spatial outcomes in the development of patterns of segregation or isolation. Majority religious groups have imposed such patterns on others, either to maintain a hegemonic social order or to protect themselves from contact with outcast religious groups. The millet system of the Ottoman Empire, for example, while providing diverse religious groups with control over their internal affairs, also maintained Islamic hegemony by institutionalizing local social boundaries and by asserting the primacy of Islamic law in conflicts between Muslims and non-Muslims. The restrictions placed on Jews by Christians in medieval Europe, on the other hand, exemplified more explicit patterns of discrimination and persecution. Legal barriers limited Jewish participation in local social space by placing constraints on political activity, occupation, and land ownership, and contributed to the residential segregation characteristic of Jewish ghettos.

Religious minorities have also defined various boundaries and barriers between themselves and the larger society, however. For such groups, self-imposed separation from society again provides defense against external influences, although it may also derive from the group's conception of the proper order of a community. Certain Anabaptist groups have thus sought isolation to protect themselves from worldly influences, but they have also structured their local communities to conform to internal religious concerns, such as the Amish belief in remaining a separate people and the Hutterite practice of communalism. Somewhat differently, in the early spread of the Islamic empire the Muslim population residing in frontier outposts often lived in isolation from conquered peoples in the local area as a means of asserting its distinct communal identity. For other minority groups, self-imposed separation reflexively expresses resistance to the hegemony of another group or of secular society. The latter pattern has been common among religious fundamentalists, who represent their isolation as a critique of the larger society. Fundamentalists have in some cases pursued this strategy by forming distinct communities, as in the Santi Asoke movement in Thailand. In other cases, fundamentalists have isolated themselves through the formation of more dispersed networks of group institutions. Christian fundamentalists in the United States have largely followed this pattern, for example, as have the less radical Islamic fundamentalists in Egypt, Pakistan, and other Muslim countries.[62]

Like many other forms of external territoriality, religious groups' efforts to articulate boundaries within local social space have frequently produced conflict. In most instances such conflict is expressed through the political contesting of control over social space. As an example, Hasidic and ultra-Orthodox Jews in the United States and Israel have used political means, both formal and informal, to control the use of social space in and around their neighborhoods in recent years. In 2001, the Satmar Hasidic community located in the Williamsburg neighborhood of Brooklyn strongly opposed the development of the adjacent Brooklyn Navy Yard into a motion picture production facility, arguing that this use would intrude on their ability to remain isolated from secular influences. The movie studio nonetheless opened in 2004. The isolationist strategies of the Satmar Hasidim residing north of New York City in the village of Kiryas Joel have also generated conflict with others in the area who oppose the continued expansion of the segregated Hasidic community within local social space, a process driven by the group's high birth rate.[63] Similar territorial conflicts have developed around the ultra-Orthodox neighborhood of Meah Shearim in Jerusalem, in addition to the controversy over street closings on the Sabbath discussed above. Residents have for many years posted signs asking women visiting the neighborhood to dress in accordance with ultra-Orthodox standards of modesty (photo 4.11). In recent decades they have also occasionally used more active methods, from public confrontation to the vandalism of automobiles, to discourage what they see as immodest dress among women working in government offices near Meah Shearim. Such actions have produced a significant tension between the meanings of public and private space in this part of Jerusalem.[64]

Christian fundamentalists have tried to impose boundaries between themselves and other groups in somewhat different ways. Their primary concern has not been the defense of residential neighborhoods. They have instead focused on the meanings that they attach to other kinds of public social space. Since the early 1990s Christian fundamentalists have opposed the organization of Gay Pride parades and Gay Days in local social space, events that welcome the social participation of gays and lesbians in various settings (photo 4.12). This controversy originally focused on the Disney Company's acceptance of an annual Gay Day organized by gay and lesbian groups at its Disney World theme park in Florida. More recently, it has extended to similar events at other sites, such as professional sporting events. Christian fundamentalists view these activities as grievous transgressions against social spaces like theme parks and sports stadiums, which they associate with traditional conceptions of family-oriented entertainment.

Photo 4.11.   Sign posted at the entrance to Meah Shearim, a major ultra-Orthodox Jewish neighborhood in Jerusalem, asking women visitors to dress in accordance with the emphasis on female modesty in the ultra-Orthodox ethos. Jerusalem, Israel, 2007.

Source: Lisa Mathon (commons.wikimedia.org/wiki/Image:Panneau_mea_shearim.jpg), under Creative Commons license (creativecommons.org/licenses/by-sa/2.5/).

The articulation of boundaries between religious groups in local social space has also resulted in more violent forms of conflict. Such violence has a long history, of course, but it persists in many contemporary contexts. Antagonisms between different religious groups have frequently given rise to sporadic, disorganized forms of local violence, such as the vandalism of places of worship, cemeteries, homes, or businesses. Although it may have complex motivations, vandalism directed at members of another

Photo 4.12.   Christian protesters at a Gay Pride parade in the Hillcrest district of San Diego. San Diego, California, 2006.

Source: Jason Mouratides (www.flickr.com/photos/scragz/205086161/), under Creative Commons license (creativecommons.org/licenses/by/2.0/).

religious group typically expresses a generalized hostility toward the presence of that other group in local social space. More specific sources of conflict, on the other hand, tend to generate more reflexive forms of violence. One common source of violence is the perception by one religious group that another group has threatened its local social space. In many contexts, missionary activity by proselytic groups has provoked violent confrontations with local indigenous populations. Hindu fundamentalists, for example, have attacked Christian missionaries in locations across India in recent years as part of a broader campaign to block the growth of Christian influence, particularly among lower-caste Hindus, untouchables, and tribal groups. Similar conflicts between Muslims and Christians have occurred in many locations across Africa. Traditional Muslim communities in the Sahel and along Africa's east coast have been particularly resistant to the expansion of Christian missionary activity in recent decades. The construction of new churches, Christian evangelism in the vicinity of mosques, and public evangelical crusades have all sparked violence, from Liberia to Kenya. In 1998, for example, Muslims in Mali destroyed a Christian church and missionary homes after the local showing of a film about Jesus.

Somewhat more broadly, unresolved antagonisms between competing religious groups within plural societies have provoked many forms of local violence associated with the articulation of religious boundaries. Outbreaks of violence may be linked to specific triggering events, but they typically occur within the context of persistent enmity between groups. Local violence between Hindus and Muslims has been commonplace in India over the past century, for example, fueled both by specific local issues and by a wider clash of cultures dating from the period of the medieval Muslim invasions. Local conflicts between Christian Orthodox Serbs and Muslim Albanians in Kosovo during the 1990s arose within a similar context of long-standing antagonism. Such patterns of violence have again taken on a more reflective character in recent times, however, through intersections among religious adherence, identity, group solidarity, and destabilizing social change. In the wake of decolonization, analogous patterns of conflict have thus developed between Muslims and Christians in Nigeria and the Philippines and between Buddhists and Muslims in Burma.

In conclusion, efforts by religious groups to extend their influence beyond their own membership into broader structures within local social space have had diverse influences. Such patterns have developed unreflexively among hegemonic groups as their beliefs and practices become naturalized within the spaces that they dominate. In more diverse contexts, however, religious groups have adopted these strategies more reflexively. In the process, some groups have sought to preserve their existing influence within social space, others have worked to transform local society, and still others have tried to protect their faith from external pressures. The frequent emergence of violence from such conflicts in part derives from the intensity with which believers pursue these goals, but it also reflects the frequent entanglement of such concerns with political, social, and cultural factors organized at other scales.

Narrower Scales

At scales narrower than the local community, external expressions of religious territoriality are less commonplace than internal expressions. The concerns of a religious group regarding the scales of body and home tend to focus primarily on the behaviors and beliefs of the group's own adherents. Because of this inward focus, most religious groups have identified relatively few issues calling for the assertion of control over spaces external to the group at these narrower scales. Within many societies, moreover, the personal practices of individuals and families are defined as part of a private realm largely closed to outside interference from nongovernmental groups. In such cases, society may have little tolerance for intrusions by religious groups into these private matters as they concern nonmembers. Nonetheless, religious groups have exerted some forms of influence over secular space at narrower scales, primarily with regard to two issues: individual religious adherence and moral behavior. Proselytic religious groups have most explicitly displayed concerns with individual religious adherence through their focus on missionary activity, but many religious groups have also tried to shape patterns of adherence through territorial controls on heterodoxy, heresy, and apostasy. Religious groups have exercised territoriality as well in seeking to force the moral behavior of outsiders to conform to the group's own religious standards.

Religious Adherence

The missionary activity of proselytic religions typically involves processes constructed at multiple scales. National or international organizations of believers often provide the funding and larger institutional structures to support extensive missionary endeavors, and frequently set the spatial strategies that determine where missionary efforts will be concentrated. Ultimately, though, proselytism focuses on a process constituted at the scale of the body: the act of conversion performed by the individual adherent. This act essentially involves a redefinition of the body space of the convert in terms of its relationship to a new system of belief, including perceived transformations in the convert's spiritual status and personal identity. The importance of these transformations at the scale of the body finds expression in specific conversion rituals. The Christian ritual of baptism explicitly involves the body in the conversion process. In Christian belief, baptism of the physical body purifies the soul, linking the convert to the body of Jesus, or to the church broadly defined, and to the Holy Spirit. Conversion to Islam requires the physical process of reciting the shahada, the declaration that there is no god but God and Muhammad is God's messenger. Judaism, although not a proselytic religion for most of its history, also incorporates body space into the conversion process through the immersion of the convert in a ritual bath and for males the act of circumcision. As discussed in chapter 2, the process of conversion involves complex patterns of agency, involving both the proselyte and the proselytizer. From the perspective of the former, conversion represents an internal process. The actions of the proselytizer, however, originate in an external expression of territoriality emphasizing action directed toward the personal space of outsiders.

The relationship between religious adherence and external territoriality at narrower scales also appears in the suppression of heterodoxy, heresy, and apostasy. The control of such phenomena by a religious group involves the complex intersection of internal and external processes, since charges of heresy or apostasy are usually directed at former members of the group itself. By the time it makes such charges, however, a religious group has defined the accused as the Other, outside the group itself, and further actions by the group therefore take the form of external control. The suppression of unacceptable beliefs has again occurred across different scales. Within the Roman Catholic Church, for example, the Inquisition in various forms provided a widespread institutional framework for uncovering and punishing doctrinal deviations in various places during the medieval period. During the twentieth century the church revised this framework, forming the Congregation for the Doctrine of the Faith to maintain doctrinal purity throughout the spatial domain of the Roman Catholic Church.

In other cases, adherents in many traditions have organized the legal and institutional suppression of heterodoxy at local and national scales. The legal systems of the Islamic states of Saudi Arabia, Iran, and Sudan, for instance, incorporate the traditional sharia punishment of death for blasphemy and for apostasy from Islam. Pakistani law also defines blasphemy as a capital offense. Again, however, the response of religious groups to heterodoxy, heresy, and apostasy has largely focused on the scale of the body through various forms of punishment; and the threat of bodily punishment provides a significant deterrent to the public expression of views unacceptable to the dominant religious group. The specific means used at the scale of the body to control deviant religious views have taken many different forms. In some cases they have been extreme, as in the use of torture to extract confessions of heresy during the medieval Inquisition or the execution of apostates in accordance with the sharia. In the early decades of Puritan New England, Baptists and Quakers likewise faced corporal and capital punishment for their deviations from Puritan orthodoxy. In other cases, however, such punishments have been less violent. In various traditions the process of excommunication provides a means of severing bonds between the group and individuals holding unacceptable beliefs. Similarly the practice of shunning, used by many Amish and by Jehovah's Witnesses, establishes significant social constraints on the body space of those being punished by isolating them from direct interactions with other believers.

Moral Behavior

Concerns with the moral behavior of individuals constitute a further motivation for religious groups to exercise external territoriality at narrower scales. Such concerns focus primarily on the assertion of religious law or moral standards at the scale of the body. Within this context too, religious groups seek to control the meaning and use of body space through strategies organized at wider scales, for example by supporting legislation that restricts certain kinds of behavior; but the primary aim of these efforts remains centered on constraints on body space itself. In some cases religious groups have sought to impose more general constraints within society as a means of preventing proscribed moral behavior. This pattern clearly appears in the restrictions placed on the body space of women, including nonadherents as well as adherents, by religious groups having a strong patriarchal tradition. Adherents impose such restrictions in part to control the sexuality of both women and men, and in the process to protect marital and familial relationships as well. Restrictions on women's body space thus have implications at the scales of the home and family in addition to that of the body. The expectation in some Muslim societies that both Muslim and non-Muslim women will wear veils in public exemplifies this kind of general restriction on female body space. Non-Muslim women in Saudi Arabia and other conservative Muslim societies thus face strong social pressures to veil themselves, for example. The above-mentioned protests of Islamic fundamentalists in Nigeria against the Miss World pageant in 2002 demonstrated a similar concern with control over the body space of nonadherents, as do the efforts of ultra-Orthodox Jews in Jerusalem to control female dress near their neighborhoods. For both traditional Muslims and ultra-Orthodox Jews, the insistence on gender segregation in public represents another significant effort to place restrictions on female body space among nonadherents and adherents alike.

In addition to these more general efforts to promote social morality outside their membership, religious groups have often targeted specific deviations from their own religious standards at the scale of the body. Opposition to abortion by many conservative Christians again represents an important example of this pattern in the United States. Although this opposition has led to action at various scales, its primary focus is a religiously grounded moral issue defined at the scale of the body, particularly through discourses focusing on the womb as an extension of social space.[65] Religious opponents of abortion have articulated two concerns at that scale: the moral responsibilities of the mother, the would-be target of control, in the divinely sanctioned act of reproduction; and the inviolable rights of the fetus as a living soul. Significantly, supporters of abortion rights have also conceptualized this issue at the scale of the body, focusing primarily on the individual rights and responsibilities of the mother. Abortion opponents have further represented the issues involved as moral absolutes, applicable not only to their own religious group but to society in general and thus requiring broader social and legal restrictions. The efforts of religious groups to control abortion also have implications at scales beyond the body, of course, again including the scales of family and home.

A similar entangling of the scales of body and home informed conservative Protestant support for the temperance movement and Prohibition during the late nineteenth and early twentieth centuries. Various Protestant groups, including most prominently the Women's Christian Temperance Union, played a central role in the campaign to spread abstinence from the consumption of alcohol. Conservative Protestants defined the basic problem of alcohol abuse at the scale of the body, characterizing it as a rejection of individual moral responsibility. They also viewed alcohol abuse as a contributing factor in various other evils, such as sexual promiscuity and domestic violence, again rooted in moral deviance at the scale of the body. At the same time, though, they emphasized the broader social consequences of these problems, particularly in terms of their destructive effects at the scale of the home. Conservative Protestants again viewed the problems that they associated with alcohol in absolute and universal terms and thus sought the establishment of broader social controls like Prohibition. As discussed above, similar concerns with alcohol use have characterized Islamic fundamentalism as well.

Finally, contemporary examples of religious opposition to perceived violations of moral standards within society have developed as well in response to the advancement of gay and lesbian interests. Members of various Hindu fundamentalist groups, including Shiv Sena and the Rashtriya Swayamsevak Sangh, protested the 2004 release of an Indian motion picture about a lesbian relationship, characterizing it as an affront to Indian culture. In addition to demanding that the movie be banned, militants in various Indian cities destroyed public advertisements for the movie and attacked theaters where it was being shown.[66] Within the United States, religious opposition to the gay rights movement has recently focused primarily on the concept of same-sex marriage. Many conservative and moderate Christians in the United States have opposed recent attempts to extend marriage or some other form of civil union to gay and lesbian couples, based in part on their conception of marriage as the sacred union between a man and a woman and in part on their more general opposition to homo-sexuality. For conservative Protestants especially, this opposition derives from religious concerns with social control constituted at the scale of the body, but it has obvious implications as well for the assertion of control at the scale of the home and family, for example by promoting the traditional family structure as the ideal context for the moral and religious socialization of children.

Wider Scales

Several factors contribute to the importance of wider scales as contexts for external expressions of religious territoriality. Perhaps most importantly, the scale of the state represents the context within which religious groups have most often used political means to extend control over secular space beyond the boundaries of their own mem-bership. The state essentially provides the most effective institutional mechanisms for establishing public expressions of religious territoriality within a heterogeneous soci-ety. In addition, conflicts between competing religious groups are often constituted at state, international, or global scales. Although individual actions within such conflicts occur locally, antagonists tend to comprehend the significance of the conflict at wider scales, in relation to more extensive, imagined communities of adherents. Finally, the scales of state and globe serve as contexts for the universal aims of religious groups seeking to transform humanity or human society generally. Again, each of these factors involves the intersection of processes constructed at multiple scales, but adherents con-ceptually link the meanings of those phenomena to broader spatial contexts. As an illustration, religious opponents of abortion in the United States seek to prevent this practice at the scale of the body, as discussed above, but in pursuing this goal they emphasize asserting control at the scale of the state through legislation or a constitu-tional amendment. Territoriality articulated at wider scales in effect provides the framework for achieving more local forms of control.

The State

At the most basic level, religious territoriality at the scale of the state focuses on the identity of the state itself. As discussed above, state religious identity has been expressed in many ways: through the formal constitution of the state as a theocracy, by the establishment of a state religion, or less formally in the implicit hegemony of a dominant religious group. As an external form of territoriality, the articulation of a state's religious identity can have far-reaching influences on religious practice. In many contexts this process has fostered the conversion of the populace to a state religion, as in the spread of Christianity after it became the Roman Empire's official religion. Similar patterns developed with regard to the diffusion of Buddhism in India follow-ing the conversion of the emperor Asoka in the third century BCE. In various states the hegemony of an official religion has contributed as well to the rise of syncretistic faiths, as among Africans in the Caribbean and South America during the period of slavery.

The formation of a state's religious identity may be a relatively uncontroversial process, particularly if the state contains a homogeneous population or if the official religion is sufficiently dominant in social or political terms. At the same time, the increasing secularization of some contemporary states has also reduced the importance of relict religious identities. The Church of England remains the established religion in England, for example, but the association between church and state has comparatively little significance in the modern era. In many contexts, however, the religious identities of states have been a significant source of conflict. The articulation of a state religious identity has frequently had negative consequences for religious minorities, who because of their religious affiliation have been subjected to various forms of discrimination or persecution. Furthermore, in many contexts competing interests have vigorously contested the definition of a state's religious identity. The often-intense concern with the latter process reflects its significance as an expression of religious territoriality, with implications for the status of different religious groups, the meaning of the state itself, the substance of government policies, and the state's external political relations. For adherents, the outcome of this process also has crucial consequences for their interpretation of the legitimacy and authority of the state.

The contesting of state religious identity has traditionally arisen from overt competition between religious groups. Such competition can develop through the conquest of an area by a group that has subsequently imposed its own religious identity on conquered territory. The persistent warfare between the Ottoman Empire and various Christian states in southeastern Europe followed this pattern, with Christian resistance emphasizing the goal of protecting Christian lands from Muslim rule or of liberating Christian areas from Muslim control. Perhaps more commonly, however, conflicts over religious identity have arisen from religious differences within existing states, resulting in competition between groups for social control. The growth of the Puritan movement in England, for example, produced competing understandings of the religious character of the state. Puritan dissatisfaction with efforts to reform the Church of England ultimately gave rise to civil war and the efforts of Oliver Cromwell and his followers to reconstitute England as a Puritan state. Of course, discord between religious groups has often been entangled with other kinds of political concerns. The French religious wars of the 1500s focused primarily on Roman Catholic efforts to suppress the expansion of Protestantism, but they were also linked to competing social and economic interests.[67]

More recent conflicts related to state religious identity have involved similar territorial concerns but have generally been more reflexive in character, developing in connection with other contemporary political trends. The impact of religious nationalism on the contesting of state identity represents one important expression of this pattern. Although connections between religion and national identity have long existed in traditional settings, the relationship between the two has become more pronounced in certain contemporary contexts with the rise of more reflexive forms of nationalism. Within such contexts, groups have represented the articulation of the state's religious identity not only as a goal in itself but also as a source of legitimacy for other nationalist objectives. This approach has in turn generated conflict as an external form of territoriality through the exclusion or suppression of other religious communities within the state.

Conflict arising from the reassertion of Serbian nationalism in recent years provides a conspicuous illustration of this process. The fall of Yugoslavia in the early 1990s resulted in a resurgence in Serbian religious nationalism, rooted in the Serbs' nineteenth-century struggle for independence from the Ottoman Empire and their older nationalist myth of martyrdom in defense of Christianity during the Ottoman invasion of the fourteenth century. This resurgence focused in territorial terms on reestablishing the Serbian Orthodox identity of areas that had been part of the pre-Ottoman Serbian state, ultimately through the expansion of modern Serbia. In pursuing this goal, Serbian nationalists targeted the Muslim inhabitants of the region, whom they portrayed as descendants of the European converts to Islam believed to have betrayed St. Lazar in his defeat by the Ottomans. Before the international community intervened, radical nationalists within the Serbian government and military undertook brutal politics of ethnic cleansing against Muslims in Serbia-controlled Kosovo and in the neighboring state of Bosnia and Herzegovina (photo 4.13).[68]

The impact of religious nationalism on state religious identity has been reinforced in recent years by its interactions with the rise of religious fundamentalism. Fundamentalist and nationalist ideologies have intersected in contexts where adherents have articulated their concern with religious tradition in relation to issues of identity, particularly in reference to the state. Concerns with such issues have typically arisen from fundamentalists' belief that the traditional status of their religious identity

Photo 4.13.   One of many Muslim cemeteries in Sarajevo dedicated primarily to people killed between 1993 and 1996 during the Siege of Sarajevo. By most estimates the siege drove 150,000 Bosnian Muslims from the city and resulted in the deaths of thousands more. The thin, white grave markers are typical of the city's Muslim cemeteries. Sarajevo, Bosnia and Herzegovina, 2006.

Source: Eürodäna/Dana (www.flickr.com/photos/djsacche/229187099/), under Creative Commons license (creativecommons.org/licenses/by-sa/2.0/).

has been undermined by the modern and postmodern rise of secularism and pluralism as political forces. The intersection of fundamentalism and nationalism has been particularly evident within the religiously pluralistic context of South Asia.[69] The emergence of Hindu fundamentalism during the 1920s reflected concerns over the potential erosion of the predominance of Hindu identity and values in India after independence. Hindu fundamentalists promoted the concept of Hindutva (or Hinduness) as the ideological basis for Indian nationalism. Hindutva encompassed all those who viewed India as their homeland, their fatherland, and their holy land. Although centered on Hinduism, this definition also made room for religions with historical ties to Hindu and Vedic traditions, including Buddhism, Jainism, and Sikhism, but it explicitly excluded Islam, Christianity, and Judaism. In political terms, Hindu fundamentalists sought to create a state whose identity would be defined by Hindutva; and after independence, they strongly opposed the constitutional definition of India as a secular, pluralistic state. The contesting of India's secular identity, repeatedly expressed through communal rioting and other forms of violence, became increasingly pronounced during the 1990s as the fundamentalist Bharatiya Janata Party (BJP) grew into one of India's principal political parties and during the period from 1999 to 2004 when the BJP led the country's ruling political coalition (map 4.6).

An analogous pattern has also developed in neighboring Sri Lanka, where Buddhist fundamentalists within the Sinhalese ethnic majority have sought to define the state's religious identity in more explicitly Buddhist terms. Sri Lanka's constitution in

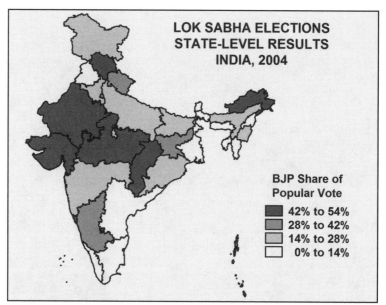

Map 4.6. Support for the Bharatiya Janata Party (BJP), a supporter of Hindu fundamentalist objectives, in the 2004 elections for representatives to India's Lok Sabha, the popularly elected lower house of its parliament. Although the BJP lost control of the Lok Sabha in 2004, it maintains particularly strong support, in percentage terms, in a large region to the south and west of the Gangetic plain. It also maintains considerable support in absolute numbers among Hindi speakers within the Gangetic plain itself.

fact identifies Buddhism as the state's foremost religion but also guarantees religious freedom to adherents of other faiths. Buddhist fundamentalists assert, however, that Sri Lanka's national identity is grounded in its historical role as a center of Theravada Buddhism. They have thus challenged pluralistic influences in Sri Lankan society, representing Hindus and other religious minorities as a threat to the state's true character. The contesting of Sri Lanka's religious identity ultimately provoked a protracted civil war, persisting since the early 1980s, that has pitted the Buddhist Sinhalese majority against Tamil Hindus and other minorities. Finally, the intersection of religious fundamentalism, nationalism, and state identity played a role in the rise of a radical Sikh nationalist movement in India during the 1980s.

The connections with religious nationalism represent only one element of the interactions between religious fundamentalism and the contesting of state religious identity. In many contexts fundamentalists seeking to influence the state's identity have in fact paid relatively little attention to nationalistic concerns. Instead, they have focused on establishing an explicitly religious polity, one whose identity is based not merely on its association with a particular nation but rather on its overt implementation of specific religious principles. Fundamentalist concerns with this issue have arisen most often in response to the perceived threats of modernism and secularism. From a fundamentalist perspective, the spread of modernism promotes the rejection of eternal religious truths and their replacement by inauthentic accommodations to contemporary thought, while secularism involves the removal of religion from public life, relegating it exclusively to the private sphere. To counter these trends, fundamentalists in various contexts have sought to reform the state so that it will conform to and reproduce basic religious principles. This objective again has implications both within and outside the religious group pursuing it. Internally, this objective relates to adherents' desire to reside within a state that in their view possesses religious authenticity and authority. As an external expression of territoriality, on the other hand, this objective reflects adherents' desire to impose their religious values on society at large, a goal that others have often contested.

Fundamentalist concepts of the Islamic state represent a significant expression of the above pattern. Although based on the historical model of the Islamic polity founded by Muhammad and drawing on various other historical examples, fundamentalist efforts to create an ideal Islamic state have taken place within the context of the modern state system.[70] The immediate goal of such efforts has not been to create a single empire encompassing the entire Muslim umma but rather to redefine existing states as strictly Islamic political entities. Some Muslims have considered such state-centered objectives to be problematic, particularly when combined with nationalism, because they create formal political divisions within the Muslim umma, which in the worldview of traditional Islam should remain unified. Others have responded to this concern by characterizing the creation of a local Islamic state as the first step in establishing a universal Islamic polity and as a realistic strategy within the context of the modern state system.

As external expressions of territoriality, however, fundamentalist efforts to redefine modern states in Islamic terms have provoked diverse forms of conflict and resistance. In some contexts, opposition has come primarily from secularist or modernist interests within the state, which may recognize the social importance of Islam but also assert that the state should be organized on secular or modernist principles. This pattern has developed within Egypt and Pakistan, for example, where secular governments have used various means, including active suppression, to curb fundamentalist influences. In other contexts, religious diversity has produced opposition to fundamentalist efforts to remake the state. After the restructuring of Sudan in Islamic terms in the late 1980s by a coalition of military leaders and members of the Sudanese Muslim Brotherhood, opposition from the country's Christian and animist minorities contributed to an extended civil war. Less commonly, fundamentalists have conceptualized the formation of an ideal Islamic state as an external form of territoriality in relation to the existing Muslim society, which they view as being inherently corrupt. The most radical wing of Islamic fundamentalism in Egypt has adopted this position, portraying itself as a revolutionary vanguard seeking to destroy the inauthentic Islam that in their view dominates Egyptian society. From this perspective, the establishment of the Islamic state represents an externally directed action involving the reconversion of the Muslim masses to true Islam.[71] Finally, the external implications of the formation of an Islamic state have become most evident in settings where fundamentalist groups have actually succeeded in achieving this goal, as in Sudan or Iran, where religious minorities have faced various forms of discrimination and persecution.

In contrast to the above examples, fundamentalist concerns have in some settings focused less on the establishment of formal theocratic structures than on their conception of a state's religious identity as a broader expression of cultural tradition. A primary example of this pattern has emerged in the United States, where Christian fundamentalists have sought to assert the country's identity as a Christian nation, although typically without supporting overtly theocratic goals. Again, this effort has arisen through fundamentalist reactions against the perceived influences of modernism and secularism, and it reflects an underlying goal of restructuring American society to conform to fundamentalist interpretations of Christian values. Fundamentalists have based this conception of the religious identity of the United States on the belief that the country was founded on Christian principles. Others have contested this belief, arguing that it contradicts the constitutional separation of church and state and inherently disadvantages non-Christians.

A very different example of a fundamentalist conception of state identity has developed in relation to religious Zionism, one of the principal forms of Jewish fundamentalism. Religious Zionists are distinguished from other Jewish fundamentalists by their identification of the modern state of Israel as the core of the Jewish Promised Land. They thus view the founding of modern Israel, and particularly its extension over all of Jerusalem and into the West Bank following the Six-Day War, as the beginning of the divine redemption of the Jewish people. Ultra-Orthodox Jewish fundamentalists, in contrast, denounce the founding of Israel as a human effort to usurp divine authority over the reestablishment of the land of Israel. The religious Zionists' perspective has had significant territorial implications external to the group because of their insistence that the West Bank, as part of the Jewish territorial patrimony, remain part of the state of Israel. To further this goal, they have been strongly committed to the formation of Jewish settlements in the West Bank and equally resistant to the idea of giving up such settlements in a peace agreement with the Palestinians. Their claim that they have a sacred right to possess these lands has obviously been vigorously contested by Palestinians.[72]

Beyond issues relating in general terms to identity, a second major focus of external territoriality at the scale of the state has been the intersection of religious concerns with specific state policies. Such patterns are not limited to theocratic contexts. They have been commonplace in societies where the beliefs of a dominant group have been incorporated, often unreflexively, into the social structures of the state. They have developed as well through the purposeful efforts of religious groups, of either majority or minority status, to shape the character of society and the state. In such cases, adherents often focus on the scale of the state because the latter provides an effective context for exerting influence over society at large. For certain groups, conversely, this scale represents the logical context for resisting efforts by the state, or by a larger society, to constrain their own religious practices. Religious groups have undertaken both formal and informal political activities at the state level. Within the context of modern states, however, this process has typically centered on the establishment of political parties, lobbying groups, or other formal organizations to advance the group's interests.

As at the scale of the community, external forms of religious territoriality at the scale of the state have reflected a variety of concerns. Perhaps most commonly, adherents have acted at the scale of the state to integrate their own religious values into public policy. Often they have done so primarily to prevent others from violating perceived moral certainties. Contemporary efforts by conservative Christians in the United States to incorporate their readings of biblical principles into public policy follow this pattern. These efforts have given rise to a variety of religiously based organizations aimed at influencing political decision making, such as the Moral Majority, the Christian Coalition, and Focus on the Family. Such groups have typically focused on specific issues, such as abortion or same-sex marriage, that to them represent violations of incontrovertible moral laws, and they seek to ban these phenomena uniformly throughout the state. Recent efforts by Hindu fundamentalists to establish a uniform, nationwide cow protection law in India reflects a similar expression of territoriality in defense of religious values.

Muslim efforts to exert religious influence at the scale of the state have frequently been broader in scope, centered on establishing the sharia. Hegemonic Muslim societies have traditionally based their law on the sharia, but in modern contexts this practice has become more contentious because of opposition from secularists and religious minorities. Official establishment of the sharia has thus become a major issue for Islamic fundamentalists in various countries. In place of a formal establishment of the sharia, fundamentalists have also pushed for constitutional affirmations of the state's commitment to Islamic values and traditions; and such statements appear in the constitutions of both Pakistan and Egypt.

Along somewhat different lines, religious groups have in some instances sought to integrate their values into public policy as a means of fulfilling their own perceived moral responsibilities as defined in their religious ethos. A primary example of this form of religious activism is Christian Democracy, a political movement that developed in Western Europe during the late 1800s to promote policies based on the social teachings of the Roman Catholic Church. The movement combined support for conservative social values with concern for the working class and issues of social welfare such as housing and health care. After World War II, state-based Christian Democratic parties became a major political force throughout much of Western Europe.[73]

The wider influence of religious groups at the scale of the state has also developed in less direct ways as they have sought to protect the integrity of their own religious values. The concern with such issues does not directly involve issues of morality or social policy. Instead, it reflects the group's desire to ensure that other cultural or political influences do not interfere with its ability to maintain its beliefs and practices. By seeking such accommodation, however, the group necessarily extends its influence beyond its own membership. In traditional contexts, hegemonic religious groups exerted such influence by asserting the centrality of their own religious system within society, often using the mechanisms of the state to marginalize or exclude other religious groups. This pattern might involve the exclusion of adherents of minority religions from positions of political power. Traditional Muslim states often imposed such restrictions, as did medieval Christian states with regard to Jews. Not until 1829 did the British government allow Roman Catholics to sit as members of the British Parliament. More generally, hegemonic groups have sought to protect their religious system by discouraging overt public displays of religious activity by other groups. Again, traditional Muslim states frequently followed this pattern, even with regard to Christians and Jews who were officially tolerated as "People of the Book."[74] Dominant religious groups have also used the state to restrict the missionary work of other groups. In some cases the state has designed such constraints to prevent local conflicts between competing religious communities, but in others the state's actions have been driven by the objections of a hegemonic religious group to the introduction of incompatible belief systems. In the most extreme cases, a hegemonic group's desire to control the religious makeup of the state has taken more severe forms, such as the elimination of an undesired religious minority. This form of external territoriality occurred, for example, in the expulsion of Jews from various European states during the medieval period, a pattern echoed in far more virulent form during modern times as the Nazi Holocaust.

Religious groups have additionally sought to maintain specific elements of their belief system through state policies. Islamic fundamentalists in Pakistan, for example, have successfully pushed for so-called blasphemy laws that prohibit the denigration of Islam by either Muslims or non-Muslims. Among the latter, Ahmadis and Christians have most often been charged under this law. Fundamentalists in Pakistan have also tried to pressure the state to drop the current use of Sunday as a weekly holiday, a practice adopted to facilitate international business relations. Fundamentalists argue that this implicit observance of the Christian Sabbath diminishes the status of Islam, although businesses are closed as well on Friday afternoons during the period of communal Islamic worship.

In a similar manner, Christian fundamentalists in the United States have sought state support for specific religious practices in connection with the issue of school prayer. Prayer had traditionally been part of the daily classroom routines of public schools in many parts of the country prior to 1962, when the Supreme Court issued a ruling prohibiting the practice. Since that time fundamentalist groups have focused considerable attention on reinstating teacher-led prayer in the classroom. At the scale of the state, this effort has concentrated in recent years on promoting an amendment to the Constitution that would permit prayer in public schools and other public places. Opponents of this proposal argue that its approval would improperly impose hegemonic Christian practices on religious minorities and persons having no religious affiliation.

As a final example, the Gush Emunim and other religious Zionists have tried to use Israeli state policies to support their effort to reclaim control of the Jewish Prom-ised Land, specifically through the formation of the settlements in the West Bank.[75] Since the mid-1970s they have succeeded in establishing scores of communities in the region with government support. Although the Israeli government has officially prohibited the creation of new Jewish settlements in the West Bank since 2001, it continues to provide various forms of financial support and subsidies to those that exist. Moreover, religious Zionists have adamantly opposed surrendering any of the places they have settled in the West Bank as an act of blasphemy against the divine redemption of the Jewish people. This expression of religious territoriality has thus had significant external implications, not only for Palestinians in the immediate vicin-ity but also for the resolution of the Israeli-Palestinian conflict.

The preceding examples have emphasized the ways in which religious groups have used the political structures of the state to exert influence beyond their own membership. External forms of territoriality have also developed as expressions of resistance to the state. This pattern has arisen among religious groups reacting against state policies that restrict their ability to practice their faith. In such contexts, territo-rial strategies organized by religious groups have focused on exerting various forms of political pressure on the state to alleviate the difficulties that they face. Groups may seek to exert conventional forms of political pressure, for example through political protest, appeals to specific political parties, or the petitioning or lobbying of govern-ment officials. Islamic fundamentalists have adopted such approaches in Turkey in recent years to protest the limitations placed on religious practice, including restric-tions on mosque construction and religious education and bans on women wearing veils in universities and government offices. Muslims in France and Singapore have similarly protested state policies against girls wearing headscarves in schools, as dis-cussed above.

In contemporary settings, many religious groups have also sought to bring inter-national pressures to bear on state policies of discrimination. Tibetan Buddhists have repeatedly called for international support in their resistance against the Chinese gov-ernment's efforts to weaken Buddhism's influence in Tibetan society, for example. Similar patterns have emerged more recently in China among adherents of Falun Dafa, a new religious movement rooted in Buddhist and Taoist principles that focuses on the practice of spiritual exercises known as Falun Gong. The Chinese government has characterized the group as a dangerous cult and has tried to suppress it.[76] Adher-ents have protested the government's actions in China, but have also sought support from foreign states and international human rights organizations.

In some instances the inability of religious groups to influence restrictive state policies has led to more violent responses, including the use of terrorism and civil war. This pattern developed in Afghanistan during the 1980s, when militant Islamic fundamentalists successfully waged a civil war against the socialist regime supported by the Soviet Union's military occupation. On a less extensive scale, Islamic militants have also used terrorism to attack the policies of various moderate or secularist govern-ments in predominantly Muslim states, such as Egypt and Algeria.

International and Global Concerns

Wider expressions of external religious territoriality have not been limited to the scale of the state, of course. Many have extended across national boundaries, even to the

global scale. For proselytic religious, missionary activity has played an especially important role in this context, serving to extend a religious group's influence across wide
expanses of secular space. The organization of widespread missionary processes has been
commonplace in both traditional and contemporary settings. In the former, proselytism frequently developed within the context of state expansion, colonialism, and trade,
as discussed in chapter 2. In more recent times, proselytic religions have increasingly
organized missionary work as a more independent activity, not directly associated with
other political and economic processes. At the same time, missionaries have made
increasing use of available technology to extend the geographical scope of their efforts.
Christian missionary groups have been particularly active in this context, developing
extensive broadcasting networks to exert religious influence on widely dispersed
regions.[77] Muslim missionaries have made use of radio as well, but on a more limited
scale. In recent years, moreover, the Internet has become an increasingly important
outlet for Christian, Muslim, and Buddhist missionary activity. The continuing vigor
of missionary work by proselytic religions has in turn generated conflict in various
locations. Such conflict has arisen out of competition between Christian and Muslim
efforts in parts of Africa, for example. Competition has also emerged within a single
tradition, between different Christian sects or between strict Islamic groups and Sufi
orders. The intensive targeting of particular regions of the world by Christian missionary groups has also generated conflict, and many countries have imposed limitations
on the number and activity of foreign missionaries within their boundaries.[78]

Religious groups have tried as well to exert broader social influences over others
beyond the scale of the state, again either by fulfilling perceived moral responsibilities
or promoting their own religious values and beliefs. A great variety of religious groups
have organized charitable and humanitarian work at the global scale, emphasizing such
issues as economic development, education, disaster relief, and health care. Such activities have on occasion generated conflict when religious groups have incorporated proselytism into their humanitarian efforts. For example, Muslim groups in Indonesia criticized the proselytic activities of some Christian aid groups participating in relief efforts
following the tsunamis that devastated areas around the Indian Ocean late in 2004.[79]

Religious groups have also been involved in various forms of social and environmental activism at wider scales. As discussed above, Engaged Buddhists have been
actively involved in promoting peace and disarmament, for example by organizing
interfaith conferences, raising funds for United Nations relief programs, developing
peace proposals and educational programs, and staging *Dhammayatra* or "peace
walks" to protest the effects of specific conflicts or to raise public consciousness regarding peace issues. Similarly, the Transcendental Meditation movement has organized
collective meditation activities in an effort to promote world peace, based on the belief
that correct meditation can have external as well as internal influences. Following the
terrorist attacks in the United States on September 11, 2001, the movement's founder,
Maharishi Mahesh Yogi, sought to organize a permanently endowed group of forty
thousand meditators to reduce global tensions. With regard to the environment,
Christian Evangelicals have become involved in various forms of activism since the
1980s, based on their reading of a number of traditional Christian concepts, including
the belief that God gave humanity stewardship of the earth, concerns with broader
humanitarian aims as they relate to environmental justice, and the principle that the
human and the natural are both part of a unitary, divine creation.[80]

In addition to focusing on such broader concerns, religious groups with sufficient national influence may seek to affect foreign policy decisions related to their religious values. Since the rise of the Christian right as a political force in the United States during the 1980s, various conservative and fundamentalist Christian groups have exerted such influence.[81] These groups have lobbied strongly for U.S. support for Israel, for example, based in part on the millennialist belief that the return of the Jewish people to Israel represents an initial step in preparation for the Second Coming of Christ. Conservative Christians have also opposed the use of U.S. foreign aid in supporting the practice of abortion in other countries, a position that was incorporated into U.S. policy in the 1980s under Ronald Reagan.

External forms of religious territoriality beyond the scale of the state have also found expression through violent conflict. The religious dimensions of warfare have a long history and have developed in many different contexts.[82] Military conquest has played a major role in the spread of certain religions and the spatial contraction of others. The overland growth of various Muslim empires and the expansion of the colonial empires of Christian European states, to cite two key examples, had major effects on the diffusion of Islam and Christianity, and in many locations contributed to corresponding declines in indigenous tribal religions. Conflicts between competing states with different religious identities have also extended the impact of religious warfare to international scales, as in the medieval conflicts between Christianity and Islam in Iberia, southeastern Europe, and the eastern Mediterranean region. The various conflicts between Israel and neighboring Arab states that have occurred since the late 1940s represent a contemporary example of the same pattern.

Since the mid-twentieth century, the rise of militant forms of Islamic fundamentalism has generated new forms of religious conflict beyond the scale of the state. One important dimension of this process has been the formation of an informal, trans-state force of Islamic militants who have engaged in conflicts in widely dispersed locations, motivated by a reflexive commitment to the defense of Islam and Islamic territory. This group fought against the establishment of Israel in the late 1940s, and in the following decade fought on the side of Egypt in the conflict with Britain and France over the Suez Canal. The war against Soviet occupation in Afghanistan provided perhaps the most important context for the further development of this group, but it also became involved in conflicts in Algeria, Bosnia, and Chechnya. This group also served as the foundation for a second key development, the emergence of international terrorist organizations, such as al-Qaeda, which have conducted violent actions against widely distributed targets. The 2001 attacks on the World Trade Center in New York and the Pentagon in Washington, D.C., represent the most egregious example of such actions.

The rise of militant Islamic fundamentalism has contributed to the post–Cold War theory that future global conflicts will develop around clashes between distinct regional civilizations, which in many cases are defined by a shared religious identity.[83] This theory has been widely criticized by political geographers as being overly simplistic in asserting the homogeneity within individual regions, however.[84] The notion that Islamic militants across the globe are now carrying out a Third World War against non-Muslim regions, for example, does not take into account the great differences that exist among the different places and groups involved. Conflicts between Christians and Muslims in Nigeria have causes, objectives, and potential outcomes very different from those of conflicts between Muslims and Hindus in Kashmir or between Muslims and Buddhists in Southeast Asia. Despite its weaknesses, however, the "clash of civilizations" theory is indicative to some extent of the continuing importance of religious differences in international conflict.

Intersections among Scales

As in the case of internal expressions of religious territoriality, external expressions typically involve complex connections across different scales. When a religious group seeks to exert influence beyond its own membership, it may be able to address concerns at one scale only by taking action at another scale. Missionary activity thus focuses most immediately at the scale of the body, but has frequently been carried out through institutions organized at much wider scales. A group's external concerns may in fact encompass a range of scales, each involving a different set of actions and potential conflicts. As an example, the opposition of many conservative Christians to the practice of abortion has implications and expressions at multiple scales. Their opposition is explicitly grounded in the scale of the body, articulated in relation to religious principles concerning the perceived meanings of sexual reproduction, individual human life, and divine law. In their view those principles incontrovertibly proscribe certain practices in body space, including abortion. At the same time, they believe that these proscriptions do not apply solely to the bodies of adherents. Rather, they apply at a universal scale essentially defined by their own worldview. To enforce the proscription against abortion and control the prenatal space of the womb, conservative Christians have therefore devised externally directed strategies at other scales. At the scale of the community, they have targeted local health institutions that provide abortions, using various forms of public protest and in a small number of extreme cases actual violence, to discourage both the providers themselves and potential patients. They have also sought to oppose abortion at the scale of the family, for instance through laws that require parental notification when a minor seeks to have an abortion. Their desire to achieve universal control of this practice in body space has further led them to address the issue at the scale of the state, most prominently by lobbying in favor of laws placing restrictions on abortions, by supporting the appointment of Supreme Court justices perceived to support the overturning of rulings allowing abortion, and by seeking the passage of a constitutional amendment banning the practice. In addition, they have sought to influence behavior outside the United States by pressuring the government to withhold funding from international organizations that promote or provide abortions. As a concern of conservative Christians, then, opposition to abortion represents a complex issue constituted at diverse scales, involving nested layers of religious territoriality.

Conclusions

This chapter has considered the importance of religious belief and practice in the efforts of culture groups to influence or control the meanings and uses of secular space. In addressing this topic, the discussion has specifically examined the varied nature of such efforts, both internal and external, and the different scales at which they have been articulated. Taken together, these expressions of territoriality represent a crucial feature of religions as cultural systems. For believers, the incorporation of religious faith into the symbols and structures of secular space signifies a primary manifestation of the connections between immediate lived experience and the abstract certainties of their worldview. Through this process, adherents express the fundamental meanings of their religious system, worldly expressions of religious authority, the ultimate foundations of their individual and communal identity, and key elements of religious experience in daily life. While efforts to influence or control secular space represent a general feature of religious systems, however, they have taken on a great variety of specific forms, reflecting essential differences in the concerns of religious groups and in the contexts in which they have enacted their beliefs. Most importantly, such efforts have in some cases focused internally on maintaining coherence between a religious group's faith and its own lived environment, and in others have focused externally on imposing consistency between a group's beliefs and a larger social context. Whatever their character, expressions of religious territoriality have contributed significantly to the cultural distinctiveness of particular places, comprising an important element of the depth of religious influence within secular space. The resulting connections between faith and place thus constitute one of the principal sources of the contextual character of religions. In this sense, religious territoriality serves to integrate the intrinsic contextuality and spatiality of religious systems.

The diversity among these expressions of territoriality further reflects many of the cultural tensions that exist in relation to religions as cultural systems. Most importantly, they reveal the complex interactions that commonly exist between processes of human agency, through which adherents continually strive to achieve accommodation between faith and daily life, and the underlying structures of religious systems rooted in a specific worldview and ethos. The exercise of religious territoriality provides a way for adherents to articulate and resolve in immediate and practical terms the meanings around which they organize their faith. Often this process has resulted in tension between innovation and tradition, or in more geographical terms between local practice and universal custom. Expressions of territoriality have also necessarily produced tensions across different geographical scales, from the individual to the community to the state and beyond, as believers have sought to establish and enforce consistency in belief and practice at all levels of experience. The practice of a religion at one scale, in other words, typically has far-reaching implications for the religious use, interpretation, and control of secular space at other scales. And in its external forms, religious territoriality has frequently provoked or reinforced tensions between distinct religious communities or between religious and secular groups. Such tensions have emerged in some instances as a group has tried to shape broader social spaces in accordance with its own beliefs and in others as a group has sought to constrain unwanted sources of external influence. Through these various processes, the exercise of territoriality by religious groups has often led to the contesting of social spaces and the meanings applied to them.

Finally, many of the examples discussed in this chapter illustrate that expressions of religious territoriality in traditional contexts have often developed unreflexively, within a local or national context dominated by a particular religious group. Some traditional forms of territoriality have in fact been more reflexive, such as scrupulous adherence to religious laws derived from scriptural sources or the purposeful discrimination of a hegemonic group against a weaker one. As contemporary examples throughout the chapter have suggested, however, the reflexivity of religious territoriality has generally increased within modern and postmodern settings, where social change has challenged traditional practices once taken for granted. Within such settings, the perceived threat of the privatization of faith and corresponding efforts to deprivatize religious belief and practice have played an especially important role in the reflexive exercise of religious territoriality.[85] The process of privatization involves an overt decline in the public role of religion as society redefines religious belief and practice as the private concerns of individuals and communities of believers. An important corollary of this process is the redefinition of the role of religious meanings in secular space.

The privatization of religion has been most pronounced in modern political states that have adopted secular or pluralistic identities, and is closely related to modern conceptions of religious freedom as a basic human right. Even in countries that have not espoused secularism or pluralism, however, adherents may be concerned with the potential threat of the process of privatization, particularly through the effects of foreign cultural influences. This pattern has developed within a number of predominantly Muslim states, for example, where the incursions of Western popular culture have reinforced some believers' concerns with exerting or reasserting religious control over social spaces, at scales from the body to the state and beyond. More generally, traditionalists in many religious traditions have opposed the process of privatization because they believe that the latter expresses a false distinction between religious concerns and other aspects of human existence. From the traditionalist perspective, religion informs all aspects of life.

Like other forms of religious territoriality, therefore, the responses of opponents to the privatization of religion seek to project religious faith into the spaces of everyday life. In the process, moreover, believers typically express a reflexive concern with the defense of their religious system from this perceived threat by ensuring that it retains concrete expressions within the meanings and uses of secular space at multiple scales. Adherents have undertaken this effort in various ways, however. Some have sought primarily to combat trends that have already weakened the public role of religion. This approach has been commonplace among fundamentalist groups in secular or pluralistic contexts, which seek to restore the influence of religious meanings across different scales of public space. Other adherents, particularly in traditional cultural settings, have tried to preserve society's acceptance of religion's role in secular space in the face of potential but not fully realized threats. Islamic fundamentalists in predominantly Muslim states have exemplified this pattern. Still other adherents have sought to adapt to the process of privatization by redefining the relationship of religious practice to secular space, largely by trying to maintain the broader social relevance of religious meanings under changing circumstances. The Christian Social Gospel, Engaged Buddhism, liberation theology, and the Christian Democracy movement represent examples of this strategy, emphasizing the public role of religion through conceptions of moral and social responsibility, enacted at various scales, rather than through strict adherence to tradition.

Despite the increasingly private character of religious belief and practice in many social contexts, then, the expression of religious territoriality at diverse scales in secular space remains a key element of the complexity of religious systems. The concern with secular space represents only one dimension of the spatiality of religious systems, however. In the following chapter, the text turns to the other principal dimension, that of sacred space.

Notes

1. Neil Smith, "Homeless/global: Scaling Places," in *Mapping the Futures: Local Cultures, Global Change*, ed. Jon Bird et al. (New York: Routledge, 1993), 87–119; Benno Werlen, "Regions and Everyday Regionalizations: From a Space-Centered towards an Action-Centered Human Geography," in *B/ordering Space*, ed. Henk van Houtum, Olivier Kramsch, and Wolfgang Zierhofer (Burlington, Vt.: Ashgate, 2005), 47–60.

2. Robert David Sack, *Human Territoriality* (New York: Cambridge University Press, 1986); David Storey, *Territory: The Claiming of Space* (London: Pearson Prentice-Hall, 2001), 9–20.

3. Clifford Geertz, "'The Pinch of Destiny': Religion as Experience, Meaning, Identity, Power," *Raritan* 18 (Winter 1999): 1–19.

4. On gender and Muslim house forms, see Daphne Spain, *Gendered Spaces* (Chapel Hill: University of North Carolina Press, 1992), 46–50; on social spaces supporting Jewish dietary practices, see Etan Diamond, "The Kosher Lifestyle: Religious Consumerism and Suburban Orthodox Jews," *Journal of Urban History* 28 (May 2002): 488–505; and on the settlement patterns of various communal religious groups, see Dolores Hayden, *Seven American Utopias: The Architecture of Communitarian Socialism, 1790–1975* (Cambridge, Mass.: MIT Press, 1976).

5. For example, see Anna J. Secor, "The Veil and Urban Space in Istanbul: Women's Dress, Mobility and Islamic Knowledge," *Gender, Place, and Culture* 9, no. 1 (March 2002): 5–22; Anna Secor, "Islamism, Democracy, and the Political Production of the Headscarf Issue in Turkey," in *Geographies of Muslim Women: Gender, Religion, and Space*, ed. Ghazi-Walid Falah and Caroline Nagel (New York: Guilford Press, 2005), 203–25.

6. J. Spencer Trimingham, *The Sufi Orders in Islam* (New York: Oxford University Press, 1971), 234.

7. Cf. Yvonne Yazbeck Haddad and Adair T. Lummis, *Islamic Values in the United States: A Comparative Study* (New York: Oxford University Press, 1987), 34–57.

8. On the internal spatiality of megachurches, see Jeanne Halgren Kilde, "Reading Megachurches: Investigating the Religious and Cultural Work of Church Architecture," in *American Sanctuary: Understanding Sacred Spaces*, ed. Louis P. Nelson (Bloomington: Indiana University Press, 2006), 225–49; for a case study of an individual megachurch, see John Connell, "Hillsong: A Megachurch in the Sydney Suburbs," *Australian Geographer* 36, no. 3 (November 2005): 315–32.

9. U.S. Department of Education, *Digest of Education Statistics, 2005* (Washington, D.C.: U.S. Government Printing Office, 2006), 13, 89.

10. Lily Kong, "Religious Schools: For Spirit, (F)or Nation," *Environment and Planning D: Society and Space* 23, no. 4 (August 2005): 615–31; Mike Castelli and Abdullah Trevathan, "The English Public Space: Developing Spirituality in English Muslim Schools," *International Journal of Children's Spirituality* 10, no. 2 (August 2005): 123–31.

11. Roger W. Stump, *Boundaries of Faith: Geographical Perspectives on Religious Fundamentalism* (Lanham, Md.: Rowman and Littlefield, 2000), 189.

12. Deryck O. Lodrick, *Sacred Cows, Sacred Places: Origins and Survivals of Animal Homes in India* (Berkeley: University of California Press, 1981).

13. Dan Stanislawski, "Dionysus Westward: Early Religion and the Economic Geography of Wine," *Geographical Review* 65 (1975): 427–44; Erich Isaac, "The Citron in the Mediterranean: A Study in Religious Influences," *Economic Geography* 35 (January 1959), 71–78.

14. The development of this symbolic practice is examined in Akeia A. Benard, "The Material Roots of Rastafarian Marijuana Symbolism," *History and Anthropology* 18, no. 1 (March 2007): 89–99.

15. Stump, *Boundaries of Faith*, 192.

16. Scott M. Manetsch, "Pastoral Care East of Eden: The Consistory of Geneva, 1568–82," *Church History* 75, no. 2 (June 2006): 274–313.

17. Stump, *Boundaries of Faith*, 142–44, 188–89.

18. Hayden, *Seven American Utopias*, 64–147.

19. David Newman, ed., *The Impact of Gush Emunim: Politics and Settlement in the West Bank* (London: Croom Helm, 1985).

20. F. W. Boal, "Belfast: Walls Within," *Political Geography* 21 (June 2002), 687–94; religious spaces do play important roles within Northern Ireland's segregated neighborhoods, as discussed in David N. Livingstone, Margaret C. Keane, and Frederick W. Boal, "Space for Religion: A Belfast Case Study," *Political Geography* 17 (February 1998), 145–70.

21. Jeff Haynes, *Religion in Third World Politics* (Boulder, Colo.: Lynne Rienner Publishers, 1993), 103–9.

22. Stump, *Boundaries of Faith*, 145–47.

23. Firuz Kazemzadeh, "The Baha'is in Iran: Twenty Years of Repression," *Social Research* 67, no. 2 (Summer 2000): 537–58; U.S. Congress, House, Committee on International Relations, and Senate, Committee on Foreign Relations, *Annual Report, International Religious Freedom, 1999*, 350–56.

24. Malise Ruthven, *Islam in the World* (New York: Oxford University Press, 1984), 276–77.

25. For a detailed examination of the internal spatial structure of Orthodox Christian monasteries, see Svetlana Popovic, "The *Trapeza* in Cenobitic Monasteries: Architectural and Spiritual Contexts," *Dumbarton Oaks Papers* 52 (1998): 281–303.

26. For detailed coverage of Christian and Buddhist monasticism, see William M. Johnston, ed., *Encyclopedia of Monasticism* (London: Routledge, 2000).

27. Smith, "Homeless/global: Scaling Places," in *Mapping the Futures: Local Cultures, Global Change*, ed. Bird et al., 102–5; Robyn Longhurst, "The Body and Geography," *Gender, Place and Culture* 2, no. 1 (March 1995): 97–106.

28. Linda Boynton Arthur, *Religion, Dress and the Body* (New York: Berg Publishers, 1999).

29. T. F. Ruby, "Listening to the Voices of Hijab," *Women's Studies International Forum* 29, no. 1 (2006): 54–66; Secor, "The Veil and Urban Space in Istanbul," 5–22.

30. Johan Wedel, *Santeria Healing: A Journey into the Afro-Cuban World of Divinities, Spirits, and Sorcery* (Gainesville: University Press of Florida, 2004).

31. For example, see Wil Gesler, "Lourdes: Healing in a Place of Pilgrimage," *Health and Place* 2 (June 1996): 95–105.

32. Catherine Vincent, "Discipline du Corps et de l'Esprit chez les Flagellants au Moyen Âge," *Revue Historique* 615 (July–September 2000): 593–614; Robert E. Lerner, "The Black Death and Western European Eschatological Mentalities," *American Historical Review* 86, no. 3 (June 1981): 533–52.

33. For example, see Michael P. Carroll, *The Penitente Brotherhood: Patriarchy and Hispano-Catholicism in New Mexico* (Baltimore: Johns Hopkins University Press, 2002).

34. Vernon James Schubel, "Karbala as Sacred Space among North American Shi'a," in *Making Muslim Space in North America and Europe*, ed. Barbara Daly Metcalf (Berkeley: University of California Press, 1996), 186–203.

35. A thorough discussion of the concept of hijra appears in Muhammad Khalid Masud, "The Obligation to Migrate: The Doctrine of *Hijra* in Islamic Law," in *Muslim Travelers: Pilgrimage, Migration, and the Religious Imagination*, ed. Dale F. Eickelman and James Piscatori (Berkeley: University of California Press, 1990), 29–49.

36. Richard P. Taylor, *Death and the Afterlife: A Cultural Encyclopedia* (Santa Barbara, Cal.: ABC-CLIO, 2000).

37. Jean-François Staszak, "L'Espace Domestique: Pour une Géographie de l'Intérieur," *Annales de Géographie* 620 (July–August 2001): 339–36; J. Douglas Porteus, "Home: The Territorial Core," *Geographical Review* 66, no. 4 (October 1976): 383–90.

38. Stump, *Boundaries of Faith*, passim.

39. Marvin Harris, "The Cultural Ecology of India's Sacred Cattle," *Current Anthropology* 7 (February 1966): 51–66.

40. Jon D. Mikalson, *Ancient Greek Religion* (Malden, Mass.: Blackwell, 2005), 160–80.

41. Ira M. Lapidus, *A History of Islamic Societies* (New York: Cambridge University Press, 1988), 230–31.

42. Lapidus, *History of Islamic Societies*, 355.

43. For an analysis of the actions of such groups and their relative impact, see Stump, *Boundaries of Faith*, 85–156.

44. Ger Duijzings, *Religion and the Politics of Identity in Kosovo* (New York: Columbia University Press, 2000), 176–202; Michael A. Sells, *The Bridge Betrayed: Religion and Genocide in Bosnia* (Berkeley: University of California Press, 1996), 37–69.

45. Parviz Daneshvar, *Revolution in Iran* (London: Macmillan, 1996), 143–45.

46. John L. Esposito, *The Islamic Threat: Myth or Reality?*, 3d ed. (New York: Oxford University Press, 1999), 135; for a more complete account of Mawdudi's influence on Islamic thought, see Seyyed Vali Reza Nasr, *Mawdudi and the Making of Islamic Revivalism* (New York: Oxford University Press, 1996).

47. Oklahoma, Tennessee, Mississippi, and Arkansas all passed state laws banning the teaching of evolution in public schools during the 1920s.

48. Derek H. Davis, "The Ten Commandments as Public Ritual," *Journal of Church and State* 44, no. 2 (Spring 2002): 221–28; John Dart, "Religious Right Rails at High Court Rulings," *Christian Century* 122 (September 6, 2005): 14; "Commandment Controversies: A Battle of Biblical Proportions," *Church and State* 54 (July/August 2001): 13.

49. John C. Blakeman, "The Religious Geography of Religious Expression: Local Governments, Courts, and the First Amendment," *Journal of Church and State* 48, no. 2 (Spring 2006): 399–422.

50. Adam Liptak, "Court Orders Removal of Monument to Ten Commandments," *New York Times*, July 2, 2003, A18.

51. Bill Rankin, "Prayers Provoke Lawsuits," *Atlanta Journal-Constitution*, August 21, 2005, 1D.

52. Stump, *Boundaries of Faith*, 193.

53. Celia W. Dugger, "A Chant to Fire Up Children, and Inflame Adults," *New York Times*, December 9, 1998, A4.

54. N. M. Thomas, "On Headscarves and Heterogeneity: Reflections on the French Foulard Affair," *Dialectical Anthropology* 29, no. 3–4 (2005): 373–86.

55. Mary Beth McCauley, "When a Triangle Affronts Religious Beliefs," *Christian Science Monitor*, May 23, 2002, 3; "Amish Win Court Case on Vehicle Emblem," *Christian Century* 113 (July 3, 1996): 689.

56. Ashutosh Varshney, *Ethnic Conflict and Civic Life: Hindus and Muslims in India* (New Haven, Conn.: Yale University Press, 2002), 197–98; Reece Jones, "Sacred Cows and Thumping Drums: Claiming Territory as 'Zones of Tradition' in British India," *Area* 39, no. 1 (March 2007): 55–65.

57. Johannes Harnischfeger, "Sharia and Control over Territory: Conflicts between 'Settlers' and 'Indigenes' in Nigeria," *African Affairs* 103 (July 2004): 431–52.

58. Faye Ginsburg, "Rescuing the Nation: Operation Rescue and the Rise of Anti-Abortion Militance," in *Abortion Wars: A Half Century of Struggle, 1950–2000*, ed. Rickie Solinger (Berkeley: University of California Press, 1998), 227–50.

59. Ebenezer Obadare, "In Search of a Public Sphere: The Fundamentalist Challenge to Civil Society in Nigeria," *Patterns of Prejudice* 38, no. 2 (June 2004): 177–98.

60. For example, see Rita M. Gross, "Toward a Buddhist Environmental Ethic," *Journal of the American Academy of Religion* 65, no. 2 (Summer 1997): 333–53; Akuppa, *Touching the Earth: A Buddhist Guide to Saving the Planet* (Birmingham, U.K.: Windhorse Publications, 2004).

61. Warren F. Ilchman, Stanley N. Katz, and Edward L. Queen, II, eds., *Philanthropy in the World's Traditions* (Bloomington: Indiana University Press, 1998).

62. Stump, *Boundaries of Faith*, 138–50.

63. Fernanda Santos, "Reverberations of a Baby Boom," *New York Times*, August 27, 2006, 23–26.

64. Tovi Fenster, "Identity Issues and Local Governance: Women's Everyday Life in the City," *Social Identities* 11, no. 1 (January 2005): 21–36; Stump, *Boundaries of Faith*, 184–85.

65. Nathan Stormer, "Prenatal Space," *Signs: Journal of Women in Culture and Society* 26, no. 1 (Autumn 2000): 109–44.

66. Lawrence Van Gelder, "Film Protest in India," *New York Times*, June 15, 2004, E2.

67. Mack P. Holt, *The French Wars of Religion, 1562–1629* (New York: Cambridge University Press, 1995).

68. Sells, *The Bridge Betrayed*; Vjekoslav Perica, *Balkan Idols: Religion and Nationalism in Yugoslav States* (New York: Oxford University Press, 2002); Roger W. Stump, "Religion and the Geographies of War," in *The Geography of War and Peace*, ed. Colin Flint (Oxford: Oxford University Press, 2005), 149–73.

69. Peter van der Veer, *Religious Nationalism: Hindus and Muslims in India* (Berkeley: University of California Press, 1994); Stump, *Boundaries of Faith*, 63–77.

70. For an analysis of the foundations of the concept of the Islamic state in Muslim political thought, see Asma Afsaruddin, "The 'Islamic State': Genealogy, Facts, and Myths," *Journal of Church and State* 48, no. 1 (Winter 2006): 153–73.

71. Stump, *Boundaries of Faith*, 145.

72. The complex relationships between religion and political sovereignty in Israel are examined in Yosseph Shilhav, "Religious Factors in Territorial Disputes: An Intra-Jewish View," *GeoJournal* 53, no. 3 (March 2001): 247–59.

73. Paolo Pombeni, "The Ideology of Christian Democracy," *Journal of Political Ideologies* 5, no. 3 (October 2000): 289–300; for patterns in the electoral support for Christian Democracy, see Christian Vandermotten and Pablo Medina Lockhart, "An Electoral Geography of Western Europe," *GeoJournal* 52, no. 2 (October 2000), 93–105.

74. Albert Hourani, *A History of the Arab Peoples* (New York: MJF Books, 1991), 47.

75. Newman, ed., *Impact of Gush Emunim*, passim.

76. On Chinese restrictions on religion generally, see Pitman B. Potter, "Belief in Control: Regulation of Religion in China," *China Quarterly* 174 (2003): 317–37.

77. Roger W. Stump, "Spatial Implications of Religious Broadcasting: Stability and Change in Spatial Patterns of Belief," in *Collapsing Space and Time: Geographic Aspects of Communications and Information*, ed. S. D. Brunn and T. R. Leinbach (London: Unwin Hyman, 1991), 354–75.

78. U.S. Congress, *International Religious Freedom, 1999*, passim.

79. David Rohde, "Mix of Quake Aid and Preaching Stirs Concern," *New York Times*, January 22, 2005, A1–A5.

80. Laurel Kearns, "Saving the Creation: Christian Environmentalism in the United States," *Sociology of Religion* 57, no. 1 (Spring 1996): 55–70; Laurel Kearns, "Noah's Ark Goes to Washington: A Profile of Evangelical Environmentalism," *Social Compass* 44, no. 3 (September 1997): 349–66.

81. Doris Buss and Didi Herman, *Globalizing Family Values: The Christian Right in International Politics* (Minneapolis: University of Minnesota Press, 2003).

82. Stump, "Religion and the Geographies of War," 149–73.

83. Samuel P. Huntington, *The Clash of Civilizations and the Remaking of World Order* (New York: Simon & Schuster, 1996).

84. For example, see Klaus Dodds, *Geopolitics in a Changing World* (Harlow, U.K.: Prentice Hall, 2000), 11–15.

85. Jeff Haynes, "Religion and Politics: What Is the Impact of September 11?" *Contemporary Politics* 9 (March 2003), 7–15; José Casanova, *Public Religions in the Modern World* (Chicago: University of Chicago Press, 1994).

CHAPTER 5

The Meanings and Uses of Sacred Space

The association of religious meaning with geographical space represents a crucial trait of religious systems. As discussed in the preceding chapter, the integration of space and meaning commonly occurs in secular contexts as adherents live out their beliefs and practices within the contexts of everyday life. This process acquires more transcendent significance, however, through believers' conceptualizations of sacred space, the focus of this chapter. Adherents understand sacred space in explicitly religious terms, in direct relation to their religion's concepts of the superhuman and the ultimate nature of reality. From their perspective, sacred space in its various forms essentially represents a manifestation of the cosmos defined in their religious worldview. It encompasses imagined, superhuman regions that exist beyond the realm of sensory experience, such as heaven, nirvana, or the spirit world. At the same time, it comprises crucial points of contact between human and superhuman domains, such as places of revelation or worship. The meanings of sacred space include abstract notions of cosmology, but they also reflect belief in the existence of spiritual discontinuities in the material world, extraordinary places where the sacred is linked to physical reality.[1] Through these meanings, sacred space itself takes on a highly charged and compelling character for adherents, expressed in a wide variety of religious obligations and worship practices. Proper interactions with sacred space are thus central to the ethos of a religious system. Through their experiences of and within sacred space, believers fully assimilate the basic motivations, expectations, and emotions associated with living their religion.

Traditional approaches to the comparative study of religions have represented beliefs concerning sacred space as expressions of universal archetypes within the religious imagination. Although this traditional view has fallen from scholarly favor in recent decades, the prevalence of concepts of sacred space in diverse religions does suggest a distinct commonality among different religious systems.[2] That commonality arises from the central importance of space in human attempts to structure and understand experience. In a general sense, culturally defined spaces provide crucial links between reality and the meanings, symbols, and signs through which people understand the worlds in which they live. Within the context of religion, the definition of sacred space serves specifically to connect the meanings of a system's worldview and ethos to recognizable spatial constructions. These constructions perform vital functions for adherents, expressing the existence of superhuman authority, demonstrating the power of the superhuman, and providing either physical or imagined access to the superhuman itself. Believers in effect use their understandings of various sacred spaces to locate transcendent meanings in definite forms within the contexts of their lived experience. In this regard, beliefs regarding sacred space represent a pervasive expression of the inherent spatiality of religious systems.

In defining the sanctity of particular spaces, adherents of different religions have drawn on varied meanings rooted in their group's traditions and experiences. Through those meanings, believers have in turn characterized the sources of the sacredness of places in diverse ways (table 5.1). Cosmological spaces represent key locations in the larger cosmic structure posited in a religion's worldview. Such places may have a mate-

Table 5.1. Categories of Sacred Space

Category	Source of Religious Significance	Examples
Cosmological	Crucial location, either real or imagined, within the cosmos	Amitabha's Pure Land Hell Mount Kailas as the axis mundi
Theocentric	Continual presence at a location of the divine or superhuman	Hindu temple as a god's dwelling place Mt. Olympus as home of the Greek gods Western Wall in Jerusalem
Hierophanic	Setting for a specific religious apparition, revelation, or miracle	Ascension of Jesus from Mount of Olives Enlightenment of Buddha at Bodh Gaya Marian apparition at Lourdes
Historical	Association with the initiating events or historical development of a religion	Bethlehem as the birthplace of Jesus Karbala as the site of Husayn's martyrdom Temple Mount in Jerusalem
Hierenergetic	Access to manifestations of superhuman power and influence	Hindu sacred rivers as a source of healing Icons in Eastern Orthodoxy Tombs of Sufi shaykhs
Authoritative	Center of authority as expressed by major religious leaders or elites	The oracular shrine to Apollo at Delphi Potala Palace as the seat of the Dalai Lama The Vatican within Roman Catholicism
Ritual	Repeated ritual usage in relation to an atmosphere of sanctity	The Buddhist pilgrimage route on Shikoku Camp meeting sites in Christianity Mosques as sites of communal prayer

rial presence, as in the Hindu belief that Mount Kailas, in western Tibet, represents the axis mundi or center of the cosmos. Cosmological places also include many locations beyond the realm of physical space, however, such as conceptions of heaven and hell or other imagined spaces associated with the afterlife.

Theocentric spaces acquire a more specific sanctity from adherents' belief in a direct association between the location in question and a deity or other superhuman figure. A common form of theocentric space is the dwelling place of a deity. Adherents may locate such places within material space. Following the diffusion of Buddhism to Japan, for example, believers understood Mount Fuji to be the abode of the celestial Buddha Dainichi Nyorai, the central deity in the Shingon school. More commonly, however, theocentric spaces exist within imagined realms. The domains inhabited by celestial Buddhas according to the Pure Land school of Mahayana Buddhism exemplify the latter pattern.

Hierophanic space represents a more explicit discontinuity within the world of lived experience, the site of a specific religious apparition, revelation, or miracle. The hierophany that defines the meaning of the site often acquires a specific material association. That association may be with a natural feature, as in the grotto and springs that form the core of the Roman Catholic shrine at Lourdes, France; or it may involve a miraculous object, most often an artwork or relic, as in the miraculous image of Mary in the Roman Catholic shrine of Our Lady of Guadalupe in Mexico. Hierophanic spaces have often developed into important sacred sites following a single revelation, or a series of related revelations; but in some instances they represent the location of repeated hierophanies, as in the ancient Greek shrine to Apollo at Delphi, whose oracles passed on revelations for perhaps a millennium, into the third century CE.

Historical spaces draw their meaning from the central role that they have played in the historical development of a religion. The meaning of historical spaces may be purely commemorative, but a space can also draw power from the events that took place there. The most fundamental expressions of historical space have associations with the founding events of a religious tradition, as exemplified by the Buddhist complex of shrines and temples at Bodh Gaya, the location in northern India where the Buddha attained enlightenment. The Christian concept of the Holy Land reflects the sanctification of space at a broader scale, subsuming many individual locations. Historical spaces may also be associated with later events in a religion's history such as acts of martyrdom, as in the Jewish sacred site at Masada.

The root sources of hierenergetic spaces frequently intersect with those of the preceding categories, but this type of sacred space is distinguished by its explicit potential for invoking or conducting divine or spiritual power. These spaces in effect provide a source of contact between adherents and supernatural entities believed to have influence over both religious and secular matters. In many cases these sites have a unique identity, often through their association with a specific deity, saint, or spirit. Jewish worship at the Western Wall in Jerusalem, for example, reflects the belief that the divine presence is particularly strong there. Similarly, Eastern Orthodox Christians attribute significant hierenergetic power to particular icons. Hierenergetic space also has more generic expressions in most religions, however. The power attributed by Buddhists to any stupa reflects this pattern, as does the power attributed to diverse local shrines in Shinto, or the power attributed to the altar in many forms of Christianity.

Authoritative spaces connect human and divine agency, acquiring their sacredness from the special role of religious leaders or other authority figures in the interpretation of divine will or superhuman events. This type of space again has many different forms of expression, from the sacred capital city of a hierarchically organized religion, such as the Vatican as the center of institutional authority in Roman Catholicism, to the site of the oracle of a particular deity, such as the aforementioned example of the shrine to Apollo at Delphi.

Finally, ritual space provides a crucial link between religious practice and the concept of sacred space.[3] The causal link between ritual and the sacredness of a place is complex. In some cases, such as an ordinary mosque, a space acquires sanctity from repeated ritual use. Muslims do not consider ordinary mosques to be intrinsically sacred in an absolute sense, for example, but a long history of use can elevate the mosque's religious meaning. In other instances, however, a space becomes used as a ritual center because of the sanctity already attributed to the location by believers. The ghats, or riverside steps, along the Ganges River that are used by Hindus for cremating the dead exemplify this pattern, as these sites derive their sanctity from the more fundamental sacredness of the Ganges itself in Hindu belief.

The categories of sacred space outlined above overlap significantly, of course, and at the same time they have found expression in a great variety of forms. Adherents also interact with these spatial centers of sacredness in many different ways, in the process linking the performance of key elements of their ethos to particular places. This chapter examines in detail the diversity inherent in conceptions of sacred space as an intrinsic element of religious systems. The discussion first focuses on the nature of sacred space, exploring the variety of forms that sacred space has taken in different religious traditions, including the various scales at which adherents have conceptualized sacred space. Believers interpret the meaning of sacred space through their understanding of divine or superhuman forces, aligning particular sacred spaces with key aspects of their more general worldview. In the process, adherents naturalize the existence of sacred space within their worldview; but seen from outside, the production and reproduction of sacred space by a religious community exhibits cultural processes of selectivity. In this sense, the diverse forms and scales of sacred space reflect the specific situations in which adherents articulate its meaning.

The second theme of this chapter relates to the uses of sacred space by believers. Adherents interact with sacred space in many different ways. Most often, such interactions take place at the scale of the local religious community, either within the context of ordinary religious practice or in relation to less frequent rituals associated with the major stages of life. Less commonly, but in some ways more importantly, adherents also interact with sacred spaces at more expansive scales. Pilgrimage spaces represent the primary material example of this type of interaction. Believers interact as well, however, with many types of imagined spaces, spaces that lie outside the material world but that have a powerful presence within the religious imaginations of adherents. All of these spaces have specific uses, and the ways in which adherents interact with them, symbolically or in daily life, play an important part in their larger religious system.

In many contexts, however, the ability of adherents to use a particular site has been threatened or prevented by outside forces. Such patterns represent the primary concern of the final theme of this chapter, the contesting of sacred space. Sacred space can be contested in diverse ways. Members of the same religious community, for example, may disagree over the meaning and uses of a particular space. More overt forms of conflict have emerged, however, in the often-violent disputes that have developed between competing religious groups over the control of a specific sacred site. In either case, the nature of the conflict illustrates the great importance that adherents place on the meaning and uses of sacred space and reinforces the intrinsic spatiality of religions.

Forms of Sacred Space

The geographical forms of sacred space recognized by believers differ greatly in their character and extent. They range in scope from imagined conceptions of the structure of the cosmos to locally constituted places of worship and even to the body of the individual adherent. They differ as well in their relation to time, as adherents attribute permanent sacred status to many sacred spaces but only temporary status to others. Similarly, many sacred sites are unique in their identity within the worldview of a religious system, while others fulfill more generic roles in everyday worship practices. And the sacred spaces recognized by adherents may include elements of either the natural or human landscape. Despite their varied geographical forms, however, sacred spaces all possess a central importance in the worldviews of believers. Through the diverse spaces that they define as sacred, adherents articulate their understanding of the universe and the role of superhuman forces within it. In so doing, adherents further establish their relation to the cosmos, their identity within humanity at large, and their own obligations and practices as followers of a particular religion. The different forms of sacred space contribute to these processes in different ways, often reflecting the interaction between a religious system and the particular context in which believers enact it. The conceptualization of sacred space, in other words, plays a crucial role in the grounding of adherents' religious beliefs in the lived spaces of daily existence.

In exploring the different forms of sacred space, the following discussion is organized primarily around the concept of scale. This organizational structure differs somewhat from the use of scale in chapter 4, which addressed the organization of social and cultural processes at various scales. As examined in chapter 4, scale referred to the spatial frames of reference within which lived religious activity takes place. In this chapter, on the other hand, scale relates more explicitly to the total scope of adherents' worldviews, thus encompassing both material and intangible spaces. The latter include spaces conceptualized at scales much broader than the global social scale, extending to the entire cosmos as defined in a religion's worldview. In addition, these intangible spaces encompass various imagined places that, although possibly quite real to adherents in terms of belief, do not exist within physical, concrete reality. Concepts like heaven and hell fall into this category, for example. In some ways, then, the geographical forms of sacred space are considerably more complex than are the secular spaces actually occupied and used by adherents. Sacred space necessarily comprises both tangible and intangible layers, including crucial locations for human interaction with superhuman forces but also the larger, imagined spaces inhabited and controlled by those superhuman forces.

The Cosmic Scale

From the above perspective, the broadest scale at which adherents conceptualize sacred space is that of the cosmos itself, encompassing both the tangible and imagined elements of the universe. The cosmographies posited in the worldviews of particular religions take different forms and incorporate varying amounts of detail. The traditional cosmography of Christianity, for example, divides the cosmos into three vertical domains: heaven, the material earth, and hell. This traditional view also commonly identified Jerusalem as the physical center of the material world, a belief reflected in the so-called O-T (*orbis terrarum*) maps produced in medieval Europe (map 5.1).[4] In contrast, classical Hinduism developed a highly detailed conception of the cosmos, divided into a great number of distinct realms having specific characteristics. The basic structure of this cosmography posited the existence of seven concentric island continents organized around Mount Meru, the center of the universe, which Hindus came to associate with Mount Kailas. The seven islands were further subdivided into different regions. One such region on the innermost island corresponded to Bharata, or India, distinguished as the one place where humans could achieve salvation. Beneath these regions lay the *Patala*, a region of seven different underworlds, and below this region according to most cosmographies were twenty-eight different hells, or *Narakas*. Above the land of daily life were the realms of the celestial bodies and of various gods and demigods. Most forms of Buddhism possess a similar cosmography, made up of seven islands surrounding Mount Meru (again associated with Mount Kailas); underworlds inhabited by the spirits of the deceased, animals, and the damned; and twenty-seven layers of heaven, each of increasing purity.

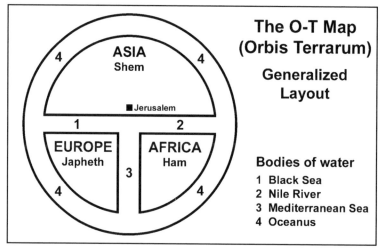

Map 5.1. Generalized layout of an O-T map, with Jerusalem at the central point where Africa, Asia, and Europe meet. Such maps typically associated each of these continents with one of the three sons of Noah: Africa with Ham, Asia with Shem, and Europe with Japheth. According to biblical tradition, all people are descended from one of Noah's sons. The association of Africa with Ham, whose son Canaan had been cursed by Noah (Genesis: 9:22–27), later provided a justification for the enslavement of Africans by Europeans during the slave trade.

In defining the structure of the cosmos, many religions have paid particular attention to the meaning of the four cardinal directions. Traditional Hindu belief, for example, associates north with human beings, south with ancestors, east with deities, and west with animals. In pre-Columbian North America, the Navajo linked the four cardinal directions with the sacred mountains that delimited the created land of order and meaning that they inhabited. They further tied the directions with four cosmically significant color phenomena: dawn (east), sky (south), twilight (west), and darkness (north).

Again, imagined places figure prominently in adherents' understanding of sacred space at the scale of the cosmos. Imagined geographies of the cosmos in many religions contain theocentric spaces identified as the abode of divine or superhuman beings. Such places typically have a key situation in the universe, occupying either a significant portion of the cosmos or a position of special importance above the human world, in the sky or atop a significant peak. Mount Olympus played such a role as the imagined abode of the principal deities of ancient Greek religion. Although Mount Olympus exists as a physical place, adherents came to believe that the deities associated with it lived not on the mountain itself but in an unreachable theocentric space above it. Similarly, Hindu beliefs identify Mount Kailas as the home of Shiva and other deities. In more abstract terms, ancient Judaism generally represented heaven as the dwelling place of Yahweh, located above the material world. Many animistic religions have a similar understanding of the skies as the residence of the most powerful deities. The pre-Hindu animism of Bali, for example, placed the primary gods in the uppermost of various sky realms, the others being inhabited by ancestors and lesser deities. Balinese ritual typically focused on "calling down" the gods from this heavenly abode, a sacred process also found in many other animistic religions.

Most religions have also associated imagined space at the cosmic scale with abodes of the dead. In some instances, these places are neutral in character, simply the cosmographic realm of deceased or unborn spirits, as in the ancient Jewish belief that the dead inhabited a common underworld known as Sheol.[5] Perhaps more commonly, however, religious cosmographies have included places of reward or punishment for the dead. By the beginning of the Common Era, for example, Jewish belief reconceptualized heaven as the abode of the deserving dead as well as of Yahweh. Christianity and Islam had similar views of heaven, as the paradise where those deemed worthy on the Day of Judgment would dwell. Based on the Quran, Islamic beliefs placed particular emphasis on the physical environment of heaven, a paradise of endless streams, gardens, fountains, fruit groves, and jewels (Quran 47: 15; 55: 46–76).

Other religions developed a more detailed set of cosmographic spaces for the dead. In ancient Aztec religion, for example, those who died in battle or through sacrifice attained a higher paradise than those who died from disease or natural disaster. A particularly elaborate system of cosmographic paradises developed within Mahayana Buddhist belief in the concept of Pure Lands or Buddha-worlds. Mahayana Buddhism posits the existence of a countless number of these transcendent worlds, each governed by its own celestial Buddha. These Buddha-worlds are not in fact abodes of the dead. Instead, they are anticipated sites of reincarnation in a coming lifetime, hoped for by believers because they are particularly conducive to the attainment of enlightenment. Ordinary Buddhists incapable of following a strict monastic existence thus pray to be reborn in a Buddha-world, which will provide both an idyllic existence and the environment for attaining nirvana in that subsequent lifetime. Of the many Buddha-worlds mentioned in Buddhist sutras, the most important is the Western Pure Land associated with Amitabha (Sanskrit, "Boundless Light," also Omito in Chinese and Amida in Japanese), the primary focus of the various Pure Land schools of Mahayana Buddhism.

In the worldviews of many religions, special cosmographic spaces also serve as places of punishment. The concept of hell appears in some form in most religions, although its character varies significantly.[6] Hell may be conceptualized as a place of physical pain or torment, a place of separation from divine blessing, or both. Hell represents an important concept in Judaism, Christianity, and Islam, defining in cosmographic terms the outcome of the Day of Judgment for those deemed unworthy of salvation. A similar pattern exists in many animistic religions, such as that of the Maya peoples of Central America who believed in a hell of nine levels where evil persons would be punished after death. In the Asian religions that incorporate belief in reincarnation, on the other hand, hell takes on a less permanent character, serving as a place of torment in atonement for past wrongdoing while at the same time providing the possibility for rebirth under better circumstances at some point in the future. Hindu writings such as the *Garuda Purana* identify up to twenty-eight Narakas, including places for those who kill cows, for those who kill women or children, for those who kill their parents, for those who steal, and so on, each hell also distinguished by the particular torments applied there. Buddhists have posited a similar variety of hells beneath the material world, places where wrongdoers undergo appropriate punishments in the much longer process of attaining nirvana.

The larger spaces that comprised the basic structure of the cosmos were most often imagined spaces existing beyond the tangible realm of human existence. Nonetheless, an important feature of these cosmographic spaces in many traditions is their intersection with or relationship to particular places on earth. The most common expression of this pattern has been the association of particular locations with the center of the cosmos or axis mundi.[7] This practice provides believers with a sense of order by linking the observable environment to cosmographic space, while it also grounds the sacred in the real by defining the transcendent significance of places with which adherents may interact. The places of contact between the imagined cosmos and the visible world take varied forms, of course. As discussed above, Hindus and Buddhists identify the remote Mount Kailas with Mount Meru, the axis around which the cosmos is organized. At a more familiar scale, some interpretations of Buddhism identify the axis mundi with the Bodhi tree at Bodh Gaya under which the Buddha attained enlightenment. In contrast to these examples involving natural phenomena, many religious groups have identified particular cities or temples as the center of the universe, as in the definition of Jerusalem as the center of the world by medieval Christians. The Incas followed a similar pattern, defining the holy city of Cuzco ("Navel of the earth"), and more specifically the city's temple of the sun, Coricancha, as the center of the cosmos. The Incas reinforced Cuzco's symbolic centrality through the creation of a system of 328 shrines arranged along 42 lines that extended outward from the city.[8]

Despite the ultimate importance of cosmographic space, adherents more commonly and frequently encounter sacred space within the context of places and phenomena grounded in the tangible world of human experience. Within this context, adherents define and reproduce sacred spaces at a variety of scales, spaces that are distinguished both by their intrinsic meanings and by their relation to religious practice. These spaces, like their imagined, cosmographic counterparts, reflect important elements of a religion's worldview but they have more immediate relevance to the ethos enacted by adherents, as discussed in greater detail in the following section of this chapter. These sacred spaces in effect represent the material settings for much of the individual adherent's religious experience, including the ordinary routines of everyday worship as well as the more profound instances associated with pilgrimage and other special religious practices.

Holy Lands

Within the confines of human environments, the idea of a holy land commonly represents the most broadly conceived expression of sacred space. This concept involves the assignment of sacredness to a significant region or territory. In terms of their particular forms and meanings, the characteristics of holy lands vary considerably among religions, and some religious traditions do not have a well-defined holy land. For those that do, however, adherents typically attribute sacredness to their holy land on the basis of one or both of two factors: the region's role in the sacred history of the adherents' religious tradition, as the site either of past sacred events or of the future fulfillment of religious prophecy; and the region's role in defining the adherents' religious identity and ethos. Within the contexts of these two factors, the specific characteristics of sacredness attributed to a holy land by adherents provide important insights into their religious tradition.

The Promised Land of Israel, or Eretz Yisrael, exemplifies the roles both of sacred events and of group identity in defining the character of a holy land. Eretz Yisrael represents the land promised to Abraham and his Israelite descendants through their covenant with Yahweh, as recounted in the Torah. The boundaries of Eretz Yisrael are not entirely clear, as their scriptural definitions vary. In the broadest terms some adherents have defined this holy land as encompassing the territory reaching from the Nile to the Euphrates. Others have articulated more confined boundaries, although usually including more territory than the present state of Israel. Within Jewish belief, Eretz Yisrael has a number of significant functions. At the most basic level, it defines the spatial context within which Judaism itself developed, and so includes a large number of more local sacred places. Theologically, it represents tangible evidence of the covenant between God and the Jewish people. It therefore serves as a physical manifestation of Jewish religious identity as "people of the covenant." As such, in Jewish belief it represents a region that should be dedicated to the worship of God and that therefore provides the optimal setting for an adherent to live a good religious life. For much of Jewish history, identification with the sanctity of the region has also made it the preferred place of burial. The significance of Eretz Yisrael also derives, however, from its key role in Jewish sacred history. For example, it represents the land within which all of the Jewish prophets dwelled. To Jews, their expulsion from the region early in the Common Era represented a catastrophe in sacred as well as secular terms, essentially transforming the nature of Judaism. The return to Israel from exile thus became an enduring theme in diasporic Judaism. For many Jews, this theme found expression in the belief in a future messianic redemption, in which God would restore the Jewish people in Eretz Yisrael and create there a perfect Jewish society that would represent a new heaven on earth. Jews have thus used Eretz Yisrael to define their identity as a distinct religious group, but they have also venerated the region as the central space in the unfolding of their sacred history.[9]

Concepts of identity and sacred history also underlie the definition of holy lands by many animistic groups. In such cases, the holy land itself typically encompasses the traditional homeland of the group, and in the latter's belief system control over that homeland has arisen from past sacred events that have occurred there. The Navajo of the southwestern United States identify their holy land as the region bounded by four sacred mountains, each associated with a cardinal direction, a particular deity, a color, plant and animal symbols, and a time of day.[10] The Navajo define their identity, in cultural terms, by their residence within the domain of these four peaks (map 5.2). In addition, however, the territory encompassed by the four peaks represents the site of the creation story in Navajo religious belief. According to this story, divine beings created the First Man and First Woman in the First World, an underworld beneath the Najavo holy land. These figures along with various deities traveled upward through different levels to that of the Fifth World, the world of material existence. In the Fourth World they created the four sacred mountains that defined the boundaries of the Navajo people, and in the Fifth World they created the Navajo people and established them in this bounded land. For most adherents of animistic religions, this type of connection between their homeland and their sacred history has developed unreflexively, as a naturalized element of the life of the group, based on belief in the relationship between a tribe's implicitly sacred territory and its ancestors or creation myth.

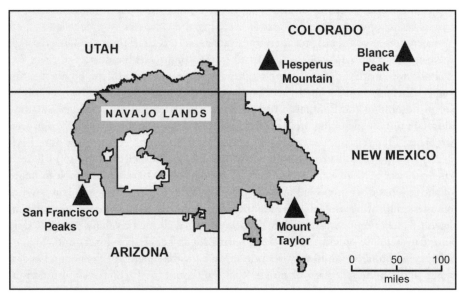

Map 5.2. Location of the sacred mountains associated with the four directions by the Navajo people, along with the current extent of the Navajo Nation's reservation lands, which contain none of the four sacred peaks. Although the Navajo lands in New Mexico are depicted as a single region, their eastern extent actually contains a mixture of many small areas of reservation and nonreservation territory.

In many contexts, however, the association of religious group identity with a holy land has become increasingly reflexive in recent centuries. Developments within Hinduism provide a prominent example of this pattern. Hindus have traditionally seen a great multitude of locations in India as being intrinsically sacred because they represent the setting for the actions and manifestations of various Hindu deities. Over time, the veneration of these locations has produced a strong sense of identification between the sacred history of Hinduism in its various forms and India itself. This connection was explicitly expressed in V. D. Savarkar's *Hindutva* ("Hinduness"), an important work of Hindu revivalism first published in 1915.[11] Savarkar argued that the land surrounded by the Indus River, the Himalayas, and the Indian Ocean represented the holy land of Hindustan, sacred to all Hindus. Similarly, he defined Hindus as those who considered Hindustan to be both their fatherland and their holy land, thus including Buddhists, Jains, and Sikhs under the umbrella of Hindutva. Savarkar thus linked the Hindu holy land not only to Hindu sacred history but to a reflexive sense of Hindu identity as well. His concept of India as a holy land has been strongly promoted in recent decades by Hindu fundamentalists, who see it as the basis for re-creating the identity of India as a modern state. In addition, Hindu fundamentalists have extended the concept of India as holy land to include future events in Hindu sacred history and specifically the establishment of a new kingdom of Rama, or *Ram Rajya*, based on the ideal kingdom established by Rama, an incarnation of Vishnu, at the end of the epic *Ramayana*. Fundamentalists see Rama's kingdom as a sacred utopia fully organized around Hindu values, and they believe that Hindus must return to this ideal both to fulfill their identity and to complete their sacred history.[12]

In contrast to the preceding examples regarding ethnic and tribal religions, the various proselytic religions place less importance on matters of group identity in relation to their holy lands. As Buddhism, Christianity, and Islam spread out of their hearths, their universalistic character made cultural identification with the original hearth unnecessary and unimportant for believers in other locations. The holy lands of these traditions thus draw their significance from their association with particular sacred events rather than from their role in defining or manifesting the specific group identity of adherents. The Holy Land of Christianity has meaning in a historical sense as the site of the birth of Christ, of the miracles attributed to him, and of his crucifixion. Many Christians also attribute significance to the Holy Land as the future site of the Second Coming of Christ. Similarly, Muslims identify the Hejaz region of western Arabia, including Mecca and Medina, as the holy land of their religion, encompassing the sites of the revelation of the Quran to Muhammad and of the original Islamic polity under Muhammad's rule. The region does not necessarily figure in beliefs concerning the future sacred history of Islam, however. Beliefs among various Islamic groups concerning the future coming of the Mahdi or messiah, who would establish a perfect Islamic society, have often located the center of that society elsewhere, for example. Similarly, the efforts by various Islamic fundamentalists over the past century to re-create an ideal society based on Muhammad's original polity have sought to do so in a variety of other locations. Buddhists likewise continue to venerate the hearth of their tradition in northern India, which remains an important pilgrimage site for believers from around the world.[13] Buddhists do not place special importance on this region's role in forming group identity or in the further unfolding of Buddhist sacred history, however. The association of these holy lands primarily with the sacred past has not lessened concerns with control over them, however. The control of the Holy Land of Christianity by Muslims represented a grave concern to medieval Christians and provided the religious rationale for the Crusades. Similarly, within Islam the control of the Hejaz and its sacred cities has been a recurring source of conflict, as discussed later in this chapter.

Natural Spaces

At scales narrower than that of a holy land, adherents have defined as sacred a great variety of more local spaces in the material world, in reference both to natural features and to human structures. The sanctification of natural features has arisen from diverse interpretations of the manifestation of superhuman power and meaning in nature. This practice is more common in religions with a strong animistic or polytheistic character than in the revealed, historical religions. Animists, for example, typically attribute sanctity to many different natural features in accordance with their belief in a densely populated spirit world. Polytheistic religions, such as most forms of Hinduism, similarly tend to recognize sacredness in varied natural spaces in part through their connections to a diverse pantheon. On the other hand, revealed, scriptural religions like Judaism, Christianity, and Islam tend to focus less on natural sacred spaces, generally emphasizing those with a particular historical association, such as a specific event in sacred history or a specific occurrence of divine revelation.

Natural sacred spaces may be quite massive, associated with major landscape features such as prominent mountains or rivers.[14] As an example, the Ganges River represents a major sacred space in Hinduism and the most important of India's sacred rivers. For Hindus, the meaning of the Ganges derives from primordial events in sacred history. According to the Puranas, the Ganges was originally a celestial river but it was brought to earth with the permission of Shiva to purify the ashes of one of the early kings of Ayodhya. In descending from heaven the river flowed through Shiva's hair to soften its fall and prevent the flooding of the earth. In the Puranas the river is also personified as the goddess Ganga, a manifestation of Shakti and one of the consorts of Shiva. The Ganges thus represents an important theocentric space in Hinduism, but functions as well as one of the religion's principal hierenergetic spaces through which divine power can influence human life. In Hindu belief, water from the Ganges has the power to heal and purify the living and the river itself represents an important site for cremation and disposal of the dead.[15]

Mount Fuji in Japan represents a somewhat different and more complex expression of natural sacred space (photo 5.1). Early Shinto belief identified the volcanic Fuji with a god of fire that required propitiation to prevent destructive eruptions. Over time, however, the mountain acquired a more beneficent aspect in Shinto belief, becoming associated with a nature goddess identified with flowering trees. After Buddhism diffused to Japan, adherents of that religion came to venerate Fuji as the abode of Dainichi Nyorai (or Vairocana in Sanskrit), the principal celestial Buddha and the incarnation of spiritual wisdom and teaching. Later Shinto cults also venerated Fuji as a principal national symbol, and in that regard worshipped the mountain as a deity in its own right.[16]

Jewish and Christian views of Mount Sinai provide a useful example of the con-

Photo 5.1. ``Asakusa Honganji in the Eastern capital,'' from the series of prints titled *36 Views of Mount Fuji* produced by Katsushika Hokusai early in the nineteenth century. This print suggests the religious significance of Mt. Fuji, its distinctive shape visible in the background, by placing the viewer at the Honganji, a Jodo Shin or True Pure Land temple, located in the Asakusa district of Tokyo, the Eastern capital. The image reproduced here derives from a print produced circa 1930 to illustrate Japanese woodblock techniques.

Source: Public domain (commons.wikimedia.org/wiki/Image:Asakusa_Honganji_temple_in_th_ Eastern_capital.jpg).

trasting way in which revealed, scriptural religions approach major natural spaces. Mount Sinai derives its importance from its identity in Judaism and Christianity as the place where God gave to Moses the stone tablets containing the Ten Commandments and, in Jewish belief, revealed to Moses the entirety of the Torah. This expression of divine agency represents one of the key initiating events in Judeo-Christian sacred history. In both traditions, however, Mount Sinai had significance not because of its own intrinsic hierenergetic power but as the locus of a principal revelation or hierophany. The revelation itself thus took precedence over the place where the revelation occurred. Jewish tradition consequently places little emphasis on Mount Sinai itself. Christians have paid somewhat more attention than Jews to the purported site of Mount Sinai, establishing a monastic center there by the middle of the first millennium CE. It remains relatively unimportant as a pilgrimage destination for Christians, however, and the surviving Orthodox Christian monastery on the site supports a relatively small community.

The ascription of sacred qualities to natural spaces occurs at more local scales as well as in reference to various landscape features. This pattern occurs widely in animistic religions, in which belief in the spirits of natural springs, trees, animals, or rocks lent sanctity to the spaces associated with these phenomena. The Baganda people of southern Uganda, for example, believe that forests represent the sacred domains of tree spirits, the principal spirit typically residing in one of the largest trees in the forest. They therefore believe that they must propitiate the appropriate spirit in the forest before cutting down a smaller tree within that spirit's domain. Animistic and polytheistic religions have also often attributed hierenergetic power to a great variety of local natural spaces. The Neolithic religion practiced in Crete, for example, apparently attributed significant power to specific caves on the island, which thus became the site of religious activity. Later, these same caves were incorporated into Greek religion as shrines for particular deities.[17] The purifying power of sacred springs also appears as a belief in many religions. Those consulting the oracle at Delphi in ancient Greece, for example, first had to bathe in the Castalian spring at the site, while the oracle herself drank from the nearby Cassotis spring.

The revealed, historical religions have also incorporated beliefs concerning local natural features, particularly within the context of folk religion but in some instances with more widespread acceptance as well. An important sacred feature in Mecca, for example, is the well of Zamzam, uncovered in the desert by the angel Jibril so that Hajar (or Hagar), the wife of Ibrahim (or Abraham) could provide water to her infant son Ismail (or Ishmael), whom Muslims regard as a patriarch. The Hajj incorporates a visit to the well as a key ritual and Muslims believe that water from the well has special healing properties. Within Christianity, adherents have identified a great variety of local natural sites as hierenergetic centers capable of bringing healing or other kinds of blessings to those who visit them.[18] Typically these Christian sites have specific historical origins, however, through links to specific saints, miracles, or apparitions. The grotto and springs at Lourdes exemplify this pattern. The site at Lourdes became a significant sacred space following the visions of Mary experienced by Marie-Bernarde Soubirous, or Bernadette of Lourdes, beginning in 1858. The site became a major pilgrimage center with official recognition from the Roman Catholic Church in 1862 and the canonization of Bernadette in 1933, based on belief in the curative properties of water from the spring.[19]

Sacred Cities

Human structures have also figured prominently in the sacred spaces recognized by religious adherents. Many religions have defined entire cities as being sacred. In such cases, the city has not served simply as the site of a particular church or shrine. Instead, the precincts of the entire city have an important religious role and thus the city as a whole takes on transcendent significance. Various overlapping factors may contribute to the sanctity of a city. Especially in the revealed religions, certain cities have acquired sacred status because of their association with key historical events in the religion's development. Muslims identify Mecca and Medina as holy cities largely because of their association with Muhammad. According to Islamic belief, these cities were the locations where Jibril revealed the Quran to Muhammad and from which Muhammad organized his idyllic Islamic state. Mecca has other religious meanings as well, as it is linked in Islamic belief to Ismail and ultimately to Adam, who created the first altar at the site of the Kaaba in the Great Mosque; and Mecca had also served as a major ritual site for the region's Arabs before the rise of Islam, as discussed in chapter 2.

Nonetheless, Mecca's historical associations with the divine revelations to Muhammad contribute most significantly to its holy status.

A similar pattern exists in Jewish, Christian, and Muslim traditions concerning Jerusalem. For all three groups Jerusalem represents a holy city, but for very different historical reasons.[20] Jerusalem represents the capital of the early Jewish kingdom, under the rule of David and Solomon, and the site of the first two Jewish temples, the centers of ancient Jewish worship. In Jewish tradition, the Western Wall adjacent to the Temple Mount represents an important link to the city's past and it remains an important pilgrimage destination. For Christians, Jerusalem has significance as the birthplace of Mary and as the location of the final days and crucifixion of Jesus, of his temporary tomb, of his ascension to heaven, and of the early organization of his followers into a coherent religious body. Muslims view the city (in Arabic, *al-Quds* or "the Holy") as an important site in their sacred history as the point from which Muhammad ascended on a miraculous "night journey" to heaven, which took him from Mecca to Jerusalem to heaven and then back to Mecca again.[21] Al-Aqsa Mosque on the Temple Mount also was one of the first important communal mosques built outside the Hejaz region, early in the eighth century.

A second factor that can contribute to the sacredness of a city is its association with particular deities, sacred figures, or manifestations of the superhuman. Returning to the example of Jerusalem, this factor contributes in part to the city's sanctity for Jews, Christians, and Muslims. According to Jewish tradition, the *Shekhinah* (or the presence of God, primarily in its feminine aspect) is particularly strong in Jerusalem, especially at the Western Wall with its connections to the earlier temples.[22] In addition, Jerusalem will be the site for the completion of Jewish sacred history through the arrival at the Mount of Olives of a messiah who will raise the dead, pass judgment on all souls, and establish an earthly kingdom of God. Many Christians also ascribe eschatological significance to Jerusalem, identifying Mount Zion as the point at which the Second Coming of Christ will take place. Muslims too have interpreted Jerusalem in this manner, believing that the Dome of the Rock will be the point at which an angel will arrive to announce the last judgment at the end of history. Beyond the examples cited, Shiite Muslims maintain belief in a number of holy cities associated with the twelve Shiite Imams or their relatives (table 5.2, map 5.3). To Shiites, a number of these cities are especially distinguished by their ability to bring blessings to those buried there, including Najaf and Karbala in Iraq and Mashhad and Qom in Iran. Each of these cities contains the tomb of one of the Shiite Imams or a relative: Najaf, that of Ali, Muhammad's son-in-law; Karbala, that of Husayn, Ali's son; Mashhad, that of the eighth Twelver Shiite Imam, Ali al-Rida; and Qom, that of Ali al-Rida's sister, Fatima, who is idealized as the model Shiite woman. The latter two cities are the most important pilgrimage destinations for Iranian Shiites. All four cities contain large cemeteries of adherents within or just outside their boundaries.

Associations between particular cities and divine or superhuman agency have developed within many other religious traditions as well. Hindu tradition identifies seven major sacred cities associated with particular deities or manifestations of superhuman agency (map 5.4). Varanasi, the most important of these, is identified as the worldly birthplace and living symbol of the god Shiva. By reciting the correct prayer at the time of death, according to Hindu belief, adherents in Varanasi will be freed from the cycle of rebirth through Shiva's agency. Similarly, three of Hinduism's sacred

Table 5.2.   Shiite Sacred Cities

City	Country	Significance
Mecca	Saudi Arabia	Initial revelation of Quran to Muhammad
Medina	Saudi Arabia	Tomb of Muhammad Tomb of the 2nd Imam, Hasan Tomb of the 4th Imam, Ali Zayn al-Abidin Tomb of the 5th Imam, Muhammad al-Baqir Tomb of the 6th Imam, Jafar al-Sadiq
Karbala	Iraq	Tomb of the 3rd Imam, Husayn
Najaf	Iraq	Tomb of the 1st Imam, Ali
Samarra	Iraq	Tomb of the 10th Imam, Ali al-Hadi Tomb of the 11th Imam, Hasan al-Askari Occultation of the 12th Imam, Muhammad al-Mahdi
Baghdad	Iraq	Tomb of the 7th Imam, Musa al-Kazim Tomb of the 9th Imam, Muhammad al-Taqi
Mashhad	Iran	Tomb of the 8th Imam, Ali al-Rida
Qom	Iran	Tomb of Fatima, sister of the 8th Imam
Tehran	Iran	Tomb of Saleh, son of the 7th Imam
Rey	Iran	Tomb of Tahir, son of the 4th Imam Tomb of Hamzeh, brother of the 8th Imam
Borujerd	Iran	Tomb of Jafar, grandson of the 4th Imam

cities are associated with incarnations of the god Vishnu: Ayodhya as the birthplace of Rama, and Mathura and Dwaraka, the birthplace and seat of power of Krishna. Two other cities, Haridwar and Ujjain, represent places where heavenly nectar fell to earth and figure prominently in the Kumbh Mela pilgrimages discussed later in this chapter. Ujjain is also particularly sacred to Shiva, while Haridwar represents the earthly point of origin of the Ganges River. A final city, Kanchipuram, acquired its sanctity from the very large number of temples constructed there, mostly in veneration of Vishnu, Shiva, and Shakti. In addition to these seven primary cities, many other Hindu cities derive sacred meaning from their association with the divine. Madurai in southern India, for example, derives its sacred status from a major temple to the local deity Meenakshi, who is understood to be a manifestation of Shakti in the form of Parvati, the consort of Shiva. Hindus similarly attribute sanctity to Janakpur in Nepal as the assumed birthplace of Sita, the consort of Rama.

As suggested by some of the preceding examples, a third factor contributing to the sacred identity of cities is their role as ritual centers. Through the repeated performance of religious rituals, cities may take on an active dimension of sacredness that goes beyond their original historical or superhuman associations. The sacred cities of Hinduism, for example, have also served as important centers of ritual activity center-

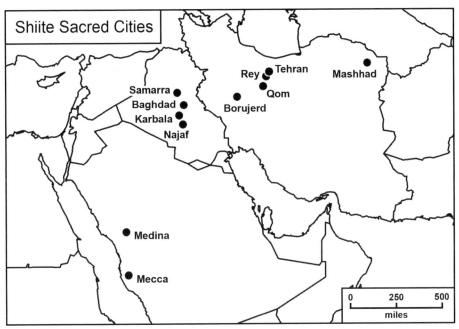

Map 5.3. The holy cities of Shia Islam. The most important of these cities are associated with the burial places of Shiite Imams, but others have acquired religious meaning as the burial sites of particular relatives of the Imams (table 5.2). Qom ranks as the most important of the latter as the resting place of Fatima, whom Shiites see as a model of female piety. All of these cities serve as important Shiite pilgrimage centers.

ing on pilgrimage, purification rituals, and the like. Much of Varanasi's importance derives from the religious significance of its location on the sacred Ganges, which draws many pilgrims to the city seeking to cleanse themselves through ritual bathing in the river. The city's holiness has also made it a major center for funerary rituals, with the remains of those cremated dispersed in the waters of the Ganges.[23] Janakpur has likewise served as a major pilgrimage center, particularly for newlyweds who come to dedicate their marriage to the ideal model established by Rama and Sita in the *Ramayana*. The Incan city of Cuzco, defined above as the center of the cosmos, also subsequently drew its sanctity in part from several centuries of ritual use, prior to the Spanish conquest of the region, as the religious focus of the Incas' hierarchical society. Cities defined as ritual centers have in some cases been quite narrow in focus. The Greek city of Delphi existed primarily as a center for the worship of Apollo, drawing ritual importance from its major temple and authoritative significance from the oracle through whom Apollo was believed to speak to adherents. In other contexts, however, ritual centers developed a much greater degree of diversity. Kyoto developed as a major ritual center in Japan, for example, through the establishment of hundreds of temples, shrines, and monasteries associated with many different schools of Buddhism and Shinto sects.[24]

The fourth and final factor related to the sacred identity of cities is their organizational role in the functioning of a religious system. Such cities essentially serve as centers of religious authority, although in the case of individual cities this factor may again overlap with any of the other factors outlined above. Rome, for example, plays

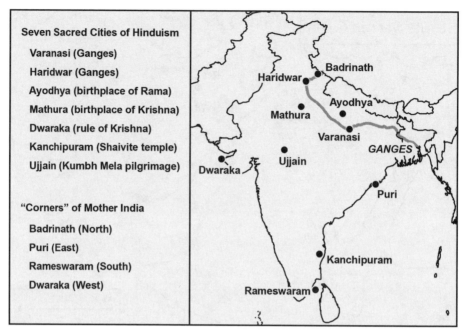

Seven Sacred Cities of Hinduism

Varanasi (Ganges)

Haridwar (Ganges)

Ayodhya (birthplace of Rama)

Mathura (birthplace of Krishna)

Dwaraka (rule of Krishna)

Kanchipuram (Shaivite temple)

Ujjain (Kumbh Mela pilgrimage)

"Corners" of Mother India

Badrinath (North)

Puri (East)

Rameswaram (South)

Dwaraka (West)

Map 5.4. The sacred cities of Hinduism, including the so-called ''seven sacred cities'' and the four cities that symbolically define the boundaries of India as the Hindu holy land.

a significant role as a holy city in Roman Catholicism as the location of that religion's sacred capital, the Vatican, where rulings concerning church doctrine and policy are made. Rome's character as a sacred city draws on other factors as well: the role that it played in the early development of Christianity; its identity as the burial place of St. Peter and St. Paul; the large number of early Christians martyred there in the Colosseum; and the extensive catacombs of early Christianity. Nonetheless, the focus of Roman Catholicism's global organizational hierarchy on the Vatican and the office of the pope lend Rome considerable importance as a center of religious authority, a factor that continues to support Rome's importance as a pilgrimage destination. Other cities within Christianity have at times played a similar role. During the sixteenth century, Calvinist Geneva acquired the reputation of being the Protestant equivalent of Rome, attracting Protestant refugees from France, England, and other locations. In nineteenth-century America, Salt Lake City, Utah, similarly emerged as the most successful of a series of sacred capitals established by the Latter-Day Saints, the earlier efforts near Independence, Missouri, and at Nauvoo, Illinois, having been abandoned in the face of external threats. As the sacred city of Mormonism, Salt Lake City serves as the headquarters of the religion's organizational structure and contains the most important Mormon temple. Finally, as discussed in chapter 4, sacred capitals have become an important feature of African Instituted Churches, mostly Christian bodies organized to be independent of external, non-African influences. Many of these churches have established a specific holy city, usually associated with the birthplace of the group's founding prophet or the place where the church first became organized; and these cities serve both as authoritative organizational centers and as pilgrimage destinations centered on healing practices.[25]

Unique Local Spaces

Local structures constructed at scales narrower than the city take two general forms: unique shrines, places of worship, or ritual places having a singular, exceptional identity; and the ordinary or generic places of religious activity with which believers interact in more routine or customary ways. The sanctity of unique sacred spaces organized at the local scale may derive from various sources. Some such spaces acquire their sacredness from their fundamental centrality, in a ritual sense, within a religious system. Such spaces include major places of worship or specific structures associated with religious authority. As an example, the Great Mosque of Mecca represents an exceptional place of worship, different from all other mosques because of its links to Muhammad, its role in the Hajj, and its distinctive internal characteristics. Most importantly, the Great Mosque houses the Kaaba, which in turn contains the black stone believed to be a remnant of the first altar constructed by Adam. The Great Mosque of Mecca thus takes precedence over all other mosques. Similarly, the Golden Temple compound in Amritsar contains the most sacred of Sikh temples or *gurdwaras* ("gateways to the guru"), the primary center of religious authority, and the principal Sikh religious organizations (photo 5.2). The same pattern of centrality traditionally characterized the Potala Palace, the principal Tibetan Buddhist monastery in Lhasa, home to the Dalai Lama before the invasion of Tibet by China in 1959, and a major pilgrimage center for Tibetans (photo 3.4).[26]

A countless number of unique sacred spaces have commonly been linked as well to specific miracles or sacred events that have occurred at the site in question, either in a historical sense or as part of the mythical elements of a religious group's sacred history. A wide variety of local places have acquired sanctity in Roman Catholicism through local hierophanies such as miracles and apparitions, for example. These places in effect represent a point of contact between the material and intangible spaces of the believer's worldview. The aforementioned apparition at Lourdes has made the site a pilgrimage center of international importance for Roman Catholics, attracting millions of pilgrims each year seeking medical cures or others forms of blessing. In North America, St. Joseph's Oratory in Montreal, Canada, known to Roman Catholics for healings linked to the shrine's early twentieth-century founder, Brother André, attracts two million visitors annually. The special miracles associated with specific local sites may also take on other forms of meaning over time. A primary example of this pattern is the miracle of Our Lady of Guadalupe in Mexico, the earliest Christian shrine in the New World. The primary focus of the shrine is an image of Mary, miraculously produced in the 1530s on the cloak of a local Aztec convert to Christianity after he collected flowers in his cloak at Mary's request. The local church built a sanctuary to house the relic, which over time took on significant meaning, not only as the sign of a Marian apparition but as a symbol of Mexican national and religious identity, particularly for those of mixed European and Native American ancestry (photo 5.3). The sanctuary housing the image thus attracts more than ten million visitors annually.[27]

Photo 5.2. The Golden Temple or Harmandir Sahib (``House of God'') is the most sacred of Sikh gurdwaras. It was the first gurdwara, completed in 1601, and since 1604 has housed the authoritative versions of the Guru Granth Sahib, the Sikh scriptures. It also serves as Sikhism's principal pilgrimage destination. The Golden Temple thus exemplifies the centralization of religious meaning in a specific local structure. Amritsar, India, no date.

Source: Jpatokal (wikitravel.org/shared/Image:HarmandirSahib_Gateway.jpg), under Creative Commons license (creativecommons.org/licenses/by-sa/1.0/).

In other religions, unique local shrines have developed in association with events within the domain of mythical sacred history. Such associations are very common in animistic and polytheistic religions, where the sanctity of specific sites may date to the original time of creation. Uluru, the massive sandstone outcrop in interior Australia also known as Ayers Rock, represents such a feature (photo 5.4). According to the Australian aboriginal worldview, this site marked the battle ending the mythical prehistoric period known as the Dreamtime or Dreaming. The red rock of Uluru itself represents the upwelling of sorrow by the earth in the aftermath of the battle. Although a major tourist destination, Uluru continues to serve as the site of initiation rites for aboriginal groups and as the location for believers to ask for food, water, and other forms of spirit blessing. As a focus of such rituals, its imposing presence in the landscape provides a tangible link to imagined, mythic realms of existence.

As a final example of unique local spaces, Hindu belief links many shrines and temples to local hierophanies and theocentric expressions. Such links find explicit expression in the Hindu concept of the *tirtha*, a "crossing place" that can help believers cross over to the state of moksha through the site's association with manifestations of a particular deity or saint.[28] Regarding a more specific expression of this concept, Hindus relate many *pithas* ("seats" or "thrones") to Shakti, specifically in her manifestation as Sati, the first consort of Shiva.[29] According to Hindu belief, Sati's father declined to invite her to an important sacrifice and in response she came to the event

Photo 5.3.   Detail from a mural on the back wall of a local business on the south side of San Antonio. The mural contains various depictions of daily life organized around a reproduction of the sacred image of Our Lady of Guadalupe, distinguished by the positions of Mary's hands and face, the bright aura radiating around her, and her position standing on the outspread wings of an angel. For people of Mexican ancestry living in Texas, Our Lady of Guadalupe serves as a powerful symbol of identity and solidarity. San Antonio, Texas, 2002.

Source: Author.

Photo 5.4.   Uluru, the large sandstone outcrop in central Australia that marks the location of events associated with the end of the Dreaming in the religious system of the aboriginal people. The site remains an important center for aboriginal rituals. Uluru, Australia, no date.

Source: Boris Gaasbeek, under Stock.xchng image license (www.sxc.hu/txt/license.-html).

anyway and killed herself there. In his subsequent rage, Shiva killed Sati's father and, carrying Sati's body, began a dance of grief so impassioned that it threatened the stability of the cosmos. Vishnu thus intervened, stopping Shiva's dance by cutting Sati's body into pieces, which he then distributed across the holy land of India. As each piece fell to earth, it established a *shakti-pitha* or throne of Shakti where the supreme goddess incarnated by Sati could be worshipped. Hindus view the temples built at these sites, each associated with a specific body part, in theocentric terms as living expressions of Shakti's presence (photo 2.1). The number of shakti-pithas varies among traditions, 51 and 108 being common enumerations. Four of the pithas also carry cosmological significance through their association with the cardinal directions.

As suggested by the preceding examples, unique local shrines also derive their significance from their role as centers for the expression of or access to divine or super-human agency. In Roman Catholic belief, for example, acceptance of the occurrence of a miracle at a particular place frequently gives rise to a strong pilgrimage site focusing on achieving access to divine blessings. The hierenergetic power of such sites is essentially cumulative, each successful application to divine aid providing added weight to the place's reputation, as evidenced by the collections of crutches, wheelchairs, and similar votive offerings that have frequently accumulated at particular sites. Many kinds of unique local spaces develop the reputation for hierenergetic power. Orthodox Christians, for example, believe that painted icons depicting important religious events and persons in fact embody the immediate, living presence of their subject matter. Orthodox Christianity thus accepts the veneration of the icons themselves and associates superhuman agency with many of them. As an example, the icon depicting Our Lady of Vladimir has for centuries been venerated by Russian Orthodox adherents, who see the icon as the protectress of Russia.[30] Although moved to a museum from its traditional place in Moscow's Assumption Cathedral, it remains an important pilgrimage destination for the Russian Orthodox. In Roman Catholicism, miraculous statues less commonly play much the same role in sanctifying particular shrines. As an example, the Shrine of Notre-Dame du Cap de la Madeleine, in Quebec, draws its significance as a sacred space from two nineteenth-century miracles: the creation of an ice-bridge over the St. Lawrence River allowing the transportation of stones from a quarry on the far side to the Cap de la Madeleine, for use in constructing an expanded chapel dedicated to Mary; and, following the dedication of the chapel, the apparition that the statue of Mary on the site opened its eyes widely to look out over the landscape. In subsequent years this site became the national shrine for Canada's Roman Catholics, and again adherents associate it with healing and other forms of blessing.

The special power of local sites also frequently derives from the enshrinement of a relic of a holy person. The use of reliquaries is widespread within Roman Catholicism but occurs in many other religions as well. Within Buddhism, for example, particular stupas and temples acquire unique sanctity from the relics that they contain, attributed either to the Buddha or to another revered Buddhist master. The Temple of the Tooth in Kandy, Sri Lanka, represents one of the most prominent instances of this pattern, believed by adherents to contain the left canine tooth of the Buddha. According to traditional Buddhist belief, the tooth itself had the power to bring rain to the country, usually sought during the summer festival of *Esala Perahera* (a procession during the month of Esala), and ownership of the tooth conferred the right of kingship. Possession of the tooth has thus become central to the religious identity of the island's Sinhalese Buddhist majority. More generally, Buddhist relics have provided believers with an important means of maintaining a sense of continuity with venerated figures, and in this sense served to ground the diffusion of Buddhism in the dispersal and preservation of physical objects. Such objects are most commonly the mortal remains of venerated Buddhists but may also take the distinctive form of *ringsel*, small spherical beads purportedly found among the cremated ashes of Buddhist teachers that contain the wisdom and spiritual essence of the deceased. The enshrinement of these and other relics in a stupa in turns lends sanctity to the place itself.[31]

Finally, the superhuman power inherent in local shrines often derives from the latter's personal association with a specific saint, spirit, or deity. This hierenergetic pattern appears very clearly in the Islamic worship of saints' tombs, particularly in North Africa or in areas dominated by Sufism or Shiism. Many Muslims believe that great saints can pass on baraka or a blessing to those who visit their tombs, and thus many saints' tombs have become important pilgrimage sites. Sufi adherents have particularly strong ties to the tombs of the early founders or leaders of their orders, giving rise to the development of major compounds, or zawiyas, near the tombs of important figures.[32] Hierenergetic shrines that draw on the power of superhuman spirits and deities are also commonplace in animistic and polytheistic religions. This pattern is exemplified by the use of so-called spirit houses in Thailand, an animistic survival among a population that is predominantly Buddhist (photo 5.5). The spirit house is a small model of a dwelling designed to attract local spirits or *phii* believed to have influence over human affairs. Thais build the spirit house in appeasement of the phii but also to gain both spiritual and material benefits from them. In a clear example of Southeast Asian syncretism, adherents built a particularly distinctive spirit house in Bangkok in the 1950s, the Erawan shrine dedicated to the Hindu deity Brahma, to protect workers constructing a large hotel. The shrine has since become a major pilgrimage destination, where adherents of various religions from across Asia seek divine influence in spiritual and material affairs.[33]

Ordinary Local Spaces

Along with places of unique importance, local, humanly constructed sacred space includes a great diversity of ordinary places of worship. These ordinary places are associated with the everyday enactment of religion in a community. Adherents frequently organize them and use them as an undifferentiated portion of their social space. Nonetheless, ordinary places of worship typically have at least an implicit degree of sanctity, and in this sense they represent the most immediate forms of sacred space with which believers interact in everyday life.

The most common form of this type of space is the communal place of worship. Such spaces possess an intrinsic sacredness in most traditions, which is typically expressed in the structure's interpretation, construction, and use. In Hindu belief, for example, temples represent the earthly dwelling places of particular gods, whose presence sanctifies the entire structure. In addition, Hindu temple architecture incorporates a variety of elements that explicitly link the structure to sacred concepts relating to cosmology or doctrine, although the resulting structures have taken on many differ-

Photo 5.5. Spirit houses for sale in northeastern Thailand. Spirit houses reflect the survival of pre-Buddhist animistic beliefs in Thailand. Believers hope to attract spirits to reside in the structures that they build. The spirit houses in turn become hierenergetic sites as resident spirits provide various spiritual and material benefits. Ubon Ratchathani, Thailand, no date.

Source: Henry Flower (en.wikipedia.org/wiki/Image:Spirithouses01.jpg), under GNU Free Documentation License, Version 1.2 (www.gnu.org/licenses/fdl.txt).

ent forms. Most commonly, the plan of the core area of a temple mirrors the design of a mandala, an abstract depiction of the structure of the cosmos organized as a set of smaller square areas within one larger square. At the center of this core area lies the temple's inner sanctuary, the *garbhagriha*, which contains the shrine to the temple's primary deity where the latter's presence is strongest. Rising above the mandala plan and centered on the garbhagriha is the *shikhara* ("peak"), a tower symbolizing Mount Meru (photo 3.1). The shikhara thus links the temple to Mount Meru's identity as the axis mundi and the abode of various Hindu deities. The preceding elements all relate the temple as sacred space to larger divine and cosmic elements. At the same time, Hindu temples typically incorporate elements symbolic of the individual believer's religious journey, usually organized east to west in a sequence from the temple entrance through a series of halls to the garbhagriha.[34]

The communal places of worship associated with a single religious tradition display considerable geographical diversity, of course; the preceding Hindu architectural traits represent widespread features but are not universal. Architectural features in general vary according to available building materials, local building traditions, and many other factors.[35] More to the point, within widely dispersed religions that encompass extensive doctrinal diversity, the communal place of worship has come to serve as a sacred expression of the distinctive faith of a particular religious tradition. The sanctity of the place of worship may be comprehensive and overt in such cases. Within the

Christian tradition, for example, Roman Catholicism, the Orthodox churches, and some forms of Protestantism explicitly consecrate parish churches and cathedrals as sacred structures devoted to God, not to be used for profane purposes, through a specific rite of consecration. Following the Reformation, on the other hand, the consecration of churches was rejected by many Protestant groups, such as Calvinists, Pietists, Anabaptists, and Separatists. These groups generally reject the intrinsic sacredness of consecrated churches as a nonbiblical innovation. Some further argued that sacredness lay in manifestations of the divine, not in places created through human action. Nonetheless, places of worship did often possess a measure of sanctity for these groups, but as worldly settings for processes of interaction with the divine rather than as inherently sacred spaces.

These divergent views of churches within Christianity also found expression in architectural patterns and internal decoration. Forms of Christianity that defined the church as a consecrated house of God generally developed more elaborate architectural and decorative forms symbolizing divine supremacy, the heavenly Jerusalem, the larger community of believers, and the sacraments.[36] Traditionally these groups also incorporated sacred symbolism into the layout of many churches, typically following the Latin-cross plan in Roman Catholicism (with one arm of the cross longer than the others) and the Greek-cross plan in Eastern Orthodoxy (with all four arms of equal length). Christian groups that rejected the formal consecration of churches, on the other hand, developed a greater emphasis on architectural plainness and simplicity, employing fewer elaborate images or structural devices, to provide a humble and sober setting for interactions with the divine.[37] Similarly, although Buddhists in both Theravada and Mahayana traditions use consecration rituals to establish the inherent sanctity of newly constructed temples, they too diverge to some extent in their decorative traditions. Mahayana temples typically have a more exoteric aspect focusing on the veneration of many different celestial and historical figures, especially through the use of elaborate symbolism and imagery depicting various Buddhas and bodhisattvas (photo 5.6). Theravada temples, in contrast, tend to contain somewhat fewer images, typically rendered in simpler styles, that depict the historical Buddha to provide a specific focus for meditation.

Within other religious traditions, believers have understood and articulated the sanctity of communal places of worships in still different ways. Jewish belief in the synagogue as sacred space developed gradually, inhibited in antiquity by belief in the Jerusalem Temple as the rightful sacred place of worship in Judaism. At the same time, the tradition of moveable sacred space established during the Proto-Judaic period prior to the nomadic Israelites' settlement in Canaan provided a model for the later sanctification of the synagogue and the subsequent decentralization of Jewish sacred space after the destruction of the Second Temple. The conception of the synagogue as sacred space that emerged in late antiquity focused in particular on its housing of the Ark that contained the local community's Torah scrolls. Through this function, the synagogue in effect acquired sacredness from the presence of the Ark.[38]

In most expressions of Islam, by way of contrast, adherents do not formally ascribe consecrated sacredness to the local mosque; the latter essentially functions as a place for prayer, which may in fact take place anywhere. In practice, however, the mosque may acquire a degree of implicit sanctity over time through the repetition of prayer rituals within it. Such rituals include ordinary communal prayer on Fridays,

Photo 5.6. Main altar in a small Buddhist temple adjacent to the Grafton Peace Pagoda. This site is maintained by an ordained nun of the Nipponzan Myohoji Order, a branch of the Nichiren school of Mahayana Buddhism and an active group within the Engaged Buddhism movement. In typical Mahayana fashion, the altar displays a diversity of venerated personages, including Nichiren, Nichidatsu Fujii (the founder of Nipponzan Myohoji), Mahatma Gandhi (a friend and collaborator of Fujii), and various bodhisattvas and Buddhas. Grafton, New York, 2001.
Source: Author.

but they also comprise more specialized practices, such as believers' performance of extended prayer cycles in search of divine inspiration or pilgrimage rites to attain access to the baraka of a local saint.[39] In addition, adherents may interpret the defacing or destruction of a mosque as a sacrilegious assault on sacred space, as discussed later in this chapter.

Local sacred spaces serve many functions other than communal worship, of course, including funerary practices, festival uses, and rites of initiation or purification. Places set apart for the dead represent a common feature of religious systems but they take highly varied forms. Some religions, such as many forms of Judaism and Christianity, consecrate pieces of land for burying the dead and consider such places to be holy ground. Adherents may also value specific locations as places of burial, from local spaces of consecrated ground to specific holy sites. In animistic religions like that of the Baganda people, described in chapter 3, the burial grounds of the deceased are located in or near family compounds and become important shrines for seeking assistance from ancestors. Religious groups that do not generally bury the dead, such as Hindus and Buddhists, may nonetheless set aside local areas as sacred space for funerary practices, as in the use of specific cremation sites. The many cremation ghats located along sacred rivers in India exemplify this pattern.

Adherents also define local sacred spaces for use in specific religious festivals. The sukkot associated with the Festival of Booths, discussed in chapter 4, represent one example, although the sanctity of the individual sukkah is largely symbolic. Within Shia Islam, adherents set aside special places of worship, known as husayniyas in Iran, for commemorating the martyrdom of Husayn, places that are of particular importance during the observance of Ashura.[40] In many religions, public spaces become temporarily transformed into sacred space through public rituals on certain festival days. Public displays of self-mortification by Shiites on Ashura follow this pattern, as does the traditional public display of a casket bearing Buddha's tooth in Kandy during the Esala Perahera. Hindus in many communities likewise sanctify a route through public streets while displaying the primary divine image or statue from a local temple, a practice also followed by many local Roman Catholic communities, usually in reference to Mary or a locally important saint.[41]

A further form of ritual associated with local sacred spaces involves practices related to purification or initiation. This type of ritual usually confines adherents to hierenergetic spaces that purify either the mind or the body, or both. The mikveh, the Jewish ritual bath, exemplifies this type of place, traditionally used to cleanse men before the Sabbath and major festivals or after contact with the dead, women after menstruation or childbirth, and persons seeking conversion to Judaism (photo 5.7). A further example appears in the sweat lodges associated with various Native American religions. The sweat lodge most commonly serves as a context for ritual purification, for example before major life events such as adulthood ceremonies and marriage; but in many Native American traditions it is also associated with healing, both physical and spiritual, and with efforts to produce sacred visions.

Photo 5.7. Entrance to the restored mikveh, or Judenbad, in Speyer, Germany. The mikveh dates at least to 1128 and thus to the early period of Ashkenazi society in Germany. Within this context it represented a crucial ritual space for local adherence to the Jewish ethos of purity and obedience to divine law. Speyer, Germany, 2006.
Source: Julia R. Stump.

Microscales

Finally, adherents have constructed many ordinary sacred spaces at very limited microscales, including the spaces of specific sacred objects and in certain contexts of the bodies of adherents themselves. Perhaps the most generally observed expression of sacred space at this narrow scale is the altar, or similar object, which serves as the center of worship itself. These objects represent the most immediate points of contact between the human and the superhuman, achieved through prayer, offerings, sacrifice, or some other form of ritual. In Roman Catholicism, the altar serves as a consecrated space whose sacredness allows it to hold the wine and wafer of the Eucharist. Traditionally, the sanctity of Roman Catholic altars was reinforced by the placement of saintly relics within them. In Hinduism, a pitha holds the physical symbol of a deity, while the *vedi* ("altar") serves as the actual point of contact with the divine through worship and offerings. In Hindu belief, the vedi symbolically represents the axis mundi where the divine enters the material world. The altar played a significant role in Proto-Judaism and Temple Judaism, but in Rabbinic Judaism has been replaced by the Ark containing a synagogue's Torah scrolls. The Ark symbolizes the original Ark of the Covenant, which contained the tablets that God gave to Moses; and as such it represents the center of sacred space in the synagogue. Again, Muslims generally do not explicitly ascribe sacredness to their mosques, but portions of the mosque may acquire an implicit sacred character by association. The *mirhab*, a niche in the wall of the mosque oriented toward the qibla or direction toward Mecca, defines the sacred orientation for those in prayer. The *kursi* or Quran stand in a mosque, from which the local imam reads during Friday prayers, also acquires a degree of sanctity from the Quran itself, the primary holy object within Islam.

In various religious traditions, sacred symbols represent an important localized form of sacred space. In Orthodox Christianity, the iconostasis represents an important symbolic form. It traditionally served as a screen separating the church's sanctuary, in which the altar is located, from the rest of the church; but it also contains a set of sacred icons depicting various biblical scenes and persons. The theocentric or hierenergetic character of certain objects representing deities also reinforces the sacredness of Hindu temples. Perhaps the most well known of such objects is the lingam, usually a stone cylinder or pillar representing the generative energy of Shiva. Often the phallic lingam is paired in temples with a yoni, usually a triangular stone symbolizing the female sex organs and divine energy of Shakti, and signifying the feminine means through which Shiva's masculine energy becomes manifest in the world. A wide variety of animistic religions also attribute hierenergetic power at microscales to diverse forms of icons and fetishes, which serve not so much as objects of worship as means of drawing on superhuman protections and powers.

In many religious traditions, the localization of sacred space extends as well to the body of the adherent. The sacredness of body space may derive from an intrinsic characteristic of the body. In the Jewish and Christian traditions, the body acquires sanctity because God created the human body in his own image. Thus, for example, John Calvin in his writings exhorted his followers to do good to all people, regardless of their merits, because they are all created in the image of God and thus carry a degree of sanctity.[42] The sacredness of the body takes a somewhat different form in the Lingayata sect, a Hindu group worshipping Shiva as the primary deity, which in accordance with the teaching of the medieval reformer Basava accepted the body itself as the true temple of Shiva worship. In other contexts, religious groups have attributed sanctity to the body within particular religious states. Various Sufi orders, for example, believe that at any given time a select group of seventy holy people, the *abdal*, serve as the foundations of the cosmos while their leader, the *qutb*, represents the axis mundi. Adherents of Hasidism and Kabbalistic Judaism similarly identify the zaddik, their devotional ideal, as the representation of the axis mundi, Zion, or the Jerusalem Temple.[43] More generally, many religious groups believe that adherents themselves embody sacred space within the context of religious practice. This pattern commonly appears in religions emphasizing spirit possession. In Vodou, to cite one example, the bodies of adherents when entranced serve as the earthly sacred spaces in which the various loa or divine spirits become manifest. Adherents of some varieties of Zen Buddhism likewise interpret the meditative state as creating an internal sacred space.

For all of the aforementioned forms of sacred space, the meaning of space derives from its association with a religious system's conception of reality. Sacred space in effect represents the manifestation, visible or imagined, of a religion's worldview. As such, sacred space in its various forms also represents a significant context for the realization of a religion's ethos. Adherents believe that the sacred meanings attributed to portions of space require many different kinds of action and response. Such interactions between adherents and sacred space represent the focus of the next section of this chapter.

Adherent Interactions with Sacred Space

Sacred space represents a crucial element of a religion's worldview, corresponding to those portions of the cosmos where superhuman manifestations, characteristics, or powers are most evident. Sacred space in effect serves to ground supernatural meanings in specific spatial contexts, either imagined or tangible. The importance of sacred space in a religion's worldview also derives, however, from its role as the setting for various forms of interaction between the human and superhuman realms of the cosmos. Sacred space, for example, may provide the believer with direct proof of the divine, with worldly evidence of superhuman influence over natural events, or with a means of gaining access to the divine. Some forms of sacred space provide contexts in which human worship is particularly meritorious or efficacious. Others serve to bring together larger communities of adherents to share a common sense of sacred identity. In all of these functions, sacred space establishes significant contexts for the enactment of a religion's ethos. Most religious groups emphasize the enactment of their ethos within secular space as well, but within sacred space this process takes on its most concentrated and definitive expressions. In this sense, the interactions between believers and sacred space represent a fundamental process in the larger cultural reproduction of a religious system.

The ways in which adherents interact with sacred space are as varied in character as is sacred space itself. In general terms, however, such interactions fall into four broad categories: the ordinary worship practices of everyday life; worship practices associated with specific life transitions or rites of passage; the exceptional worship events associated with various forms of pilgrimage; and the imagined practices associated with the afterlife or reincarnation. Again, adherents' understanding of or participation in these different types of interaction serves to ground the transcendent meanings of sacred space within the accessible domains of religious practice. These interactions thus lend sacred space a recognizable human dimension even while it remains linked to the superhuman elements defined by a religion's worldview.

Ordinary Worship Practices

In enacting the ordinary practice of a religion, adherents interact with sacred space primarily through local places of worship. At the most basic level, such places exist within the household itself as family or domestic shrines. Indeed, in many ancient and animistic religions, household shrines served as the primary site of everyday religious activity. Family shrines or altars devoted to the spirits of ancestors are a common feature of dwellings within the context of animistic religions, providing a means of contact between adherents and their forebears. The family shrine may also extend conceptually to space outside the dwelling devoted to a family cemetery plot. In these contexts, the family shrine typically represents the medium through which adherents receive aid or protection from ancestral spirits. Adherents may also establish household shrines to domestic gods believed to oversee the fortunes of an individual family, as in the example of the worship of domestic lares, or household deities, in ancient Rome. In contrast, adherents in many traditions devote home shrines to widely worshipped deities or saints, although individual families or family members may nonetheless feel a special, personal bond to the particular object of worship. In Hinduism, for example, adherents typically maintain a household shrine devoted to specific deities, which serves as the focus of regular family worship. Similar practices exist in most forms of Buddhism as well.

In most of the major world religions, however, communal places of worship represent a more common setting for everyday interactions between adherents and sacred space. Although their specific forms vary widely, such communal structures typically organize space to support the adherent's interaction with the sacred and the rituals associated with it. The traditional layout of Christian churches, for example, is designed so that the congregation faces the eastern end of the structure, where the altar, Lord's Table, or pulpit is located. The east in this context also represents the sacred direction from which the Second Coming of Christ will occur. In Jewish synagogues, the congregation faces the Ark, the focus of local sacred space, which by tradition is situated so that those looking toward it also face in the direction of Jerusalem. Similarly, Muslim mosque design places the mirhab niche in one wall to designate the direction of Mecca toward which the assembled congregation faces in prayer. Mosque design also incorporates an outer area where adherents may perform ritual ablutions so that they can enter the mosque proper in a state of ritual cleanliness. Hindu temples can be quite complex in layout, but generally focus on the square beneath the temple's main tower, which symbolizes Mount Meru. The tower also serves to bring the deity to whom the temple is consecrated into the space below it and thus into contact with adherents.

The interactions between adherents and the sacred spaces associated with ordinary religious practice are reinforced by a wide variety of customs enacted at the scale of the body.[44] Within such contexts, the intersection of body space and sacred space serves as the foundation for immediate religious experience. In most religious traditions, adherents believe for example that ordinary interactions with sacred space require processes of religious concentration, as in prayer or meditation. Religious groups have thus practiced various means of controlling the body within the setting of everyday worship to achieve a desired religious state. Many such practices have focused in particular on the performance of specific bodily attitudes or poses. Early Christians most commonly prayed in church while standing with arms uplifted or outspread to express gratitude for divine blessings, but they also adopted the practice of kneeling during worship services as a bodily expression of repentance. The early Christian church banned kneeling on Sundays, during which interactions with the sacred were to be devoted to divine reverence rather than to penitence. Over time, however, kneeling became widely adopted as the most common attitude of prayer within western Christianity, although many forms of standing prayer continue to be practiced as well. Prayer in Islam involves a more detailed set of practices related to sacred space, including a sequence of bows and prostrations in the direction of Mecca during the formal prayer itself. Individual prayers of supplication, on the other hand, fall outside of this more formal pattern and are made with the palms facing the divine space above to receive God's blessings. The practice of meditation in many Buddhist forms of worship typically involves more exacting methods of bodily control aimed at quieting the body to foster mental concentration. A common practice includes sitting with legs crossed in the *padmasana* or lotus position, resting the right hand on top of the left with palms up, with the torso vertically aligned.

Religious traditions have also commonly incorporated more active expressions of interaction with the sacred spaces of ordinary worship. Often the action simply involves a physical expression of reverence or veneration toward the sacred, such as the Roman Catholic and Eastern Orthodox practice of making the sign of the cross when entering the sanctuary of a church, before praying, and in various other contexts. Specific religious rituals frequently focus on bodily involvement in sacred space, a process that is crucial in the believer's assimilation of ritual knowledge or power.[45] The Christian practice of receiving communion reflects this pattern at various scales. By ingesting the Eucharistic bread and wine, adherents are bodily linked to the divine space of the bread and wine itself, the sanctity of the local altar or Lord's Table, and the imagined sacred spaces associated with the Christian doctrines of salvation and resurrection. This act represents the central sacrament in the Christian tradition. The act of ritual purification represents a further example of ordinary interactions with sacred space, as in Islamic performance of ablutions before entering the mosque or Jewish use of the mikveh. Finally, adherents of many religions have used asceticism and mortification of the body to achieve states of sacred communion with the superhuman or the divine. Such practices have a significant history in Christian mysticism, for example, in which adherents have used bodily pain to attain union with Christ as savior.[46]

More active use of the body is also frequently central to communal acts of worship in local sacred space. Dance represents a particularly distinctive expression, found in many traditions, of the use of body in ordinary rituals. Dance provides a fundamental means of using body space to incorporate the believer into dynamic spatial patterns of religious meaning. In tribal religions, dance represents a central element of shamanistic rites, contributing to the realization of trance states or the possession of the adherent by totem animals whose behavior the dance reproduces. The dervishes of the Sufi Mawlawiya order similarly have used dance in their communal worship services to achieve ecstatic states of divine communion. In North America, the Shakers used dance during worship in their otherwise quite plain meetinghouses as a means of invoking the freedom of heavenly space while still on earth.[47] Dance, in both folk and elite forms, also represents an important element of the communal celebration of festivals within Hinduism (photo 5.8). The religious use of body space in dance may also take on more formal elements, however, as in the reproduction of sacred narratives in traditional Hindu temple dancing, a pattern that survives in Indian classical dance.

Life Transitions

Beyond the regular interactions between adherents and sacred space that occur during ordinary worship practices, religious systems typically identify a variety of less frequent interactions associated with more specific events or obligations. Practices associated

Photo 5.8. Dancers celebrating the Tamil festival of *Adi Perukku*, which honors the sacred Kaveri River deified as a goddess for providing life-sustaining water. This festival is generally restricted to the Kaveri Valley in Karnataka and Tamil Nadu states and is celebrated primarily by women. Because of its association with fertility, believers use the festival to seek blessings for newlyweds and the soon-to-be-wed. The dance depicted here is the Kolattam, or stick dance, which is widely associated with Tamil festivals held during the month of Adi, including Adi Perukku. Chennai, India, 2006.

Source: Kumarrajendran (commons.wikimedia.org/wiki/Image:Chennai_dancers.jpg), placed in the public domain.

with significant life transitions, including birth, maturation, initiation, and death, represent one such context for the interaction between adherents and sacred space. Baptismal rituals within Christianity exemplify this type of practice as it relates to birth, although the exact form of such rituals varies considerably. In Roman Catholicism, Orthodoxy, and numerous Protestant churches, the baptism of infants acquires its meaning from sacred space defined by the use of a baptismal font and consecrated holy water in initiating the infant into the church. Sacred space is perhaps more widely relevant to rituals associated with rites of passage to adulthood, which are found in many different religious traditions. In animistic religions, such rituals typically focus on the initiate's interaction with a sacred space believed to possess significant hierenergetic power, especially with regard to the production of visions. Various Native American tribes of the northern Great Plains, for example, have used the Black Hills of South Dakota as the site for vision quests carried out by young men entering adulthood. Typically this process involves ritual purification in a sweat lodge followed by a prolonged period of fasting during which the power of the spirits inhabiting the mountains reveals a vision containing insights into the youth's future.

Rites of passage may also make use of more formally defined sacred spaces, such as altars in the Christian rite of confirmation or the Ark and Torah scrolls in the Jewish bar mitzvah. The Hindu *upanayana* ceremony, also known as the sacred thread ritual, makes particular use of the sacrificial fire, a survival from the earliest forms of Vedic religion. By tradition, this ceremony ritually marks the transition of young males from childhood to the beginning of serious religious study under a guru, a transformation symbolized by the donning of a sacred thread around the torso. During the complex ritual itself, the youth symbolically contacts the sacred by standing on a stone representing perseverance. At the end of the ritual, the youth also circumambulates the central sacred space of the sacrificial fire as a sign of the completion of his initiation. More selective rites of initiation make similar uses of sacred space. As an example, the Buddhist *abhiseka* ("anointing") ritual initiates students into Tantric rites, particularly within Tibetan Buddhism. After a complex process of preparation involving a number of different ceremonies, the initiate has power bestowed upon him after entering the sacred space of a mandala, a representation both of the cosmos generally and of the body, speech, and mind of a specific Buddha.

The most important life transition involving interactions with sacred space, however, is the death of an adherent. Religious systems have specified many particulars concerning the treatment of the body of the deceased and its proper disposal, as discussed in chapter 4. Much of the concern with the latter focuses on the relationship between the corpse and sacred space. Religions holding to a unitary view of the body and soul and to belief in physical resurrection of the body, including Judaism, Christianity, and Islam, place considerable importance on burial of the deceased's remains in an appropriate location. These religions have thus emphasized burial in a cemetery that is restricted to the deceased's religious group or that has been consecrated in some way. Specific sacred locations have also emerged within these religions as preferred burial sites. Seeking burial in Israel has been and remains an important practice in traditional forms of Judaism, based on the belief that burial in the Eretz Yisrael will ease both the pain of death and the ultimate process of resurrection. This belief has led to the establishment of services that supervise the burial of Jews from other parts of the world in Israeli cemeteries. Shiite Muslims have similarly sought burial in close proximity to the shrines of important Imams, for example at Karbala in Iraq and Mashhad in Iran, based on the belief that this practice will ensure their ultimate entry into paradise. Regardless of their place of burial, Muslims and Christians have also emphasized the correct orientation of the interred corpse in alignment with a sacred direction. According to Islamic belief, the body should be buried lying on its right side facing Mecca; and according to Christian tradition the body should be placed in an east-west alignment, with the feet to the east, the direction from which the dead will receive the final call to judgment.

Concerns with the proper disposition of corpses appear as well among religious groups adhering to a dualistic conception of the individual, according to which the soul survives independently of the body. The methods of disposition differ from those of religions holding a unitary view, however. As discussed in chapter 4, such religions generally use methods of disposal that result in the destruction of the body itself, such as cremation or, less commonly, exposure to predators. Nonetheless, issues of location remain a significant concern in the funerary practices of these religions. Within Hinduism, for example, cremation normally takes place in close proximity to a river, where the cremated remains are commonly placed; and the Hindu cremation ritual involves placement of the body with the head oriented northward. Particular sites have acquired special significance in this context as well. Most notably, Hindu belief posits that adherents may achieve release from the cycle of reincarnation by dying and being cremated in the sacred city of Varanasi along the Ganges River. Based on this belief, tens of thousands of cremations take place at Varanasi every year. Funeral rites take many different forms among the diverse varieties of Buddhism. In places with a strong tradition of ancestor worship before the arrival of Buddhism, as in parts of Southeast and East Asia, the placement of the deceased's remains in a consecrated cemetery or family shrine has traditionally been common. Buddhist temples play a particularly important role in conducting funerary rites and in housing cemeteries in Japan, where Buddhism traditionally superseded Shinto in matters concerning death.

Pilgrimage

Adherents interact most frequently with sacred space at the local scales of everyday life, primarily through ordinary worship practices and various rituals of transition. Their most intense and profound interactions with sacred space may occur more rarely, however, and are especially associated with exceptional forms of worship, forms that take place outside of the ordinary realms of daily existence. Rites of passage often incorporate a degree of this exceptionality, as do local religious festivals and other periodic forms of worship. The exceptionality of worship becomes most pronounced, however, within the context of the pilgrimage, in which adherents come into most extensive contact with sacred space beyond the geographical and temporal boundaries of their everyday lives. For many believers, the completion of a pilgrimage thus represents a pinnacle of religious experience during their lifetime. The effort and resources expended by adherents in achieving this objective clearly reflect the cultural significance of the pilgrimage, as does the increase in social status that in many cultures is attributed to those who have completed this sacred process.

Pilgrimage rituals themselves are highly diverse in character, differing significantly in the definition of the ritual process and the motivations for participation, as well as in their specific destinations. As a result, some scholars have argued that the concept of pilgrimage is so diverse in meaning that it has little analytical value. Others have argued, however, that sufficient similarities exist among different pilgrimage traditions to make the concept a useful one in understanding the geographical dimensions of religion.[48] The latter argument, adopted here, identifies a cluster of features that pilgrimages generally share in common. Most importantly, as already suggested, pilgrimage is distinguished as a form of religious ritual by its inherent exceptionality. It is exceptional in large part because it involves the believer's interaction with unique, and presumably unusually potent, expressions of sacred space. In some cases, that interaction follows a converging pattern, with adherents from diverse origins gathering at a single location; in others it follows a prescribed pattern in which pilgrims follow a defined route or sacred path, typically visiting a sequence of sacred places.[49] The exceptional character of a pilgrimage further derives from its location beyond the local spaces of the adherent's everyday life, necessitating commitments of time and travel not usually required for religious practice. In this sense pilgrimages represent rare events, departures from the normal routine of religious life. The pilgrimage is also exceptional in the sense that it attracts the participation of significant numbers of believers, either in large congregations or in frequent smaller groups dispersed over time or along a sacred path. Pilgrimage, in effect, is a fundamentally communal activity. And finally, the pilgrimage draws its exceptionality as a form of worship from the motivations of the adherents who undertake it. These motivations are highly diverse, as outlined below, but they generally share a special weight or importance different from the factors associated with ordinary religious observance.

Access to Divine Power or Guidance

In making a pilgrimage to a sacred place of special meaning, adherents often seek to gain access to sources of hierenergetic power. A common motivation underlying such efforts is the desire to acquire some significant form of divine or superhuman intervention in the material world, such as healing. In ancient Greek religion, for example, shrines associated with Asclepius, the god of healing, were frequent destinations for pilgrims seeking cures, particularly the major healing temple located at the cult center of Epidaurus. Based on the belief that Asclepius produced cures in dreams, pilgrims to his temple slept inside in a sacred dormitory to gain access to his power.[50] To cite a more modern example, the Roman Catholic site at Lourdes also typifies the pattern of seeking hierenergetic healing through pilgrimage. Although it attracts a wide variety of pilgrims and tourists, every year tens of thousands of adherents in search of healing make the pilgrimage to the grotto where Bernadette experienced a Marian apparition, particularly from the waters of the spring at the site, which Bernadette revealed as having miraculous, curative properties during one of her visions. The baths at Lourdes, which use waters from the miraculous spring, are a particularly important destination for adherents who are ill and infirm, although some subsequently dispute the waters' ability to cure.[51] The Roman Catholic Church maintains that the baths are primarily purifying, but it does not deny their role in producing miraculous cures.

Adherents in most traditions also use pilgrimage practices to gain access to a great variety of superhuman interventions other than healing, relating both to spiritual and material affairs. This type of pattern is very common, for example, within the practice of maraboutism among North African Muslims. This practice focuses on the belief that adherents have access to the baraka or holy power of a marabout, a local saint or Sufi shaykh, at the site of his tomb and that through this power the marabout can influence the material world or serve as an intermediary between the believer and God (photo 5.9). A strong tradition of pilgrimage has thus developed around the tombs of major saints and shaykhs, taking place throughout the year but commonly reaching a peak on the anniversary of the marabout's death. Pilgrims to these sites seek many different kinds of blessings, in some cases focusing on spiritual merit but also relating to a wide variety of familial, financial, social, and other worldly concerns. Similar practices developed in parts of North Africa among Sephardic Jews in relation to the burial sites of zaddikim, a pattern that Sephardic migrants brought to Israel during the twentieth century.[52]

In addition to seeking superhuman intervention, pilgrimage motivations for seeking access to sources of hierenergetic power also focus on the goal of acquiring divine or superhuman insight into issues of concern to the believer. In many religious cultures this type of pilgrimage focuses on oracular spaces, typically a location where an oracle, a human intermediary, transmits superhuman messages in response to the questions or requests of pilgrims. This form of ritual differs from the similar but more commonplace practice of divination in the importance of the questions asked of the oracle, the difficulty of achieving access to the oracle, and the linking of the oracle to a specific shrine sacred to a particular deity. The Apollonian oracle at Delphi represents a primary example of this type of pilgrimage site. Pilgrimage to the site at Delphi typically followed well-defined interactions with the sacred space there. Pilgrims were required to begin by making an appropriate offering to Apollo and to purify themselves in a sacred spring. The oracle, an older woman, also purified herself before entering the sacred cell from which she made her pronouncements. The Delphic oracle was particularly important in Greek culture as a source of advice on political matters, but addressed the varied personal concerns brought to her by pilgrims as well.

Photo 5.9.   The tomb of a marabout in southern Morocco. Such tombs typically have whitewashed exteriors and thus stand out dramatically in North Africa landscapes. Morocco, 2006.

Source: Chrumps (commons.wikimedia.org/wiki/Image:Grobowiec_Marabuta-Maroko.jpg), under Creative Commons license (creativecommons.org/licenses/by/2.5/).

In contrast to the preceding examples, hierophanic pilgrimage sites have had more specific uses in some other contexts. In Tibetan Buddhism, for example, pilgrimages by senior monastic officials to the sacred lake of Lhamo Latso, located in a remote area of southern Tibet southeast of Lhasa, have played a crucial role in the identification of tulkus, the reincarnations of past lamas. In Tibetan Buddhist belief, pious adherents in a proper meditative state, after having devoted several days to making the appropriate prayers and offerings, may observe hierophanic visions reflected in the surface of the lake itself. The most important use of the lake involves the identification of clues concerning the identity or location of young tulkus, such as the reincarnates of the Dalai Lama and Panchen Lama.[53] This process of revelation may require an extended stay by the side of the lake but has been considered essential to the correct recognition of the reincarnated leaders of Tibetan Buddhism. With many monastic leaders living in exile since the Chinese occupation of Tibet in the 1950s, the lack of access to Lhamo Latso has become a potential problem for the Tibetan Buddhist community.

Proximity to the Divine

Pilgrimages to sites associated with a superhuman presence do not focus solely on seeking divine intervention or insight. Pilgrims may also visit such sites simply to achieve proximity to the divine at theocentric spaces, without necessarily seeking to engage divine power in addressing their own concerns. This pattern is characteristic of Jewish pilgrimage to the Western Wall in Jerusalem, an ancient structure standing along a portion of the western side of the Temple Mount. The latter was the site of the two ancient Jewish temples in Jerusalem, the first of which according to Jewish belief housed the Ark of the Covenant within an inner sanctuary, the Holy of Holies. Because of the Western Wall's association with the ancient temple, Jewish tradition holds that the Shekhinah, or presence of God, is particularly strong there. Pilgrims thus come to worship before the sacred space of the Western Wall to interact with the divine presence. Orthodox Jews follow strict patterns of observance in support of this practice, including concentrated forms of prayer associated with repeated rocking motions and the division of the area in front of the wall into separate spaces for men and women (photo 5.10). Many pilgrims to the Western Wall also seek divine blessings of various kinds, traditionally by inserting requests written on pieces of paper into the cracks between the stones that make up the wall.[54]

Pilgrimages seeking proximity to the divine presence at theocentric spaces appear in many other religions as well. In Christianity, such pilgrimages developed as early as the fourth century CE around sites in the Christian Holy Land that were associated with Jesus, Mary, and various biblical saints. The popularity of these pilgrimages grew out of the overwhelming sense of awe that believers felt in the presence of sacred sites believed to offer visible proof of the sacred history of Christianity.[55] Important sites in the Holy Land pilgrimage include, among others, the Basilica of the Annunciation in Nazareth, where the archangel Gabriel announced to Mary that she would bear the son of God; the Basilica of the Nativity in Bethlehem, where Jesus was born; the route of the Stations of the Cross in Jerusalem, which follows Jesus' movements from his condemnation through his crucifixion to his entombment; the Church of the Holy Sepulcher in Jerusalem, believed to contain the tomb of Jesus; and the Chapel of the

Photo 5.10. Jewish women praying at the Western Wall in Jerusalem early in the twentieth century. As depicted here, women have traditionally prayed at the southern portion of the Western Wall, apart from male worshippers. Jerusalem, Israel, no date.

Source: G. Eric and Edith Matson Photograph Collection, Prints and Photographs Division, U.S. Library of Congress.

Ascension on the Mount of Olives, identified as the location of the resurrection of Jesus. A significant cartographic tradition has developed around the production of pilgrimage maps to assist travelers in visiting these various places.[56]

Similar sites in the life of the Buddha play an important role in Buddhist pilgrimage, although the different branches of this tradition disagree on whether the Buddha was human or divine. Regardless, pilgrims travel to Buddhism's sacred hearth in Nepal and northern India to experience the sense of awe produced by immediate contact with the sites associated with the Buddha's enlightenment, including Lumbini, his birthplace in Nepal; Bodh Gaya, the site of his enlightenment; the Deer Park at Sarnath, the site of his first sermon; and Kushinagar, where he died, passing into nirvana. According to the Mahaparinibbana Sutta, part of the Pali canon, at Kushinagar the Buddha himself recommended that adherents complete pilgrimages to these four sites to foster reverence for and attentiveness to the goals of their faith. Most pilgrims to these sites also visit a second set of locations tied to miracles associated with the Buddha.

In quite different ways, the journey to spaces containing a divine presence has also appeared within contemporary contexts in less formal expressions of pilgrimage, for example in relation to New Age religious movements. Such activities often develop outside of organized religious structures. They may selectively incorporate traditional beliefs and practices but generally do not do so in an exclusivist sense, instead merging influences from different sources into a more diffuse or general sense of spirituality. These activities also are more frequently individualistic than communal in character, a departure from standard pilgrimage patterns. Perhaps the most common expressions of this form of unconventional pilgrimage focus on the wilderness or particular natural sites as locations for encountering a divine or spiritual presence. In a similar manner, Neo-Pagan groups have used pilgrimage to ancient sacred spaces from diverse traditions as a means of arriving at eclectic or universal experiences of the superhuman.[57]

Veneration of Devout Believers and Saints

Somewhat related to pilgrimages involving theocentric space are those that involve the simple veneration of particularly devout or significant persons at sites associated with them. This pattern characterizes the orthodox interpretation of Islamic pilgrimage to the tomb of Muhammad at the Great Mosque in Medina, often carried out subsequent to the Hajj. Islamic orthodoxy insists on an absolute monotheism in which God alone should be worshipped. Since gaining control of the sacred cities of the Hejaz, the Wahhabi sect has been particularly concerned with preventing worship activities at the tomb of Muhammad that would elevate him above human status. To prevent such a deviation from orthodoxy they have, for example, posted signs prohibiting the act of prostration before the tomb.[58] The pilgrimage to Medina represents the primary form of a more widespread type of Islamic pilgrimage known as the *ziyara* ("visit"), which in addition to Medina involves pilgrimages to the tombs of local saints, Sufi shaykhs, or Shiite Imams.[59] The ziyara does not possess the status of the more central institution of the Hajj, but because of the wider distribution of destinations provides a more accessible form of pilgrimage for those who cannot afford the journey to Mecca. Simple veneration of important shaykhs represents an important part of the ziyara, although as in the aforementioned case of maraboutism the pilgrim also frequently requests favors from the holy person buried at the pilgrimage site. Many specific instances of ziyara exist in different regions. In Egypt, for example, a primary example of ziyara involves pilgrimage to the tomb of Ahmed al-Badawiya, a thirteenth-century shaykh who founded the Sufi order that carries his name, one of the most popular and important in Egypt. The main feature of the annual pilgrimage to his shrine is the adherent's recitation of Sufi *dhikr* or ritual prayers in remembrance of the shaykh. Although counter to orthodox teachings, in popular worship believers consider participation in this ritual to carry nearly the spiritual weight of the Hajj.

Similar kinds of pilgrimages, held in commemoration of important or devout persons, have appeared in many other religious traditions. A form of pilgrimage particularly important in Christianity, for example, focuses on sacred sites associated with martyrs. Such pilgrimages played an important role in the diffusion of formally approved pilgrimage traditions outside of the Holy Land, first throughout Europe and then to other parts of the world. Rome has traditionally been an important pilgrimage center in this regard because of the large number of Christians martyred there in the first two centuries CE. Further afield, the National Shrine of the North American Martyrs in central New York, which commemorates the martyrdom of three Jesuit saints, has been a principal Roman Catholic pilgrimage site in North America.

Personal Religious Transformation

Along with superhuman agency, proximity to the divine, and simple practices of veneration, pilgrimage also provides a vehicle for adherents to influence or transform their own personal religious situation or condition. In its various forms, this type of pilgrimage tends to be somewhat more demanding than those already discussed, involving some sort of sacrifice on the part of the believer in return for a marked change in religious status. Perhaps the simplest expressions of this type of pilgrimage involve the completion of a complex set of rituals to gain spiritual merit. The Kumbh Mela pilgrimages are the world's largest in terms of the number of adherents involved, in some cases drawing as many as fifteen million participants. These pilgrimages are held every three years, rotating among four different sites (Allahabad, Nashik, Ujjain, and Haridwar) located on four sacred rivers, with the pilgrimage at Allahabad representing the climax of the cycle. They are based on the Hindu belief that a battle between gods and demons caused a vessel containing the nectar of immortality to spill onto earth at the four sites of the pilgrimage cycle. The focus of each pilgrimage is an exact astrological moment when the nectar becomes manifest in the river in question, generating great religious merit for the adherent bathing there through both bodily and spiritual purification. That merit increases with the successful completion of the entire Kumbh Mela cycle.

Somewhat different pilgrimages of this type have emerged in the vicinity of Varanasi, the most important of Hinduism's sacred cities. The most demanding and most sacred of these pilgrimages is the *Panchkoshi Parikrama*, which involves following a sacred path around the city approximately 50 miles in length and marked by worship at 108 different shrines and temples. Again, completion of the pilgrimage serves primarily to bring spiritual merit to the individual adherent. An analogous but more prolonged process appears in one of Japan's most important Buddhist pilgrimages, that of the Eighty-Eight Temples of Shikoku.[60] This pilgrimage involves following a clockwise sacred path over seven hundred miles in length that connects temples across the island of Shikoku. The time involved may now be shortened by the use of motor vehicles, but many Buddhists continue to perform the pilgrimage on foot. In Buddhist belief, prayer in each of the eighty-eight temples along the sacred path will release the pilgrim from the cycle of karmic rebirth. A parallel tradition has developed through which pilgrims can stand in for others, through their own actions freeing dead relatives from the process of reincarnation.

The difficult pilgrimage around Mount Kailas in western Tibet represents another important means of generating spiritual merit for Hindus, Buddhists, Jains, and followers of the Tibetan Bon religion (map 5.5). This pilgrimage is complicated by the extreme remoteness of Mount Kailas. The mountain can only be reached through many days of overland travel from the nearest major road; and the pilgrimage path, running clockwise around the base of the mountain for thirty-two miles, itself contains few amenities. By tradition, one circuit of the mountain removes the effects of one lifetime's accumulated sins, but many pilgrims seek to make the circuit multiple times. Again by tradition, a lifelong total of 108 circuits brings final enlightenment to the pious believer.[61]

Within modern contexts especially, finally, the process of personal transforma-

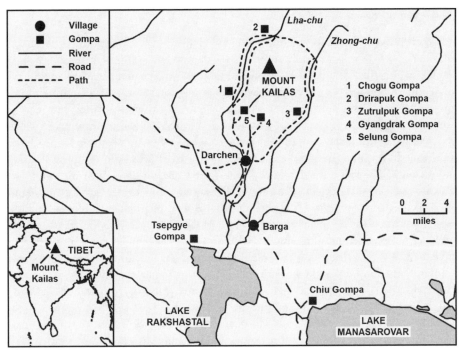

Map 5.5. The pilgrimage route around Mount Kailas in southern Tibet. Darchen serves as the starting point of the pilgrimage. During the Cultural Revolution the Chinese destroyed the *gompas*, or monasteries, that lie along the route, but these structures have since been rebuilt and again serve pilgrims to the region. The pilgrimage to Mount Kailas traditionally ends with a visit to Lake Manasarovar. Adherents of Hinduism, Buddhism, Jainism, and Tibet's Bon religion hold the lake to be sacred, fostering a widely held belief that its waters (only a few degrees above freezing at an elevation of 15,000 feet) cleanse the individual of sin.

tion associated with pilgrimage may relate not to the accumulation of spiritual merit but rather to the actualization or progression of other social meanings. The pilgrimage to the shrine of Our Lady of Guadalupe in Mexico, for example, has provided a means for individuals to reproduce their identification with a larger sense of group solidarity, first in relation to peasant resistance to hegemonic powers within Mexico and, somewhat later, to populist forms of nationalism. In the 1980s the Marian shrine at Medjugorje, located in Bosnia and Herzegovina, acquired a similar but somewhat more reflexive meaning among Croatians, although it also became an important pilgrimage destination for non-Croatian Roman Catholics as well. For Croat pilgrims, the journey to Medjugorje combines the usual religious meanings with the sanctification of Croatian nationalism, while the latter in turn brings greater immediacy and reality to the shrine's religious identity. Other types of political consciousness and communal identity may also be actualized or advanced by pilgrimage. Within the Goddess movement, a fusion of feminist thought and Neo-Pagan practices that emerged in the 1970s, pilgrimage exemplifies this pattern by fostering the believer's identification with the goals of feminism, with a re-imagined sense of her own body, with other believers, and with diverse sacred landscapes.[62]

Fulfillment of Religious Obligation

Another form of pilgrimage relating to the adherent's personal religious status centers on the concept of religious obligation. In this context, the ethos of a religious system explicitly prescribes that believers, if able, should participate in a particular pilgrimage of central importance to the belief system. Such pilgrimages in part serve to reinforce in the believer's mind the principal ideals of the religious system's ethos, but serve as well to strengthen the sense of community shared by the religion's adherents. A principal example of this form of pilgrimage is the Hajj (map 5.6).[63] According to the Quran (2: 196), all Muslims physically and financially able to do so should complete the Hajj at least once. The Hajj is held annually during the twelfth lunar month and comprises a variety of stages lasting roughly a week. These stages link the adherent to Muhammad, as they correspond to his actions during his final pilgrimage to Mecca. In addition, they articulate key elements of the ethos of Islam. Preparation for the pilgrimage includes the declaration of the intent to perform the ritual and entrance into the purified state of ihram. Men don two plain white garments, a uniformity of dress that reinforces the humility and equality of all believers. Women don clothing that covers them completely, except for their face and hands. Although not required, many women wear white robes. The pilgrimage process itself involves following a distinct sacred path beginning in the Great Mosque in Mecca with the *Tawaf*, in which adherents circumambulate the Kaaba seven times and if possible kiss the black stone embedded in the Kaaba, followed by the *Say*, a ritual display of mercy following the path of Hajar in the search for water for her infant son Ismail, ending at the Zamzam well. To complete the Say ritual, pilgrims also drink water previously collected from the well. The pilgrims then leave Mecca for a stay at nearby Mina where they pray in

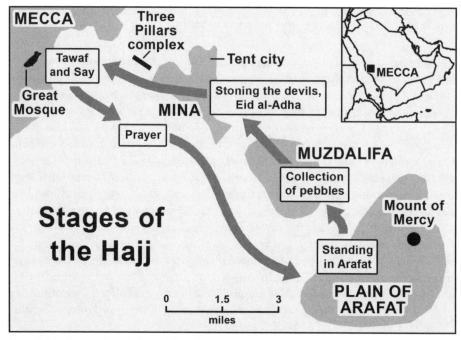

Map 5.6. Generalized plan of the stages of the Hajj.

preparation for the pilgrimage's climax on the plain of Arafat. On the following day they reach Arafat by midday and then begin the ritual known as standing in Arafat, in commemoration of Muhammad's final sermon. During this ritual, they stand facing Mecca in prayer until sunset. Although not the end of the pilgrimage, with the completion of this stage the pilgrim has satisfied the formal obligation to observe the Hajj. After the standing at Arafat, pilgrims move back toward Mecca, spending the night at Muzdalifa where they collect pebbles to use the next day. On the following morning they return to Mina, where in imitation of Muhammad they cast the pebbles they collected earlier at three stone pillars, a ritual known as stoning the devils, as a symbolic rejection of evil, temptation, and wrongdoing. This ritual is repeated on the two following days. While in Mina the pilgrims also celebrate *Eid al-Adha*, the major sacrifice observed at that time by Muslims around the world. Because in modern times the Hajj has attracted so many pilgrims, regularly numbering in the millions, accommodations have been made to prevent the necessity for the public sacrifice of so many animals, including the establishment of a large slaughterhouse that will sacrifice animals for others and then prepare the meat produced for distribution to the poor in other countries. This stage of the pilgrimage thus reinforces both the ethos of thankfulness for wealth received and generosity to those having less. The path of the Hajj ends with the return to Mecca and a repetition of the Tawaf and Say in the Great Mosque. Finally, after completing the Hajj pilgrims in various cultures have used specific means to signify the accompanying change in their religious status, such as the wearing of a white "hajji" cap by men or decorating house exteriors with paintings representing the pilgrimage.[64]

Obligatory pilgrimages like the Hajj, although not common, have also appeared in other traditions. According to Shinto belief, adherents have the obligation to make the pilgrimage to Ise, Shinto's most important shrine, at least once in their lifetime. This pilgrimage practice acquired widespread currency starting in the fifteenth century as part of the recurring effort to rebuild and renew the shrine at Ise, a process that took place every twenty years from the 600s to the 1600s and every twenty-one years since then. Ise thus became the most important Shinto pilgrimage destination. It draws millions of adherents annually, with somewhat larger numbers during the periods of reconstruction. The inner shrine within a larger sacred compound at Ise is dedicated to Amaterasu, the sun goddess and chief figure in the Shinto pantheon. Shinto belief also identifies Amaterasu as the progenitor of Japan's imperial family. The shrine at Ise has thus been particularly sacred to them, and the interior of the shrine compound is in fact accessible only to members of the imperial household. The shrine holds special duties for the imperial family, such as the annual blessing of the rice harvest; but for common adherents, the pilgrimage to Ise represents a simpler, obligatory display of faith in the practice of Shinto, although some adherents believe that this ritual also serves to strengthen the Japanese nation.

Demonstration of Penance

Finally, in addition to generating merit or satisfying obligation, pilgrimage may affect the adherent's religious status by serving as a demonstration of penance. One example of this pattern occurs in the Shiite Muslim pilgrimage to Karbala for Ashura, a holiday held on the tenth day of the first month of the Islamic lunar calendar. Ashura was originally designed by Muhammad as a day of atonement, similar in function to Judaism's Yom Kippur, although it no longer plays a significant role in the Sunni sacred calendar. Shiites later transformed the holiday into a commemoration of the martyrdom of Husayn, Muhammad's grandson, at the hands of his Sunni enemies at Karbala. Shiites celebrate Ashura everywhere, but the holiday focuses especially on Karbala, also the site of Husayn's tomb. The pilgrimage to Karbala during Ashura thus represents a major sacred event for Shiites. Participants express sorrow over Husayn's martyrdom but also repent for their own sins during the pilgrimage, a practice that takes its most dramatic form in public processions incorporating displays of self-flagellation, during which pilgrims draw blood from their heads and torsos by beating themselves with chains or cutting themselves with knives. The association of Ashura with intense forms of penitence originated shortly after Husayn's death, when Shiites from nearby areas sought to sacrifice themselves in battle with the Sunnis in penance for not having come to Husayn's aid. Late in the twentieth century the Ashura pilgrimage to Karbala was largely suppressed by Saddam Hussein, particularly after the rise of politicized Shiism in neighboring Iran in the late 1970s. After Hussein's fall, however, the pilgrimage resumed its importance for both Iraqi and Iranian Shiites and has attracts hundreds of thousands of participants.

Pilgrimages focusing on penance have also developed in other traditions. A primary example from Christianity is the pilgrimage known as the Camino de Santiago de Compostela or Way of St. James (map 5.7).[65] This pilgrimage dates to the ninth century, when Christians in northwestern Spain had a vision of a "field of stars" (*compostela*) on a site later believed to hold the remains of St. James the Apostle, or Santiago in Spanish. The site became a major symbol of Christian resistance to Moorish rule and following the Christian reconquest of Iberia became the third most important pilgrimage destination for Christians, following Jerusalem and Rome. Because of the relative remoteness of the site, the pilgrimage developed into the form of a sacred path, or actually a series of sacred paths beginning in different parts of Spain, Portugal, and France. The primary Spanish route runs from Roncesvalles in the Pyrenees to Santiago, a distance of roughly five hundred miles by foot. Since the medieval period pilgrims have undertaken the entire pilgrimage for various reasons, including the fulfillment of a vow or the acquisition of spiritual merit, but the difficulty of the pilgrimage, commonly lasting three months or more, has made it an especially important ritual of penance. During the medieval period, moreover, judges in Spain often sentenced wrongdoers to completion of the pilgrimage as part of their punishment. Although this pilgrimage has generally declined in significance over time, several hundred thousand adherents continue to undertake the ritual annually.

*   *   *

Adherents may undertake pilgrimages for reasons other than those already outlined, including the giving of thanks for a divine favor that has been bestowed or the fulfillment of a vow made in praying for some event to occur. Particularly in modern times, adherents may also mix the religious objectives of pilgrimage with secular interests in tourism and travel to unfamiliar locations.[66] Moreover, the motivations outlined above are not mutually exclusive. Many adherents engage in pilgrimages for more than one religious reason. The ziyara of a North African Muslim to the tomb of an important Sufi shaykh may thus reflect a general reverence for the holy figure, identification with

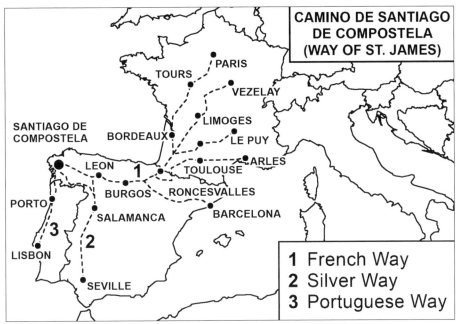

Map 5.7. The Camino de Santiago de Compostela or Way of St. James, a major Christian pilgrimage route since the eighth century. Pilgrims may take any of several routes to Santiago de Compostela. The most important of these, the French Way, runs across northern Spain from the Pyrenees. The French Way extends back into France along four major routes and many pilgrims in fact begin their journey from even more distant locations, following less well-traveled routes across Europe to one of the four French routes and from there to Santiago de Compostela. In modern times, pilgrims typically undertake these longer pilgrimages in sections, at a series of different times, rather than as one continuous journey.

a particular tariqa, and specific requests for help in material matters. Similarly, a Buddhist pilgrim to the Deer Park in Sarnath may be motivated by simple reverence for the Buddha, participation in the larger community of Buddhists, and the desire to earn religious merit. Nonetheless, the various motivations and examples discussed above serve to illustrate both the diversity of pilgrimage as a form of spatially meaningful ritual and the usefulness of the concept of pilgrimage in understanding some of the similarities among these diverse interactions with sacred space in different traditions.

Imagined Spaces

The interactions between adherents and sacred space discussed thus far have all involved material manifestations of sacred space, those related to the practice of ordinary worship, life transition rituals, and pilgrimage. A final, somewhat more complex dimension of sacred space with which adherents interact involves the imagined spaces, like heaven and hell, which they believe to exist beyond the material world. Such spaces represent a crucial part of adherents' worldviews in a cosmographic sense in that they represent the portion of the cosmos that comprises the ultimate spaces of the individual's fate. Believers interact with these spaces in ways very different from the types of sacred space already considered, however. Most importantly, adherents do not interact directly with imagined spaces within the context of their material lives. Instead, they prepare themselves in various ways for future interactions with these spaces. Such preparations in fact represent an important manifestation of a religious system's ethos, and may involve the manner in which adherents interact with other people, the extent to which they adhere to the specific laws and rules of their faith, and their completion of specific religious tasks. Because believers understand these preparations to be a lifelong effort, however, they may pay little attention to them in the short term. In the long term, however, believers accept the notion that their actions will ultimately influence how they interact with the imagined sacred spaces that exist beyond the material world.

Religious systems generally define interactions with such imagined spaces in one of two forms, linear or cyclical. Linear interpretations, often associated with a unitary view of body and soul, posit that after life in the material world the adherent will move, immediately or at some later point in sacred history, to a specific imagined space. In many cases, two or more such spaces exist and the movement of adherents to any particular space derives from a process of judgment and a subsequent pattern of reward or punishment. On the other hand, in religions comprising belief in a cyclical pattern of life after death, and typically a dualistic view of body and soul as well, adherents believe that they will experience a process of reincarnation. Generally in this process some aspect of the adherent's soul will be reborn into a new body and a new life, a pattern that may occur again and again over many lifetimes. This process is not endlessly cyclical, however. The reborn aspect of the believer may improve its spiritual merit from one lifetime to the next, being rewarded with rebirth in improved spiritual circumstances. This process may eventually end, therefore, when the reborn entity achieves full enlightenment or oneness with God and attains freedom from the cycle of reincarnation. Again, in both linear and cyclical interpretations, adherence to the ethos of the religious system represents the primary means available to the adherent for ensuring desired interactions with imagined spaces in the future.

The linear interpretation of the movement of adherents through the spaces of life and death is characteristic of Judaism, Christianity, and Islam. Judaism originally did not place much emphasis on this process, identifying heaven as a domain above the earth where God and the angels dwelled and Sheol as the common destination of the dead. This interpretation gradually changed, however, with heaven being redefined as the world to come following the earthly arrival of the Messiah, after which those judged to be righteous, including the resurrected dead, would live in the kingdom of God. Those who are judged to be undeserving of heaven would be condemned to burn in Gehenna or hell. Depending on one's actions in life, however, the interaction with Gehenna varies. For some, the burning provides purification as well as torment and these adherents are eventually cleansed to the point that they can enter heaven. The truly wicked, on the other hand, remain perpetually in Gehenna.

This interpretation of the afterlife in many ways resembles those of Christianity and Islam. Christianity has traditionally placed special emphasis on the role of judgment in the afterlife, linking it to the concept of Jesus's atonement for humanity's sins and to the Second Coming. Interactions between the believer and the afterlife are complicated in Christianity, moreover, by two theological views of judgment: the judgment that occurs with the Second Coming, at the end of time, when all people are judged; and the personal judgment applied to individuals at their time of death. A traditional resolution of these interpretations in many forms of Christianity posits an immediate judgment of the soul after death and the rejoining of the soul with the resurrected body in the appropriate space of reward or punishment following the Second Coming. Within the Christian afterlife individuals are generally directed to heaven or hell based on the righteousness of their lives. Roman Catholicism, like Judaism, also incorporates a temporary place of punishment in purgatory, where individual souls are purified before being admitted to heaven. The specific requirements for admission to heaven are defined very differently in different strains of Christian thought, ranging for example from Universalism, which argues that all people will be saved, to the Jehovah's Witnesses, who believe that only an anointed 144,000 adherents will reign in heaven with God. The nature of hell itself has also been described in different ways, from physical torment to eternal separation from God. Within Islamic belief, the righteous and the wicked are identified on a day of judgment at the end of sacred history, with the former entering heaven and the latter being consigned to hell. The Quran identifies different levels of hell for different kinds of evildoers, each with an appropriate set of punishments. At the same time, the Quran suggests that some of those consigned to hell may be released if God so chooses.

Finally, a linear interpretation of the relationship between life and death has also characterized many ancient and animistic religions, which have generally envisioned a relatively simple afterlife. In some instances, the dead simply inhabit an undifferentiated underworld and have relatively little to do with the material world. In many animistic religions, however, the dead become an active part of the spirit world and may continue to interact with the material world. Dead ancestors play an important role in the belief system of the Baganda, for example, by acting to support their descendants.

Cyclic interpretations of the individual's movement through the spaces of life and death characterize the religions incorporating belief in reincarnation, including Hinduism, Buddhism, Jainism, and Sikhism. For these traditions, in contrast to Judaism, Christianity, and Islam, the final objective of life is not to enter an imagined heavenly location after death but rather to attain nirvana, a sort of sacred placelessness that marks the extinction of the self, liberation from the cycle of reincarnation, and an undifferentiated oneness with the universe. Sikhism differs from the other Indic traditions, however, by reinterpreting this objective in a theocentric context as the attainment of the heavenly *Sach Khand*, or "Realm of Truth," where the adherent achieves unity with God.

Within the Indic religions, much of the ongoing cycle of reincarnation takes place, repeatedly, in the material world. In various ways, however, these religions have also incorporated significant beliefs concerning imagined spaces through which aspects of the adherent's soul pass during the intervals between periods of material existence. Tibetan Buddhists believe that following death aspects of the adherent's soul pass through a state, or series of states, known as *bardo*, during which the circumstances of rebirth are determined. For the prepared soul, this state can in fact provide the context for achieving moksha, or freedom from the cycle of rebirth and thence nirvana. For both Buddhists and Hindus, reincarnation does not necessarily involve immediate rebirth into the material world. In a pattern resembling purgatory, those who have lived ignominious lives may be reborn into one of the Narakas, or levels of hell, included in the cosmographies of Hinduism and Buddhism. The severity of life in the different levels accords with the nature of the misdeeds of those consigned there. Adherents may be reborn into the lower domains for many lifetimes, atoning for their accumulation of negative karma, before achieving rebirth in the material world. On the other hand, those who have led exemplary lives may be reborn into a higher domain in preparation for the ultimate attainment of nirvana. In Hinduism, a commonly sought destination is *Svarga*, a heavenly realm ruled by the god Indra, where according to some Hindu texts the reincarnated can themselves become godlike. In Mahayana Buddhism, the most commonly sought destination is one of the Pure Lands, and particularly the Western Pure Land ruled by Amitabha. According to the Pure Land school, adherents born into a Pure Land can never be reborn in a lesser domain and will instead live in an environment that in every way supports the attainment of nirvana. Even more rarified than the Western Pure Land is Tushita, into which only bodhisattvas are reborn before their final incarnation on earth during which they will achieve nirvana. Maitreya, also known as the Buddha-to-be, rules this special Buddha-world. Adherents of Jainism and Sikhism adhere to beliefs concerning the process of reincarnation that are generally similar to those of Hinduism and Buddhism, although Jains place greater belief on an unchanging, eternal soul.

Out of concern with the difficulties faced by the dead in their encounters with the imagined spaces of the afterlife, many religious groups have developed traditions aimed at preparing individuals for the journey after death or helping the deceased make their way. In some religions such efforts have taken the form of guides to dying. Essays on *ars moriendi*, or the art of dying well, became a popular form of devotional literature in late medieval Europe, for example, beginning with the *Tractatus artis bene moriendi* ("Managing the art of dying well") published in 1415.[67] The primary purpose of this literature was to lead the reader away from the paths leading to damnation and toward the path leading to heaven. Within Tibetan Buddhism, the *Bardo Thodol* ("Book of the Dead") provided detailed instructions on how to achieve liberation from rebirth during different stages in the period of bardo, or failing that on how to achieve a favorable rebirth.[68] Funerary practices also often reflected efforts to assist the dead in the imagined space of the afterlife. Many religions orient the burial site in a certain direction as a form of assistance. Christian graves, for example, are laid out with the feet to the east so that the body of the deceased can arise facing the direction of the Second Coming. In animistic religions, the orientation of burial sites frequently reflected the association of a particular direction with the underworld, thus pointing the deceased in the appropriate direction. Along different lines, the practice of embalming in ancient Egypt reflected the belief that the deceased would require an intact body to successfully navigate the world of the dead. Many religious groups also supply provisions for the deceased in the journey after life, as in the Greek practice of placing coins in the mouth or on the eyelids of the deceased to pay for the ferry across the river Styx to the underworld.

*   *   *

All of the aforementioned interactions between adherents and sacred space play crucial roles in the religious lives of adherents. For believers, interactions with sacred space contribute at fundamental levels to the realization of their worldview. Such interactions make the sacredness in and of the world tangible and authentic. Moreover, the many roles of believers in enacting ritual within sacred space reinforce the compelling character of their religious ethos. The ritual relationships between adherents and sacred space in effect articulate the most basic values and meanings of a religious system, expressing the religious objectives that adherents seek to attain both in everyday and extraordinary settings. Through the many ways in which they interact with particular sacred spaces, adherents in turn become deeply concerned with preserving the sanctity of the latter. In diverse contexts, such concerns have contributed to various forms of conflict over the meaning and control of sacred space, the central theme of the final section of this chapter.

Sacred Space as Contested Space

Believers assign great significance to the sacred spaces with which they interact. Such spaces represent the most compelling physical manifestations of a religious system's worldview and provide crucial contexts for adherents to enact fundamental expressions of their ethos. Believers consequently exert a strong degree of territoriality over the sacred spaces with which they interact, seeking to protect and preserve those spaces' meanings and uses. In varied contexts, however, such concerns have for a number of different reasons contributed to conflicts concerning sacred space. Perhaps most fundamentally, conflicts have emerged when a religious group has considered a particular space to be so central to its worldview and ethos that it cannot countenance any threat to or deviation from its traditional meanings or uses. Conflict emerges in such cases when the sanctity of the space faces some form of external threat, typically either from a different religious group or from secular influences. The contesting of sacred space may also develop when different groups, either from within the same tradition or from entirely different traditions, lay claim to the same sacred space but seek to control or use it in different ways. In this type of situation, each group sees the other as a threat to the sanctity of the space in question. Finally, conflicts involving sacred space may extend beyond purely religious concerns into broader political or cultural matters, particularly when a sacred space takes on secular symbolic meanings. Through the influence of these factors, sacred spaces have often been strongly contested as cultural artifacts by opposing groups. This contesting of the meanings and uses of sacred space contrasts dramatically with the adherent's belief in the transcendence or permanence of the space in question. That contrast makes the conflict over sacred space all the more important to the adherent, however. Instead of undermining belief in the sanctity of the space, the conflict is more likely to strengthen the adherent's sense of religious dedication or obligation. The contesting of sacred space in essence becomes a conflict over religious truth, which tends to reinforce the contrasts between opposing groups rather than weaken them.

In examining the contesting of sacred space, the following discussion classifies conflicts according to the nature of the groups contesting the space in question. The first category focuses on conflicts between religious groups from separate traditions. Conflicts in this category typically involve the most violent disputes over sacred space as well as the most difficult to resolve. The second category includes conflicts between different groups within the same tradition. Such conflicts, although usually less violent, are in many ways more complex than those of the first category, since they are often based on more detailed issues of religious authority and interpretation. The third category, finally, includes conflicts between religious groups and secular forces. Conflicts in this category have become increasingly common over the past century but vary significantly in their scope and meaning.

Conflicts between Religious Groups

The contesting of sacred space between adherents from different traditions has frequently arisen from traditional patterns of military conquest and imperial expansion. The destruction of sacred sites or their conversion into new places of worship for the invading force's religion has been a widely used strategy of conquest. To cite one example, in the century following the destruction of the Jewish Temple in Jerusalem in 70 CE, the emperor Hadrian established a new temple to Jupiter on the site as part of a policy aimed at the suppression of Judaism. Because they are so commonplace, such patterns in the contesting of sacred space have given rise to a variety of distinctive conflicts in specific contexts. One such conflict that has emerged over broad spatial and temporal scales has involved the control of Palestine, which contains sacred sites for Judaism, Christianity, and Islam. The Crusades represent one important manifestation of that conflict. Beginning in 1095, the Crusades comprised over two centuries of conflict between Christian Europe, with the strong encouragement of the papacy, and Muslim empires in southwest Asia. Many factors contributed to the Crusades, but the discourses disseminated by the Roman Catholic Church, starting with Pope Urban II at the end of the eleventh century, focused on three concerns relating to sacred space in the Christian Holy Land: the question of access for Christian pilgrims to the region's sacred sites, the possible desecration of the sites by Muslims, and the safety and freedom of Christians already living in the region.[69] Prior to the Crusades, the Holy Land of Christianity had in fact been ruled by Muslims for several centuries but without great hardship for pilgrims or threats to the sacred sites themselves. As a result, the Holy Land had become one of the major pilgrimage destinations for European Christians. Following the conquest of Jerusalem by the Turkish Seljuk Empire in the eleventh century, however, European Christians perceived a greater degree of threat to the Holy Land, especially since the Seljuks posed an increasing threat to the Orthodox Byzantine empire. The First Crusade (1095–1099), backed by papal promises of the remission of sins, succeeded in freeing Jerusalem from Muslim rule in 1099. As a consequence, Muslims then experienced the same concerns for their holy sites and pilgrims in Jerusalem, arguing that this portion of their sacred space should be liberated from the control of Christians. In 1143, Jerusalem returned to Muslim control and Europe's Second Crusade (1145–1149) failed to win it back. Despite further efforts continuing into the next century, the Holy Land remained largely under Muslim control into the twentieth century and pilgrimages to the region declined in number for several centuries.

In recent decades, the contesting of sacred spaces in Palestine has again become pronounced but now predominantly between Jews and Muslims, although some conflicts involving Christians have emerged as well. The contesting of sacred space by Jews and Muslims in the region must be considered within the broader context of the

Israeli-Palestinian political conflict. The concerns of these groups with the meanings and uses of sacred space go beyond political symbolism, however, focusing on basic issues of territorial control over places deemed to be of essential religious significance. The primary focus of conflict between Jews and Muslims has been the Temple Mount in the old city of Jerusalem. For Jews, this site represents the location of the two ancient Jerusalem temples established when Jewish kingdoms ruled the region. For Muslims, it represents al-Haram al-Sharif ("the Noble Sanctuary"), a sacred compound containing two key shrines: al-Aqsa Mosque, in Islamic tradition the second-oldest Abrahamic place of worship after the mosque in Mecca; and the Dome of the Rock, which houses the stone from which Muhammad ascended to heaven during his "night journey." Conflict over the site became most intense after the Six-Day War in 1967, when Israel took control of all of Jerusalem. Since then Israeli authorities have allowed the existing Muslim waqf or endowment to continue its traditional management of the sacred sanctuary atop the Temple Mount, although the site itself is under Israeli jurisdiction.

Under these circumstances, conflicts between fundamentalist Muslims and Jews have become increasingly pronounced as each side has asserted its claim to the site. Religious Zionists, who represent a branch of Jewish fundamentalism that sees the founding of the modern state of Israel as part of the divine redemption of the Jews, have repeatedly sought to reclaim control of the Temple Mount as part of that process of redemption. Extremists within the group plotted in the 1980s to destroy the Dome of the Rock and al-Aqsa Mosque, but were arrested by Israeli authorities before carrying out their plot. During the 1990s the Temple Mount Faithful, a major religious Zionist organization, repeatedly held demonstrations near the Temple Mount displaying a large block of stone, which they identified as the intended cornerstone of a new Jewish Temple to be built on top of the Temple Mount. Such efforts have in turn produced repeated protests and demonstrations by Muslims, who see the religious Zionists as a direct threat to preservation of the sacred shrines within al-Haram al-Sharif. Many such protests have led to conflicts with the Israeli police. In 2005 the religious Zionists developed a new plan of seeking to hold major rallies within al-Haram al-Sharif itself to promote their cause of reclaiming the site, a strategy that has again provoked major protests from Muslim Palestinians.[70]

Conflicts over sacred space in Israel have not been limited to the Temple Mount. A similar contesting of space has developed in the West Bank city of Hebron focusing on the Tomb of the Patriarchs. Jews and Muslims both consider the tomb to be a sacred site, the burial place of the biblical patriarchs Abraham, Isaac, and Jacob, and in most traditional accounts of their wives, Sarah, Rebecca, and Leah. Both Jews and Muslims consider these patriarchs to be important figures in their tradition's sacred history. For centuries a medieval Islamic structure, al-Ibrahimi Mosque, has been located over the cave in which the tomb itself is situated, and the site itself has been accessible primarily to Muslims. During the Six-Day War, however, Israel took control of Hebron. Religious Jews then began to settle in Hebron, demanding access to the holy site. Muslims have argued that their traditional control of the site gives them exclusive use of it, while Jews have insisted that they will not give up the right to worship there. The conflict became violent in 1994 when a lone Jewish settler killed twenty-nine Muslims praying at the site. Since that time, authorities have devised various means of separating Jewish and Muslim worshippers at the site, but the site itself remains contested.

The Six-Day War also initiated the contesting of space at a somewhat broader scale as well after Israel regained control of the West Bank, including the ancient regions of Judea and Samaria. Religious Zionists saw the occupation of these areas as part of the divine redemption of the Jews, a reshaping of the boundaries of Israel to conform more closely to those of the Jewish Promised Land. To maintain Jewish control over these areas, the religious Zionist organization Gush Emunim ("Bloc of the Faithful") initiated in the 1970s an extensive campaign of settlement in the West Bank. These areas do not have special sacred significance for Muslims in the region, so the contesting of this space has immediate religious connotations primarily for one side in the conflict. Nonetheless, the future of these Jewish settlements in the West Bank, and of the West Bank itself, remains a religiously charged issue within the broader Israeli-Palestinian conflict. Because religious Zionists see this territory as part of their sacred patrimony, they have been strongly opposed to any form of compromise regarding control of the settlements they have founded.[71]

Finally, although religious conflicts in this region have focused most prominently in recent years on disputes involving Jews and Muslims, Christian concerns regarding sacred space also continue to arise. As an example, in recent years a persistent conflict has developed concerning the use of space around the Basilica of the Annunciation, the sacred Christian site marking the announcement to Mary that she would bear the Son of God. Muslims in Nazareth have sought to build a mosque in a plaza adjacent to the basilica, with the mosque to be dedicated to a Muslim hero in the fight against the Crusades. Christians assert that the presence of the mosque will desecrate the sacred space of the basilica, while Muslims assert that mosque and basilica are compatible land uses since they too believe in the sanctity of the Annunciation. The Israeli government has ruled against construction of the mosque, however, demolishing a makeshift mosque erected in the plaza in 2003.[72]

As the above conflicts suggest, the contesting of sacred space can have significant political and historical dimensions even when couched in primarily religious terms. Another important example of this pattern has developed in India over the past fifty years in relation to a site contested by Hindus and Muslims in the northern Indian city of Ayodhya. The site in question for nearly five centuries was the location of a mosque dedicated to the Mughal ruler Babur, who ordered it built in the early 1500s. According to Hindu tradition, however, the mosque occupied the location of an older temple, one of many destroyed during the period of Mughal conquest. Hindus thus continued to worship at the site, which by tradition was identified with the birthplace of the Hindu deity Rama, hero of the *Ramayana* epic and an incarnation of Vishnu. At a local scale, Hindus and Muslims continued to contest the meaning and use of the site into the period of British colonial rule. Following Indian independence, however, Hindus became more aggressive in their demands for control of the site. To prevent violence, the government closed the site to both Hindus and Muslims in 1949.

The Babri Mosque again became the center of controversy in the 1980s, however, with the rising influence of a militant Hindu fundamentalist movement. Fundamentalists singled out control of the site in Ayodhya as a major concern both in real terms, in relation to their focus on the worship of Rama, and in symbolic terms, in relation to their desire to strengthen the role of Hinduism in the secular Indian state.

Fundamentalists demanded that the Babri Mosque be destroyed and that a major new temple to Rama be erected in its place as the mark of a new period of rule according to Hindu principles. After a series of massive demonstrations in Ayodhya, the fundamentalists themselves tore down the mosque in 1992, an action that provoked extensive communal violence across India. Since then, Hindu fundamentalists have been fabricating bricks, pillars, and other architectural elements needed to construct a new temple to Rama; and the fundamentalist Bharatiya Janata Party (BJP) and allied organizations have made the establishment of the temple on the site in Ayodhya a principal goal of their political agenda (photo 5.11). Even as the head of a ruling coalition in the Indian parliament from 1992 to 2004, however, the BJP was unable to get judicial approval for this action. The contesting of the meaning and use of the site in Ayodhya therefore persists. For conservative Hindus, the conflict involves concerns with the appropriate veneration of a site associated with a major religious hero and with the preservation of what they view as the essential Hindu character of Indian society. For the Muslim minority, on the other hand, the conflict raises issues about their status within Indian society while also setting a precedent for the possible destruction of other historic mosques across northern India. For both sides of the conflict, the potential outcomes are thus fraught with religious meaning.[73]

The examples discussed thus far have focused on cases in which competing groups have both defined a contested space as having significant sanctity for them. In

Photo 5.11.   Members of the Bajrang Dal, a Hindu youth organization, marching with a model of the temple to Rama proposed for construction in Ayodhya, part of a larger demonstration celebrating the anniversary of the destruction of Ayodhya's Babri Mosque in 1992. Bajrang Dal is one of a number of organizations that collectively make up the Sangh Parivar (''Family of Associations''), the institutional framework of Hindu fundamentalism, which also includes the Bharatiya Janata Party. Amritsar, India, 2006.

Source: Narinder Nanu/AFP/Getty Images.

such cases, both groups typically contest not only control of the site itself but also the ultimate meaning of the site as sacred space. In many instances, however, this symmetry of concerns regarding a contested space does not exist, usually because one group associates the space with a much greater degree of religious meaning than does the other. Such has been the case, for example, in the conflict in recent years over control of Kosovo, a region in southeastern Europe.[74] This conflict has its roots in the rise of Serbian nationalism between the twelfth and fourteenth centuries, a process strongly connected to the establishment early in the thirteenth century of an autonomous Serbian Orthodox Church, primarily centered in Kosovo. In Serbian culture, the region of Kosovo came to be regarded as the sacred hearth of Serbian Orthodoxy. The religious significance of Kosovo was reinforced in the fourteenth century, moreover, during the conquest of the Serbs by the expanding Ottoman Empire. The key event in that process was the defeat and death of the Serbian prince Lazar in the Battle of Kosovo in 1389. During the subsequent period of Ottoman rule over the Serbs, lasting into the nineteenth century, the Serbs came to interpret Lazar's defeat in mythic terms as analogous to the crucifixion of Christ, brought on in part by what they saw as the Judas-like betrayal of Lazar by Slavs siding with the Ottomans. More generally, they also viewed Kosovo as the site of their martyrdom as a people as they sought to halt the spread of Islam. These views strongly reinforced the sanctity of Kosovo in Serbian culture. The Serbs in effect came to see Kosovo as a national holy land that had to be reclaimed, a process which some Serbs compared to the resurrection of Christ. The creation of an independent Serbia in the late 1800s and again, after the fall of Yugoslavia, in the late 1900s led to sustained Serbian efforts to incorporate Kosovo into their national territory. The widespread migration of Albanian Muslims into Kosovo during the period of Ottoman rule complicated this process, however, as did the centuries-old animosity of the Serbs toward Muslims, particularly those of Slavic origin descended from converts following Ottoman conquest. Many Serbs believed that they had a religious obligation to take control of Kosovo and that this goal could only be achieved by weakening the presence of Muslims in the region. As a result, the Serbian government under Slobodan Milosevic carried out a campaign of ethnic cleansing and genocidal warfare against the Albanian Kosovars in the late 1990s, killing thousands of ethnic Albanians and destroying many of the region's mosques before NATO intervened. For the ethnic Albanians, the contested space of Kosovo did not have transcendent religious meaning; but for many Serbs the retaking of Kosovo represented the reclaiming of a crucial sacred space.

Conflicts within a Religious Tradition

Although believers consider their sacred spaces to be intrinsically and essentially holy, the character of any sacred space is subject to varied interpretations, as is the case with other elements of religions as cultural systems. Adherents of the same tradition may therefore develop conflicting understandings of a sacred space, based on differing interpretations of religious authority and experience. These differences may occur in relation to the meaning of a sacred space and the source of legitimacy on which its sanctity is based. Such differences often reflect divergences between centralized sources of authority and local religious practices, and thus in some cases between clergy and laity. Differences may also reflect contrasting ideas regarding the proper use of a sacred space in accordance with a particular authority. Such differences often arise over differing conceptions of orthodoxy and its role in religious practice. In all of these situations, the inherent contextuality of religions contributes to the contesting of sacred space.

Such conflicts have emerged in a number of settings within the Roman Catholic Church. Of particular significance in this context has been the recurring tension between local practice and centralized authority within the church. By the early medieval period, for example, the veneration of the shrines of local saints had proliferated widely within the church, often without official approval. For the laity, the sacred sites associated with local saints provided an immediate, concrete link to broader, more abstract conceptions within the Roman Catholic worldview and ethos. At the same time, however, these local sites often supported various expressions of heterodoxy, such as unapproved belief in a local saint's miracles or other local traditions concerning magic and the supernatural. To the Roman Catholic hierarchy, these local shrines therefore represented a challenge to doctrinal orthodoxy and the authority of the church. Throughout the medieval period, the Roman Catholic Church responded to this proliferation of local sacred spaces by placing greater ritual emphasis on the mass and by supporting a more universal devotion to Mary rather than to local saints, as discussed in chapter 3.

Over time, however, local shrines to Mary devoted to various apparitions perceived by adherents again came to challenge the centralized authority of the church hierarchy over sacred space. The church approved the authenticity of some such apparitions, such as the one at Lourdes that produced a major shrine there. The proliferation and heterodoxy of Marian apparitions since the mid-1800s, however, have led the church to withhold approval or actively condemn a number of such shrines. As an example, an unofficial shrine to Mary has developed in Bayside, New York, focusing on a series of visions purportedly experienced by a woman there between 1970 and 1994.[75] These visions included various messages typical of Marian apparitions, addressing issues of faith and prophesying future events. The Roman Catholic hierarchy condemned the visions as inauthentic and contrary to church doctrine and ordered that adherents should not visit or support the shrine. Adherents continue to visit the shrine nonetheless.

The same pattern has developed in more recent years with regard to the pilgrimage site at Medjugorje in Bosnia and Herzegovina. This site too arose around visions of Mary, first purportedly received by six young Croats in 1981 and over time by many other believers visiting the site. Again, the messages focused on faith and prophecy. Yugoslavia's Communist government sought to suppress the site during the 1980s, but its reputation as a contemporary sacred space continued to grow. In recent years Medjugorje has in fact become one of the most frequently visited Marian shrines in the world. As discussed above, it has also become a significant religious focus of Croatian nationalism. Nonetheless, the Roman Catholic Church has not approved the authenticity of the messages received at the site and it has forbidden church institutions from staging organized pilgrimages to the site. Many other unofficial pilgrimage sites devoted to Mary have developed despite the lack of support, or even active opposition, from the Roman Catholic hierarchy, a pattern that clearly reflects the contesting of religious legitimacy between formal institutions and lay believers.

Within Islam, conflicts focusing on religious authority and orthodoxy have developed in various contexts between members of the Wahhabi movement and other Muslims. The Wahhabis maintain an ethos of strict adherence to Islamic orthodoxy and opposition to any form of innovation, an ethos that has found expression in relation to sacred space in a number of ways. Since their origins in the 1700s, they have opposed the control of the holy cities of Mecca and Medina by rulers they deem to be religiously corrupt. Early in the nineteenth century, they rejected the right of the Ottoman Empire to rule over Mecca and Medina, a position based on their belief that the empire had deviated from true Islam and consequently had no religious legitimacy. They therefore joined with the Saud dynasty in its first attempt, only temporarily successful, to take control of the Hejaz and its holy cities. Early in twentieth century, the Wahhabis used the same discourse in supporting the Saudis' renewed effort to expand their kingdom into the Hejaz, in this instance challenging the religious legitimacy of Sharif Husayn, who had gained control over the Hejaz during World War I with backing from the British.

A further concern of the Wahhabis relating to sacred space focuses on their opposition to the creation or identification of spaces for the worship of anyone other than God. This concern arises from their strict interpretation of the absolute monotheism of Islam expressed in the Quran, the belief that there is no god but God. They have therefore opposed the popular transformation of the tombs of important religious figures into sites of veneration. In the expansion of the Saudi kingdom during the early 1800s, for example, the Saudis expanded northward into present-day Iraq, taking control of sites sacred to the Shiites. In the city of Karbala the Wahhabis destroyed the tomb of Husayn to prevent Shiites from worshipping there, based on the belief that the veneration of Husayn represented an unacceptable deviation from orthodox practice. They subsequently applied the same rationale to sacred sites in the Hejaz as Saudi control extended westward. The Wahhabis destroyed a number of Sunni tombs and shrines to local saints in the region, again arguing that these spaces violated Islamic orthodoxy. They also dismantled the sepulcher of Muhammad in Medina, asserting that its presence too promoted unorthodox patterns of devotion; and to reinforce this point, they sought to prevent Muslims who had performed the Hajj from traveling to Medina to worship at Muhammad's tomb. In Mecca, they further insisted on the removal of all ornamentation from the Kaaba. When the Saudis regained control of the Hejaz in the twentieth century, Wahhabi orthodoxy again became the rule within the sacred cities and indeed across Saudi Arabia; and from this base Wahhabism has spread widely to other Muslim societies. In addition, the Hajj itself has provided a mechanism for the diffusion of elements of Wahhabism through pilgrims exposed to its teaching in Mecca. As a result, Wahhabis in a variety of Muslim countries have sought to promote Islamic orthodoxy by discouraging practices such as worshipping at the tombs of local saints.[76] In most locations, however, such practices have continued through the strength of local custom.

Concerns among Muslims over the control of Mecca and Medina have produced more recent conflicts as well, but focusing on the legitimacy of the Saudi regime's stewardship of the holy sites, primarily because of its interactions with Western interests. During a failed rebellion in 1979, on the first day of the Islamic new year, more than four hundred members of a militant Saudi sect forcibly took over the Great Mosque of Mecca, also taking hundreds of worshippers hostage. These militants were members of a strict rejectionist sect that opposed participation in Saudi society and espoused belief in the coming of the Mahdi, apparently in the form of the group's leader, who would establish a pure Islamic state. Once in control of the mosque, the militants issued a manifesto rejecting the legitimacy of the rulers of Saudi Arabia as guardians of Islam's holy cities, decrying the erosion of traditional Islam in the country and demanding that the government eliminate the contaminating effects of Western influences on Saudi society. Portions of the mosque remained under the militants' control for two weeks, but Saudi forces eventually retook it and the government later executed the sect's leaders. Nonetheless, their contesting of sacred space remained an important symbolic event for other rejectionists and in the twenty-first century for more radical Islamic groups.[77]

In the following decades, the legitimacy of Saudi Arabia's stewardship of the sacred cities was again challenged, in this instance by Iran. This conflict arose in 1987 after Iranian pilgrims participating in the Hajj clashed with Saudi government forces during an Iranian demonstration against the United States, Israel, and the Soviet Union, all identified as enemies of Islam. The clash occurred when demonstrators tried to enter the Great Mosque, despite orders from the Saudi forces to remain out-side, resulting in the deaths of hundreds of Iranian pilgrims. The Iranian government strongly protested and Ayatollah Khomeini declared the Saudi ruling family unfit to govern Mecca and Medina, in part because of the violence but also in part because the Saudis had allowed a contaminating American presence within Saudi Arabia. Iran subsequently ceased diplomatic relations with Saudi Arabia and enforced an Iranian boycott of the Hajj for a number of years.[78]

Some of the objections of the Saudi Mahdists and of Iran to Saudi Arabia's control of the sacred cities have been echoed in more recent years, finally, by al-Qaeda in its discourse of violence against threats to Islam. The group's 1998 manifesto, "Jihad Against Jews and Crusaders," explicitly lists the American military presence in Saudi Arabia as one of the grievances underlying its campaign of violence, asserting that the presence of the United States in the Arabian Peninsula has polluted sacred Islamic territory and that all Muslims have the obligation to use violence to liberate the region's sacred sites from American influence.[79] In all three of these examples, then, Muslims have contested the status quo of Saudi responsibility for Mecca and Medina, arguing that the sacred hearth of Islam has been polluted because it has not been properly protected from external influences. These challenges to the status quo have focused, however, less on physical threats to Mecca and Medina, which remain inaccessible to non-Muslims, than on the moral authority of the Saudi government and perceptions of its adherence to genuine Islamic principles.

Somewhat different examples of conflict over the proper use of sacred space have developed among adherents of Judaism, again in reference to the Temple Mount. The haredim, or ultra-Orthodox Jews, have three primary concerns with Jewish use of the Temple Mount, all focusing on preventing desecration of the site through improper actions. First, they strongly oppose any efforts, such as those of religious Zionists, to take control of the Temple Mount or even to enter the space on top of it occupied by al-Haram al-Sharif. To the haredim, such an attempt would challenge the view of sacred history inherent in their worldview. They believe that the sacred space of the Temple Mount will be returned to full Jewish control through divine intervention rather than human action. As a result, efforts by believers to reclaim the site would represent heretical intrusions on divine authority.

The haredim secondly oppose the entry of any Jews into the sacred space atop the Temple Mount for fear that the latter would inadvertently desecrate the space, now unidentified, occupied by the Holy of Holies during the period of Temple Judaism. The haredim believe that the strict ritual and spiritual preparations required to enter in the Holy of Holies according to Jewish law are no longer available. According to tradition, these preparations require water of purification containing ashes from the sacrifice of an unblemished red heifer, none of which are now known to exist. Concern over contamination of the Holy of Holies, it should be noted, is not limited to the haredim. The Chief Rabbinate of Israel has in fact prohibited Jews from having access to the top of the Temple to prevent contamination of the space that once housed the Ark of the Covenant. Some religious Zionist rabbis have argued against this ban, however, as long as believers take the proper precautions, including ritual purification and avoidance of areas thought to lie within the boundaries of the ancient Temple. Religious Zionists have argued in favor of access to the site to advance Jewish control of the Temple Mount as a whole.[80]

Finally, the haredim also have strong concerns with proper religious behavior at the Western Wall along the western side of the Temple Mount. As a major Jewish sacred site, the Western Wall attracts Jewish pilgrims from diverse origins, including many Reform and Conservative Jews whose religious systems do not maintain many of the traditions to which Orthodox and ultra-Orthodox Jews adhere. One such tradition is the insistence on gender segregation in public spaces, a tradition that the haredim believe to be particularly important within the contexts of sacred space. The haredim have therefore insisted on the physical separation of men and women at the Western Wall. They further insist, based on tradition, that within this sacred space women's voices must remain inaudible to men engaged in prayer and that women may not read aloud from the Torah or wear prayer shawls. Reform and Conservative Jews visiting the site have often rejected these restrictions on women, asserting that they should have the right to worship at the Western Wall in ways consistent with their own interpretations of Judaism. Their efforts to do so have resulted in demonstrations by the haredim, however, who insist that those who do not observe traditional practices are desecrating the sacred space of the Western Wall. Israel's courts have generally supported the haredi position. In 2003, for example, the Supreme Court upheld the ban on women reading from the Torah at the Western Wall and recommended an alternative worship site for women who chose not to adhere to traditional practice.[81]

Conflicts between Religious and Secular Groups

With the growth of secularist states and social perspectives during the modern era, conflicts over the meanings and uses of sacred space have increasingly pitted the interests of religious adherents against those of secular institutions or groups. In extreme instances, such conflicts have developed through the deliberate efforts of states to suppress the use of particular sacred sites, usually because the state construes the actions of a religious group as a threat to social unity or stability. Such a pattern developed in

Yugoslavia in relation to the abovementioned Medjugorje pilgrimage space, for example, as the country's socialist government originally sought to suppress activity at the site. The government's antagonism toward the Medjugorje apparition derived in part from the official promotion of atheism but also reflected official concern that the shrine would weaken the state by supporting the strengthening of nationalism among the country's Croatian minority.

A more extensive and destructive example of government suppression of religion occurred in Tibet following its invasion and annexation by China in the 1950s. In seeking to maintain control in Tibet, the government has vigorously suppressed Buddhism as a competing source of authority. In the process, the Chinese government has closed, damaged, or destroyed thousands of Tibetan Buddhist sacred spaces, including temples, monasteries, and other shrines. The devastation of these sacred sites became particularly intense in the late 1960s and early 1970s during China's Cultural Revolution, a brutal campaign aimed at eradicating traditional cultures and customs, as well as non-Maoist intellectual trends, from Chinese society. The desecration during this period of Tibet's preeminent Buddhist structure, the Jokhang Temple, included converting portions of it to house Chinese soldiers and farm animals.[82] The government also destroyed the monasteries and shrines associated with Mount Kailas, one of the most important pilgrimage sites in the region. In more recent years, the Chinese government has provided funding to restore some of the damaged sites, primarily to foster tourism. Nonetheless, it has also asserted administrative control over most Tibetan monasteries and has recently closed some that have been centers of Buddhist resistance to Chinese rule.[83] In recent years the government has also limited access to temples and monasteries by lay adherents, particularly those who are employed by the state.

As a final example of government suppression, the pattern of intentional abuses of sacred space was even more pronounced in Cambodia during the 1970s under the Maoist Khmer Rouge. The primary tragedy of that period was the massive destruction of life as the Khmer Rouge murdered more than 1.5 million Cambodians, including members of various religious groups, intellectuals, homosexuals, and other perceived enemies. In the process, the regime eliminated a fifth of the Buddhist population and tens of thousands of Buddhist monks and nuns. Most other monks and nuns were forced to abandon their monastic life and adopt a secular life. In addition, the campaign of violence carried out by the Khmer Rouge also destroyed most of the country's monastic communities and a majority of its Buddhist temples.

Conflicts between religious and secular groups over sacred space have not been as violent or destructive in most other contexts, however. Many such conflicts have developed not because secular forces seek to eliminate sacred space as a threat but rather because religious and secular groups value a particular space for different reasons, usually based on significant contrasts in worldview and ethos. This type of pattern has developed in many parts of the world, for example, where indigenous peoples have been displaced from lands that they traditionally occupied. That process of displacement has often resulted in subsequent threats to sites that the group considers sacred, typically resulting from the intrusion of incompatible land uses. For example, the Black Hills of South Dakota have traditionally been an important sacred place for a number of Plains Indian tribes in the United States, as mentioned earlier in the chapter. The sanctity of this region has repeatedly been threatened, however, by external secular forces and especially by economic interests seeking to exploit the region. The discovery of gold in the 1870s brought a significant influx of European Americans, contrary to earlier treaty agreements; and despite the subsequent Native American victory at the Battle of Little Big Horn, external economic interests became entrenched in the area. In more recent years, the primary concern of tribal groups has been tourist development, particularly in reference to the expansion of tourist destinations like casinos outside of areas that have already undergone development.

Similar conflicts have developed in many other parts of the United States. One such conflict has focused on Devils Tower National Monument in Wyoming, a site considered sacred by a variety of Native American tribes who have inhabited that region. Native Americans have objected to the use of Devils Tower for recreational climbing, particularly when it interfered with their tribal religious ceremonies. In 1995 the National Park Service thus ruled that recreational climbing was to be discouraged during the month of June to allow for undisturbed religious activities on the sacred site, a ruling later upheld in the courts. More recently, a similar conflict has emerged in the southwestern United States over use of the San Francisco Peaks north of Flagstaff, Arizona, which the Navajo identify as their sacred mountain of the west, one of the defining points in their cosmos. The Navajo have for decades objected to the commercial use of the peaks for skiing, but had failed in a number of court cases to prevent this activity since the peaks lie outside of their reservation. In 2005 they renewed their claim that the sacred site was being desecrated, however, after the U.S. Forest Service approved the expansion of a commercial ski site on the peaks involving the generation of artificial snow through the use of recycled sewage water. To the Navajo this project would be an unacceptable desecration of one of their most sacred spaces. Although the Navajo lost their original suit attempting to block the project, they won their case on appeal in 2007.[84]

Conflicts between adherents and secular interests may also focus on more commonplace sacred spaces. To cite a widespread instance, believers in many different religious contexts have sought to protect the sanctity of cemeteries, tombs, and other burial places from sources of desecration. This concern represents a recurring source of contention between the haredim and secular Israeli society, for example. The haredim insist on the absolute sanctity of Jewish gravesites, no matter how old, based on orthodox beliefs that the dead should be allowed to rest in peace and that the body must remain intact until the final resurrection of the dead at the end of sacred history. These beliefs in effect sanctify gravesites and cemeteries, making them spaces of obligation for the living, who are responsible for their care. At the same time, these beliefs have placed haredi Jews in conflict with Israeli society in various ways. The haredim have strongly opposed the excavation of archaeological sites containing ancient graves, even though Israeli law requires that Israel's Department of Religious Affairs promptly reinter excavated remains. As a result, many Israeli archaeologists in turn view haredi opposition as a threat to their field of study. The haredim have also opposed a large number of road building and construction projects that in their view risk the desecration of ancient cemeteries or gravesites. They have repeatedly expressed their opposition to such projects through forceful and in some cases violent demonstrations, for example by blocking traffic or interfering with construction.

Indigenous peoples in various places have similarly sought protection for gravesites as sacred spaces, again seeking protection from both archaeological projects and miscellaneous secular sources such as land development. In the United States, support for Native American concerns regarding this issue led to passage of the Native American Graves Protection and Repatriation Act by the U.S. Congress in 1990. This act requires federal agencies and all institutions receiving federal funding to return human remains and other artifacts taken from gravesites to the appropriate tribal group if so requested. Comparable restrictions on private organizations, such as corporations, land developers, and local governments, do not exist, however. Conflicts over the disposition of Native American gravesites have thus occurred in locations across the country.

Finally, the concerns of religious groups with defending sacred space from secular influences can develop around issues of cultural politics. Such conflicts arise when a secular group seeks to use sacred space to advance its own cultural agenda but in the process offends adherents who consider that agenda to be incompatible with the sacred space in question. In some ways this type of conflict mirrors conflicts in which religious adherents seek to insert religious meanings into spaces that others consider to be purely secular, as in the erection of Christmas nativity scenes in front of public buildings in the United States. In both types of conflict, groups seek to use the meaning of space to legitimize and actualize their beliefs. The two types of conflict typically differ, however, in the specific objectives adopted by the offending group. Religious groups seeking to give religious meaning to secular space typically do so to promote their understanding of the status quo in which their group predominates. Secular groups making use of sacred space to promote their agenda, on the other hand, frequently do so as an explicit form of transgression, in which their departure from normal practices concerning a sacred space draws attention to the significance and implications of their message. At the same time, however, this strategy of transgression provokes greater opposition from believers seeking to defend the sacred space at issue.

Recent instances of this type of conflict have developed, for example, in response to efforts by gay and lesbian organizations to hold events in locations considered sacred by a religious group. Organizers of World Pride, an international gay festival, met with vigorous opposition from the Roman Catholic Church after selecting Rome as the event's location for the year 2000. Those staging the event intentionally chose Rome as a provocative location as a means of publicizing their message. The Roman Catholic hierarchy countered by arguing that Rome, as a sacred city, should not be the site of an event celebrating behavior that the church considered to be sinful. The Vatican objected more specifically to plans for the event's gay pride parade to run adjacent to the Colosseum, a site of particular sanctity because of the large number of Christians martyred there in ancient Rome. In the Vatican's view, the parade would desecrate this important sacred space. Church leaders further objected to the scheduling of the event during the Great Jubilee of 2000, a holy year celebrating religious commitment and divine forgiveness. City officials thus denied the organizers permission to march past the Colosseum, although many participants did so nonetheless. Pope John Paul II himself subsequently expressed anger at these events, asserting that the festival represented an attack on Christian values.[85]

A similar controversy arose in 2005 when World Pride organizers sought to hold their event in Jerusalem. In this case, however, the proposed event drew strong criticism from the city's Haredi Jewish community and from a number of different religious leaders and groups as well, including the two Chief Rabbis of Israel, the Vatican ambassador, the Greek Orthodox and Armenian Orthodox churches, and conservative Muslim clerics, all of whom considered the event to be a threat to the sanctity of Jerusalem. Israeli authorities also were concerned about diverting police resources to the event to prevent possible violence against the parade and thus cancelled the event for 2005. Organizers hoped that with additional planning the parade could be staged in Jerusalem in the following year, but authorities again banned the event in 2006. Organizers finally succeeded in staging the parade in 2007, with the police significantly outnumbering the participants.[86]

*   *   *

In all of the conflicts discussed above, the sacred spaces in question hold great meaning for believers. In part the significance of such spaces is symbolic. The meanings and uses of sacred space reflect important issues of religious authority, legitimacy, and orthodoxy. A religious group's territorial control over its sacred spaces is a crucial symbolic expression of the authority of its religious system, while loss of control connotes a weakening of that authority. Similarly, a religious group's insistence on the proper treatment of its sacred space signifies in more general terms the insistence that others acknowledge the legitimacy of that group's religious system. And articulation of the ways in which sacred space can be properly used provides an important means for representing the group's understanding of orthodoxy and obligation. At the same time, however, conflicts over sacred space are not only of symbolic importance. For adherents engaged in these conflicts, the sacred spaces in question are crucial expressions of the fundamental worldview and ethos that they enact in everyday life. These spaces represent real, tangible manifestations of religious truth, serving as the means through which superhuman influences and forces are grounded in the world of human experience. For religious adherents the defense of these sacred spaces therefore frequently takes on a genuine and profound sense of urgency. The loss of such spaces is not merely an abstraction but rather a direct challenge to the lived faith of a religious system. The protection of such spaces, conversely, represents the fulfillment of an essential religious obligation.

Conclusions

The various examples discussed in this chapter illustrate the diversity of phenomena encompassed by the concept of sacred space. Again, most scholars no longer hold the view that expressions of sacred space derive from a universal archetype intrinsic to all religious traditions. Sacred space instead represents a distinct but varied manifestation of more general human concerns with the organization and interpretation of space. Nonetheless, the examples presented in this chapter demonstrate that spatial representations of religious significance, both real and imagined, are a crucial element of religions as cultural systems. Adherents use conceptions of sacred space in part to define and understand the basic structure of their worldview. They see sacred space as a naturalized part of the world around them, linked not only to symbolic meanings but to the actual workings of the universe as well. Sacred space comprises the primary centers of power in the cosmos as believers know it, where the divine or the superhuman is manifested most clearly. It likewise encompasses the places of greatest significance in the unfolding of a religious group's sacred history, including the sites of formative events in the origins of their religious system along with the imagined places that will persist beyond the end of history. Adherents further relate sacred space to their religious ethos, to the particular beliefs and emotions that they enact in living their religion. In this regard, sacred space helps to define significant elements of the structure of adherents' lives, both within the context of everyday routine and in relation to less ordinary events, such as a pilgrimage or a rite of passage. Through such processes, sacred space in effect connects the human to the superhuman. It provides settings where adherents can actively relate their own concerns to their larger religious universe through acts of worship, ritual, or obligation. Although conceptions of sacred space have taken many different forms, in sum, at a fundamental level they reflect a degree of commonality among the spatial imaginations of diverse religious groups.

Because of its centrality as an element of religion systems, however, sacred space has also been a recurrent focus of religious, social, and political conflict. The profound meanings of particular sacred spaces compel adherents to defend them against external influences or sources of desecration. The contesting of sacred space often arises, for example, from believers' conviction that a particular space represents a crucial feature of their sacred history or identity and that possession or control of the space is therefore necessary for the group to maintain its own integrity as a sacred community. In other cases, conflicts involving sacred space have focused on more practical issues such as physical access to specific sacred sites, especially in situations where access to a specific site is essential to the performance of a particular religious rite or custom. Whatever the source of the conflict, however, disputes over sacred space generally differ in a crucial way from more worldly disputes over secular space because the former involve the contesting of spaces perceived, by at least one of the groups involved, to possess absolute significance through their transcendent meaning and power. Believers view the spaces involved not merely as pieces of territory but as repositories of truth, authority, and legitimacy. Because they hold such views, believers are likely to oppose any form of compromise in conflicts over sacred space, often making such conflicts quite resistant to resolution. Again, compromise would result in the yielding not only of territory but of religious authenticity as well.

In the varied ways addressed in this chapter, then, the importance that believers place on sacred space reflects both the contextuality and the spatiality of religions. The meanings and behaviors associated with specific sacred places vary considerably among different contexts, and even among adherents of the same tradition. Within those diverse contexts, however, conceptions of sacred space in all of their diverse forms are central to the manner in which believers understand and enact a religious system.

Notes

1. Mircea Eliade, *The Sacred and the Profane* (New York: Harcourt & Brace, 1959), 20.
2. Eliade, *The Sacred and the Profane*, 20–65, provides a classic examination of sacred space from the traditional perspective of comparative religion; for a critique of the comparative method, see N. Ross Reat, "Insiders and Outsiders in the Study of Religious Traditions," *Journal of the American Academy of Religion* 51, no. 3 (September 1983): 459–76; for a reassessment

of comparative approaches, see Kimberly C. Patton and Benjamin C. Ray, eds., *A Magic Still Dwells: Comparative Religion in the Postmodern Age* (Berkeley: University of California Press, 2000).

3. An influential examination of the relationship between ritual and space appears in Jonathan Z. Smith, *To Take Place: Toward Theory in Ritual* (Chicago: University of Chicago Press, 1987).

4. Yi-Fu Tuan, *Topophilia: A Study of Environmental Perception, Attitudes, and Values* (Englewood Cliffs, N.J.: Prentice-Hall, 1974), 40–41.

5. J. Edward Wright, *The Early History of Heaven* (New York: Oxford University Press, 2000), 85–88.

6. Alice K. Turner, *The History of Hell* (New York: Harcourt Brace and Co., 1993).

7. For an analysis of the development of this concept, see Frank J. Korom, "Of Navels and Mountains: A Further Inquiry into the History of an Idea," *Asian Folklore Studies* 51, no. 1 (1992): 103–25.

8. Brian S. Bauer, *The Sacred Landscape of the Inca: The Cusco Ceque System* (Austin: University of Texas Press, 1998).

9. Gwyn Rowley, "The Land of Israel: A Reconstructionist Approach," in *The Impact of Gush Emunim: Politics and Settlement in the West Bank*, ed. David Newman (London: Croom Helm, 1985), 125–36; Arie Morgenstern, *Hastening Redemption: Messianism and the Resettlement of the Land of Israel* (New York: Oxford University Press, 2006); regarding the complexity of Jewish views concerning Eretz Yisrael, see Yosseph Shilhav, "Religious Factors in Territorial Disputes: An Intra-Jewish View," *GeoJournal* 53, no. 3 (March 2001): 247–59.

10. Stephen C. Jett, "The Navajo Homeland," in *Homelands: A Geography of Culture and Place across America*, ed. Richard L. Nostrand and Lawrence E. Estaville (Baltimore: Johns Hopkins University Press, 2001), 173; Klara Bonsack Kelley and Harris Francis, *Navajo Sacred Places* (Bloomington: Indiana University Press, 1994), 20–21.

11. Vinayak Damodar Savarkar, *Hindutva: Who Is a Hindu?* (New Delhi: Hindi Sahitya Sadan, 2003); Jyotirmay Sharma, *Hindutva: Exploring the Idea of Hindu Nationalism* (New Delhi: Viking, 2003).

12. Roger W. Stump, *Boundaries of Faith: Geographical Perspectives on Religious Fundamentalism* (Lanham, Md.: Rowman and Littlefield, 2000), 196.

13. John Guy, "The Mahabodhi Temple: Pilgrim Souvenirs of Buddhist India," *The Burlington Magazine* 133 (June 1991): 356–67.

14. For a general survey of sacred mountains in different traditions, see Edwin Bernbaum, *Sacred Mountains of the World* (Berkeley: University of California Press, 1998).

15. J. L. Brockington, *The Sacred Thread*, 2d ed. (Edinburgh: Edinburgh University Press, 1996), 200; David R. Kinsley, *Hindu Goddesses: Visions of the Divine Feminine in the Hindu Religious Tradition* (Berkeley: University of California Press, 1986), 187–96.

16. Norbert C. Brockman, *Encyclopedia of Sacred Places* (Santa Barbara, Cal.: ABC-CLIO, 1997), 190.

17. Mircea Eliade, *A History of Religious Ideas*, 3 vols. (Chicago: University of Chicago Press, 1978–1985), I:129–31.

18. Mary Lee Nolan and Sidney Nolan, *Christian Pilgrimage in Modern Western Europe* (Chapel Hill: University of North Carolina Press, 1989), 307.

19. Gisbert Rinschede, "The Pilgrimage Town of Lourdes," *Journal of Cultural Geography* 7, no. 1 (1986): 21–34.

20. Lee I. Levine, ed., *Jerusalem: Its Sanctity and Centrality to Judaism, Christianity, and Islam* (New York: Continuum, 1999).

21. The Quran (17: 1) mentions Muhammad's night journey but the details of the story derive from the hadith; see J. R. Porter, "Muhammad's Journey to Heaven," *Numen* 21, no. 1 (April 1974): 64–80.

22. Stuart Charmé, "The Political Transformation of Gender Traditions at the Western Wall in Jerusalem," *Journal of Feminist Studies in Religion* 21, no. 1 (Spring 2005): 9–10.

23. Jonathan P. Parry, *Death in Banaras* (New York: Cambridge University Press, 1994).

24. Hiroshi Tanaka, "Landscape Expression of the Evolution of Buddhism in Japan," *Canadian Geographer* 28, no. 3 (1984): 240–57.

25. Such cities characterize the "communal" form of prophetic-healing churches as discussed in H. W. Turner, "A Typology for African Religious Movements," *Journal of Religion in Africa* 1, no. 1 (1967): 32–33.

26. Peter Bishop, "Reading the Potala," in *Sacred Spaces and Powerful Places in Tibetan Culture*, ed. Toni Huber (Dharamsala, India: Library of Tibetan Works and Archives, 1999), 376–85.

27. D. A. Brading, *Mexican Phoenix: Our Lady of Guadalupe: Image and Tradition across Five Centuries* (New York: Cambridge University Press, 2001); Patricia Harrington, "Mother of Death, Mother of Rebirth: The Mexican Virgin of Guadalupe," *Journal of the American Academy of Religion* 56, no. 1 (Spring 1988): 25–50.

28. Surinder Mohan Bhardwaj, *Hindu Places of Pilgrimage in India: A Study in Cultural Geography* (Berkeley: University of California Press, 1973), 80–96; Diana L. Eck, "India's Tirthas: 'Crossings' in Sacred Geography," *History of Religions* 20, no. 4 (May 1981): 323–44.

29. Kinsley, *Hindu Goddesses*, 184–87; Bhardwaj, *Hindu Places of Pilgrimage*, 99.

30. David B. Miller, "Legends of the Icon of Our Lady of Vladimir: A Study of the Development of Muscovite National Consciousness," *Speculum* 43, no. 4 (October 1968): 657–70; on sacred space and Russian icons generally, see Oleg Tarasov, *Icon and Devotion: Sacred Spaces in Imperial Russia*, trans. and ed. Robin Milner-Gulland (London: Reaktion Books, 2002).

31. Dan Martin, "Pearls from Bones: Relics, Chortens, Tertons and the Signs of Saintly Death in Tibet," *Numen* 41, no. 3 (September 1994): 273–324; John Strong, *Relics of the Buddha* (Princeton, N.J.: Princeton University Press, 2004).

32. For a classic case study of this pattern, see Dale F. Eickelman, *Moroccan Islam: Tradition and Society in a Pilgrimage Center* (Austin: University of Texas Press, 1976).

33. Sheila Tefft, "Thai Spirit Houses," *Christian Science Monitor*, August 30, 1991, 13.

34. For detailed treatments of the complexities of Hindu temple form and meaning, including its regional stylistic variations, see R. Champaalakshmi, *The Hindu Temple* (New Delhi: Roli Books, 2001); George Michell, *The Hindu Temple: An Introduction to Its Meaning and Forms* (London: Elek, 1977).

35. A detailed examination of such variations in reference to the mosque appears in Martin Frishman and Hasan-Uddin Khan, eds., *The Mosque: History, Architectural Development and Regional Diversity* (New York: Thames and Hudson, 2002).

36. See, for example, Laurence Hull Stookey, "The Gothic Cathedral as the Heavenly Jerusalem: Liturgical and Theological Sources," *Gesta* 8, no. 1 (1969): 35–41.

37. Among such groups the nature of church architecture has varied over time, however, in association with changes in religious ideology, as examined in reference to Mennonites in the United States in Charles Heatwole, "Sectarian Ideology and Church Architecture," *Geographical Review* 79, no. 1 (January 1989): 63–78.

38. Seth Daniel Kunin, *God's Place in the World: Sacred Space and Sacred Place in Judaism* (New York: Cassell, 1998), 11–63; Steven Fine, *This Holy Place: On the Sanctity of the Synagogue during the Greco-Roman Period* (Notre Dame, Ind.: University of Notre Dame Press, 1997).

39. Annemarie Schimmel, *Deciphering the Signs of God: A Phenomenological Approach to Islam* (Albany: State University of New York Press, 1994), 52.

40. Masoud Kheirabadi, *Iranian Cities: Formation and Development* (Austin: University of Texas Press, 1991), 62–84.

41. For Roman Catholic examples, see Joseph Sciorra, "Religious Processions in Italian Williamsburg," *The Drama Review: TDR* 29, no. 3 (Autumn 1985): 65–81.

42. See chapter 2, part VI in John Calvin, *Golden Booklet of the True Christian Life* (Grand Rapids, Mich.: Baker Books, 1952), 37–38.

43. Arthur Green, "The Zaddiq as Axis Mundi in Later Judaism," *Journal of the American Academy of Religion* 45, no. 3 (September 1977): 327–47.

44. For a survey of this topic, see Sarah Coakley, ed., *Religion and the Body* (New York: Cambridge University Press, 1997).

45. Theodore W. Jennings, "On Ritual Knowledge," *The Journal of Religion* 62, no. 2 (April 1982), 115–16.

46. See, for example, Maureen Flynn, "The Spiritual Uses of Pain in Spanish Mysticism," *Journal of the American Academy of Religion* 64, no. 2 (Summer 1996): 257–78.

47. Dolores Hayden, *Seven American Utopias: The Architecture of Communitarian Socialism, 1790–1975* (Cambridge, Mass.: MIT Press, 1976), 71.

48. Simon Coleman and John Elsner, *Pilgrimage: Past and Present in the World Religions* (Cambridge, Mass.: Harvard University Press, 1995), 196–98; Surinder M. Bhardwaj, "Geography and Pilgrimage: A Review," in *Sacred Places, Sacred Spaces: The Geography of Pilgrimages*, ed. Robert H. Stoddard and Alan Morinis (Baton Rouge: Geoscience Publications, Dept. of Geography and Anthropology, Louisiana State University, 1997), 1–23; Robert H. Stoddard, "Defining and Classifying Pilgrimages," in *Sacred Places, Sacred Spaces*, ed. Stoddard and Morinis, 41–60.

49. Stoddard, "Defining and Classifying Pilgrimages," 52–53.

50. Wilbert M. Gesler, *Healing Places* (Lanham, Md.: Rowman and Littlefield, 2003), 21–42.

51. Gesler, *Healing Places*, 65–82.

52. Alex Weingrod, "Saints and Shrines, Politics, and Culture: A Morocco–Israel Comparison," in *Muslim Travelers: Pilgrimage, Migration, and the Religious Imagination*, ed. Dale F. Eickelman and James Piscatori (Berkeley: University of California Press, 1990), 217–35.

53. Isabel Hilton, *The Search for the Panchen Lama* (New York: W.W. Norton, 2000), 39–40 and passim.

54. The various meanings of the Western Wall for believers are addressed in Mordecai Roshwald, "The Wall of Communication," *Judaism* 35, no. 4 (Fall 1986): 483–86.

55. In recent times, psychiatrists have identified delusional manifestations arising from this intense sense of awe in the presence of sacred space as the Jerusalem syndrome; see Yair Bar-El, Rimona Durst, Gregory Katz, Josef Zislin, Ziva Strauss, and Haim Y. Knobler, "Jerusalem Syndrome," *British Journal of Psychiatry* 176 (January 2000): 86–90.

56. Rehav Rubin, "One City, Different Views: A Comparative Study of Three Pilgrimage Maps of Jerusalem," *Journal of Historical Geography* 32, no. 2 (April 2006): 267–90; Noga Collins-Kreiner, "Cartographic Characteristics of Current Christian Pilgrimage Maps of the Holy Land," *Cartographica* 34, no. 4 (Winter 1997): 45–54.

57. On pilgrimage to natural sites, see William Cronon, "The Trouble with Wilderness; or, Getting Back to the Wrong Nature," in *Uncommon Ground: Toward Reinventing Nature*, ed. William Cronon (New York: W.W. Norton and Co., 1995), 69–90; Lynn Huntsinger and María Fernández-Giménez, "Spiritual Pilgrims at Mount Shasta, California," *Geographical Review* 90, no. 4 (October 2000): 536–58; on Neo-Pagan pilgrimage, see Jenny Blain and Robert J. Wallis, "Sacred Sites, Contested Rites/Rights," *Journal of Material Culture* 9, no. 3 (November 2004): 237–61; Kathryn Rountree, "Performing the Divine: Neo-Pagan Pilgrimages and Embodiment at Sacred Sites," *Body and Society* 12, no. 4 (December 2006): 95–115.

58. Coleman and Elsner, *Pilgrimage*, 61.

59. Surinder M. Bhardwaj, "Non-Hajj Pilgrimage in Islam: A Neglected Dimension of Religious Circulation," *Journal of Cultural Geography* 17, no. 2 (Spring/Summer 1998): 69–88.

60. Hiroshi Tanaka, "Geographic Expression of Buddhist Pilgrim Places on Shikoku Island, Japan," *Canadian Geographer* 21, no. 2 (1977): 111–32.

61. Brockman, *Encyclopedia of Sacred Places*, 191–93.

62. On Our Lady of Guadalupe, see Victor Turner and Edith Turner, *Image and Pilgrimage in Christian Culture: Anthropological Perspectives* (New York: Columbia University Press, 1978), 40–103; on Medjugorje and Croatian nationalism, see Zlatko Skrbi, "The Apparitions of the Virgin Mary of Medjugorje: The Convergence of Croatian Nationalism and Her Apparitions," *Nations and Nationalism* 11, no. 3 (2005): 443–461; on the pilgrimage in the Goddess move-

ment, see Kathryn Rountree, "Goddess Pilgrims as Tourists: Inscribing the Body through Sacred Travel," *Sociology of Religion* 63, no. 4 (Winter 2002): 475–96.

63. A comprehensive examination of the character and development of the Hajj appears in F. E. Peters, *The Hajj: The Muslim Pilgrimage to Mecca and the Holy Places* (Princeton, N.J.: Princeton University Press, 1994); for a historical survey of literary accounts of the Hajj by pilgrims, see Michael Wolfe, *One Thousand Roads to Mecca: Ten Centuries of Travelers Writing about the Muslim Pilgrimage* (New York: Grove Press, 1997); on the centripetal effects of the Hajj on the Islamic community, see Gwyn Rowley, "The Centrality of Islam: Space, Form and Process," *GeoJournal* 18, no. 4 (June 1989): 351–59.

64. Ann Parker and Avon Neal , *Hajj Paintings: Folk Art of the Great Pilgrimage* (Washington, D.C.: Smithsonian Institution Press, 1995).

65. Conrad Rudolph, *Pilgrimage to the End of the World: The Road to Santiago de Compostela* (Chicago: University of Chicago Press, 2004).

66. For case studies from various traditions, see Ellen Badone and Sharon R. Roseman, eds., *Intersecting Journeys: The Anthropology of Pilgrimage and Tourism* (Urbana: University of Illinois Press, 2004); Dallen J. Timothy and Daniel H. Olsen, *Tourism, Religion and Spiritual Journeys* (London: Routledge, 2006).

67. A survey of this motif appears in Paul Binski, *Medieval Death: Ritual and Representation* (Ithaca, N.Y.: Cornell University Press, 1996), 33–47.

68. W. Y. Evans-Wentz, ed., *The Tibetan Book of the Dead* (New York: Oxford University Press, 2000).

69. On the social and economic factors underlying the Crusades, see Marcus Bull, "Origins," in *The Oxford Illustrated History of the Crusades*, ed. Jonathan Riley-Smith (New York: Oxford University Press, 1995), 13–33.

70. On the general conflict over the Temple Mount, see Stump, *Boundaries of Faith*, 159–66; regarding more recent discord, see "Palestinians Say Jerusalem Holy Site 'Stormed' by Israeli 'Extremists,'" *BBC Monitoring Middle East–Political*, October 19, 2005, *LexisNexis Academic* (accessed July 24, 2007); "Attempt by 'Jewish Extremists' to Storm Al-Aqsa Mosque Reportedly Foiled," *BBC Monitoring Middle East–Political*, August 4, 2006, *LexisNexis Academic* (accessed July 24, 2007).

71. Stump, *Boundaries of Faith*, 167–68.

72. Greg Myre, "In a Christian-Muslim Dispute, Israel Blocks a New Mosque," *New York Times*, July 2, 2003, 8(A).

73. Stump, *Boundaries of Faith*, 168–72.

74. Michael A. Sells, *The Bridge Betrayed: Religion and Genocide in Bosnia* (Berkeley: University of California Press, 1996), 37–69; Laura Silber and Allan Little, *The Death of Yugoslavia* (New York: Penguin Books, 1996), 72; Thomas A. Emmert, *Serbian Golgotha: Kosovo, 1389*, East European Monographs Series, no. 278 (New York: Columbia University Press, 1990).

75. Michael W. Cuneo, *The Smoke of Satan: Conservative and Traditionalist Dissent in Contemporary American Catholicism* (New York: Oxford University Press, 1997), 152–77.

76. Cf. the interactions between Wahhabism and various expressions of African Islam discussed in David Westerlund and Eva Evers Rosander, eds., *African Islam and Islam in Africa: Encounters between Sufis and Islamists* (Athens: Ohio University Press, 1997).

77. Thomas Hegghammer and Stéphane Lacroix, "Rejectionist Islamism in Saudi Arabia: The Story of Juhayman al-'Utaybi Revisited," *International Journal of Middle East Studies* 39, no. 1 (February 2007): 103–22.

78. Stump, *Boundaries of Faith*, 173–74.

79. World Islamic Front, *Jihad Against Jews and Crusaders*, www.fas.org/irp/world/para/docs/980223-fatwa.htm (accessed December 4, 2006).

80. Motti Inbari, "Religious Zionism and the Temple Mount Dilemma–Key Trends," *Israel Studies* 12, no. 2 (Summer 2007): 29–47.

81. Charmé, "Political Transformation of Gender Traditions," 5–34; Stump, *Boundaries of Faith*, 164.

82. On the impacts of the Cultural Revolution in Tibet, see Brockman, *Encyclopedia of Sacred Places*, 136; Tséring Shakya, *The Dragon in the Land of Snows: A History of Modern Tibet Since 1947* (New York: Columbia University Press, 1999), 314–47.

83. U.S. Congress, House, Committee on International Relations, and Senate, Committee on Foreign Relations, *Annual Report, International Religious Freedom, 1999*, 110–14.

84. Todd Wilkinson, "Skis Carve a Path of Controversy in Arizona," *Christian Science Monitor*, March 30, 2005, 3; Randal C. Archibold, "National Briefing West: California: Bar On Snowmaking at Indian Sites," *New York Times*, March 13, 2007, 17.

85. Alessandra Stanley, "Pope Declares His 'Bitterness' Over Gay Event," *New York Times*, July 10, 2000, A(11); Pierpaolo Mudu, "Repressive Tolerance: The Gay Movement and the Vatican in Rome," *GeoJournal* 58, no. 2–3 (October 2002): 189–96.

86. Etgar Lefkovits, "Holy Land Clerics Warn of Backlash to Gay Parade," *Jerusalem Post*, March 31, 2005, 2; Etgar Lefkovits, "International Gay Parade Rescheduled to 2006," *Jerusalem Post*, May 16, 2005, 4; Etgar Lefkovits, "Gay Pride Parade Canceled," *Jerusalem Post*, July 28, 2006, 25; Etgar Lefkovits, "Gays Hail Symbolic Victory in a Brief, Colorful J'lem Parade," *Jerusalem Post*, June 22, 2007, 1.

CHAPTER 6

Religion and Human Geography

The primary concerns of this text have been the interactions of place and space with expressions of religious faith and the importance of these interactions in understanding religions as cultural systems. The central argument has been that geographical perspectives provide significant insights into the study of religions as expressions of human culture. This final chapter, on the other hand, turns that argument around, asserting that the study of religion represents an important part of human geography. Many others writers have effectively made the case for the importance of religion in human geography and so that case will not be examined in detail here. Rather, this chapter will briefly review the general rationale for the geographical study of religion, as related to the arguments presented in the preceding chapters, and will then conclude with a discussion of the relevance of religion to the geographical study of several contemporary issues.

Studying Religion

Within the past forty years, religion has tended to be marginalized somewhat as an area of study within many of the social sciences, including human geography.[1] The more economically based social and political theories that have dominated much of social science over this period have tended to de-emphasize the importance of religious activity, casting it as part of the cultural flotsam produced by more fundamental social and political forces. Thus, for example, most of the work on urban and behavioral geography since the 1960s has more or less ignored religion as a salient theme.[2] Through the 1970s many social scientists also readily accepted secularization theory, the thesis that processes of modernization would inevitably undermine the influence of religion in society and ultimately lead to its irrelevance in most dimensions of social life. The universal applicability of secularization theory has largely been rejected in recent decades.[3] In this writer's view, however, the influences of secularization on social scientists themselves may have contributed as well to the de-emphasizing of the study of religion during this period. Many social scientists have taken the position that religion has become less influential in society, that it has lost its position of centrality within daily life, and that its concerns are removed from those of contemporary scholarship. In more direct terms, to the extent that academics have believed that religion has little bearing in their own lives, they may also have become less likely to study it. As a result, during much of the last third of the twentieth century, the study of religion in most of the social sciences increasingly (and often mistakenly) came to be perceived by those working outside the area as the domain of individuals having a strong commitment to religion in their personal lives, a perception that then further reinforced the marginalization of this area of study.[4]

The logic of this perception does not necessarily follow, however. My own concern with religious themes, for example, derives simply from the conclusion that religion plays a crucial role in the cultural life of different groups and places, and more specifically that it is integrated in complex ways into the beliefs, actions, and experiences of believers and that its effects cannot be reduced merely to secondary manifestations of more basic socioeconomic and political trends.[5] Religion, from this perspective, represents an important focus of study because it is an influential and distinct expression of culture not entirely reducible to other phenomena. Stated somewhat differently, this view recognizes that the worldview and ethos espoused by a community of believers can be vital, although generally not exclusive, sources of social agency.[6] This perspective does not stipulate the intrinsic truth of religious systems but rather acknowledges the significance that believers attribute to them. Of course, many geographers hold this and other views concerning the importance of religion as an object of inquiry, and the above-described de-emphasis on religion has obviously not eliminated the geography of religion as a field of study. Quite on the contrary, a significant and increasingly coherent body of geographical work in this area has continued to develop in recent decades, as discussed in chapter 1. Nonetheless, one cannot help but conclude that the study of religion has remained something of a byway in human geography. For example, three important texts dealing with the "new" cultural geography of the late 1980s, 1990s, and 2000s, each informed by and extending the body of geographical thought associated with cultural studies and critical theory, make virtually no mention of religion.[7]

Despite past trends, various reasons can be cited in support of religion as a focus of study, both in the social sciences generally and in human geography specifically. Most importantly, religions as cultural systems play a crucial role in the grounding of existence within larger meanings, specifically through the concepts of worldview and ethos. These meanings link adherents to the dimensions of life that they find most important, to realms of transcendence not essential to other forms of cultural expression. Because these meanings take on compelling importance for the adherent, they find expression in many different aspects of cultural life, material and nonmaterial alike. Reductionist interpretations that cast religious concerns purely in terms of material benefits miss this compelling character of religious belief as a factor in human behavior. Similarly, interpretations that de-emphasize the importance of individual intention in the study of culture, as in the articulation of religious belief and practice, miss the phenomenological significance of religion as a source of meaning to the adherent and, more generally, the disparate effects of internal motivations on individual behavior. The behavior of a Muslim who sacrifices a major portion of his wealth to make the Hajj to Mecca, for example, cannot be explained solely in reference to materialist factors or larger structural processes of which he is unaware. In part, at least, a satisfactory explanation of his behavior must include reference to his internal articulation of religious belief as a source of agency. To cite a different example, the concern of a Native American over the desecration of her ancestors' burial sites makes little sense if interpreted solely in material terms without reference to her religious system and how she understands its significance. In these and countless other examples, the logic of Occam's razor would seem to apply. If adherents themselves, reflexively or not, understand and legitimize their own thoughts and actions in relation to their religious system, additional models or assumptions seeking explanations from nonreligious factors may be neither necessary nor useful. At a minimum, believers' acceptance of certain religious truths should not be discounted as salient explanatory factors in understanding their behavior.

Because adherents' beliefs and practices become implicated in many dimensions of their lives, moreover, religion serves as a key cultural marker, signifying an important indicator and source of difference between culture groups. The contextuality of religions, the product of their continual reproduction and contesting by particular culture groups in specific local circumstances, thus offers basic insights into geographical variations in culture and cultural identity. For example, the distinctiveness of the African Instituted Churches, which developed following the spread of Christianity to Africa, provides a meaningful focus for exploring local intersections of African and European cultures and the syncretistic processes through which adherents in different locations establish their distinctive identity through their own understandings of Christianity. The cultural differences that emerge from contextual interpretations of religious systems also reveal the importance of lived experience in processes of cultural reproduction. Again, adherents typically understand their religious system as a set of eternal truths, applicable everywhere; and yet at the same time adherents constantly adapt and reproduce their religious system to fit their particular circumstances. The resulting diversity among religious systems derived from the same source powerfully illustrates the importance of the local in cultural systems. The relationships between contextual interpretations of religious systems and the places where they are enacted further reveal the role of scale in culture, in particular by demonstrating how local practices develop through intersections with cultural processes organized at both wider and narrower scales. The practice of Hasidic Judaism in Brooklyn, for example, typically reflects the dominant beliefs and practices articulated within a local Hasidic neighborhood, but those beliefs and practices intersect with processes organized at many other scales, from the individual patriarchal household to the larger branch of Hasidism following a particular leader and ultimately to the historical traditions of Judaism as a whole.

In integrating religious beliefs and practices into their lives, adherents also create and use various kinds of spaces, both sacred and secular and both material and imagined. These processes provide telling illustrations of the complex cultural relationships between meaning and space. One critical dimension of this relationship is the influence of religious meanings on the creation of religiously significant spaces. The identification of Mount Kailas as the abode of Shiva in Hindu scriptures, for example, has defined the mountain and its surroundings as a distinct space in religious terms and as an integral part of the Hindu worldview. Once established as an important site, the imagined space comprising Mount Kailas and its environs has in turn shaped the ways in which it has actually been used by adherents and the meanings that adherents have associated with those uses. Over time this space was thus transformed into an important, if remote, pilgrimage center by the development of the shrines and monasteries that traditionally surrounded the mountain to provide support for pilgrims. And for pilgrims, the journey to the site has in large part taken its meaning from their personal encounter with the space itself, and in particular from the lived narrative of following the sacred path that circles the mountain. Through such interactions of meaning, use, and action, religions as cultural systems again possess an intrinsic and illustrative spatiality. Moreover, the religious spaces identified and reproduced by adherents have frequently had significance far beyond the realms of religious worship or belief. Such spaces have often been involved in the articulation of much broader social and cultural concerns, as illustrated by the various conflicts involving secular and sacred space discussed in chapter 5.

In all of these ways, then, religion represents an essential element of culture. Indeed, for many adherents of different traditions religion represents the most important facet of their culture in terms of the breadth and depth of its articulation within their lives. And despite the predictions of secularization theory, the salience of religion in the geographical study of culture and society has not declined in contemporary settings. On the contrary, religion remains a key factor in a great variety of cultural and social phenomena relevant to the concerns of human geography. This chapter concludes with a brief survey of the relationships of religion to three such themes: the articulation of cultural identity, the politics of fundamentalism, and the impacts of globalization.

The Articulation of Cultural Identity

Within contemporary, postmodern settings, the articulation of cultural identity has become an increasingly significant and reflexive process, rooted in basic conceptions of similarity and difference but linked as well to the complex social and cultural contexts associated with everyday life. The expression of cultural identity increasingly extends across different scales as well, from the local to the global, particularly as individuals reflexively identify with widely dispersed culture groups. Processes relating to the articulation of identity have important implications for geography because they continue to link identity to place, although in ever-changing ways, and because they play an important role in the formation and reproduction of distinctive cultural spaces.

Religion in particular remains a crucial factor in the articulation and reproduction of cultural identity throughout much of the world. The significance of religious systems in this context derives in part from their integration of a totalizing ideology, extending to all domains of life, which provides a source of cultural grounding for adherents living in places that are undergoing periods of social, political, and economic change. Within such contexts, the adherent who espouses an identity defined in religious terms gains a significant measure of stability, through the acceptance of religious truths, through participation in a local community practicing a common set of social and cultural norms, through access to a variety of local institutions, and ultimately through a sense of unity with a wider community of coreligionists in other places. The process of religious identification thus firmly grounds adherents within their community, their larger world, and the cosmos.

Such a pattern has clearly developed, for example, for many inhabitants of the Central Asian republics since the demise of the Soviet Union, an event that produced a sudden social vacuum as existing social structures and government policies disintegrated. Many Muslims responded by reflexively adopting an identification with the region's older Islamic traditions, both as a reassertion of their connection to persistent sources of cultural meaning and as a response to post-Soviet social disorder. Through that process of identification, believers achieved a sense of continuity with pre-Soviet traditions, a sense of common cause shared by others in the local community, and a significant bond with coreligionists in more distant locations. Following decades of Soviet policies suppressing or restricting the practice of Islam, the republics have therefore generally experienced a flourishing of expressions of Islamic identity. Scholarly opinion varies regarding the extent to which popular Islam in fact remained active and cohesive under Soviet rule. In addition, Soviet control and suppression of Islam severely weakened traditional institutions and the authentic reproduction of Islamic practices, thus leading to the contesting of Islamic identity since the early 1990s among the populace, Islamic leaders, and governments of the Central Asian republics. Regardless, the articulation of Islamic identity has become far more open and widespread since independence, as seen for example in the increasing construction of mosques and the rising enrollments at madrassas (photo 6.1). By most accounts, this process of identity formation is likely to remain a crucial political and cultural force in the Central Asian republics for the foreseeable future.[8]

The persistent significance of religious systems in the spatial articulation and reproduction of cultural identity also derives from their relevance to the formation of ideologies of resistance in specific places, in particular for culture groups whose material circumstances are dominated by an external force.[9] In such instances, the religious system provides both a rationale for resistance, by defining the group's relationship to a transcendent and incontestable reality, and a means of carrying out acts of resistance

Photo 6.1.   A new mosque built near the village of Changon in central Tajikistan. Mosque construction has proceeded at a rapid pace since Tajikistan became independent in 1991, both in reaction against decades of Soviet suppression of Islam and to reassert pre-Soviet identities and traditions. Changon, Tajikistan, 2007.

Source: Brian Harrington Spier (www.flickr.com/photos/brianharringtonspier/50785 3262/), under Creative Commons license (creativecommons.org/licenses/by-sa/2.0/).

in specific places and through particular behaviors and group institutions. As an example, Buddhism has played a central role in the resistance of Tibetans to the Chinese occupation of their homeland since the 1950s. Despite significant government efforts to limit religious activity and to integrate the region into China, Tibetans have continued to use Buddhist practices and institutions as a means of resisting assimilation and asserting their distinct identity. One contested practice has been the display of pictures of the Dalai Lama, a traditional custom based on veneration of the Dalai Lama as the reincarnation of Chenrezig or Avalokitesvara, the bodhisattva of compassion. The sale of his picture is forbidden, as is its public display; and Chinese authorities in the region consider even the private possession of his picture to be evidence of antigovernment sentiments. Nonetheless, his picture is widely displayed in private homes. Within this context, Tibetan Buddhists have focused on the private spaces of their homes as centers of cultural meaning, displaying the Dalai Lama's picture as an act of Buddhist identity, of veneration for the Tibetan leader, and of resistance against the Chinese. The linking of religion, identity, space, and resistance has occurred among many other minorities or disempowered groups as well. The ties between Islamic identity and resistance to Israel articulated by Muslim Palestinian groups such as the Islamic Resistance Movement (or Hamas) represent an important example. The latter group has articulated its resistance in violent terms, however, as in the use of suicide bombers in acts of terrorism. The latter strategy in effect articulates spaces of resistance and identity at the scale of the body, as individual suicide bombers sacrifice themselves to inflict damage on their enemy and to define themselves as martyrs.

A third factor underlying the significance of religious traditions as contemporary sources of identity is their relative stability at wider spatial scales, despite their great diversity at narrower scales. This factor has been particularly significant for members of diasporic groups. The concept of diaspora focused originally on the dispersion of the Jews across the Roman Empire following the destruction of the second Jewish temple in Jerusalem in 70 CE. In recent years, the term has also come to be applied to a wide variety of culture groups who have dispersed from their homeland to various locations, who have not widely assimilated in their new places of residence, and who maintain a strong sense of identity with their place of origin. Living in diaspora makes it difficult for migrants to retain their cultural identity intact, however. Many migrants therefore reflexively emphasize particular elements of their original identity as they redefine it within diasporic spaces. The articulation of a new, often hybrid, identity can be quite complex and takes varied forms, but in many cases diasporic groups have focused on religion as the central factor in the process.

The articulation of identity by Hindu migrants to Great Britain and North America, for example, has typically focused more on religion than on language or ethnicity. Religion represents a practical and socially acceptable source of identity in these places and maintains for the individual a strong sense of connection to the certainties of a familiar worldview and ethos. For Hindus, moreover, religious identity often provides the foundation for a larger diasporic community at local scales than would language or ethnicity. At the same time, the articulation of a common Hindu identity often brings together individuals whose traditional expressions of Hinduism have differed, the result being processes of simplification, homogenization, or innovation in religious practice as believers emphasize the commonalities in their understandings of tradition.[10] Contrary to practices in India, for example, a single diasporic

Hindu temple is often dedicated to more than one deity or used by practitioners of more than one Hindu sect (photo 6.2). Along somewhat different lines, the emphasis on religion in identity may also serve to heighten the religious concerns of those in diaspora relative to those who have remained in a group's homeland. Sikhs living in Great Britain and North America, for example, have become the primary proponents of an independent Sikh homeland in recent years, identifying more strongly with their Sikh traditions than with their larger homeland of India.[11]

As the preceding examples illustrate, religion may play a crucial role in the contemporary formation of cultural identities in diverse contexts. This role derives in part from traditional, unquestioned uses of religion as a means of distinguishing between different culture groups. Within many contexts, however, groups have also reflexively articulated their identity in religious terms because religion represents an accepted, and often protected, element of cultural difference. Most importantly, in either situation religious systems themselves provide the very meanings around which believers can construct their identity, including concepts of power, authority, legitimacy, and obligation. The compelling nature of these concepts accounts for their great potency within processes of identity formation.

The Politics of Fundamentalism

The rise of the Christian right in U.S. politics, of the Bharatiya Janata Party in India, and of different varieties of political Islam in many predominantly Muslim countries represent three distinct examples of a widespread process: the increasing interaction

Photo 6.2. The Shiva Vishnu Temple of Greater Cleveland. The twin shikharas or towers, one for each of the temple's two principal deities (Shiva and Vishnu), reflect the broad view of Hinduism characteristic of many diasporic communities, combining the worship of multiple deities into a unified conception of tradition. Parma, Ohio, 2002.

Source: Author.

between religious belief and political action in various parts of the world in recent years. These phenomena have generally been characterized as expressions of fundamentalism.[12] The latter term has frequently been contested by those to whom it applies, and by some scholars as well who see the term as being too imprecise. The concept of fundamentalism has proven useful, however, in articulating significant commonalities among diverse religious movements.[13] These commonalities include an insistence on the exclusive legitimacy of their interpretation of traditional sources of religious authority; a sense of urgency in seeking to protect idealized traditions and the spaces associated with them from specific contemporary threats; and openness to using various modern, secular strategies and technologies to further the movement's objectives. Some movements characterized as fundamentalist, it should be noted, pursue their objectives through patterns of isolation from the rest of society. Those that do not, which are much greater in number, have typically cast at least their immediate goals in explicitly political terms, either through engagement with a state's existing political structures or in more extreme cases through violent conflict. As a result, fundamentalism as a global phenomenon represents a major factor in understanding a variety of issues relevant to political geography at different spatial scales.

At the scale of the individual state, the rise of fundamentalism as a political force has often mirrored other forms of political cleavage.[14] In particular, it resembles certain center-periphery cleavages that pit a dominant culture against a minority culture. In expressing their position in such conflicts through political discourse, however, fundamentalists have in some instances represented themselves as the majority but in others as the minority. Within the United States, for example, Christian fundamentalists in recent decades have cast themselves as the dominant group, the "moral majority," within what they characterize as an essentially Christian nation (photo 6.3). In the twenty-first century, this position has especially become associated with the more conservative wing of the Republican Party and the Bush presidency. In the summer before the 2004 presidential elections, for example, the Texas Republican Party explicitly included a statement in its election platform identifying its belief in the United States as a Christian nation organized according to biblical principles.[15] In other instances of political cleavage, fundamentalist movements have acknowledged their minority status while still seeking to bring about political change. The religious Zionist movement in Israel, for example, has since the 1970s sought to influence government policies toward settlements in the West Bank, a region that they view as sacred space but which to the Palestinians represents occupied territory.

Despite their superficial similarities to political groups associated with center-periphery cleavages, however, fundamentalist movements differ from such groups in one significant way: fundamentalists by definition believe that their political legitimacy derives from transcendent and unchanging religious truth to which they alone have access. This emphasis on religious truth in effect negates the possibility of compromise on certain key issues. Moreover, fundamentalists' objectives do not focus solely, or even primarily, on ordinary issues of political contention; instead, their concerns ultimately involve much more basic issues of authority, legitimacy, and morality as defined by their worldview and ethos. These characteristics underlie the absolutism and the sense of urgency that are typical of fundamentalist groups. Together, such perspectives have important implications for the political process, since fundamentalists tend to characterize their opponents not just in political terms but also as the

Photo 6.3.   A monument to the Ten Commandments that had been on display in Alabama's state courthouse before a federal district court ordered that it be removed, in 2003. Here, the monument is on display in Longview, Texas. The controversy surrounding this monument highlights the concern among Christian fundamentalists with recognition of the United States as a Christian nation. After the monument's removal from the Alabama state courthouse, it was physically transported and publicly displayed on a tour of 164 locations in 21 states by the American Veterans in Domestic Defense, a Christian fundamentalist veterans' group. Longview, Texas, 2004.

Source: Mario Villafuerte/Getty Images.

enemies of faith and truth. This Manichean division between truth and error, or good and evil, produces a distinctively charged political atmosphere around fundamentalist movements. Within some movements it has further promoted the use of martyrdom as a political strategy, as in the case of contemporary terrorist groups that have derived their ideology from radical Islamic thought, discussed below.

Fundamentalists have also played an important role in broader conflicts in recent years; and again, such conflicts take on a distinctive character because those involved on one or both sides define their concerns in absolutist, transcendent terms. The Israeli-Palestinian conflict would presumably be difficult to resolve even if it were limited to purely secular concerns, but the added dimension of fundamentalist interpretations of space and legitimacy, particularly with respect to the West Bank and the holy sites in Jerusalem, renders the conflict vastly more complex. This religious dimension in particular makes compromise exceedingly difficult because the views of the fundamentalists on either side are ineluctably absolute. For religious Zionists, no successful peace plan can sacrifice the Temple Mount or the biblical lands of Judea and Samaria; for Palestinian Islamic fundamentalists, no successful peace plan can sacrifice the sacred sites within al-Haram al-Sharif. Less absolutist parties on each side may ultimately prevail, but in the meantime these fundamentalist perspectives have contributed significantly to the difficulty of establishing a workable peace. To cite a different example, the actions of Hindu fundamentalists in India and of Islamic fundamentalists in Pakistan during certain periods have lent a particularly strident tone to the political relations between those two countries. The razing of the Babri Mosque in Ayodhya in 1992, for example, led to pointed exchanges between the governments of Pakistan and India, each sensitive to the necessity of placating fundamentalist responses within their own countries. Nonetheless, the event prompted fundamentalists in both countries to engage in further communal violence and the destruction of additional places of worship, actions that provoked each side to further criticize the other. Again, the absolutism of the fundamentalists on both sides has significantly complicated their relations with one another.

Finally, the rise of fundamentalism has contributed as well to the emergence of new kinds of political conflicts articulated at transnational scales, outside the traditional political structures of the state system. The most important example of this trend is the emergence of various forms of militant Islamic fundamentalism as a political force. It can be argued that the terrorism committed by al-Qaeda and similar extremists falls outside the definitional scope of fundamentalism because it is so egregious in its character and impacts.[16] Certainly most forms of fundamentalism have not adopted violence at such scales in pursuing their objectives. Moreover, the characterization of Islamic militancy as a single, unitary phenomenon is highly problematic as this phenomenon has in fact taken very different forms in different locations, as discussed in chapter 3.[17] Putting aside these issues, however, it is clear that militant political Islam has developed a strong transnational dimension in recent decades as theoreticians and activists from various locations have sought to act in the defense of Islam. Such actions, characterized by fundamentalists as a basic religious obligation, have taken diverse forms. At the most extreme, they have involved an irregular cadre of militants from various origins in a series of violent conflicts, including the Palestinian uprising against British rule in the 1930s; the Israeli war of independence; the Egyptian conflict with the British over the Suez Canal; and later conflicts in Afghanistan, Bosnia, Kosovo, Eritrea, Chechnya, and Iraq.[18] Other extreme examples have focused on a more broadly defined struggle against Western hegemony, rather than on an ongoing conflict in a specific location, as in al-Qaeda's attacks on New York and Washington, D.C., in 2001 or in the terrorist attacks on public transit and airports in the United Kingdom in 2005 and 2007. Again, the meanings and implications of all of these uses of violence cannot be fully understood without reference to the religious imaginations of those involved in them, who understand the defense of Islam in absolutist and Manichean terms. Of course, fundamentalist actions in the defense of Islam have taken less extreme forms as well. For example, the development of global fundamentalist institutions such as charities and missionary organizations has also furthered the political influence of militant Islam, although usually at more local scales, especially through the construction of contexts for the reproduction of fundamentalist thought such as schools and mosques.

Fundamentalism, in sum, represents a diverse but highly influential force in contemporary politics, at local, state, and global scales. Fundamentalist movements achieve their influence in part through their ability to link their specific interests to broader political concerns, and in this sense they resemble many contemporary forms of political activism. The distinctiveness of fundamentalist movements as political agents derives, however, from the transcendent foundations of their ideologies. All fundamentalist groups ultimately link their actions in this world to inflexibly defined truths rooted in their worldview and ethos, and their actions must therefore be construed in reference to such connections. Moreover, fundamentalists' religious certainties have significant and distinctive effects on the manner in which they pursue political objectives. As discussed above, they generally define the contesting of political objectives in explicitly Manichean terms, as a struggle between absolute expressions of good and evil. This position in turn supports a characteristic unwillingness to compromise, since for fundamentalist groups the terms of any compromise would require an intolerable accommodation of evil. At the same time, the definition of conflict in Manichean terms fosters a commitment to the idea of individual sacrifice, particularly as a temporal action that will be rewarded in the afterlife or in some other future existence as specified by a group's worldview. It should be noted that while the suicide bombers associated with radical Islamic groups represent the most conspicuous example of this pattern, less violent expressions of sacrifice, such as the donation of material wealth, the risking of imprisonment, or self-imposed isolation from society, exist among most fundamentalist groups. Finally, the relationship between political goals and transcendent ideals has supported fundamentalists' perseverance in pursuing their objectives. By placing their objectives within a larger transcendent context, fundamentalists in effect articulate their own actions in reference to the broad temporal scope of sacred history rather than to the more constrained timeline of worldly events.

The Impacts of Globalization

The process of globalization has perhaps been most widely discussed in economic terms as the development of various kinds of economic interactions and activities organized at a global scale or without reference to state borders. At the same time, geographers have readily recognized that globalization has important consequences outside the realm of economics, including far-reaching impacts on cultures and cultural processes. These impacts include the global expansion of cultural interactions among elite groups as well as at the popular level; the development of an increasingly global culture, predominantly rooted in Western and, more specifically, American sources; and the rise of a global civil society that fosters both the international acceptance of cultural differences and the establishment of universal norms of behavior, as in the Universal Declaration of Human Rights adopted by the United Nations. At the same time, the rise of cultural globalization has provoked strong counter-responses, particularly at more local scales by groups who see the expansion of a global culture as a threat to their particular values or who seek to preserve the identity of their local context while accommodating the effects of global processes.[19] From a geographical perspective, the impacts of globalization are thus quite complex, extending across a variety of spaces and scales.

Religions have intersected in a number of significant ways with the above processes of cultural globalization. Many non-Western and fundamentalist religious groups have perceived the spread of Western popular culture, with its secular outlook and emphasis on individualism, as a major threat to the customary worldview and ethos of their own cultural space. Indeed, one could argue that globalization has been a major factor in the growth of fundamentalist movements in recent decades. Explicit examples of the concern over cultural globalization developed, for example, in Iran following the Islamic Revolution and in Afghanistan under the Taliban as clerics banned satellite television dishes and foreign publications as sources of corrupting influences. Similarly, in 2002 Nigerian Muslims protested the staging of the Miss World pageant in their country, characterizing the event as an affront to local Islamic values. In a particularly telling example of protests linked to the cultural dimensions of globalization, Hindu militants held a number of demonstrations against McDonald's restaurants in New Delhi and Mumbai in 2001 to protest the use of beef fat in preparing French fries not in India but in McDonald's outlets in the United States (photo 6.4).[20] These protests clearly revealed the local manifestation of a global perspective, focusing on the religious meaning of spatially remote events; but they also represented the local articulation of an absolutist worldview intolerant of external deviations, however distant in space, from the group's own religious norms. It should be added that opposition to global popular culture has been voiced within Western settings as well, especially by Christian fundamentalists in the United States. One well-known example involved Jerry Falwell, leader of the Moral Majority organization, who in 1999 warned his followers against allowing their children to watch the *Teletubbies*, an internationally distributed children's television program, because in his view one of the costumed characters represented a gay role model and symbol of gay pride.[21]

The intersections between religions and processes of globalization have not focused solely on perceived threats associated with global culture, however. An equally important form of interaction has developed as the processes and technologies of globalization have facilitated the diffusion of particular religious movements. Such factors

Photo 6.4.   A member of the Bharatiya Janata Party protesting in Mumbai against McDonald's restaurants based on the concern of Hindus in the United States that beef fat had been used in the preparation of French fries there. In a telling expression of opposition to the consumption of beef, of antagonism toward alien cultural influences, of Hindu belief in the sacredness of the cow, and of respect for the products such as milk and manure that cattle provide within Hindu culture, the protestor is smearing cow dung on a likeness of Ronald McDonald, the mascot of the McDonald's chain. Mumbai, India, 2001.

Source: AFP/Getty Images.

have clearly contributed to the spread of Islamic fundamentalism, for example. During the 1970s and 1980s, cassette tapes of the sermons of particular clerics became an important means of spreading their message, a function that in more recent years has increasingly been taken over by the Internet. The ease of travel across the globe has also played a role. The number of pilgrims attending the Hajj in a given year has grown dramatically, from tens of thousands a century ago to more than two million by the beginning of the twenty-first century.[22] This increase in pilgrimage has drawn increasing numbers of Muslims into contact with the Wahhabi orthodoxy that dominates Saudi Arabia. Many pilgrims have thus returned to their place of origin with a more universal and orthodox understanding of Islam, and some of those have in turn gone on to form organizations to spread Wahhabism locally. Moreover, such organizations have frequently relied on external sources of support, linking local adherents to transnational or global Islamic organizational structures. This process has been particularly noticeable in Africa, where groups stressing Islamic orthodoxy have increasingly sought to weaken the influence of the region's more heterodox Sufi brotherhoods.[23]

A second major example of religious diffusion within the context of globalization has been the rapid spread of popular Protestantism in recent decades.[24] Popular Protestantism comprises a variety of churches and religious movements, most of which originated in the United States during the 1800s and early 1900s. These groups generally place a strong emphasis on personal religious experience, the process of salvation, and strict moral behavior in everyday life as a sign of personal sanctification. The most significant expression of this phenomenon is Pentecostalism, a movement encompassing many specific denominations that emphasize speaking in tongues, prophecy, healing, and other religious phenomena as evidence of baptism in the Holy Spirit and of salvation. Other important examples of popular Protestantism include the Latter-Day Saints, Seventh-Day Adventists, Jehovah's Witnesses, and many of the African Instituted Churches. Together the adherents of these groups number well into the hundreds of millions worldwide. Their rapid growth in recent decades has been closely tied to globalizing processes, including missionary activity originating in the United States and, perhaps more importantly, the widespread use of radio, television, and the Internet to reach potential converts. The Joshua Project, a transdenominational effort to bring Christianity to all parts of the world by establishing self-sustaining Christian churches among all distinct ethnic groups, exemplifies this global missionary objective (map 6.1). The similar World By Radio group, an association of Christian broadcasters, seeks to make religious radio programming available to all the people of the world in languages that are intelligible to them.[25] For these groups, the process of globalization has special religious significance based on the New Testament teaching (Mark 13:10) that the Second Coming of Christ will occur only after the gospel of Christianity has been spread to all nations of the world.

A final intersection between religion and globalization centers on the issue of religious tolerance and acceptance at the global scale. The growth of global interactions in all realms of life to some extent requires the diminution of conflict between distinct religious groups. The possibility for such conflict in effect limits the effectiveness of globalizing processes. Scholars have addressed this issue in part by focusing on the potential emergence of a global civil religion, which would smooth over the religious differences that exist among places. This global civil religion would have two primary characteristics: the belief that all religions share some features in common,

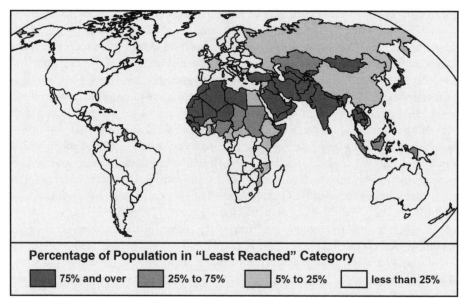

Percentage of Population in "Least Reached" Category

| ■ 75% and over | ■ 25% to 75% | ■ 5% to 25% | □ less than 25% |

Map 6.1. Distribution of the ''least reached people'' of the world, in terms of their exposure to the teachings of Christianity as defined by the Joshua Project (www. josh-uaproject.net). The Joshua Project, a group founded by conservative evangelical Protestants, focuses on the task of global evangelism as a precondition for the Second Coming of Christ.

such as compassion and ethical behavior; and an agreement to set aside absolutist understandings of religious truth in interactions between adherents from different traditions. This global religious system would not possess a common worldview but would focus instead on the concept of individual religious freedom. As an intermediary step, versions of civil religion may develop within larger traditions. One could argue, for example, that elements of the religious right in the United States have focused on asserting a Judeo-Christian civil religion. Similarly, moderate Islamic movements in Indonesia have supported what is essentially an Islamic civil religion. Ultimately, however, a global civil religion would have to be part of a broader global civil society, which through its institutions would support the goal of religious freedom. The foundations of such a global civil society have in fact already emerged in the realm of international law and in the actions of diverse international organizations and institutions.

Nonetheless, significant obstacles remain to the widespread acceptance of a global civil religion.[26] At the most basic level, the incompatibilities between the worldviews of different religions present a major obstacle in reaching common ground. Indeed, the unwillingness to surrender the claim to possession of the absolute truth has been a major feature of religious fundamentalism, and one that in many cases has emerged as a response to globalization. A second inhibiting factor revolves around the issue of proselytism. The right to convert to a different religion is clearly spelled out in the Universal Declaration of Human Rights. Many religious groups view proselytism directed at their own members as a significant threat, however. Not only does active proselytism draw converts away from their original religion, it also implicitly expresses a difference in status between religions. The proselytizing group essentially represents its religion as being superior to that of the potential convert. Many religious groups have thus perceived proselytism to be a form of cultural imperialism. This perception is reinforced, moreover, by the prominent role of American churches and organizations in missionary activity worldwide. And the issues of status and religious superiority gain additional significance from the nature of globalization itself. To date, economic processes of globalization have produced distinct winners and losers; different parts of the world have benefited to different degrees, as have different groups within the same country. Many adherents believe, implicitly or explicitly, that similar patterns may emerge in cultural terms through processes of global interaction. As a result, many religious groups have actively protested the presence of other groups seeking converts and many countries have passed legislation limiting or banning proselytism.[27]

Conclusions

The discussions of the three preceding topics provide brief illustrations of the relevance of religion to geographical issues broader in scope than the particulars of religious belief and practice. In addition, they reiterate some of the basic themes of this text. They clearly reveal, for example, that religion as a form of cultural expression remains widely integrated into the concerns of adherents in diverse locations, concerns relating to issues ranging from cultural identity and political resistance to foodways and sexual behavior. Religious systems, from this perspective, provide a framework of meanings through which adherents understand their place in the cosmos and through which they interact, across different scales, with varied aspects of the world around them.

Moreover, the preceding examples again illustrate the recurrent agency of believers in the reproduction and refinement of those religious meanings, resulting in the continuous diversification of religious systems in specific places. As seen throughout this text, the intrinsic mutability of religions has several major effects. Most obviously, it produces significant variations in the enactment of a religious tradition among different contexts. The practice of Hinduism in North America or Great Britain, for example, necessarily differs from the practice of Hinduism in India. Perhaps more importantly, however, adherents use this mutability to preserve the relevance of their religious system within their particular surroundings. Thus Hindu immigrants in diasporic contexts have preserved core elements of their belief system even while reshaping others to fit their new cultural environment. The mutability of religious systems also relates to the role of scale as an interpretive concept in human geography. The reproduction of religions in diverse contexts, for example, supports the construction of varied scales of identity within an individual tradition, from the local to the global. The Islamic tradition clearly illustrates this intersection of scale and identity, emphasizing the unity of all Muslims but also encompassing many different local expressions.

The central theme of the religious construction and use of diverse spaces also reappears throughout the examples discussed in this chapter. Tibetan Buddhists have used the local space of the household, where they preserve pictures of the Dalai Lama, as a center of resistance against the efforts of the Chinese government to weaken the role of Buddhism in Tibetan culture and, more generally, against the broader intrusion of external cultural influences as Tibet has become more accessible to the outside world. For many Jews, and for religious Zionists in particular, the broader territory of Eretz Yisrael contains meanings crucial to understanding the relationship between the modern state of Israel and the unfolding of sacred history. Such meanings are central to the ways in which these believers have responded to conflicts over control of the West Bank and Jerusalem, ultimately casting these conflicts in religious rather than secular political terms. Evangelical Christians have conceptualized the interaction of space and religious meanings over a much wider expanse through their notion of the global mission field, a concept that is central to the organization of various missionary efforts but that also reflects an understanding of the fulfillment of sacred history through the articulation of Christian beliefs to all peoples of the world.

Finally, the preceding examples, along with countless others throughout the text, reveal the basic cultural importance of religion, for instance as a source of identity, as a foundation for the structuring of society, and as a key factor in the interactions of believers with diverse global processes. Religion differs from most other expressions of culture, however, because believers use it to articulate ultimate, transcendent concerns. Religious systems therefore carry a distinctive authority and legitimacy for their adherents that most other expressions of culture do not. At the same time, the preceding examples further illustrate that adherents do not understand their religious systems solely as a set of remote or abstract concepts. Instead, they experience religion in direct and immediate ways relating to the manifold dimensions of human existence. For adherents, religious systems thus serve in basic ways to ground the sacred within the world of everyday life. For all of the above reasons, then, religion in its many different expressions represents a complex and vital issue in the geographical study of humanity.

Notes

1. James Proctor, "Introduction: Theorizing and Studying Religion," *Annals of the Association of American Geographers* 96, no. 1 (March 2006): 165–68; N. J. Demerath, III, "A Sinner among the Saints: Confessions of a Sociologist of Culture and Religion," *Sociological Forum* 17, no. 1 (March 2002): 1–19.

2. Wilbur Zelinsky, "The Uniqueness of the American Religious Landscape," *Geographical Review* 91, no. 3 (July 2001): 566–67.

3. William H. Swatos, Jr., and Kevin J. Cristiano, "Secularization Theory: The Course of a Concept," *Sociology of Religion* 60 (Fall 1999): 209–28; Peter L. Berger, "The Desecularization of the World: A Global Overview," in *The Desecularization of the World: Resurgent Religion and World Politics*, ed. Peter L. Berger (Washington, D.C.: Wm. B. Eerdmans, 1999), 1–18.

4. This issue is raised in the context of sociology in Demerath, "A Sinner among the Saints," 6–7, 18–19.

5. Daniel Pals, "Reductionism and Belief: An Appraisal of Recent Attacks on the Doctrine of Irreducible Religion," *The Journal of Religion* 66, no. 1 (January 1986): 18–36; various psychological foundations for this view of religion are examined in Benjamin Beit-Hallahmi and Michael Argyle, *The Psychology of Religious Behaviour, Belief and Experience* (London: Routledge, 1997).

6. A cogent review of the issues involved here appears in Susan Rosa and Dale Van Kley, "Religion and the Historical Discipline: A Reply to Mack Holt and Henry Heller," *French Historical Studies* 21, no. 4 (Autumn 1998): 611–29.

7. Peter Jackson, *Maps of Meaning: An Introduction to Cultural Geography* (London: Unwin Hyman, 1989); Don Mitchell, *Cultural Geography: A Critical Introduction* (Oxford: Blackwell, 2000); David Atkinson et al., eds., *Cultural Geography: A Critical Dictionary of Key Concepts* (New York: Palgrave Macmillan, 2005).

8. Jeff Haynes, *Religion in Global Politics* (London: Longman, 1998), 148–67; T. Jeremy Gunn, "Shaping an Islamic Identity: Religion, Islamism, and the State in Central Asia," *Sociology of Religion* 64, no. 3 (Fall 2003): 389–410.

9. Jeff Haynes, "Religion and Political Transformation," in *Culture and Global Change*, ed. Tracey Skelton and Tim Allen (London: Routledge, 1999), 223–31.

10. Steven Vertovec, *The Hindu Diaspora: Comparative Patterns* (New York: Routledge, 2000), 30–31; Carolyn V. Prorok, "Evolution of the Hindu Temple in Trinidad," *Caribbean Geography* 3, no. 2 (1991): 73–93; Surinder M. Bhardwaj and Madhusudana N. Rao, "The Temple as a Symbol of Hindu Identity in America?" *Journal of Cultural Geography* 17, no. 2 (Spring/Summer 1998): 125–43.

11. Darshan Singh Tatla, *The Sikh Diaspora: The Search for Statehood* (Seattle: University of Washington Press, 1999).

12. Roger W. Stump, *Boundaries of Faith: Geographical Perspectives on Religious Fundamentalism* (Lanham, Md.: Rowman and Littlefield, 2000).

13. Martin Riesebrodt, "Fundamentalism and the Resurgence of Religion," *Numen* 47, no. 3 (2000): 266–87.

14. Seymour Martin Lipset, *Consensus and Conflict: Essays in Political Sociology* (New Brunswick, N.J.: Transaction, 1985), 113–85.

15. "Christian Platform Ripped as Offensive," *Washington Times*, June 13, 2004, A1.

16. William D. Dinges, "On Naming Religious Extremists: The 'Fundamentalist' Factor," in *Democracy and Religion: Free Exercise and Diverse Visions*, ed. David W. Odell-Scott (Kent, Ohio: Kent State University Press, 2004), 243–68; Roger W. Stump, "Fundamentalism, Democracy, and the Contesting of Meaning," in *Democracy and Religion*, ed. Odell-Scott, 185–202.

17. Stump, *Boundaries of Faith*, 48–63, passim.

18. Cf. Roger W. Stump, "Religion and the Geographies of War," in *The Geography of War and Peace*, ed. Colin Flint (Oxford: Oxford University Press, 2005), 149–73.

19. For a review of recent work relating to these themes, see Katharine N. Rankin, "Anthropologies and Geographies of Globalization," *Progress in Human Geography* 27, no. 6 (December 2003): 708–34.

20. Luke Harding, "Hindus Angered by Burger Chain's Beef Lie," *The Guardian (London)*, May 25, 2001, 13.

21. Michael Ellison, "Tinky Winky Falls Foul of the Moral Majority," *The Guardian (London)*, February 11, 1999, 3.

22. F. E. Peters, *The Hajj: The Muslim Pilgrimage to Mecca and the Holy Places* (Princeton, N.J.: Princeton University Press, 1994), 337.

23. Michael Watts, "Mapping Identities: Place, Space, and Community in an African City," in *The Geography of Identity*, ed. Patricia Yaeger (Ann Arbor: The University of Michigan Press, 1996), 59–97.

24. Peter L. Berger, "Religions and Globalisation," *European Judaism* 36 (Spring 2003): 4–10.

25. Roger W. Stump, "Spatial Implications of Religious Broadcasting: Stability and Change in Spatial Patterns of Belief," in *Collapsing Space and Time: Geographic Aspects of Communications and Information*, ed. S. D. Brunn and T. R. Leinbach (London: Unwin Hyman, 1991), 354–75; Stump, *Boundaries of Faith*, 223–25.

26. George M. Thomas, "Religions in Global Civil Society," *Sociology of Religion* 62 (Winter 2001): 515–33.

27. See the individual country reports in U.S. Congress, House, Committee on International Relations, and Senate, Committee on Foreign Relations, *Annual Report, International Religious Freedom, 1999*.

Glossary

African Instituted Churches (AICs). Christian denominations established in Africa as bodies independent of missionary churches and usually characterized by emphases on experiential religion, prophecy, and healing, and in some cases incorporating survivals from older animistic traditions.

ahimsa. In Hinduism, Buddhism, and Jainism, veneration of and nonviolence toward all living things.

al-Haram al-Sharif ("Noble Sanctuary"). The portion of the Temple Mount sacred to Muslims, containing the Dome of the Rock and al-Aqsa Mosque.

Alvars (the "Immersed"). A school of Tamil devotional poetry devoted to Vishnu that played a major role in the spread of bhakti devotionalism.

arahant (Pali) or arhat (Sanskrit). One who, following the teachings of the Buddha, attains complete enlightenment and liberation from the cycle of reincarnation.

Ashkenazim. The Jewish community that developed primarily in Germany and Eastern Europe during the medieval period.

Ashura. A major holy day in Shia Islam commemorating the martyrdom of Imam Husayn by Sunni forces at Karbala.

atman. The Upanishadic concept of the eternal self or soul that unites the individual with universal, transcendent reality.

axis mundi. The central point or axis of the cosmos, at which different worldly and cosmological realms meet.

Baal Shem Tov ("Master of the Good Name"), abbreviated in acronymic form as Besht. An appellation of Israel ben Eliezer, the founder of Hasidism, recognizing his esoteric knowledge of the ineffable name of God and his ability to use the power of that knowledge.

Bahaism. A heterodox nineteenth-century sect based on the teachings of Husayn Ali Nuri, who claimed to have superseded Islam with a new religion that unified all world faiths in a single religion of God.

baraka. The divine blessing received and accumulated by a Sufi saint, or wali, which can then be transmitted to others.

bardo. In Tibetan Buddhism, the states between death and rebirth during which the circumstances of the adherent's rebirth, including the possibility of attaining moksha, are determined.

bhakti. In Hinduism, personal devotion to a particular deity.

Bodhi tree. The bo tree in Bodh Gaya under which the Buddha attained enlightenment.

bodhisattva. A Buddhist who has approached the state of nirvana but has held back from achieving that goal to remain active in the material world, helping others to achieve nirvana instead; a central concept in Mahayana Buddhism.

brahman. The power of the Vedic fire sacrifice to compel divine action, and the ritual utterances used to invoke such power.

Brahman. The Upanishadic concept of the omnipresent essence of reality.

387

Brahmanas. Vedic writings produced early in the first millennium BCE that explicate the ritual elements associated with the Vedas.

Buddha. One who has attained complete achievement and nirvana, including the historical Gautama Buddha as well as a large number of material and celestial Buddhas.

cenobitic monasticism. A collective form of monasticism organized around the religious meanings of the life of the entire community.

Dar al-Harb. The "Realm of War," comprising areas not ruled by Muslims.

Dar al-Islam. The "Realm of Islam," including all areas where the sharia is followed.

dawah. The obligation of Muslims to invite others to convert to Islam.

dharma. The observance of Hindu customs and religious duties, and the way of life based on such observance.

Dharmashastras. Hindu texts compiled between 200 BCE and 400 CE that provide instructions concerning the obligations associated with a believer's caste and stage of life.

dhikr. In Sufism, ritual prayers through which adherents achieve unity with God and commemorate the shaykhs of their tariqas.

Eid al-Adha ("Feast of the Sacrifice"). The major Islamic feast held toward the end of the Hajj by Muslims worldwide, commemorating the willingness of Ibrahim (or Abraham) to sacrifice his son Ismail (or Ishmael) to God.

Eid al-Fitr ("Feast of Breaking the Fast"). The major Islamic feast celebrating the successful completion of Ramadan, the month during which Muslims fast during daylight hours and scrupulously observe rules of correct Islamic behavior.

Eretz Yisrael. In traditional Jewish belief, the Promised Land of Israel to which the Jews will be restored through their divine redemption.

eruv ("mixture," pl. eruvin). The shared private domain of an Orthodox Jewish community, comprising a mixture of private and public spaces and bounded by cords and various architectural structures, which allows observant Jews to move easily throughout their neighborhood without contravening the prohibition in Jewish law against carrying objects outside their private domain on the Sabbath.

Esala Perahera. A major Buddhist festival in Sri Lanka centering on the procession of the casket for the Buddha's tooth relic, traditionally containing the tooth itself, through Kandy to foster popular veneration of the Buddha.

esoteric. Relating to religious beliefs and rituals grounded in sources of special knowledge that are often accessible only to an elite minority.

ethnic religion. A religion whose membership is generally limited to individuals who share a particular ethnic identity.

ethos. A system of values, motivations, and emotions through which adherents realize consistency between their own lives and their worldview.

exoteric. Relating to popular religious beliefs and rituals that are widely accessible to believers and that often involve public and demonstrative practices.

Faqih. Following the Islamic Revolution, the title used by Iran's supreme religious leader, designating his role as the preeminent Islamic jurist and religious scholar.

feng shui. Various magical practices in traditional Chinese folk religions aimed at creating harmony between superhuman forces and human activities and artifacts, including graves, houses, and cities.

gathered church. A religious group whose membership is limited to individuals who have explicitly accepted the group's beliefs and have purposefully sought union with fellow believers.

ghat. Riverside steps that provide a context for Hindu rites alongside a sacred waterway, including ritual bathing and cremation of the dead.

gurdwara ("gateway to the guru"). A Sikh temple.

hadith. An account of a statement, action, or expression of approval attributed to Muhammad accompanied with a demonstration of the authority of the account based on the specific sequence of its provenance from various written and oral sources, brought together into a number of canonical collections during the ninth and tenth centuries.

Hajj. The pilgrimage to Mecca, defined in the Quran as a religious obligation for Muslims.

halakhah. Jewish religious law derived from the Torah and other written and oral traditions.

halal ("permissible"). Relating to that which is permitted under the sharia, most often used to describe permitted foods or foods prepared in a prescribed manner.

Hanafi legal school. One of the four schools of Islamic law, distinguished by its acceptance of the legitimate role of the qadi's individual judgment, reasoning by analogy, and local tradition in the rendering of legal decisions.

Hanbali legal school. The strictest of the four schools of Islamic law, emphasizing the exclusive legitimacy of the Quran, Sunna, and hadith as primary sources of insight into the sharia.

haredim ("those who tremble" at the word of God). Ultra-orthodox Jews who adhere strictly to traditional laws and customs.

Hasidism. A traditionalist Jewish movement established in Eastern Europe in the eighteenth century that stresses religious zeal and mysticism.

heterodoxy. Deviation from or diversity in established patterns of religious doctrine or belief.

hijra ("migration"). As a religious concept, the migration of Muslims, considered obligatory by some religious scholars, from Dar al-Harb to Dar al-Islam.

Hijra. Muhammad's early migration from Mecca to Medina to escape his enemies in the former and to establish the first Islamic polity in the latter.

Hindutva. The sense of Hinduness or Hindu identity attributed to those who consider the traditional geographical domain of Hindu culture to be their homeland as well as their holy land.

husayniya. A Shiite place of worship for commemorating the martyrdom of Imam Husayn, especially during Ashura.

idiorrhythmic monasticism. A form of monasticism organized around the religious life of the individual living in strict isolation.

ihram. Preparation for performing the Hajj by adopting simple clothing, always white among men, and performing various acts of purification.

ijma. Consensus among the Muslim umma as a whole or, more conservatively, among religious scholars, as a legitimate source of insight in interpreting the sharia.

ilm ("knowledge"). In Shiism, the comprehensive knowledge that an Imam passes on to his chosen successor.

imam. In Sunni Islam, a local ruler or religious leader.

Imam. In Shia Islam and some Kharijite sects, the supreme religious leader of the entire group.

jihad ("struggle"). A complex Islamic concept encompassing, in various contexts, the individual's struggle to lead an authentically Islamic life, the struggle of believers to spread Islam through missionary activity, and the struggle of believers to defend Islam against those who would attack it.

Kaaba ("Cube"). A cubical structure within the Great Mosque of Mecca that in Islamic belief marks the center of the cosmos and contains a portion of the first altar erected by Adam.

Kabbalah. An esoteric school of Jewish thought concerned with the nature of God, creation, evil, and the human soul.

kakars. The five expressions of faith for male Khalsa Sikhs, also known as the five Ks, including kesh, uncut hair and beard; kanga, kara, and kacha, a wooden comb, an iron bracelet, and breeches worn by the adherent; and kirpan, a small sword carried by the adherent.

karma. The doctrine in Indic religions that all past actions have future consequences, which must be resolved before the individual can achieve moksha or liberation from reincarnation.

Khalsa Sikhs. The "community of the pure," those baptized Sikhs who adhere to a strict set of rules of conduct.

Kharijites ("Seceders"). A radical Islamic sect formed during the seventh century in opposition to both the Sunnis and the Shiites, emphasizing strict adherence to Quranic principles, severe treatment of apostates, and the legitimacy of rebellion against corrupt leaders.

koan. Paradoxical anecdote or statement used in Ch'an or Zen Buddhism to provoke the abandonment of conventional thought as a means of attaining enlightenment.

Kumbh Mela. A major Hindu pilgrimage cycle, completed every twelve years, made up of individual pilgrimages every three years to one of a sequence of four sacred cities on four sacred rivers which, at the time of a pilgrimage, become transformed in Hindu belief into a divine nectar spilled during a primeval battle between gods and demons.

lingam ("sign"). An abstract or aniconic phallus-shaped object, usually made of stone, which symbolizes the generative energy of the Hindu god Shiva.

loa. In Vodou, the divine spirits that interact with the world of humanity through the possession of adherents and through actions arising from rituals of propitiation.

lubaale. The hero gods of the Baganda people, associated with particular phenomena central to Baganda life such as fertility, wealth, the hunt, the elements, war, hunger, and disease.

madrassa. A traditional Islamic religious school.

Mahabharata. A major Hindu epic containing a variety of historical narratives, legends surrounding deities within the Hindu pantheon, and discussions of Hindu philosophy.

Mahavamsa. A Buddhist chronicle dating from the fifth century that describes the origins of the Sinhalese people and the coming of Buddhism to Sri Lanka.

Mahdi. In Shia Islam, the last Imam whose messianic return at the end of sacred history will reunite religious and secular authority in a perfected Islamic society; in Sunni Islam, a messianic leader who will create a just Islamic state.

Maliki legal school. One of the four schools of Islamic law, distinguished by its emphasis on traditional practices followed in Medina, the site of Muhammad's original Islamic state, as legitimate sources of insight into the interpretation of the sharia.

mandala. In Indic religions, an abstract or symbolic depiction of the structure of the cosmos, varying among contexts from simple geometrical representations to highly complex arrangements of religious iconography.

maraboutism. A form of Sunni Islam practiced in North Africa that focuses on the veneration of local saints or Sufi shaykhs, known as marabouts, who serve as intermediaries between the believer and God and whose tombs provide a context for the transmission of divine blessing to the believer.

mezuzah. In Judaism, a text from the Book of Deuteronomy contained within a small case that is attached to the doorpost of a house or room in observance of the Torah's commandment that adherents mark their religious identity with God on their houses.

mikveh. A Jewish ritual bath used by men before the Sabbath and major festivals or after contact with the dead, by women after menstruation or childbirth, and by those seeking conversion to Judaism.

mirhab. A niche in the wall of a mosque that is oriented toward the qibla, the direction toward Mecca, to be faced by Muslims during prayer.

Mishnah. The Rabbinic codification of Jewish law as handed down through the teachings of the oral Torah, interpreted through commentaries compiled in the *Gemara*.

moksha. In Indic religions, liberation from the cycle of reincarnation through the attainment of ultimate enlightenment or salvation.

Mount Meru. In Indic religions, the axis mundi around which the different vertical layers of the cosmos are organized.

Namu Amida Butsu. A Japanese phrase signifying "I take refuge in Amida Buddha" whose constant repetition (a practice known as nembutsu) represents the primary ritual of Pure Land Buddhism in Japan.

nass ("designation"). In Shiism, the divinely guided process through which an Imam designates his successor.

nat. A local spirit or divine guardian requiring ritual propitiation in Burmese folk religion, the belief in which persists as an animistic survival within Burmese Theravada Buddhism.

Nayanars ("Masters"). A school of Tamil devotional poetry devoted to Shiva that played a major role in the spread of bhakti devotionalism.

niddah ("separation"). Jewish laws of purity, most commonly referring to the requirement that women erase their separation from ritual purity during menstruation by subsequently performing a ritual bath or mikveh.

night journey of Muhammad. Other than the revelation of the Quran, the only miraculous event associated with Muhammad, during which he traveled on a winged steed from Mecca to Jerusalem (the portion of the journey known as *Isra*) and from there ascended to heaven before returning to Mecca (the portion of the journey known as *Miraj*).

nirvana. In Indic religions, a state of eternal and undisturbed oneness with the true reality that marks the extinction of the self and liberation from the cycle of reincarnation.

orisha. One of the deities venerated in Santeria, each of which is associated with both a Yoruba deity derived from African traditions and a Roman Catholic saint or appellation of Mary, and which are the focus of beliefs and practices relating to possession and divination.

orthodoxy. Correctness in matters of religious doctrine and belief.

orthopraxy. Correctness in matters of religious practice and action.

phi (pl. phii). A local spirit in Thai folk religion that believers typically propitiate through the provision of a spirit house, a practice that persists as an animistic survival within Thai Theravada Buddhism.

pitha ("seat"). A sacred site representing a worldly seat or throne of a Hindu deity at which worshippers have access to the deity's presence, most widely exemplified by the shakti-pithas associated with Shakti.

proselytic religion. A religion whose membership is in theory open to individuals of any background and that spreads in part through proselytism, or efforts to attract converts into the faith.

puja. Ceremonial worship based on bhakti or devotion to a particular deity.

Puranas. Hindu narratives, generally set down in written form between 200 CE and 500 CE, which address the process of creation, the sacred history of the Hindu pantheon, genealogies of kings and sages, and other cosmological and philosophical themes.

purdah. The seclusion of women from public view, practiced in Islam and in some varieties of Hinduism.

Pure Land. In Buddhist belief, any of a large number of separate worlds, each governed by a Buddha and various bodhisattvas, which possess optimal conditions for the attainment of nirvana by all of those reborn into the world, the primary objective of Pure Land Buddhism.

qadi. A local religious jurist employed by a ruler to interpret and apply the sharia, normally within the framework of a specific Islamic legal school.

qibla. The sacred direction toward the Kaaba in Mecca, which Muslims must face in prayer.

qiyas. In Islam, reasoning by analogy from principles in the Quran, the Sunna, and the hadith in applying the sharia to cases with no established precedent.

Ramayana. A Hindu epic describing the adventures of Rama, the seventh incarnation of the Hindu god Vishnu.

rock edicts. Statements of Buddhist morals and ethics carved in local languages into stone pillars, cliff faces, and cave walls across India during the third century BCE by order of the emperor Asoka.

Saivism. A major devotional tradition within Hinduism that focuses on the veneration of Shiva.

sangha. A Buddhist monastic order or, more broadly, the Buddhist community.

Sanskritization. As used in this text, the process through which the written Indo-Aryan traditions of Vedism, early Hinduism, and the Brahmin caste merged with the folk religions of local communities, especially within the Dravidian region of southern India.

Sefer ha-Zohar. A commentary on the Torah produced by the Sephardic scholar Moses de Leon in the thirteenth century, focusing on Kabbalistic concerns rather than on the more conventional explication of religious law.

Sephardim. The Jewish community that developed primarily in Iberian Europe during the medieval period.

Sevener Shiism. A Shiite sect that recognizes only seven Imams, with the Imamate passing from a father to his eldest son as follows: Ali, Hasan, Husayn, Ali Zayn, Muhammad al-

Baqir, Jafar, Ismail (not counted as an Imam because he predeceased Jafar), and Muhammad ibn Ismail (the future Mahdi).

Shafii legal school. The second most conservative of the four schools of Islamic law, after the Hanbalis, distinguished by its emphases on ijma, or the consensus of the ulama, and on reasoning by analogy, as well as by its opposition to the qadi's use of individual judgment or discretion.

shahada. The Islamic declaration of faith, one of the Five Pillars of Islam, in which the believer asserts that there is only one God and that Muhammad was his final messenger.

Shaktism. A major devotional tradition within Hinduism that focuses on the veneration of Shakti in all of her manifestations as the preeminent deity and the female personification of divine creative energy.

sharia. Islamic law based on the Quran and the Sunna.

shaykh. A Sufi master who serves as a teacher for his followers, as an important link in the spiritual lineage of his tariqa, and often as a source of baraka for followers during and after his lifetime.

Shekhinah ("Dwelling"). In Judaism, the presence of God, usually in its feminine aspect associated with spiritual joy and wisdom, manifest in a particular location or divine dwelling place.

stupa. A Buddhist shrine, originally constructed as a simple mound but later commonly built with a spire and other detailed features, and usually acquiring special sanctity from the ashes or other relics of a Buddhist master that are contained within it.

sukkah ("booth," pl. sukkot). In Judaism, a temporary booth or hut created in emulation of structures built by the Israelites during the Exodus and serving during Sukkot as the location for all meals and often as a place for sleeping as well.

Sukkot. The Jewish Festival of Booths, combining a traditional celebration of the autumn harvest with commemoration of the wandering of the Israelites in the Sinai desert.

Sunna. Islamic traditions associated with Muhammad and his companions; after the Quran, the most important source of Islamic law.

sutra (Sanskrit) or sutta (Pali). In Hinduism (sutra only), a text articulating a specific interpretation of philosophical or cosmological concerns; in Buddhism (sutra and sutta), a canonical text that records specific oral teachings of Gautama Buddha.

Talmud. Rabbinic commentaries on Jewish law and tradition, including the Mishnah and Gemara.

Tantrism. A variety of esoteric practices and rituals aimed at accelerating the attainment of enlightenment, typically through the use of arcane mental and physical processes but in some cases incorporating transgressive elements such as sexual practices.

tariqa ("path"). In early usage the means or path by which Sufi mystics achieved unity with God, but later the whole system of beliefs and practices that a Sufi shaykh taught to his followers, and ultimately, in its most common contemporary meaning, the entire community of believers that practice the teachings of a lineage of shaykhs.

tawhid ("unity"). The Islamic belief in strict monotheism, expressed as the absolute unity of God.

Temple Mount. The site in Jerusalem believed to have been the location of Judaism's Second Temple, as well as the location of important Muslim shrines within al-Haram al-Sharif.

theocracy. A political state that functions as a religious entity through the merging of political ideology and religious belief, either under the direct rule of religious leaders (a strict theocracy) or under the rule of secular leaders who receive some form of guidance from religious leaders (a limited theocracy).

theodemocracy. An Islamic political concept describing a polity in which the system of government incorporates democratic institutions which, by acting in accordance with divine will, enable the state to function as a divine instrument.

tilak. In Hinduism, a mark usually painted on the forehead indicating devotion to a particular deity, and especially to Vishnu, Shiva, or the Mother Goddess.

Tipitaka. Also known as the Pali canon, the canonical scriptures of Theravada Buddhism, including the *Vinaya pitaka*, describing ethical principles and the rules of monastic life; the *Sutta pitaka*, describing the Buddha's oral teachings; and the *Abhidhamma pitaka*, providing analyses of various aspects of Buddhist thought.

tirtha ("ford"). In Hinduism and Jainism, a sacred location that can foster the efforts of believers to cross over to the state of moksha, or ford the boundary between the material world and nirvana, through the site's association with manifestations of a particular deity or saint.

tirthankaras ("ford-makers"). Twenty-four Jain teachers who have achieved liberation from reincarnation and have sought to define a path for others to follow toward the same end, and the last of whom was Vardhamana, the founder of the Jain religion.

tribal religion. A religion whose membership is generally limited to members of a specific, localized tribal group.

Tripitaka. Originally the Sanskrit version of the Tipitaka, but in later usage among some Mahayana Buddhists any canonical collection of Buddhist texts, including those containing texts not found in the Tipitaka.

tulku. The reincarnation of a deceased leader of Tibetan Buddhism, usually identified in childhood through an elaborate investigation of potential candidates.

Twelver Shiism. The majority group within Shiism defined by its recognition of twelve Imams, with the Imamate passing from a father to his eldest living son, as follows: Ali, Hasan, Husayn, Ali Zayn, Muhammad al-Baqir, Jafar, Musa, Ali al-Rida, Muhammad al-Jawad, Ali al-Hadi, Hasan al-Askari, Muhammad al-Mahdi (the future Mahdi).

ulama. The community of Islamic religious and legal scholars, often responsible for operating local Islamic educational systems and administering other religious institutions.

umma. The community of all Muslims.

Upanishads. Commentaries on the Vedas produced during the first millennium BCE that shifted the focus of Vedic thought away from the fire sacrifice and toward more philosophical concerns relating to the nature of reality and the self, such as the concepts of karma and moksha.

Vaishnavism. A major devotional tradition within Hinduism that focuses on the veneration of Vishnu and his avatars.

varna. One of the four castes of Vedism, including Brahmins (priests and scholars), Kshatriyas (warriors and rulers), Vaishyas (merchants, artisans, farmers, and herders), and Shudras (serfs and servants).

Vedas ("**Books of Knowledge**"). The scriptures of Vedism, which address the correct performance of public Vedic rituals, especially the fire sacrifice (in the *Rig-veda*, the *Sama-veda*, and *Yajur-veda*), and various domestic rituals (in the *Atharva-veda*).

Wahhabism. An eighteenth-century Islamic revivalist movement that emphasizes absolute monotheism, strict interpretation and observance of the Quran, and adherence to the Hanbali school of Islamic law.

wali. Any Sufi saint who possesses superhuman abilities and serves as a repository of baraka, or divine blessing, which can be transmitted to others even after the saint's death.

waqf. In Islam, a charitable foundation, most often funded primarily through local donations, that provides support for the maintenance of a local religious structure or institution.

Wicca. A group of Neo-Pagan religious movements articulated during the twentieth century but incorporating a diverse array of older practices and beliefs drawn from various pagan religious traditions, as in the worship by many Wiccans of the Goddess, a universal deity that has taken different forms in many different cultural contexts.

worldview. A system of beliefs concerning the essential nature of reality and the ultimate sources of causality, including superhuman forces.

yoga. In Hinduism, various meditative and ascetic practices intended to promote spiritual insight through mental or physical discipline.

yoni ("**womb**" or "**female sex organs**"). In Hinduism, an abstract or aniconic object, usually triangular and made of stone, representing the generative energy of Shakti.

zaddik. The model of religious behavior in the Jewish Talmud; more specifically, a spiritual leader of the Hasidic branch of Judaism.

zawiya. A local Sufi lodge, which may serve as a monastic community, a center of religious instruction, a public setting for interactions between a shaykh and his followers, a burial place for a local shaykh, and a pilgrimage destination for believers seeking access to baraka at a shaykh's tomb.

ziyara ("**visit**"). An Islamic pilgrimage to a destination other than Mecca, most often to Medina and Muhammad's tomb or to the tomb of a local saint, Sufi shaykh, or Shiite Imam.

Selected Bibliography

Reference Works

Barrett, David B., George T. Kurian, and Todd M. Johnson, eds. *World Christian Encyclopedia: A Comparative Survey of Churches and Religions in the Modern World.* Oxford: Oxford University Press, 2001.

Bowker, John, ed. *The Oxford Dictionary of World Religions.* New York: Oxford University Press, 1997.

Brockman, Norbert C. *Encyclopedia of Sacred Places.* Santa Barbara, Cal.: ABC-CLIO, 1997.

al Faruqi, Isma'il Ragi, and David E. Sopher, eds. *Historical Atlas of the Religions of the World.* New York: Macmillan, 1974.

Gaustad, Edwin Scott, and Philip L. Barlow, eds. *New Historical Atlas of Religion in America.* New York: Oxford University Press, 2000.

Johnston, William M., ed. *Encyclopedia of Monasticism.* London: Routledge, 2000.

Jones, Lindsay, ed. *Encyclopedia of Religion*, 2d ed., 15 vols. Detroit: Macmillan Reference USA, 2005.

Smart, Ninian, ed. *Atlas of the World's Religions.* Oxford: Oxford University Press, 1999.

Taylor, Richard P. *Death and the Afterlife: A Cultural Encyclopedia.* Santa Barbara, Cal.: ABC-CLIO, 2000.

General Historical and Theoretical Works

Beit-Hallahmi, Benjamin, and Michael Argyle. *The Psychology of Religious Behaviour, Belief and Experience.* London: Routledge, 1997.

Eliade, Mircea. *The Sacred and the Profane.* New York: Harcourt Brace & Company, 1959.

————. *A History of Religious Ideas*, 3 vols. Chicago: University of Chicago Press, 1978–1985.

Geertz, Clifford. *Interpretation of Cultures: Selected Essays.* New York: Basic Books: 1973.

Idinopulos, Thomas, and Brian C. Wilson, eds. *What is Religion? Origins, Definitions, and Explanations.* Leiden: Brill, 1998.

Lawson, E. Thomas, and Robert N. McCauley. *Rethinking Religion: Connecting Cognition and Culture.* Cambridge: Cambridge University Press, 1990.

Pals, Daniel L. *Seven Theories of Religion.* New York: Oxford University Press, 1996.

Patton, Kimberly C., and Benjamin C. Ray, eds. *A Magic Still Dwells: Comparative Religion in the Postmodern Age.* Berkeley: University of California Press, 2000.

Smith, Huston. *The World's Religions: Our Great Wisdom Traditions*, rev. ed. San Francisco: HarperCollins, 1991.

Smith, Jonathan Z. *Imagining Religion: From Babylon to Jonestown.* Chicago: University of Chicago Press, 1982.

Stark, Rodney, and William Sims Bainbridge. *A Theory of Religion.* New York: Peter Lang, 1987.

General Works on the Geography of Religion

Deffontaines, Pierre. *Géographie et Religions*. Paris: Gallimard, 1948.
Geographies of Religions and Belief Systems. gorabs.org/journal/index.htm (accessed June 25, 2007).
Park, Chris C. *Sacred Worlds: An Introduction to Geography and Religion*. London: Routledge, 1994.
Sopher, David E. *Geography of Religions*. Englewood Cliffs, N.J.: Prentice-Hall, 1967.

Comparative Studies of Religious Belief and Practice

Arthur, Linda Boynton. *Religion, Dress and the Body*. New York: Berg Publishers, 1999.
Bernbaum, Edwin. *Sacred Mountains of the World*. Berkeley: University of California Press, 1998.
Coakley, Sarah, ed. *Religion and the Body*. New York: Cambridge University Press, 1997.
Coleman, Simon, and John Elsner. *Pilgrimage: Past and Present in the World Religions*. Cambridge, Mass.: Harvard University Press, 1995.
Gesler, Wilbert M. *Healing Places*. Lanham, Md.: Rowman and Littlefield, 2003.
Levine, Lee I., ed. *Jerusalem: Its Sanctity and Centrality to Judaism, Christianity, and Islam*. New York: Continuum, 1999.
Stoddard, Robert H., and Alan Morinis, eds. *Sacred Places, Sacred Spaces: The Geography of Pilgrimages*. Baton Rouge: Geoscience Publications, Dept. of Geography and Anthropology, Louisiana State University, 1997.
Szarmach, Paul E., ed. *An Introduction to the Medieval Mystics of Europe: Fourteen Original Essays*. Albany: State University of New York Press, 1984.
Turner, Alice K. *The History of Hell*. New York: Harcourt Brace and Co., 1993.
Wright, J. Edward. *The Early History of Heaven*. New York: Oxford University Press, 2000.

Contemporary Religious Phenomena

Berger, Peter L., ed. *The Desecularization of the World: Resurgent Religion and World Politics*. Washington, D.C.: Wm. B. Eerdmans, 1999.
Bruce, Steve. *Religion in the Modern World: From Cathedrals to Cults*. Oxford: Oxford University Press, 1996.
Buss, Doris, and Didi Herman. *Globalizing Family Values: The Christian Right in International Politics*. Minneapolis: University of Minnesota Press, 2003.
Casanova, José. *Public Religions in the Modern World*. Chicago: University of Chicago Press, 1994.
Haynes, Jeff. *Religion in Global Politics*. London: Longman, 1998.
Ilchman, Warren F., Stanley N. Katz, and Edward L. Queen, II, eds. *Philanthropy in the World's Traditions*. Bloomington: Indiana University Press, 1998.
Stump, Roger W. *Boundaries of Faith: Geographical Perspectives on Religious Fundamentalism*. Lanham, Md.: Rowman and Littlefield, 2000.
Varshney, Ashutosh. *Ethnic Conflict and Civic Life: Hindus and Muslims in India*. New Haven, Conn.: Yale University Press, 2002.

Buddhism

Akuppa. *Touching the Earth: A Buddhist Guide to Saving the Planet*. Birmingham, U.K.: Windhorse Publications, 2004.

Conze, Edward. *Buddhism: A Short History*. Oxford: Oneworld Publications, 2000.

Dumoulin, Heinrich, ed. *Buddhism in the Modern World*. New York: Macmillan, 1976.

Huber, Toni, ed. *Sacred Spaces and Powerful Places in Tibetan Culture*. Dharamsala, India: Library of Tibetan Works and Archives, 1999.

Keown, Damien. *A Dictionary of Buddhism*. New York: Oxford University Press, 2003.

Ling, Trevor. *The Buddha: Buddhist Civilization in India and Ceylon*. London: Temple Smith, 1973.

Morgan, Kenneth W., ed. *The Path of the Buddha: Buddhism Interpreted by Buddhists*. New York: Ronald Press, 1956.

Pardue, Peter A. *Buddhism*. New York: Macmillan, 1971.

Ray, Reginald A. *Indestructible Truth: The Living Spirituality of Tibetan Buddhism*. Boston: Shambhala, 2000.

Strong, John. *Relics of the Buddha*. Princeton, N.J.: Princeton University Press, 2004.

Zürcher, E. *The Buddhist Conquest of China: The Spread and Adaptation of Buddhism in Early Medieval China*, 2 vols. Leiden: E. J. Brill, 1972.

Christianity

Badone, Ellen, ed. *Religious Orthodoxy and Popular Faith in European Society*. Princeton, N.J.: Princeton University Press, 1990.

Conkin, Paul Keith. *American Originals: Homemade Varieties of Christianity*. Chapel Hill: University of North Carolina Press, 1997.

Gifford, Paul. *African Christianity: Its Public Role*. Bloomington: Indiana University Press, 1998.

Hardwick, Susan Wiley. *Russian Refuge: Religion, Migration, and Settlement on the North American Pacific Rim*. Chicago: University of Chicago Press, 1993.

Hefner, Robert W., ed. *Conversion to Christianity: Historical and Anthropological Perspectives on a Great Transformation*. Berkeley: University of California Press, 1993.

Miller, Daniel R., ed. *Coming of Age: Protestantism in Contemporary Latin America*. Lanham, Md.: University Press of America, 1994.

Nolan, Mary Lee, and Sidney Nolan. *Christian Pilgrimage in Modern Western Europe*. Chapel Hill: University of North Carolina Press, 1989.

Riley-Smith, Jonathan, ed. *The Oxford Illustrated History of the Crusades*. New York: Oxford University Press, 1995.

Tarasov, Oleg. *Icon and Devotion: Sacred Spaces in Imperial Russia*, trans. and ed. Robin Milner-Gulland. London: Reaktion Books, 2002.

Turner, Victor, and Edith Turner. *Image and Pilgrimage in Christian Culture: Anthropological Perspectives*. New York: Columbia University Press, 1978

Wallace, Peter G. *The Long European Reformation: Religion, Political Conflict and the Search for Conformity, 1350–1750*. New York: Palgrave Macmillan, 2003.

Hinduism

Bhardwaj, Surinder Mohan. *Hindu Places of Pilgrimage in India: A Study in Cultural Geography*. Berkeley: University of California Press, 1973.

Bhargava, Manohar Lal. *The Geography of Rgvedic India*. Lucknow: The Upper India Publishing House, 1964.

Brockington, J. L. *The Sacred Thread: Hinduism in Its Continuity and Diversity*, 2d ed. Edinburgh: Edinburgh University Press, 1996.

Burghart, Richard, ed. *Hinduism in Great Britain: The Perpetuation of Religion in an Alien Cultural Milieu*. London: Tavistock Publications, 1987.

Chaudhuri, Nirad C. *Hinduism: A Religion to Live By*. New York: Oxford University Press, 1979.

Flood, Gavin. *An Introduction to Hinduism*. Cambridge: Cambridge University Press, 1996.

Kinsley, David R. *Hindu Goddesses: Visions of the Divine Feminine in the Hindu Religious Tradition*. Berkeley: University of California Press, 1986.

Lodrick, Deryck O. *Sacred Cows, Sacred Places: Origins and Survivals of Animal Homes in India*. Berkeley: University of California Press, 1981.

Michell, George. *The Hindu Temple: An Introduction to Its Meaning and Forms*. London: Elek, 1977.

Sharma, Jyotirmay. *Hindutva: Exploring the Idea of Hindu Nationalism*. New Delhi: Viking, 2003.

Vertovec, Steven. *The Hindu Diaspora: Comparative Patterns*. New York: Routledge, 2000.

Islam

Eickelman, Dale F., and James Piscatori, eds. *Muslim Travelers: Pilgrimage, Migration, and the Religious Imagination*. Berkeley: University of California Press, 1990.

Esposito, John L. *Islam: The Straight Path*, 3d ed. New York: Oxford University Press, 1998.

———. *The Islamic Threat: Myth or Reality?*, 3d ed. New York: Oxford University Press, 1999.

Falah, Ghazi-Walid, and Caroline Nagel, eds. *Geographies of Muslim Women: Gender, Religion, and Space*. New York: Guilford Press, 2005.

Frishman, Martin, and Hasan-Uddin Khan, eds. *The Mosque: History, Architectural Development and Regional Diversity*. New York: Thames and Hudson, 2002.

Hodgson, Marshall G. S. *The Venture of Islam: Conscience and History in a World Civilization*, 3 vols. Chicago: University of Chicago Press, 1974.

Lapidus, Ira M. *A History of Islamic Societies*. New York: Cambridge University Press, 1988.

Peters, F. E. *The Hajj: The Muslim Pilgrimage to Mecca and the Holy Places*. Princeton, N.J.: Princeton University Press, 1994.

Trimingham, J. Spencer. *The Sufi Orders in Islam*. New York: Oxford University Press, 1971.

Vertovec, Steven, and Ceri Peach. *Islam in Europe: The Politics of Religion and Community*. New York: St. Martin's Press, 1997.

Westerlund, David, and Eva Evers Rosander, eds. *African Islam and Islam in Africa: Encounters between Sufis and Islamists*. Athens: Ohio University Press, 1997.

Judaism

Bartal, Israel. *The Jews of Eastern Europe, 1772–1881*, trans. Chaya Naor. Philadelphia: University of Pennsylvania Press, 2005.

Blau, Joseph L. *Modern Varieties of Judaism*. New York: Columbia University Press, 1966.

Cohn-Sherbok, Dan. *Atlas of Jewish History*. London: Routledge, 1994.

———, ed. *Holocaust Theology: A Reader*. New York: New York University Press, 2002.

Finkelstein, Israel, and Neil Asher Silberman. *The Bible Unearthed: Archaeology's New Vision of Ancient Israel and the Origin of Its Sacred Texts*. New York: The Free Press, 2001.

Hundert, Gershon David, ed. *Essential Papers on Hasidism: Origins to Present*. New York: New York University Press, 1991.

Kunin, Seth Daniel. *God's Place in the World: Sacred Space and Sacred Place in Judaism*. New York: Cassell, 1998.

Morgenstern, Arie. *Hastening Redemption: Messianism and the Resettlement of the Land of Israel*. New York: Oxford University Press, 2006.

Newman, David, ed. *The Impact of Gush Emunim: Politics and Settlement in the West Bank*. London: Croon Helm, 1985.

Sigal, Phillip. *Judaism: The Evolution of a Faith*. Grand Rapids, Mich.: William B. Eerdmans Company, 1988.

Wertheimer, Jack, ed. *The Uses of Tradition: Jewish Continuity in the Modern Era*. New York: Jewish Theological Seminary of America, 1992.

Other Religious Traditions

Bauer, Brian S. *The Sacred Landscape of the Inca: The Cusco Ceque System*. Austin: University of Texas Press, 1998.

Beard, Mary, John North, and Simon Price. *Religions of Rome*, 2 vols. Cambridge: Cambridge University Press, 1998.

Fernandez Olmos, Margarite, and Lizabeth Paravisini-Gebert. *Creole Religions of the Caribbean: An Introduction from Vodou and Santeria to Obeah and Espiritismo*. New York: New York University Press, 2003.

Heissig, Walther. *The Religions of Mongolia*. Berkeley: University of California Press, 1980.

Kelley, Klara Bonsack, and Harris Francis. *Navajo Sacred Places*. Bloomington: Indiana University Press, 1994.

Mikalson, Jon D. *Ancient Greek Religion*. Malden, Mass.: Blackwell, 2005.

Tatla, Darshan Singh. *The Sikh Diaspora: The Search for Statehood*. Seattle: University of Washington Press, 1999.

Wedel, Johan. *Santeria Healing: A Journey into the Afro-Cuban World of Divinities, Spirits, and Sorcery*. Gainesville: University Press of Florida, 2004.

Index

About the Author

Roger W. Stump is professor of geography and religious studies at the University at Albany, State University of New York. His publications include *Boundaries of Faith: Geographical Perspectives on Religious Fundamentalism*, published in 2000 by Rowman & Littlefield, as well as a variety of articles and book chapters focusing primarily on the geography of religion. His current interests include the intersections between religious doctrine and political ideology, particularly with regard to fundamentalist and reformist movements, and the religious meanings of the spatial practices and behaviors of schismatic and unorthodox religious groups.